ANNUAL EDITIONS

Violence and Terrorism
08/09

Eleventh Edition

EDITOR

Thomas J. Badey
Randolph-Macon College

Thomas J. Badey is an associate professor of Political Science and the director of the International Studies Program at Randolph-Macon College in Ashland, Virginia. He received a BS in Sociology from the University of Maryland (University College) in 1986 and an MA in political science from the University of South Florida in 1987. In 1993 he received a PhD in political science from the *Institut für Politische Wissenschaft* of the *Ruprecht-Karls Universität* in Heidelberg, Germany. He served as a security policeman in the United States Air Force from 1979 to 1988 and was stationed in the United States, Asia and the Middle East. Dr. Badey regularly teaches courses on international terrorism and has written a number of articles on the subject. He is also the editor of the McGraw-Hill Contemporary Learning Series *Annual Editions: Homeland Security*.

McGraw-Hill Higher Education

Boston   Burr Ridge, IL   Dubuque, IA   New York   San Francisco   St. Louis
Bangkok   Bogotá   Caracas   Kuala Lumpur   Lisbon   London   Madrid   Mexico City
Milan   Montreal   New Delhi   Santiago   Seoul   Singapore   Sydney   Taipei   Toronto

ANNUAL EDITIONS: VIOLENCE AND TERRORISM, ELEVENTH EDITION

Published by McGraw-Hill, a business unit of The McGraw-Hill Companies, Inc., 1221 Avenue of the Americas, New York, NY 10020. Copyright © 2009 by The McGraw-Hill Companies, Inc. All rights reserved. Previous edition(s) 1997–2008. No part of this publication may be reproduced or distributed in any form or by any means, or stored in a database or retrieval system, without the prior written consent of The McGraw-Hill Companies, Inc., including, but not limited to, in any network or other electronic storage or transmission, or broadcast for distance learning.

Some ancillaries, including electronic and print components, may not be available to customers outside the United States.

Annual Editions® is a registered trademark of the McGraw-Hill Companies, Inc.
Annual Editions is published by the **Contemporary Learning Series** group within the McGraw-Hill Higher Education division.

1 2 3 4 5 6 7 8 9 0 QPD/QPD 0 9 8

ISBN 978–0–07–339776–4
MHID 0–07–339776–8
ISSN 1096–4274

Managing Editor: *Larry Loeppke*
Managing Editor: *Faye Schilling*
Developmental Editor: *Dave Welsh*
Editorial Assistant: *Nancy Meissner*
Production Service Assistant: *Rita Hingtgen*
Permissions Coordinator: *Shirley Lanners*
Senior Marketing Manager: *Julie Keck*
Marketing Communications Specialist: *Mary Klein*
Marketing Coordinator: *Alice Link*
Project Manager: *Jean Smith*
Design Specialist: *Tara McDermott*
Senior Administrative Assistant: *DeAnna Dausener*
Senior Production Supervisor: *Laura Fuller*
Cover Design: Kristine Jubeck

Compositor: Laserwords Private Limited
Cover Images: U.S. Marine Corps photo by Lance Cpl. Jessica N. Aranda
U.S. Army photo/Spc. Micah E. Clare

Library in Congress Cataloging-in-Publication Data
Main entry under title: Annual Editions: Violence and Terrorism. 2008/2009.
  1. Violence and Terrorism—Periodicals. I. Badey, Thomas J., *comp.* II. Title: Violence and Terrorism.
658'.05

www.mhhe.com

Editors/Advisory Board

Members of the Advisory Board are instrumental in the final selection of articles for each edition of ANNUAL EDITIONS. Their review of articles for content, level, currentness, and appropriateness provides critical direction to the editor and staff. We think that you will find their careful consideration well reflected in this volume.

EDITOR

Thomas J. Badey
Randolph-Macon College

ADVISORY BOARD

Kristian Alexander
University of Utah

Robert M. Carter
*United States Military Academy
(Major General, Retired)*

Robert Cassinelli
American River College

Cynthia C. Combs
University of North Carolina–Charlotte

John George
University of Central Oklahoma

David Gray
University of Denver

Michael M. Gunter
Tennessee Technological University

Charles Loftus
Arizona State University

Jane D. Matheson
Northeastern University

George Michael
*The University of Virginia's
College at Wise*

Richard Pearlstein
Southeastern Oklahoma University

James M. Poland
California State University–Sacramento

Todd Sandler
University of Texas–Dallas

John E. Santosuosso
Florida Southern College

Donna M. Schlagheck
Wright State University

Peter C. Sederberg
University of South Carolina

Stephen Sloan
University of Central Florida

Brent Smith
University of Arkansas

Paul Wallace
University of Missouri–Columbia

Preface

In publishing ANNUAL EDITIONS we recognize the enormous role played by the magazines, newspapers, and journals of the public press in providing current, first-rate educational information in a broad spectrum of interest areas. Many of these articles are appropriate for students, researchers, and professionals seeking accurate, current material to help bridge the gap between principles and theories and the real world. These articles, however, become more useful for study when those of lasting value are carefully collected, organized, indexed, and reproduced in a low-cost format, which provides easy and permanent access when the material is needed. That is the role played by ANNUAL EDITIONS.

Successful elections in Afghanistan and Iraq failed to bring about peace or reduce the threat of terrorism, and continuing violence in Latin America and Europe and new violence in Asia and Africa reminds us that the global war on terrorism is far from over. Violence and terrorism affect our lives and will continue to affect our lives well into this century. Political, economic, social, ethnic and religious strife, fueled by the availability of weapons, advances in technology, and an ever-present international media, set the stage for the future of violence and terrorism. The only real defense against terrorism is to try to understand terrorism. Thus, *Annual Editions: Violence and Terrorism 08/09* continues to address some basic questions: Why does terrorism occur? How does it occur? Who are the terrorists? How can or should governments respond?

The selections for this edition of *Annual Editions: Violence and Terrorism* were chosen to reflect a diversity of issues, actors, and points of view. This revision incorporates many new articles that reflect the changes that have occurred since the previous edition was published. While, as always, influenced by recent events, this volume endeavors to maintain sufficient regional and topical coverage to provide students with a broad perspective as a basis for understanding contemporary political violence. Articles for this introductory reader were chosen from a variety of sources and reflect diverse writing styles. It is our hope that this broad selection will provide easy accessibility at various levels and will thus stimulate interest and discussion. In addition to the aforementioned considerations, elements such as timeliness and readability of the articles were important criteria used in their selection.

This anthology is organized into ten units. Unit 1 attempts to address the complex task of conceptualizing terrorism. It underlines the difficulty of finding a commonly accepted definition of the problem. Unit 2 examines the methods employed by terrorists. It focuses on current terrorist tactics used by terrorist organizations. Unit 3 examines the role of state sponsors in international terrorism. Focusing primarily on so called "rogue states," this unit sheds light on the complex and changing relationship between sponsor states and terrorist organizations. Unit 4 provides an overview of some of the major actors in contemporary international terrorism. Shifting the focus to the domestic front, Unit 5 examines terrorism in America. In addition to articles on domestic terrorism, it highlights the potential impact of policies to combat terrorist threats to personal freedom and civil liberties. Unit 6 focuses on the role that the media plays in terrorism and points to potential consequences of increased terrorist-media interaction. Unit 7 examines the complex relationship between terrorism and religion and how religion is used to justify contemporary political violence. Unit 8 looks at the role of women, who continue to play an important and increasingly active role in contemporary political violence. Unit 9 examines the methods and policies governments use to counter the threat of terrorism. Finally, Unit 10 explores trends, projections, and future threats in international terrorism.

This anthology provides a broad overview of the major issues associated with political violence and terrorism. It is our hope that *Annual Editions: Violence and Terrorism* will introduce students to the study of terrorism and serve as a stimulus for further exploration of this vital topic.

I would like to thank the many scholars who provided feedback and submitted suggestions for articles to be included in this volume. I am also grateful to Jessica Kuehn, who worked as my research assistant on this project. She helped review the numerous articles that were submitted for consideration, provided valuable insights, and above all provided a critical students' perspective, which made my job much easier. I hope that you, the reader, will take the time to fill out the article rating form in the back of this anthology so we can continue to improve future editions.

Thomas J. Badey
Editor

Contents

Preface	iv
Topic Guide	xi
Internet References	xiii

UNIT 1
The Concept of Terrorism

Unit Overview   xvi

1. **Ghosts of Our Past,** Karen Armstrong, *AARP Modern Maturity,* January/February 2002

   In order to *fully understand the War on Terrorism,* it is necessary to explore the past incidents that have served as catalysts over time. We cannot understand the present crisis without taking into account the painful process of modernization and the effects of the "Great Western Transformation" on the Muslim world.   2

2. **An Essay on Terrorism,** Marc Nicholson, *American Diplomacy,* Vol. 8, No. 3, 2003

   Former diplomat Marc Nicholson provides a quick overview of contemporary political violence. He describes terrorism as a "tool of the weak, used by disaffected groups or minorities to oppose the rule and (as they see it) the oppression of an established and militarily superior power."   6

3. **The Origins of the New Terrorism,** Matthew J. Morgan, *Parameters,* Spring 2004

   Matthew J. Morgan examines what he considers to be a "new" and more "evolved" type of terrorism. He argues that cultural, political, and technological factors have shaped its development.   9

4. **The Myth of the Invincible Terrorist,** Christopher C. Harmon, *Policy Review,* April/May 2007

   Christopher Harmon uses examples to highlight potential vulnerabilities of terrorist organizations. Focusing on the tactical, technological, strategic, and ideological obstacles faced by these groups, he challenges the notion that terrorists are invincible.   17

UNIT 2
Tactics of Terrorism

Unit Overview   26

5. **Paying for Terror,** David E. Kaplan, *U.S. News & World Report,* December 5, 2005

   Terrorist organizations are exploring new ways to fund operations. David Kaplan examines how organized crime and drug trafficking provide the financing that terrorists seek. He also discusses scams, identity theft, and extortion as new sources of revenue.   28

6. **Toy Soldiers,** Cheryl Benard, *Current History,* January 2007

   Cheryl Benard argues that demographic changes in the Middle East have led to the increased recruitment of youth by terrorist organizations. She believes that immature brain development, thrill seeking behavior, and misperceptions of reality make this group particularly vulnerable.   34

The concepts in bold italics are developed in the article. For further expansion, please refer to the Topic Guide.

UNIT 3
State-Sponsored Terrorism

Unit Overview   38

7. **Iran's Suicide Brigades,** Ali Alfoneh, *Middle East Quarterly,* Winter 2007

   This article examines Iran's use of "martyrdom-seekers" against internal and external threats. It describes the training and command of these units, their use in internal power struggles, and their impact on Iran's relationship with its neighbors.   40

8. **Hizballah and Syria,** Emile El-Hokayem, *The Washington Quarterly,* Spring 2007

   This article assesses the changing relationship between Syria and Hizballah. It discusses the historical development of the relationship between the "state" and its "client," arguing that Hizballah is becoming increasingly more autonomous.   45

9. **Guerrilla Nation,** Thor Halvorssen, *The Weekly Standard,* January 26, 2005

   Thor Halvorssen offers evidence of a potential connection between Venezuelan President Hugo Chavez and the Armed Revolutionary Forces of Colombia (FARC). Halvorssen argues that, despite Chavez's consistent denials, he continues to support the FARC.   54

10. **The Growing Syrian Missile Threat: Syria after Lebanon,** Lee Kass, *Middle East Quarterly,* Fall 2005

    Lee Kass focuses on Syria's ambitions to develop its weapons of mass destruction (WMD) capability. He points to Syria's links with terrorist organizations and argues that it will become more difficult to confront Syrian sponsorship of international terrorism.   56

UNIT 4
International Terrorism

Unit Overview   62

11. **Colombia and the United States: From Counternarcotics to Counterterrorism,** Arlene B. Tickner, *Current History,* February 2003

    Colombia's terrorist network and its drug trade are impossible to separate. Arlene Tickner argues that U.S. policies to address these issues have been defined primarily in military terms and have ". . . taken precedence over equally significant political, economical, and social considerations."   64

12. **Wounded But Still Dangerous,** *The Economist,* June 16, 2007

    Despite Indonesia's recent successes against Jemaah Islamiah, the group remains a significant threat. While there have been no large-scale attacks against foreigners since the Bali bombings in 2005, there are indications that JI may be rearming and reorganizing.   72

13. **Peace at Last?,** Joshua Hammer, *Smithsonian,* January 2007

    Joshua Hammer explores the roots of the conflict in the Basque region of Spain. While skepticism remains high on both sides, there is some hope that the latest cease fire will lead to a peace agreement, ending decades of separatist violence.   74

14. **Root Causes of Chechen Terror,** Alon Ben-Meir, *The World & I,* December 2004

    The Chechen struggle offers an example of how misguided policy can lead to tragic consequences. Ben-Meir argues that as long as Russia continues to ignore the root causes of Chechen terrorism, there is no chance of diminishing or eliminating it.   78

15. **End of Terrorism?,** Meredith Moore, *Harvard International Review,* Summer 2005

    Meredith Moore argues that, despite Basque's calls for peace, the lack of action on both sides of the conflict will lead to a continuation of violence in Spain.   80

The concepts in bold italics are developed in the article. For further expansion, please refer to the Topic Guide.

UNIT 5
Terrorism in America

Unit Overview   82

16. **Homegrown Terror,** Michael Reynolds, *Bulletin of the Atomic Scientists,* November/December 2004

    Reynolds contends that the preoccupation with Islamic terrorism has caused the government and the media to ignore the potential threat posed by extremists and right-wing groups in the United States. He asserts that, Joseph Konopka and William Krar, two U.S. citizens prosecuted in 2002 and 2003 were in possession of " . . . far more chemical weapons than have been found in post-war Iraq."   84

17. **Green Rage,** Matt Rasmussen, *Orion,* January/February 2007

    Sympathetic to the cause, Rasmussen looks at the motives behind attacks carried out by radical environmentalists in the United States. He blames harsh sentencing on the efforts of an overzealous administration trying to distract from its failings " . . . to counter real terrorism."   90

18. **Echoes of the Future,** Daveed Gartenstein-Ross and Kyle Dabruzzi, *The Weekly Standard,* June 7, 2007

    The authors discuss some of the details of a recent terror plot targeting New York's John F. Kennedy airport. They argue that evidence from the plot may indicate a potential change in terrorists' *modus operandi.*   96

19. **Casting a Wider Net,** Allan Lengel and Joby Warrick, *The Washington Post National Weekly Edition,* October 2–8, 2006

    The Federal Bureau of Investigation has expanded its pool of potential suspects in the anthrax attacks immediately after 9/11. New information about the quality of the anthrax has caused the FBI to cast a "wider net" in its efforts to determine who may be responsible for these attacks.   98

20. **Speaking for the Animals, or the Terrorists?,** Scott Smallwood, *The Chronicle of Higher Education,* August 5, 2005

    Smallwood covers the story of Steven Best, an associate professor at the University of Texas-El Paso, who is a spokesperson and advocate for the Animal Liberation Front (ALF). The article questions whether vocal support for a terrorist organization and its objectives constitutes terrorism.   100

21. **José Padilla and the War on Rights,** Jenny S. Martinez, *The Virginia Quarterly Review,* Fall 2004

    Martinez, a counsel for José Padilla, an American citizen detained as an "enemy combatant," describes the legal hurdles Padilla's lawyers have faced while trying to ensure due process. She uses Padilla's case to illustrate how civil liberties have been sacrificed in the name of security.   104

UNIT 6
Terrorism and the Media

Unit Overview   110

22. **A Violent Episode in the Virtual World,** John Gray, *New Statesman,* July 18, 2005

    John Gray shows how media portrayals of terrorist acts can shape reality. Through the media, each terrorist incident becomes a problem of the global community: a problem that must be solved.   112

The concepts in bold italics are developed in the article. For further expansion, please refer to the Topic Guide.

vii

23. **Terror's Server,** David Talbot, *Technology Review,* February 2005

The Internet has become an integral part of terrorist organizations' communications, recruitment, and funding strategies. David Talbot explores the extent to which tighter security and regulation of Web page content could aid the war on terror. **114**

24. **The Globe of Villages,** Feisal Mohamed, *Dissent,* Winter 2007

Feisal Mohamed discusses the role of the Internet in disseminating radical Islamic ideas. He argues that the medium of dissemination is as important as the content of the messages. **119**

25. **Congress and the "YouTube War,"** Michael A. Cohen and Maria Figueroa Küpçü, *World Policy Journal,* Winter 2006/2007

The rise of stateless enemies and Internet organization heralds a new type of war. Cohen and Küpçü argue that the 110th Congress must implement legislation that addresses this change in warfare. **122**

UNIT 7
Terrorism and Religion

Unit Overview **126**

26. **Qutbism: An Ideology of Islamic-Fascism,** Dale Eikmeier, *Parameters,* Spring 2007

Eikmeier highlights the importance of understanding the enemy's ideology. In his article he describes the basic tenets of Qutbism and ways to defeat it. **128**

27. **The Madrassa Scapegoat,** Peter Bergen and Swati Pandey, *The Washington Quarterly,* Spring 2006

Bergen and Pandey argue that Western countries have falsely attributed the training of terrorists to Islamic schools. A study of the five worst anti-Western terrorist attacks in the past 15 years shows that while many of the terrorists involved were highly educated, only a few had attended religious schools. **134**

28. **Holy Orders,** Mark Juergensmeyer, *Harvard International Review,* Winter 2004

Juergensmeyer argues that religious terrorism is a tool of the powerless in their struggle against the secular state. Religion provides the moral basis for the individual's struggle for identity in the increasingly complex modern world. **138**

UNIT 8
Women and Terrorism

Unit Overview **142**

29. **Female Suicide Bombers: A Global Trend,** Mia Bloom, *Daedalus,* Winter 2007

Bloom examines the motives of women who choose to become suicide bombers. She discusses potential reasons for recruitment of women by terrorist organizations, and concludes that these women are not likely to become "portents of gender equality." **144**

The concepts in bold italics are developed in the article. For further expansion, please refer to the Topic Guide.

viii

30. **Cross-Regional Trends in Female Terrorism,** Karla J. Cunningham, *Studies in Conflict & Terrorism,* 2003

Karla Cunningham examines the roles of female terrorists in various regions around the world, focusing on what motivates women to engage in political violence. Cunningham concludes with a discussion of the future of women in international terrorism. **150**

31. **Explosive Baggage: Female Palestinian Suicide Bombers and the Rhetoric of Emotion,** Terri Toles Patkin, *Women and Language,* Fall 2004

Patkin discusses the role of women in the context of contemporary religious violence. Focusing on women in Palestine, she argues that it is the culture of martyrdom and the lack of opportunity that motivates women to become suicide bombers. **166**

32. **The Bomb Under the Abaya,** Judith Miller, *Policy Review,* June/July 2007

Judith Miller interviews two would-be women suicide bombers in Hasharon prison in Israel. Based on her interviews and a review of the expert literature on the subject, she explores how governments can best respond to this threat. **176**

33. **Picked Last: Women and Terrorism,** Alisa Stack-O'Connor, *Joint Force Quarterly,* Issue 44, 1st Quarter 2007

Alisa Stack-O'Connor examines how and why terrorist organizations use women in their attacks. Focusing on their propaganda value, the obstacles they face, and the tactical advantage they provide, she emphasizes the importance of women to terrorist organizations. **184**

UNIT 9
Government Response

Unit Overview **190**

34. **The Eye of the Storm,** Kevin Whitelaw, *U.S. News & World Report,* November 6, 2006

Whitelaw provides a first look into the day-to-day activities of the National Counterterrorism Center and identifies some of the problems that its staff has encountered. **192**

35. **Port Security Is Still a House of Cards,** Stephen E. Flynn, *Far Eastern Economic Review,* January/February 2006

Stephen Flynn argues that efforts to secure domestic ports and monitor foreign points of origin have not been successful. Flynn highlights three important weaknesses of the maritime security apparatus and offers policy recommendations designed to address these issues. **196**

36. **Are We Ready Yet?,** Christopher Conte, *Outlook,* October 2005

This article discusses efforts by various public health agencies to prepare local communities for bioterrorism. Conte argues that preparations for bioterrorism are drawing resources away from more pressing health crises. **200**

37. **Held Without Trial in the USA,** A.C. Thompson, *The Progressive,* March 2007

Thompson discusses the case of Ali Saleh Kahlah al-Marri, a man accused of collaboration with al-Qaeda. Labeled an "enemy combatant" four years ago, al-Marri was stripped of all legal rights, including the right to trial. **203**

The concepts in bold italics are developed in the article. For further expansion, please refer to the Topic Guide.

UNIT 10
Future Threats

Unit Overview   **206**

38. **From the War on Terror to Global Counterinsurgency,** Bruce Hoffman, *Current History,* December 2006

    Hoffman describes a shift in Al Qaeda's operations. He argues that the U.S. Government must "adjust and adapt its strategy, resources and tactics to counter the threat."

39. **The Terrorism to Come,** Walter Laqueur, *Policy Review,* August/September 2004

    Walter Laqueur provides a broad overview of the world of terrorism, focusing on potential challenges that we will face in the 21st century.   **214**

Test-Your-Knowledge Form   **222**
Article Rating Form   **223**

The concepts in bold italics are developed in the article. For further expansion, please refer to the Topic Guide.

Topic Guide

This topic guide suggests how the selections in this book relate to the subjects covered in your course. You may want to use the topics listed on these pages to search the Web more easily.

On the following pages a number of Web sites have been gathered specifically for this book. They are arranged to reflect the units of this *Annual Edition*. You can link to these sites by going to the student online support site at *http://www.mhcls.com/online/*.

ALL THE ARTICLES THAT RELATE TO EACH TOPIC ARE LISTED BELOW THE BOLD-FACED TERM.

Africa
30. Cross-Regional Trends in Female Terrorism

Al Qaeda
37. Held Without Trial in the USA
38. From the War on Terror to Global Counterinsurgency

Asia
12. Wounded But Still Dangerous
15. End of Terrorism?

Biological terrorism
16. Homegrown Terror
19. Casting a Wider Net
36. Are We Ready Yet?

Civil rights and civil liberties
17. Green Rage
23. Terror's Server
37. Held Without Trial in the USA

Counterterrorism
11. Colombia and the United States: From Counternarcotics to Counterterrorism
34. The Eye of the Storm
35. Port Security Is Still a House of Cards
36. Are We Ready Yet?

Culture
24. The Globe of Villages
27. The Madrassa Scapegoat
33. Picked Last: Women and Terrorism

Cyberterrorism
23. Terror's Server
24. The Globe of Villages

Domestic terrorism
16. Homegrown Terror
17. Green Rage
18. Echoes of the Future
19. Casting a Wider Net
20. Speaking for the Animals, or the Terrorists?
21. José Padilla and the War on Rights

Europe
15. End of Terrorism?
39. The Terrorism to Come

Funding
5. Paying for Terror
9. Guerrilla Nation

Future threats
38. From the War on Terror to Global Counterinsurgency
39. The Terrorism to Come

Government response to terrorism
21. José Padilla and the War on Rights
25. Congress and the "YouTube War"
32. The Bomb Under the Abaya
34. The Eye of the Storm
35. Port Security Is Still a House of Cards
36. Are We Ready Yet?
37. Held Without Trial in the USA

History of terrorism
3. The Origins of the New Terrorism
8. Hizballah and Syria
33. Picked Last: Women and Terrorism

International terrorism
11. Colombia and the United States: From Counternarcotics to Counterterrorism
12. Wounded But Still Dangerous
13. Peace at Last?
14. Root Causes of Chechen Terror
15. End of Terrorism?
27. The Madrassa Scapegoat

Jihad
12. Wounded But Still Dangerous

Latin America
9. Guerrilla Nation
11. Colombia and the United States: From Counternarcotics to Counterterrorism
33. Picked Last: Women and Terrorism

Law and terrorism
3. The Origins of the New Terrorism
16. Homegrown Terror
17. Green Rage
21. José Padilla and the War on Rights
25. Congress and the "YouTube War"
37. Held Without Trial in the USA

Media and terrorism
22. A Violent Episode in the Virtual World
23. Terror's Server
24. The Globe of Villages
25. Congress and the "YouTube War"

Middle East
6. Toy Soldiers
7. Iran's Suicide Brigades
10. The Growing Syrian Missile Threat: Syria after Lebanon
26. Qutbism: An Ideology of Islamic-Fascism
27. The Madrassa Scapegoat
31. Explosive Baggage: Female Palestinian Suicide Bombers and the Rhetoric of Emotion

Osama bin Laden
26. Qutbism: An Ideology of Islamic-Fascism

Psychology of terrorism
- 6. Toy Soldiers
- 29. Female Suicide Bombers: A Global Trend
- 31. Explosive Baggage: Female Palestinian Suicide Bombers and the Rhetoric of Emotion
- 32. The Bomb Under the Abaya

Religious extremism
- 7. Iran's Suicide Brigades
- 26. Qutbism: An Ideology of Islamic-Fascism
- 27. The Madrassa Scapegoat
- 28. Holy Orders: Religious Opposition to Modern States

State-sponsored terrorism
- 7. Iran's Suicide Brigades
- 8. Hizballah and Syria
- 9. Guerrilla Nation

Technology
- 3. The Origins of the New Terrorism
- 10. The Growing Syrian Missile Threat: Syria after Lebanon
- 23. Terror's Server
- 34. The Eye of the Storm
- 36. Are We Ready Yet?

Terrorism, defined
- 1. Ghosts of Our Past
- 2. An Essay on Terrorism

- 3. The Origins of the New Terrorism
- 4. The Myth of the Invincible Terrorist

Terrorist tactics
- 5. Paying for Terror
- 6. Toy Soldiers
- 12. Wounded But Still Dangerous
- 18. Echoes of the Future
- 29. Female Suicide Bombers: A Global Trend

War on Terrorism
- 4. The Myth of the Invincible Terrorist
- 22. A Violent Episode in the Virtual World
- 23. Terror's Server
- 39. The Terrorism to Come

Weapons of mass disruption
- 19. Casting a Wider Net
- 35. Port Security Is Still a House of Cards
- 36. Are We Ready Yet?

Women and terrorism
- 29. Female Suicide Bombers: A Global Trend
- 31. Explosive Baggage: Female Palestinian Suicide Bombers and the Rhetoric of Emotion
- 32. The Bomb Under the Abaya
- 33. Picked Last: Women and Terrorism

Internet References

The following Internet sites have been carefully researched and selected to support the articles found in this reader. The easiest way to access these selected sites is to go to our student online support site at *http://www.mhcls.com/online/*.

AE: Violence and Terrorism 08/09

The following sites were available at the time of publication. Visit our Web site—we update our student online support site regularly to reflect any changes.

General Sources

DefenseLINK (U.S. government)
http://www.defenselink.mil

The Department of Defense's public affairs online service provides DoD news releases and other public affairs documents. This is a gateway to other DoD agencies (i.e., Secretary of Defense, Army, Navy, Air Force, Marine Corps).

International Network Information Center at University of Texas
http://inic.utexas.edu

This gateway has many pointers to international sites, organized into African, Asian, Latin American, Middle East, Russian, and East European subsections.

U.S. Central Intelligence Agency Home Page
http://www.cia.gov

This site includes publications of the CIA, such as the *1996 World Fact Book; 1995 Fact Book on Intelligence; Handbook of International Economic Statistics, 1996;* and *CIA Maps.*

U.S. White House
http://www.whitehouse.gov

This official Web page for the White House includes information on the President and Vice President and what's new. See especially The Virtual Library and Briefing Room (today's releases) for hot topics and latest federal statistics.

UNIT 1: The Concept of Terrorism

MIPT Terrorism Knowledge Base
http://www.tkb.org/Home.jsp

Developed by the National Memorial Institute for the Prevention of Terrorism (MIPT), the Terrorism Knowledge Base offers in-depth information of terrorist incidents, groups, and trials.

Political Science Resources/International Relations
http://www.lib.umich.edu/govdocs/psintl.html

The Documents Center of the University of Michigan contains material relation to violence and terrorism under several headings, including Peace and Conflict and Human Rights. This site includes simulations.

Terrorism: Background and Threat Assessment Links
http://www.fas.org/irp/threat/terror.htm

This site provides documents covering a broad range of topics on Terrorism.

The Terrorism Research Center
http://www.terrorism.com

The Terrorism Research Center is dedicated to informing the public of the phenomena of terrorism and information warfare. This site features essays and thought pieces on current issues, as well as links to other terrorism documents, research, and resources. Navigate the site by clicking on the area of interest.

UNODC—Terrorism Definitions
http://www.unodc.org/unodc/terrorism_definitions.html

The lack of agreement on a definition of terrorism has been a major obstacle to meaningful international countermeasures. Cynics have often commented that one state's "terrorist" is another state's "freedom fighter." This site provides the consensus on the definition of "terrorism" by the United Nations Council.

UNIT 2: Tactics of Terrorism

FrontPage Magazine—Ecoterrorism and Us
http://www.frontpagemag.com/Articles/Printable.asp?ID=1277

Columnist Robert Locke examines the motivations behind modern ecoterrorism and signals a warning for possible future terrorist actions.

JCSS Military Resources
http://www.tau.ac.il/jcss/lmas.html

The Jaffe Center for Strategic Studies at Tel-Aviv University lists five different groups of Web site Directories on low-intensity warfare and terrorism.

UNIT 3: State-Sponsored Terrorism

Council for Foreign Relations
http://www.cfr.org/issue/458/state_sponsors_of_terrorism.html

This site provides a regional update on terrorist activities around the world. It provides an overview to a country's/region's ties to terrorism and more.

International Institute for Terrorism and Counterterrorism
http://www.ict.org.il/inter_ter/st_terror/State_t.htm

ICT is unique in that it focuses solely on the subject of counterterrorism. All of its efforts and resources are dedicated to approaching the issue of terrorism globally—that is, as a strategic problem that faces not Israel but other countries as well.

State Department's List of State Sponsors of Terrorism
http://www.state.gov/s/ct/rls/crt

This site contains the U.S. Department of State's list of State Sponsors of Terrorism.

www.mhcls.com/online/

UNIT 4: International Terrorism

Arab.Net Contents
http://www.arab.net/sections/contents.html

Web links to 22 Arab countries ranging from Algeria through Yemen. It includes a search engine.

International Association for Counterterrorism and Security Professionals
http://www.iacsp.com/index.html

The International Association for Counterterrorism and Security Professionals was founded in 1992 to meet security challenges facing the world as it enters an era of globalization in the twenty-first century. The Web site includes a detailed overview of state-sponsored terrorism.

The International Policy Institute for Counter-Terrorism
http://www.ict.org.il

ICT is a research institute and think tank dedicated to developing innovative public policy solutions to international terrorism. The Policy Institute applies an integrated, solutions-oriented approach built on a foundation of real-world and practical experience.

International Rescue Committee
http://www.intrescom.org

Committed to human dignity, the IRC goes to work in the aftermath of state violence to help people all over the world. Click on Resettlement Problems, IRC Fact Sheet, Emergency Preparedness and Response, and links to other sites.

United Nations Website on Terrorism
http://www.un.org/terrorism

This site gives information on what the United Nations is doing to counter terrorism.

United States Institute of Peace
http://www.usip.org/library/topics/terrorism.html

This site contains links by topical categories to resources primarily in English providing information on terrorism/counter-terrorism.

UNIT 5: Terrorism in America

America's War Against Terrorism
http://www.lib.umich.edu/govdocs/usterror.html

This Web site by the University of Michigan provides a news chronicle of the September 11, 2001 attacks and the war against terrorism.

Department of Homeland Security
http://www.dhs.gov/dhspublic/index.jsp

The home page for the Department of Homeland Security includes up-to-date news and information.

FBI Homepage
http://www.fbi.gov

The home page for the Federal Bureau of Investigation includes up-to-date news and information and a section on terrorism.

ISN International Relations and Security Network
http://www.isn.ethz.ch

This is a one-stop information network for security and defense studies.

The Militia Watchdog
http://www.adl.org/mwd.m1.asp

This page is devoted to monitoring U.S. right-wing extremism, including abortion clinic bombings and neo-Nazi militias.

The Hate Directory
http://www.bcpl.lib.md.us/~rfrankli/hatedir.htm

This site has a list of hate groups on the Web, groups that advocate violence against, separation from, defamation of, deception about, or hostility toward others based on race, religion, ethnicity, gender, or sexual orientation.

UNIT 6: Terrorism and the Media

Institute for Media, Peace and Security
http://www.mediapeace.org

This Web page from the University for Peace is dedicated to examining interactions between media, conflict, peace, and security.

Terrorism Files
http://www.terrorismfiles.org

This is an up-to-date Web source for news and editorials covering terrorism and current events.

The Middle East Media Research Institute
http://www.memri.org

The Middle East Media Research Institute (MEMRI) explores the Middle East through the region's media. MEMRI bridges the language gap, which exists between the West and the Middle East, providing timely translations of Arabic, Persian, and Turkish media, as well as original analysis of political, ideological, intellectual, social, cultural, and religious trends in the Middle East.

UNIT 7: Terrorism and Religion

FACSNET: "Understanding Faith and Terrorism"
http://www.facsnet.org/issues/faith/terrorism.php3#

This site is guided by the most current research from the nation's top institutions. FACS translates their knowledge and tailors it specifically for the educational needs of journalists.

Islam Denounces Terrorism
http://www.islamdenouncesterrorism.com

This Web site was launched to reveal that Islam does not endorse any kind of terror or barbarism and that Muslims share the sorrows of the victims of terrorism. It includes many references to the Koran that preaches tolerance and peace.

Religious Tolerance Organization
http://www.religioustolerance.org/curr_war.htm

This site provides some insight on civil unrest and warfare caused by religious belief.

SITE Institute
http://www.siteinstitute.org/

SITE provides interested parties with well-documented and comprehensive reports on terrorist entities and the individuals and organizations supporting them.

www.mhcls.com/online/

UNIT 8: Women and Terrorism

Free Muslims Against Terrorism Jihad
http://www.freemuslims.org/news/articles.php?article-140

This site provides information and links such as Press Corner; Resources; and a Blog on the Muslim community.

Foreign Policy Association—Terrorism
http://www.fpa.org/newsletter_info2478/newsletter_info.htm

This page is a comprehensive source of information about terrorism and a gateway to the vast amount of information on the subject.

Israel Ministry of Foreign Affairs—The Exploitation of Palestinian Women for Terrorism
http://www.mfa.gov.il/mfa/go.asp?MFA0//10

This official Web site of the Israeli government chronicles the use of women by Arab terrorists as agents of terror.

Women, Militarism, and Violence
http://www.iwpr.org/pdf/terorrism.pdf

Dr. Amy Caiazza's paper, "Why Gender Matters in Understanding September 11: Women, Militarism, and Violence," analyzes women's roles as victims, supporters, and opponents of violence, terrorism, and militarism and proposes policy recommendations.

UNIT 9: Government Response

Counter-Terrorism Page
http://counterterrorism.com

This site contains a summary of worldwide terrorism events, terrorist groups, and terrorism strategies and tactics, including articles from 1989 to the present of American and international origin, plus links to related Web sites, pictures, and histories of terrorist leaders.

ReliefWeb
http://www.reliefweb.int

This is the UN's Department of Humanitarian Affairs clearinghouse for international humanitarian emergencies. It has daily updates.

The South Asian Terrorism Portal
http://www.satp.org/

This site provides the current happenings of the intelligence community in South Asia.

UNIT 10: Future Threats

Centers for Disease Control and Prevention—Bioterrorism
http://www.bt.cdc.gov

The CDC Web site provides news, information, guidance, and facts regarding biochemical agents and threats.

Nuclear Terrorism
http://www.nci.org/nci/nci.nt.htm

The Nuclear Control Institute's Web site includes a Quick Index to articles on nuclear terrorism and a bibliography.

We highly recommend that you review our Web site for expanded information and our other product lines. We are continually updating and adding links to our Web site in order to offer you the most usable and useful information that will support and expand the value of your Annual Editions. You can reach us at: *http://www.mhcls.com/annualeditions/*.

UNIT 1

The Concept of Terrorism

Unit Selections

1. **Ghosts of Our Past,** Karen Armstrong
2. **An Essay on Terrorism,** Marc Nicholson
3. **The Origins of the New Terrorism,** Matthew J. Morgan
4. **The Myth of the Invincible Terrorist,** Christopher C. Harmon

Key Points to Consider

- Why is developing a common definition of terrorism so difficult?
- Do terrorists' means justify their ends?
- What are the components of the "new terrorism"?
- Can terrorist organizations be defeated?

Student Web Site
www.mhcls.com/online

Internet References
Further information regarding these Web sites may be found in this book's preface or online.

MIPT Terrorism Knowledge Base
  http://www.tkb.org/Home.jsp
Political Science Resources/International Relations
  http://www.lib.umich.edu/govdocs/psintl.html
Terrorism: Background and Threat Assessment Links
  http://www.fas.org/irp/threat/terror.htm
The Terrorism Research Center
  http://www.terrorism.com
UNODC—Terrorism Definitions
  http://www.unodc.org/unodc/terrorism_definitions.html

US Navy photo

Defining and conceptualizing terrorism is an essential first step in understanding it. Despite volumes of literature on the subject, there is still no commonly agreed upon definition of terrorism. The application of former Supreme Court Justice Potter Steward's famous maxim, "I know it when I see it," has led to definitional anarchy. The U.S. government, in its efforts to fight a Global War on Terrorism, has further confounded the definitional problem by a myriad of confusing statements and policies.

Terrorists have also exacerbated this problem. They often portray themselves as victims of political, economic, social, religious, or psychological oppression. By virtue of their courage, their convictions, or their condition, terrorists see themselves as the chosen few, representing a larger population, in the struggle against the perceived oppressors. The actions of the oppressor, real or imagined, against the population they claim to represent, serve as motivation and moral justification for their use of violence. Existing institutional mechanisms for change are deemed either illegitimate or are in the hands of the oppressors. Hence, the terrorists portray themselves as freedom-fighters, as violence becomes the primary means of asserting their interests and the interests of the people they claim to represent.

While arguments among academics and policymakers about how terrorism should be defined continue, most would agree that terrorism involves three basic components: the perpetrator, the victim, and the target of the violence. The perpetrator commits violence against the victim. The victim is used to communicate with or send a message to the intended target. The target is expected to respond to perpetrator. Fear is used as a catalyst to enhance the communication and elicit the desired response.

Defining the problem is an essential first step in the accumulation of statistical data. Definitions impact not only the collection and collation of data, but also their analysis and interpretation. Ultimately, definitions have a profound effect on threat perceptions and policies developed to counter terrorist activities.

The articles in this section provide some insights into terrorists' motivations and the potential causes of violence. The first article introduces the reader to the role the past plays in the present geopolitical situation. Article two explores the potential causes of violence and provides a broad overview of terrorism and political violence. Article three by Matthew Morgan examines what has been described by some as the "new terrorism." Morgan argues that cultural political and technological factors have influenced the development of terrorism. In the last article of this section, Christopher Harmon addresses some of the myths about terrorism.

Ghosts of Our Past

To win the war on terrorism, we first need to understand its roots.

KAREN ARMSTRONG

About a hundred years ago, almost every leading Muslim intellectual was in love with the West, which at that time meant Europe. America was still an unknown quantity. Politicians and journalists in India, Egypt, and Iran wanted their countries to be just like Britain or France; philosophers, poets, and even some of the *ulama* (religious scholars) tried to find ways of reforming Islam according to the democratic model of the West. They called for a nation state, for representational government, for the disestablishment of religion, and for constitutional rights. Some even claimed that the Europeans were better Muslims than their own fellow countrymen since the Koran teaches that the resources of a society must be shared as fairly as possible, and in the European nations there was beginning to be a more equitable sharing of wealth.

So what happened in the intervening years to transform all of that admiration and respect into the hatred that incited the acts of terror that we witnessed on September 11? It is not only terrorists who feel this anger and resentment, although they do so to an extreme degree. Throughout the Muslim world there is widespread bitterness against America, even among pragmatic and well-educated businessmen and professionals, who may sincerely deplore the recent atrocities, condemn them as evil, and feel sympathy with the victims, but who still resent the way the Western powers have behaved in their countries. This atmosphere is highly conducive to extremism, especially now that potential terrorists have seen the catastrophe that it is possible to inflict using only the simplest of weapons.

Even if President Bush and our allies succeed in eliminating Osama bin Laden and his network, hundreds more terrorists will rise up to take their place unless we in the West address the root cause of this hatred. This task must be an essential part of the war against terrorism.

We cannot understand the present crisis without taking into account the painful process of modernization. In the 16th century, the countries of Western Europe and, later, the American colonies embarked on what historians have called "the Great Western Transformation." Until then, all the great societies were based upon a surplus of agriculture and so were economically vulnerable; they soon found that they had grown beyond their limited resources. The new Western societies, though, were based upon technology and the constant reinvestment of capital. They found that they could reproduce their resources indefinitely, and so could afford to experiment with new ideas and products. In Western cultures today, when a new kind of computer is invented, all the old office equipment is thrown out. In the old agrarian societies, any project that required such frequent change of the basic infrastructure was likely to be shelved. Originality was not encouraged; instead people had to concentrate on preserving what had been achieved.

So while the Great Western Transformation was exciting and gave the people of the West more freedom, it demanded fundamental change at every level: social, political, intellectual, and religious. Not surprisingly, the period of transition was traumatic and violent. As the early modern states became more centralized and efficient, draconian measures were often required to weld hitherto disparate kingdoms together. Some minority groups, such as the Catholics in England and the Jews in Spain, were persecuted or deported. There were acts of genocide, terrible wars of religion, the exploitation of workers in factories, the despoliation of the countryside, and anomie and spiritual malaise in the newly industrialized mega-cities.

Successful modern societies found, by trial and error, that they had to be democratic. The reasons were many. In order to preserve the momentum of the continually expanding economy, more people had to be involved—even in a humble capacity as printers, clerks, or factory workers. To do these jobs, they needed to be educated, and once they became educated, they began to demand political rights. In order to draw upon all of a society's resources, modern countries also found they had to bring outgroups, such as the Jews and women, into the mainstream. Countries like those in Eastern Europe that did not become secular, tolerant, and democratic fell behind. But those that did fulfill these norms, including Britain and France, became so powerful that no agrarian, traditional society, such as those of the Islamic countries, could stand against them.

In the West, we have completed the modernizing process and have forgotten what we had to go through. We view the Islamic countries as inherently backward and do not realize we're seeing imperfectly modernized societies.

Today we are witnessing similar upheaval in developing countries, including those in the Islamic world, that are making their own painful journey to modernity. In the Middle East, we see constant political turmoil. There have been revolutions, such as the 1952 coup of the Free Officers in Egypt and the Islamic Revolution in Iran in 1979. Autocratic rulers predominate in this region because the modernizing process is not yet sufficiently advanced to provide the conditions for a fully developed democracy.

In the West, we have completed the modernizing process and have forgotten what we had to go through, so we do not always understand the difficulty of this transition. We tend to imagine that we have always been in the van of progress, and we see the Islamic countries as inherently backward. We have imagined that they are held back by their religion, and do not realize that what we are actually seeing is an imperfectly modernized society.

The Muslim world has had an especially problematic experience with modernity because its people have had to modernize so rapidly, in 50 years instead of the 300 years that it took the Western world. Nevertheless, this in itself would not have been an insuperable obstacle. Japan, for example, has created its own highly successful version of modernity. But Japan had one huge advantage over most of the Islamic countries: It had never been colonized. In the Muslim world, modernity did not bring freedom and independence; it came in a context of political subjection.

Modern society is of its very nature progressive, and by the 19th century the new economies of Western Europe needed a constantly expanding market for the goods that funded their cultural enterprises. Once the home countries were saturated, new markets were sought abroad. In 1798, Napoleon defeated the Mamelukes, Egypt's military rulers, in the Battle of the Pyramids near Cairo. Between 1830 and 1915, the European powers also occupied Algeria, Aden, Tunisia, the Sudan, Libya, and Morocco—all Muslim countries. These new colonies provided raw materials for export, which were fed into European industry. In return, they received cheap manufactured goods, which naturally destroyed local industry.

This new impotence was extremely disturbing for the Muslim countries. Until this point, Islam had been a religion of success. Within a hundred years of the death of the Prophet Muhammad in 632, the Muslims ruled an empire that stretched from the Himalayas to the Pyrenees. By the 15th century, Islam was the greatest world power—not dissimilar to the United States today. When Europeans began to explore the rest of the globe at the beginning of the Great Western Transformation, they found an Islamic presence almost everywhere they went: in the Middle East, India, Persia, Southeast Asia, China, and Japan. In the 16th century, when Europe was in the early stages of its rise to power, the Ottoman Empire [which ruled Turkey, the Middle East, and North Africa] was probably the most powerful state in the world. But once the great powers of Europe had reformed their military, economic, and political structures according to the modern norm, the Islamic countries could put up no effective resistance.

Muslims would not be human if they did not resent being subjugated this way. The colonial powers treated the natives with contempt, and it was not long before Muslims discovered that their new rulers despised their religious traditions. True, the Europeans brought many improvements to their colonies, such as modern medicine, education, and technology, but these were sometimes a mixed blessing.

Thus, the Suez Canal, initiated by the French consul Ferdinand de Lesseps, was a disaster for Egypt, which had to provide all the money, labor, and materials as well as donate 200 square miles of Egyptian territory gratis, and yet the shares of the Canal Company were all held by Europeans. The immense outlay helped to bankrupt Egypt, and this gave Britain a pretext to set up a military occupation there in 1882.

Railways were installed in the colonies, but they rarely benefited the local people. Instead they were designed to further the colonialists' own projects. And the missionary schools often taught the children to despise their own culture, with the result that many felt they belonged neither to the West nor to the Islamic world. One of the most scarring effects of colonialism is the rift that still exists between those who have had a Western education and those who have not and remain perforce stuck in the premodern ethos. To this day, the Westernized elites of these countries and the more traditional classes simply cannot understand one another.

After World War II, Britain and France became secondary powers and the United States became the leader of the Western world. Even though the Islamic countries were no longer colonies but were nominally independent, America still controlled their destinies. During the Cold War, the United States sought allies in the region by supporting unsavory governments and unpopular leaders, largely to protect its oil interests. For example, in 1953, after Shah Muhammad Reza Pahlavi had been deposed and forced to leave Iran, he was put back on the throne in a coup engineered by British Intelligence and the CIA. The United States continued to support the Shah, even though he denied Iranians human rights that most Americans take for granted.

Fundamentalists are convinced that modern, secular society is trying to wipe out the true faith and religious values. When people feel that they are fighting for their very survival, they often lash out violently.

Saddam Hussein, who became the president of Iraq in 1979, was also a protégé of the United States, which literally allowed him to get away with murder, most notably the chemical attack against the Kurdish population. It was only after the invasion in 1990 of Kuwait, a critical oil-producing state, that Hussein incurred the enmity of America and its allies. Many Muslims resent the way America has continued to support unpopular rulers, such as President Hosni Mubarak of Egypt and the Saudi royal family. Indeed, Osama bin Laden was himself a protégé of the West, which was happy to support and fund his fighters in the struggle for Afghanistan against Soviet Russia. Too often, the Western powers have not considered the long-term consequences of their actions. After the Soviets had pulled out of Afghanistan, for example, no help was forthcoming for the devastated country, whose ensuing chaos made it possible for the Taliban to come to power.

When the United States supports autocratic rulers, its proud assertion of democratic values has at best a hollow ring. What America seemed to be saying to Muslims was: "Yes, we have freedom and democracy, but you have to live under tyrannical governments." The creation of the state of Israel, the chief ally of the United States in the Middle East, has become a symbol of Muslim impotence before the Western powers, which seemed to feel no qualm about the hundreds of thousands of Palestinians who lost their homeland and either went into exile or lived under Israeli occupation. Rightly or wrongly, America's strong support for Israel is seen as proof that as far as the United States is concerned, Muslims are of no importance.

In their frustration, many have turned to Islam. The secularist and nationalist ideologies, which many Muslims had imported from the West, seemed to have failed them, and by the late 1960s Muslims throughout the Islamic world had begun to develop what we call fundamentalist movements.

Fundamentalism is a complex phenomenon and is by no means confined to the Islamic world. During the 20th century, most major religions developed this type of militant piety. Fundamentalism represents a rebellion against the secularist ethos of modernity. Wherever a Western-style society has established itself, a fundamentalist movement has developed alongside it. Fundamentalism is, therefore, a part of the modern scene. Although fundamentalists often claim that they are returning to a golden age of the past, these movements could have taken root in no time other than our own.

Fundamentalists believe that they are under threat. Every fundamentalist movement—in Judaism, Christianity, and Islam—is convinced that modern, secular society is trying to wipe out the true faith and religious values. Fundamentalists believe that they are fighting for survival, and when people feel their backs are to the wall, they often lash out violently. This is especially the case when there is conflict in the region.

The vast majority of fundamentalists do not take part in acts of violence, of course. But those who do utterly distort the faith that they purport to defend. In their fear and anxiety about the encroachments of the secular world, fundamentalists—be they Jewish, Christian, or Muslim—tend to downplay the compassionate teachings of their scripture and overemphasize the more belligerent passages. In so doing, they often fall into moral nihilism, as is the case of the suicide bomber or hijacker. To kill even one person in the name of God is blasphemy; to massacre thousands of innocent men, women, and children is an obscene perversion of religion itself.

Osama bin Laden subscribes roughly to the fundamentalist vision of the Egyptian ideologue Sayyid Qutb, who was executed by President Nasser in 1966. Qutb developed his militant ideology in the concentration camps in which he, and thousands of other members of the Muslim Brotherhood, were imprisoned by Nasser. After 15 years of torture in these prisons, Qutb became convinced that secularism was a great evil and that it was a Muslim's first duty to overthrow rulers such as Nasser, who paid only lip service to Islam.

Bin Laden's first target was the government of Saudi Arabia; he has also vowed to overthrow the secularist governments of Egypt and Jordan and the Shiite Republic of Iran. Fundamentalism, in every faith, always begins as an intra-religious movement; it is directed at first against one's own countrymen or co-religionists. Only at a later stage do fundamentalists take on a foreign enemy, whom they feel to lie behind the ills of their own people. Thus in 1998 bin Laden issued his fatwa against the United States. But bin Laden holds no official position in the Islamic world; he simply is not entitled to issue such a fatwa, and has, like other fundamentalists, completely distorted the essential teachings of his faith.

The Koran insists that the only just war is one of self-defense, but the terrorists would claim that it is America which is the aggressor. They would point out that during the past year, hundreds of Palestinians have died in the conflict with Israel, America's ally; that Britain and America are still bombing Iraq; and that thousands of Iraqi civilians, many of them children, have died as a result of the American-led sanctions.

None of this, of course, excuses the September atrocities. These were evil actions, and it is essential that all those implicated in any way be brought to justice. But what can we do to prevent a repetition of this tragedy? As the towers of the World Trade Center crumbled, our world changed forever, and that means that we can never see things in the same way again. These events were an "apocalypse," a "revelation"—words that literally mean an "unveiling." They laid bare a reality that we had not seen clearly before. Part of that reality was Muslim rage, but the catastrophe showed us something else as well.

In Britain, until September 11, the main news story was the problem of asylum seekers. Every night, more than 90 refugees from the developing world make desperate attempts to get into Britain. There is now a strong armed presence in England's ports. The United States and other Western countries also have a problem with illegal immigrants. It is almost as though we in the First World have been trying to keep the "other" world at bay. But as the September Apocalypse showed, if we try to ignore the plight of that other world, it will come to us in devastating ways.

So we in the First World must develop a "one world" mentality in the coming years. Americans have often assumed that they were protected by the great oceans surrounding the United States. As a result, they have not always been very well-informed about other parts of the globe. But the September Apocalypse and the events that followed have shown that this isolation has come to an end, and revealed America's terrifying vulnerability. This is deeply frightening, and it will have a profound effect upon the American psyche. But this tragedy could be turned to good, if we in the First World cultivate a new sympathy with other peoples who have experienced a similar helplessness: in Rwanda, in Lebanon, or in Srebrenica.

We cannot leave the fight against terrorism solely to our politicians or to our armies. In Europe and America, ordinary citizens must find out more about the rest of the world. We must make ourselves understand, at a deep level, that it is not only Muslims who resent America and the West; that many people in non-Muslim countries, while not condoning these atrocities, may be dry-eyed about the collapse of those giant towers, which represented a power, wealth, and security to which they could never hope to aspire.

We must find out about foreign ideologies and other religions like Islam. And we must also acquire a full knowledge of our own governments' foreign policies, using our democratic rights to oppose them, should we deem this to be necessary. We have been warned that the war against terror may take years, and so will the development of this "one world" mentality, which could do as much, if not more, than our fighter planes to create a safer and more just world.

KAREN ARMSTRONG is the author of *The Battle for God: A History of Fundamentalism* and *Islam: A Brief History*.

From *AARP Modern Maturity*, January/February 2002, pp. 44–47, 66. Copyright © 2002 by Karen Armstrong. Reprinted by permission of Felicity Bryan Literary Agency.

An Essay on Terrorism

Terrorist movements have rarely, if ever, succeeded militarily; when they succeeded, it was by bringing a superior power to the bargaining table....

MARC E. NICHOLSON

We reflexively condemn terrorism after each new outrage—in Northern Ireland, Israel, Indonesia, and elsewhere—without a real attempt to understand and dissect it. Dissection is clinical, stripped of emotion, and does not imply approval: I emphasize the point lest any be tempted to view this essay as an apologia. It is not. It is an attempt to examine how some terrorists pursue a political goal beyond pure malice; why their tactics, if bloody, may be the most effective path open to them and have worked on occasion; how the familiar Western distinction between civilian and military combatants is ethically questionable in the modern age; and how, above all, we must distinguish in the future between movements we may be able to address by negotiation and those which we must annihilate.

Do terrorists' means justify their ends? That is a moral question with an answer that differs little in practical context from the decision by a national state to wage war. Such a state decision entails the unintended but wholly predictable consequence of the deaths by "collateral damage" of many civilians, as well as the equally predictable demise of enemy and friendly soldiers who are no less human than the civilian targets of terrorism.

It is a moral fiction to draw a sharp distinction between resort to force by states and employment of force by subnational, including terrorist, groups. Both cases bring death and entail the use of violence. The chief distinction is a surface legitimacy to the state premised on little more than its greater longevity and organized control of territory. Thus these varied actors—state and non-state—are better judged and distinguished ultimately by the morality of their ends, not by their a priori "status." If it were otherwise, would not the insurgents of the American Revolution have been damned in their time?

A separate but closely related issue: the stress on the distinction between human beings called soldiers (the first casualties of warring states) and civilians (the frequent first casualties of terrorist groups) is to deem the former as dispensable cannon fodder while asserting Marques of Queensbury rules protecting the latter. That violates modern morals. All lives are precious, and the fact that soldiers in theory "accept the risk" of the job is no dispensation for their lives. In a modern democratic state, soldiers can be categorized as civilians, not a separate caste. The civilian electorates who govern the state more than soldiers are responsible for the decisions of the government they elect, for its application of armed force, and thus for the negative consequences, and thus also for the fact that they are the logical targets of pressure for change.

This, of course, raises the question of means vs. ends and is at the core of the conventional moral critique of terrorism; indeed, terrorism's means define it. To the extent a consensus definition of terrorism exists, it may be described as the deliberate killing of non-military personnel in order to pursue a claimed political goal through exertion of pressure on a society. The literature is rife with other definitions, but their core comes down to this: murderous attacks on civilians for political purposes.

Terrorists who lash out from hatred but without concrete and achievable political goals, including those whose political goals are so sweeping as to be delusional—such as Al-Qaeda members "acting out" the multiple failures of Middle Eastern societies—are practically, if not philosophically, nihilists with nowhere to go. Their acts are pointless. They are a psychotic, not a political, phenomenon and the only reasonable answer is the use of force to kill or incarcerate them, while seeking in the longer term to address the social pathologies which produce new recruits.

But there are other "terrorist" movements now and in history with genuinely political aims, which resorted to violent tactics because the latter were the most effective available. The anti-colonial struggles of the 1950s and '60s that gave birth to numerous new nations in some instances relied in part on terrorism.

The "grand daddy" of such groups was none other than the Irgun faction of the Zionist movement in Israel, which engaged in bombings and assassinations (including of a senior UN official) to press the end of British occupation. The Irgun was far from the decisive factor in achieving Israeli independence, and was opposed by many in the Zionist movement, but it made a contribution and that contribution to independence eventually absolved its leader of his past and he went on to become prime minister of Israel, Menachem Begin.

The pattern is familiar. Terrorist movements have rarely, if ever, succeeded militarily; when they succeeded, it was by bringing a superior power to the bargaining table; and if the movement's leaders were ultimately successful and judged to be on the right side of history, they were cleansed of their past.

Who resorts to terrorism and why? Terrorism is the tool of the weak, used by disaffected groups or minorities to oppose the rule and (as they see it) the oppression of an established and militarily superior power. Because it is resistance on the cheap, terrorism often emerges out of civil society rather than state sponsorship, because oppressed civilian groups, lacking control over governmental machinery, can summon little or no regular military force able to confront their "oppressor" in conventional military terms.

Thus they resort to "hit and run" or even suicidal attacks, and may choose soft non-military targets to pressure the government they seek to influence. Whatever the morality of slaughtering innocents, this strategy can make sense in military/political terms: why fail in frontal armed assault against a far superior state-sponsored military apparatus? The goal instead is to so upset the civilian economic and social life of an adversary state as to force negotiations on more equal terms.

The specific methods of a given terrorist group depend on the nature of the regime it opposes. In democracies (e.g., the conflict in Northern Ireland), terrorists seek to wear down the voting majority until it is so sick of strife and uncertainty as to consent to a political solution by meeting the minority's demands in part or in whole. (Of course, there is always the possibility of backlash, as is evident in the case of Israel, where terrorism against the body politic successfully put the PLO on the map but more recently proved self-defeating by feeding Israeli doubt that Palestinians could ever be appeased short of the destruction of the Israeli state.)

In autocratic states (e.g., Egypt), which are less subject to public opinion and relatively indifferent to civilian casualties, terrorist groups seek more to disrupt national economies—in particular by scaring off foreign tourism and investment—to the point where governments are goaded to concessions because the damage to the nation's economic life threatens the (corrupt) elites' ability to sustain their rule.

While autocratic states may eventually crack under such strains, democratic governments are more immediately susceptible to terrorism, at least if the "cause" is plausible, because terrorism strikes common people who in democracies have influence to prod their governments towards negotiation if the pain becomes too great and the minority's grievances are perceived as not unreasonable, even if their methods are condemnable. Thus, though it seems perverse, one may argue that terrorism in some cases is more justified, or at least more effective, when directed against democratic governments. Terrorist movements in such states typically arise from confrontation between an oppressed minority and a dominant majority (e.g., Northern Ireland; Israel/Palestine).

Civilians guide such a state, the state commands the military, the military applies force, including death, to its opponents. Should the ultimate civilian authors of those consequences be exempt from pressure while their military servants (in fact their fellow citizens) take the brunt of the polity's decisions? The democratic nation in the modern age, certainly since World War I, is a nation in arms. Every citizen has a role in deciding its fate through the vote or by military effort expressed in mass mobilization or industrial support of the war machine. Thus, every citizen must accept the consequences of state policies.

We resist that notion of equal responsibility and we hate the idea of terrorism. Why? Because terrorism seeks to alter the status quo and shake complacent (dominant) populations or elites out of their complacency. It threatens our comfortable and insulated everyday lives ... including the moral barrier we have sought to erect by the increasingly strained distinction between military combatants and the civilians who ultimately direct them in a democratic state. It puts electorates squarely up against the lethal consequences of their own voting decisions.

Or, if you prefer, it acknowledges the civilian electorate as politically influential agents who are targeted by terrorists seeking to influence or blackmail their political decisions. In the democratic West, terrorism is a handmaiden of democracy: everyman has the power, so everyman is now a target. And stoically accepting that fact, accepting our responsibility as citizens without whimpering or whining as potential combatants and agents of resistance is, in my view, required now as an act of patriotism on the part of participants in the modern democratic state. To plead overly the distinction between military combatants and civilian "victims" is an abdication of our responsibility as citizens. In that respect we are coming closer to the model of the ancient Greek city states which gave birth to democracy: our physical safety is more directly bound to the future of our polity than it has been in a long time ... and it should be.

All governments condemn terrorism. But they sometimes give in to it and even later, if sometimes grudgingly, applaud its exponents, provided the latter's underlying cause was just and politically successful: Witness the ANC and Nelson Mandela in South Africa.

There is a life cycle to successful terrorist movements. They begin weak in their actions and condemned by "responsible" authorities. If they represent a serious and widely shared grievance, they may grow stronger, more effective (more lethal), and still more condemned. At some point, that very effectiveness can turn condemnation into reluctant acceptance of them by states as a negotiating partner. They have won a place at the table by the classic means any actor ever has in politics: by demonstrating the capacity to exert force or other influence.

That is a critical moment for such terrorist movements. Can their leadership shift from the role of hunted opponents to the role of accepted statesmen; can they shift from a narrow military/terrorist focus to a broader political vision, which inevitably implies compromise rather than maximalist rhetoric? That in the past has defined the difference between the success or failure of a number of such movements. An example of success: Nelson Mandela in South Africa. An example of failure: Yassir Arafat in Israel/Palestine. The roles of guerrilla leader and visionary statesman call for different qualities in an individual; not all terrorist/guerrilla leaders are personally capable of the transition.

The classic era of terrorists with a nationalist vision appears on the decline, since many of them have realized their goals in the post-World War II period. Increasingly we confront instead violently psychotic millenialist groups which must be extirpated rather than engaged. Nonetheless, some ethnic-based movements will continue to arise, perhaps with terrorist components, seeking in the traditional mode independence or autonomy for more or less narrowly defined populations. It behooves us to recognize the difference between those movements and irreconcilable millenialist groups and, where appropriate, to suspend our moral qualms and adopt our tactics and even negotiate with the former.

We will have enough on our hands as it is in dealing with the "wretched of the earth" in the coming century: given the ever-widening gap between rich and poor, we can expect many more terrorist movements based on pure frustration and psychosis. We will have to put them down insofar as they affect us. So, as a matter of pure economy, it behooves us to recognize where we are dealing instead with genuine political movements, albeit using terrorist means, which may be dealt with more cheaply (if holding our noses) by negotiation.

Born in California in 1950, **MARC E. NICHOLSON** graduated from Yale University, served in the U.S. Army in West Germany, and entered the Foreign Service in 1975. He had tours as a political and political/military officer in Brasilia, Lisbon, Bangkok, and Washington before retiring in 2000 to Washington, DC, where he now lives and works as a part-time consultant.

From *American Diplomacy*, Vol. 8, No. 3, 2003. Copyright © 2003 by American Diplomacy. Reprinted with permission.

Article 3

The Origins of the New Terrorism

MATTHEW J. MORGAN

The suicidal collision of hijacked commercial airliners into the World Trade Center and the Pentagon on 11 September 2001 was the most destructive terrorist attack in world history. Before the deaths of approximately 3,000 people in those attacks, the most devastating single terrorist attack had claimed the lives of about 380 people. The 2001 disaster took place at a time when experts had been defining a new form of terrorism focused on millennial visions of apocalypse and mass casualties. The catastrophic attacks confirmed their fears.

The State Department's *Patterns of Global Terrorism,* published in early 2002, revealed that terrorist attacks have scaled back in number in recent years, even though more casualties have occurred.[1] The late 1980s were a high point for the number of terrorist attacks, with the incidence of attacks exceeding 600 annually in the years 1985–88. With the exception of 1991, the number of terrorist attacks after 1988 decreased to fewer than 450 every year, reaching their recent low point in the years 1996–98, when the number of attacks was about 300. The number of attacks has increased slightly since 1998, when there were 274 attacks, but the level has not reached the number realized in any of the years of the 1980s. This report is not a linear progression from a large number to a small number of attacks, but the trend revealed is one of a decreasing incidence. Yet even if the frequency has decreased, the danger has not.

Osama bin Laden and the al Qaeda network of international terrorists are the prime examples of the new terrorism, but Islamic radicalism is not the only form of apocalyptic, catastrophic terrorism. Aum Shinrikyo, the Japanese religious cult, executed the first major terrorist attack using chemical weapons on a Tokyo subway in 1995. The bombing of the Murrah Federal Building in Oklahoma revealed similar extremism by American right-wing militants. Other plots by Christian Identity terrorists have shown similar mass-casualty proclivities.

Nadine Gurr and Benjamin Cole labeled nuclear-biological-chemical (NBC) terrorism as the "third wave of vulnerability" experienced by the United States beginning in 1995. (The first two waves were the Soviet test of the atomic bomb in 1949 and the escalating nuclear arms race that followed.[2]) David Rapoport made a similar assessment that religiously motivated modern terrorism is the "fourth wave" in the evolution of terrorism, having been preceded by terrorism focused on the breakup of empires, decolonization, and anti-Westernism.[3]

The National Commission on Terrorism found that fanaticism rather than political interests is more often the motivation now, and that terrorists are more unrestrained than ever before in their methods.[4] Other scholarly sources have reached similar conclusions. Terrorism is increasingly based on religious fanaticism.[5] Warnings about the dangers of nontraditional terrorism were raised frequently in pre-2001 literature.[6] For instance, Ashton Carter, John Deutch, and Philip Zelikow declared in the pages of *Foreign Affairs* in 1998 that a new threat of catastrophic terrorism had emerged.[7] Earlier concerns about alienating people from supporting the cause are no longer important to many terrorist organizations. Rather than focusing on conventional goals of political or religious movements, today's terrorists seek destruction and chaos as ends in themselves. Yossef Bodansky's *Bin Laden* quotes from S. K. Malik's *The Quranic Concept of War:*

> Terror struck into the hearts of the enemies is not only a means, it is in the end in itself. Once a condition of terror into the opponent's heart is obtained, hardly anything is left to be achieved. It is the point where the means and the ends meet and merge. Terror is not a means of imposing decision upon the enemy; it is the decision we wish to impose upon him.[8]

Today's terrorists are ultimately more apocalyptic in their perspective and methods. For many violent and radical organizations, terror has evolved from being a means to an end, to becoming the end in itself. The National Commission on Terrorism quoted R. James Woolsey: "Today's terrorists don't want a seat at the table, they want to destroy the table and everyone sitting at it.[9]

Some analysts argue that the evolution of terrorism represents continuity rather than change, that mass-casualty bombings have long been characteristic of terrorist methods, and that radical extremism has always dominated terrorist motivations.[10] Walter Laqueur's most recent book warns against trying to categorize or define terrorism at all because there are "many terrorisms," and he emphasizes the particularities of various terrorist movements and approaches.[11] (Laqueur, however, recognizes some evolving strains of terrorism, especially the Islamist variant.) Bruce Hoffman discussed the definition of terrorism at length in his 1998 book, *Inside Terrorism,* and his final definition includes "political change" as the desired end-state of terrorist activity.[12] This would be more consistent with traditional means-end constructions of terrorism. Richard Falkenrath pointed out in a pre-9/11 article that mass-casualty terrorism is still an aberrant occurrence.[13] A recent survey of terrorism suggests historical and intellectual links between the fascism of fanatical Islamist terrorism today and the totalitarian movements of the 20th century, further emphasizing continuity rather than change.[14]

Most recent scholarship, however, has taken the perspective that contemporary terrorism represents a significant departure from the past. Various factors have led to the development of this new type of terrorism. Paul Wilkinson pondered the increase in indiscriminateness among terrorists, and he posited several possible reasons accounting for this upsurge.[15] First, the saturation of the media with images of terrorist atrocity has raised the bar on the level of destruction that will attract headline attention. Second, terrorists have realized that civilian soft targets involve lower risk to themselves. Finally, there has been a shift from the politically-minded terrorist to the vengeful and hard-line fanatic.

While Wilkinson's factors accurately describe developments in terrorist strategy and tactics, there are more fundamental forces at work. The world has undergone a variety of changes on several levels. While it is impossible to link all social changes to terrorism today, it is possible to track several distinct factors that have converged to evolve a form of terrorism that is unprecedented in the level of threat it poses around the world. This article will explore these factors from cultural, political, and technological perspectives.

Cultural Factors

Islamic radicalism is the most notorious form of the new culture of terrorism, but it is far from the only variety of cultural trends motivating terrorist activity. Numerous cults, whose emergence in many cases has been synchronized with the turn of the new millennium, have also posed an increasing threat. Finally, the American religious right has been active with escalating and destructive objectives, although law enforcement presence has restrained these groups.

> "Islamic radicalism is not the only form of apocalyptic, catastrophic terrorism."

It is important to distinguish religious terrorists from those terrorists with religious components, but whose primary goals are political. Religiously motivated terrorist groups grew sixfold from 1980 to 1992 and continued to increase in the 1990s. Hoffman asserted that "the religious imperative for terrorism is the most important characteristic of terrorist activity today."[16] This may not be as much an entirely new phenomenon as a cyclic return to earlier motivations for terror. Until the emergence of political motives such as nationalism, anarchism, and Marxism, "religion provided the only acceptable justifications for terror."[17] However, terrorism in modern times has not, until recent years, been so dominated by religious overtones. At the time when modern international terrorism first appeared, of the 11 identifiable terrorist groups, none could be classified as religious.[18]

Today's terrorists increasingly look at their acts of death and destruction as sacramental or transcendental on a spiritual or eschatological level. The pragmatic reservations of secular terrorists[19] do not hold back religious terrorists. Secular terrorists may view indiscriminate violence as immoral. For religious terrorists, however, indiscriminate violence may not be only morally justified, but constitute a righteous and necessary advancement of their religious cause. In addition, the goals of secular terrorists are much more attuned to public opinion, so senseless violence would be counterproductive to their cause, and hence not palatable to them. As Hoffman observed, the constituency itself differs between religious and secular terrorists. Secular terrorists seek to defend or promote some disenfranchised population and to appeal to sympathizers or prospective sympathizers. Religious terrorists are often their own constituency, having no external audience for their acts of destruction.[20]

Aum Shinrikyo has been included in typologies of terrorism that include radical Islamists as part of a group of religiously motivated organizations that attack symbols of the modern state.[21] In many ways, the dynamics of cultist followings make groups such as Aum Shinrikyo (also known as Aleph) more dangerous than religious terrorists rooted in conventional and broadly based religious traditions or denominations. There is no constituency of more moderate adherents to share common beliefs with the radical group while at the same time posing a restraining influence. For the fundamentalist Islamic or Christian radical, authoritative figures from either of those religions can condemn violence and de-legitimize the terrorist, at least in the eyes of the average faithful.

Another feature of religious cults that makes them incredibly dangerous is the personality-driven nature of these groups. Cultist devotion to one leader leaves followers less able to make their own moral decisions or to consult other sources of reasoning. If that leader is emotionally or mentally unstable, the ramifications can be catastrophic. The more dangerous religious terrorist groups from traditional faiths may often share this feature of the cult: a charismatic leader who exerts a powerful influence over the members of the group.

According to many analysts, Aum Shinrikyo demonstrated its comparatively more threatening potential in its sarin attack in the Tokyo subway. As D.W. Brackett wrote, "A horrible bell had tolled in the Tokyo subway.... Terrorists do not follow rules of engagement in their operations but they do absorb the lessons to be learned from successful acts of violence."[22] If for no other reason than providing an example to others, Aum Shinrikyo has gained notoriety as one of the more dangerous terrorist elements. Despite setbacks such as the incarceration of key leadership figures, the group continues to pose future threats. The ability of Aum Shinrikyo to recruit individuals with a high level of education and technical knowledge also has been a significant aspect of the threat posed by the cult.[23]

In the past, cults were not viewed as national security threats; they were more dangerous to unwary individuals who might succumb to the cult's influence. Even the emergence of cultist mass suicides did not alter this perception. However, the recent appearance of cults willing and able to adopt destructive political goals has revised the more benign view of the cult phenomenon. Since cults are often fundamentally based on the violence of coercion, they can be accustomed to the mindset necessary to adopt terrorist methods. Although cults more often practice a mental violence with psychological control and extreme invasions of privacy, they do occasionally engage in physical abuse. The most dangerous cults are also fascinated by visions of the end of the world—which, like radicals from more mainstream religions, cultists often believe that they are instrumental in bringing about. The nature of the cult's mythical figure can also be indicative of the level of threat. A vengeful deity is more threatening than a suffering savior. This sign is somewhat unpredictable, however, because cults can switch their principal myths as circumstances change.[24] In summary, cults are a particularly dangerous form of religious terrorism because they can appear quickly without warning, have no rational goals, and can become agitated due to the apprehension and hostility with which they are viewed by the society at large.

Whether initiated by cultists or by extremists from more established religions, the violence of religious terrorists can be particularly threatening in comparison with that of the political terrorists of earlier years. As Hoffman notes, "For the religious terrorist, violence is a divine duty . . . executed in direct response to some theological demand ... and justified by scripture."[25] Religion can be a legitimizing force that not only sanctions but compels large-scale violence on possibly open-ended categories of opponents.[26] Terrorist violence can be seen as a divinely inspired end in itself. One explanation that has been proffered to account for violent Islamic extremism views revenge as the principal goal of the terrorists.[27] This reasoning makes political change or conventional political objectives irrelevant, and it is consistent with observations that violence is itself the objective. Fundamentalist Islam "cannot conceive of either coexistence or political compromise. To the exponents of Holy Terror, Islam must either dominate or be dominated."[28] A recent study that traced the Islamic theological doctrine to the Middle Ages noted recent philosophical developments that explain the preponderance of religious mass-casualty terrorism coming from adherents of Islam.[29]

Remarkably, a recent analysis of bin Laden's fatwa, published in *Studies of Conflict and Terrorism,* found that the content of the fatwa was "neither revolutionary nor unique, as it encapsulates broad sentiments in the Muslim world, especially that of Islam's being on the defensive against foreign secular forces and modernization."[30] However, some of the content of the fatwa does fall directly within the paradigm of contemporary religious terrorism. Consider the following excerpts:

> Praise be to God, who revealed the book, controls the clouds, defeats factionalism, and says in his book: "But when the forbidden months are past, then fight and slay the pagans wherever ye find them. . . ."

> On that basis, and in compliance with God's order, we issue the following fatwa to all Muslims:

Article 3. The Origins of the New Terrorism

> The ruling to kill the Americans and their allies—civilians and military—is an individual duty for every Muslim who can do it in any country in which it is possible to do it.[31]

In an article published shortly after 9/11, Steven Simon and David Benjamin noted that many al Qaeda attacks, including the major planning phase of the 9/11 attacks, took place during favorable times for the Palestinians in the Middle East peace process, and that no foreign policy changes by the US government could possibly have appeased the bin Ladenist radical.[32]

While Islamic terrorists are the most notorious of today's violent radicals, others such as right-wing Christian extremists also exhibit many characteristics of the new terrorism. Mark Juergensmeyer, in his book *Terror in the Mind of God: The Global Rise of Religious Violence,* identified three elements that Islamists, radical Christians, and other religious terrorists share: They perceive their objective as a defense of basic identity and dignity; losing the struggle would be unthinkable; and the struggle is in deadlock and cannot be won in real time or in real terms.[33]

In the past, right-wing Christian terrorists conducted racially motivated or religiously motivated acts of violence discriminately against chosen victims, and confrontation with the state was limited to instances when the state interfered with the political or religious agenda of the terrorist groups.[34] Today, some such groups are directly hostile to the government, which adherents believe is engaged in a widespread conspiracy threatening the existence of the "white Christian way of life." A recent FBI strategic assessment of the potential for domestic terrorism in the United States focused on such groups as Christian Identity and other ultraconservative movements associated with Christian fundamentalism.[35] The most extreme of these fanatics attribute a subhuman status to people of color, which in their eyes mitigates any moral compunction to avoid harming such individuals. In addition, they view themselves in a perpetual battle with the forces of evil (as manifested through non-white races and a powerful, sinister government) that must culminate in the apocalyptic crisis predicted by the Book of Revelations. The Christian terrorists view it as their duty to hasten the realization of this divine plan, which permits and even exhorts them to greater levels of violence. That violence is directed against existing social structures and governments, which are viewed to be hopelessly entangled with such "dark forces" as Jewry, enormous financial conglomerates, and international institutions trying to form an ominous "new world order."

While Christian violence in the United States has been discriminately focused for decades against racial minorities and "immoral" targets, it recently has expanded into attempted bombings and poisoning municipal water supplies.[36] These indiscriminate attacks demonstrate a willingness to tolerate greater levels of collateral damage in efforts to generate mass levels of casualties. The bombing of the Murrah Federal Building in Oklahoma City was the pinnacle of this trend, and although Timothy McVeigh accepted responsibility for that attack, some speculate that there was additional involvement by other conservative militia or Christian terrorists.[37] Effective domestic law enforcement in the United States has largely prevented these groups from achieving widespread violence on the level of Oklahoma City, making that incident a tragic exception among a larger number of foiled plots.

> "At the same time that globalization has provided a motivation for terrorism, it has also facilitated methods for it."

While there is certainly no cooperation between foreign Islamist and US-domestic Christian radicals, there is a disquieting similarity in their views. August Kreis of the paramilitary group Posse Comitatus responded to the collapse of the World Trade Center towers with this disconcerting rant: "Hallelu-Yahweh! May the WAR be started! DEATH to His enemies, may the World Trade Center BURN TO THE GROUND!"[38] Jessica Stern's recent book, *Terror in the Name of God: Why Religious Militants Kill*, which compiles interviews with international terrorists conducted over five years, does not begin with an example from the Guantanamo Bay detention facility or the streets of the Middle East.[39] Her introductory example is a former Christian terrorist in a Texas trailer park. While Islamic terrorism is the most salient threat to the United States, it is not the only danger posed by the new trend of a culture of religious violence and extremism.

A cluster of several cultural features among new international terrorist groups indicates the high level of threat. These aspects include a conception of righteous killing-as-healing, the necessity of total social destruction as part of a process of ultimate purification, a preoccupation with weapons of mass destruction, and a cult of personality where one leader dominates his followers who seek to become perfect clones.[40] These aspects taken together represent a significant departure from the culture of earlier terrorist groups, and the organizations that these characteristics describe represent a serious threat to the civilized world.

Political and Organizational Factors

A number of developments on the international scene have created conditions ripe for mass-casualty terrorism. Gross inequalities in economic resources and standards of living between different parts of the world are a popular reason given for the ardency and viciousness of contemporary terrorists,[41] although governmental collapse in "failed states" as a breeding ground for terrorists presents a more convincing variation on this logic.[42] However, there is no "comprehensive explanation in print for how poverty causes terror," nor is there a "demonstrated correlation between the two."[43] The intrusion of Western values and institutions into the Islamic world through the process of free-market globalization is an alternative explanation for the growth of terrorism, which is the weaker party's method of choice to strike back.[44] The process of globalization, which involves the technological, political, economic, and cultural diminution of boundaries between countries across the world, has insinuated a self-interested, inexorable, corrupting market culture into traditional communities. Many see these forces as threatening their way of life. At the same time that globalization has provided a motivation for terrorism, it has also facilitated methods for it.

One of the major consequences of globalization has been a deterioration of the power of the state.[45] The exponential expansion of non-governmental organizations (NGOs), regional alliances, and international organizations has solidified this trend. Although certainly not a conventional humanitarian-based NGO like the Red Cross or Doctors without Borders, al Qaeda has distinguished itself as among the most "successful" of non-governmental organizations in pursuing its privately-funded global agenda. The trend among terrorists to eschew direct connections with state sponsors has had several advantages for the enterprising extremist. Terrorist groups are more likely to maintain support from "amorphous constituencies," so extreme methods are more acceptable because such methods can be used without fear of alienating political support.[46] Harvey Kushner described this development as a growth of "amateur" groups as direct state sponsorship has declined.[47] Lawrence Freedman pointed out that the Taliban-ruled Afghanistan was not so much a state sponsor of terrorism as it was a "terrorist-sponsored state."[48]

Terrorists do, however, continue to enjoy the benefits of indirect state sponsorship. Although the opportunity for state sponsorship has arguably diminished as a result of the Bush Administration's war on terror that has been prosecuted in the aftermath of the 9/11 attacks, state sponsorship remains widespread. In fact, developments in counterterrorist measures may propagate some dangerous trends of modern terrorism. When terrorists cannot rely on direct state sponsorship, they may become less accountable and harder to track. States must conceal their involvement by exercising less control and thus maintain less-comprehensive intelligence of radical terrorist organizations. Many states have been on the US government list of state sponsors for more than a decade, including Cuba, Iran, Iraq, North Korea, Libya, and Syria. More recently, Sudan and Afghanistan became government sponsors of terrorism. Many state sponsors cooperate with one another to promote terrorist violence, making terrorist activity further disconnected from the foreign policy of any single state. Iran has funded training camps in Sudan, and the Palestinian Islamic Jihad has received support from both Iran and Syria.[49]

Further exacerbating the problem is the method of funding, which often has no measures for accountability. Iran's support for terrorist organizations can include no particular target selection, and it occasionally results, with the funds disappearing, in no terrorist attacks.[50] This unpredictability is tolerated by state sponsors because of the occasional destructive payoff and the obfuscation of evidence connecting the state to the terrorist. Iran has consciously created a decentralized command structure because of these advantages.[51] A further advantage of maintaining arm's length from extremist operatives is for self-protection. The government intelligence organization of Sudan evidently monitored Osama bin Laden while he lived in that country, apparently to prevent his activists from eventually doing harm to even that extremist government.[52]

While the American operations in Afghanistan and Iraq have diluted the threat from those states, other sponsors have possibly been left off official lists for political reasons. (It has been frequently argued that inclusion of a state on the list of state sponsors of terrorism reflects its relationship with the United States.[53]) Pakistani intelligence reportedly has been involved in sponsoring violent terrorists, both in Afghanistan and in the contentious Kashmir. Additionally, the Kingdom of Saudi Arabia has been at the center of controversy over sponsorship and proliferation of radicalism and violence. Laurent Murawiec, an analyst at the RAND Corporation, attracted public attention by pointing out the dangers of Saudi support for radical Islamists and specifically Osama bin Laden in a briefing to the Defense Policy Board in 2002. While no official publication of the RAND Corporation documents this analysis, Murawiec highlighted evidence of Saudi support for the Islamist agenda through Islamic educational venues and financial backing.

So while globalization has helped remove many of the restraints that state sponsorship once imposed, terrorists can still enjoy the funding and protection that sponsorship provides. Another factor of globalization that benefits terrorism is targeting: "In today's globalizing world, terrorists can reach their targets more easily, their targets are exposed in more places, and news and ideas that inflame people to resort to terrorism spread more widely and rapidly than in the past."[54] Among the factors that contribute to this are the easing of border controls and the development of globe-circling infrastructures, which support recruitment, fund-raising, movement of materiel, and other logistical functions.

In addition to international political changes, developments in organizational practice have enhanced the lethality of terrorists. As corporations have evolved organizationally, so have terrorist organizations. Terrorist groups have evolved from hierarchical, vertical organizational structures, to more horizontal, less command-driven groups. John Arquilla, David Ronfeldt, and Michele Zanini note that terrorist leadership is derived from a "set of principles [that] can set boundaries and provide guidelines for decisions and actions so that members do not have to resort to a hierarchy—'they know what they have to do.'" The authors describe organizational designs that may "sometimes appear acephalous (headless), and at other times polycephalous (Hydra-headed)."[55] Paul Smith observed that the multi-cellular structure of al Qaeda gave the organization agility and cover and has been one of its key strengths.[56] This flexibility has allowed al Qaeda to establish bases using indigenous personnel all over the world. It has infiltrated Islamic nongovernmental organizations in order to conceal operations.[57] Jessica Stern recently commented on al Qaeda's ability to maintain operations in the face of an unprecedented onslaught:

> The answer lies in the organization's remarkably protean nature. Over its life span, al Qaeda has constantly evolved and shown a surprising willingness to adapt its mission. This capacity for change has consistently made the group more appealing to recruits, attracted surprising new allies, and—most worrisome from a Western perspective—made it harder to detect and destroy.[58]

Technological Factors

In addition to the cultural and religious motivations of terrorists and the political and organizational enabling factors, technology has evolved in ways that provide unprecedented opportunities for terrorists. The collapse of the Soviet Union and the possibility of proliferation of nuclear weapons to non-state users is the primary factor that has significantly increased the danger of nuclear terrorism.[59] However, nonnuclear weapons of mass destruction and information technology also have created opportunities for terrorists that are in many ways more threatening than radiological terrorism because these alternatives are more probable.

Some theorists have argued that weapons of mass destruction do not represent a weapon of choice for most terrorists, even in these changing times. Stern writes that "most terrorists will continue to avoid weapons of mass destruction (WMD) for a variety of reasons," preferring the "gun and the bomb."[60] Brian Jenkins agreed that most terrorist organizations are technologically conservative, but he also noted that the self-imposed moral restraints which once governed terrorist actions are fading away.[61] As the trends in the preceding sections reach fullness, increasing the proclivity toward mass-casualty terrorism, terrorists may turn more to these weapons that will better fit their objectives and moralities.

Walter Laqueur's *New Terrorism* emphasizes the availability of very powerful weapons of mass destruction as the major current danger facing the industrialized world.[62] Aside from the nuclear variety of WMD, biological and chemical weapons pose serious dangers. Biological weapons are limited because human contact is required to spread the effects, but as the Asian brush with Severe Acute Respiratory Syndrome (SARS) demonstrated, the associated panic and uncertainty can take a large economic and political toll—not to mention the cost in human suffering for those exposed to the pathogen, perhaps without knowing how or even whether they have been infected. Biological weapons can come in a variety of forms, including viruses, bacteria, and rickettsia (bacteria that can live inside host cells like viruses).

Chemical toxins differ from biological weapons in that they are nonliving pathogens and require direct infection and contact with the victim. This negates the continual spread of the weapon, but it entails more direct and possibly more damaging effects. Chemical agents appear in several types: choking agents that damage lung tissue, blood agents that cause vital organs to shut down, blister agents (also known as vesicants) that damage the skin, and—most lethal—nerve agents. Various methods allow the agent to infect its victim, including inhalation, skin absorption, and ingestion into the digestive tract. Exacerbating the danger is the fact that many deadly chemicals, or their components, are commercially available.

The State Department's annual report on terrorism asserted that the events of 11 September 2001 confirmed the intent and capability of terrorist organizations to plan and execute mass-casualty attacks. The report also stated that these unprecedented attacks may lead to an escalation of the scope of terrorism in terms of chemical, biological, radiological, or nuclear methods.[63]

The report further cited evidence discovered in military raids of Afghan terrorist facilities, the use of poison by Hamas to coat shrapnel in improvised explosives, and an unnamed group arrested in Italy with maps of the US embassy and possessing a compound capable of producing hydrogen cyanide. Activities of cults such as Aum Shinrikyo and American terrorist plans to poison municipal water facilities provide further evidence of the WMD threat.

Another key development is recent advances in communications and information technology. This technology provides both assistance to the terrorists and an opportunity for targeting as industrialized societies place greater reliance on information infrastructures. Terrorists will likely avoid dismantling the internet because they need the technology for their own communication and propaganda activities. Accordingly, terrorists may be more interested in "systemic disruption" rather than the total destruction of information networks.[64] While the consequences of a major disruption of American or global information infrastructures could be catastrophic financially or socially, terrorists have not shown the inclination or capability to undertake massive strikes in this area. There have been limited attacks along these lines, but the major use of information technology has been as an aid for terrorists rather than as a target of their activity. The reported use of the internet and e-mail by al Qaeda to coordinate the strikes on the World Trade Center and the Pentagon provides a dramatic example of this sort of coordination. As Paul Pillar noted, "Information technology's biggest impact on terrorists has involved the everyday tasks of organizing and communicating, rather than their methods of attack."[65]

Technology also has increased the ability of terrorists to conduct mass-casualty attacks. As noted earlier, the worst single terrorist attack before 9/11 claimed the lives of about 380 people. The yield of contemporary radiological, chemical, and biological weapons could dwarf that number, given the goals of today's terrorists as exemplified by the World Trade Center and Pentagon attacks, the Oklahoma City bombing, the sarin gas attack on the Tokyo subway, and other, less-successful attacks of the past decade. Technological developments and their availability as spread by the globalized market economy have unavoidably expanded the dangers of terrorism in the new century.

Conclusions

The practice of terrorism has undergone dramatic changes in recent years. The categorical fanaticism that is apparent in terrorist organizations across a spectrum of belief systems is a major part of this change. In the past, terrorists were more likely to be dominated by pragmatic considerations of political and social change, public opinion, and other such factors. Today, a phenomenon that was a minute rarity in the past—terrorists bent on death and destruction for its own sake—is more commonplace than ever. In addition, the statelessness of today's terrorists removes crucial restraints that once held the most extreme terrorists in check or prevented them from reaching the highest levels in their organizations. Terrorists can still enjoy the funding and shelter that only a national economy can mobilize, but they are on their own to a greater degree in greater numbers than in the past. Organizationally, terrorists are using the non-hierarchical structures and systems that have emerged in recent years. Finally, the potential availability of nuclear, chemical, and biological WMD technology provides the prospect that these trends could result in unprecedented human disasters.

Terrorism has quantitatively and qualitatively changed from previous years. Whether it is Gurr and Coleman's "third wave of vulnerability" or Rapoport's "fourth wave of terrorism," contemporary terrorism is a significant departure from the phenomenon even as recently as during the Cold War. The US *National Security Strategy* has recognized terrorism, in the memorable phrase "the crossroads of radicalism and technology," as the predominant security threat in the post-Cold War world. The cataclysmic impact of 9/11 on both the American strategic consciousness and the international security environment can scarcely be overstated. Those attacks resulted from a combination of cultural, political, and technological factors and were a revelation to the world of the emergence of the new terrorism.

Notes

1. US Department of State, *Patterns of Global Terrorism 2001* (Washington: GPO, May 2002), p. 171. The statistical review in the State Department's report does not cover total casualties; it tracks only Americans, and the casualty reporting is not as longitudinal as the number of attacks. The casualties of terrorist incidents are tracked for the previous five years versus the previous 20 years.
2. Nadine Gurr and Benjamin Cole, *The New Face of Terrorism: Threats from Weapons of Mass Destruction* (New York: I. B. Tauris, 2002).
3. David C. Rapoport, "The Fourth Wave: September 11 and the History of Terrorism," *Current History,* December 2001, pp. 419–24.
4. National Commission on Terrorism, *Countering the Changing Threat of International Terrorism: Report of the National Commission on Terrorism* (Washington: GPO, 2000).
5. Walter Laqueur, "Terror's New Face," *Harvard International Review,* 20 (Fall 1998), 48–51.
6. Richard A. Falkenrath, Robert D. Newman, and Bradley A. Thayer, *America's Achilles' Heel: Nuclear, Biological, and Chemical Terrorism and Covert Attack* (Cambridge, Mass.: MIT Press, 1998); Philip B. Heymann, *Terrorism and America: A Commonsense Strategy for a Democratic Society* (Cambridge, Mass.: MIT Press, 1998); Bruce Hoffman, *Inside Terrorism* (New York: Columbia Univ. Press, 1998); Brad Roberts, ed., *Terrorism with Chemical and Biological Weapons: Calibrating Risks and Responses* (Alexandria, Va.: Chemical and Biological Arms Control Institute, 1997); and Jessica Stern, *The Ultimate Terrorists* (Cambridge, Mass.: Harvard Univ. Press, 1999).
7. Ashton Carter, John Deutch, and Philip Zelikow, "Catastrophic Terrorism," *Foreign Affairs,* 77 (November/ December 1998), 80–94.
8. S. K. Malik, *The Quranic Concept of War* (Lahore, India: Wajidalis, 1979), quoted in Yossef Bodansky, *Bin Laden* (Roosevelt, Calif.: Prima Publishing, 1999), p. xv.

9. National Commission on Terrorism, *Countering the Changing Threat*, p. 2.
10. Chris Quillen, "A Historical Analysis of Mass Casualty Bombers," *Studies in Conflict and Terrorism*, 25 (September/October 2002), 279–92.
11. Walter Laqueur, *No End to War: Terrorism in the Twenty-First Century* (New York: Continuum, 2003).
12. Bruce Hoffman, *Inside Terrorism* (New York: Columbia Univ. Press, 1998).
13. Richard Falkenrath, "Confronting Nuclear, Biological and Chemical Terrorism," *Survival*, 40 (Autumn 1998), 52.
14. Paul Beuman, *Terror and Liberalism* (New York: W. W. Norton, 2003).
15. Paul Wilkinson, *Terrorist Targets and Tactics: New Risks to World Order*, Conflict Study 236 (Washington: Research Institute for the Study of Conflict and Terrorism, December 1990), p. 7.
16. Hoffman, *Inside Terrorism*.
17. David C. Rapoport, "Fear and Trembling: Terrorism in Three Religious Traditions," *American Political Science Review*, 78 (September 1984), 668–72.
18. Bruce Hoffman, "'Holy Terror': The Implications of Terrorism Motivated by a Religious Imperative," *Studies in Conflict and Terrorism*, 18 (October–December 1995), 271–84.
19. Brian M. Jenkins, *The Likelihood of Nuclear Terrorism*, P-7119 (Santa Monica, Calif.: RAND, July 1985).
20. Hoffman, "'Holy Terror," p. 273.
21. Mark Juergensmeyer, "Terror Mandated by God," *Terrorism and Political Violence*, 9 (Summer 1997), 16–23.
22. D. W. Brackett, *Holy Terror: Armageddon in Tokyo* (New York: Weatherhill, 1996), pp. 5–7.
23. David Kaplan and Andrew Marshall, *The Cult at the End of the World* (New York: Crown Publishers, 1996), p. 74.
24. Stern, *The Ultimate Terrorists*, p. 72.
25. Hoffman, *Inside Terrorism*, p. 20.
26. Hoffman, "'Holy Terror," p. 280.
27. Gavin Cameron, *Nuclear Terrorism* (Basingstoke, Eng.: Macmillan, 1999), p. 139.
28. Amir Taheri, *Holy Terror: The Inside Story of Islamic Terrorism* (London: Hutchinson, 1987), p. 192.
29. Daniel Benjamin and Steven Simon, *The Age of Sacred Terror* (New York: Random House, 2002).
30. Magnus Ranstorp, *Studies in Conflict & Terrorism*, 21 (October–December 1998), 321–32.
31. Shaikh Osama Bin Muhammad Bin Laden, Ayman al Zawahiri, Abu-Yasir Rifa'I Abroad Taha, Shaikh Mir Hamzah, and Fazlul Rahman, "The World Islamic Front's Statement Urging Jihad Against Jews and Crusaders," *London al-Quds al-Arabi*, 23 February 1998.
32. Steven Simon and Daniel Benjamin, "The Terror," *Survival*, 43 (Winter 2001), 12.
33. Mark Juergensmeyer, *Terror in the Mind of God: The Global Rise of Religious Violence* (Berkeley: Univ. of California Press, 2000).
34. Gurr and Cole, *The New Face of Terrorism*, p. 144.
35. Federal Bureau of Investigation, *Project Megiddo* (Washington: GPO, 20 October 1999), http://permanent.access.gpo.gov/lps3578/www.fbi.gov/library/megiddo/megiddo.pdf.
36. Gurr and Cole, *The New Face of Terrorism*.
37. See Gore Vidal, *Perpetual War for Perpetual Peace: How We Got to Be So Hated* (New York: Verso, 2002) for an exposition of the point of view that the Murrah Federal Building bombing could not have possibly occurred without a larger support structure.
38. Daniel Levitas, *The Terrorist Next Door: The Militia Movement and the Radical Right* (New York: Thomas Dunne Books, 2002).
39. Jessica Stern, *Terror in the Name of God: Why Religious Militants Kill* (New York: HarperCollins, 2003).
40. Robert J. Lifton, *Destroying the World to Save It: Aum Shinrikyo, Apocalyptic Violence, and the New Global Terrorism* (New York: Metropolitan Books, 1999).
41. James D. Wolfensohn, "Making the world a Better and Safer Place: The Time for Action is Now," *Politics*, 22 (May 2002), 118–23; Andrew S. Furber, "Don't Drink the water …" *British Medical Journal*, 326 (22 March 2003), 667; Jan Nederveen Pieterse, "Global Inequality: Bringing Politics Back In, *Third World Quarterly*, 23 (December 2002), 1023–46.
42. Karin von Hippel, "The Roots of Terrorism: Probing the Myths," *Political Quarterly*, 73 (August 2002), 25–39.
43. Michael Mousseau, "Market Civilization and Its Clash With Terror," *International Security*, 27 (Winter 2003), 6.
44. Mousseau, "Market Civilization"; Audrey Kurth Cronin, "Behind the Curve: Globalization and International Terrorism," *International Security*, 27 (Winter 2003), 30–58.
45. Charles W. Kegley, Jr., and Gregory A. Raymond, *Exorcising the Ghost of Westphalia: Building World Order in the New Millennium* (Upper Saddle River, N.J.: Prentice Hall, 2002).
46. Stern, *The Ultimate Terrorists*.
47. Harvey W. Kushner, ed., *The Future of Terrorism: Violence in the New Millennium* (Thousand Oaks, Calif.: Sage Publications, 1998).
48. Lawrence Freedman, "The Third World War?" *Survival*, 43 (Winter 2001), 61–88.
49. James Adams, *The New Spies* (London: Hutchinson, 1994), pp. 180, 184.
50. Ibid., p. 180.
51. Taheri, *Holy Terror*, pp. 100–01.
52. Frank Smyth, "Culture Clash, bin Laden, Khartoum and the War Against the West," *Jane's Intelligence Review*, October 1998, p. 22.
53. Adrian Guelke, *The Age of Terrorism* (London: I. B. Tauris, 1998), p. 148.
54. Paul R. Pillar, "Terrorism Goes Global: Extremist Groups Extend their Reach Worldwide," *The Brookings Review*, 19 (Fall 2001), 34–37.
55. John Arquilla, David Ronfeldt, and Michele Zanini, "Networks, Net war, and Information-Age Terrorism," in *Countering the New Terrorism*, ed. Ian O. Lesser et al., MR-989-AF (Santa Monica, Calif.: RAND, 1999), p. 51.

56. Paul J. Smith, "Transnational Terrorism and the al Qaeda Model: Confronting New Realities," *Parameters,* 32 (Summer 2002), 37.
57. Ibid., p. 37.
58. Jessica Stern, "The Protean Enemy," *Foreign Affairs,* 82 (July/August 2003).
59. Brian M. Jenkins, "Will Terrorists Go Nuclear? A Reappraisal," in Kushner, *The Future of Terrorism,* pp. 225–49.
60. Stern, *The Ultimate Terrorist,* p. 70.
61. Jenkins, "Will Terrorists Go Nuclear?"
62. Walter Laqueur, *The New Terrorism: Fanaticism and the Arms of Mass Destruction* (New York: Oxford Press, 2000).
63. US Department of State, *Patterns of Global Terrorism,* p. 66.
64. Arquilla, Ronfeldt, and Zanini, "Networks, Net war, and Information-Age Terrorism."
65. Pillar, "Terrorism Goes Global."

Captain **MATTHEW J. MORGAN** is the Commander of the Headquarters and Headquarters Operations Company (HHOC), 125th Military Intelligence Battalion, at Schofield Barracks, Hawaii. Following command, Captain Morgan will deploy to Operation Enduring Freedom in Afghanistan on the Joint Task Force intelligence staff.

From *Parameters,* Spring 2004, pp. 29–43. Copyright © 2004 by U.S. Army War College. Reprinted by permission of the publisher and author.

The Myth of the Invincible Terrorist

CHRISTOPHER C. HARMON

We are in a hard march in rough country. The "Global War on Terrorism" requires patience and perseverance, and yet notes of pessimism have become audible among our ranks as citizen-soldiers. This is not surprising. After five years we still have not caught up with fugitive Osama bin Laden. Hard-working military officers wonder aloud if the polity back home will keep supporting its military services. Politicians sound more and more partisan. Academics are no better: A professor at Harvard declares that the president's war on terror has been a "disaster," while at a conference in Washington in September two well-known national security analysts say we are "losing" the war on terror.

In fact, there are good reasons to judge that we are winning this global war against terrorists. And not only because we have arrested or killed two-thirds of the middle- and lower-level leaders, as well as some of their superiors and commanders. It is because terror groups all have vulnerabilities. They are human organizations with human problems; al Qaeda is no exception. For all the talk of the new "flatter" al Qaeda organization, rarely does anyone ever mentions that a *flatter* organization means *less* organization, and that in global war, that cannot help Osama bin Laden.

The history of counterterrorism and counterinsurgency is rich, and the last four or five decades offer good lessons in terrorism's vulnerabilities and counsel on how to exploit them. What follows here is a review of some of those.

Human Factors and Personnel

Terror group leaders have large egos, as they must to order the deaths of multitudes who are innocent and whom they have never met. The more famous and successful terrorist leaders become, the more these egos are likely to swell. The Kurdistan Worker's Party's Abdullah Ocalan, Shining Path's Abimael Guzman, Abu Nidal—these are example of outsized and ferocious egos. But that fact of character has disadvantages, of which one can be fatal. Ego may prevent such leaders from mentoring successors. And, struggle being as it is, when the leader and his cult of personality succumb to arrest or death, the entire organization may collapse.

In September 1992 this came to pass with the arrest of Sendero Luminoso's leader, Dr. Guzman, who called himself "The Fourth Sword of Marxism." His organization had been winning control of immense swaths of the Peruvian countryside. His capture doomed this progress and began a swift regression. Soon the group could boast only a few thousand fighters, and today it is down to a few hundred. Guzman had surrounded himself with female lieutenants but readied none to command in his absence. Only one likely male successor appeared, a field commander, soon caught by the army. Now the group manages an occasional terrorist attack, but its profile has shrunk beyond belief.

Something similar took place with the Kurdistan Worker's Party. Abdullah Ocalan built it from the ground up over a quarter century. He controlled both the military and political wings and made all key decisions. His successes against the Republic of Turkey and its armed forces were impressive and advanced the dream of an independent Kurdistan. But he was caught in early 1999, and the buoyant balloon of his nationalist and Marxist hopes hissed to near-empty. PKK congressed, deciding initially they would not appoint a successor. They then renamed themselves and promised pacific politics. Later, terrorism was renewed; some goes on in southern Turkey now. But PKK/Kongra Gel is not what it once was. It commanded some 30,000 guerrillas but now can muster less than a sixth as many.

These cases support "decapitation" strategies by opponents of terrorism. Former Defense Secretary Caspar Weinberger posed a question in an article a few years back: "Can We Assassinate the Leaders?" His answer was that we can and should assassinate some terror leaders. Whether death by martial or judicial means is necessary, and whether rendering death is even as prudent as capturing a terror group leader, are other questions. What is clear is that decapitation strategies might indeed work. In some cases, they have. The approach uses the terrorist group's most apparent strength against it; if "the great leader" is the center of gravity, then when he is imprisoned, so is the movement.

In the case of the guerrilla and terrorist supergroup "Tamil Tigers," LTTE of Sri Lanka, it is evident that founder and leader, Velupillai Prabhakaran, is the center of gravity, or "the hub of all power and movement," as Clausewitz wrote. A formidable organization under his control, with elaborate finance and logistical networks, a fierce army, a navy, capable suicide bombers, etc.—yet it could all dissipate without Prabhakaran. Members swear loyalty to him, not to LTTE, or the concept of a free land of the Tamils. The clan of the Tigers could dissolve were he killed, or jailed and publishing a plea for peace (as Guzman and Ocalan both did from jail). The master of LTTE apparently has no designated successor. Tamil nationalism is not so strong that it could be certain of holding its militant and terrorist form in his absence.

Decapitating al Qaeda by removing bin Laden and al Zawahiri isn't impossible, but it's likely to be difficult.

Unfortunately, al Qaeda is better structured. It was a stroke of brilliance, shortly before the 9/11 assaults, to merge the Afghans and others at "The Base" controlled by Osama bin Laden with the Egyptians of Ayman al Zawahiri, himself already a practiced terrorist leader. If today one or the other of these two men were to be taken, his counterpart would carry on ably. In this they enjoy some of the strength of an authentic Communist Party, instead of the weakness of a caricature of one, such as Romania's Nicolae Ceausescu ran before his destruction in 1989. Decapitation of al Qaeda by removing both bin Laden and al Zawahiri is not impossible, but it is likely to remain difficult. And if it were achieved, possibly their old friend, the Taliban chief and favored mullah, Mohammad Omar, would cobble together some of the old organization and take command. Efforts to capture or kill the top leaders should continue, but al Qaeda is most likely to be defeated by other means.

A second problem in terror group personnel management goes through all the levels of an organization and is most intense at the lowest. Underground life has unattractive qualities, and some brutish ones. Terrorism means years on the run, eating poor food, and enduring primitive medical care, with all the stresses of campaigning and doubts about one's family back home. There is, as well, for at least some, the problem of conscience over the horrific things the group is doing to innocent people. It adds up to immense stress and strain. I once had an opportunity to ask Oxford historian Michael Howard how it is that terrorist groups end. "Fatigue," he replied.

Terrorists' memoirs recur to these strains of underground life. Red Brigades depositions published by RAND are one example of how continuous and complex are the pressures of secrecy and attention to details of self-protection. Marc Sageman, a psychologist and analyst of Muslim terrorists, writes of how personal attitudes may change, too, as the years slip by. Once-powerful motives to join do not always translate into certainty about staying.

The German neo-Nazi Ingo Hasselbach was a rising star in the underground after 1988. He had charisma when the sputtering movement needed it, fighting spirit, and organizational skills. But he gradually became sickened. He felt the total absence of normal friendships, and he disapproved of a lethal 1992 firebombing of an immigrants' hostel in Molln. Hasselbach simply dropped out. On the far left, in Germany's underground, the once-formidable Baader-Meinhof crowd experienced its own fatigue. The threat of jail and the patient press of German police operations wore down some outside; jail in Stanheim prison had its own effects on leaders inside the justice system. The "Red Army Faction"—the last generation of these violent radicals—did not formally quit until 1992, but by then their East German aid and their operational abilities had waned, along with their zeal for the mission and any sense they were making progress with the German public.

I once had an opportunity to ask historian Michael Howard how it is that terrorist groups end. "Fatigue," he replied.

This means that counterterrorists must have well-evolved methods for encouraging defections. Dropouts like Hasselbach are absolutely perfect for the public cause of counterterrorism. They mean a confession of some sort, which itself is a media spectacle. They mean a certain amount of public healing; a defector does not just reject something, he affirms something. They are a body blow to the particular political cause the terrorist once represented. And for intelligence officers, a defector—especially when he or she talks before the illegal organization is able to react defensively—can be priceless.

Against rebellions in the Philippines, captives and defectors have had great public value. The U.S. war of a century ago was not won by butchery on Samar so much as by the ruse of an American general who captured nationalist leader Emilio Aguinaldo. Caught in 1901, he wrote extensively and toured the U.S., a picture of defeat which discredited the notion of resisting the U.S. authorities. A half century later came the Hukbalahap—Marxist-Leninists who emerged within the Philippines after World War II under the command of Luis Taruc. Taruc became worn down and worn out, later writing two books that reveal much about the rebels' problems and inadvertently affirm much about Filipino democracy. Today we see a third kind of example: the Philippines' military intelligence organization has a new top officer, Victor Corpus, a defector from the New People's Army. After coming over to the government side, he became an invaluable asset to the military for all that he knows, and to the public for all that his defection represents. Now he commands a sizeable structure dealing with guerrilla and terrorist opponents of the republic. Meanwhile, the NPA is intact, but largely inactive militarily.

Some assume, perhaps encouraged by TV shows and dashes of history, that captives from terror movements might be mined for information by torture. But that practice is foolish, as well as immoral. Skilled commanders think that stress, or cleverness, or understanding the person's greatest psychological needs, are better sources of information. Even kindness may elicit information from certain prisoners. A Nepalese brigadier general told me he has been surprised at how sometimes sitting down to tea with a prisoner could elicit cooperation. Perhaps this is because the Maoist cadres have been briefed to expect barbarities or death if they are captured; perhaps it is because others in Nepal's army who first acquired the captive were less kind than the general; perhaps there are always complex motives affecting each prisoner. The point is that counterterrorist forces need strategies for encouraging defections. Then they need a good system for questioning or interrogation. It must be done promptly and thoroughly, by experts. Then the intelligence must be disseminated quickly to those who can act on it before the terrorist group morphs to accommodate its loss. Defectors, when well-managed, can be gems, whether or not their conversions are full. At the very least, they cause the deepest kinds of doubts within their old clandestine organization.

Internal strife is an important factor of undergrounds, but it has largely been ignored, even by analysts of terrorism.

Internal strife is another human factor of undergrounds—though it has largely been ignored, even by terrorism analysts. The grounds for terror group strife may be political, financial, personal, or other. Bloody and sometimes large-scale battles and purges have sometimes gripped the guts of a terrorist organization or larger insurgency. These episodes should give hope to legitimate states fighting to protect sovereignty and citizens.

Before he was mysteriously and repeatedly shot in Iraq four years ago, Sabri al Banna (a.k.a. Abu Nidal) ran a tight ship called "Black June" or Fatah—The Revolutionary Council. Abu Nidal captained a tight ship in part because he was an effective organizer and in part because he was a demented paranoid. In 1987, however, concerns over defectors or leaks swept through the Abu Nidal Organization (ANO)—or swept through the head of Sabri al Banna. In Lebanon and in Libya, ANO murdered its own, most of them young Palestinian men. This formidable organization, "credited" with some 900 external victims throughout the world, was already small; it can only have been wrecked internally by this self-destruction of 600 personnel—more than a third of its strength. Even surviving cadres could be crippled psychologically or operationally by such "discipline," in the way Stalin's army was wrecked by the crazed purges of the mid-1930s. There are several reasons why ANO became almost inoperative in its last years, and surely one of them is the climate of terror *inside*. Counterterrorist psychological operations should further such obsessions.

Other groups making frequent use of terrorism as a strategy have undergone large purges or defections. Even the disciplined, highly-successful LTTE Tigers have been battling a defecting commander named Karuna since April 2004. The dissidents killed four dozen LTTE personnel in 2005. Could it be that Sri Lankan intelligence helped engineer or aggravate this split? Past cases of insurgencies wracked by internal pangs in the 1980s include such communist groups as FARC, or Revolutionary Armed Forces, in Colombia, and the Filipino New People's Army. This September, police uncovered yet another mass grave from the NPA's self-inflicted wounds of the 80s, this time in southern Leyte. The Japanese Red Army staged a self-indulgent bloodbath in December 1971 called the "Snow Murders." It unfolded in (and under) a safe house in the mountains during a Japanese winter when both human isolation and police pressure were afflicting the group. The members were mostly university students with a penchant for fierce debate and Maoist self-criticism. One session of this became particularly nasty. After confessing, or declining to do so sufficiently, loyal members were beaten to death or left outside, bound, to freeze from exposure. The group's founder, a woman named Fusako Shigenobu, had shown fire and charisma, and certainly the Japanese left was well-stocked with Marxist-Leninists ready to fight capitalist success. But imagine how recruiting efforts might go after this kind of news seeped out. The Japanese Red "Army" remained platoon-sized, and today it does not operate.

Terror is ugly, terrorists are morally ugly; this ugliness is weakness in the struggle for public opinion.

Relativists do not understand the depths of their error when they pronounce that "terrorism is just a word for violence we don't like," or "terrorism is a Westerners' epithet." Terrorists are living, breathing men and women using vile but calculated means to make political gains, and it is vital that politicians and academics and police chiefs continue pointing that out. Terror is ugly, making terrorists morally ugly; this ugliness is weakness in the struggle for public opinion. More must be made of that, in the service of truth and of counterterrorism. Another lesson flows from the facts above: Groups and their leaders may well be vulnerable to psychological operations. As circumstances allow, counterterrorism can play up rivals around the leaders, or create fissures between working partners, or throw doubt over loyalties of old comrades.

Violent organizations have pressure points; our challenge is to find and use them. Against the Huks, there were clever psy-ops by Defense Secretary Ramon Magsaysay and American advisor Edward Lansdale of the new CIA, and some of these fueled internal divisions among the communist militants. An example was their handling of "bounties," which states often proffer for bringing in a wanted man "dead or alive." The Philippines published many such offers. But they added with care a few sums which were deliberately lower than the monetary level the targeted terrorists could find honorable. In lowballing rewards for certain fugitives, the government counted on provoking and angering and embarrassing them. Such movements may seem too subtle for war, but Sun Tzu advised that the essence of war is not destroying the enemy but throwing him off balance.

At least one further weakness haunts terror organizations: personal foibles and corruption.

Today, the Abu Sayyaf Group in the Philippines is a rattled outfit. Its founding leader A.A. Janjalani was killed in a government shootout in December 1998. Filipino army pursuit has been relentless, and ASG has lost two more leaders. Almost comically, 19 defections were induced in an April 2002 incident in which the armed forces promised good treatment and air-delivered cheeseburgers to a starving Abu Sayyaf section. Ransom monies, once a source of ASG's power, have become something over which members have had fights, at least once with guns. ASG is no longer a regional apple of Osama's eye; the Saudi benefactor became disillusioned with the organization. He has turned to courting another veiled Filipina, MILF, or Moro Islamic Liberation Front.

At least one further weakness in personnel matters haunts terror organizations: personal foibles and corruption. These can be pointed to, and attacked, whether publicly or covertly, to destroy terrorists' reputations, enhance illusions, spread dissension, create rivalries, and the like.

Michael J. Waller of the Institute of World Politics has rightly called for further use of ridicule in our political warfare. Several cases in counterterrorism come to mind which might support Waller's approach. Apparently that mysterious and terrifying man Abimael Guzman was somewhat demystified in Peruvian eyes after the release of a single videotape: the great man was caught looking silly, dancing drunkenly, at the wrong kind of "party gathering." The prospect for undermining a cocky terrorist in Iraq arose in June 2006 with the surfacing of outtakes of footage for an Abu Musab al Zarqawi video. The cutting-room material showed the insurgent fumbling ignorantly with a weapon he was using as a prop in his hagiographical video. Both examples show that limited release of personal details, or description of a particular unsavory episode in the media, or magnification of these through private channels, may damage a leader's credibility. Quite possibly, ridicule or bad publicity could prod an arrogant terrorist into reckless action, the sort that would blow his cover or reveal something new about his organization.

Cowardice is an underused but potent charge. "Commanders" of terror groups often stash themselves in safety for years in comfortable villas in states such as Syria and Iran, while their troops get fired upon or die in distant operations. What could goad a terrorist leader more easily than a charge of cowardice? And one must not forget sex. Sexual misconduct was one of the firing points that nearly immolated the Japanese Red Army in 1971. Sex is a vulnerable point for certain terror group leaders. A senior officer may be an abuser; a mid-level commander of an insurgency may be one of those who takes virtual sex slaves. Such practices, especially by organizations posturing as religious or ideologically pure, can harm the group if revealed. There are dozens of other kinds of corruption or personal lapses which might be publicly or secretly used against terror group leaders. Yet our media and government often do little to publicize such facts.

Iraq is a regime that was on the U.S. list of state sponsors of terrorists for decades. Yet, I remember exactly where I was when learning for the first time that Saddam Hussein's two sons controlled their own apparatus of personal terrorism. They abducted women, had opponents shot, ordered the torture of Olympic athletes who disappointed Iraq's audiences, etc. Such information profoundly affects one's view of a regime; the information sticks hard. Before war came in March 2003, why did we not do more to publicize such facts as these for Iraqi audiences? The same holds for Abu Musab al Zarqawi, the recently-deceased insurgent. He did jail time in Jordan for pimping and other acts of petty crime. Such a case history is not unusual. Ali La Pointe, a famed terrorist for the FLN during the Battle of Algiers, had exactly that same profile—pimp and petty criminal—before time and choices remade him as a "nationalist" and "fedayeen." Criminals are in fact commonplace in political undergrounds; Mao wrote of how to understand and use them; we should use their pasts to discredit them.

Tactics and Technology

A second area in which the vulnerabilities of terrorists are evident, and may be exploited, is the tactical and the technical. Terror group leaders are often well-educated, but this does not mean they are good military planners or adept handlers of technology. Even the very good may be deceived by someone more clever.

One top commander of the Algerian FLN forces of the 1950s lusted after a modern radio to control his battles and his men. Learning this, French counterinsurgents obliged him, "mistakenly" leaving behind such a device during their own army operations in the target's sector. The treasured radio was immediately brought to the FLN commander in his cave. Many loyalists died when the French bomb inside detonated. In a second case, French intelligence made skilled use of a defector who called himself Safy-le-Pur. This defector maintained his top-level FLN communications, and coaxed one group of leaders to a "conference"—at which they were all arrested by the French. The tactic had strategic effects: Amirouche, the guerrilla leader most affected by the disaster, began an infuriated hunt for informers that left many dead loyalists in his own region. The purges extended into the adjoining guerrilla region, and hundreds of insurgents killed hundreds of other insurgents. It was all most economical for the French—and disastrous for the FLN. Terrorists are prone to such manipulation.

Sometimes, the terrorists fool themselves. The Irish Republican Army is a deep reservoir of martial skill and lethality. Yet these same "Provos" have had many failures with technology and tactics. Indeed, they have had so many bitter experiences with their own bombs detonating during manufacture, or prematurely during transit, that there is an expression for the disaster—"own goals." The metaphor is taken from the soccer mistake of accidentally knocking the ball into your own net. Sean O'Callaghan, the best-known defector from the IRA, describes a day on which he nearly blew himself up in his bomb-making shop. Three Weathermen once did exactly that, burning down a New York City townhouse.

Terrorist "commanders" often stash themselves in villas while their troops die in distant operations.

In war, counterinsurgents sometimes sabotage arms and arrange to get them into terrorist hands. France did this systematically to the FLN by influencing arms factories in Spain and Switzerland where they knew the FLN was buying weapons. The results on insurgent morale can be profound. In the Philippines, during the Huk rebellion, observers of the location of a rebel ammo dump sometimes put sabotaged shells into the collection, knowing the rebels would recover and use the stuff, wounding themselves. Such tricks also cast doubts on all ammo caches, even those untouched by state agents. This is insidious and effective. One can imagine Afghans using such tricks in their war with al Qaeda and the Taliban in remote border regions.

Under calmer circumstances, or in peacetime efforts against a small terrorist group, such actions might be illegal or inappropriate. What can always be tried, however, within bounds in a democratic society, is *neutralization* of weapons, rather than their sabotage. Technical failing in arms and shells is not at all unusual, and so it need not arouse a conviction among the terrorists that their stores have been tampered with. And yet technical failings can wreck tactical attacks, embarrass the users, lead to the exposure and capture of the gunmen, or provoke internal dissent about the "idiots down in logistics."

It appears that the FBI may have done this to snuff one Libyan ploy of the 1980s. Tripoli was paying a black Chicago street gang called El Rukns to make trouble within the United States, and at some point the group tried to use a shoulder-launched weapon against an airplane at O'Hare Airport. The missile was inert. A series of later cases has come to light as varied groups pursue ground-to-air weapons to destroy airliners. In the U.S. and Britain, for example, individual buyers or technicians for the IRA have repeatedly been foiled as they've sought to acquire means of shooting down British helicopters. Stings by undercover G-men have often been the reason.

Terrorist failings may easily disable a good plan. A timely leak from inside a terror cell can wreck a tactical plan months or years in preparation. It is stunning to consider what could have occurred had we properly questioned and jailed even two of the foreign hijackers "sleeping" here before 9/11 but stopped by police on driving charges or for other petty infractions. With luck, we might have had a red-hot warning, or at least "connected some dots." Instead, al Qaeda's plotting continued.

Stings by undercover G-men have kept the IRA from acquiring the means to shoot down British helicopters.

It is clear that having an agent inside a terror organization can foil operations. Once Sean O'Callaghan weakened in his IRA convictions, he did not try to poison others' morale, or shoot his comrades, but he did make sure important plots failed. He disabled a 1983 attempt on the lives of the Charles and Diana. In the next year, O'Callaghan betrayed the arriving arms ship *Valhalla* carrying $2 million worth of arms to the IRA from Boston. He did this without blowing uncovered as an informer for the Irish police. American examples of such penetrations and disruptions include the work of Larry Grathwohl, who got inside the Weathermen, neutralized several of their operations, and walked away to write memoirs (*Bringing Down America,* Arlington House, 1976). Not many have such coolness and skill. But this is skill that can be developed by intelligence agencies that demand results and have political support to attain results.

A very different sort of tactical vulnerability attends the management of guerrilla armies. Insurgents frequently use terrorism but also irregular combat forces. When they do, they must master the difficult problem of when to risk forces in positional fighting against better-prepared and better-armed government forces. Some always decline. Others accept battle and pay a huge price. The challenge always lies before such modern groups as the Taliban, al Qaeda, the LTTE, and FARC. They may prefer murder of soft targets one day but choose battle against a company of soldiers or police the next. A venerated teacher of strategy, Harold W. Rood (*Kingdoms of the Blind,* Carolina Academic Press, 1980), likes to say that the greatest problem in counterinsurgency is bringing the guerrilla to battle, but that once you do, you may well have your way with him. This was true in Vietnam, where General Giap's army (as against Ho Chi Minh's terrorists) too early brought about pitched battles with the French, in the Red River Valley, and were beaten. It was true again at Tet, in 1968, when Viet Cong guerrillas were ordered into positional fighting throughout Vietnam, and were worse than decimated by the contact. These dangers help explain why many aspiring guerrillas can never transition into a real national army.

Bin Laden, normally self-controlled, crowed visibly on videotape over the extent of damage he did to the Twin Towers, saying that as an engineer he could not have hoped for both to tumble down after the planes hit. But he did no crowing on camera about the arrival of American forces in Afghanistan in October and November of 2001. It had been his prized sanctuary. He clearly believed in the myths of guerrillaism. He was wrong. The White House was determined to oust the regime in Afghanistan, a country that has always been a candidate for the most remote and unappealing in the world. No fear, no legacy of Red Army defeat, no terror of further suicide bombings, kept President Bush from ordering the action. The U.S. worked well with Afghan allies, central to the larger coalition. Bin Laden, vaunted "guerrilla" leader, must have aged notably seeing his men and Taliban troopers dying in masses in static trenches while unseen American guerrillas with radios directed the fall of aerial bombs. Instead of extending the Afghans' legacy of victory over conventional force, the Arabs of al Qaeda and the Pakistanis and Afghans of the Taliban were smashed and driven from Afghanistan in one of modern history's fastest campaigns. It took years, and foreign refuge and Pakistani help, for the Taliban to recover. Al Qaeda has not recovered; it is running on half-power.

No fear, no legacy of Red Army defeat, no terror of further suicide bombs, kept President Bush from ordering action.

Far smaller groups than the Taliban risk the same fate when they take a stand against trained and established forces with mechanisms for command and control. Self-described guerrillas and Castroites of Peru, MRTA/Tupac Amaru, had quite a profile and many small successes with "hit and run" actions and terrorism. Then they seized the Japanese ambassador's residence in Lima in 1996. Their Latin teledrama was good press for MRTA/Tupac Amaru for many months. But President Fujimori was a tough man, and his brother was a captive in the residence. He did not yield. MRTA found that staking 14 terrorists' lives on holding this building was harder than, say, shooting unsuspecting citizens in a public marketplace. Once Peru's commandos were ordered in, in April 1997, all the terrorists quickly got shot. MRTA has gone dead quiet since.

The new technical requirements for contemporary terrorism bring many challenges and problems for the groups. For example, reconnaissance on targets used to entail surveillance as well as quiet work in libraries and clipping newspapers. Today terrorists videotape a great deal. This has the disadvantage of placing them on the attack site more often. Terrorists may be observed when they are observing, as have several Muslims in the U.S. since 9/11. Even if the resultant questioning does not led to arrest, or if the arrest does not lead to conviction, they can be inhibited and obstructed by police attention and perhaps public exposure. A security expert for the contractor Blackwater advises me after years in Iraq that many times, terrorists and insurgents were shot or captured while trying to videotape their next target. Yet they press on: to operational and tactical requirements for such tape there is added a new custom in the Middle East of making propaganda pictures of their own attacks for later release. And while that videotape is good publicity for the terrorists, it also reveals things about the operation: the time of year and day on which the reconnaissance was made; the place from which the attack was made; details about the camera and its crew, etc. Videotape might also be captured before it is edited, revealing far more.

> **Prominent groups now brief cadres on how to resist police tricks and torture, because they assume they will be caught.**

The same principle applies to other terrorist intelligence operations and record-keeping. It can produce a counterintelligence nightmare for them. Consider what authorities learned from the personal computer of Ramzi Youssef, caught in the Philippines with plans for terrorizing air operations over the Pacific. Consider what they might have learned from the same computer had they been smarter and shared intelligence better. The machine on which the terrorist worked up and preserved his plans became a terrible vulnerability. Some of the most exciting material ever seen about the inner workings of al Qaeda was captured in Afghanistan by a reporter, Alan Cullison, who bought two al Qaeda PCs from a thief in Kabul just days after looters sacked a headquarters. Recall the undisguised enthusiasm of U.S. forces discovering documents in the rubble of al Zarqawi's rural safehouse in July 2006.

Finances are now computerized by such groups as Colombia's National Liberation Army, or ELN. There were advantages of going from ledgers—which can erode or mold in that climate or be burned in fires—to diskettes, copies of which can be dispersed and better protected. But police found a stash of diskettes on one occasion, and it bore the entire record of ongoing ELN collections from peasants, cattle farmers, oil companies meeting ELN extortion demands, and kidnapping. The catch detailed the wealth of the group. More important, it revealed the workings of the organization and the range of its operations. In counterintelligence it was a body blow to ELN.

With sufficient trained manpower, it is practical to use even everyday policing and police technologies to obstruct and pursue undergrounders. Terrorists must engage in criminal practices, such as document fraud and robbery, and thus may expose themselves to alert police. Today the "GWOT" is more about policing than it is about armies. Adept policing yields more arrests and causes other operational problems for terrorists. Several prominent groups now thoroughly brief their cadres on how to resist police tricks and torture, because they assume their members will be caught. The IRA published a *Green Book* which displays the dangers members face under interrogation and coaches them in responding to British inquisitors. The al Qaeda manual *Military Studies in the Jihad Against the Tyrants* has detailed pages on such matters for the "Brothers." The Greek terrorists of "Revolutionary Organization November 17th" were invisible to police eyes for a quarter-century. But in 2002 when a member suffered an "own goal" and ended up in a hospital, he talked to authorities. Now, all are caught and jailed. November 17th is gone. It is a fact of the underground that secrecy is hard to maintain and easy to lose.

Strategies

Terrorism is a sword with two cutting edges. While it frightens, it may frighten the wrong people. When it frightens, it risks cutting into the group's popular support. Terrorist acts may prove political potency, or they can appear nihilistic. This is another reason that successfully leading a terrorist group is harder than it appears.

One reads in histories of the Malayan Emergency that "Communist Terrorists" fighting British rule after 1948 overused terrorism and alienated the people they sought to win over. In our day, Algerians of the Armed Islamic Group (GIA) may have done the same in their country. They are famous, but they have not won over most of the population, and they have certainly not defeated the Algerian government. Indeed, when the other prominent Algerian Muslim terrorist group, the Front for Islamic Salvation, made a pact with Algiers, GIA became isolated politically.

Abu Musab al Zarqawi, a Jordanian, was enormously successful with terrorism while in Iraq. There he was a hero, capitalizing on Iraqi troubles and divisions, fears for the future, and the unwelcome coalition presence. If Jordanians next door were troubled by his massacres, they did not loudly say so. But then

Zarqawi dared to strike his native Jordan. He blew up tourist hotels, killing many Muslims and creating horrors and problems for the authorities. His "poll numbers" dropped dramatically. He angered Jordan. Jordanian intelligence agents reportedly did the work that allowed the precision air strike that killed Zarqawi in June 2006.

Zarqawi made a strategic mistake and made himself appear shameful. The terrorism weapon always comes with such risks, and governments may often exploit them publicly through well-aimed rhetoric. By definition, terrorists' horrific actions open them to charges of murdering the innocent. Varied and good arguments present themselves, even if Washington has usually had a tin ear for them, or failed to marshal them well. U.S. strategy for public diplomacy should combat the strategy of terrorism by throwing light (and statistics) on the realities of terrorism: (1) Muslim terrorists have usually killed more Muslims than Jews or Christians. (2) The prime reason for Shiite deaths in Iraq today is terrorism by Sunni minorities, not the U.S. occupation. (3) When al Qaeda "struck at America" in 1998, its two embassy bombs killed and wounded thousands of East Africans while killing exactly 12 Americans. Such "targeting" is morally sick; it can only damage al Qaeda's image in Africa—if the truth is well-told and the good arguments are well-marshaled by skilled officers of public affairs and public diplomacy.

Terrorists themselves, being calculating, recognize this danger, and do hold debates about strategy. *Inside Al Qaeda* (Diane Publishing, 2004) by Algerian journalist and infiltrator Mohamed Sifaoui is the latest book to show how some members of even the most hardened terrorist organization will dissent, or argue, or otherwise oppose killing the innocent and civilians. There are often advocates for alternative approaches, violent or nonviolent. Sean O'Callaghan developed a bad conscience over a particular murder the IRA performed, and began to turn. Marc Sageman's book *Understanding Terror Networks* (University of Pennsylvania Press, 2004) shows how a debate on strategy split up the Egyptians of "Jihad" or al Jihad, which had murdered Anwar Sadat.

Sean O'Callaghan developed a bad conscience over a particular murder committed by the IRA, and began to turn.

Public pressures by adept political figures may create or enhance such internal disputes, increasing fissures. Skilled penetrators—if we have them—can begin internal debates where they do not yet exist. There are ways to advance internal confusion and dissension, and they should be used when the stakes are so high and the essential activity of the terror group is by nature repugnant and dangerous. It sounds odd to suggest promoting debate within terrorist organizations. But even terrorists can have, or develop, conscience. And terrorists also are well-attuned to self-interest. No one should forget the damage done to the Italian Red Brigades by once-loyal insiders when authorities offered "repentants" good deals with prosecutors. Many terrorists talked, and it tore out the guts of the once-clandestine networks in Italian cities.

Terrorists' morale has also been beaten by brilliant counterterror operations. This is denied by the errant who speak endlessly and only of the "root causes" of terrorism. We have already seen how MRTA in Peru saw its star fall from the skies in a few minutes, shot down by the guns of Peruvian commandos retaking the Japanese residence in Lima. Similar violence was done to the hopes of the Baader-Meinhof chiefs counting time in jail in Germany in 1977. They planned on a Lufthansa hijacking to free them, in a bargain with authorities. But German authorities had recovered from the indulgence and incompetence shown at Munich in 1972. The new GSG-9 counterterror force flew after the plane to Mogadishu, broke into it on the ground, killed the terrorists, and rescued the hostages. The moral effect was strategic: four of the Baader-Meinhof leaders attempted suicide, three succeeding. While all red dreams did not die with them in Germany, neither did this group recover. War is an interactive process, as Clausewitz taught. Governments can break terrorists' will; governments need not themselves always be the ones broken.

State support for terrorism is another problem at the strategic level, and it, too, can be countered. State support to transnational "substate" killers is intolerable under international law, both traditional and modern. That means it can be exposed and then politically opposed—by capitals and their allies. Military pressure may also stop state sponsors. Turkey endured years of Kurdish PKK training in Syrian safe havens, but when it finally mobilized troops within Turkey over the matter, Abdullah Ocalan was sent packing—and could then be caught in Kenya by the Turks. The effect on PKK capabilities as a guerrilla force was dramatic.

Political Ideologies

Hannah Arendt and other experts on totalitarian regimes felt they look as invulnerable as sheet steel from the outside, but that once cracked slightly, they could fall apart like broken glass. We later watched this happen to the Soviet bloc. Terror groups may be vulnerable to political complexities and errant decisions. Certainly they are vulnerable to what communists criticize as "splittism"—the terrifying risk of ideological division, sometimes over rather minor matters. Small groups can be vulnerable to frustration in political obscurity as the minority of all minorities. The "White Power" movement within the U.S. showed at least two signs of division in the past year or so. One was open and ideological—over the question of whether "Jews are *the* enemy," or whether all minorities are the enemy. The second case was physical, at a "Nordic Fest" in Kentucky, when the National Socialist Movement found its members bloodily assaulted by another faction of neo-Nazis—over personal insults at a speech.

By contrast, moderation and democracy have many natural human allies and natural international appeal. It is a simple truth—not a simplistic one—that in most matters of terrorism, U.S. counterterrorists are far more on the side of virtue than of vice. Set aside Abu Ghraib for a moment and the several military scandals in Iraq. In the overall global war on terrorism, during the past five years, and in far larger matters of political philosophy and our role in the world, democracy does not have much to apologize for. Terrorism does. So if we use the right arguments abroad we will have some political effect. Instead, as all of Washington knows, our public diplomacy has seemed absent for years at a time, or has been ham-handed when it should be a firm, communicative handshake. And even when public diplomacy can be good, as in sending American speakers and nongovernmental experts abroad as citizens representing our country, such efforts are so inadequately funded that they cannot reach very many hearts and minds.

Who is the enemy in Iraq? The otherwise powerful insurgency in Iraq is totally open to charges of incoherence and aimlessness and contradictory positions. Yet when did we last see U.S. diplomats, or the Iraqi government, forcefully point this out? The Achilles heel of the Iraqi insurgency is that its elements have no unified platform of the sort the Algerian FLN published when starting its war in November 1954. That document guided the FLN's work over the years to complete victory in 1962. It created some consensus where there had been none and committed a mix of interests and parties to submit to discipline in ways once foreign. It was an essential political instrument. The Iraqi terrorists today have no counterpart. This is an opening through which we should be driving a truck.

President Bush is right to decry Muslim militancy that spills innocent blood as a repudiation of true religion.

Or consider religion and the global war on terrorism. Religion is by definition idealistic. It is a different form of ideology from, say, political realism. Therefore if the actions of "religious" terrorists can be shown to be base, or self-serving, or contrary to the religion, the terrorists can be discredited.

For that reason, President Bush and others are right to decry Muslim militancy that spills innocent blood as a repudiation of true religion. But their point demands expansion and elaboration. Bin Laden should be ridiculed for his self-assumption of clerical authorities; the man never studied at a seminary. There is every reason to point to the shocking arrogance of published fatwas which cast legitimate imams into the shadows while dictating who should be killed. And when moderate Muslims condemn terrorism, as they have in Spain, Britain, and the United States, their judgments deserve respect—and much better press and official attention.

Specific vulnerabilities also lie within the heart of each terrorist ideology. Classical fascism, for example, lacked the advantages of internationalism—in appeal, and in operations. Japan's self-centered world view left her with almost no partners during World War II, while democracies in the "The Atlantic Charter" could hold hands naturally, no matter how wide the seas between them. Neofascism today is hobbled by the thorough discrediting of its doctrine in the eyes of most of the world by or before 1945. Becoming a fascist in 1927 was dramatic, revolutionary, interesting—it even showed optimism of an odd sort. Becoming a fascist in 2007 is to be a pariah in most social or political sitting rooms. It means no coalitions or weak coalitions with other parties, less money, and regular ill treatment by the press. Today a convinced southern Austrian neo-Nazi might say encouraging things about Danish storm troopers, but that does not mean he'll tender a third of his party treasury to them to watch them start up more cells. Actual cooperation, let alone joint planning, between neofascists from different nations is very unusual. There is as well the discredit of one's intellectual heroes, for example David Irving, who lost in a court opportunity to prove his case. The most important neo-Nazi group in recent times, at Hayden Lake, Idaho, has been broken by a lawsuit; its "church" and compound are plowed under. The lawyer who did it, Morris Dees, is a national hero, which points to another problem for American neofascists: public resistance. In America it has been true for several decades that the Ku Klux Klan or the neo-Nazis can usually get a permit to march; but then they are met by five or ten times as many counterdemonstrators. A neofascist march in the United States is a tiny parody of the demonstrations of power once seen in downtown Munich or Nuremberg.

Bin Laden should be ridiculed for his self-assumption of clerical authorities; he never studied at a seminary.

Consider an opposite case. Al Qaeda's internationalism is its most important characteristic, after its lethality. Internationalism is a source of power—ideologically, operationally, and for recruiting. Do opportunities for us lie within that center of gravity? Might there be exploitable grievances? There might. About where the new caliphate would be sited, and what territories it could cover—and exclude. About whether Asian al Qaeda members get the same credit and respect as Arabs with bin Laden's organization. About what geographical theaters get emphasis from the logistical comptrollers at "The Base" while others might go relatively hungry, or even starve. About whether large cash contributions from known donors are being well spent by management, or whether some are wasted, or hiding in foreign banks for individuals planning to depart the revolution. About the places al Qaeda chooses to fight: surely some of al Zawahiri's Egyptians must resent these protracted efforts across the globe which—let's face it—have created *no change* at home in Egypt.

Today's Islamofascism, as Mohamed Sifaoui and Francis Fukuyama call it, has another specific failing: It leaves out most Muslims. Our world is home to more than a billion Muslims, but only 100,000 to 200,000 may really believe that the murder, maiming, and menacing of the innocent to inspire fear and create a new political force will actually strengthen Islam. Still fewer count on a new caliphate. The willpower and current enthusiasm of the minuscule minority seem important to us, and they are; but they can wane, as surely as Baader-Meinhof/Red Army faction pretensions to popularity gave way over time to the sober views and desires of tens of millions of Germans. Isolating the terrorists may take years, but it can and must be done.

Another vulnerability that must keep terrorism's planners up at night is the difference between Shiite and Sunni. Zarqawi enjoyed exploiting those deep divisions in Iraq, up to the point of his death, but for many terror group leaders, inter-Islamic warfare would be a horrid prospect and a dangerous weapon. Using terror to start internal war can be akin to using a grenade made in a back street shop—it is just as likely to hurt you as whomever you throw it at. The strategists of internecine Muslim warfare expect to defeat the infidels first and then deal later with their closer Muslim enemies. But there are political disadvantages to such an approach, and most terror leaders lack the skill of an Osama bin Laden, long known for building alliances.

Other ideologies have their own inherent vulnerabilities that weaken political militancy and beg for exploitation. Anarchism was potent a century ago, yet it suffers from the ineradicable problem that anarchists do not want to organize! And in their diversity, defeat awaits. Contemporary anarchism has some political muscle but no instinct for the kill, and no well-developed doctrine of militancy. Anarchists today illuminate certain causes, such as antiglobalism and the environment. They are little threat to government. When anarchist gunmen appear, they may succeed in firing an opening scatter of shots, but the movement is most unlikely in our day to be able to mount a pitched battle.

Tamil Tigers in Sri Lanka and the FARC in Colombia have only totalitarian communism to offer to populations well accustomed to democracy. Since democracy works well in most parts of both those very different countries, democracy has a natural credibility with voters and citizens. Communism's promise to overthrow it in favor of a now-discredited system of economics and politics is not the strongest suit of these contemporary terrorists. Their appeal is limited. Colombia is the second oldest democracy in this hemisphere. The alternative is an offshoot of Castroite communism in a year when Fidel is 80. That cannot much impress sober Colombians.

We are indeed in a hard march through rough country. No one is quite sure how long it will take to defeat al Qaeda. But as a determined Englishman said when his people were on a "stony road" during 1942, some things are not to be doubted. "We have reached a period in the war when it would be premature to say that we have topped the ridge, but now we see the ridge ahead. . . . We shall go forward together." If anything is clear, it is that his war was far harder than our own.

CHRISTOPHER C. HARMON holds the Kim T. Adamson Chair of Insurgency and Terrorism at Marine Corps University. He is author of *Terrorism Today* (Taylor & Francis). He writes in his personal capacity and is not a representative of the U.S. government.

From *Policy Review,* April/May 2007, pp. 57–74. Copyright © 2007 by Christopher C. Harmon. Reprinted by permission of The Hoover Institution, Stanford University and Christopher C. Harmon. www.policyreview.org

UNIT 2
Tactics of Terrorism

Unit Selections
5. **Paying for Terror,** David E. Kaplan
6. **Toy Soldiers,** Cheryl Benard

Key Points to Consider
- What motivates suicide bombers?
- How do terrorists fund their organizations?
- Why are youths in conflict zones particularly susceptible to terrorist recruitment?
- What is the difference between a tactic and a strategy?

Student Web Site
www.mhcls.com/online

Internet References
Further information regarding these Web sites may be found in this book's preface or online.

FrontPage Magazine—Ecoterrorism and Us
http://www.frontpagemag.com/Articles/Printable.asp?ID=1277

JCSS Military Resources
http://www.tau.ac.il/jcss/lmas.html

The tactics of terrorism appear to be universal. While ideologies and motivations vary, terrorist organizations in different parts of the world often use similar methods to instill fear and wreak damage. It's unclear whether this is the consequence of increased communications among terrorist organizations, or the result of greater access to information in this age of global media. Some argue that terrorists simply tend to be conservative in their selection of tactics, relying on tactics that have proven successful rather than risking failure. Regardless of the underlying reasons, the tactics used by terrorists have remained remarkably consistent. While they have increased in size and sophistication, bombs are still the primary tool employed by terrorist organizations. On average, bombs are used in over two-thirds of all terrorist attacks around the world. In addition to bombings, kidnapping, hostage taking, hijacking, armed attacks, and arson are tactics commonly employed by terrorist organizations. To finance these activities terrorists are increasingly resorting to organized crime and drug trafficking.

The articles in this unit highlight some contemporary terrorist tactics. David Kaplan examines how organized crime and drug trafficking provide the financing that terrorists seek. In the second article Cheryl Benard argues that demographic changes in the Middle East have led to the increased recruitment of youths by terrorist organizations. She believes that immature brain development, thrill seeking behavior, and misperceptions of reality make this group particularly vulnerable.

NATA photo

Paying for Terror

How jihadist groups are using organized-crime tactics—
and profits—to finance attacks on targets around the globe.

DAVID E. KAPLAN

The first blast struck at 1:25 P.M., shattering the walls of the Bombay Stock Exchange, leaving a grisly scene of broken bodies, shattered glass, and smoke. Next to be hit was the main office of the national airline, Air India, followed by the Central Bazaar and major hotels. At the international airport, hand grenades were thrown at jets parked on the tarmac. For nearly two hours the carnage went on, as unknown assailants wreaked havoc upon one of the world's largest cities. In all, 10 bombs packed with plastic explosives rocked Bombay, killing 257 and injuring over 700.

What happened in Bombay on that day, March 12, 1993, was a chilling precursor to the 9/11 terrorist attacks, a careful choreography of death and destruction, aimed at the heart of a nation's financial center and intended to maximize civilian casualties. Engineered by Muslim extremists, the attacks were meant to exact revenge for deadly riots by Hindu fundamentalists that had claimed over a thousand lives, most of them Muslim. But more than vengeance was at work in Bombay. Indian police later recovered an arsenal big enough to spark a civil war: nearly 4 tons of explosives, 1,100 detonators, nearly 500 grenades, 63 assault rifles, and thousands of rounds of ammunition. Within days of the attacks, police had gotten their first break by tracing an abandoned van filled with a load of weapons. The trail soon led to a surprising suspect: not a terrorist but a gangster. And not just any gangster but an extraordinary crime boss, a man known as South Asia's Al Capone.

Virtually unknown in the West, Dawood Ibrahim is a household name across the region, his exploits known by millions. He is, by all accounts, a world-class mobster, a soft-spoken, murderous businessman from Bombay who now lives in exile, sheltered by India's archenemy, Pakistan. He is India's godfather of godfathers, a larger-than-life figure alleged to run criminal gangs from Bangkok to Dubai. Strong-arm protection, drug trafficking, extortion, murder-for-hire—all are stock-in-trade rackets, police say, of Dawood Ibrahim's syndicate, the innocuously named D Company.

Dawood, as he is known in the Indian press, is very much on Washington's radar screen today. Two years ago, the Treasury Department quietly designated Ibrahim a "global terrorist" for lending his smuggling routes to al Qaeda, supporting jihadists in Pakistan, and helping engineer the 1993 attack on Bombay. He is far and away India's most wanted man, his name invoked time and again by Indian officials in their discussions of terrorism with U.S. diplomats and intelligence officers. As a result of those discussions, the FBI and the Drug Enforcement Administration each have active investigations into Dawood's far-flung criminal network, *U.S. News* has learned.

> "The world is seeing the birth of a new hybrid of organized-crime-terrorist organizations."

Understanding Dawood's operations is important, experts say, because they show how growing numbers of terrorist groups have come to rely on the tactics—and profits—of organized criminal activity to finance their operations across the globe. An inquiry by *U.S. News,* based on interviews with counterterrorism and law enforcement officials from six countries, has found that terrorists worldwide are transforming their operating cells into criminal gangs. "Transnational crime is converging with the terrorist world," says Robert Charles, the State Department's former point man on narcotics. Antonio Maria Costa, the head of the United Nations Office on Drugs and Crime, agrees: "The world is seeing the birth of a new hybrid of organized-crime-terrorist organizations. We are breaking new ground."

Blood Money

Some scholars argue that terrorists and traditional crime groups both now exist on a single, violent plane, populated at one end by politically minded jihadists and at the other by profit-driven mobsters, with most groups falling somewhere in between. Mafia groups and drug rings in Colombia and the Balkans, for example, commit political assassinations and bomb police and prosecutors, while terrorist gangs in Europe and North Africa traffic in drugs and illegal aliens. Both crime syndicates and terrorist groups thrive in the same subterranean world of black markets and laundered money, relying on shifting networks and secret cells to accomplish their objectives. Both groups have similar needs: weapons, false documentation, and safe houses.

But some U.S. intelligence analysts see little evidence of this melding of forces. Marriages of convenience may exist, they say, but the key difference is one of motive: Terrorist groups are driven by politics and religion, while purely criminal groups have just one thing in mind—profit. Indeed, associating with terrorists, particularly since 9/11, can be very bad for business—and while crime syndicates may be parasitical, most do not want to kill their host.

What many intelligence analysts do see today, however, is terrorist organizations stealing whole chapters out of the criminal playbook—trafficking in narcotics, counterfeit goods, illegal aliens—and in the process converting their terrorist cells into criminal gangs.

The terrorist gang behind the train bombings in Madrid last year, for example, financed itself almost entirely with money earned from trafficking in hashish and ecstasy. Al Qaeda's affiliate in Southeast Asia, Jemaah Islamiyah, engages in bank robbery and credit card fraud; its 2002 Bali bombings were financed, in part, through jewelry store robberies that netted over 5 pounds of gold. In years past, many terrorist groups would have steered away from criminal activity, worried that such tactics might tarnish their image. But for hard-pressed jihadists, committing crimes against nonbelievers is increasingly seen as acceptable. As Abu Bakar Bashir, Jemaah Islamiyah's reputed spiritual head, reportedly said: "You can take their blood; then why not take their property?"

The implications are troubling because organized crime offers a means for terrorist groups to increase their survivability. A Stanford University study conducted after the 9/11 attacks looked at why some conflicts last so much longer than others. One key factor: crime. Out of 128 conflicts, the 17 in which insurgents relied heavily on "contraband finances" lasted on average 48 years—over five times as long as the rest. "If the criminal underworld can keep terrorist coffers flush," says Charles, the former State Department official, "we will continue to face an enemy that would otherwise run out of oxygen."

The terrorists behind the Madrid train bombings paid their way by selling drugs.

The growing reliance on crime stems from the end of the Cold War, when state sponsorship of terrorism largely faded along with communism, forcing groups to become much more self-sufficient. Accelerating the trend, analysts say, is the crackdown since 9/11 on fundraising by Islamic radicals from mosques and charities, which has pushed their operations further toward racketeering. "The bottom line is if you want to survive today as a terrorist, you probably have to support yourself," says Raphael Perl, a counterterrorism specialist at the Congressional Research Service. The drug trade, in particular, has proved irresistible for many. Nearly half of the 41 groups on the government's list of terrorist organizations are tied to narcotics trafficking, according to DEA statistics.

Scams

The new face of terrorism can best be seen in western Europe. "Crime is now the main source of cash for Islamic radicals in Europe," says attorney Lorenzo Vidino, author of the new book *Al Qaeda in Europe*. "They do not need to get money wired from abroad like 10 years ago. They're generating their own as criminal gangs." European police and intelligence officials agree: The Continent's most worrisome cells, composed largely of immigrants from Morocco and Algeria, have in effect become racketeering syndicates. Their scams are as varied as the criminal world: Drugs, smuggling, and fraud are mainstays, but others include car theft, selling pirated CDs, and counterfeiting money. One enterprising pair of jihadists in Germany hoped to fund a suicide mission to Iraq by taking out nearly $1 million in life insurance and staging the death of one in a faked traffic accident. Some cells are loosely bound and based on petty crime; others, like the group behind the Madrid bombings, suggest a whole new level of sophistication.

The terrorists behind the Madrid attacks were major drug dealers, with a network stretching from Morocco through Spain to Belgium and the Netherlands. Their ringleader, Jamal "El Chino" Ahmidan, was the brother of one of Morocco's top hashish traffickers. Ahmidan and his followers paid for their explosives by trading hashish and cash with a former miner. When police raided the home of one plotter, they seized 125,800 ecstasy tablets—one of the largest hauls in Spanish history. In all, authorities recovered nearly $2 million in drugs and cash from the group. In contrast, the Madrid bombings, which killed 191 people, cost only about $50,000.

Similar reports of drug-dealing jihadists are coming out of France and Italy. In Milan, Islamists peddle heroin on the streets at $20 a hit and then hand off 80 percent of the take to their cell leader, according to Italy's *L'Espresso* magazine. The relationship, surprisingly, is not new. As early as 1993, says Vidino, French authorities warned that dope sales in suburban Muslim slums had fallen under the control of gangs led by Afghan war veterans with ties to Algerian terrorists. What is new is the scale of this toxic mix of jihad and dope. Moroccan terrorists used drug sales to fund not only the 2004 Madrid attack but the 2003 attacks in Casablanca, killing 45, and attempted bombings of U.S. and British ships in Gibraltar in 2002. So large looms the North African connection that investigators believe jihadists have penetrated as much as a third of the $12.5 billion Moroccan hashish trade—the world's largest—a development worrisome not only for its big money but for its extensive smuggling routes through Europe.

Along with drug trafficking, fraud of every sort is a growth industry for European jihadists. Popular scams include fake credit cards, cellphone cloning, and identity theft—low-level frauds that are lucrative but seldom attract the concerted attention of authorities. Some operatives are more ambitious, however. Officials point to the case of Hassan Baouchi, a 23-year-old ATM technician in France. Baouchi told police last year that he'd been held hostage by robbers who forced him to empty six ATMs of their cash—about $1.3 million. Investigators didn't quite buy Baouchi's story and soon put him under arrest; the money, they believe, has ended up with the Moroccan Islamic Combatant Group—the al Qaeda affiliate tied to the bombings in Casablanca and Madrid.

Another big racket for European jihadists is human smuggling. "North Africa and western Europe are somewhat like Mexico and the United States," says a U.S. counterterrorism agent. "But now imagine if Mexico were Muslim and jihadist cells were the ones moving aliens across the border." Jihadists do not dominate Europe's lucrative human smuggling trade, but they are surely profiting by it. Authorities in Italy suspect that one gang of suspected militants made over 30 landings on an island off Sicily, and that it moved thousands of people across the Mediterranean at some $4,000 a head. Particularly active is the Salafist Group for Call and Combat, an Algerian al Qaeda affiliate known by its French acronym, GSPC. Two years ago, German authorities dismantled another group moving Kurds into Europe, tied to al Qaeda ally Ansar al-Islam, a fixture of the Iraq insurgency. A recent Italian intelligence report notes that jihadists' work in human smuggling has brought them into contact with domestic and foreign criminal organizations. One partner in the trade, sources say, is the Neapolitan Camorra, the notorious Naples-based version of the Mafia, which operates safe houses for illegal aliens. Italian court records show contact between Mafia arms dealers and radical Islamists as early as 1998.

Prison Recruits

The prime training ground for Europe's jihadist criminals may well be prison. There are no hard numbers, but as much as half of France's prison population is now believed to be Muslim. In Spanish jails, where Islamic radicals have recruited for a decade, the number has reached some 10 percent. Ahmidan, leader of the Madrid bombing cell, is thought to have been radicalized while serving time in Spain and Morocco. Prison was also the recruiting center for many of the 40-plus suspects nabbed by Spanish authorities last year for plotting a sequel to the Madrid bombings—an attack with a half ton of explosives on Spain's national criminal court. Nearly half the group had rap sheets with charges ranging from drug trafficking to forgery and fraud.

Al Qaeda's leadership, however, has proved more wary about jumping into the drug trade. Holed up in the forbidding mountain refuges of the Pakistan-Afghanistan border, Osama bin Laden and his remaining lieutenants have steered clear of the largest horde of criminal wealth in years: the exploding Afghan heroin trade. Press reports of bin Laden's involvement in the drug trade are flat wrong, say counterterrorism officials. Long ago, al Qaeda strategists reasoned that drug trafficking would expose them to possible detection, captives have told U.S. interrogators. They also don't trust many of the big drug barons, intelligence officials say, and have encouraged their members not to get involved with them.

Bin Laden continues to come up with funds raised from sympathetic mosques and other supporters, but the money no longer flows so easily. Pakistan and Saudi Arabia have banned unregulated fundraising at mosques, and western spy agencies now watch closely how the money flows from big Islamic charities. One result: Cash-strapped jihadists in the badlands of the border region are staging kidnappings-for-ransom and highway robberies, Pakistani officials tell *U.S. News*. "Those people are now feeling the pinch," says Javed Cheema, head of the Interior Ministry's National Crisis Management Cell. "We see a fertile symbiosis of terrorist organizations and crime groups." Some jihadists have joined in wholesale pillaging of Afghanistan's heritage by smuggling antiquities out of the country—a trade nearly as lucrative as narcotics. Among the items being sold clandestinely on the world market: centuries-old Buddhist art and other works from the pre-Islamic world. Apparently, al Qaeda's interest is not new; before 9/11, hijack ringleader Mohamed Atta approached a German art professor about peddling Afghan antiquities, Germany's Federal Criminal Police Office revealed this year. Atta's reason, reports *Der Spiegel* magazine: "to finance the purchase of an airplane."

"You can take their blood; then why not take their property?"

Al Qaeda may be avoiding the heroin trade, but nearly everyone else in the region—from warlords to provincial governors to the Taliban—is not. The reasons are apparent: Afghanistan's opium trade is exploding. The cultivation of opium poppies, from which heroin is made, doubled from 2002 to 2003, according to CIA estimates. Then, last year, that amount *tripled*. Afghanistan now provides 87 percent of the world's heroin. "We have never seen anything like this before," says Charles, the former State Department narcotics chief. "No drug state ever made this much dope and so quickly." The narcotics industry now makes up as much as half of Afghanistan's gross domestic product, analysts estimate, and employs upward of 1 million laborers, from farmers to warehouse workers to truck drivers. And now Afghans are adding industrial-level amounts of marijuana to the mix. U.N. officials estimate that some 74,000 to 86,000 acres of pot are being grown in Afghanistan—over five times what is grown in Mexico.

Corruption

And if al Qaeda itself is staying out of drugs, its allies certainly are not. The booming drug trade has given a strong second wind to the stubborn insurgency being waged by the Taliban and Islamist warlords like Gulbuddin Hekmatyar. Both the Taliban and Hekmatyar's Hezb-i-Islami army control key smuggling routes out of the country, giving them the ability to levy taxes and protection fees on drug caravans. Crime and terrorism experts are also alarmed over the corrosive, long-term effects of all the drug money, not just within Afghanistan but across the region. The ballooning dope trade is rapidly creating narco-states in central Asia, destroying what little border control exists and making it easier for terrorist groups to operate. Ancient smuggling routes from the Silk Road to the Arabian Sea are being supercharged with tons of heroin and billions of narcodollars. Within Afghanistan, drug-fueled corruption is pervasive; governors, mayors, police, and military are all on the take. A raid this year in strategically located Helmand province came up with a whopping 9½ tons of heroin—stashed inside the governor's own office.

The smuggling routes lead from landlocked Afghanistan to the south and east through Pakistan, to the west through Iraq, and to the north through central Asia. Throughout the region the amounts of drugs seized are jumping, along with rates of crime, drug addiction, and HIV infection. Particularly hard hit are Afghanistan's impoverished northern neighbors, the former Soviet republics of Kirgizstan and Tajikistan. Widely praised demonstrations in Kirgizstan this year, which overthrew the regime of strongman Askar Akayev, have brought to power an array of questionable figures. "Entire branches of government are being directed by individuals tied to organized crime," warns Svante Cornell of the Central Asia-Caucasus Institute at Johns Hopkins University. "The whole revolution smells of opium."

"If you want to survive today as a terrorist, you probably have to support yourself."

Neighboring republics are little better off. Central Asia's major terrorist threat, the Islamic Movement of Uzbekistan, has largely degenerated into a drug mafia, officials say. In Kazakhstan the interior minister tried to investigate corruption by going undercover in a truck packed with 9 tons of watermelons, motoring 1,200 miles from the Kirgiz Republic to the Kazakh capital. His team had to pay bribes to 36 different police and customs officials en route—some as little as $1.50. (Others merely accepted their bribe in melons.) The cargo was never inspected. What is happening in Iran, meanwhile, is "a national tragedy," according to the U.N.'s Costa. So much Afghan dope is being shipped into the country that it now has the world's highest per capita rate of addiction. The ruling mullahs in Tehran have taken it seriously; Iranian security forces have fought deadly battles with drug traffickers along their border, losing some 3,600 lives in the past 16 years. But even as their troops fight, the corruption has reached high officials of the Iranian government, who are using drug profits as political patronage, sources tell *U.S. News*. "There are indications," says Cornell, "that hard-line conservatives are up to their ears in the Afghan opium trade."

Nor has Russia escaped the heroin boom's impact. From central Asia, growing amounts of Afghan heroin are entering the south of the country; drug-control officials report that large numbers of Russian military are on the take, even trucking the stuff in army vehicles. The level of corruption has, in turn, raised concern over the ultimate black market: in radioactive materials. Russia's "nuclear belt"—a chain of nuclear research and weapons sites—runs directly along those heroin smuggling routes. How bad are conditions in the area? Bemoans one intelligence expert: "We know so little."

"Even if a little bit ends up in insurgent hands, it doesn't take a lot to build a truck bomb."

Iraq, too, is starting to see its share of narcotics, but drugs are but a bit player in an insurgency that has also blurred the lines between terrorism and organized crime. Within Iraq's lawless borders exists an unsavory criminal stew composed of home-grown gangsters, ex-Baathists, and jihadists. "Terrorists and insurgents are conducting a lot of criminal activities, extortion and kidnapping in particular, as a way to acquire revenues," Caleb Temple of the Defense Intelligence Agency testified to Congress this July. Among the biggest cash cows: The insurgents take part in the wholesale theft of much of Iraq's gasoline supply, earning millions of dollars in a thriving black market. Extortion and protection are also rife, and kidnapping for ransom has ballooned into a major industry, with up to 10 abductions a day. Among those targeted: politicians, professors, foreigners, and housewives. Those with political value may find they've been sold to militants.

The insurgents are also key players in the graft and corruption that have enveloped Iraq. So much foreign aid money has disappeared that two U.S. intelligence task forces are now investigating its diversion to the insurgency, *U.S. News* has learned. Western aid agencies, Islamic charities, and U.S. military supply programs all have been targeted, analysts believe. Occupation authorities cannot account for nearly $9 billion of oil revenues it had transferred to Iraqi government agencies between 2003 and 2004, according to an audit by a special U.S. inspector general set up by Congress. "Even if a little bit ends up in insurgent hands," says one official, "it doesn't take a lot to build a truck bomb." The implications are troubling: The insurgents may be using America's own foreign aid to fund the killing of U.S. troops.

Back at home, U.S. officials are looking warily at the growing rackets of terrorist groups overseas and voice concern that the trend will grow here. "We see a lot of individual pockets of it in the United States," says Joseph Billy, deputy chief of the FBI's counterterrorism division. "Left unchecked, it's very worrisome—this is one we have to be aggressive on." Federal investigators have uncovered repeated scams here largely involving supporters of Hamas and Hezbollah, and they have traced tens of thousands of dollars back to those groups in the Middle East. "There's a direct tie," says Billy. The list of crimes includes credit card fraud, identity theft, the sale of unlicensed T-shirts—even the theft and resale of infant formula. Most of these U.S. rackets have been low level, but some, involving cigarette smuggling and counterfeit products, have earned their organizers millions of dollars.

Foreign Fish

The big fish—the Indian mobsters, Moroccan hash dealers, and Afghan drug barons—are swimming overseas, however, and U.S. law enforcement is starting to train its sights on the worst of them. After being shut out of Afghanistan for two decades, the Drug Enforcement Administration is making progress in going after top Afghan traffickers tied to the Taliban. DEA agents are applying the same sort of "kingpin strategy" that helped to break the Medellin and Cali cartels in Colombia by targeting whole trafficking organizations. The agency has identified some 10 of these "high-value targets," led by Afghans who have amassed fortunes of as much as $100 million, officials say. Two already have fallen this year: In April, agents nabbed a man they've dubbed "the Pablo Escobar of Afghanistan," Taliban ally Bashir Noorzai, by enticing him to a New York meeting. Noorzai is said to have helped establish the modern Afghan drug trade, and so lucrative were his operations that the indictment against him calls for the seizure of $50 million in drug proceeds. Then in October, the Justice Department announced the extradition of Baz Mohammad, another alleged "Taliban-linked narcoterrorist," charged with conspiring to import over $25 million worth of heroin into the United States and other countries. Mohammad, according to an indictment, boasted that "selling heroin in the United States was a 'jihad' because they were taking the Americans' money at the same time the heroin was killing them." He is now awaiting trial, in a New York jail.

The DEA's experience, however, illustrates some of the problems in grappling with the nexus between organized crime and terrorism. Despite post-9/11 calls for cooperation, the DEA's ties to other U.S. agencies are often strained; the drug agency is not even considered part of the U.S. intelligence community. Pentagon officials, worried over "mission creep," routinely refuse to give DEA agents air support in Afghanistan. Other turf issues still plague the FBI, CIA, Homeland Security, and other agencies, making collaborative work on the crime-terrorism issue problematic. The intelligence community, for example, remains leery of seeing its people or information end up in court. "It's the same wall we saw between law enforcement and the intelligence world," says one insider. "Only now it's between terrorism and other crimes."

"We have stovepiped battling terrorism and organized crime," agrees Charles, the State Department's former top cop. "You cannot meet a complex threat like this without a similar response. And we don't have one." Indeed, interviews with counterterrorism and law enforcement officials in a half-dozen federal agencies suggest that cooperation across the government remains episodic at best and depends most often on personal relationships. "The incentives are all still against sharing," complains one analyst. "The leadership says yes, the policies say yes, but the culture says no. The bureaucracy has won."

Washington looks like a model of cooperation compared with Europe, however, where the walls between agencies and across borders stand even higher. "If we don't get on top of the criminal aspect and the drug connections, we will lose ground in halting the spread of these [terrorist] organizations," warns Gen. James Jones, head of the U.S. European Command, who has watched the rise in terrorist rackets with mounting concern. "You have to have much greater cohesion and synergy."

For a brief moment in the early '90s, American cops, spies, and soldiers did come together on a common target of crime and terrorism—Pablo Escobar and his Medellin cocaine cartel. Escobar's killers were blamed for the murder of hundreds of Colombian officials and the bombing of an Avianca airliner that killed 110. To get Escobar, firewalls between agencies came down, information was shared, and money and people were focused on destroying one of the world's most powerful crime syndicates. During the 1990s, transnational crime continued to be seen as a national security priority, but it fell off the map after 9/11. Until January of this year, the federal government's chief interagency committee on organized crime hadn't even met for three years. The intelligence community's reporting on the area, although boosted in the past year, remains a near-bottom priority. One knowledgeable source called the quality of work overseas on crime "sorely lacking" and said the best material comes from other governments. Domestically, meanwhile, years of neglect by the FBI of analysis and information technology have left the agency without much useful information in its files. "Everyone thinks we've got huge databases with all our materials on organized crime," says one veteran. "We've got nothing close."

Still, the growing criminal inroads by terrorist groups have raised alarms among a handful of tough-minded policymakers in Washington, and they are pushing for change. The National Security Council has begun work on a new policy on transnational crime that promises to make the crime-terrorism connection a top priority. The CIA's Crime and Narcotics Center is spearheading the work of a dozen agencies in revamping the government's overall assessment of international crime; their report, with special attention to the nexus with terrorism, is scheduled for release early next year. One program that has caught U.S. attention is underway in Great Britain, where London's Metropolitan Police now routinely monitor low-level criminal activity for ties to terrorism, checking over reports of fraud involving banks, credit cards, and travel documents. Similar work is being done by the feds' Joint Terrorism Task Forces in some U.S. cities. And Immigration and Customs Enforcement has prioritized cracking rings smuggling people from high-risk countries, with good success.

"Draining the Swamp"

In some ways, the deeper involvement by terrorists in traditional criminal activity may make it easier to track them. Criminal informants, who can be tempted with shortened prison time and money, are much easier to develop than the true believers who fill the ranks of terrorist groups. Acts of crime also attract attention and widen the chances that terrorists will make a mistake. Take, for example, a case uncovered this July, in which four men allegedly plotted to wage a jihad against some 20 targets in Southern California, including National Guard facilities, the Israeli Consulate, and several synagogues. Prosecutors said the planned attacks, led by the founder of a radical Islamic prison group, were being funded by a string of gas station robberies.

The break in the case came not by an elite counterterrorist squad but by local cops who found a cellphone one of the robbers had lost during a gas station stickup.

Jihadists don't dominate Europe's human-smuggling trade, but they profit from it.

Getting a handle on terrorism's growing criminal rackets will not prove easy, however. "Draining the swamp," as counterterrorism officials vow to do, may require more than even a seamless approach by intelligence and law enforcement can offer. Many of the worst groups owe their success to a pervasive criminality overseas, to failed states and no man's lands from Central Asia to North Africa to South America, where the rule of law remains an abstract concept. In other places, it is the governments themselves that are the criminal enterprises, so mired in corruption that entire countries could be indicted under U.S. antiracketeering laws. Together, they help make up a criminal economy that, like a parallel universe, runs beneath the legitimate world of commerce. This global shadow economy—of dirty money, criminal enterprises, and black markets—has annual revenues of up to $2 trillion, according to U.N. estimates, larger than the gross domestic product of all but a handful of countries. Without its underground bankers, smuggling routes, and fraudulent documents, al Qaeda and its violent brethren simply could not exist. But taking on a worldwide plague of crime and corruption might be more than the public bargained for. "Ultimately, cracking down means trying to impose order where there's instability, good governance where there's corruption and crime, and economic growth where there's poverty," says the University of Pittsburgh's Phil Williams, a consultant to the United Nations on crime and terrorism finance. "As long as the only routes of escape are violence and the black market, then organized crime and terrorism will endure as global problems."

From *U.S. News & World Report*, December 5, 2005, pp. 40–54. Copyright © 2005 by U.S. News & World Report, L.P. Reprinted by permission.

Toy Soldiers
The Youth Factor in the War on Terror

"Membership in a clandestine terrorist cell; online linkages with glamorous, dangerous individuals; the opportunity to belong to a feared and seemingly heroic movement complete with martyrs—all of this is inherently appealing to young people."

CHERYL BENARD

"About the time of Easter . . . , many thousands of boys, ranging in age from six years to full maturity, left the plows or carts which they were driving, the flocks which they were pasturing, and anything else which they were doing . . . [and] put up banners and began to journey to Jerusalem. . . . They [said] that they were equal to the Divine will in this matter and that, whatever God might wish to do with them, they would accept it willingly and with humble spirit. Some were turned back at Metz, others at Piacenza, and others even at Rome. Still others got to Marseilles, but whether they crossed to the Holy Land or what their end was is uncertain. One thing is sure: that of the many thousands who rose up, only very few returned."

—*From a description of the so-called Children's Crusade in* Chronica Regiae Coloniensis Continuatio prima, *translated by James Brundage*

Much has been made of an ominous demographic reality prevalent in the Middle East. Although the exact number varies from country to country, any speaker who mentions the proportion of the population below age 20, or below age 16, can count on receiving gasps of surprise from Western audiences. Fifty percent of the population below age 19! Sixty-five percent below age 25! And no functioning economy to absorb them. It is clear even to a layperson that this spells trouble.

Experts will point out that it could also spell prosperity—in theory. In theory, a young population has the potential to be productive and to bless its society with a low dependency ratio: that is, with a larger segment of productive workers supporting a smaller segment of the elderly, the very young, the incapacitated, and otherwise nonproductive individuals who must count on tapping into the income of others. In reality, though, cultural, political, and economic factors can—and throughout much of the Islamic world do—stand in the way of productivity and prosperity. The youth overhang, instead of constituting a motor for growth, becomes what Isobel Coleman of the Council on Foreign Relations has called a potential "youthquake" and a "massive demographic tsunami."

Many young people in the Middle East, especially the famously more volatile young males, are deprived of sensible activities, bereft of real hope for a happy and independent future, unschooled in practical modes of thinking, and sexually frustrated in their strict and puritanical societies. Many are hammered with the rousing appeals of radical preachers and ideologues. Others are simply bored and purposeless. Clearly this is not a promising recipe for stable social advancement.

All of these social conditions and their implications in the region are being discussed and fretted over, and with good cause. But another variable in the situation has received less attention: the underlying mindset and mental development of young adults generally. I would argue that, beneath many of the conflicts tearing at the Middle East today, including the "war on terror," the Palestinian intifada against Israel, and the insurgency in Iraq—as indeed underneath probably most instances of major violence throughout history—there lies an unspoken, disturbing social contract in which older people pursue agendas by deploying the volatile weapon of mentally not-yet-mature younger men.

The Immature Brain

While this issue has important ethical dimensions, the question is raised more neutrally by recent neurological and developmental findings that in turn are the product of improved medical technology. Increasingly sophisticated Magnetic Resonance Imaging (MRI) of brains, in combination with research in experimental psychology, indicates that maturation may take place more gradually and conclude later than formerly presumed. A number of studies suggest that mental and behavioral development continues to be in considerable flux until somewhere between the ages of 22 and 24; that before this time, young people and particularly young men are inclined to show particular responses, behaviors, and mind-sets; and that these are of high relevance to their own personal safety and well-being and to those of others around them.

The findings can be summed up as follows: young men are strongly inclined to seek out situations of risk, excitement, and danger; and they also are likely to make fallacious judgments about their own abilities, overestimating their capacities and underestimating objective obstacles and dangers. In a variety of important interactive contexts, as a result, their reactions predictably veer toward the impulsive taking of unwise risks. All of this affects their ability not so much to understand, but to process and "believe in" the potential for negative outcomes and even catastrophic consequences of their decisions.

Not much of this, of course, really comes as a surprise. That young people are impulsive and that young men like to test themselves in situations of high risk is well known. Recent research, however, provides a much more specific window into the mechanics of youthful responses and decisions, as well as the situations that represent a particular risk for reactions that can be harmful to the individual or to others. It also reveals the inherence of some of these behaviors, which are not individual failings or errors but flow from a natural developmental process to which all individuals are subject—and which others might exploit.

The first conclusion that suggests itself from current research in neurological development is that adolescence and young adulthood conclude later than formerly assumed. Brain development is of course an ongoing process. Adolescence, however, is a time of particularly high change. Longitudinal studies following changes in the prefrontal cortex indicate that the changes do not wind down until age 22 or even later. The prefrontal cortex is jovially referred to by experts in this field as the "area of sober second thought." This is the part of the mind that carefully considers the consequences of a decision, weighs the pros and cons, reflects, and, depending on the evidence, may come to reconsider. In the absence of a fully developed prefrontal cortex, an individual will be more inclined to follow through on a spontaneous, impulsive decision.

In a 2004 study titled "Adolescent Brain Development and Drug Abuse," Ken Winters of the University of Minnesota noted that three brain structures that undergo maturation during youth—the nucleus accumbens, amygdale, and prefrontal cortex—have important implications for understanding adolescent behavior. "An immature nucleus accumbens is believed to result in preferences for activities that require low effort yet produce high excitement.... The amygdale is the structure responsible for integrating emotional reactions to pleasurable and aversive experiences. It is believed that a developing amygdale contributes to two behavioral effects: the tendency for adolescents to react explosively to situations rather than with more controlled responses, and the propensity for youth to misread neutral or inquisitive facial expressions of others as a sign of anger. And one of the last areas to mature is the prefrontal cortex . . . responsible for the complex processing of information, ranging from making judgments to controlling impulses, foreseeing consequences, and setting goals and plans. An immature prefrontal cortex is thought to be the neurobiological explanation for why teenagers show poor judgment and too often act before they think."

Better-adjusted male teenagers satisfy their craving for excitement with video games; those who belong to a disaffected minority may be drawn to the real thing.

Recent MRI and brain mapping research has also focused on the cerebellum, a part of the brain formerly thought to relate primarily to physical movement, but now found to coordinate a variety of cognitive processes and to enable individuals to "navigate" social life. As Jay Giedd of the National Institute of Mental Health, among others, has pointed out, this portion of the brain is not fully developed until well into the early twenties.

Besides magnetic resonance imaging, a second strand of research employs experiments to measure the responses and the decision making of individuals in relation to an assortment of variables, among them, age and gender. These include tests that place an individual in simulated decision-making scenarios, such as a driving situation in which he or she must make a split-second decision on whether or not to proceed through an intersection; tests that require the individual to override a physical reflex, for example by deliberately not looking in the direction of a suddenly bright light; gambling tasks that measure risk aversion; and many more. Young men perform very poorly on all of these tasks.

Thrill Seekers

In turn, outcomes suggested by the findings of both of these research methods are reflected in broader social data. Changes that begin with adolescence and conclude at the end of young adulthood incline young people, and young men in particular, to seek excitement, to misjudge situations, and to dismiss danger. These inclinations are clearly readable in morbidity rates, which increase by a dramatic 200 to 300 percent between childhood and full adulthood.

Roadside accidents, for example, are one arena in which this plays itself out. In a 2005 study commissioned by the Allstate Foundation, accident fatalities and car-related injuries to young drivers were studied in collaboration with Temple University, which brought neuropsychiatric and experimental findings to bear in an analysis of accident causation. The study noted that "key parts of the brain's decision-making circuitry do not fully develop until the mid-20s. So, in actual driving situations, teens may weigh the consequences of unsafe driving quite differently than adults do. This, combined with the increased appetite for novelty and sensation that most teens experience at the onset of puberty, makes teens more disposed to risk-taking behind the wheel—often with deadly results."

Males below the age of 24 have nearly three times as many accidents as their older counterparts; their accidents are significantly more likely to be fatal; and accident analysis reveals that the young men are almost always at fault. This is not attributable, as some might suppose, to a lack of experience or technical skill. Rather, the problem lies in the propensity of young men to take risks, to misjudge or ignore danger, and to make erroneous split-second decisions on the basis of factually unwarranted optimism and overconfidence. Young people are also substantially more likely to make the decision to drive while under the influence of alcohol or drugs.

The Allstate study found that conventional drivers' education programs are not effective in countering these dangerous youthful inclinations. They can enhance skill levels and convey information, including warnings about dangers and advice about safer decisions, but they do not affect the underlying impulses and motivators. Interestingly, the expedient of placing a female passenger in the vehicle with the young male driver effects more improvement in safe driving than a lecture or a class. Having him joined by another young male, on the other hand, will increase the likelihood of reckless driving.

Another example of how young adulthood differs from both childhood and full adulthood can be found in recent research on Post Traumatic Stress Disorder—in particular, a study published in the October 2006 issue of the *American Journal of Psychiatry*. Research conducted at Walter Reed Army Medical Hospital on veterans of combat in Afghanistan and Iraq found that soldiers below age 25 are 3.4 times more likely to experience Post Traumatic Stress Disorder than older soldiers. This is in accordance with other research showing that adolescence and young adulthood are a time of particular vulnerability to stress, and an age at which grief and loss are felt with enhanced severity.

A few caveats are in order before speculating on the political significance of these insights into young people's mentality. First, this research is fairly young and we may come, at some future point, to challenge or even reverse its findings. Second, the determinism of responses and behaviors varies. The mere fact that inclinations or reflexes push an individual in a certain direction does not mean that he or she is unable to override them; it just means that this may be more difficult.

Finally, the point being made by the research is that maturation is a process. The findings do not mean that individuals are irresponsible and volatile until, at some arbitrary point, be it 18 or 21 or 22 or 24, they suddenly emerge as mature and sober adults. Maturation unfolds at different rates and to different degrees; it seems reasonable to presume, though this has not yet been studied, that much will also depend on the surrounding societal circumstances, on education, and on other variables affecting the life circumstances and influences operating on the individual young adult.

It remains nonetheless a telling fact that, within the Middle East and Muslim communities worldwide, young males constitute the most numerous participants in violent behavior and pose the greatest security threat to Western societies. Indeed, Western European security agencies report that radicalization among European Muslim minority communities is manifesting itself at ever-younger ages, with 14 and 15 now the typical age at which young people are drawn into extremism. (The most effective recruiting tool today is the Internet.)

It is not difficult to see that propensities inherent in this age group, and effective until age 24 or so, make this subpopulation an ideal audience for radical recruitment. Membership in a clandestine terrorist cell; online linkages with glamorous, dangerous individuals; the opportunity to belong to a feared and seemingly heroic movement complete with martyrs—all of this is inherently appealing to young people. And membership comes with flaming speeches, weapons, face-masks, and all the accoutrements of a forbidden armed struggle. Better-adjusted male teenagers satisfy their craving for excitement with video games; those who belong to a disaffected minority may be drawn, at least in some instances, to the real thing.

How Real Is Real?

After all, when you are an adolescent, how real is real? The question cannot yet be scientifically measured, but we can glimpse an answer in some of the Muslim suicide bomber videos circulating on the Internet. Do not look, for the moment, at the chanting group of celebrants surrounding the prospective bomber. Ignore the splendid, resolute text he is reading from his notes. Look instead at his face, and take note of the momentary expression of surprise, even shock. Did this young man, when he signed up to become a suicide bomber, truly understand that this moment would come, that it would feel like this, that it would be real and irreversible? His expression suggests otherwise, but there is no turning back, not with the video camera rolling and his cheering comrades ready to pack him into the truck—where in many cases, to strengthen his resolve, he will be handcuffed to the steering wheel.

Similarly, the teenagers who place improvised explosive devices (IEDS) on the streets of Baghdad may not have thought very far beyond the money, or the approbation of their clique, with which this act is rewarded. us intelligence officers report seeing children, including a 14-year-old girl, placing roadside IEDS. Iraqi officials report capturing near the Syrian border a 10-year-old boy who had "come to wage jihad."

This is not to dismiss the more elaborate, complex approaches that are being put forward to explain and respond to the threat of Islamist radicalism, global terrorism, and the insurgency in Iraq. Certainly, political and ideological and cultural and ethnic and economic and perhaps religious reasons play a part. But with all of that, it would be a mistake to forget that most of the minds involved are very young and acting on impulses and a logic that any proposed solutions should take into account.

It is necessary to mention, as well, that the same is true on the other side of this conflict. If America's adversaries in Iraq, for example, are primarily young, then so are the soldiers that the United States is sending forward to confront them. There is some difficulty in criticizing Islamist recruitment videos aimed at teenage viewers, when the online game "America's Army" similarly seeks to rope in 14-year-olds for subsequent service. This multi-player interactive online game is a recruiting tool created by the us military. It is popular because of its excellent graphics and because it is free. Research conducted by the us military shows that the game is instrumental in the decision of numerous young people to join the actual armed services.

The point here obviously is not to equate the goal of these two "recruiting agencies." The point is that 14-year-old males are largely vulnerable to the promise of thrills and danger and largely oblivious to risk, and that—if the research cited above is correct—they will not have changed enough by 17 or 18 years of age to assure that their decision to join a war and risk death and dismemberment has been judicious, thoughtful, and taken in full understanding of what it can entail. Research on young people's brain development also implies that militaries ought, at a minimum, to consider some of the revealed inclinations and predispositions of young adults in their training and deployment of younger soldiers. Thus, a propensity to interpret facial expressions as reflecting hostility can clearly be detrimental in interactions with civilian populations, for example in house searches.

More generally, developmental research raises provocative questions for a us intervention in Iraq in which the largest proportion of casualties is borne by troops aged 21 and below. Do optimistic risk assessments and split-second decisions in favor of the more dangerous path play a role? Does the United States really have a "volunteer army" if very young adults have an impaired ability to judge the consequences of their decisions? And perhaps most intriguingly of all: What would the "war on terror" look like if neither side could deploy large numbers of young men with high affect, operating on hair-trigger responses, and low on "sober second thought"?

CHERYL BENARD *is a senior political scientist with the RAND Corporation and director of RAND's Initiative on Middle East Youth. She is the author of* Civil Democratic Islam *(Rand, 2004).*

Reprinted from *Current History,* January 2007, pp. 27–30. Copyright © 2007 by Current History, Inc. Reprinted with permission.

UNIT 3
State-Sponsored Terrorism

Unit Selections
7. **Iran's Suicide Brigades,** Ali Alfoneh
8. **Hizballah and Syria,** Emile El-Hokayem
9. **Guerrilla Nation,** Thor Halvorssen
10. **The Growing Syrian Missile Threat: Syria after Lebanon,** Lee Kass

Key Points to Consider
- How has the creation of suicide brigades affected Iran's neighbors?
- What is the relationship between Syria and *Hezbollah*?
- Is there a link between Hugo Chavez and the FARC?
- How has the relationship between terrorist organizations and their state sponsors changed?

Student Web Site
www.mhcls.com/online

Internet References
Further information regarding these Web sites may be found in this book's preface or online.

Council for Foreign Relations
   http://www.cfr.org/issue/458/state_sponsors_of_terrorism.html
International Institute for Terrorism and Counterterrorism
   http://www.ict.org.il/inter_ter/st_terror/State_t.htm
State Department's List of State Sponsors of Terrorism
   http://www.state.gov/s/ct/rls/crt

The role of states in international terrorism has long been the subject of debate. It is clear that states often support foreign groups with similar interests. This support can take a number of forms. States may provide political support, financial assistance, safe havens, logistical support, training, or in some cases even weapons and equipment to groups that advocate the use of political violence. State support for terrorist organizations, however, does not necessarily translate into state *control* over terrorism. As Martha Crenshaw has noted, "while terrorists exclude no donors on principle . . . the acceptance of support does not, however, bind clients to the wishes of their patrons."

Nevertheless, since the passage of the Export Administration Act of 1979, the U.S. government has sought to hold some states responsible for the actions of groups they support. Section 6 (j) of the Export Administration Act requires the publication of an annual list of state sponsors of terrorism and thus provides the basis for contemporary U.S. anti-terrorism and sanctions policy. This list currently includes Cuba, Iran, Libya, North Korea, Sudan, and Syria. Not surprisingly, this list includes only states perceived to be, for wide variety of reasons, a threat to U.S. interests. States in which the United States has significant political or economic interests are, regardless of their record on terrorism, deliberately excluded.

In the first article in this unit, Ali Alfoneh examines Iran's use of "martyrdom-seekers" against internal and external threats. He describes the training and command of these units, their role in internal power struggles, and their potential impact on Iran's relationship with its neighbors. Next, Emile El-Hokayem assesses the

U.S. AID photo

changing relationship between Syria and Hizbollah. He examines the historical development of the relationship between Syria and its "client," arguing that Hizballah is becoming increasingly more autonomous. Next, Thor Halvorssen discusses evidence of a potential connection between Venezuelan President Hugo Chavez and the Armed Revolutionary Forces of Colombia (FARC). He argues that, in spite of Chavez's consistent denials, he continues to support the FARC. Finally, Lee Kass focuses on Syria's ambitions to develop its weapons of mass destruction (WMD) capability. He points to Syria's links to terrorist organizations and argues that it will become more difficult to confront Syria's sponsorship of international terrorism.

Iran's Suicide Brigades
Terrorism Resurgent

ALI ALFONEH

More than five years after President George W. Bush's declaration of a global war against terrorism, the Iranian regime continues to embrace suicide terrorism as an important component of its military doctrine. In order to promote suicide bombing and other terrorism, the regime's theoreticians have utilized religion both to recruit suicide bombers and to justify their actions. But as some factions within the Islamic Republic support the development of these so-called martyrdom brigades, their structure and activities suggest their purpose is not only to serve as a strategic asset in either deterring or striking at the West, but also to derail domestic attempts to dilute the Islamic Republic's revolutionary legacy.

Such strategy is apparent in the work of the Doctrinal Analysis Center for Security without Borders (*Markaz-e barresiha-ye doktrinyal-e amniyat bedun marz*), an Islamic Revolutionary Guard Corps think tank.[1] Its director, Hassan Abbasi, has embraced the utility of suicide terrorism. On February 19, 2006, he keynoted a Khajeh-Nasir University seminar celebrating the anniversary of Ayatollah Ruhollah Khomeini's *fatwa* (religious edict) calling for the murder of British author Salman Rushdie. As Khomeini often did, Abbasi began his lecture with literary criticism. He analyzed a U.S. publication from 2004 that, according to Abbasi, "depicts the prophet of Islam as the prophet of blood and violence." Rhetorically, he asked, "Will the Western man be able to understand martyrdom with such prejudice? [Can he] interpret Islam as anything but terrorism?" The West sees suicide bombings as terrorism but, to Abbasi, they are a noble expression of Islam.

So what is terrorism if not suicide bombing? To Abbasi, terrorism includes any speech and expression he deems insulting to Islam. According to press coverage of his lecture, Abbasi noted that "[German chancellor] Merkel and [U.S. president] Bush's support of the Danish newspaper, which insults Islam's prophet, has damaged their reputation in the Islamic world and has raised the question of whether Christianity, rather than Islam, is of terrorist nature."[2] From the Iranian leadership's perspective, therefore, *Jyllands-Posten*'s cartoons are evidence of Christian terrorism.

By Abbasi's definition, Iran may not sponsor terrorism, but it does not hesitate to promote suicide attacks. He announced that approximately 40,000 Iranian *estesh-hadiyun* (martyrdom-seekers) were ready to carry out suicide operations against "twenty-nine identified Western targets" should the U.S. military strike Iranian nuclear installations.[3]

Such threats are not new. According to an interview with Iran's Fars News Agency released on Abbasi's weblog, he has propagated *haras-e moghaddas* (sacred terror) at least since 2004. "The front of unbelief," Abbasi wrote, "is the front of the enemies of God and Muslims. Any deed which might instigate terror and horror among them is sacred and honorable."[4] On June 5, 2004, he spoke of how suicide operations could overcome superior military force: "In 'deo-centric' thought, there is no need for military parity to face the enemy . . . Deo-centric man prepares himself for martyrdom while humanist man struggles to kill."[5]

Abbasi's rise to prominence in the state-controlled Iranian media coincides with the growth of a number of organizations that have constrained those prone to moderation within the Islamic Republic. Take, for example, the Headquarters Commemorating the Martyrs of the Global Islamic Movement (*Setad-e Pasdasht-e Shohada-ye Nehzat-e Eslami*), an organization founded in 2004 as a protest against President Mohammad Khatami's attempts at improving Iran's relations with Egypt.[6]

The organization's prominence continued to grow throughout the year. On June 5, 2004, the reformist daily *Shargh* granted Mohammad-Ali Samadi, Headquarters' spokesman, a front page interview.[7] Samadi has a pedigree of hard-line revolutionary credentials. He is a member of the editorial boards of *Shalamche* and *Bahar* magazines, affiliated with the hard-line Ansar-e Hezbollah (Followers of the Party of God) vigilante group, as well as the newspaper *Jomhouri-ye Eslami*, considered the voice of the intelligence ministry.[8] Samadi said he had registered 2,000 volunteers for suicide operations at a seminar the previous day.[9] Copies of the registration forms show that the "martyrdom-seekers" could volunteer for suicide operations against three targets: operations against U.S. forces in the Shi'ite holy cities in Iraq; against Israelis in Jerusalem; and against Rushdie. The registration forms also quote Khomeini's declaration that "[I]f the enemy assaults the lands of the Muslims and its frontiers, it is mandatory for all Muslims to defend it by all means possible [be it by] offering life or property,"[10] and current supreme leader Ali Khamene'i's remarks that "[m]artyrdom-seeking operations mark the highest point of the greatness of a nation and the peak of [its] epic. A man, a youth, a boy, and a girl who are prepared to sacrifice their lives for the sake of the interests of the nation and their religion is the [symbol of the] greatest pride, courage, and bravery."[11] According to press reports, a number of senior regime officials have attended the Headquarters' seminars.[12]

Suicide Units

The Iranian officials appeared true to their word. During a September 2004 speech in Bushehr, home of Iran's declared nuclear reactor, Samadi announced the formation of a "martyrdom-seeking" unit from Bushehr while Hossein Shariatmadari, editor of the official daily *Keyhan,* called the United States military "our hostage in Iraq," and bragged that "martyrdom-operations constitute a tactical capability in the world of Islam."[13]

Then, on November 23, 2004, in response to the U.S. campaign against Iraqi insurgents in Fallujah,[14] Samadi announced the formation of the first suicide unit. Named after the chief bombmaker of Hamas, Yahya Ayyash, also known as Al-Muhandis (The Engineer) assassinated on January 5, 1996, it consisted of three teams of unknown size: the Rim Saleh ar-Riyashi team, named after Hamas's first female suicide bomber; the Mustafa Mahmud Mazeh team, named after a 21-year-old Lebanese who met his death in a Paddington hotel room on August 3, 1989, priming a book bomb likely aimed at Salman Rushdie; and the Ahmad Qasir team, named after a 15-year-old Lebanese Hezbollah suicide bomber whose operation demolished an eight-story building housing Israeli forces in Tyre, southern Lebanon, on November 11, 1982.[15] Samadi said there would be an additional call for volunteers at Tehran's largest Iran-Iraq war cemetery, the Behesht-e Zahra, the following week,[16] and even promised to consider establishing special elementary schools to train for suicide operations.[17]

He kept his word. On December 2, 2004, the Headquarters gathered a crowd in the Martyr's Section of Behesht-e Zahra,[18] where those who conducted suicide operations are honored. According to the Iranian Mehr News Agency, the organization unveiled a memorial stone commemorating the "martyrs" killed in the 1983 Hezbollah attacks on the U.S. Marine and French peacekeepers' barracks in Beirut. They set the stone next to one commemorating Anwar Sadat's assassin. Samadi concluded the ceremony with a raging speech, declaring, "The operation against the Marines was a hard blow in the mouth of the Americans and demonstrated that despite their hollow prestige and imagined strength . . . they [have] many vulnerable points and weaknesses. We consider this operation a good model. The cemeteries in which their dead are buried provide an interesting view and cool the hearts of those Muslims who have been stepped upon under the boots of the Yankees while they were ignored by the international community."[19]

The suicide corps continued to expand even though there is no evidence that their patrons have made them operational. In April 2005, the semi-official daily *Iran* announced convocation of a unit of female suicide bombers nicknamed the Olive Daughters.[20] The *Baztab* news website, which is associated with Mohsen Rezai, head of the Islamic Revolutionary Guard Corps from 1981 to 1997 and since secretary of the Expediency Council, cited one Firouz Rajai-Far, who said, "The martyrdom-seeking Iranian women and girls . . . are ready to walk in the footsteps of the holy female Palestinian warriors, realizing the most terrifying nightmares of Zionists."[21] Rajai-Far, a former hostage taker at the U.S. Embassy in Tehran, holds the license for *Do-Kouhe* (*Two Mountains,* referring to one of the fiercest battlegrounds of the Iran-Iraq war) magazine, which is affiliated with the vigilante organization Ansar-e Hezbollah.[22]

Ayatollah Hossein Nouri Hamedani bestowed theological legitimacy upon such suicide terror operations in a written message to the gathering.[23] Attendance at the rally indicates some endorsement and a support network for suicide operations. Attending the rally were Palestinian Hamas representative Abu Osama al-Muata; Muhammad Hasan Rahimian, the supreme leader's personal representative to the powerful Bonyad-e Shahid (The Martyr Foundation); Mehdi Kuchakzadeh, an Iranian parliamentarian; Mustafa Rahmandust, general secretary of the Association for Support to the People of Palestine; and model female fighter Marziyeh Hadideh Dabbagh.[24]

More vocal expressions of solidarity are limited, however. The Mehr News Agency reports only a single declaration of solidarity from the spokesman of the University Basij at the Tehran branch of Islamic Azad University, who compared contemporary suicide operations with the "revolutionary deeds" of Mirza-Reza Kermani, the assassin of Nasser al-Din Shah, a nineteenth-century king vilified by the Islamic Republic, and with Navvab Safavi, founder of the Fadayian-e Islam and famous for assassinating the liberal nationalist author and historian Ahmad Kasravi.[25] Still, that a group at the Islamic Azad University endorsed the organization is significant. Founded to broaden the reach of education after the Islamic Revolution, the university has several dozen satellite campuses across the country and today is the largest higher education system in Iran.

On May 13, 2005, officials declared the second suicide terror unit, the so-called "Martyr Shahada unit," consisting of 300 martyrdom-seekers, to be ready.[26] Some months later, there was a gathering of the "martyrdom-seekers" at Shahrud University. While the invited Hamas representative did not attend, they watched Mahmoud Ahmadinejad's speech from the "World without Zionism" conference on screen.[27] While the status of the third and fourth suicide brigades remains unclear, new suicide units continue to declare their readiness. In May 2006, a fifth "martyrdom-seeking" unit, named after Commander Nader Mahdavi, who died in a 1988 suicide mission against the U.S. Navy in the Persian Gulf, declared itself ready to defend Iran. The Headquarters even claims to have recruited "thirty-five foreign Jews" for suicide attacks.[28]

Lebanese Hezbollah's abduction of two Israeli soldiers on July 12, 2006, provided another press opportunity for Iranian suicide brigades. On July 17, 2006, Arya News Agency reported an expedition of two "martyrdom-units," one consisting of eighteen and the second consisting of nine "martyrdom-seekers," to Lebanon.[29] At demonstrations in Tehran and Tabriz ten days later, sixty Iranian volunteers declared their readiness for holy war.[30] There was also a rally in Rasht, capital of the Caspian province of Gilan, on July 29.[31] But despite the bravado, Iranian police stopped a caravan of self-described "martyrdom-seekers" at the Turkish border. A leftist weblog quoted the governor of the West Azerbaijan province in which the border crossings with Turkey lie as saying he received a telephone call from Ahmadinejad asking him to stop the suicide units.[32]

Training and Command

While the Iranian government seeks propaganda value out of announcements of new suicide units, it remains in doubt just how committed recruits are. When an Iranian youth magazine interviewed Rajai-Far, an organizer of the Olive Daughters, she remained elusive about how serious her recruits were about suicide.[33]

Despite its rhetoric and the occasional rally, there is little evidence that the Iranian government has established camps to train suicide terrorists. While the Revolutionary Guards operate a network of bases inside Iran, there is little coverage—at least in open source newspapers and Iranian media—of actual training of those recruited by the Headquarters. There have been two mentions of a military exercise for the suicide brigades around the Karaj Dam. Muhammad-Reza Ja'afari, commander of the Gharar-gah-e Asheghan-e Shahadat (Congregation of the Lovers of Martyrdom) training camp, referred to one exercise as the "Labeik Ya Khamene'i" (We are responding to your call, Khamene'i).[34] With the exception of the representation of Hamas in the early development of the Iranian "martyrdom-seekers," there is little proof of organizational links to external terrorist organizations.

Nor does the training of any unit mean that the Iranian government is prepared to deploy such forces. In June 2004, Samadi explained that the "activities of the Headquarters will remain theoretical as long as there is no official authorization, and martyrdom-seeking operations will not commence unless the leader [Khamene'i] orders them to do so."[35]

But command and control remain vague. Hussein Allah Karam, a well-known figure from Ansar-e Hezbollah without formal ties to the "martyrdom-seekers," stresses that Khamene'i need not grant permission for any exercises since the trainees are not armed. Evading the question of what need there is to create "martyrdom-seeking" units parallel with the Basij, Karam responded, "Martyrdom-seeking groups are nongovernmental organizations,"[36] not part of Iranian officialdom.

The Basij, a paramilitary militia of irregulars loosely charged with defending the revolution, has not been happy with the competition. Basij Commander Mohammad Hejazi condemned the Headquarters' declaration that it sought to dispatch suicide units to Lebanon. "Such actions have absolutely no link to [Iran's] official apparatus and only serve propaganda aims," he declared. In an indirect critique of the suicide units' leadership, he added: "Some seemingly independent groups are trying to attract . . . the youth with no coordination with official institutions and without the approval of the command structure for propaganda purposes. Their goals might be noble, but their means are not correct."[37] Government spokesman Gholam-Hussein Elham underlined this argument.[38]

The nongovernmental status of the Headquarters and the "martyrdom-seekers" was reinforced in comments of an anonymous Revolutionary Guards commander to *Shargh*. He explained, "Since the Headquarters . . . is a nongovernmental organization, the organization does not look for orders from the military in case they should take action. Their operations are to be compared with the martyrdom-operations of the Palestinians which are not related to the government of Iran."[39] The foreign ministry, which under Khatami was more reformist than the hard-line Revolutionary Guards, referred to the Headquarters members as "irresponsible elements" who did "not reflect the line of government,"[40] and, on August 3, 2006, Iranian parliamentarian Mehdi Kuchekzadeh called the Headquarters an NGO during a rally at Behesht-e Zahra.[41]

Baztab reacted angrily to the publication of advertisements for "martyrdom operations" in *Partov*, the hard-line monthly of the Imam Khomeini Research Institute in Qom, accusing the publication, the Headquarters, and the director of the institute, Ayatollah Mohammad Taghi Mesbah Yazdi—perhaps the most radical of the Islamic Republic's religious theoreticians—of enabling outsiders more easily to label Iran as a terror sponsor.[42] Vice President Mohammad Ali Abtahi expressed similar sentiments. "Martyrdom-operations against the interests of other states must remain secret . . . The public exposure of such gatherings is the very proof that they are not going to do anything," he wrote. Abtahi accuses Yazdi of harming the national interests of Iran, and more seriously, of attempting to create parallel institutions in the Islamic Republic in order to eliminate internal opposition to his political interests.[43] Such attacks called member of the parliament Shokrollah Attarzadeh to the defense of Mesbah Yazdi. Attarzadeh said that volunteers without connection to the ayatollah organized the "martyrdom operations," which he claimed, at any rate, to be purely defensive.[44]

An Instrument for Power Struggles

Baztab's hostility toward Mesbah Yazdi is significant. The Islamic Republic of Iran has long sanctioned widespread use of terror and vigilante justice to keep its citizens in line. Perhaps the most prominent example was the 1997–99 serial killings in which the Iranian secret services systematically liquidated Iranian intellectuals with the aim of intimidating dissidents. This case has been subject to extensive debate, causing a considerable uproar among the Iranian public. The Iranian Ministry of Intelligence and National Security claims that the murders were committed by rogue cells in the ministry. However, Iran's most famous journalist and political dissident, Akbar Ganji, accuses the former minister of intelligence, Ali Fallahian, and Khamene'i of responsibility for the killings.[45]

During the 2005 presidential campaign, the reformist daily *Rooz* warned of the formation of a new Forghan,[46] a radical Islamist group from the early days of the Islamic Revolution.[47] Ali Yunesi, minister of intelligence, and Abtahi both seconded such concerns.[48] Baqir Nobakht, spokesman for Ali Akbar Hashemi Rafsanjani's election campaign, criticized Yazdi by suggesting that he sought to use the "army of martyrdom-seekers" for operations against his political enemies inside Iran.[49]

For more than a century, hard-line officials have turned to vigilante groups during periods of political upheaval.[50] Their political influence is noticeable.[51] The 1979 Islamic revolution only strengthened such tendencies, and there is no doubt that the patrons of the "martyrdom-seekers" have used the Headquarters as a tool to maintain revolutionary values against those that might ameliorate them.

Here, the crisis regarding the change in Iran's policy towards Egypt is instructive. From almost the start of the Islamic Republic, there has been considerable tension between Tehran and Cairo. Ayatollah Khomeini objected to Egyptian president Anwar Sadat's recognition of and peace treaty with Israel. After Sadat's assassination, Iranian authorities named a street after his assassin, Khaled Islambouli. For years after, this action has been an irritant in Egyptian-Iranian relations.[52] But in January 2004, toward the end of Muhammad Khatami's presidency, the Mehr News Agency reported that the Iranian government had asked Tehran's city council to change the street name.[53] The city council acquiesced, renaming it "*Intifada* Street." Foreign Ministry spokesman Hamid-Reza Asefi attributed the decision to improving Egyptian-Iranian relations.[54]

The Headquarters protested, sending a letter to then-mayor Mahmoud Ahmadinejad.[55] Ahmadinejad defended the decision in the name of promoting unity among Muslim countries "in order to face the global Zionist front."[56] The Headquarters responded with a press release,[57] and a demonstration against the decision.[58] Mehdi Chamran, the Tehran city council chairman and brother of the late commander of the Revolutionary Guard, Mostafa Chamran, said that the foreign ministry had imposed the decision but that he preferred to honor Islambouli.[59] In an Iranian-style compromise, the street was finally called Mohammad al-Durrah Street after a 12-year old boy who was caught in crossfire and killed in the opening days of the second *intifada*.[60] But the Headquarters was successful in scuttling rapprochement with the largest Arab state to make peace with Israel. On January 28, 2004, the London-based Arabic daily *Asharq al-Awsat* announced that Egyptian president Hosni Mubarak would not visit Iran due to the presence of a picture of Khaled Islambouli on public display in Tehran.[61]

Those associated with the Headquarters appear willing to use irregular forces against enemies not only foreign but also domestic. Groups connected to Mesbah Yazdi roughed up Rafsanjani on June 5, 2006, in Qom.[62] In the past, vigilantes directed such attacks against reformers or free thinkers, but now the first generation of the Iranian revolutionaries such as Rafsanjani receive the same treatment.

And as in the past, the violence is connected to the same groupings in Iranian politics: the *Keyhan* editor Shariatmadari, now close to the Headquarters, as the intellectual proponent of violence against liberal elements,[63] and Hussein Allah Karam of Ansar-e Hezbollah, now also linked to the "martyrdom-seekers"[64] and, more directly, with Ansar-e Hezbollah itself, which publishes advertisements for the Headquarters and interviews with their spokesmen.[65]

Conclusions

Since 9-11, the increased focus on international terror has amplified fear of terrorism. By forming suicide terrorists units, Tehran can, at a minimum, exploit such fear. Already, Western policymakers warn that any strike against Iran could spark a resurgence of Iranian-backed terror. That the Islamic Republic has already formed suicide bomber brigades underscores that point. But the fact that the Iranian leadership must embrace such nonconventional deterrents may suggest that Tehran recognizes that the Iranian military is weaker than Iranian figures admit.

However, the suicide units may serve a dual function. They are, in effect, the most radical factions' guns-for-hire, unquestioning loyalists who are willing to die to preserve revolutionary values. As such, Iranian hard-liners can use them to saber-rattle as well as to keep reformers and liberals at bay. This may pose the more immediate threat since the willingness of Iranian hard-liners to use violence against their internal political opponents, could pose an almost insurmountable impediment to those who might seek to liberalize the Islamic Republic from within.

Notes

1. Doctrinal Analysis Center for Security without Borders website, accessed Aug. 8, 2006.
2. *Shargh* (Tehran), Feb. 20, 2006.
3. *Shargh,* Feb. 20, 2006.
4. Hassan Abbasi weblog, June 5, 2004, accessed Aug. 6, 2006.
5. Abbasi weblog, June 5, 2004.
6. Mehr News Agency (Tehran), Jan. 5, 2004.
7. *Shargh,* June 5, 2004.
8. *Shargh,* June 5, 2004.
9. *Shargh,* June 5, 2004.
10. Ruhollah Khomeini, *Tawzih al-Masa'il,* 9th ed. (Tehran: Entesharat-e Iran, 1999), pp. 454–5.
11. Ali Khamene'i, May 1, 2002 speech.
12. Mehr, Oct. 16, 2004.
13. *Iran* (Tehran), Sept. 11, 2004.
14. *Iran,* Nov. 20, 2004.
15. Mehr, Nov. 29, 2004.
16. Mehr, Nov. 23, 2004.
17. *Iran,* Sept. 11, 2004.
18. For a pictorial report, see Mehr, Dec. 2, 2004.
19. Mehr, Dec. 3, 2004.
20. *Iran,* Apr. 19, 2005.
21. *Baztab* (Tehran), Apr. 21, 2005.
22. *Shargh,* June 5, 2004.
23. *Baztab,* Apr. 21, 2005.
24. *Baztab,* Apr. 21, 2005; *Shargh,* Apr. 23, 2005.
25. Mehr, Dec. 5, 2004.
26. Mehr, May 13, 2005.
27. *Rooz* (Tehran), Nov. 18, 2005.

28. *Shargh,* May 27, 2006.
29. Arya News Agency, July 17, 2006.
30. CNN, July 27, 2006.
31. *Shargh,* July 30, 2006.
32. *Peik Net* (Tehran), Aug. 3, 2006.
33. *Javan* (Tehran), July 9, 2005.
34. *Javan,* Aug. 16, 2005.
35. *Shargh,* June 5, 2004.
36. *Iran,* Sept. 5, 2005.
37. *Shargh,* July 22, 2006.
38. *Jahan-e Eghtesad* (Tehran), July 25, 2006.
39. *Shargh,* June 5, 2004.
40. *Shargh,* Aug. 17, 2004.
41. *E'temad* (Tehran), Aug. 3, 2006.
42. *Baztab,* July 24, 2005.
43. See Mohammad Ali Abtahi, *Webnevesht* website, July 27, 2005.
44. *Shargh,* July 31, 2005.
45. Akbar Ganji, *Tarik-khaneh-ye ashbah. Asibshenasi-ye gozar be dowlat-e democratic-e tosé-gara* (Tehran: Tarh-e No, 1999), pp. 408–10; idem, *Alijenab-e sorkhpoush va alijenaban-e khakestari: Asibshenasi-ye gozar be dowlat-e demokratik-e tose'e-gara* (Tehran: Tarh-e No, 2000), pp. 210–8.
46. *Rooz,* June 21, 2005.
47. For more information, see Rasoul Ja'farian, ed., *Jaryan-ha va sazeman-ha-ye mazhabi-siyasi. Sal-ha-ye 1320–1357* (Tehran: Markaz-e Asnad-e Enghelab-e Eslami, 2004), pp. 568–82; Michael Rubin, *Into the Shadows. Radical Vigilantes in Khatami's Iran* (Washington, D.C.: The Washington Institute for Near East Policy, 2001), pp. 21–2.
48. Iranian Students' News Agency (ISNA), July 16, 2005 ; Abtahi, *Webnevesht,* July 27, 2005.
49. *Iran,* June 22, 2005.
50. Richard Cottam, *Nationalism in Iran* (Pittsburgh: University of Pittsburgh Press, 1964), pp. 37–8; Marvin Zonis, *The Political Elite of Iran* (Princeton: Princeton University Press, 1971), p. 348.
51. Rubin, *Into the Shadows,* p. xviii.
52. Shahrough Akhavi, "Egypt: Political and Religious Relations in the Modern Period," *Encyclopaedia Iranica Online,* accessed Aug. 23, 2006; William Millward, "Egypt and Iran: Regional Rivals at Diplomatic Odds," *Commentary,* May 1992; *Neshat Daily* (Tehran), June 6, 1999, in *BBC Summary of World Broadcasts,* June 8, 1999; *Al-Hayat* (London), June 7, 1999, in *BBC Summary of World Broadcasts,* June 9, 1999.
53. *Mehr,* Jan. 5, 2004.
54. *Mehr,* Jan. 6, 2004.
55. *Mehr,* Jan. 7, 2004.
56. *Mehr,* Jan. 7, 2004.
57. *Mehr,* Jan. 9, 2004.
58. *Mehr,* Jan. 9, 2004.
59. *Mehr,* Jan. 9, 2004.
60. *BBC News,* Jan. 5, 2004.
61. *Mehr,* Jan. 28, 2004.
62. For a pictorial account of the attack against Rafsanjani, see ISNA, June 5, 2006.
63. *Iran,* Sept. 11, 2004.
64. *Iran,* Sept. 5, 2005.
65. Firouz Rajai-Far, interview, *Ya Lesarat al-Hossein* (Ansar-e Hezbollah, Tehran), May 10 and 17, 2006; see advertisements for "martyrdom operations," *Ya Lesarat al-Hossein,* Apr. 12, 2006.

ALI ALFONEH is a PhD fellow in the department of political science, University of Copenhagen, and a research fellow at the Royal Danish Defense College. He thanks Henrik Joergensen and Thomas Emil Jensen, both from the Institute for Strategy at the Royal Danish Defense College, for their input.

Article 8

Hizballah and Syria
Outgrowing the Proxy Relationship

EMILE EL-HOKAYEM

Terms such as "proxy" and "client" are often used to characterize the power dynamic between Hizballah and its allies Iran and Syria. These states' vital resources and indispensable political sponsorship elevated Hizballah to the position it enjoys today. They each played a central role in past decisions of momentous importance for Hizballah. Today, however, this image of Hizballah as a client of Iran and Syria has become obsolete due to the power base the Shi'ite group has nurtured and expanded in Lebanon and the growing political capital it has acquired in the Middle East thanks to at least the perception of its military victories, be they real or not, particularly in the summer 2006 war against Israel.

By holding its ground against Israel, the region's strongest military, Hizballah demonstrated its capacity to shake the Lebanese and regional political landscape. Hizballah resisted Israel's onslaught without substantive Syrian support. By partnering with Hizballah, Syria hoped to defy isolation and reclaim its role as a pivotal power in the region, as well as give the Asad regime a new lease on life. The shifting dynamics of this relationship, however, with Hizballah asserting itself as a more-autonomous actor, have considerable implications for policies aimed at engaging or isolating Syria, as well as for dealing with the Hizballah challenge.

Hizballah has acquired a degree of autonomy and flexibility in recent years vis-à-vis Syria. Long gone are the days when Damascus's rules and influence determined Hizballah's activities, guaranteeing the predictability and restraint that prevented full-blown war. Hizballah has emerged as a more-independent player able to operate in Lebanon and the wider Middle East on its own terms.

Syria and Hizballah maintain complex relations that have evolved considerably over the past 25 years, shifting to fit their strategic interests and ideological agendas. Yet, two crucial changes, one in the early 1990s when Syria established itself as the unquestioned dominant player in Lebanon and the other ongoing since 2000 as Hizballah gradually grows stronger, have redefined how they interact and led them to reassess their relative positions. Hizballah has acquired enough confidence and prestige to become more than just a pawn for Syria to manipulate. Today, for strategic and ideological motives, Syria is more pro-Hizballah than Hizballah is pro-Syria.

Hizballah's Initial Volatile Relationship with Syria in the 1980s

Lebanon's Hizballah was born from a long process of Shi'ite awakening made possible by the political activism of charismatic clerics and by urbanization and rose from the chaos of the Lebanese civil war. It has emerged as the foremost and most famed Shi'ite organization in the Sunni-dominated Arab world.[1] The Islamic Republic of Iran's commitment to exporting its revolution and Israel's 1982 invasion of Lebanon to dismantle the Palestinian guerrilla infrastructure in Lebanon and install a friendly regime gave Hizballah its central and crucial raison d'etre—*muqawama,* or resistance against a formidable occupier, Israel—that would transcend political and sectarian rifts and shape its political outlook.

Syria had a direct but not determining role in Hizballah's birth, allowing Iranian units to enter Lebanon to provide organizational, logistical, and operational support for guerrilla operations. An in-depth examination of the Hizballah-Iran connection falls outside the scope of this paper,[2] but unlike Tehran, Damascus did not anticipate Hizballah's evolution into Lebanon's foremost guerrilla organization, nor was it comfortable with the prospect of managing an Islamist organization with clear transformational goals. Given its own experience with Islamists, Damascus was concerned about a potential loss of control over this new movement.[3] Hizballah's ideology, Iranian political sponsorship, independent resources, and tight discipline made it problematic for Syria to exert the kind of control it had over its other Lebanese clients, including Amal, the Shi'ite community's initial champion and Syria's favorite proxy.

Yet, after the weakening of Syria's position in Lebanon following the Israeli invasion and the deployment of the multinational force composed of U.S. and European troops, Hizballah was instrumental in facilitating Syria's reentry into the Lebanese arena. Lacking a strategy and resources, Damascus was in no position to confront the multinational force and Israeli occupation forces in Lebanon head-on to protect its Western flank and interests in Lebanon. It therefore relied on local allies to reestablish influence, and many willingly cooperated. Hizballah complied mostly on tactical grounds because its interests intersected with those of Syria. It did not initially accept the Syrian logic of co-opting or coercing Lebanese leaders from all political and religious persuasions into accepting its domination without questioning Lebanon's sectarian-based political system. Nonetheless, Syria appreciated the potency of Hizballah's asymmetric warfare and willingness to spearhead both the anti-Israeli resistance and efforts to expel the multinational force. At the same time, Syria went to great lengths to avoid irrevocably alienating Western powers by posing as a moderating force and cultivating deniability, especially during the hostage crisis.[4] What Syria would not do, Hizballah and others did.

This image of Hizballah as a client of Iran and Syria has become obsolete.

Syria's uneasiness with Hizballah showed in its efforts to sideline the group's political outreach. Hizballah was notably absent from several unsuccessful efforts to negotiate a comprehensive settlement of the Lebanese war, including the Syria-engineered Tripartite Agreement of December 1985. Hizballah was also involved in deadly clashes with Syria and Syrian allies over control of West Beirut in the 1980s. By the end of the decade, Hizballah's future was still far from guaranteed. Much would hinge on the nature and quality of its relations with Syria, by then the dominant player in Lebanon, whose strategic environment and preferences were quickly changing with the rise of the United States as the uncontested external power in the Middle East.

Hizballah Adapts to Syrian Domination in the 1990s

Major regional realignments and international acceptance of Syrian domination of Lebanon in the early 1990s paved the way for the first turning point in Syrian-Hizballah relations. Persuaded by U.S. diplomacy, Syria joined both the U.S.-led coalition against Iraq and the Arab-Israeli peace process in 1991. Almost simultaneously, the death of Ayatollah Ruhollah Khomeini in 1989 and Iranian fatigue of revolutionary radicalism resulted in a pragmatic reorientation of Iranian foreign policy that gave Syria a freer hand to maneuver regionally. Syria became the uncontested power in Lebanon.

Syria's Strategic Leverage

The official framework for Syria's presence in Lebanon was based on the 1989 Taif Agreement, which reaffirmed the centrality of Lebanon's sectarian power-sharing structure while calling for its deconfessionalization. The agreement crushed Hizballah's idealistic goal of an Islamic state and should have spelled its end as an armed organization, as it also required the disarmament of all militias. Hizballah's conundrum was that Syria had become the Taif Agreement's godfather, and rejecting it would inevitably lead to confrontation. This new political reality compelled Hizballah, after intense internal debates, to accept Lebanon's confessional system and to work out an arrangement with Syria to preserve its weaponry.[5] Conveniently, Syria had a use for this arrangement. Syrian president Hafiz al-Asad sought to recover the Golan Heights lost to Israel in 1967 and to obtain a peace agreement that acknowledged Syria's pivotal role in the region. Hafiz had few avenues for exerting pressure, and he quickly grasped the value of relying on Hizballah as an armed group to improve Damascus's negotiating position vis-à-vis Israel.

Syria's departure from Lebanon presented Hizballah with challenges and opportunities.

The writings of prominent U.S. and Israeli peace negotiators as well as interviews with Syrian officials confirm that Hafiz sincerely desired a negotiated settlement with Israel, contingent on the full recovery of the Golan Heights in exchange for a flexible mechanism for its return, including mutual security guarantees, water arrangements, and diplomatic relations.[6] Although Hafiz hoped to orchestrate an Arab front to strengthen his own negotiating position, the collapse of the elusive Arab front after the 1993 Oslo accords and the 1994 Israeli-Jordanian peace agreement forced Syria to look elsewhere for leverage.

Lebanon, firmly anchored in the Syrian orbit, served as Damascus's strategic depth. It guaranteed good-faith negotiations over the Golan Heights from a position of relative strength. The Western and Israeli assumption underlying Syrian-Israeli talks was that Damascus would constrain and eventually disarm Hizballah once peace was reached. As former Western and Arab diplomats put it, there was an informal understanding that once peace between Syria and Israel was signed, a treaty between Israel and Lebanon would follow, providing a framework for Hizballah's disarmament and the integration of its fighters into Lebanon's regular armed forces.[7] Yet, Hizballah's future was never explicitly put on the table, and there is no clear indication that Syria was asked to offer written guarantees to that end. Hizballah's own statements were contradictory enough to wonder whether its leadership even knew the endgame. Hizballah's ambiguous rhetoric might have been aimed at augmenting pressure on Israel and increasing its own value as a Syrian asset.[8]

Syria's official position on Hizballah's activities in Lebanon relied on the disingenuous argument that Hizballah was a legitimate actor operating with the full consent of the Lebanese nation without Syrian intervention. Syria thus could not determine the post-peace future of Hizballah for Lebanon or publicly acknowledge any need for continued Hizballah attacks against Israel if Israel withdrew unconditionally from southern Lebanon under UN Security Council Resolution 425. In reality, to preserve the linkage with the Golan Heights, Syrian leverage on Israel through Hizballah depended on the continued Israeli occupation of southern Lebanon. This explains why the Lebanese government and Hizballah, with heavy Syrian prompting, raised the contentious issue of the Shebaa Farms, a strip of land whose real ownership remains unclear but which Lebanon claims. This delicate and confusing game on Lebanon contrasted with the clarity of the Syrian position regarding bilateral Israeli-Syrian issues, especially the necessity for Israel to return the Golan Heights.

The informal understanding on Hizballah's future after a peace settlement fell short of a guarantee that Hizballah would disarm. Given the absence of a simultaneous Israeli-Lebanese negotiation track, which was deemed unnecessary because Syria called the shots, Lebanon could not assure Israel and the United States that Hizballah would relinquish its weapons. Moreover, even if Syria were prepared to enforce Hizballah's disarmament in principle, former Syrian officials are at loss to describe what steps, if any, Syria would take to promote and facilitate this implementation or whether Syria felt confident that it could deliver on such a commitment.[9] Would Syria's presence, under the pretext of negotiating its end, be even more entrenched by linking it to an effective and permanent disarmament of Hizballah? Would renouncing Hizballah's weapons require a new negotiation over power-sharing in Lebanon to give the Shi'ite community a greater share of power? Could the Lebanese polity cope with such dramatic changes without being closely associated with their formulation? Hafiz probably hoped that Syria's role in Lebanon could continue beyond a peace settlement to prevent the Shi'ite militia from becoming a spoiler.[10] Therefore, Hizballah would have served as a pretext for perpetuating Syrian control over Lebanon, which remained the ultimate prize for Damascus.

Hizballah embraced the label of national resistance to circumvent the Taif Agreement and to differentiate itself from other militias. This meant that Syria had to manage two conflicting projects in Lebanon.[11] Hassan Nasrallah, the young and charismatic secretary-general of Hizballah, articulated an agenda of steadfast resistance against Israel aimed at transcending Lebanon's political and sectarian divisions. On the other hand, Rafik Hariri, a wealthy businessman and prime minister from 1992 to 1998 and 2000 to 2004, envisioned Lebanon as a hub for regional trade and finance and a prime real estate market, as well as a magnet for tourism, and relied on the expectation of imminent regional peace.

Syria resolved this quandary by facilitating an informal bargain.[12] Hizballah obtained autonomy and absolute exclusivity in carrying out its resistance against Israel from Lebanese territory with official cover but agreed to minimize its participation in Lebanese economic and political affairs. Hariri was given considerable authority over reconstruction and domestic and economic policies but little or no say over resistance strategy and policy.

This deal had obvious limitations for these Lebanese actors. Whenever Israel and Hizballah clashed, the fighting jeopardized Hariri's economic plans by reminding international investors and donors of the continuous instability plaguing Lebanon.[13] Tensions between Hizballah and Hariri were frequent, sometimes erupting in public arguments that were quickly contained by Damascus.[14] Yet, despite the difficulty of managing this arrangement and the need to preserve a clear but delicate division of roles, it served Syrian interests well. Damascus relied on Hariri to project a reassuring image to the West, other Arab states, and much of the Lebanese public and to generate revenue and growth in Lebanon, which would sustain Syria's own economy. Hizballah's growing power also checked Hariri's ambitions, most notably by limiting government reach into Hizballah-controlled areas and serving as a reminder of Syria's overriding authority. By retaining a decisive say in all security and foreign policy matters, Syria acted as the ultimate arbiter of disputes.

At the same time, support for Hizballah and other Damascus-based Palestinian groups allowed Syria to play up its pan-Arab, anti-Israeli credentials and avoid harsh criticism for its involvement in the peace process. Importantly, Hafiz demonstrated calculated caution, being careful not to meet personally or in public with Nasrallah and relying heavily on his intelligence apparatus to run Hizballah. This approach was primarily shaped by Hafiz's prudence, distrust of Hizballah's ideology, and genuine investment in peace negotiations with Israel.

Hizballah Struggles for a Future

Hizballah was expected to channel and moderate the frustrations of its Shi'ite constituency. It did so by developing an extensive network of social services that reflected its social vocation (*da'wa*) and compensated for the lack of government resources and presence, instead of promoting Shi'ite rights within the framework of the state. Doing so would have created friction with other Lebanese sects and jeopardized the Syrian-engineered consensus on the muqawama. This arrangement ironically boosted Hizballah's domestic profile over time, shielding it from the Lebanese population's wide rejection of the corrupt Lebanese political elites, highlighting its principled agenda compared to their parochial interests, and allowing for gradual political integration without sharing the blame for the country's many ills. Therefore, instead of contributing to the country's reform, Hizballah subordinated significant Lebanese concerns to its resistance agenda, arguably a priority given the continued Israeli occupation of southern Lebanon.

Syria's withdrawal from Lebanon has eroded its capacity to constrain or disarm Hizballah.

Hizballah remained closely aligned with Syrian diplomatic posturing, alternating lulls and uptakes in armed conflict as needed. It drew comfort from the fact that Syria differentiated between the concepts of peace and normalization. Whereas peace meant the end of the state of war and the establishment of normal diplomatic relations, normalization went further, calling for broader cooperation on a variety of economic, cultural, and social issues. The hope was that a peace with Israel would allow Hizballah to endure as a national guard. If Hizballah could no longer resist Israel militarily, its carefully nurtured society and culture of resistance would prevent the rapprochement of Israeli, Syrian, and Lebanese societies, keeping Israel regionally ostracized despite a formal end to war.[15]

Midlevel Hizballah officials were naturally concerned about the future of their movement when the much-publicized land-for-peace formula assumed the dismantlement of its armed branch. Yet, they also held a belief, born from Hizballah's political successes, that Hizballah could genuinely transform itself into a political party if need be.[16] Ironically, while Hizballah's military successes in 1993 and 1996 raised its value as a Syrian asset in negotiations, they also gradually transformed it into a more autonomous player with enhanced Lebanese and regional prestige, creating some confidence that it would survive any Syrian-Israeli peace.

Ultimately, of course, there was no grand bargain between Syria and Israel. In its place, after repeated Israeli failures to degrade Hizballah and to break Syria's linkage of southern Lebanon to the Golan Heights, a set of rules were formulated in 1993 and formalized in 1996 to manage the escalation of violence and enforce redlines in Lebanon. Hizballah agreed to limit its attacks on Israeli forces and their surrogates in southern Lebanon, while Israel pledged not to strike Lebanese civilians. These rules augmented Syria's leverage by formalizing its role as a guarantor of stability in the area.

Bashar's Search for Legitimacy since 2000

The second major turning point in Syrian-Hizballah relations came at the turn of the century with a change in Syrian leadership. Israeli prime minister Ehud Barak had hoped to break the Syria-created linkage between the Golan Heights and southern Lebanon when he ordered an unconditional withdrawal from southern Lebanon in May 2000, only to see Hafiz al-Asad's death in June and the unexpected issue of the Shebaa Farms thwart this calculus. Syria's ability to reach peace heavily depended on Hafiz's power and commitment. Bashar al-Asad, Hafiz's younger son not cultivated for statecraft, came to power with no serious leadership or management experience and no anti-Israeli or military credentials. He lacked legitimacy and credibility at home as well as in the region. To be sure, his youth and softer image quickly endeared him to the Syrian public, but this hardly granted him the authority or strength to guarantee his hold on power and to pursue peace. To compensate, he sought to acquire these traits by associating himself with allies whose regional prestige was built on a record of anti-U.S. and anti-Israeli opposition.

Hizballah's power is not just a result of the high-technology weaponry supplied by Iran and Syria.

Enter Hizballah, the Lebanese guerrilla movement and political party that had scored its biggest victory to date, Israel's withdrawal, just weeks before Hafiz died and months before Bashar succeeded him. The group could easily provide Bashar with the credentials that he needed to gain credibility, initiating a process of legitimization by association. By associating himself with Hizballah's strength and resolve, Bashar hoped to counter perceptions that he was either a weak leader manipulated by hidden interests or an aggressive one prone to strategic miscalculations.[17] Bashar reasoned that if the victorious Nasrallah was thanking him for Syria's support of efforts that led to Israel's withdrawal from southern Lebanon, the Syrian and Arab publics would view him as the legitimate heir to his father's legacy. To justify his own attitude on major regional developments, including his opposition to the U.S. invasion of Iraq, Bashar relied heavily on Hizballah's own principled hostility to U.S. designs.

Breaking with his father's cautious handling of Hizballah, Bashar cultivated a close personal relationship with Nasrallah and made certain that the praise they lavished on each other was well publicized. Perhaps the most trivial but revealing illustration of this shift has been the sudden flurry of posters featuring Hafiz, Bashar, and Nasrallah plastered across Syria and Lebanon since 2000. A former regime insider, now a low-key critic of Bashar, remarked half-jokingly that the senior Asad, were he able to rise from the dead, would use these posters as fuel to burn his own son.[18]

To be fair, Bashar's decision may have been vital to his regime's ability to overcome the many domestic and regional crises he has faced since his ascent to power. What some have branded a necessary learning curve or a typical consolidation of power, however, has in fact been a slow but willing conscription of Bashar as Hizballah's ideological partner. Pressed by deteriorating regional conditions, from the second Palestinian intifada to the U.S. invasion of Iraq, Bashar grew from a follower of Hizballah by necessity into a faithful admirer and willing captive of Hizballah's confrontational outlook when

U.S. pressure on Syria intensified in 2003. By overtly partnering with the region's steadfast resistance group par excellence, Bashar lost the plausible deniability that his father had cherished so much. With that, he jeopardized Syria's ability to maneuver diplomatically without dangerously alienating his Western partners and Israel.

Nasrallah's influence on Bashar is apparent in the latter's public remarks. Bashar borrows from Nasrallah's repertoire, rhetorically espousing Hizballah's worldview, appealing to audiences beyond Syria, and framing his resolute opposition to U.S. policy as part of a larger struggle against imperialistic oppression. Bashar has also revived a waning pan-Arab, nationalist, and strongly anti-Western rhetoric in an attempt not only to recast himself as his father's legitimate successor but also to defy U.S.-allied Arab leaders and pander to their anti-U.S. publics.

Syria's mostly symbolic gains from its partnership with Hizballah became tangible and political ones in 2004. After the September 2004 passage of UN Security Council Resolution 1559, which demanded Hizballah's disarmament and Syria's withdrawal from Lebanon, and the February 2005 assassination of Hariri, Syria relied heavily on Hizballah's outrage to counter rising U.S. and French pressure and to portray the resolution as an international diktat with no Lebanese or Arab legitimacy.

During this tense period, Hizballah emerged as Syria's honorable and reliable ally. Under heavy scrutiny from Western and Arab countries as well as intense criticism inside Lebanon, Syria could not resort to its usual unsavory proxies to mount a credible defense of its record in Lebanon. A Syrian official remarked in May 2005, "Many of our allies in Lebanon have thrived since 1990 thanks to Syria, but they have lost their credibility with their people. Not Hizballah."[19] Nasrallah stood out as Syria's champion, organizing a massive "good-bye but thank you" demonstration on March 8, 2005, and presenting the departing head of Syrian intelligence with a peculiar if telling gift of gratitude for Syria's support for the resistance: an Israeli rifle seized by Hizballah.[20] The photo op served to mitigate the humiliation of Syria's forced withdrawal and to shore up Bashar's profile at home. The positive relationship with Hizballah, a Shi'ite party with a seemingly nonsectarian attitude and a glorious anti-Israeli record, became the key achievement that Bashar wanted to highlight domestically and regionally. His eagerness to do so demonstrated that the tables had turned. Rather than Hizballah deriving great benefits from Syria's support, Syria now reaped more benefits from its association with Hizballah.

Hizballah Today

Syria's departure from Lebanon considerably changed the strategic environment in which Hizballah operates and presented it with challenges and opportunities. The key challenge was to preserve a consensus on its weapons and retain a special status in Lebanese politics. The key opportunity was to finally overcome its image as a Syrian pawn and capitalize on its achievements and credibility. This process was fraught with considerable difficulties, and domestic and regional developments conspired against it.

Hizballah's actions since the 2005 Syrian withdrawal from Lebanon are often presented as an extension of Syrian and Iranian policy.[21] To be sure, its interests often coincide and reinforce those of Syria and Iran, but many overestimate the influence that they have over Hizballah's decisionmaking and preferences. Syria today is more pro-Hizballah than Hizballah is pro-Syria. Hizballah is no longer a card or a proxy; it has become a partner with considerable clout and autonomy.

Paradoxically, there is little love today for Syria among Hizballah's supporters.[22] They see Syria as having constrained Hizballah's political potential. The Lebanese Shi'ite community also suffered from Syrian workers competing for the same jobs. Furthermore, Hizballah owes no particular heritage to Syria, contrary to Iran, which remains a supreme religious and ideological reference. An anecdote making the rounds in Beirut has Hizballah militants comparing Syria to a ring and Iran as a finger on Hizballah's hand. The ring can fall off or be taken off willingly, whereas the finger can only be severed.[23] This contrasts with the attitude of the Syrian public, which identifies with Hizballah. Syrians view the Lebanese as fractious, greedy, and ungrateful for Syrian sacrifices in Lebanon, but they see Hizballah as righteous and animated by a just, pan-Arab cause.

Hizballah's objectives are often misunderstood. Hizballah's raison d'etre has become the very idea of perpetual but not necessarily active muqawama against Israel. A former Hizballah activist put it this way: "Resistance is like a one-wheel[ed] bike that Hizballah is riding. If it stops pedaling, it falls."[24] Yet, the muqawama refers not only to guerrilla operations, but also to a culture of resistance based on social mobilization and an associated political and social discourse that transcends religion, territoriality, and nationalism, although it is rooted in all three. Therefore, Hizballah has no tangible ultimate objective such as advancing Shi'ite demands, reforming Lebanon's governance system, or liberating Israeli-occupied Arab territories. It will undoubtedly accept those as valuable by-products of its resistance efforts, but they do not constitute Hizballah's core purpose.

Contrary to its initial goals and to the fears of many, Hizballah no longer actively seeks to impose an Islamic agenda on Lebanon and even prefers not to govern the country if it can rely on amenable allies from various sects in parliament and government.[25] Hizballah has genuinely adjusted to the sectarian fabric of Lebanon's society, gradually emphasizing muqawama instead of Islamism in its rhetoric and ideology. Hizballah has not abandoned its Islamist ideal, but to the extent that this goal complicates its ability to pursue muqawama or erodes its image, Hizballah is willing to do away with it.

Syria is in no position to respond constructively to potential U.S. overtures.

What Hizballah today wants most is to ensure that nothing, especially Lebanese domestic considerations, can constrain its ability to conduct its resistance agenda in the time frame and form of its choosing. It developed a two-tiered political strategy to anchor Lebanon firmly in a rejectionist axis formed by Iran, Syria, and radical Palestinian groups. It has placed itself within Lebanese society through its political activities and much-praised social services. It has simultaneously positioned itself above society by defining muqawama, preferably but not necessarily endorsed by a national consensus, as a fundamentally supranational vocation.[26] In practical terms, this focus on resistance shapes how Hizballah operates as a political actor, determining its degree and nature of political involvement, its choice of alliances, and even the decision and timing of its operations against Israel.

Hizballah, which thrived as a guerrilla force mostly equipped with small and light weaponry to resist Israeli occupation, became a more-sophisticated force as its main mission shifted to deterrence based on rocket and missile capabilities. Syria's departure from Lebanon meant that Hizballah could no longer count on an external enforcer to protect its weapons. This left Hizballah with three options: build alliances with other forces and deepen its political engagement to eventually govern the country, manipulate sectarian politics to create a Shi'ite shield, or a combination of the two. All of these options are highly dissatisfying. They turn Hizballah into a political party like the others and conflict with the nonsectarian image it cultivates for national and regional purposes.

This fear of the end of a national consensus over its armament prompted Hizballah to enter the Lebanese government for the first time in 2005 and to obtain a formal Cabinet statement endorsing the resistance as "a sincere and natural expression of the Lebanese people's right to defend its land and dignity in the face of Israeli aggression, threats, and ambitions as well as of its right to continue its actions to free Lebanese territory." Hizballah's concern was quickly validated as its rationale for remaining armed came under heavy domestic criticism. The necessity of reaffirming the value of its arsenal led Hizballah to launch the fateful July 12 operation that started the summer 2006 war with Israel with the stated objective of obtaining the liberation of the remaining Lebanese prisoners in Israeli jails. For its supporters, the war validated the need to preserve Hizballah as a militia to defend Lebanon. For its critics, it illustrated the dangers of Hizballah's continued resistance.

In the aftermath of the summer war, constrained by new strategic realities, namely the deployment of Lebanese and UN-mandated troops in southern Lebanon, and undoubtedly exhausted by the fight, Hizballah redirected its efforts toward Beirut, hoping to capitalize on its "divine victory." Faced with the reluctance of the anti-Syrian Lebanese parliamentary majority to offer the expected substantive political gains, angry at the government's alleged connivance with Israel, and concerned that Hizballah's victory would bring no tangible results and leave it weakened in southern Lebanon and in Beirut, a victorious yet apprehensive and frustrated Hizballah stepped up the pressure on the central government to obtain a government reshuffle and a veto right.[27] A senior Hizballah official confirmed this in December 2006: "Now we are demanding [a greater government share] because our experience during the war and the performance of the government has made us unsure. On several occasions they pressured us to lay down our weapons while we were fighting a war."[28]

The U.S. government and others, including Lebanese politicians, misrepresent Hizballah's push to obtain more governmental power as a Syrian- and Iranian-engineered attempt to overthrow the Lebanese government. True, Syria in particular benefits from paralyzing Lebanese government activity as it seeks to obstruct the international tribunal that will try the suspects in the Hariri and other assassination cases and to avoid the institutionalization and expansion of its isolation under a UN umbrella. Yet, Hizballah pursues this objective for a different motive: guaranteeing an institutional cover for the resistance by seizing a veto over government decisions in order to prevent a further erosion of its domestic position. The confluence of the two crises means that the vital interests of Damascus are intrinsically linked to those of Hizballah, even though it abhors being identified with a Syrian goal.

Engaging Syria?

The deteriorating U.S. situation in Iraq and the summer war in Lebanon have given new life to the idea of enlisting Syria to help stabilize Iraq and restrain Hizballah. Powerful voices have called for a more-inclusive diplomatic strategy in the Middle East. Those advocating engaging Syria stress the value of luring Damascus away from Tehran, thereby countering Iran's spreading influence in the region.[29] Former U.S. secretary of state James Baker, the architect of the peace process in the 1990s, confidently argues, "If you can flip the Syrians, you will cure Israel's Hizballah problem."[30] At the same time, a piecemeal approach runs the risk of being turned down. The International Crisis Group argues that "[i]f the idea [of engagement] amounts to politely asking what up to now has been curtly demanded, [it is] better not even to try."[31] In any case, the Bush administration remains loath to pursue such a course due to the fear of projecting weakness by engaging foes and due to the high price Syria would be expected to extract. Nevertheless, engaging Syria might be worth trying on its own merits, but only if assumptions about peace talks are revised, the relative power of the parties is well understood, and expectations are kept low.

Syria will not sacrifice its ties to Iran and Hizballah.

The summer 2006 war reinforced Syria's position on several levels. Syria derived much pride and prestige from the perceived achievements of Hizballah. It hoped that the war illustrated the pacifying role that Syria had played in Lebanon since 1990 and persuaded many of the mistakes of pushing it out of Lebanon. The war also reminded Israel of Syria's enduring power of nuisance when ignored or mistreated. Nevertheless, the reasoning behind engaging Syria should not be uniquely driven by the hope that it can somehow stabilize Lebanon in a durable manner.

If talks were to begin, Bashar would be expected to demonstrate his willingness and ability to constrain Hizballah and then to disarm it once an agreement is reached. Syria's withdrawal from Lebanon has eroded its capacity to deliver on both counts. Syria could theoretically cut off the supply of Iranian weapons to Hizballah as required by UN Security Council Resolution 1701, which ended the summer 2006 war with Israel. Further, Hizballah could still be negatively affected by changes in Damascus, particularly if Bashar awakes to the precariousness of his position. To be sure, Damascus retains leverage over Hizballah because it receives logistical support from Syria. Yet, although Hizballah and Iran give Bashar short-term legitimacy and strategic confidence, they cannot offer him regional and international acceptance or much-needed economic assistance.

The Syrian regime, despite some bombastic statements during the summer war, cannot embrace Hizballah-style resistance because it has a lot more to lose to an Israeli attack than Hizballah does. Syria is also nervous about growing Iranian power in the Levant, a powerful constraint on its diplomatic options. Such a course of action, however, ignores the reality that Hizballah thrives as a guerrilla force; its power is not just a result of the high-technology weaponry supplied by Iran and Syria. It would also be politically dangerous for Bashar to try to outsmart his Iranian ally. Moreover, Hizballah could turn the tables on Syria if it felt outmaneuvered, most likely by provoking Israel without Syrian knowledge but at Syrian expense. Testing Syrian intentions without a clear process and end goal could therefore backfire.

Reaching a political accommodation with Hizballah, as unpleasant as it may be, is essential.

In reality, despite encouraging signs from Damascus, including high-profile interviews of Bashar in Western media and meetings with U.S. senators, Syria is in no position to respond constructively to potential U.S. overtures anyway. A Syrian list of demands and apparent readiness to talk do not amount to a coherent and encouraging negotiating posture. Bashar welcomes the process of dialogue mainly because it replaces the narrative of 2005 as Bashar having systematically miscalculated with a new one of Bashar having correctly positioned Syria to take advantage of the rapidly changing landscape in the Middle East. Moreover, calling for dialogue while knowing that the other side will not respond makes Damascus seem open to compromise and makes Washington look intransigent and arrogant. Bashar may well calculate that, were he to survive the next two years and wait for the next U.S. administration to adjust to the many U.S. failures in the Middle East, he would emerge on top, stronger and vindicated.

Although Syria could negotiate peace in good faith during the 1990s because of its strong strategic position, the loss of Lebanon as its economic and political depth and the apparent international consensus on preventing its return to Lebanon suggest that Syria will not sacrifice its ties to its few remaining strategic partners, Iran and Hizballah. Bashar is prisoner to the radical outlook he has espoused in order to gain domestic and regional legitimacy. He can hardly jump ship in the current regional environment. Syria is in a position of relative weakness vis-à-vis its partners. Bashar does not enjoy the same degree of popular legitimacy as Nasrallah, Iranian president Mahmoud Ahmadinejad, Hamas political leader Khaled Meshaal, or Palestinian Prime Minister Ismail Haniyeh, all of whom are either elected leaders or leaders of successful political parties legitimized by elections. Regime survival against domestic challengers, though weak and divided, continues to top Bashar's priorities. His narrow sectarian base, though loyal, is hardly expandable; and Syria's crippling economy, sectarian fabric, and domestic discontent are a recipe for internal instability.

The new relationship between Syria and Hizballah profoundly impacts how peace should be pursued in the region. Seeing Hizballah only through a regional prism and assuming that Syria will systematically determine Hizballah's behavior is flawed. Lebanon's fabric and conditions must inform Hizballah-specific policies. As counterintuitive and cliché as it seems, the priority should be political reform. As long as Hizballah subordinates everything to its resistance agenda, it will not play a positive role in reforming Lebanon. This paradoxically provides an opportunity to expose Hizballah's dilemma. Although many Shi'ites see Hizballah as their champion, the latter, to preserve its raison d'etre, does not prioritize Shi'ite demands, a dilemma one Shi'ite intellectual calls Hizballah's "schizophrenia." Even within Hizballah, there is a rift between a powerful core committed to permanent resistance and the midlevel political cadre willing to focus exclusively on political participation.

The underlying assumption that Israeli peace with Syria will lead to Hizballah's disarmament must also be reassessed. There is no more symmetry in what to expect from Syria with regard to Hizballah. Today, Syria probably retains the power to ignite Hizballah and hopefully to restrain it, but it has lost the power to disarm it. This prospect alarms Israeli strategic thinkers and explains their measured enthusiasm for the Syrian withdrawal from Lebanon. The summer 2006 war between Israel and Hizballah even suggested to some that the predictability of a deterrable Syria controlling Lebanon is better than the alternative of an unbound Hizballah.

What Next for Hizballah?

Despite its summer 2006 victory, Hizballah's position in Lebanon remains precarious, with a risk that it might overplay its hand. Its domestic alliances might not outlast the current cycle of political unrest for tactical and ideological reasons. Its Christian allies do not adhere to Hizballah's strong anti-Western outlook and would not settle for an indefinite postponement of a discussion over Hizballah's weapons.[32] Sectarian dynamics have forced Hizballah to resort to its Shi'ite shield, eroding its cross-sectarian appeal in Lebanon and hurting its image in the Arab world.

More recently, however, Hizballah has tried to regain a wider support base by publicly articulating political and economic demands instead of focusing exclusively on the muqawama. Further, in the midst of deadly clashes in Lebanon in early 2007, Nasrallah offered to widen the ranks of the muqawama to include non-Shi'ite factions in an attempt to polish its Lebanese credentials and counter sectarian criticism. Hizballah seems willing to part with its cherished monopoly over anti-Israeli resistance in order to regain national, multisectarian cover and legitimacy.

The need to avoid domestic strife, which would durably taint Hizballah, could lead it to respond positively to Iranian or Arab pressure to accept an unsatisfactory political compromise, although Syria could emerge as an obstacle to such a settlement. If a compromise is not reached, a politically weakened Hizballah could redirect its efforts to the south and pressure the UN peacekeeping forces there. Hizballah is also in the process of reframing muqawama to include the United States, now seen as an existential threat to be countered. Given this emerging reality, an overly aggressive U.S. posture will only reinforce Hizballah's rationale for pursuing the muqawama instead of undermining it. This is why reaching a political accommodation with Hizballah, as unpleasant as it may be, is so essential.

The fates of Syria and Hizballah are intertwined, but addressing the challenges they pose requires differentiated approaches. Hoping that Syria is the key to Hizballah ignores the reality that although Syria retains some influence, Hizballah has gained leverage and independence over its former patron. Although Syrian and Iranian nods, as unlikely as they may be, would go a long way in containing Hizballah, confrontation by proxy is no longer enough. Rather, only the Lebanese political process, as messy and imperfect as it is, can constrain Hizballah. Political reform and progress on some of Hizballah's demands, including those related to the Lebanese-Israeli track, will undermine its main levers of power and influence. This is of course fraught with considerable risks and is premised on the capacity of the Lebanese polity to demonstrate adaptability and farsightedness. Nonetheless, this is the approach that the international community should promote to prevent another dramatic explosion of violence.

Notes

1. For a discussion of Shi'ite awakening and rise in Lebanon, see Fouad Ajami, *The Vanished Imam: Musa Al-Sadr and the Shia of Lebanon* (Ithaca, N.Y.: Cornell University Press, 1986); Augustus Richard Norton, *Amal and the Shi'a: Struggle for the Soul of Lebanon* (Austin: University of Texas Press, 1987).
2. For a discussion of the Iran-Hizballah relationship, see Graham E. Fuller, "The Hizballah-Iran Connection: Model for Sunni Resistance," *The Washington Quarterly* 30, no. 1 (Winter 2006–07): 139–150.
3. Former Syrian intelligence officer, interview with author, Beirut, summer 2003.
4. See Magnus Ranstorp, *Hezbollah in Lebanon: The Politics of the Western Hostage Crisis* (New York: St. Martin's Press, 1997).
5. See Amal Saad-Ghorayeb, *Hizbu'llah: Politics and Religion* (Sterling, Va.: Pluto Press, 2002); Nizar Hamzeh, "Lebanon's Hizballah: From Revolution to Parliamentary Accommodation," *Third World Quarterly* 14, no. 2 (1993): 321–337.
6. Dennis Ross, *The Missing Peace: The Inside Story of the Fight for Middle East Peace* (New York: Farrar, Straus, and Giroux, 2004); Itamar Rabinovich, *Waging Peace* (Princeton, N.J.: Princeton University Press, 2004); Helena Cobban, *The Israeli-Syrian Peace Talks: 1991–96 and Beyond* (Washington, D.C.: USIP Press Books, 1999).
7. European and Arab diplomats, interviews with author, Paris, Beirut, and Damascus, summer 2003 and May 2005; former U.S. negotiator, interview with author, Washington, D.C., December 2006.
8. Eli Carmeli and Yotan Feldner, "Lebanon and the Armed Struggle After Israel's Withdrawal," *MEMRI Inquiry and Analysis Series*, no. 26 (March 31, 2006), http://memri.org/bin/articles.cgi?Page=archives&Area=ia&ID=IA2600.
9. Syrian official, interviews with author, Beirut, summer 2003; former Syrian official, interview with author, Europe, November 2006.
10. European and Arab diplomats, interviews with author, Paris, Beirut, and Damascus, summer 2003 and May 2005.
11. Nadim Shehadi, "Riviera vs. Citadel: The Battle for Lebanon," openDemocracy.net, August 22, 2006, http://www.opendemocracy.net/conflict-middle_east_politics/riviera_citadel_3841.jsp#.
12. Judith Palmer Harik, *Hezbollah: The Changing Face of Terrorism* (New York: I.B. Tauris, 2004), p. 47.
13. Ibid.
14. Ibid.
15. For an examination of the society and culture of resistance, see Mona Harb and Reinoud Leenders, "Know Thy Enemy: Hizbullah, 'Terrorism,' and the Politics of Perception," *Third World Quarterly* 26, no. 1 (February 2005): 173–197.
16. Hizballah officials, interviews with author, Beirut, July 2003.
17. Syrian analyst, interview with author, Damascus, May 2005.

18. Former Syrian official, interview with author, Paris, November 2006. See Volker Perthes, "The Syrian Solution," *Foreign Affairs* 85, no. 6 (November/December 2006): 33–40.
19. Syrian regime insider, interview with author, Damascus, May 2005.
20. Seth Colter Walls, "Striking a Syrian Pose?" *Weekly Standard*, November 17, 2005, http://www.weeklystandard.com/Content/Public/Articles/000/000/006/369xrvlb.asp?pg=1.
21. See Office of the Press Secretary, The White House, "Statement on Condemnation of Hizballah Kidnapping of Two Israeli Soldiers," July 12, 2006, http://www.whitehouse.gov/news/releases/2006/07/20060712.html.
22. Hizballah militants, interview with author, Beirut, May 2005.
23. See also Augustus Richard Norton, "Hizballah in a National and Regional Context, From 2000 to 2006," *Journal of Palestine Studies*, no. 141 (Fall 2006), http://www.palestine-studies.org/final/en/journals/issue.php?iid=141&jid=1&vid=XXXVI&vol=203.
24. Former Hizballah activist, interview with author, Beirut, November 2006.
25. "Nasrallah New TV Interview Excerpts," Mideastwire.com, September 4, 2006, http://www.mideastwire.com/topstory.php?id=10401.
26. Emile El-Hokayem, "Hizbollah's Enduring Myth," *Arab Reform Bulletin* 4, no. 9 (November 2006), http://www.carnegieendowment.org/publications/index.cfm?fa=view&id=18857&prog=zgp&proj=zme#hizbollah.
27. Hizballah official, interview with author, Beirut, November 2006.
28. Scheherezade Faramarzi, "Hezbollah Seeks More Power in Lebanon," Associated Press, December 15, 2006.
29. Itamar Rabinovich, "Courting Syria," *Ha'aretz*, November 30, 2006, http://www.haaretz.com/hasen/spages/791583.html.
30. David E. Sanger, "Dueling Views Pit Baker Against Rice," *New York Times*, December 8, 2006, http://www.nytimes.com/2006/12/08/world/middleeast/08diplo.html?th&emc=th.
31. Robert Malley and Peter Harling, "Talks With Iran and Syria Will Not Be an Easy Ride," *Financial Times*, December 13, 2006, http://www.ft.com/cms/s/f03dea38-8ad8-11db-8940-0000779e2340.html.
32. Christian demonstrators allied with Hizballah, interview with author, Beirut, December 2006.

EMILE EL-HOKAYEM is a research fellow at the Henry L. Stimson Center in Washington, D.C.

Guerrilla Nation

The arrest of FARC terrorist Ricardo Granda sheds new light on Hugo Chavez's ongoing support of terrorism.

THOR HALVORSSEN

Simon Trinidad is the *nom de guerre* of Ricardo Palmera, a high-ranking terrorist of the Fuerzas Armadas Revolucionarias de Colombia (FARC), the deadliest and largest terrorist organization in the world. Thanks to Colombia's president, Alvaro Uribe, Trinidad was extradited to the United States last month. He now awaits trial for a lengthy list of crimes involving the recent kidnapping and murder of American citizens in Colombia. Trinidad's capture was a victory in the fight against global terror (see **Note**), but it is unlikely that the FARC terrorists will be defeated as long as Venezuelan president Hugo Chavez continues to use his government to harbor, equip, and protect them.

Since assuming the presidency of Venezuela in 1999, Lieutenant Colonel Hugo Chavez has often sympathized with global terrorism. Not only has he proclaimed his "brotherhood" with Saddam Hussein and bestowed kind words on the Taliban, but he also maintains close economic and diplomatic ties with the leaders of Iran and Libya. Moreover, President Chavez is increasingly identified with the FARC terrorists. Although the full extent of Chavez's involvement with FARC is unknown, he has been accused of everything from sympathizing with the group to providing it with weapons and monetary support. The allegations against Chavez are numerous and it is likely that some of them are either exaggerated or untrue. Even so, President Chavez's activities reveal a consistent pattern of sympathy for terrorists.

The FARC terrorist group has been fighting the democratic government of Colombia for almost 40 years. Founded as the armed wing of the Colombian Communist party, this 16,000-strong terrorist force recruits children and funds its activities with billions of dollars collected as taxes on the cocaine trade. The group's explicit objective is to take Colombia by force. In pursuing its mission, FARC terrorists have kidnapped, extorted, and executed thousands of innocent civilians, bombed buildings, assassinated hundreds of political leaders, and, with two other local terrorist organizations, have turned Colombia into one of the most violent and dangerous countries in the world. All in all, FARC has caused the deaths of more than 100,000 people.

The U.S. Department of State has designated FARC a Foreign Terrorist Organization—yet FARC leaders are welcomed in Venezuela and treated as heads of state. The prominent FARC leader Olga Marin, for example, spoke on the floor of Venezuela's National Assembly in the summer of 2000, praising Hugo Chavez as a hero of the rebel movement and thanking the Venezuelan government for its "support." Weeks later, the Colombian government announced that it had confiscated from terrorists more than 400 rifles and machine guns bearing the insignia of the Venezuelan armed forces. Although President Chavez claimed this was a smear campaign against him and that many of those weapons could have come into terrorist hands as a result of border skirmishes with Venezuelan armed forces, his explanation was less than plausible, since some of the guns had sequential serial numbers and were therefore likely part of a unified arms shipment.

In February 2001, months after the Chavez government denied supporting FARC, the capture of a Colombian terrorist revived the debate. Jose Maria Ballestas, a leader of Colombia's other left-wing terrorist organization, the National Liberation Army (ELN), was captured in Venezuela's capital by Interpol operatives working in conjunction with the Colombian police. Although Ballestas was wanted for a 1999 commercial airliner hijacking, he was immediately released from custody by order of the Chavez government. As the Colombian media cried foul, Chavez officials denied that Ballestas had ever been arrested and claimed that "news" of his arrest was actually a story concocted by enemies of the Chavez government. When Colombian officials responded by releasing a video of the arrest, the Chavez government tried to claim that Ballestas was seeking asylum from political persecution in Colombia. As diplomatic tension reached a fever-pitch, Venezuela re-arrested Ballestas and grudgingly extradited him to Colombia.

Seeking to repair relations with Colombia's president, President Chavez paid a state visit to Colombia in May 2001. While there, he allowed a FARC associate, Diego Serna, to serve as his personal bodyguard. Serna was arrested months later and told the magazine Cambio (published by Nobel laureate Gabriel Garcia Marquez) that President Chavez was in constant and secret touch with the FARC leadership. Serna remarked that in Colombian television broadcasts of the presidential summit "you can see not only our closeness, but also the confidence and the comments he made to me on various occasions." Indeed, the footage shows Chavez laughing, jostling, and whispering in Serna's ear.

Three months after diplomatic tension over the Serna incident died down, the Chavez-FARC connection surfaced again when Venezuela's intelligence chief, Jesus Urdaneta, publicly denounced Chavez for supporting FARC. A lifelong friend and military colleague of President Chavez, Urdaneta publicized documents showing that the Chavez government offered fuel, money, and other support to the terrorists. The documents included signed letters from a Chavez aide detailing an agreement to provide support for FARC. That aide later became Chavez's minister of justice, a position which gave him oversight of the entire Venezuelan security apparatus.

Less than a week after Urdaneta went public, a group of female journalists released a video showing meetings between Venezuelan military leaders and FARC guerilla commanders. The next day, hundreds of miles away, the Colombian Air Force captured a Venezuelan plane loaded with ammunition. Colombian intelligence established that the supplies were meant for the FARC terrorists.

The Colombian Government is currently embroiled in the most momentous FARC-related matter since Simon Trinidad's extradition. On December 14, 2004, Ricardo Granda, widely known as FARC's "foreign secretary," was arrested on the Colombian border. One of the most senior, well connected, and highly skilled political strategists in FARC's history, Granda had been living in Venezuela's capital.

In Caracas Granda enjoyed Venezuelan citizenship (granted by government decree), took advantage of state-supplied protection, and even, on December 8, participated in a government-sponsored networking conference attended by Chavez, Daniel Ortega, and other revolutionary socialists. Today, Chavez expresses fury that Granda was captured, lamenting that Granda was apprehended in Caracas, stuffed in the trunk of a car, and driven to Colombia where he was then given to Colombian authorities by junior Venezuelan military and police officers working for cash rewards. The Venezuelan government has announced it will issue arrest warrants for the Colombian Defense secretary and for the Colombian attorney general, who are to be charged with "kidnapping."

The Colombian Government has understandably become exasperated by the impunity with which Chavez has permitted terrorists to use Venezuela as a safe haven and justifies its actions by claiming that the United Nations forbids members to harbor terrorists in either an "active or passive" manner. Last week the Colombian foreign secretary went public with a list of senior FARC terrorists living in Venezuela.

Thus far, the U.S. State Department has been exceedingly tame with the Venezuelan government. Perhaps the Granda case will spur the new secretary of state to focus more on terrorist threats plaguing our own hemisphere. Should she do so, she will effect a necessary and long overdue shift in U.S.-Venezuela relations.

THOR HALVORSSEN, a human rights and civil liberties advocate, is First Amendment Scholar at the Commonwealth Foundation. He lives in New York.

Note—FARC terrorist Simon Trinidad's indictment last month includes information about the murder and kidnapping of American citizens in Colombia last year. Trinidad's actions were not exceptional; killing Americans is routine for FARC. For example, in 1999 FARC terrorists killed three American activists who were in Colombia on a humanitarian mission. They were Terence Freitas, 24; Ingrid Washinowatok, 41; and Lahe'ena'e Gay, 39.

Apprehended after attending a religious ceremony on an Indian reservation, Freitas, Washinowatok, and Gay were initially held for ransom but were later taken into Venezuela and executed in cold blood. Washinowatok, a New Yorker, was the head of the Fund for Four Directions, a Rockefeller-supported charity which helps indigenous peoples. Lahe'ena'e Gay was an award-winning Hawaiian photographer. Terry Freitas was an environmental activist from California. All three progressive activists had colorful life stories. Washinowatok, for example, was a Menominee Indian from Minnesota, daughter of a tribal chieftain, and personal friend of Nobel Peace Prize laureate Rigoberta Menchu. She studied in Havana and is described by her friends as a champion of the oppressed. Her lifeless body, found just inside the Venezuelan border, was impossible to identify since her face had been destroyed by gunshot. The autopsy revealed that she had been forced to march barefoot through the jungle for several days despite having been bitten by a poisonous spider. She was only identified when her foundation's American Express card was found hidden in her clothing. Washinowatok and her friends were executed for one chilling reason: They were Americans.

From *The Weekly Standard*, January 26, 2005. Copyright © 2005 by The Weekly Standard. Reprinted by permission.

The Growing Syrian Missile Threat: Syria after Lebanon

Lee Kass

Even though international pressure succeeded in forcing Damascus to withdraw its troops from Lebanon, the Syrian regime remains in the cross hairs of U.S. defense and intelligence concern about four other Syrian activities. First, the Syrian regime has continued its attempts to acquire sophisticated surface-to-surface missiles. Second, U.S. intelligence officials remain concerned that the Syrian government has become custodian to Iraq's biological and chemical weapons. Third, questions remain about whether Damascus benefited from the network of Abdul Qadir Khan, the Pakistani nuclear scientist who sold nuclear secrets to a number of rogue regimes. Lastly, Bashar al-Assad continues to flirt with international terrorism. The young president shows no inclination to cease the behavior that has for more than a quarter century led the U.S. government to designate Syria a state-sponsor of terrorism.

Left unresolved, such questions about Syrian proliferation ambitions, coupled with the regime's demonstrated willingness to use terrorism to advance its goals, will make any rapprochement between Washington and Damascus impossible.

A Syrian Ballistic Missile?

Much of Syria's arsenal consists of Cold War remnants received from the Soviet Union. The Syrian military has already begun upgrading its tanks, acquiring the faster, tougher T-72s from a cash-starved Russian military industry.[1] Analysts believe that Damascus acquired the tanks for their speed—to maneuver and advance more effectively on the Golan Heights. The Syrian regime has also sought to upgrade its air force. While much of the fleet is old, the Syrian military still has enough planes to saturate Israeli air defenses and conduct a significant strike against the Jewish state. Still, the Israeli air force remains far superior, and because Syrian air defenses are old and lack complete interoperability,[2] Jerusalem still maintains a large advantage.

Perhaps to compensate for this weakness, the Syrian regime has sought to upgrade its weapons capability. When Israeli warplanes struck a Palestinian Islamic Jihad base ten miles northwest of Damascus in October 2003 following the terrorist group's suicide bomb attack in a Haifa restaurant, Iraqis who were in Damascus at the time said Syrian air defense did not react.

The Syrian regime's efforts to upgrade its missile capability threaten U.S., Israeli, and Turkish interests. With a stronger Syrian missile capability, the Assad regime could launch either a preemptive strike or, more likely, feel itself secure enough in its deterrent capability to encourage terrorism without fear of consequence.

> **Launched from Damascus, the Iskander-E could reach Tel Aviv in less than three minutes.**

Syrian officials have sought to obtain the advanced SS-X-26 surface-to-surface missiles, also known as Iskander-Es, from Russia, but Russian president Vladimir Putin cancelled the deal after learning from his experts that Israel would not have a capability to intercept the missiles.[3] With a range of 174 miles (280 kilometers), the Iskander-E could have hit cities such as Tel Aviv, Jerusalem, and Haifa. While a significant threat due to the proximity of Israeli population centers, the missiles fall under the 186 mile (300 kilometer) range subject to the Missile Technology Control Regime to which Russia, the United States, and thirty-two other countries are subject. It is unclear from unclassified sources whether countries that obtain Iskander-Es can extend the missiles' range, but if so, they would pose an enhanced threat to Turkey, Jordan, and Iraq as well.[4] Regardless, the chance that the Syrian government might provide the missile to terrorists or other rogue states undermines both the spirit and the effectiveness of the Missile Technology Control Regime and other nonproliferation agreements.

The Iskander-E would be a particularly dangerous upgrade. Unlike Scuds, Iskander-Es have solid fuel propellants. Solid propellants are less complicated because the fuel and oxidizer do not need to travel through a labyrinth of pumps, pipes, valves, and turbo-pumps to ignite the engines. Instead, when a solid propellant is lit, it burns from the center outward, significantly reducing launch preparation time.

Immediately after launch, Iskander-Es perform maneuvers that prevent opponents from tracking and destroying the launchers. Once in flight, the Iskander-Es can deploy decoys and execute unpredictable flight paths to confuse missile defense systems.[5] Moreover, they are fast. According to Uzi Rubin, former head of Israel's Arrow-Homa missile defense program, the Iskander can fly at 1,500 meters per second, equivalent to 3,355 miles (5,370 kilometers) per hour,[6] Launched from Damascus, the Iskander-E could reach Tel Aviv in less than three minutes, sooner if the Iskanders' mobile launchers were moved closer to the border. This capability might prevent Israel's multi-tiered missile defense shield from adequately protecting the country.

Even though Iskander-Es lack the range to hit many strategic targets, their accuracy and varied warhead types make them an adaptable military system. The missile was intended to obliterate both stationary and mobile targets, particularly short-range missile launchers, ports, command and control facilities, factories, and hardened structures. Such flexibility would allow Syria to destroy an enemy's existing military capabilities and its ability to wage a future war.[7]

These concerns have led both the U.S. and Israeli governments to criticize the Syrian regime's attempts to acquire the new technology. One U.S. official stated, "We don't think that state sponsors of terrorism should be sold weapons of any kind.[8] Israel's government is focused on the possibility that Palestinian terrorists might obtain the equipment.[9] According to the State Department's *Patterns of Global Terrorism,* Syria supports or provides safe-haven to a number of terrorist groups, including Islamic Jiliad. Hamas, and the Popular Front for the Liberation of Palestine-General Command.[10]

Russian defense minister Sergey Ivanov acknowledged such concerns when he announced, at least temporarily, that Moscow would halt export of the missile to Syria.[11] At an April 2005 meeting with senior Israeli officials, Russian president Vladimir Putin confirmed that he cancelled the Syrian Iskander contract because Israel lacks the ability to intercept those missiles.[12]

Instead, Putin said that the Russian government would only authorize sale of Strelet surface-to-air systems that are unable to penetrate Israel.[13] While a nominal downgrade, even with a range of just three miles (five kilometers),[14] the system can pose a significant threat to Israel. These missiles can proliferate to Hezbollah and other terrorist organizations supported by the Syrian regime. In such hands, the Strelets could endanger passenger planes on descent to Ben Gurion International Airport, outside Tel Aviv and just four miles from the West Bank.[15] Russian officials say they will only sell Damascus the vehicle-mounted version and not the shoulder-held type, but Western defense officials say operators can easily dismantle Strelets to make them transportable.[16]

Augmenting concern was the Israeli disclosure of a Syrian launch of three Scud missiles on May 27, 2005.[17] The tests were the first since 2001 and represented a significant milestone in the country's missile program—the three carried airburst warheads. This capability reinforced Israeli concerns that Syria could use the Scuds to deliver chemical weapons. One of the missiles launched was an older Scud B, with a range of about 185 miles (300 kilometers), while the remaining two were newer Scud-Ds with a range of approximately 435 miles (700 kilometers).[18] The greater range not only gives Syria greater reach but also allows launches from deeper within Syrian territory, making it more difficult to undertake a preemptive aerial attack on the launchers.

Questions about a possible transfer of Iraqi weapons to Syria remain unanswered.

U.S., Israeli, and other Western governments' concerns over Russian missile sales to Syria will likely go unheeded. After all, international security concerns have not stopped Russian support for the Iranian nuclear program.[19] Sergey Kazannov, head of the Russian Academy of Sciences World Economics and International Relations Institutes' Geopolitics Division, said that in Soviet times, political reasons and the need to maintain the Soviet defense industry motivated Moscow's arms sales.[20] The post-Cold War climate undercut opportunities for the Russian defense industry. He elaborated, "Seventy percent of our defense complex's output goes for export. And depriving ourselves of that factor under our unenviable conditions is almost tantamount to death." He also added that the missile sales allow Moscow, Damascus, and other regional actors the independence to develop policies without regard to U.S. pressure.[21] As relations between Putin and the West worsen, such political calculations might re-enable the Iskander-E sale.

Iraqi Weapons in Syria?

White Western governments were able to pressure Moscow to alter its weapons shipments, Bashar al-Assad may not have limited himself to over-the-counter weapons purchases. The Syrian military's unconventional weapons arsenal already has a significant stockpile of sarin. The Syrian regime has also attempted to produce other toxic agents in order to advance its inventory of biological weapons.[22]

Several different intelligence sources raised red flags about suspicious truck convoys from Iraq to Syria in the days, weeks, and months prior to the March 2003 invasion of Iraq.[23]

These concerns first became public when, on December 23, 2002, Ariel Sharon stated on Israeli television, "Chemical and biological weapons which Saddam is endeavoring to conceal have been moved from Iraq to Syria."[24] About three weeks later, Israel's foreign minister repeated the accusation.[25] The U.S., British, and Australian governments issued similar statements.[26]

The Syrian foreign minister dismissed such charges as a U.S. attempt to divert attention from its problems in Iraq.[27] But even if the Syrian regime were sincere, Bashar al-Assad's previous statement—"I don't do everything in this country,"[28]—suggested that Iraqi chemical or biological weapons could cross the Syrian frontier without regime consent. Rather than exculpate the Syrian regime, such a scenario makes the presence of Iraqi weapons in Syria more worrisome, for it suggests that Assad might either eschew responsibility for their ultimate custody or may not actually be able to prevent their transfer to terrorist groups that enjoy close relations with officials in his regime.

Two former United Nations weapon inspectors in Iraq reinforced concerns about illicit transfer of weapon components into Syria in the wake of Saddam Hussein's fall. Richard Butler viewed overhead imagery and other intelligence suggesting that Iraqis transported some weapons components into Syria. Butler did not think "the Iraqis wanted to give them to Syria, but ... just wanted to get them out of the territory, out of the range of our inspections. Syria was prepared to be the custodian of them."[29] Former Iraq Survey Group head David Kay obtained corroborating information from the interrogation of former Iraqi officials. He said that the missing components were small in quantity, but he, nevertheless, felt that U.S. intelligence officials needed to determine what reached Syria.[30]

Baghdad and Damascus may have long been rivals, but there was precedent for such Iraqi cooperation with regional competitors when faced with an outside threat. In the run-up to the 1991 Operation Desert Storm and the liberation of Kuwait, the Iraqi regime flew many of its jets to Iran, with which, just three years previous, it had been engaged in bitter trench warfare.[31]

Subsequent reports by the Iraq Survey Group at first glance threw cold water on some speculation about the fate of missing Iraqi weapons, but a closer read suggests that questions about a possible transfer to Syria remain open. The September 30, 2004 Duelfer report,[32] while inconclusive, left open such a possibility. While Duelfer dismissed reports of official transfer of weapons material from Iraq into Syria, the Iraq Survey Group was not able to discount the unofficial movement of limited material. Duelfer described weapons smuggling between both countries prior to Saddam's ouster.[33] In one incident detailed by a leading British newspaper, intelligence sources assigned to monitor Baghdad's air traffic raised suspicions that Iraqi authorities had smuggled centrifuge components out of Syria in June 2002. The parts were initially stored in the Syrian port of Tartus before being transported to Damascus International Airport. The transfer allegedly occurred when Iraqi authorities sent twenty-four planes with humanitarian assistance into Syria after a dam collapsed in June 2002, killing twenty people and leaving some 30,000 others homeless.[34] Intelligence officials do not believe these planes returned to Iraq empty. Regardless of the merits of this one particular episode, it is well documented that Syria became the main conduit in Saddam Hussein's attempt to rebuild his military under the 1990–2003 United Nations sanctions,[35] and so the necessary contacts between regimes and along the border would already have been in place. Indeed, according to U.S. Defense Department sources, the weapons smuggling held such importance for the Syrian regime that the trade included Assad's older sister and his brother-in-law. Assaf Shawqat, deputy chief of Syria's military intelligence organization. Numerous reports also implicate Shawqat's two brothers who participated in the Syrian-Iraqi trade during the two years before Saddam's ouster.[36]

While the Duelfer report was inconclusive, part of its failure to tic up all loose ends was due to declining security conditions in Iraq, which forced the Iraq Survey Group to curtail its operations.[37] The cloud of suspicion over the Syrian regime's role in smuggling Iraq's weapons—and speculation as to the nature of those weapons—will not dissipate until Damascus reveals the contents of truck convoys spotted entering Syria from Iraq in the run-up to the March 2003 U.S.-led invasion of Iraq.[38] U.S. intelligence officials and policymakers also will not be able to end speculation until Bashar al-Assad completely and unconditionally allows international inspectors to search suspected depots and interview key participants in the Syrian-Iraqi weapons trade. Four repositories in Syria remain under suspicion. Anonymous U.S. sources have suggested that some components may have been kept in an ammunition facility adjacent to a military base close to Khan Abu Shamat, 30 miles (50 kilometers) west of Damascus.[39] In addition, three sites in the western part of central Syria, an area where support for the Assad regime is strong, are reputed to house suspicious weapons components. These sites include an air force factory in the village of Tall as-Sinan; a mountainous tunnel near Al-Baydah, less than five miles from Al-Masyaf (Masyat); and another location near Shanshar.[40]

While the Western media often focus on the fate of Iraqi weapons components, just as important to Syrian proliferation efforts has been the influx of Iraqi weapons scientists. *The Daily Telegraph* reported prior to the 2003 Iraq war that Iraq's former special security organization and Shawqat arranged for the transfer into Syria of twelve mid-level Iraqi weapons specialists, along with their families and compact disks full of research material on their country's nuclear initiatives. According to unnamed Western intelligence officials cited in the report, Assad turned around and offered to relocate the scientists to Iran, on the condition that Tehran would share the fruits of their research with Damascus.[41]

The Weapons Proliferation Hydra

The Iraqi government may not have been Bashar al-Assad's only source of advanced weapons technology. Following his January 29, 2002, State of the Union speech. Bush launched the Proliferation Security Initiative.[42] Participation grew quickly to include over sixty countries. Participants seek to deter rogue states and non-state actors from obtaining material for weapons of mass destruction and ballistic missile initiatives through various activities—interdiction of suspicious shipments, streamlined procedures to analyze and disseminate information, and strengthened national and international laws and regulations. Liberia and Panama's participation marked a key development because vessels registered from both countries account for approximately 50 percent of the world's total shipping.[43]

The Syrian government remains convinced that U.S. efforts to isolate it will fail.

In 2003, cooperation between U.S. and British intelligence and coordination with their militaries led to the seizure of a Libya-bound ship that carried material for its nuclear weapons program. The capture partly led to Tripoli's agreement to dismantle and destroy its weapons of mass destruction capabilities.[44] Additionally, it was the seizure of this ship that unraveled Pakistani nuclear scientist Abdul Qadir Khan's clandestine nuclear proliferation network. While the exposure of the network drew international attention, the limelight did not eradicate the program. As one former aid of Khan's acknowledged, "The hardware is still available, and the network hasn't stopped."[45]

Khan visited various countries throughout Europe, Africa, and Asia. While no credible evidence yet links Khan's network to Damascus, Western diplomats said that he gave numerous lectures on nuclear issues in late 1997 and early 1998 in Damascus. According to sources, starting in 2001, meetings with the Syrians were held in Iran to avoid any possible linkages between Damascus and Khan's nuclear network. One senior U.S. official stated that an experimental electronic monitor recognized the unique patterns of operational centrifuges in Syria in early to mid-2004. The source reaffirmed Washington's suspicion that the technology originated from Khan's nexus.[46]

The Pakistani government has been unwilling to cooperate fully in the investigation of Khan's activities. As Pakistani president Pervez Musharraf explained, "This man is a hero for the Pakistanis, and there is a sensitivity that maybe the world wants to intervene in our nuclear program, which nobody wants . . . It is a pride of the nation."[47] In addition to safeguarding the nuclear weapons program, some analysts note that Islamabad fears Khan might disclose the extent of support he obtained from the Pakistani military. Further complicating efforts to determine what assistance, if any, the Khan network provided Syria. Pakistan's interior ministry denied exit visas to over a dozen technicians who worked in the country's nuclear weapons program. The officials were also barred from meeting or exchanging information with any foreigner.[48] Such unknowns about the extent of weapons know-how and material acquired from Iraq and Pakistan may not equate to proof, but they raise serious concerns about Syrian intentions, all the more so because Damascus has not been forthcoming with explanations and simultaneously has worked to acquire potential delivery systems from Russian firms.

Assad's Terrorist Game

U.S. concerns about Syrian weapons ambitions are magnified by the Syrian regime's flirtation with terrorism as a method to advance policy. According to the 2004 *Patterns of Global Terrorism* report, the Syrian regime provides Hezbollah, Hamas, Islamic Jihad, and other groups both logistical and financial assistance.[49]

Syrian willingness to encourage terrorism, not only against Israel but also against other neighbors, is well documented.

The Syrian government denies harboring terrorists although much of this denial is based on unwillingness to recognize terrorist groups as such. Damascus views many terrorists as soldiers in its war against Israel. Syrian-backed terrorists have attacked Israel, often from Syrian-occupied Bekaa Valley in neighboring Lebanon.[50] Even though the Syrian military has officially ended its occupation of Lebanon under terms of U.N. Security Council Resolution 1559,[51] the Syrian intelligence presence remains significant.[52]

Syrian willingness to encourage terrorism, not only against Israel but also against other neighbors, is well documented. Until 1999, the Syrian regime provided Kurdistan Workers Party (PKK) terrorists safe-haven from which to strike at Turkey.[53] Syrian intelligence or its proxies remain the chief suspect in the February 14, 2005 assassination of former Lebanese Prime Minister Rafik Hariri.[54]

The Syrian regime has also played a double game with regard to Iraq. General John Abizaid, the commander of U.S. forces in the Middle East, commented that although Damascus made some progress in the curtailment of insurgents entering Iraq, "I don't regard this effort as being good enough . . . I cannot tell you that the level of infiltration has decreased."[55] CIA director Peter Goss concurred. In March 2005, he told the U.S. Senate Armed Services Committee, "Despite a lot of very well-intentioned and persistent efforts to try and get more cooperation from the Syrian regime, we have not had the success I wish I could report."[56] Syrian support for terrorism combined with its lack of support for the new Iraqi government make more troubling the possibility that the Syrian regime became custodian to Iraq's chemical and biological weapons capability in the final days of Saddam Hussein's regime.

The confluence of weapons of mass destruction ambitions and Syrian willingness to sponsor terrorism make Syrian ambitions particularly dangerous. In April 2004, for example, Jordanian authorities intercepted, arrested, or killed several al-Qaeda-sponsored terrorists who planned to attack the U.S. embassy and Jordanian targets in Amman with chemical weapons. The terrorists gathered their materials in Syria and used that country as a base from which to infiltrate Jordan.[57] While the Syrian government denies any role, the implication that it participated in such a potentially catastrophic tragedy underlines Damascus's opposition to the war on terrorism.

The Syrian government may feel that it can ameliorate or outlast U.S. concerns about its flirtation with terrorist groups. In the aftermath of 9-11, Syrian officials detained some alleged al-Qaeda operatives, but they allowed U.S. officials only to submit questions in writing, not to interrogate the suspects directly.[58] Realists within the Bush administration did not sanction such a la carte for the war on terrorism. Deputy Secretary of State Richard Armitage, for example, remarked. "If you oppose terrorism, you oppose all terrorism."[59] Secretary of State Condoleezza Rice's new lineup at the State Department shows no sign of deviating from such positions.

The Syrian government may also believe that Washington is not able to back its rhetoric against Syria with action. With more than 100,000 U.S. troops committed in Iraq, looming crises over the Iranian and North Korean nuclear programs, and European Union cynicism, the Syrian government remains convinced that U.S. efforts to isolate Damascus will fail. As Assad recently told the Italian newspaper *La Repubblica,* "Sooner or later [the Americans] will realize that we are the key to the solution. We are essential for the peace process, for Iraq. Look, perhaps one day the Americans will come and knock on our door."[60]

But, Assad's belief that Washington needs his cooperation may be a significant misread of U.S. policy. Partly in response to Damascus's refusal to cooperate completely in the war on terrorism. President Bush signed the "Syria Accountability and Lebanese Sovereignty Restoration Act of 2003."[61] Under terms of the act, American firms cannot export any products to Syria beyond food and medicine. The president can wave this provision for an unspecified duration provided he determines that it would further U.S. national security and he submits justification for the waiver to the appropriate Congressional committees.[62] However, Bush increasingly shows little inclination to waive such provisions. In late February 2005, some U.S. government officials suggested that the Bush administration was exploring additional measures against Syria. Under the Syrian Accountability Act, Bush could cut off Syrian access to U.S. banks, limit the travel of Syrian diplomats within the United States, and freeze Syrian assets.[63] Other provisions call for the secretary of state to submit to Congress an annual report on provisions relating to the prevention of dual-use technologies that Damascus could use to advance its ballistic missiles and weapons of mass destruction projects; such reports will also prevent questions over Syrian compliance to fade from policymakers' attention.[64]

Future Policy

In a recent interview. Bashar al-Assad stated, "I am not Saddam Hussein. I want to cooperate."[65] Evidence indicates otherwise. Syrian attempts to obtain a sophisticated Russian ballistic missile undermine Washington's ability to prevent terrorist sponsors from advancing their military capabilities. Damascus's failure to come clean regarding prewar Iraqi convoys and immigration of Iraqi weapons personnel, as well as its flirtation with Abdul Qadir Khan, raise questions about Assad's sincerity.

The Syrian withdrawal from Lebanon has neither changed basic Syrian behavior nor altered its regional ambitions.

The unknowns regarding Syria's weapons programs are especially worrisome given Assad's continued rejection of international norms of behavior. Syrian obstructionism and attempts to augment its weapons of mass destruction stock make expansion and enforcement of the Proliferation Security Initiative imperative, a strategy supported by U.S. defense secretary Donald Rumsfeld.[66] Offering economic or political incentives to Yemen, Turkey, Egypt, and other countries which retain close relationships with Syria might help shut down avenues which the Syrian regime uses to advance its weapons projects although the damage to counter-proliferation efforts caused by Abdul Qadir Khan's network suggests that there should be a verification mechanism beyond simple diplomatic assurance.

Failure to counter Syrian weapons ambitions could undercut U.S. democracy and antiterror initiatives. The Syrian withdrawal from Lebanon has neither changed basic Syrian behavior nor altered its regional ambitions. The combination of a ballistic missile capability, chemical and biological weapons, and a willingness to arm or turn a blind-eye to terrorists—including those targeting the U.S. presence in Iraq—might lead to bolder terror initiatives, like the attempt in Amman in April 2004, as well as embolden rejectionism by a Syrian regime feeling its arsenal sufficient to deter a U.S. response. Only with sustained pressure can Washington prevent the Syrian regime from such a miscalculation.

Notes

1. *Yedi'ot Ahronot* (Tel Aviv), Sept. 16. 1994.
2. *Syria Primer,* Virtual Information Center, Apr. 24, 2003, p. 38, 47.
3. Associated Press, Apr. 28, 2005.
4. "The SS-26," The Claremont Institute, accessed June 8, 2005.
5. Ibid.
6. *Ha'aretz* (Tel Aviv), Jan. 13, 2005.
7. "The SS-26," The Claremont Institute.
8. Agence France-Presse, Feb. 16, 2005.
9. Radio Free Europe/Radio Liberty, Jan. 13, 2005.
10. "Overview of State-Sponsored Terrorism," *Patterns of Global Terrorism, 2004* (Washington, D.C.: U.S. Department of State, Apr. 2005).
11. *Agenlstvo Voyennykh Novostey* (Moscow), Mar. 25, 2005.
12. Associated Press, Apr. 28, 2005.
13. Associated Press, Apr. 21, 2005.
14. Associated Press, Apr. 26, 2005.
15. Yaakov Amidror, "Israel's Requirements for Defensible Borders," *Defensible Borders for a Lasting Peace* (Jerusalem: Jerusalem Center for Public Affairs), p. 33.
16. Reuters, Apr. 21, 2005.
17. *The Jerusalem Post,* June 5, 2005.
18. *The New York Times,* June 4, 2005.
19. *BBC News,* May 21, 2005.
20. *Potitkum.ru* (Moscow), Feb. 21, 2005.
21. Ibid.
22. "Unclassified Report to Congress on the Acquisition of Technology Relating to Weapons of Mass Destruction and Advanced Conventional Munitions, 1 July through 31 Dec. 2003," CIA, Nov. 2004, p. 6.
23. *The Washington Times,* Oct. 28, 2004.
24. Israel's Channel 2, Dec. 23, 2002.
25. *Petah Tiqva,* Yoman Shevu'i supplement (Tel Aviv), Feb. 21, 2003.
26. "Syria's Weapons of Mass Destruction and Missile Development Program," testimony of John R. Bolton. U.S. undersecretary of arms control and international security, before the House International Relations Committee, Subcommittee on the Middle East and Central Asia, Sept. 16. 2003; *BBC News,* Apr. 14, 2003; Alexander Downer, Australian minister of foreign affairs, news conference, Canberra, June 5, 2003.

27. *Agence France-Presse,* Apr. 17, 2003.
28. *Time,* Mar. 14, 2005.
29. *Agence France-Presse,* Apr. 15, 2003.
30. *Sunday Telegraph* (London), Jan. 25, 2005.
31. *Los Angeles Times,* Oct. 8, 1991.
32. Complied by Charles Duelfer, special advisor for strategy to the director of Central Intelligence.
33. *Comprehensive Report of the Special Advisori- to the DCI on Iraq's WMD,* vol. 1 (Washington, D.C.: CIA, Sept. 30, 2004), hereafter, Duelfer report, p. 104.
34. *The Times* (London), June 17, 2002.
35. Duelfer report, p. 239.
36. Dueller report, p. 104.
37. *Addendums to Comprehensive Report of the Special Advisor to the DCI on WMD,* Mar. 2005, accessed on June 8, 2005.
38. *The Washington Times,* Oct. 28. 2004.
39. *Petah Tiqva,* Yoman Shevu'i supplement, Feb. 21, 2003.
40. *De Telegraaf* (Amsterdam), Jan. 5, 2004.
41. *The Daily Telegraph* (London), Sept. 26, 2004.
42. State of the Union Address, Jan. 29, 2002.
43. "The Proliferation Security Initiative," U.S. Department of State, Bureau of Nonproliferation, July 28, 2004.
44. *The Washington Times,* Dec. 23, 2004.
45. *Time,* Feb. 14, 2005.
46. *Los Angeles Times,* June 25, 2004.
47. *Los Angeles Times,* Dec. 6, 2004.
48. *The News* (Islamabad), Jan. 5, 2005.
49. *Pattern of Global Terrorism,* 2004, p. 93.
50. *Patterns of Global Terrorism,* 2003 (Washington, D.C.: U.S. Department of State, Apr. 2004), p. 93.
51. U.N. Security Council Resolution 1559, S/RES/1559 (2004), Sept. 2, 2004.
52. Reuters, May 20, 2005.
53. Ben Thein, "Is Israel's Security Barrier Unique?" *Middle East Quarterly,* Fall 2004, p. 29.
54. *Agence France-Presse,* Mar. 25, 2005.
55. Associated Press, Mar. 1, 2005.
56. Reuters, Mar. 17, 2005.
57. *CNN News,* Apr. 26, 2004.
58. *The Washington Post,* June 19, 2002.
59. U.S. Embassy news release, Sept. 10, 2004.
60. *BBC NEWS,* Feb. 28, 2005.
61. "Fact Sheet: Implementing the Syria Accountability and Lebanese Sovereignty Restoration Act of 2003," White House news release, May 11, 2004.
62. Ibid.
63. *The Washington Post,* Feb. 17, 2005.
64. "Fact Sheet," May 11, 2004.
65. *Time,* Mar. 14, 2005.
66. *The Washington Times,* Dec. 23, 2004.

LEE KASS is an analyst in the research and analysis division of Science Applications International Corporation (SAIC). The views expressed in this article are his own.

From *Middle East Quarterly,* Fall 2005, pp. 25–34. Copyright © 2005 by Middle East Forum. Reprinted by permission. www.MEQQuarterly.org

UNIT 4

International Terrorism

Unit Selections

11. **Colombia and the United States: From Counternarcotics to Counterterrorism,** Arlene B. Tickner
12. **Wounded But Still Dangerous,** *The Economist*
13. **Peace at Last?,** Joshua Hammer
14. **Root Causes of Chechen Terror,** Alon Ben-Meir
15. **End of Terrorism?,** Meredith Moore

Key Points to Consider

- What factors have led to the reemergence of the Taliban?
- What are the causes of the crisis in Colombia? What affect have U.S. policies had on Colombia's problems?
- How successful has the Indonesian government been in dealing with Jemaah Islamiah?
- What contributed to the Basque conflict? Will the current cease-fire lead to peace?

Student Web Site
www.mhcls.com/online

Internet References
Further information regarding these Web sites may be found in this book's preface or online.

Arab.Net Contents
http://www.arab.net/sections/contents.html

International Association for Counterterrorism and Security Professionals
http://www.iacsp.com/index.html

The International Policy Institute for Counter-Terrorism
http://www.ict.org.il

International Rescue Committee
http://www.intrescom.org

United Nations Website on Terrorism
http://www.un.org/terrorism

United States Institute of Peace
http://www.usip.org/library/topics/terrorism.html

International terrorism has changed significantly over time. Simply said, it has become more complex. Increased organizational complexity, improved communications, and an increased willingness to cause mass casualties, pose new challenges for the international community.

Individuals and small groups dominated international terrorism in the 1970s. Larger groups and organizations played a critical role in international terrorism in the 1980s. More complex multinational terrorist networks emerged in the 1990s. More recently, small independent groups of individuals, of local origin, have emerged to carry out attacks in their home countries in support of broad global movements. Now, all four generations and levels of organizational structure appear to exist. Sometimes terrorists act locally or regionally to pursue independent agendas. At other times they take advantage of cross-national links to obtain greater access to weapons, training, or financial resources. On occasion, they may even temporarily set aside local interests and objectives to cooperate within loosely connected international networks to pursue broader ideological agendas. At a given point in time international terrorists can be engaged in activities at all levels, posing unique challenges to those engaged in the study of and struggle against international terrorism.

Modern communications technologies have changed the way international terrorists operate. The cellphone and the laptop computer have become as important as the bomb and the AK-47 in the terrorist arsenal. The internet has provided terrorists with instant access to global communications, has enhanced their ability to exchange information, and provides them with an effective vehicle to rally their supporters. Almost all major international terrorist organizations operate their own Web sites and communicate via the internet.

A particularly disturbing trend in contemporary international terrorism is the increasing willingness by some terrorists to cause mass casualties to innocent victims. While the potential causes of this trend are subject to debate, this trend has elevated terrorism to the top of the international agenda. While over the past several decades, the number of international terrorist incidents has declined, the casualties caused by international terrorism have steadily increased. More importantly, this trend has focused international attention on terrorist methods deemed unlikely only a few years ago. Potential threats posed by biological, chemical, or radiological weapons are again at the forefront of international concern.

The five selections in this unit reflect some of the diversity in international terrorism. The first article examines the shift in U.S. policy in Colombia "from counternarcotics to counterterrorism." The

The McGraw-Hill Companies Inc./Christopher Kerrigan, photographer

second article argues that despite Indonesia's recent successes against Jemaah Islamiah, the group remains a significant threat. While there have been no large-scale attacks against foreigners since the Bali bombings 2005, there are indications that JI may be rearming and reorganizing. Next, Joshua Hammer explores the roots of thes conflict in the Basque region of Spain. While skepticism remains high on both sides there is some hope that the latest cease-fire will lead to a peace agreement ending decades of separatist violence. In the fourth article, Alon Ben-Mier argues that as long as Russia continues to ignore the root causes of Chechen terrorism, there is no chance of diminishing or eliminating it. Finally, Meredith Moore maintains that despite calls for peace, inaction on both sides will lead to a continuation of Basque violence in Spain.

Colombia and the United States: From Counternarcotics to Counterrorism

"The worldview that has molded Washington's twin wars on drugs and terrorism constitutes an extremely narrow framework through which to address the complex problems Colombia faces. National security, defined exclusively in military terms, has taken precedence over equally significant political, economic, and social considerations."

ARLENE B. TICKNER

During the past several years, United States foreign policy toward Colombia has undergone significant transformations. Long considered a faithful ally in the fight against drugs, as well as showcasing Washington's achievements in this camp, Colombia became widely identified as an international pariah in the mid-1990s during the administration of Ernesto Samper because of the scandal surrounding the president's electoral campaign, which was said to have been funded by drug money. Although the inauguration in 1998 of President Andrés Pastrana—a man untainted by drugs—marked the official return to friendly relations with the United States, Colombia came to be viewed as a problem nation in which the spillover effects of the country's guerrilla war threatened regional stability. The events of September 11, combined with the definitive rupture of the Colombian government's peace process with the rebels in February 2002, have converted this country into the primary theater of United States counterterrorist operations in the Western Hemisphere today.

The Perverse Effects of the "War on Drugs"

Any discussion of United States policy in Colombia must begin with drugs. Since the mid-1980s, when illicit narcotics were declared a lethal threat to America's national security, the drug issue has been central to relations with Colombia. Washington's counternarcotics policies have been based on repressive, prohibitionist, and hard-line language and on strategies that have changed little in the last few decades. The manner in which Colombia itself has addressed the drug problem derives substantially from the United States approach, with most of Bogotá's measures to fight drug trade the result of bilateral agreements or the unilateral imposition of specific strategies designed in Washington.[1] These American-guided efforts to combat illegal drugs "at the source" have produced countless negative consequences for Colombia, aggravating the armed conflict that continues to consume the country and forcing urgent national problems such as the strengthening of democracy, the defense of human rights, the reduction of poverty, and the preservation of the environment to become secondary to countering the drug trade.

Perhaps the most perverse result of the United States–led "war on drugs" is that it has failed to reduce the production, trafficking, and consumption of illicit substances. Between 1996 and 2001, United States military aid to Colombia increased fifteenfold, from $67 million to $1 billion.[2] During this same period, data from the United States State Department's annual *International Narcotics Drug Control Strategy* report show that coca cultivations in Colombia grew 150 percent, from 67,200 to 169,800 hectares (1 hectare = 2.471 acres). Clearly, the high levels of military assistance received by Colombia have had little effect on illicit crop cultivation in the country.

Efforts to eradicate coca cultivation, primarily through aerial spraying, have also increased progressively in Colombia. In 1998, for example, 50 percent more hectares were fumigated than in 1997; in 2001 the Colombian National Police fumigated nearly two times more coca than in 2000. In both instances, fumigation had no effect or even an inverse effect on the total number of hectares cultivated.

Intensive aerial fumigation—particularly in southern Colombia, where Plan Colombia efforts are concentrated—has created public health problems and led to the destruction of licit crops. According to exhaustive studies conducted by Colombia's

The "Realist" Approach to Drugs and Terrorism

With the end of the cold war the United States lost its most significant "other," the Soviet Union; it also lost a clear sense of the national security interests of the United States. Drugs, long considered a threat to United States values and society, became an obvious target. Viewed in this light, the "threat" represented by illegal drugs in the United States is not an objective condition; rather, narcotics constitute one of the "cognitive enemies" against which United States national identity attempted to rebuild, albeit only partially, until September 11. In this sense, drugs are seen as "endangering" the American way of life and social fabric, much like the challenge posed by the communist threat to America's values during the bipolar conflict.

Given the sense of moral superiority that has traditionally characterized United States relations with the rest of the world, drug consumption is understood as being prompted by the availability of illegal drugs, which are concentrated, unsurprisingly, in the countries of the periphery; it is not seen as a problem originating in the demand for drugs in the United States or in the prohibitionist strategies that have traditionally characterized America's handling of this issue. While this rationale clearly runs contrary to commonsense economic rules of supply and demand, it tends to reinforce the underlying assumption of moral purity on which America's sense of self is partly based.

The terrorist attacks of September 11, 2001 and the United States–led retaliation mirror this perspective on drugs. Just as the drug issue fails to conform to typical notions of security and threat from a realist perspective, so September 11 challenges traditional views of international relations. The attacks came from within America's borders, not without, and were perpetrated by nonstate actors with little or no military power.

But terrorism, rather than being seen as a diffuse, nonterritorial problem, has been associated by the Bush administration with state-based territories—Afghanistan and the entire "axis of evil"—and personified in figures such as Osama bin Laden and Saddam Hussein. The exercise of military power in countries threatening "freedom" and "justice" in the world constitutes the cornerstone of the United States strategy. And the zealous language accompanying the fight against terrorism—"those who are not with us are against us"—eerily recalls the cold war period.

The similarities between the wars on drugs and terrorism and the war on communism notwithstanding, a crucial difference exists: the enemies of these new wars are not readily identifiable, making victory nearly impossible. Hence, any explanation of the role of drugs and terrorism in United States domestic and international politics must necessarily return to the concepts of danger and threat. Although the policies implemented by the United States have failed in reducing the availability of illegal substances—and will most likely be unsuccessful in erasing terrorism from the globe—drugs and, more important, terrorism occupy a crucial discursive function in support of American identities and values. Both are considered lethal threats to United States security—and the political costs associated with directly challenging existing policies in Washington are extremely high. At the same time, the need to persevere in the war on drugs has received an additional push from the war on terrorism; the financing of terrorist activities with drug money has received much greater attention in United States policymaking circles in the aftermath of September 11.

A.B.T.

---

national human rights ombudsman in 2001 and 2002, aerial spraying with glyphosate has not only killed the legal crops of many communities in southern Colombia but has also caused health problems associated with the inhalation of the pesticide and contact with human skin.[3] On two separate occasions, the ombudsman called for a halt to aerial fumigation until its harmful effects could be mitigated. Echoing similar concerns, in late 2001 the United States Congress, as a precondition for disbursing the aerial-fumigation portion of the 2002 aid bill to the Andean region, requested the State Department to certify that drug-eradication strategies currently employed in Colombia do not pose significant public health risks. On September 4, 2002 the State Department issued its report, arguing that no adverse effects had been found. Members of the scientific community and environmental nongovernmental organizations in the United States and Europe criticized the report, primarily on methodological grounds.

Eradication efforts also have not affected the costs to users: in November 2001 the United States Office of National Drug Control Policy acknowledged that the price of cocaine in principal American cities has remained stable during the past several years. Yet Washington and Bogotá continue to insist that the war on drugs can be won simply by intensifying and expanding current strategies.

The United States war on drugs is nearly inseparable from counterinsurgency efforts in Colombia.

The "War on Drugs" and Counterinsurgency

The cold war's end saw drugs replace communism as the primary threat to United States national security in the Western Hemisphere. Military assistance to Latin America became concentrated in the "source" countries, particularly Colombia. At the same time, the definition of "low-intensity conflict"—the term used to describe the political situation in Central America during the 1980s—was expanded to include those countries in which drug-trafficking organizations threatened the stability of the state. And the strategies applied in the 1980s to confront low-intensity conflict in the region were subsequently adjusted in the 1990s to address the new regional threat: drugs.

In Colombia this view of the drug problem, and of the strategies needed to combat it, is especially troublesome, given that illegal armed actors, especially the leftist Revolutionary Armed Forces of Colombia (FARC) and the paramilitary United Self-Defense Force of Colombia (AUC), maintain complex linkages with the drug trade. At conceptual and practical levels, the United States war on drugs is nearly inseparable from counter-insurgency efforts in Colombia.[4]

The conflation of low-intensity counterinsurgency tactics with counter-narcotics strategies was facilitated initially through the "narcoguerrilla theory" (a term first made popular in the 1980s by former United States Ambassador to Colombia Lewis Tambs, who accused the FARC of sustaining direct links with drug traffickers). However, the fact that paramilitary organizations, most notably MAS (Muerte a Secuestradores, or Death to Kidnappers), were created in the early 1980s and financed by drug traffickers in retaliation for guerrilla kidnappings, seemed to belie the theory's validity. Yet by the mid-1990s, references to the "narcoguerrilla" slowly began to find their way into the official jargon of certain sectors of the United States and Colombian political and military establishment. Robert Gelbard, United States assistant secretary of state for international narcotics and law enforcement, referred to the FARC as Colombia's third-largest drug cartel in 1996. During his administration, President Ernesto Samper himself began to use the narcoguerrilla label domestically in an attempt to discredit the FARC, given the group's unwillingness to negotiate with a political figure that the guerrilla organization considered illegitimate.

Ironically, when the Colombian military during the Samper administration tried to convince Washington that the symbiosis between guerrillas and drug-trafficking organizations was real, and that counternarcotics strategies needed to take this relationship into consideration, the United States argued against the idea that the guerrillas were involved in the drug traffic. Indeed, although Tambs and others had made the accusation, the United States had never categorically associated Colombian guerrilla organizations with the latter stages of the drug-trafficking process. Only in November 2000 did the State Department accuse the FARC of maintaining relations with Mexico's Arellano-Félix Organization, one of the most powerful drug cartels in that country; it also argued that "since late 1999 the FARC has sought to establish a monopoly position over the commercialization of cocaine base across much of southern Colombia." One week later, United States Ambassador to Colombia Anne Patterson affirmed that both the FARC and the paramilitaries had "control of the entire export process and the routes for sending drugs abroad" and were operating as drug cartels in the country.

In principle, the "narcoguerrilla theory," as employed in Colombia, argues that: 1) the FARC controls most aspects of the drug trade, given the demise of the major drug cartels in the mid-1990s; 2) the Colombian state is too weak to confront this threat, primarily due to the inefficacy of the country's armed forces; and 3) United States military support is warranted in wresting drug-producing regions from guerrilla control.

The events of September 11 and America's war on terrorism have introduced an additional ingredient to United States policy in Colombia: counterterrorism.

Although bearing a certain degree of truth, this description grossly oversimplifies the Colombian situation. For example, while a general consensus exists that the FARC derives a considerable portion of its income from the taxation of coca crops and coca paste and that members of this organization have participated in drugs for arms transactions, the involvement of the FARC in the transportation and distribution of narcotics internationally is still uncertain. (Contrary to the claims made by the United States State Department and its representative in Colombia, for example, the Drug Enforcement Agency has never directly accused the FARC of operating as an international drug cartel.)

The involvement of paramilitaries in drug-related activities clouds this picture even further. According to some sources, paramilitary expansion in southern Colombia during late 2000, in particular in the Putumayo region, was largely financed by drug-trafficking organizations in response to the FARC-imposed increases in the price and taxation of coca paste. This is not surprising, since the leader of the AUC, Carlos Castaño, has personally acknowledged since March 2000 that a large percentage of this organization's revenues, especially in the departments of Antioquia and Córdoba, are derived from participation in the drug trade.

Yet even with evidence that the "narcoguerrilla theory" is simpleminded, it seems to have informed many United States and Colombian political and military actors in the search for policy options in the country, while also lending credence to those who argue that counterinsurgency techniques used in other low-intensity conflicts can be applied successfully in Colombia.

September 11 and Counterterrorism

The events of September 11 and America's war on terrorism have introduced an additional ingredient to United States policy in Colombia: counterterrorism. On the day of the attacks, United States Secretary of State Colin Powell was to have visited Bogotá on official business. Although Washington's concern about the FARC's abuse of a swath of Colombia designated as a demilitarized zone created to facilitate peace talks was clear (the FARC was accused of using the zone to cultivate coca, hold kidnapping victims, and meet with members of the Irish Republican Army, allegedly to receive training in urban military tactics), some members of the American government were beginning to express reservations about the depth and nature of

United States involvement in Colombia and the effectiveness of counternarcotics strategies in the country. To a large degree, the incidents of the day facilitated shifts in United States policy that had begun taking shape much earlier.

> **Colombia's insertion into the global antiterrorist dynamic leaves scant room for autonomous decision-making by the new president.**

In a congressional hearing held on October 10, 2001, Francis Taylor, the State Department's coordinator for counterterrorism, stated that the "most dangerous international terrorist group based in this hemisphere is the Revolutionary Armed Forces of Colombia." Both Secretary of State Colin Powell and United States Ambassador to Colombia Patterson also began to refer to Colombian armed actors, in particular the FARC, as terrorist organizations that threaten regional stability.[5] Given that the global war on terrorism has targeted the links that exist among terrorism, arms, and drugs, a new term was coined, "narcoterrorism," to describe actors such as the FARC and the AUC that fund terrorist-related activities with drug money.

The Colombian government's termination of the peace process with the FARC on February 20, 2002 placed Colombia squarely within Washington's new counterterrorist efforts. Until that day, the government of President Andrés Pastrana had never publicly referred to the guerrillas as terrorists. In a televised speech announcing his decision to call off the peace talks, however, Pastrana made this association explicit. Echoing this change, the presidential electoral battle of 2002 centered on the issues of counterterrorism and war, and led to the election of hard-liner Álvaro Uribe on May 26.

Colombia's insertion into the global war on terrorism has been reflected in concrete policy measures in the United States. In simple terms, Colombia is now viewed through the lens of counterterrorism. Public officials from both countries must frame Colombia's problems along antiterrorist lines to assure continued United States support. This shift in terminology has led to the complete erasure of differences between counternarcotics, counterinsurgency, and counterterrorist activities that formerly constituted the rhetorical backbone of United States policy in Colombia. For many years, Washington stressed the idea that its "war" in Colombia was against drug trafficking and not against the armed insurgents. As was noted, some began to openly advocate reconsideration of this policy as early as November 2000. Tellingly, United States Representative Benjamin Gilman (R., N.Y.), in a letter written that month to drug czar Barry McCaffrey that criticized the militarization of counternarcotics activities in Colombia, suggested the need for public debate concerning counterinsurgency aid to the country. A RAND report published in March 2001 also affirmed that Washington should reorient its strategy in Colombia toward counterinsurgency to help the local government regain control of the national territory.[6]

On March 21, 2002 President George W. Bush presented a supplemental budgetary request to the United States Congress totaling $27 billion for the war on terrorism and the defense of national security. The request solicited additional funding for Colombia as well as authorization to use counternarcotics assistance already disbursed to the country. The antiterrorist package finally approved by Congress in July contains an additional $35 million for counterinsurgency activities in Colombia as well as authority to use United States military assistance for purposes other than counternarcotics—namely, counterinsurgency and counterterrorism.

In its 2003 budget proposal submitted to Congress on February 4, 2002, the Bush administration also requested, for the first time, funding for activities unrelated to the drug war in Colombia. The aid package, which totals over $500 million, includes a request for approximately $100 million to train and equip two new Colombian army brigades to protect the Caño Limón-Coveñas oil pipeline, in which the American firm Occidental Petroleum is a large shareholder.

Militarization and Human Rights

One of the most severe challenges to United States policy derives from the human rights situation in Colombia. According to the United States State Department *Report on Human Rights* for 2001, political and extrajudicial actions involving government security forces, paramilitary groups, and members of the guerrilla forces resulted in the deaths of 3,700 civilians; paramilitary forces were responsible for approximately 70 percent of these. During the first 10 months of 2001, 161 massacres occurred in which an estimated 1,021 people were killed. Between 275,000 and 347,000 people were forced to leave their homes, while the total number of Colombians displaced by rural violence in the country during only the last five years grew to approximately 1 million. More than 25,000 homicides were committed, one of the highest global figures per capita, and approximately 3,041 civilians were kidnapped (a slight decline from the 3,700 abducted in 2000).

Although Colombian security forces were responsible for only 3 percent of human rights violations in 2001 (a notable improvement over the 54 percent share in 1993), the report notes that government security forces continued to commit abuses, including extrajudicial killings, and collaborated directly and indirectly with paramilitary forces. And although the government has worked to strengthen its human rights policy, the measures adopted to punish officials accused of committing violations and to prevent paramilitary attacks nationwide are considered insufficient. In the meantime, paramilitary forces have increased their social and political support among the civilian population in many parts of the country. Increasingly, Colombians sense that the paramilitaries constitute the only force capable of controlling the guerrillas' expansion. The AUC have also adopted parastate functions in those regions in which the government's presence is scarce or nonexistent.

Because of the questionable human rights record of the Colombian armed forces as well as Bogotá's unwillingness to denounce this publicly, United States military assistance to the country was severely limited during much of the 1990s. Nevertheless, the United States continued to provide the armed forces with military training, weapons, and materials. In 1994 the United States embassy in Colombia reported that counternarcotics aid had been provided in 1992 and 1993 to several units responsible for human rights violations in areas not considered to be priority drug-producing zones. As a result, beginning in 1994 the United States Congress anchored military aid in Colombia directly to antidrug activities. The Leahy Amendment of September 1996—introduced by Senator Patrick Leahy (D., Vt.)—sought to suspend military assistance to those units implicated in human rights violations that were receiving counternarcotics funding, unless the United States secretary of state certified that the government was taking measures to bring responsible military officers to trial.

The Colombian government itself began in 1994 to adopt a stronger stance on human rights and in January 1995 publicly claimed responsibility in what became known as the Trujillo massacres (committed between 1988 and 1991): more than 100 assassinations carried out by government security forces in collaboration with drug-trafficking organizations. Other measures directly sponsored by the Samper government in this area included the creation of a permanent regional office of the UN High Commissioner for Human Rights; the ratification of Protocol II of the Geneva Conventions; and the formalization of an agreement with the International Red Cross that enabled this organization to establish a presence in the country's conflict zones. Unfortunately, as the Colombian newsweekly *Semana* noted, "Little by little, the novel proposals made at the beginning of the Samper administration became relegated to a secondary status, given the government's need to maintain the support of the military in order to stay in power."

The moderate changes implemented by the Colombian government in its handling of human rights issues—combined with the intensification of the armed conflict and the military's need for greater firepower and better technology—facilitated the signing of an agreement in August 1997 in which the Colombian armed forces accepted the conditionality imposed by the Leahy Amendment. In the past, the Colombian military had repeatedly refused United States military assistance on the grounds that such unilateral impositions "violated the dignity of the army." But the marked asymmetries between United States aid earmarked for the Colombian National Police (CNP), which immediately accepted human rights conditionalities, and assistance specifically designated for the Colombian army constituted a strong incentive for the military to finally accept the conditions attached by the United States. Until the late 1990s the CNP was Washington's principal ally in the war on drugs, receiving nearly 90 percent of United States military aid given to Colombia. The 2000–2001 Plan Colombia aid package, however, reversed this trend completely: while the Colombian army received $416.9 million, primarily for the training of several counternarcotics battalions, police assistance only totaled $115.6 million.[7] In the 2002 and 2003 aid packages, the Colombian army continues to be the primary recipient of United States military assistance.

With the approval of the first Plan Colombia aid package in June 2000, the United States Congress specified that the president must certify that the Colombian armed forces are acting to suspend and prosecute those officers involved in human rights violations and to enforce civilian court jurisdiction over human rights crimes, and that concrete measures are being taken to break the links between the military and paramilitary groups. This legislation, however, gives the president the prerogative to waive this condition if it is deemed that vital United States national interests are at stake. On August 22, 2000 President Bill Clinton invoked the waiver. And although human rights organizations, the UN High Commissioner for Human Rights, and the State Department affirm that little or no improvements have been made in satisfying the human rights requirements set forth in the original legislation, President George W. Bush certified Colombia in 2002.

With the end of the peace process, human rights in Colombia have been further marginalized. (President Pastrana called off the process with the FARC on February 20, 2002, after continuous setbacks and halts in the peace talks, as well as late 2001 attempts on the part of the United Nations and several countries to serve as intermediaries and revive the process.) Several components of President Álvaro Uribe's national security strategy have caused alarm in human rights circles. Shortly after taking office on August 7, 2002, Uribe declared a state of interior commotion (*Estado de Conmoción Interio*), a constitutional mechanism that allows the executive to rule by decree. In addition to expanding the judicial powers of the police and military, plans to increase the size of the armed forces, create a network of government informants, and build peasant security forces are already under way. In a letter to the Colombian president on August 26, 2002, UN High Commissioner for Human Rights Mary Robinson expressed concern about Colombia's lack of human rights progress and suggested that some of the security measures adopted by the Uribe administration may be incompatible with international humanitarian law. In its November 2002 report on Colombia, Human Rights Watch also criticized the recent reversal of several investigations of military officers suspected of collaborating with paramilitaries.

Weakening the State

Inherent to America's growing concern with Colombia is the perception that the state has become "weak" when it comes to confronting the domestic crisis and maintaining it within the country's national boundaries. (The new National Security Strategy of the United States, made public in September 2002, explicitly identifies weak states as a threat to global security because of their propensity to harbor terrorists.) Thus, in addition to combating drugs and terrorism and reducing human rights violations, another stated goal of United States policy is to enable the Colombian military to reestablish territorial control over the country as a necessary step toward state strengthening.

Although state weakness has been a permanent aspect of Colombian political history, during the 1990s the country's deterioration quickened—with the logic of United States "drug war" imperatives playing a direct role in this process. The expansion and consolidation of drug-trafficking organizations in Colombia during the 1980s were intimately related to increasing United States domestic consumption of illegal substances, as well as the repressive policies traditionally applied to counteract this problem. America's demand for drugs and Washington's prohibitionist strategies created permissive external conditions in which the drug business in Colombia could flourish. The appearance of these organizations coincided with unprecedented levels of corruption in the public sphere, growing violence, and decreasing levels of state monopoly over the use of force.

The dismantling in the mid-1990s of the Medellín and Cali drug cartels—the two main drug-trafficking organizations in the country—gave way to fundamentally different drug-trafficking organizations that combined greater horizontal dispersion, a low profile, and the use of a more sophisticated strategy that made them even more difficult to identify and eradicate. Part of the void created by the disappearance of these two cartels was filled by the FARC and the AUC, which became more directly involved in certain aspects of the drug business between 1994 and 1998. As a result, one might also conclude—correctly—that United States drug consumption and its counternarcotics strategies have also exacerbated the Colombian armed conflict, providing diverse armed actors with substantial sources of income without which their financial autonomy and territorial expansion might not have been as feasible.

The propensity of the United States to interpret the drug problem as a national security issue, in combination with the use of coercive diplomatic measures designed to effectively confront this threat, has forced the Colombian state to "securitize" its own antidrug strategy. One underlying assumption of this "war" is that the use of external pressure is a crucial tool by which to achieve foreign policy objectives in this area, and that United States power is an enabling condition for the success of coercive diplomacy. But realist-inspired counternarcotics efforts ignore that policy orientations in source countries must necessarily answer to domestic as well as international exigencies. If domestic pressures are ignored on a systematic basis, growing state illegitimacy and state weakness can result; in an already weak state, this strategy can accelerate processes of state collapse.

With the Samper administration, the United States drug decertifications of 1996 and 1997 and the continuous threat of economic sanctions combined with domestic pressures that originated in Samper's lack of internal legitimacy to force the government to collaborate vigorously with the United States.[8] As noted, between 1994 and 1998 the Colombian government undertook an unprecedented fumigation campaign that, while returning impressive results in terms of total coca and poppy crop eradication, saw coca cultivation itself mushroom during the same period. More significantly, the fumigation campaign had tremendous repercussions in those parts of southern Colombia where it was applied. In addition to provoking massive social protests in the departments of Putumayo, Caquetá, Cauca, and (especially) Guaviare, guerrilla involvement with drugs heightened during this period, and the FARC strengthened its social base of support among those peasants involved in coca cultivation. The absence of the Colombian state in this part of the country largely facilitated the assumption of parastate functions (administration of justice and security, among others) by the guerrillas. Paramilitary activity also increased with the explicit goal of containing the guerrillas' expansion. The result was the strengthening of armed actors and the intensification of the conflict. Although the United States was clearly not directly responsible for creating this situation, the excessive pressure placed on the Samper government to achieve United States goals did make it worse.

At the same time, Samper, because of the taint of drug money, was ostracized by the United States; increasingly, Colombia became identified as a pariah state within the international community.[9] The political costs of the country's reduced status globally were significant; during his term in office Samper received only two official state visits to Colombia, by neighboring countries Venezuela and Ecuador. On an official tour through Africa and the Middle East in May 1997, the Colombian president was greeted in South Africa by news that President Nelson Mandela had been unable to meet him. Equally considerable were the economic costs. Colombia was precluded from receiving loans from international financial institutions during the time in which the country was decertified by the United States, while United States foreign investment was dramatically reduced.

The "Renarcotization" of Relations

Confronted with growing evidence that it had aggravated Colombia's domestic crisis, Washington became increasingly sensitive to the issue of state weakness and attempted to develop a more comprehensive strategy toward the country when Andrés Pastrana was elected president in 1998. This shift in policy partly explains the initial willingness of the United States to adopt a "wait-and-see" strategy regarding the peace process Pastrana initiated with the FARC in early November 1998. Moreover, because of the marked deterioration in the political sphere, it became difficult to ignore the calls of an increasingly strong civil movement for a negotiated solution to the country's armed conflict. Thus, during the first year of his government, Pastrana was able to effectively navigate between domestic pressures for peace and United States exigencies on the drug front. But less than a year later, the assassination in early March 1999 of three United States citizens at the hands of the FARC, along with growing difficulties in the peace process itself, led to a change in both the United States and the Colombian postures and facilitated the ascendance of the drug-war logic once again.

This "renarcotization" of the bilateral agenda saw the emergence of Plan Colombia in late 1999. At home the Colombian government was able to circumvent domestic pressures by manipulating information about its intentions. This was achieved mainly through the publication of distinct versions for public consumption (in both Colombia and Europe) of arguments in which peace (and not the drug war) were adeptly presented as the centerpiece of Plan Colombia's strategy. Public statements by the government downplaying the strong emphasis the United States version of the plan placed on the drug problem reinforced this idea. When the United States Congress approved the Colombian aid package in mid-2000, sustaining this argument became increasingly difficult, primarily due to the large military component (80 percent of the total) that was designated for the drug war. Instead, the Pastrana government attempted to highlight the approximately $200 million earmarked for initiatives related to alternative development, assistance to displaced persons, human rights, and democracy, while discouraging public debate concerning the significant weight attached to the military and counternarcotics aspects of the package.

Just as war-weary Colombians welcomed Andrés Pastrana's proposal for peace in 1998, a country tired of the failed peace process overwhelmingly elected Álvaro Uribe on a national security and war platform in 2002. Uribe's plans for reestablishing state control over the national territory and for crushing militarily those armed actors unwilling to negotiate on the government's terms—goals widely supported by the Colombian population—rely heavily on United States military assistance. The use of that aid for counterinsurgency and counterterrorism is conditioned on a series of measures with which the Colombian government must comply. In addition to adopting explicit commitments in the "war on drugs," including fumigation efforts that surpass those of previous administrations, the Uribe government must implement budgetary and personnel reforms within the military and apportion additional national funding for its own war on drugs and terrorism. Some of these monies will be accrued through the creation of new taxes and reductions in the size of the state, but social spending is likely to be reduced as well. In early August 2002, Washington also requested a written statement from Bogotá conferring immunity for United States military advisers in Colombia as a precondition for the continuation of military aid.

Although at first glance Colombia and the United States share a common objective—winning the war against armed groups in the country—Colombia's insertion into the global antiterrorist dynamic leaves scant room for autonomous decision-making by the new president. In the future, the hands-on, take-charge attitude that has won Uribe a high public approval rating could be blocked by decisions made in Washington. For example, the September 2002 request for the extradition to the United States of a number of paramilitary leaders and several members of the FARC on charges of drug trafficking may work at cross-purposes with future peace talks. Although it is highly unlikely that negotiations with the FARC will resume anytime soon, on December 1, 2002 a cease-fire was declared by the paramilitaries, who have said they would like to negotiate with the government. The United States has been reluctant to state whether the extradition requests, or its classification of Colombia's armed groups as terrorists, would be revoked in the event of new peace negotiations.

The Wrong Profile

United States policy in Colombia has worked at cross-purposes in terms of reducing the availability of illegal substances, confronting human rights violations, and strengthening the state. In all these areas, United States actions may actually have made an already grave situation worse. The worldview that has molded Washington's twin wars on drugs and terrorism constitutes an extremely narrow framework through which to address the complex problems Colombia faces. National security, defined exclusively in military terms, has taken precedence over equally significant political, economic, and social considerations. Until this perspective undergoes significant change, United States policy will continue to be ill equipped to assist Colombia in addressing the root causes of its current crisis.

Notes

1. For a discussion of the role of drugs in United States–Colombian relations from 1986 to the present, see Arlene B. Tickner, "Tensiones y contradicciones en los objetivos de la política exterior de Estados Unidos en Colombia," *Colombia Internacional,* nos. 49–50, May–December 2000; and "U.S. Foreign Policy in Colombia: Bizarre Side-Effects of the 'War on Drugs,'" in Gustavo Gallón and Christopher Welna, eds., *Democracy, Human Rights, and Peace in Colombia* (Notre Dame: University of Notre Dame Press, Kellogg Series, forthcoming).

2. The first disbursement of United States aid for Plan Colombia, a multipronged strategy presented by the Pastrana administration to address problems of peace, state building, poverty, drugs, and the rule of law in the country, was made in fiscal year 2000–2001.

3. The United States and the Colombian governments argue that Roundup Ultra, which is a type of glyphosate and is used for aerial fumigation in Colombia, does not have secondary effects in human beings or surrounding plant life. But the manner in which Roundup is used in Colombia is troubling because it is applied in concentrations that exceed the technical specifications established by the manufacturer and sprayed from planes at a great distance as a defensive measure against ground fire; moreover, an additive mixed with the glyphosate to make it better stick to coca leaves also causes it to adhere to human skin and other plants.

4. In the mid-1990s, before United States military assistance to Colombia began to increase, government officials often admitted that, for Colombia, counternarcotics and counterinsurgency were essentially the same. In a 1996 interview conducted by Human Rights Watch with Barry McCaffrey, then head of the United States Southern Command, McCaffrey conceded that these facets constituted "two sides of the same coin."

5. All three of Colombia's largest armed groups, FARC, the leftist National Liberation Army (ELN), and the AUC, are classified by the United States State Department as terrorist organizations.

6. Angel Rabasa and Peter Chalk, *Colombian Labyrinth: The Synergy of Drugs and Insurgency and Its Implications for Regional Stability* (Santa Monica, Calif.: RAND, 2001).

7. An additional $330 million in police and military aid was provided through the counternarcotics budgets of the State and Defense Departments.

8. The decertifications occurred because every March the president of the United States is required to present a report

Article 11. Colombia and the United States: From Counternarcotics to Counterterrorism

to Congress certifying whether a country involved in the drug trade is in compliance with United States counternarcotics efforts. Colombia was found to be in noncompliance and thus "decertified."

9. On June 20, 1994, one day after Samper won the second round of the presidential elections, Andrés Pastrana, the conservative party candidate, released an audiotape in which Cali cartel leaders Gilberto and Miguel Rodríguez Orejuela were overheard offering several million dollars to the Samper campaign. A series of accusations and denials concerning this allegation, labeled "Proceso 8,000," ensued.

ARLENE B. TICKNER is the director of the Center for International Studies and professor of international relations at the Universidad de los Andes, Bogotá, Colombia. She is also a professor of international relations at the Universidad Nacional de Colombia.

Reprinted from *Current History,* February 2003, pp. 77–85. Copyright © 2003 by Current History, Inc. Reprinted with permission.

Wounded But Still Dangerous

Indonesia has struck a blow against the Jemaah Islamiah terror group—but it remains a threat and its plans are a mystery.

When Jemaah Islamiah (JI), a South-East Asian Islamist group, bombed nightclubs on the Indonesian island of Bali in 2002, killing 202 people, it exposed the poor state of the country's anti-terrorist intelligence and policing. And the attack did not seem to lead to much improvement. The bombers struck again in 2003, at an American-run hotel in Jakarta, and in 2004 at the Australian embassy there. In 2005 they returned to Bali to attack three tourist restaurants. Of late, however, Indonesia's security forces seem to have gained the upper hand over JI.

No large-scale attacks have taken place since 2005. With the help of their Australian and American counterparts, Indonesia's national police have greatly improved their tracking of militants and have rounded up some of JI's top leaders. This culminated on June 13th with confirmation that they had arrested Abu Dujana, a JI leader whom police had recently begun to describe as their "most wanted".

Mr Dujana is said to have fought in Afghanistan and hobnobbed with Osama bin Laden. He is believed to have taken charge of one of JI's military wings, and control of its weapons and explosives, after the death of the group's chief bomb-maker, Azahari Husin, in a shoot-out with police in 2005. It has even been suggested that Mr Dujana is JI's emir, or paramount leader. Another leading figure, Noordin Muhammad Top, is still on the run. But the capture of Mr Dujana and several other terrorists in recent days follows the discovery of a huge arsenal of guns and bomb-making materials in March. It marks a "very significant" blow against JI, says Sidney Jones, in Jakarta for the International Crisis Group (ICG), a think-tank.

Indonesia's arrests came shortly after Singapore revealed that it was detaining four JI members, arrested between last November and April, and freeing five detained earlier who had "responded positively to rehabilitation." However, the Philippines' army admitted last weekend that another JI leader, known as Dulmatin, suspected of involvement in the 2002 Bali bombs, had again escaped its clutches. The army believes he is hiding in the Tawi-Tawi Islands, off Borneo. He and other fugitives in the southern Philippines are suspected of teaching local Islamist militants how to make bombs.

Indonesia's recent policing successes are a tribute to two new units set up after the 2002 bombings. One, which has stayed out of the spotlight, is an intelligence-gathering task-force. The other, Detachment 88, is a high-profile anti-terrorist squad, trained by American and Australian federal police in making arrests and gathering forensic evidence. Since their formation Indonesia's terror-fighting capabilities have "come on in leaps and bounds," says Nigel Inkster, an analyst at the International Institute for Strategic Studies in London and until recently the deputy head of the British external-intelligence service, MI6. Indonesia's army and its domestic-intelligence agency, BIN, are not much good at anti-terrorism work, says Mr Inkster, so until the new police units were formed, foreign agencies had no competent Indonesian counterparts.

Despite Detachment 88's successes, Ms Jones says the unit is too small. When it raids terrorist bases it must rely on help from Brimob, a poorly trained paramilitary-police unit. In January, for example, the two forces combined to storm a JI hideout on Sulawesi, an Indonesian island plagued by conflict between Muslims and Christians. Fifteen suspected militants and one policeman died. An ICG investigation found that the heavy casualties made local Muslims see the extremists as victims. Such incidents are counter-productive, encouraging civilians to shelter JI militants.

Another worry is lenient sentencing by Indonesia's courts. JI's spiritual leader, Abu Bakar Basyir, was let out of jail after serving 26 months of a 30-month sentence for his alleged involvement in the 2002 bombings. The courts later overturned his conviction altogether. The country's prisons, riddled with corruption and incompetence, may serve as recruiting and training centres for JI. Bringing terrorism convicts together in a specially built new jail, as is planned, may simply make the job of JI's "tutors" easier.

For all the success in tracking down JI's military leaders, the group's current plans and the extent of its network remain something of a mystery. Unlike many terrorist groups worldwide, JI lacks an overground political wing to elaborate its demands. A study by the ICG last month reckoned the group may still have around 900 members. But the scale of its recruitment in universities and Islamic boarding schools is unclear. There are signs that, as its bomb-planting and fund-raising activities are more successfully curbed, the group is simply turning to cheaper and easier forms of terrorism, such as assassinations.

Along with the arrests and the seizure of weapons in March, Indonesian police found a handwritten diagram showing that

JI operatives on Java, Indonesia's most populous island, had been reorganised into a sariyah (possibly meaning "platoon"), implying that this was part of a new military structure covering South-East Asia. But there have recently been few signs of activity outside the group's Indonesian heartland. Last week a general in Thailand's military-backed government implied that Cambodian Muslims linked to JI were somehow involved in the insurgency in Thailand's mainly Muslim southern provinces. But he backtracked after the Cambodian government furiously denounced his comments.

There has been little recent evidence that JI or, for that matter, al-Qaeda, has a hand in the Thai south's rising violence. But it is just the sort of strife-torn place, full of alienated, angry Muslims, where those seeking to organise jihad find fertile ground. Police have pruned JI's top ranks. But its roots may still be spreading.

Peace at Last?

Home to glittering beaches, robust wines, piquant foods and Bilbao's sparkling new Guggenheim Museum, the Basque Country of northern Spain has been riven by separatist violence for decades. Though political tensions linger, terrorists agreed to a cease-fire this past March. Will it mean peace at last?

JOSHUA HAMMER

The first blast reverberated through the old quarter of San Sebastián at one o'clock in the afternoon. It rattled the windows of the ornate buildings around the 18th-century Santa Maria del Coro church and sent a flock of pigeons into the sky. We were standing in a cobblestone plaza outside one of the town's most famous *pintxos*—tapas—bars, La Cuchara de San Telmo, eating braised rabbit and sipping red Rioja wine when we heard it. A minute later came a second explosion, and then a third. "Let's go see what's happening," said my companion, Gabriella Ranelli de Aguirre, an American tour operator married to a San Sebastián native, who has been living there for nearly 20 years.

I didn't know what to think. This was Basque Country, after all, the homeland of Euskadi Ta Askatasuna, or ETA (Basque for "Basque Homeland and Freedom"), which has been waging a violent campaign for independence from Spain for nearly four decades. True, the group, which has killed some 800 people and maimed hundreds more, had not carried out a bombing or shooting for three years, and momentum appeared to be building toward a lasting peace.

This past March, in a communiqué that stunned Spain and the world, the group had even declared a "permanent cease-fire" and said it was committed to promoting "a democratic process." Batasuna, ETA's political arm—which had been banned by the Spanish supreme court in 2003—has engaged in quiet talks with the Basque Nationalist Party and other Basque political parties about establishing a road map to a permanent peace. And, in another sign of changing times, Gerry Adams, the head of Sinn Fein, the IRA's political wing, and Gerry Kelly, a convicted bomber turned Sinn Fein deputy, traveled to the Basque Country last spring to give Batasuna advice on peace negotiations. The Sinn Fein leaders, who once gave ETA counsel on bomb-making technology, have also been lobbying the Spanish government to drop charges against top Basque separatists, legalize Batasuna and move 700 ETA prisoners held in Spanish and French jails closer to their families. "We are approaching the beginning of the end of ETA," Prime Minister José Luis Rodríguez Zapatero declared in February 2006.

But as Ranelli and I raced toward the harbor, I had to wonder if the group had returned to its old tactics. Then I saw the cause of the commotion: a white-haired man wearing a blue Napoleonic military uniform with epaulets and brandishing a musket was firing into the air. He belonged, he explained, to Olla Gora, one of San Sebastián's dozens of "eating societies," male-only clubs dedicated to the pursuit of socializing and gastronomic indulgence. "It's our [society's] centennial," he said, and its members were reenacting the Napoleonic battles that raged here in the 19th century As Ranelli and I made our way back down through the quaint alleys of the old quarter—rebuilt after 1813, when British and Portuguese troops burned down almost all of it—she said my reaction was all too common. "San Sebastián is a wonderful town," she went on, "but the violence has eclipsed everything else. A lot of my friends have had the impression that this is a scary place—another Beirut."

Comparisons to Lebanon may be exaggerated. But this rugged region in the shadow of the Pyrenees has long been an anomaly—an enclave marked by an ancient language, a tradition of fine food and wine, and a political culture soaked in blood. Feeding on Basque pride and decades of repression by Spanish dictator Francisco Franco, ETA's campaign of terror turned elegant cities such as San Sebastián and Bilbao into caldrons of fear and violence. At the height of its violent campaign for independence, in 1980, the separatists murdered 91 people, and countless business enterprises have fallen victim to ETA extortion over the past four decades. "Everybody in Basque Country has a cousin or an uncle who has either been a victim or a member of the group," one Basque journalist told me.

Now ETA is widely regarded as an anachronism, a holdover from the days when radical groups such as Italy's Red Brigades and West Germany's Baader-Meinhof gang were recruiting European youth with their Marxist-Leninist rhetoric and desperado chic. In 1997, the United States government designated ETA a foreign terrorist organization. Since then, a number of developments—the Basque Country's growing prosperity; a post 9/11 crackdown on terrorist groups; widespread revulsion at violent tactics in the aftermath oral Qaeda's 2004 Madrid train bombing (for which ETA was initially blamed); arrests of ETA fugitives in both Spain and France; and a waning enthusiasm for ETA's aim of independence—have drained the movement of much of its vigor.

The peace process, however, is still fragile. In recent years, ETA has declared other cease-fires, all of which collapsed. The main Spanish opposition party, led by former prime minister José María Aznar, has urged the government not to negotiate. The peace initiative is being challenged by victims of ETA terror, and any deal is likely to leave unresolved the still contentious issue of Basque independence. Zapatero, in June 2006, warned that the process would be "long, tough and difficult," saying that the government would proceed with "prudence and discretion."

Then, a series of setbacks jolted the Spanish government and raised fears of a return to violence. First, in August, ETA publicly criticized the Spanish and French governments for "continuous attacks" against the Basques, apparently referring to the arrests and trials of ETA members that have gone on in spite of the cease-fire. Three hooded ETA members read a communiqué at a pro-independence rally in late September, confirming the group's "commitment to continue fighting, arms in hand, until independence and socialism is achieved in Euskal Herria [Basque Country]." A week later, a hiker in the woods in French Basque Country, near the Spanish border, stumbled across hidden weapons—including guns and chemicals for bomb-making—sealed in plastic bins, evidently intended for ETA. Later in October, some 350 guns disappeared from a gun store in Nîmes, France; it was suspected that ETA had engineered the theft. It was perhaps the starkest indication yet that the group could be preparing for the collapse of negotiations, and the resumption of attacks.

But despite all the obstacles, the mood is upbeat. Traveling around Basque Country, from the avenues of San Sebastian to mountain villages deep in the Basque heartland, I encountered a sense of optimism—a belief that the Basques have a real chance of a lasting peace for the first time in decades. "I still remember the day I heard the news [about the cease-fire]. It gave me goose pimples," says Alejandra Iturrioz, mayor of Ordizia; a mountain town where a dozen citizens have been killed by the group since 1968.

In Bilbao, Basque Country's biggest city and an emerging cultural capital (home to architect Frank Gehry's Guggenheim Museum), the change is already being felt. "More people came this summer than ever before," says Ana López de Munain, the communications director for the striking titanium-and-glass creation. "The mood has become more relaxed. We just hope it stays that way."

Nowhere are the benefits of waning tension more evident than in San Sebastián, a cosmopolitan seaside resort that comfortably straddles the Basque and Spanish worlds. Twelve miles west of the French border, along a rugged, horseshoe-shaped bay facing the Bay of Biscay, San Sebastian was a Basque fishing and trading town until the mid-19th century; in 1845 Spanish queen Isabel II, stricken with a skin ailment, came to bathe in the Bay of Concha on her doctor's orders. Aristocrats from Madrid and Barcelona followed, throwing up beachfront cabanas and Belle Epoque villas, wedding-cake structures adorned with turrets and spires. Along the Rio Urumea, a tidal river that empties into the Bay of Concha and divides the city in two, I strolled the Paseo de Francia—a faux stretch of the Ile St. Louis, with a Seine-like promenade.

San Sebastian itself has been the scene of political violence: in 1995, an ETA gunman walked into a downtown bar and shot dead one of the city's most popular politicians, Gregorio Ordoñez. Six years later, thousands marched silently through the streets to protest the murder of newspaper executive Santiago Oleaga Elejabarrieta. But there hasn't been a shooting or bombing here in years. Real estate is booming, with two-bedroom condominiums facing the sea fetching up to a million euros.

I went to lunch in the affluent Gros neighborhood with Gabriella Ranelli and her husband, Aitor Aguirre, a 39-year-old former professional player of pelota, similar to the sport better known in the United States as jai alai, the indoor game played with a hard rubber ball and gloves with basket-like extensions. (Pelota is the most popular sport in Basque Country) We stopped by Aloña Berri, a pintxos bar known for its exquisite food miniatures, and ordered plates of Chipiron en Equilibria, a tiny square of rice infused with squid broth, served with sugar crystals spun around a wooden stick that spears a baby squid. Sophisticated establishments like this one have transformed San Sebastian into one of the culinary centers of Western Europe. Aguirre told me that these days the city is dedicated far more to the pursuit of good times than political agitation. "The roots of the Basque problems are in the provinces, where Basque culture is strongest, the language is spoken all the time and people feel that their identity is more threatened," he added. "Here, on the coast, with the cosmopolitan influence, we don't feel it as much."

Still, San Sebastian remains distinctly Basque. About 40 percent of its population speaks Basque; identification with Spain is not strong. Here, separatist politics still stir emotions. Spanish director Julio Medem's documentary *La Pelota Vasca* (*The Basque Ball*), featuring interviews with 70 Basques about the conflict, created a furor at the 2003 San Sebastian film festival. And memories of Franco's brutalities are etched into the city's psyche. The palace, where Franco vacationed for 35 years, has been shuttered since his death in November 1975; the city still debates whether to turn it into a museum, a hotel or a memorial to his victims.

One rainy afternoon, after taking in an exhibition of Russian paintings at Bilbao's Guggenheim Museum, I made the 30-minute drive to Gernika, set in a narrow riverine valley in Vizcaya Province. Gernika is the spiritual capital of the Basques, whose ancient culture and language, some believe, date back several thousand years. From medieval times, Castilian monarchs met here, beneath a sacred oak, to guarantee the Basques their traditional rights, or fueros, including special tax status and exemption from serving in the Castilian army. But in 1876, at the end of the second Carlist War in Spain, these guarantees were finally abrogated, and the Basques' dreams of autonomy or independence from Spain were indefinitely deferred.

I parked my car at the edge of town and walked to the main square, the site of the Gernika Peace Museum, which commemorates the event that has come to define the town. When the Spanish Civil War broke out in 1936, the Basques allied themselves with the Republican government, or Loyalists, against the fascists, led by Franco. On April 26, 1937, the Italian and German Air Forces, on Franco's orders, carpet-bombed and strafed Gernika, killing at least 250 people, an event immortalized by Picasso's painting named for the town. (The artist used an alternate spelling.) "Gernika is seared into the heart of every Basque," I was told by Ana Teresa Núñez Monasterio, an archivist at the city's new Peace Museum, which features multimedia displays chronicling the bombing.

Franco's fascist forces defeated the Loyalists in 1939; from then on, the dictator waged a relentless campaign to erase Basque identity. He drove the leadership into exile, banned the Basque flag and traditional dancing, and made even speaking Basque punishable by a prison term. Some families reverted to speaking Spanish, even in the privacy of their homes; others taught the language to their children in secret, or sent them to clandestine schools, or *ikastola*. Children caught speaking Basque in regular schools were punished; teachers would pass a steel ring from one student caught speaking Basque to the next; the last one to hold the ring each day would be whipped. Margarita Otaegui Arizmendi, the director of the language center at the Deusto University in San Sebastian, recalls, "Franco was very successful in instilling fear. A lot of the children grew up without a knowledge of Basque—we call them "the generation of silence."

After Franco's death, King Juan Carlos took power and legalized the Basque language; in 1979, he granted autonomy to the three Spanish Basque provinces, Alava, Guipúzcoa and Vizcaya. (Basque separatists also regard the Spanish province of Navarra as part of their homeland.) In 1980, a Basque parliament elected a president and established a capital at Vitoria-Gasteiz, beginning a new era. But ETA, founded by a small group of revolutionaries in 1959, has never given up its goal-full independence for the Spanish Basque provinces and unification with the three Basque-speaking provinces on the French side (where the nationalist movement is less fervent). For many Spanish Basques, the goal of independence has come to seem meaningless. "There's a whole generation of people under the age of 30 who have no memories of Franco," a Basque journalist told me. "We have prosperity, we have autonomy; we're pretty well off on all counts."

The journey from San Sebastián to Ordizia takes only 30 minutes by road through rugged hills cloaked in forests of oak, apple and pine, but it bridges a gap as wide as that between, say, Washington, D.C. and Appalachia. It had been raining nonstop for three days when I set out; the mist shrouding the slopes and red-tile-roofed villages conveyed a sense of a world cut off from Europe. Located in the highlands of Guipúzcoa, regarded as the most "Basque" of the three provinces, Ordizia is a town of 9,500 that was founded in the 13th century. When I arrived, crowds were flocking to the market in the town square, beneath an Athenian arcade-style roof supported by a dozen Corinthian columns. Elderly men wearing traditional wide, black berets, known as *txapelas*, browsed through piles of fresh produce, wheels of Idiazabal sheep cheese, olives and chorizo sausages. Outside rose green hills covered by concrete high-rises; Franco had ordered them built in the 1960s and packed them with workers from the rest of Spain—a strategy, many in Ordizia say, intended to weaken Basque identity.

With almost no unemployment and fertile highlands, Ordizia is one of the wealthiest corners of Spain. Yet almost everybody here has been touched by violence: there is the Basque policeman, posted out of town, who keeps his job secret from his neighbors for fear of being killed, the stationery store owner whose daughter, a convicted ETA bomb-maker, languishes in a Spanish prison hundreds of miles away in a seedy bar clubhouse in one of the high-rises on the outskirts of town, I met Iñaki Dubreuil Churruca, a Socialist town councilman: in 2001, he narrowly escaped a car bomb explosion that killed two bystanders. I asked him how many people from Ordizia had been murdered by ETA, and he and a friend began counting, rattling off a dozen or so names: "Isidro, Ima, Javier, Yoye.... We knew them all," he said.

Later I walked through the town center to a flagstone plaza, where a single rose painted on a tile marked Ordizia's most notorious killing: that of María Dolores González Catarain, known as Yoyes. An attractive, charismatic woman who joined ETA as a teenager, Yoyes tired of life in the group and, with her young son, fled into exile in Mexico. After several years she grew homesick and, reaching out to ETA's leaders, received assurances she would not be harmed if she came back. In 1986 she moved to San Sebastián and wrote a critical memoir about her life as a terrorist. That September, she returned to Ordizia for the first time since her exile to attend a fiesta and, in a crowded plaza, was shot dead in front of her son. David Bumstead, an English teacher who ran a language school in the town, later observed the scene. "I remember seeing her body, covered in a sheet, lying on the cobblestones," he says, recalling that "sadness enveloped the town."

Though Yoyes' murder caused widespread revulsion in Ordizia, enthusiasm for Basque independence has never flagged here. In 1991, Batasuna received 30 percent of the votes in municipal elections and came close to naming the town's mayor. (A coalition of other political parties formed a majority and blocked the appointment.) In a dank, smoke-filled bar beside the town's marketplace I met the man who nearly won the post, Ramon Amundarain, a grizzled former Batasuna politician. He told me that 35 percent of the highland population favored independence. "I didn't even speak Spanish until I was 10," he said. "I don't feel Spanish at all." He pulled an Euskal Herria ID card out of his wallet. "I carry it in protest," he told me. "I could be arrested for it." When I asked whether he believed violence was an acceptable way of achieving his goal, he answered, cautiously, "We did not reject it."

The next day I drove farther south into the province of Alava, part of the Rioja wine-producing region. Alava is considered the least Basque, and most Spanish, of the Basque Country's three provinces. Here, the weather cleared, and I found myself in an arid, sun-splashed valley framed by gray basalt mountains. Jagged mesas loomed over groves of cypress trees and a rolling sea of vineyards, and medieval walled villages climbed hillsides; the landscape, the climate, all seemed classically Spanish.

The 12th-century village of Laguardia was having one of its summer fiestas, this one celebrating San Juan, the town's patron saint. Then I heard a distant clattering of hoofs, and I leapt into a doorway just as half a dozen bulls roared down the main street. I had stumbled into one of the hundreds of "running of the bulls" festivals that take place every summer across Spain—this one, unlike Pamplona's a few dozen miles to the northeast, relatively unspoiled by tourists.

Later that morning, I made my way to Bodega El Fabulista, a wine cellar owned by Eusebio Santamaría, a third-generation winemaker. Santamaría has chosen to keep his operation small—he produces 40,000 bottles a year, entirely for local distribution—and he makes most of his money from the private tours of his cellar he conducts for tourists. Since the ETA cease-fire, he told me, the number of visitors had grown significantly "The atmosphere across the Basque Country has changed," he said. I asked him whether people felt their Basqueness strongly here, and he laughed. "It's a mixture of identities here, Rioja, Alava and Navarra," he said. "I say I belong to all of them. Wine does not understand or care about politics."

But people do, and everywhere I traveled in Basque Country, debates Over Basque identity and independence still raged. In Vitoria-Gasteiz, a modern city on the arid plains of Alava Province and the Basque capital, María San Gil vented her contempt for the cease-fire declaration. San Gil, 41, a gaunt, intense woman, saw the separatists' brutality firsthand in 1995, when an ETA gunman walked into a bar in San Sebastian and shot to death her colleague Gregorio Ordoñez, a popular, conservative Basque politician. Soon after that, she entered politics as a candidate for San Sebastián's city council, and is now president of the Populist Party in the Basque Country San Gil has likened Batasuna's leader, Arnaldo Otegi, to Osama bin Laden and, despite ETA's truce, remains adamantly opposed to any negotiations. "These people are fanatics, and one cannot legitimize them at the political table," San Gil told me. She dismissed comparisons between ETA and the IRA, whose cease-fire call in 1997 was embraced by the British government. "Ours is not a war between two legitimate adversaries. It's a war between terrorists and democrats, so why do we have to sit down with them? It's like sitting down with Al Qaeda. We have to vanquish them."

Others, however, see such intransigence as self-defeating. Gorka Landaburu, the son of a leading Basque politician who fled into exile in France in 1939, also knows the extremists' brutality firsthand. Landaburu, 55, grew up in Paris and moved to San Sebastián in his 20s. There he began writing for French and Spanish newspapers and became a leading voice of ETA opposition. "My parents were Basque nationalists, but I've never been," he told me as we sat in a café in front of San Sebastián's Hotel Londres, a whitewashed, early-20th-century landmark with filigreed iron balconies and French windows, overlooking the seafront promenade. "We have our own taxation, our own laws, our own government. What do we need independence for? Money? We have the euro. Frontiers? The borders are open. Army? It's unnecessary."

Landaburu's critiques made him an enemy of the separatists. "I got my first warning in 1986—an anonymous letter, with the ETA seal"—a serpent coiled around an ax—"warning me to 'keep quiet,'" he said. "I ignored it." In the spring of 2001, a parcel bearing his newspaper's return address arrived at his home. While heading out the door to work the next morning, he opened the letter; five ounces of dynamite blew up, mangling his hands, destroying the vision in his left eye and lacerating his face. "I remember every second—the explosion, the burst of fire," he told me. He staggered out the door covered in blood; a neighbor took him to a hospital. "Every time I pick up a drink, button my shirt, I think about the attack, but I can't let it dominate me or I'd go insane," Landaburu said.

In the months after I spoke to Landaburu, increasingly belligerent pronouncements by ETA, increased incidents of street violence and the theft of the handguns in Nîmes seemed to strengthen the arguments of hard-liners such as Maria San Gil. But it was difficult to know whether ETA's vows to carry on the struggle were rhetorical or whether they foreshadowed another campaign of terror. Nor was it out of the question that a radical splinter group sought to sabotage the peace process—the Basque equivalent of the Real IRA, which killed 29 people in a car bombing in Omagh, Ireland, in August 1998 in reaction to the IRA's cease-fire the previous year.

Landaburu told me that he expected setbacks: the bitterness and hatred caused by decades of violence were too deeply engrained in Basque society to be overcome easily Even so, he was willing to give peace a chance. "I'm not going to forgive, I'm not going to forget, but I'm not going to oppose the process," he told me. He took a sip of *orujo blanco,* a strong liquor distilled from white grapes, and gazed upon the Bay of Concha—the crescent of beach, the azure waters framed by forested cliffs, the hundreds of people strolling the promenade at sunset. "After 40 years of Franco's dictatorship, and 40 years of a dictatorship of terror, we want to live in a world without threats, without violence," Landaburu said. "I want peace for my kids, for my grandkids. And for the first time, I think we are going to get it."

Writer **JOSHUA HAMMER** lives in Berlin.

From *Smithsonian,* January 2007, pp. 43–50. Copyright © 2007 by Joshua Hammer. Reprinted by permission of the author.

Root Causes of Chechen Terror

ALON BEN-MEIR

Although terrorism is without exception reprehensible, as long as the United States and other powers, including Russia, continue to ignore its root causes, the prospects for diminishing and eventually eliminating it will remain practically nonexistent.

Intelligence estimates originating in the United States, Israel, and Europe, as well as experiences on the ground have shown that in the past three years the ranks of terrorist organizations have dramatically swelled. That is, for every terrorist killed or captured, two or more are joining one terrorist group or another.

The stubborn refusal by the U.S. government, and now Russia's, to acknowledge that the use of force to combat terrorism, albeit necessary at times, will neither reduce or eradicate the scourge of terrorism only adds to the problem. For anything real to be accomplished, far greater attention must be focused on the social, economic, political, and ethnic/religious conflicts and grievances that create the environment for and the motivation to commit acts of terror.

The terrorism in Russia, the direct result of the Chechens' struggle, offers a stark example of how a terribly misguided policy leads to increasingly tragic consequences when the root causes of the struggle are ignored. Chechens, recognized as a distinct people since the seventeenth century, bitterly opposed Russia's conquest of the Caucasus, which began in 1818 and was completed in 1917. They were and are of an entirely different ethnicity than the rest of Russia, with a separate culture, religion, and historic background.

After Soviet rule was reestablished in 1921, the autonomous region of Chechen was created in 1922. In 1934 it became part of the Chechen-Ingush region and was made into a republic in 1936. The Chechen collaboration with the Germans in World War II prompted the Soviets to deport many Chechens to Central Asia. After the war, most of the deportees were gradually repatriated, and in 1956, the republic of Chechnya was reestablished.

During the Soviet regime, the Chechens suffered greatly from discrimination, cruelty, and institutionalized abuse. With the collapse of the Soviet Union in 1991, the Chechen Parliament seized the opportunity and declared the republic's independence. The tensions between Russia and Chechen President Dzhokhar Dudayev escalated into warfare in 1994. Grozny, the capital was totally devastated by the Russian army and tens of thousands of Chechens killed. This national tragedy affected every man, woman, and child in Chechnya. For much of the past 10 years, Russian military and security forces have continued to persecute the Chechens. According to several major human rights watch groups, abuses in Chechnya are as rampant as they were under Stalin, with disappearances, rape, imprisonments, abductions, and other severe violations commonplace.

The terrorist attacks that recently indiscriminately killed innocent children at a Beslan school, and elsewhere in Russia, airplane passengers, subway commuters, and theater audiences are abhorrent acts that must be condemned in the strongest terms. But Chechen terrorism, however abhorrent, must be seen through the prism of what has befallen the Chechen people. To view them as pure wanton acts of terrorism rather than in their historical context defies logic and will only contribute to even greater tragedies in the future.

It is true that Chechen militants are influenced by Wahhabism, a strict form of Sunni Islam practiced in Saudi Arabia, and are aided by Islamist terrorist groups, especially al-Qaida. This, however, should neither make the war against Chechnya a war against terrorism, nor blind the Russian government to its own role in what has happened and to accepting its responsibility to deal with the Chechens' legitimate grievances.

Chechen terrorism will not end because of more repression and preemptive strikes against the Chechen people. It will end when the Russian government admits it made terrible mistakes in the past, rectifies these injustices by recognizing the rights of the Chechen people, and reaches a political settlement through negotiation. A settlement leading to Chechen self-rule while at the same time safeguarding Russia's national security and economic interests (oil and gas) is not impossible. In fact, the two go hand-in-hand. They can be realized only if the Russian government and the Chechen rebels recognize each other's legitimate requirements and national interests.

Russian President Vladimir Putin's fears that allowing the Chechens self-rule will have a domino effect throughout the Caucasus, are legitimate only to the extent that Chechnya becomes completely independent and ceases to be a part of the Russian federation. As reported by the New York Times, the Chechen rebels presented extreme demands during their seizure of the school in Beslan, including the withdrawal of Russian troops from Chechnya, the inclusion of Chechnya as a separate state within the commonwealth of the former Soviet states, and the restoration of order in the region. But the Times also reported that these demands, according to Ruslan Aushev (president of Ingushetia from 1993 to 200), who was sent by the Kremlin to Beslan to negotiate with the rebels, could have formed the basis for a negotiated settlement. And only negotiations that address the Chechen grievances, he added, can prevent future war.

Putin does not have only two choices: that of giving Chechnya complete independence or of permanently subjugating its people. (In fact, there is nothing in the history of this conflict, which spans more than two centuries, to indicate that the Chechens will ever submit to Russian domination.) Rather, given the historical reality and present situation, the only realistic solution is for Chechnya to remain part of the Russian Federation yet be permitted to run its own internal affairs as it sees fit.

For Putin to equate negotiating with the Chechen rebels to negotiating with al-Qaida, as he did recently, is both disingenuous and dangerously misleading. He may wish to find a common cause with President Bush by looking at the terrorism phenomenon in black-and-white terms. That perspective, however, will not solve the problem of the terrorism he faces any more than it has solved it for the United States. Putin will sooner than later have to answer to the Russian people about how many more of them will die before he recognizes that his strategy has failed. He should learn from the Bush administration's failure in confusing Saddam Hussein with al-Qaida and from the Israeli-Palestinian conflicts, which have claimed the lives of many thousands with no end in sight, that root causes cannot be ignored. By amassing more power under the pretext of fighting terrorism and trampling on democracy in Russia, Putin will not solve the Chechen problem or lessen the Russian people's pain over their terrible losses now or in the future.

Only a negotiated settlement with the Chechens will stop the vicious cycle and prevent this war from spreading into other republics in the region, a situation that could set the south of Russia and perhaps the entire Caucasus on fire.

ALON BEN-MEIR is the Middle East project director at the World Policy Institute and a professor of international relations at the Center for Global Studies at New York University.

As seen in *World & I Journal,* December 2004. Copyright © 2004 by United Press International. Reprinted by permission of FosteReprints.

End of Terrorism?
ETA and the Efforts for Peace

MEREDITH MOORE

A nationalist hard-line party of the Basque region, which consists of northern Spain and parts of southwestern France, has asserted Basque independence for the past 40 years. This party, known as Batasuna or *Soziidistii Abvnzjileak,* has been fighting for the autonomy of three of northern Spain's Basque provinces, but it has been declining in power since being formally banned by the conservative People's Party government in 2003. The organization that is commonly assumed to be its military wing, *Eitskadi Ta Askatasuna* (ETA), has been responsible for the deaths of over 800 people since 1968. After decades of struggle, top Batasuna officials appear to want to achieve their goals through more political means, yet the new Socialist government of Spain under Prime Minister Jose Luis Rodriguez Zapatero remains skeptical. The question is whether Batasuna's proposed political methods will bring peace to this troubled region and whether the Spanish government, which has long been debating the issue of Basque self-determination, will ever believe Batasuna's claims.

Due to the increased cooperation of the Spanish and French police forces, several key Batasuna and ETA figures have been arrested. The two states have made a concerted effort to combine their forces and intelligence in an effort to disrupt potential violent attacks. As a result, an open letter from several jailed Batasuna leaders in August 2004 encouraged ETA to use diplomacy as a method to pursue its goals, since terrorism, according to them, "was not serving any purpose." In October 2004, a major raid netted Mikel "Antza" Albizu Iriarte, one of the alleged leaders of ETA, and he and other top officials have also begun to urge the party to end its violent tactics.

These numerous arrests (over 400 ETA members are currently in prison) seem to have greatly shaken the internal structure of Batasuna, and the October raid was a very serious blow for the separatist party. There have been no deaths attributed to ETA since 2003, and some government officials have taken this fact as a sign that Batasuna is losing ground and becoming increasingly weaker due to party in-fighting and conflicting goals.

Nevertheless, there have been several bombings in public places, such as outside office buildings and in public parks, causing material damage; these disturbances show that there is still some terrorist activity. In November 2004, Batasuna released a proposal to negotiate peace with the Spanish government that involved demilitarization. Arnaldo Otegi, the leader of Batasuna, has hinted that ETA intends to "let the weapons fall silent" and is "seeking a definitive peace scenario." In February 2005 Batasuna even sent an open letter to French President Jacques Chirac asking him to speak with ETA and commence negotiations, but the appeal has not been answered.

The People's Party, which was in power until March 2004, also refused negotiations with ETA due to its unwillingness to renounce the use of violence. They banned Batasuna in 2003 due to its ties to the terrorist group, and although support for Batasuna and ETA remained strong in the Basque region, the government claimed to have scored a significant victory. Indeed, there have been no deaths attributed to ETA since the outlawing of its supposed political arm. The People's Party, however, did not completely ignore Basque complaints. It strove to find a solution to the question of Basque sovereignty and proposed giving the region some autonomous powers, while keeping it tied to Spain. These concessions were not enough for the Basque people, and the problem remains unsolved.

Although Spain elected to replace the People's Party with the Socialists in March 2004, largely due to the premature and false accusation made by the People's Party that a terrorist attack on several Madrid trains was committed by ETA, the current Socialist administration also refuses to negotiate with ETA, and the government's policy towards and dealings with the terrorist group did not change with the election. Justice Minister Fernando Lopez Aguilar stated, "We do not want a single word with ETA or anything that moves in its entourage." Despite the group's attempts at peace, the Socialists remain skeptical, especially since these peaceful overtures have been disagreeable to the younger members, led by Garikoitz Aspiazu, of the active forces of ETA. This disagreement is an ominous foreshadowing of continual terrorism and militancy in the region. Moreover, ETA has continued to plant minor bombs around the country', as the November proposals also did not overtly declare that ETA would end its violent tactics, an omission that the Socialist Spanish government lamented. Zapatero remarked this past December, "ETA knows that is has only one destiny and that is to end violence and throw down its weapons." Thus, terrorism and the conflict between ETA and Spanish authorities will not end until ETA itself formally renounces using violence to achieve its goals. Even a majority of Basque inhabitants told pollsters in February that they prefer that the government begin talks with ETA only after it makes this formal renunciation.

The lack of clarity in Batasuna's overtures and the internal squabbles have definitely weakened its credibility. Thus the only apparent path toward peace remains with ETA; until it pledges to put down its weapons, the Spanish government will continue to doubt ETA's supposed wish for peace and Batasuna's claim that it will end ETA's terrorist ways. For Spain, the lack of action on both sides unfortunately might mean continued violence in the region and throughout the country.

From *Harvard International Review*, Summer 2005, pp. 12–13. Copyright © 2005 by the President of Harvard College. Reprinted by permission.

UNIT 5
Terrorism in America

Unit Selections
16. **Homegrown Terror,** Michael Reynolds
17. **Green Rage,** Matt Rasmussen
18. **Echoes of the Future,** Daveed Gartenstein-Ross and Kyle Dabruzzi
19. **Casting a Wider Net,** Allan Lengel and Joby Warrick
20. **Speaking for the Animals, or the Terrorists?,** Scott Smallwood
21. **José Padilla and the War on Rights,** Jenny S. Martinez

Key Points to Consider
- Why does "homegrown" terrorism receive less attention than international terrorism?
- Should radical environmentalists be treated as terrorists?
- Does the JFK airport plot indicate a change in the terrorist *modus operandi*?
- Why has the FBI been unable to solve the deadliest bioterrorism attack in U.S. history?

Student Web Site
www.mhcls.com/online

Internet References
Further information regarding these Web sites may be found in this book's preface or online.

America's War Against Terrorism
http://www.lib.umich.edu/govdocs/usterror.html

Department of Homeland Security
http://www.dhs.gov/dhspublic/index.jsp

FBI Homepage
http://www.fbi.gov

ISN International Relations and Security Network
http://www.isn.ethz.ch

The Militia Watchdog
http://www.adl.org/mwd.m1.asp

The Hate Directory
http://www.bcpl.lib.md.us/~rfrankli/hatedir.htm

Domestic terrorism remains a difficult topic for many in the United States. While Americans are willing to believe in "evil forces" with origins in other countries, many become uncomfortable at the thought of U.S. citizens as a source of political violence. Many refuse to believe that a system as free, open, and democratic as ours can spawn those who hate and wish to destroy the very system that has bestowed on them tremendous individual freedoms, including the right to political dissent.

American reactions to domestic terrorists vary. While many Americans are outraged by domestic terrorism, some terrorists, like Eric Rudolph, responsible for four bombings, including attacks on the Olympics in Atlanta, two women's clinics, and a bar, have achieved cult-hero status, with bumper stickers and T-shirts popularizing Rudolph's near-legendary flight from law enforcement officials. Groups like the Animal Liberation Front (ALF) and the Earth Liberation Front (ELF) continue to attract apologists searching for ways to justify or explain the violent behavior of otherwise 'good Americans.' Even the case of Timothy McVeigh, who was prosecuted and executed for the Oklahoma City bombing, has attracted some that continue to believe in an international conspiracy with origins in the Middle East, despite evidence to the contrary. This apparent schizophrenia is echoed in media reporting, public opinion, and public policy.

While the media demonizes the foreign terrorist, it tends to humanize native U.S. terrorists. Stories of American terrorists often emphasize a human-interest perspective. Stories about Minnesota's middle-class soccer mom, Jane Olson, or the young, idealistic, and obviously misguided "American Taliban," John Walker, or even the psychologically unbalanced log-cabin-recluse, Ted Kaczynski, make good copy and are designed to elicit sympathy or empathy in a larger audience. In its efforts to explain how or why 'good' Americans have gone 'bad,' the violence and victims are often ignored.

Public opinion and public policy are also subject to this apparent dissonance. While the American public and U.S. policy makers appear to care little about the legal rights or physical detention of foreigners suspected of association with terrorist organizations, the legal rights of domestic terrorists are often the subject intense public scrutiny and debate.

The six selections in this unit look at the problem of terrorism in the United States. The first article looks at right-wing groups.

U.S. Customs and Border Protection photo by James R. Tourtellotte

Michael Reynolds argues that, preoccupied with the pursuit of Islamic terrorists, the U.S. government has downplayed the threat posed by extremists within the right-wing groups. In the second article sympathetic to the cause, Matt Rasmussen looks at the motives behind attacks carried out by radical environmentalists in the United States. He blames harsh sentencing on the efforts of an overzealous administration trying to distract from its failings " . . . to counter real terrorism."

The third article examines the recent terror plot targeting New York's John F. Kennedy airport. It argues that evidence from the plot may indicate a potential change in the terrorist *modus operandi*. The next article focuses on the FBI's investigations of the anthrax attacks immediately after 9/11. New information about the quality of the anthrax has caused the FBI to cast a "wider net" in its efforts to determine who may be responsible for these attacks. In the fourth article, Scott Smallwood examines the role of a professor at the University of Texas-El Paso, who is a spokesman and advocate for the Animal Liberation Front (ALF). Smallwood questions whether vocal support for a terrorist organization and its objectives constitutes terrorism. In the last article, Jenny Martinez, a lawyer for Jose Padilla, an American citizen detained as an "enemy combatant," describes the legal hurdles Padilla's lawyers have faced while trying to ensure due process. She uses Padilla's case to illustrate how civil liberties have been sacrificed in the name of security.

Homegrown Terror

A bomb is a bomb. A chemical weapon is a chemical weapon.
It won't matter to the victims whether their attacker's name is Ahmed or Bill.

MICHAEL REYNOLDS

On April 10, 2003, a team of federal agents armed with a search warrant entered a storage unit in a small Texas town and were stunned to find a homemade hydrogen cyanide device—a green metal military ammo box containing 800 grams of pure sodium cyanide and two glass vials of hydrochloric acid. The improvised weapon was the product of 62-year-old William Joseph Krar, an accomplished gunsmith, weapons dealer, and militia activist from New Hampshire who had moved his operations to east central Texas just 18 months earlier.

That same day the *New York Times*'s Judith Miller reported from south of Baghdad that the U.S. Army Mobile Exploitation Team had "unearthed . . . precursors for a toxic agent . . . banned by chemical weapons treaties." That turned out not to be the case. What the army team found was fewer than two dozen barrels of organophosphate used in pesticides.

In Chicago a month earlier, Joseph Konopka, a 26-year-old anarcho-terrorist had been sentenced on one count of possession of a chemical weapon. In March 2002, Konopka, who had appropriated an abandoned Chicago Transit Authority storage room under downtown Chicago, was found and arrested in a tunnel beneath the University of Illinois at Chicago. Konopka was a fugitive from federal charges in Wisconsin, where he had hit power substations, radio transmitters, and utility facilities in a 1999 firebombing campaign that caused 28 power outages.

An accomplished systems programmer and hacker, Konopka had assumed the online moniker of "Doc Chaos" and recruited bright teenage accomplices into a cadre he called the "Realm of Chaos." One of these accomplices was arrested with him. In a search of Konopka's subterranean outpost, authorities found nearly a pound of sodium cyanide along with substantial amounts of potassium cyanide, mercuric sulfate, and potassium chlorate.

The young man never gave a reason for why he had stockpiled the deadly chemicals, except to say they were not for "peaceful purposes."[1] He is now serving more than 21 years in federal prison for sabotage and possession of a chemical weapon.

By the time Krar pleaded guilty to one count of possession of a chemical weapon on November 11, 2003, two U.S. citizens—Krar and Konopka—were accountable for far more chemical weapons than have been found in post-war Iraq.

Chemical Capers

Without diminishing the significance of Konopka's attacks on local infrastructure in Wisconsin, Krar's is the more disturbing case, given the size and capabilities of his arsenal, his history, his ideology, his discipline, and his expertise. Despite that, his case attracted little national media attention. There were no press conferences called by Attorney General John Ashcroft and FBI Director Robert Mueller, even though Krar presented the most demonstrably capable terrorist threat uncovered in the United States since September 11, 2001.

Krar's cyanide apparatus was only the most dramatic component of an extraordinary arsenal Krar and his common-law wife, Judith Bruey, had stashed in their Texas storage facility.

Along with the sodium cyanide, hydrochloric acid, acetic acid, and glacial acetic acid, Krar and Bruey's armory included nearly 100 assorted firearms, three machine guns, silencers, 500,000 rounds of ammunition, 60 functional pipe bombs, a remote-controlled briefcase device ready for explosive insertion, a homemade landmine, grenades, 67 pounds of Kinepak solid binary explosives (ammonium nitrate), 66 tubes of Kinepak binary liquid explosives (nitromethane), military detonators, trip wire, electric and non-electric blasting caps, and cases of military atropine syringes.[2]

Although Krar presented the most capable terrorist threat since 9/11, there were no press conferences called by Attorney General John Ashcroft or FBI Director Robert Mueller.

The storage unit also contained an extensive library of required reading for the serious terrorist: U.S. military and CIA field manuals for improvised munitions, weapons, and unconventional warfare; handbooks on assault rifle conversions to full-auto and manufacturing silencers; formulas for poisons and chemical and biological weapons; descriptions of safety precautions in handling; and information on means of deployment. Many of the same easily acquired, open-source materials, translated into Arabic, were found in Al Qaeda terrorist manuals recovered in Afghanistan and Europe.

As for Krar's cyanide device, according to investigators, the blueprint and formula for the weapon were in the form of a computer printout and handwritten notes that Krar either took down from the internet or obtained from another source.

Margaret Kosal, an analyst of chemical and biological weapons at Stanford University's Center for International Security and Cooperation, determined that Krar had enough sodium cyanide, combined with hydrochloric acid, to produce enough hydrogen cyanide gas to kill more than 6,000 people under optimal conditions for attack.

According to Kosal, such a device, if employed in a $9 \times 40 \times 40$-foot conference room, would probably kill half of the room's occupants within one minute of inhalation. If the room was crowded, *immediate* fatalities could number as many as 400. More fatalities would probably follow as a result of age or ill health.

If the cyanide gas were dispersed in a larger space, say an enclosed shopping mall, hotel lobby, or school, the number of deaths would be diminished. In any case, the psychological impact on the public of a successfully deployed improvised chemical weapon in the United States would be enormous.

Kosal observed that it was not that difficult to obtain substantial amounts of sodium cyanide and acid. "While [sodium cyanide] is a DEA [Drug Enforcement Administration]-controlled compound," any notion that it "can only be acquired legally for specific agricultural or military projects is wrong," Kosal pointed out. The price of 2.5 kilograms purchased over the web "is only $105 . . . without an educational discount."[3]

In statements made to the FBI after his arrest, Krar claimed he obtained his sodium cyanide and acids from a gold-plating supply house.

Found by a Fluke

Krar's admission about how he acquired chemicals may be one of the few straightforward statements he has made to federal authorities since they stumbled upon him nearly two years ago.

On January 24, 2002, a UPS package was misdelivered to a family on Staten Island, New York. After inadvertently opening the packet, Michael Libecci discovered all array of identification documents with different names, all of which featured a photograph of the same man. Libecci turned over the packaging and its contents to the Middletown, New Jersey, police, who called the FBI in Newark.

The documents included a North Dakota birth certificate for "Anthony Louis Brach," a Social Security card for "Michael E. Brooks," a Vermont birth certificate for Brooks, a West Virginia birth certificate for "Joseph A. Curry," a Defense Intelligence Agency identification card, and a U.N. Multinational Force Observer identification card. The package was addressed to Edward S. Feltus in Old Bridge, New Jersey. The return address was for William J. Krar at a mailbox in Tyler, Texas. Along with the bogus IDs was a letter from Krar to Feltus.

"Hope this package gets to you O.K.," wrote Krar. "We would hate to have this fall into the wrong hands."

Seven months went by before FBI agents finally talked to Feltus, a 56-year-old employee of the Monmouth County Department of Human Services. On August 8, 2002, Feltus admitted that the forged documents were intended for him, saying he wanted "an ace in the hole" against some future "disaster" or government crackdown. The documents, he said, would allow him to travel "freely in the United States."

Feltus told the agents that he was a member of the New Jersey Militia, an anti-government right-wing paramilitary group permeated with white nationalism. FBI agents later discovered that after he requested the false IDs from Krar, Feltus had stored more than 100 rifles and pistols at a fellow militia member's residence in Vermont. Seven months after the Oklahoma City bombing, leaders of the New Jersey Militia traveled to central New Hampshire on November 22, 1995, to meet with representatives from militias in Rhode Island, Massachusetts, Maine, Connecticut, and New Hampshire, to form the New England Regional Militia. Its purpose, according to the New Jersey Militia Newsletter, was to "establish an operational framework" to "develop and implement tactical contingency plans" that would include "supply, training, public relations, and intelligence gathering."[4] A key player in the New Hampshire militia at the time was William J. Krar.

Nothing Unusual?

Born in 1940, Bill Krar grew up in Connecticut, learning all about guns from his father, a gunsmith for Colt Firearms. Although he didn't serve in the military, weapons and militaria were his life's centerpiece and primary source of income. His formal education ended after a few semesters in community college. He married and had a son, but later divorced.

Exactly when Krar was drawn into the American radical-right constellation of illegal weapons dealing, shadowy paramilitaries, white nationalism, and anti-Semitic global conspiracies is unknown. According to some who knew him at the time, Krar was active in the movement by the mid-1980s. In 1984 he was dealing guns without a federal firearms license under the name of International Development Corporation (IDC) America, listed at his home address in Bedford, New Hampshire. Krar continued using IDC America as the front for his gun dealing for the next 18 years.

From 1984 to 1985, Krar was ostensibly working as a sales representative for a home-building distributorship in the nearby town of Hooksett, near Manchester. But a co-worker recalls Krar as a highly secretive man who always had a pistol at his side and stacks of *Soldier of Fortune* in his office—and who had almost no knowledge or experience of the construction business.

In an interview, this fellow employee remembered Krar and another colleague disappearing for weeks at a time, heading

Unusual Suspects?

March 2000—Larry Ford, biochemist, gynecologist, and anti-government paramilitary activist, kills himself in his suburban southern California home, where police find buried caches of machine guns, assault rifles, thousands of rounds of ammunition, C-4 explosives, and canisters of ricin. In Ford's refrigerators agents discover 266 vials of assorted pathogens including salmonella, cholera, botulism, and typhoid. Ford also seemed to have some kind of working relationship with South Africa's apartheid-era bioweapons program, Project Coast.

November 2000—James Dalton Bell, anti-government militant and MIT-trained chemist, violates his parole and is charged with threatening Internal Revenue Service (IRS) agents. Bell had been convicted and sentenced to prison in 1998 on charges of attacking a Portland, Oregon, IRS office with a "stink bomb." While searching Bell's home lab, federal agents find three assault rifles, explosives, sodium cyanide, and precursor chemicals for the production of sarin nerve gas. Bell claims he had successfully manufactured a small amount of sarin. On one of Bell's computers authorities find the names and home addresses of more than 100 IRS and FBI agents along with those of local law enforcement personnel.

October 2001—Envelopes containing high-grade anthrax are mailed to a tabloid media office in Boca Raton, Florida, to major media offices in New York City, and to two Democratic senators' offices in Washington, D.C. Five die and scores are hospitalized. Although the case remains unsolved, some investigators believe the primary suspect or suspects are likely from within the American anti-government extremist movement.

March 2002—Joseph Konopka, a 25-year-old anarcho-hacker and anti-government extremist, is arrested in Chicago and charged with possession of a chemical weapon, sodium cyanide.

October 2002—Members of the Idaho Mountain Boys, an anti-government paramilitary group, are charged with possession of machine guns, plotting to kill a federal judge and a police officer, and helping fellow members escape from jail. The leader of the group, Larry Eugene Raugust, is also charged with possessing numerous bombs and booby-trap devices. Raugust is one of the leaders of the U.S. Theater Command, a nationwide militia network formed in 1997.

April 2003—William J. Krar, Judith Bruey, and Edward Feltus are arrested after Krar's weapons and chemical weapon cache are found in a Texas storage facility. Krar and Bruey are charged with possession of a chemical weapon.

October 2003—Norman Somerville, a 44-year-old anti-government militiaman is arrested. Near his rural Michigan home agents find an underground bunker stocked with 13 machine guns, thousands of rounds of ammunition, hundreds of pounds of gunpowder, and manuals on guerrilla warfare, "booby traps," and explosives. On the walls are pictures of President George W. Bush and Defense Secretary Donald Rumsfeld with the crosshairs of a rifle scope drawn over them. Somerville had also outfitted his van and Jeep Cherokee with machine guns. Somerville and his comrades had planned to use these "war wagons" in attacks on law enforcement agents. The men had been spurred by the killing of fellow militia member Scott Woodring in a shoot-out with police, who were attempting to arrest him for the shooting death of a state trooper. At the time of his arrest, Somerville warns of a "quiet civil war" brewing in rural Michigan. On August 10, 2004, Somerville pleads guilty to possession of machine guns and pledges "to cooperate in the hunt for shadowy rebels." Two other members of his group also enter guilty pleas to federal weapons charges.

June 2004—A Bureau of Alcohol, Tobacco, and Firearms (ATF) raid uncovers a cache of castor beans, formulas for extracting ricin from the beans, and bomb-making materials in the suburban apartment of Boston-area anti-government activist Michael Crooker. Crooker, once convicted for fraud and possession of a machine gun, had come under scrutiny by the U.S. Postal Service for shipping a silencer to a compatriot in Ohio.

July 2004—After his arrest in south Florida in November 2003, Michael Crooker. John Jordi, a Christian anti-abortion zealot and ex-U.S. Army Ranger, is sentenced to five years in prison for plotting to bomb abortion clinics, gay bars, and certain churches. U.S. District Judge James Cohn rules that Jordi is not a terrorist because federal laws require that plots have an international component to be considered terrorism.

August 2004—Two young Tennessee leaders of a dozen-member anti-government paramilitary cell called the American Independence Group (AIG) are charged with attempted bank robbery and possession of assault weapons. The AIG had intended to use the money from the bank robbery to fund their operations. According to federal agents, the AIG hated the federal government and select ethnic groups and talked of declaring war on law enforcement and killing President Bush.

Also in August, a 66-year-old convicted counterfeiter and antigovernment activist, Gale Nettles, is charged with plotting to build an ammonium nitrate/fuel oil truck bomb and use it to attack the federal courthouse in Chicago. According to federal agents, Nettles had stored 500 pounds of ammonium nitrate in a Chicago-area storage facility and was seeking more from an FBI informant. The informant also stated that Nettles was looking to make contact with either Al Qaeda or Hamas.

off to Costa Rita and other locations in Central America, even though the building supply company had no dealings beyond New England. Krar's mysterious travel activities and gun dealing occurred at the height of the Reagan administration's "private sector" paramilitary and weapons operations in support of the *contras*.[5]

It was also in 1985 that Krar was arrested by New Hampshire state police and charged with impersonating a police officer. He entered a no-contest plea, paid a fine, and was released. Three years later, in 1988, the building supply company where Krar worked went out of business following a fire that destroyed its building. That same year, Krar stopped filing federal income taxes and effectively dropped out of the system.

In April 1995 Krar became the subject of an FBI–Bureau of Alcohol, Tobacco, and Firearms (ATF) investigation stemming from a thwarted kidnapping and bombing plot concocted by white supremacist paramilitaries in Tennessee.

Following the arrest of Timothy McVeigh, Sean Patrick Bottoms and his brother Brian became outraged by media coverage of the Oklahoma City bomber and plotted to kidnap or kill Nashville television newscaster John Siegenthaler, now with MSNBC.[6]

After an informant tipped law enforcement to the plot, the Bottoms brothers fled to east Texas, where they were arrested on April 30, 1995. During a search of the brothers' residences, FBI and ATF agents found pipe bombs, large amounts of explosives, illegal weapons, thousands of rounds of ammunition, and a business card for "William J. Kaar" of IDC America. When questioned, Sean Bottoms told agents that "William Kaar" was in fact William J. Krar. Bottoms said he had lived in Manchester in late 1994 and early 1995 and had used Krar's IDC address on his driver's license.

After his indictment on explosives charges, Bottoms said that Krar, using the alias "Bill Franco," was active in the militia movement and that Krar said he had known about the Oklahoma City bombing before it happened. Krar had also said there were more attacks to come.

In July 1995, ATF agents questioned Krar, who told them that all he had done was sell some ammo and military surplus to Bottoms. Bottoms was then given a polygraph examination, which he failed.

Krar continued his involvement with the militia movement in New England. He later told FBI agents that this was when he first obtained sodium cyanide and began working with it, though there is no evidence to support the claim.

In a separate but simultaneous FBI–ATF investigation in Boston, Krar was under scrutiny for his role in a militia with "strong/violent antigovernment views." According to an FBI affidavit, a federal law enforcement source advised that Krar was a "white supremacist due to the anti-Semitic and anti-black literature" seen at his IDC America business in Manchester, where Krar hosted militia meetings. The source went on to say that Krar was "a good source of covert weaponry for white supremacist and anti-government militia groups."

Bruey, who was president of Krar's IDC operation at the time, told an undercover federal agent of her hatred of "U.S. government policies toward its citizens" and that she believed the government was afraid "military surplus would end up in the hands of citizens rejecting their government."

Despite this report and evidence from the Bottoms case that Krar was illegally selling firearms without a federal license, Krar and Bruey were left free to soldier on until they ran afoul of federal agents in 2001.[7]

Self-store Stockpiles

For a decade Krar conducted his operations out of multiple mail drops and storage units. According to investigators, he had no permanent shop, but would work in the storage units, running in electrical cords to power his tools and run lights. In June 2001 there was a fire at one of the two self-storage facilities Krar and Bruey were using in New Hampshire. Firemen discovered that Krar's unit contained thousands of rounds of ammunition and numerous firearms. ATF agents were called in and found among the weapons an assault rifle converted to full-auto. Krar said the weapons and ammo were the property of his employer, Ed Cunningham of Eagle Eye Guns, who had a federal firearms license. Krar and Bruey packed up the weapons and ammo and left, moving their stockpiles to another self-storage unit.

The manager of the new storage facility, Jennifer Gionet, recalled Krar vividly, describing him as "wicked anti-American."

According to an FBI affidavit, Gionet said that Krar told her "the U.S. government was corrupt" and that he "hated [it] and all of the cops." Krar went on to say he "hated Americans because they are 'money-hungry grubs." He also told Gionet he had several businesses in Costa Rita and offered to set her up with some "financial investments" down there. On September 11, 2001, Krar told Gionet that he knew the attacks in New York and Washington were going to happen and that there would be more in Los Angeles or Manchester. Gionet immediately reported this conversation to the local police, who notified the FBI.

Having drawn the ATF's attention in June, Bruey and Krar moved their operations to Flint, Texas, in October 2001. A young woman, Dawn Philbrick, who had become Krar's lover, accompanied them. Bruey rented two units at Noonday Storage, opened a mail drop at Mail Boxes Etc., and rented a secluded rural house. Krar was soon back at work in one of the storage units fabricating explosive devices and silencers and converting assault rifles to machine guns. He was also fabricating hundreds of magazines and receivers for Bushmaster Firearms in Maine, manufacturer of the civilian models of the AR-15 assault rifle, one of whose weapons was used by John Mohammed and Lee Malvo, the D.C. sniper team. Krar had done similar work for Bushmaster since at least 1998.

On his home computer, Krar was applying another of his skills—counterfeiting identification documents for his compatriots in the antigovernment paramilitary underground. He was as accomplished with counterfeiting as he was with guns and bombs. Over the years Krar used at least seven aliases with four different Social Security numbers and numerous business fronts. Some he used in the gun trade, some within the anti-government movement or offshore. According to investigators, Krar didn't sell counterfeit documents on the open market but gave them away to others in the white supremacist and anti-government movements. It is not known how many sets of documents Krar distributed.

The investigation into Krar and his bogus IDs was slow in developing. It took the FBI until November 2002, 10 months after opening the case, to begin surveillance on Krar, even though they had his address.

Busted... for Drugs

His activities were being monitored when, on January 11, 2003, Krar was arrested by a Tennessee state trooper in the course of a routine traffic stop on the outskirts of Nashville. Searching Krar's rental car, Trooper William Gregory found a plastic bag containing "seven marijuana cigarettes, one syringe of unknown substance, one white bottle with an unknown white substance, 40 wine-like bottles of unknown liquid," as well as two pistols, 16 knives, a stun gun, a smoke grenade, three military-style atropine injections, 260 rounds of ammunition, handcuffs, thumb cuffs, fuse ropes, binoculars, and "other various close hand-to-hand combat items." Gregory also found Krar's passport, a birth certificate, a California credit union card for "William Fritz Hoffner," and a Christian missionary identification card with Krar's photo and the name "W. F. Hoffner." There were also other documents, letters to IDC America, and four pages of what appeared to be a clandestine operations plan for cross-country travel and communications. Gregory busted Krar on marijuana possession, took him into custody, and impounded the car.

The Tennessee state police then called the local FBI, which in turn contacted its Tyler, Texas officer to inform him that Krar had been arrested. Nashville FBI Special Agent David McIntosh, who interviewed Krar that day in the local jail, said that Krar told the FBI that the weapons and ammo were his and that the other material was part of his stock as a gun dealer who worked gun shows. Krar said he was moving back to New Hampshire to help his girlfriend get out of a bad divorce, and that he didn't know that the bag contained marijuana—that it was something a waitress had left beside his plate that he had just stuffed into his pocket.[8]

Krar bonded out of jail the next day, leaving his property behind, and drove west out of Nashville. Trooper Gregory opened the jar of white powder, took a whiff, assumed it was cocaine, and threw it into an evidence locker. After the discovery of Krar's chemical weapon four months later, the powder was brought to the FBI lab, where it tested positive as sodium cyanide. Federal authorities have not released information as to what liquid was found in the 40 wine bottles.

Neither Krar nor Bruey gave up any information following their arrest. Krar accepted a plea agreement on possession of a chemical weapon in exchange for Bruey getting a lighter sentence—five years. Otherwise, all the leads federal agents were able to generate were through documents obtained in the searches of Krar and Brucy's storage units, house, and vehicles. The FBI and Justice Department say the case is still under investigation.

The Face of Terror

Krar was no mere "yarn-spinner," as his defense attorney once portrayed him. The federal agents and prosecutors who interviewed Krar described him as highly intelligent, dedicated, well organized, extremely manipulative, and very dangerous. His radical right, anti-government commitment clearly grew out of the gun and paramilitary culture that spread rapidly following the Gun Control Act of 1968 and the white backlash to civil rights that arose the same year.

Krar carried copies of *Hunter* and *The Turner Diaries*, the fictional *ur*-texts for white American revolution and terrorism written by the late neo-Nazi William L. Pierce under the pseudonym Andrew McDonald. The books have been favorites of white nationalist and anti-government terrorists for more than two decades. McVeigh carried stacks of the Diaries with him during his army days and later sold them at gun shows, pressing copies into the hands of potential allies in the years running up to the Oklahoma City bombing. When federal agents searched McVeigh accomplice Terry Nichols's home in Kansas after the bombing, they found copies of the *Diaries* and *Hunter*.

Krar had a copy of *Hunter* with him when he was stopped in Nashville. *The Turner Diaries* was found in his Texas storage unit along with all four volumes of Henry Ford's classic anti-Semitic conspiracy text, *The International Jew*, and Holly Sklar's left-wing expose of the "new world order," *Trilateralism*. Like McVeigh, Krar drew his anti-government worldview from across the spectrum of right and left.

A terrorist with limited resources would probably consider Krar's chemical weapon an attractive tool. The equipment needed is simple, and the chemicals are readily available from chemical supply houses. Procedures are easily obtained in the open literature, including on the internet. Unlike the more stringent requirements for production of satin or other nerve agents, fabricating hydrogen cyanide devices demands no greater skills beyond those needed to construct an ammonium nitrate-anhydrous hydrazine truck bomb like that used in Oklahoma City.

There is no doubt that Krar was capable of producing such devices. He had the means and technical information to do so. He was well organized, disciplined, highly skilled, and comfortable in the production of improvised explosive devices.

Would he have used such a weapon? FBI agents and Justice officials who interviewed Krar don't think so. But their assessment is not reassuring.

"I don't believe Krar would've used this himself," said Brit Featherston, assistant U.S. attorney and Justice's anti-terrorism coordinator for the Eastern District of Texas. But, "If Krar came across a Tim McVeigh or an Eric Rudolph [now facing trial for fatal bombings at the Atlanta Olympics and an abortion clinic] it would be a disaster. I don't believe he'd have a problem with putting this into their hands and sending them on their way."[9]

FBI Special Agent Bart LaRocca, lead agent in the Krar investigation, agrees. "Krar was a facilitator and a provider," said LaRocca. "There was no indication that he was marketing his bombs or chemical devices. They were intended to be used against the government or in the event of 'martial law.' They were for those willing to use them or those he could manipulate into using them."[10]

An attack with such a weapon on an office building, an abortion clinic, a large auditorium, or a shopping mall could be managed by a single, disciplined individual. A terrorist cell armed with several devices could deliver a coordinated attack at different locations. Either scenario would have a tremendous psychological impact that would go far beyond immediate casualties. The bombings in Oklahoma City and during the Atlanta

Olympics are stark examples of how homegrown terrorists are just as willing to indiscriminately kill men, women, and children as are their radical Islamic counterparts elsewhere in the world.

Ashcroft's Justice Department has shown almost no interest in what was, until the calamitous events of September 11, the primary domestic terrorism threat—the white nationalist, anti-government militia movement and its corollaries with theocratically driven terrorism, primarily abortion-related assassinations and bombings.

The upheavals in U.S. counter-terrorism and anti-terrorist intelligence agencies after the 2001 attacks on the World Trade Center and the Pentagon have not resulted in more nimble thinking about domestic terrorist threats. Apart from the FBI's longtime obsession with environmental and animal rights extremists, the Bureau's primary target for surveillance, investigation, and detention seems to be either immigrants of Arab descent or those who profess Islam as their religion. Although this focus is understandable, it is not commendable.

Had a similar sodium cyanide device been found in a storage unit rented by someone named Khalid or Omar, there is little doubt that Ashcroft and Mueller would have conducted a press conference and that it would have been the story of the week. For some reason, the Krar case was not deemed important—even though the facts of the case show that no other case has demonstrated a comparable and immediate threat. Certainly not the case of Jose Padilla, the small-time thug who merely *talked* in vague terms about a radiological bomb, or that of the young Muslims who thought it might be a good idea to travel to Pakistan for jihad training. Those incidents have been front page fodder, touted by the FBI as cases involving "significant" terrorism. Homegrown terrorists with functional cyanide gas devices are surely as serious a threat.

While Al Qaeda has no need to reach out to indigenous terrorist cells within the United States—or vice versa—a tactical confluence between them would not be surprising. Many anti-government extremists hold beliefs compatible with Islamic terrorist factions worldwide. They are violently against the "new world order," especially with regard to U.S. government and corporate policies. They are uniformly anti-Semitic or anti-Israel and are totally opposed to the war in Iraq.[11]

Apart from the one-off attack in September 2001 by 19 young foreigners, most of them Saudis, the country's most deeply entrenched and most persistent domestic terrorist threat has come from within its own borders and at the hands of its own citizens. It would be folly to believe that the American terrorist underground, after 15 years of sustained and bloody action, has somehow just given up and disappeared.

Perhaps Ashcroft and Mueller called no press conferences because the discovery of Krar's arsenal was a fluke. It was not the result of a proactive federal anti-terrorism intelligence effort targeting the American right-wing paramilitary movement.

Just like Ashcroft and the FBI, the press thinks of "angry white guys" like McVeigh, Nichols, and Rudolph as old news.

Well, maybe Bill Krar and his compatriots don't fit the politically marketable paradigm, the post-9/11 face and faith of terrorism—non-white and Muslim. But such thinking may prove unnecessarily fatal in times to come. Consider the Krar case fair warning.

Notes

1. Affidavit of FBI Special Agent Leslie Lahr, *United States of America v. Joseph Konopka,* Case No. 02CR, March 9, 2002.
2. Plea Agreement, *United States of America v. William J. Krar,* Case No. 6:03CR36, November 13, 2003; Plea Agreement, United States of America v. Judith L. Bruey, Case No. 6:03CR36 (02), November 7, 2003.
3. Interview and e-mail exchanges with Margaret E. Kosal, July 6, 2004.
4. *New Jersey Militia Newsletter,* January 1996.
5. Interview with former co-worker of William Krar, August 26, 2004.
6. Interview with John Siegenthaler, August 20, 2004.
7. Affidavit of PB1 Special Agent Bart LaRocca, *United States of America v. William J. Krar,* Case No. 6:03M12, April 3, 2003.
8. Interview with FBI Special Agent David McIntosh, Nashville, Tennessee, July 20, 2004.
9. Interview with Brir Featherston, assistant U.S. attorney, Tyler, Texas, August 4, 2004.
10. Interviews with FBI Special Agent Bart LaRocca, Tyler, Texas, July 7, July 22, 2004.
11. Michael Reynolds, "Virtual Reich," *Playboy,* February 2002.

MICHAEL REYNOLDS writes on political and religious extremism and terrorism. He has contributed to *Playboy, U.S. News & World Report, Rolling Stone, 60 Minutes,* and *Newsweek.* He was senior analyst at the Southern Poverty Law Center's Intelligence Project from 1994 to 2000.

From *Bulletin of the Atomic Scientists,* November/December 2004, pp. 48, 50–57. Copyright © 2004 by Bulletin of the Atomic Scientists, Chicago, IL 60637. Reprinted by permission of the Bulletin of the Atomic Scientists: The Magazine of Global Security, Science and Survival.

Green Rage

Radical environmentalists are caught between their love of the Earth, trespass of the law, and the U.S. government's war on terror.

MATT RASMUSSEN

People like to think of the courtroom as a crucible of justice, but to me it's always seemed a diluter of passions. The atmosphere is restrained, so respectful and genteel it's easy to forget that people's lives hang in the balance. The system has a way of straining out emotion. It is designed to objectify, to control the soaring passions that created the need for the courtroom in the first place. The perpetrators and the victims pour their passions into the settling ponds of the attorneys, and the attorneys, in turn, pour the diluted stuff into the deep vessel of the judge, and, by extension, into the even deeper water of The System.

If you sat in the gallery of a federal courtroom in my hometown of Eugene, Oregon, last summer and watched as six young men and women entered guilty pleas in a string of environmentally motivated arsons—crimes that the federal government describes as the most egregious environmental terrorism in the nation's history—you might have wondered where the passion had gone. One by one, in a windowless chamber, the defendants answered perfunctory questions posed by Judge Ann Aiken, who sat Oz-like in the highest chair. One by one, they listened to descriptions of the crimes they were accused of committing. One by one, they accepted the government's offer of plea bargains, and one by one, they said the word.

"Guilty."

Kevin Tubbs, thirty-seven, an animal rights activist who migrated to Eugene from Nebraska, mumbled the word and shook his head. Kendall Tankersley, twenty-nine, who holds a degree in molecular biology, choked it out through a gathering sob. Stanislas Meyerhoff, twenty-nine, who wants to study auto mechanics, said it with an odd sort of let's-get-this-over-with politeness. They addressed Judge Aiken as "your honor" and "ma'am."

In the gallery, reporters scribbled. Federal prosecutors with American flag pins affixed to somber blue suits looked on dispassionately. Sentencing dates were set, and the prosecutors, seeking lengthy terms, asked the judge to employ guidelines issued under counter-terrorism laws when considering how much time each should serve.

The crimes to which the six confessed included seventeen attacks, all but one of them arson or attempted arson. The actions took place in five western states between 1996 and 2001. No one was injured. Sport utility vehicles were burned at a Eugene car dealership. So was a meat-packing plant in Redmond, Oregon. Other targets included federal facilities in Wyoming and California and Oregon, where wild horses and burros were let loose and buildings burned down. And in the most notorious action, a spectacular nighttime blaze high in the Rockies destroyed several structures at the Vail ski area. Many of the attacks were followed by communiqués issued under the banner of the Earth Liberation Front, a shadowy, leaderless offshoot of the group Earth First!, and by its sister group, the Animal Liberation Front.

Prosecutors say those who did the crimes took extraordinary means to conceal their involvement. They met in secret gatherings they called "book club" meetings, discussing details such as computer security, target surveillance, and lock-picking. They required that each attendee describe actions they took to avoid detection while traveling to the meeting sites. They used nicknames and code words. They called their criminal actions "camping trips," and dubbed the timing devices they attached to incendiary bombs "hamburgers."

"Terrorism is terrorism—no matter the motive," FBI director Robert Mueller said in January 2006, after the Bush administration announced indictments in an investigation it calls Operation Backfire. "The FBI is committed to protecting Americans from all crime and all terrorism, including acts of domestic terrorism on behalf of animal rights or the environment."

Many were appalled. How could anyone possibly use that singularly loaded word to describe these acts? Where is the moral equivalence between burning an SUV in the dead of night (and doing as much as you can, given the nature of the business at hand, to see that no one gets hurt) and ramming a 767 into a skyscraper? When Eugene's daily newspaper, the *Register-Guard*, used the word *eco-terrorism* to describe the investigation, at least one reader took its editors to task, writing that the paper "appears to confuse arson occurring within the context of a nonviolent campaign with terrorism." The paper opted for the softer-sounding *eco-sabotage* thereafter.

Chelsea Dawn Gerlach is twenty-nine now. Under the terms of her plea bargain, she'll likely spend ten years in prison—assuming she cooperates with government prosecutors as they continue their investigation. If she had been found guilty at trial of all the government had accused her of, she could have been given a life sentence. (Federal prosecutors are seeking life sentences for the majority of those indicted in the Operation Backfire investigation, yet, according to the U.S. Sentencing Commission, the average sentence for arsonists in 2003 was just around seven years.) Along with Meyerhoff, Gerlach is an alum of South Eugene High, a school with a sterling reputation in the heart of Eugene's liberal, affluent south side. In fact, all six of those who entered guilty pleas had close ties to Eugene, as did four others who awaited trial at the time of this writing and three more who had fled the country.

By the time she was in her early twenties, Gerlach had come to believe that Western culture was having a ruinous effect on the global environment, that the Earth faced environmental catastrophe. She felt compelled to do something about it. At some point, passion and frustration drove her over the boundary of her country's laws. Playing by the rules, it seemed, was doing no damn good. At some point, according to the details of her plea bargain, she found herself at the base of Vail Mountain, watching flames light the night sky, awaiting the return of another ELF operative, Bill Rodgers, who had set the fires. Two days later, she found herself at the Denver Public Library, composing a claim of responsibility on a computer that couldn't be traced to her. The message said ELF took the action "on behalf of the lynx," whose habitat would be harmed by an expansion at Vail. "For your safety and convenience, we strongly advise skiers to choose other destinations until Vail cancels its inexcusable plans for expansion," Gerlach wrote.

Skiers did not stop coming to Vail. The arson attack sparked a wildfire of popular condemnation that was directed toward those responsible and, by unfair association, toward more mainstream environmentalists who had also been fighting the expansion. Ultimately, Vail's owners got $12 million from their insurers and the expansion whistled through.

Last summer, in that Eugene courtroom, Gerlach reached her day of reckoning with the system. She, too, said the word. "Guilty." Then she asked the judge if she could read a statement. Gerlach, who has straight black hair and a round, welcoming face, gathered herself and took a deep breath. The words tumbled out in a rush:

"These acts were motivated by a deep sense of despair and anger at the deteriorating state of the global environment and the escalating inequities within society. But I realized years ago this was not an effective or appropriate way to effect positive change. I now know that it is better to act from love than from anger, better to create than destroy, and better to plant gardens than to burn down buildings."

Gerlach admitted to participating in nine of the seventeen attacks described in the government's indictment. In addition to the Vail arson, she served as a lookout as other operatives put incendiary devices next to a meat-packing plant in Eugene; she tried to burn down a Eugene Police Department substation; she participated in an ELF arson that did more than $1 million in damage at an Oregon tree farm that grew genetically modified poplar trees; she helped topple an electrical transmission tower in the sagebrush-and-juniper country east of Bend. And on Christmas night in 1999, she sat in a van that she and her friends had named "Betty" and served as lookout as others placed buckets of diesel fuel next to a Boise Cascade office in Monmouth, Oregon. The buckets ignited and destroyed an eight-thousand-square-foot building, doing $1 million in damage. Then Gerlach sent out an ELF communiqué: "Let this be a lesson to all greedy multinational corporations who don't respect ecosystems. The elves are watching."

The first time I came to Eugene I wondered what all the fuss was about. I knew its reputation well—a university town, a hotbed of liberal activism, home to Ken Kesey and other '60s holdouts. But when I drove through the arterials and back streets on the north side of the city I realized that much of Eugene is just plain old suburbia—ranch homes, tidy lawns, and conservative values.

After a decade of living and working in Eugene, I know this about the place: It's a slice of America, profoundly divided along fault lines of politics, values, and culture. On the south side of the Willamette River, which bisects the city, you'll find the liberal Eugene of renown, full of University of Oregon faculty and tie-dyed hippies who attend the freewheeling Oregon Country Fair each July. Conservative Eugene is on the north side of the river, full of satellite dishes and American flags and folks who favor the traditional charms of the Lane County Fair in August.

There are divisions within the divisions, just as there are in America at large. There are monied fiscal conservatives and working-class Bush supporters. There are affluent liberals who vote Democrat and there are the more disheveled activists who have no patience for the compromises made by mainstream liberals. Those who committed the ELF arsons, and their supporters, come from this latter milieu.

If there is a physical heart of the radical environmental movement in Eugene, it is a leafy precinct of old wooden houses just west of downtown, known as the Whiteaker neighborhood. An outsider—someone from, say, Cedar Rapids, Iowa, or St. Petersburg, Florida, or Provo, Utah, or from any of a thousand bastions of conventional American culture, including many corners of Eugene—might fixate on a curbside cardboard box offering "free stuff," or a do-your-own-thing piece of art in a front yard, a dreadlocked couple strolling hand in hand, a FUCK BUSH sign, a flash of tattooed flesh, a braless woman, a pair of ratty Carhartt cutoffs, a pierced tongue, eyebrow, nose, belly button, or neck, and feel a skosh uncomfortable.

Whiteaker rose to national prominence in 1999, after perhaps a couple dozen of its residents—young adults who described themselves as anarchists—helped foment the lawlessness at the World Trade Organization conference in Seattle. Suddenly "the Eugene anarchists" were a cause célèbre.

Reporters from the BBC, the *Los Angeles Times*, CNN, the *Wall Street Journal*, and other major outlets descended on Eugene, their editors demanding analysis pieces explaining what the hell had happened in Seattle. In Eugene, there was a good deal of uneasy eye-rolling. Local civic leaders reacted with a mix of revulsion and denial to the notion that their city was Anarchy Central. The consensus was that the whole thing had been blown out of proportion.

No one knows how many anarchists there really are in Whiteaker; they don't keep membership rolls. At least some of those who donned black garb in Seattle were kids doing what kids the world over often do: immerse themselves in an adrenaline-charged cause that's greater than oneself. Not all of Eugene's anarchists are callow youths, though. Some are genuine, steadfastly committed, and deep-thinking.

Eugene's brand of anarchy is "green anarchy." Unlike old-style industrialist anarchists, green anarchists are primarily concerned with the effects of civilization on the global environment. They are more radical in their thought than, say, Marxists are. They would certainly agree that capital accumulates in a fashion that creates a wealthy elite at the expense of the exploited masses, but their critique goes far beyond that. Their central precept is not that civilization needs to be reconstructed, but rather that it needs to be overthrown in its entirety and never replaced. Things started to go wrong, they contend, when humans first domesticated plants and animals.

The nexus between the green anarchists, the Earth Liberation Front, and those ensnared in the government's investigation is not perfect. Several of the defendants don't claim to be advocates of the green anarchy movement now, if they ever were. And some of them, it seems, had not thought through the intellectual justifications of their actions in a formal sense—perhaps they just felt in their gut that things like SUVs and animal slaughterhouses and plantations that grow genetically modified trees were wrong. Whatever their motivations, their actions and rhetoric match up quite well with the principles of the green anarchist philosophy.

If they are in need of intellectual mentorship, Eugene's green anarchists have a resource close at hand. John Zerzan is in his sixties, a graduate of Stanford and San Francisco State University and one of the foremost anticivilization thinkers in the world. In the '60s he was a Marxist and a Maoist and a Vietnam protester and a devotee of the Haight-Ashbury psychedelic scene. He now believes that Paleolithic humans and the few remaining primitive cultures provide the best models for how humans should subsist. His books include *Elements of Refusal, Future Primitive,* and *Against Civilization: Readings and Reflections.* He is an editor of *Green Anarchy*, which calls itself "an anticivilization journal of theory and action." He was a confidant of Theodore Kaczynski during the Unabomber trial.

On a sunny afternoon last summer, I sat down with Zerzan on his shady back deck. His house is small and tidy, a wooden bungalow that sits near a busy one-way just south of the Whiteaker neighborhood. I asked him if he thought too much had been made of the Eugene anarchists after the WTO riots.

"*60 Minutes* was here. You can't say that would have happened just because we have a good idea," he said. Then he switched to the recent indictments. "All of the people who have been arrested in this thing used to live here in Eugene. There was a lot happening here, and that whole neighborhood [Whiteaker] was the key part. Now it's quieter."

I had never before spoken with Zerzan, although I knew that he lived in Eugene; around town, he's taken for granted in the way that minor celebrities who live in small cities often are. He has a salt-and-pepper beard, straight bangs, and a quiet, almost patrician demeanor that I found disarming. He seems younger than his age.

I asked him if he thought the arsons outlined in the government's indictment had done any good. He pointed out that most of the actions were followed by anonymous communiqués explaining precisely why the actions were taken. The combination of action and explanation can be quite powerful, he said.

Zerzan clearly struggles with the question of violence. Of Kaczynski, he said he found him "lacking in the basic kind of human connection that most people have." He hopes that the anticivilization movement will prevail without great bloodshed, although he quickly adds "my anarchist friends mainly laugh at me for being too hopeful." Humans, he believes, may very well forge a new way of living on Earth, or, rather, return to old ways of living on Earth, before utter environmental collapse imposes a Malthusian end.

"You can't make the revolution happen by promising people less," he said. Then he swept his hand out in front of him, taking in his house, the sound of cars and trucks hurtling past, the hum of the city, of human civilization. "You can't say all of this is more. This is becoming more sterile and cold and fucked up by the minute."

Down at Sam Bond's Garage, in the heart of Whiteaker, organic beer is served up in old jam jars. Tots in hemp smocks frolic on the wooden floor. A black t-shirt hangs on a wall sporting a skull and crossbones on the front and "Whiteaker" in pirate scrawl beneath.

It's a Sunday night in June, and the place is filling up fast. There's a disco ball hanging from old wooden rafters in the eatery's barnlike interior space. Two large ceiling fans beat the air, but a thermometer on the wall reports eighty-three degrees nonetheless. The usual customers, the ones who just came by for beers or a bite to eat or to chat with friends, seem a bit bewildered by the gathering crowd. A middle-aged man shoulders up to the bar to settle his tab and a young woman inquires if he's here for the rally. When the man asks what rally, she says, "It's for Free Luers. He got twenty-three years for burning up three SUVs." Soon the hall is full, a standing-room-only crowd of perhaps two hundred.

Jeffrey "Free" Luers is a skinny kid from suburban Los Angeles who is serving his fifth year in prison. In 2000, when he was twenty-one, Luers and an accomplice were arrested for setting fire to three SUVs in the middle of the night at a car lot near the University of Oregon (a separate action from those included in the Operation Backfire indictment). A Eugene judge sentenced Luers, who refused all of the government's plea bargain offers, to nearly twenty-three years in prison. The authorities say they made an example of Luers to forestall further crimes; activists say they made a martyr of him. Luers remains unrepentant. In a recent message to his supporters, he said, "I got careless, I got sloppy. I slipped up. I got caught."

I find a seat at the bar and order an ale. An acquaintance recognizes me and squeezes over to say hello. He points to a man sitting at a table in the center of the hall. Amid the young tattooed-and-pierced set and the older pony-tailed-and-sandaled set, this man is conspicuous. He looks as if he just walked in from an engineering convention. He has a conservative haircut, wears chino slacks, and keeps his reading glasses tucked in his left shirt-pocket. He's perhaps in his late sixties, and sits next to his tastefully dressed, bespectacled wife.

"That's Luers's dad," my friend says, and then pauses. "Just think—he'll probably never see his son out of prison again."

The elder Luers, whose name is John, shuffles up to a small stage at one end of the room. He leans on a cane as he walks. Rallies for his son have been held annually for the past few years, and Luers notes that this is one of forty-three around the world on this day. "The crowds just keep getting bigger," John Liters says. "We are so grateful for the support you have shown our son."

I introduce myself later and ask if he speaks with writers and he says politely but firmly, "No we don't."

There are other speakers. Jeffrey Luers may be the poster child of the government's crackdown on so-called environmental terrorists, but this night most are preoccupied with the recent arrests. This crowd refers to the government's Operation Backfire investigation as The Green Scare, seeing it as an all-out effort to discourage environmental activism and dissent. Many have been interrogated by FBI agents, and many believe their phones are tapped.

One of the organizers of the rally speaks up and says "we know what real terrorism is" to loud applause. Misha Dunlap of the Civil Liberties Defense Center, a Eugene nonprofit that has lent assistance to Luers and to the more recent defendants, gives an update. Then anticivilization author and thinker Derrick Jensen takes the stage. He asks any FBI agents in the audience to please raise their hands. When no one does, he shrugs and says, "Worth a try." Then he says, "What you're doing is wrong and I plan on seeing you brought to justice." More applause and a few boisterous hoots. Jensen speaks for more than an hour about environmental holocaust and resistance, and the audience is rapt.

When someone mentions the name Jake Ferguson, the room erupts in a chorus of hisses. Ferguson, a former Whiteaker insider, is the government's primary informant in the Operation Backfire case. He has not been charged in any of the crimes, but has admitted to being a key operative in many of them. He agreed to wear hidden recording devices when speaking with fellow activists, and now his name is anathema in Whiteaker—a stop sign just a few blocks from Sam Bond's has been defaced to read STOP JAKE.

Ferguson may bear the epithet "snitch," but many radical activists consider the six who have accepted plea bargains to be snitches too. Still, there is an unmistakable aroma of violence in the green anarchists' attitude toward Ferguson. A typical posting on the Portland Independent Media Center website, which has served as a clearinghouse among activists for information and commentary on the Operation Backfire case, described Ferguson as "the worst type of scum on earth." Another writer added, "jake admitted being a snitch to people in the community after the story broke. why he can still talk is a good question." (It's worth noting, though, that Ferguson had suffered no physical harm at the time of this writing, at least not to my knowledge. The talk may be streetwise and tough, but the vast majority of Eugene's radical activists would never intentionally harm another person or animal.)

I leave Sam Bond's before the music starts—a hip-hop duo is on the bill. Outside, the night air is cool. It feels good to be out of that space, not just because of the stifling heat, but because of the intensity in the room.

I find my car and drive through the quiet streets of Whiteaker. Downtown is empty except for a trio of homeless youths hanging out on a corner by the city library. The curtains are drawn in most of the homes in my own south side neighborhood. The crowd at Sam Bond's may be ready for the revolution, but the rest of the world just seems to want a good night's sleep.

The operation backfire indictment is sixty-five pages long and identifies the first building the Eugene arsonists burned down as the Oakridge Ranger Station, just up the road from Eugene. On the night of October 30, 1996, a motorist saw the flames and called 911. When firefighters drove into the parking lot, nails stuck in the tires of their trucks. The building was too far gone to save. By morning, it was a pile of cinders.

The Oakridge arson was one of the first subjects I wrote about after returning to my native Northwest. I had just left a job as a newspaper reporter on the East Coast, and had taken another job, editing a small magazine that covers National Forest issues. Nothing like this had ever happened in Oregon. People were shocked.

Within the region and throughout the federal government the presumption was immediate. This was the work of environmental extremists. Two nights earlier, someone had torched a Forest Service pickup truck at a ranger station seventy miles to the north, and had left graffiti including "Forest Rapers" and "Earth Liberation Front." They had also scrawled the letter A with an extended crossbar—the symbol of the anarchist movement. No one claimed responsibility for the Oakridge fire, but many people assumed both acts were done by the same people.

Dan Glickman, President Clinton's Secretary of Agriculture, who oversaw the Forest Service, told reporters then that he had "absolutely no tolerance for individuals or groups that engage in terrorism." Jack Ward Thomas, who was chief of the Forest Service, said, "This is what people do who do not understand how to operate in a democracy."

But to me, and to many in the mainstream environmental community, these assumptions made no sense. At the time of the arson, environmentalists had just scored a major victory in the steep forestlands just a few miles away from Oakridge.

In the early 1990s, the Forest Service had proposed a salvage-logging project on the slopes bordering nearby Warner Creek. The area had burned in 1991, leaving behind a patch-work of both blackened wood and healthy trees. When a Eugene judge ruled the Forest Service's plan legal under the notorious Salvage Logging Rider in 1995, protesters sprang into action. They built barricades, dug trenches, and fashioned makeshift structures to keep logging equipment out. Then, in the summer of 1996, after activists had maintained the blockade for nearly a year, the Clinton administration ordered the Forest Service to shelve its plans to log Warner Creek (and more than 150 other controversial sales around the West).

So why would an environmentalist of any stripe decide, just months later, to burn down the Oakridge Ranger Station?

Aboveground activists did all they could to distance themselves from the act. The Oregon Natural Resources Council, fearing a public relations disaster, offered a $1,000 reward to anyone who provided information leading to the conviction of those responsible.

Years passed with no arrests. There were rumors that the fire had been an inside job, the work of a disgruntled employee. The Forest Service built another ranger station, a fetching structure with two stories and broad eaves, in exactly the same spot where the other had stood. Then, last summer, Kevin Tubbs, one of the six who accepted the government's plea bargain offer, owned up to the deed.

At the Warner Creek blockade, Tubbs, curly-haired and deeply committed to the cause, had kept vigil atop a structure built from logs; if anyone tried to move the thing, he said, it would collapse and send him falling down the steep mountain-side to his death. In Eugene's federal courtroom, wearing standard-issue Lane County Jail garb, with close-cropped hair, and looking a little middle-aged, he admitted to this:

> On the night of the arson, he drove two fellow activists, Ferguson and Josephine Sunshine Overaker, east from Eugene to the vicinity of the Oakridge Ranger Station and dropped his passengers off. According to the account read in court by U.S. assistant attorney Stephen Peifer, Ferguson and Overaker placed incendiary devices around the ranger station. They threw nails onto the parking lot to slow down emergency responders and then the three drove back toward Eugene. They took back roads to avoid detection. They paused at a covered bridge near the town of Lowell and tossed the gloves they had used while committing the crime into the dark waters of a reservoir. The incendiary devices worked as intended and the ranger station was destroyed.

Despite Tubbs's confession, Timothy Ingalsbee, one of the leaders of the Warner Creek effort, still has trouble accepting the notion that environmentalists burned down the ranger station. Tall and lanky and gentle of manner, Ingalsbee holds a doctorate in environmental sociology from the University of Oregon. After the Warner Creek battle, he had wanted to work with the Forest Service to establish the site as a permanent wildfire research station within the National Forest system. "What the fire did was to destroy that opportunity," he said. "I had excellent professional relationships with the Oakridge Forest Service staff, and after the fire that ended."

Mainstream environmentalists reacted with the same sense of puzzlement and disgust to the majority of the attacks described in the Operation Backfire investigation. And while many on the left are critical of the aggressiveness with which the federal government has pursued the case—viewing the millions spent as evidence of the Bush administration's overzealousness in its war on terror and a convenient distraction from the failings of the administration to counter real terrorists—virtually no one in the environmental community believes the attacks have done anything but harm.

"It's bad for our cause all around. It stinks," Rocky Smith told *High Country News* in the days after the Vail attack. Smith, a Colorado environmentalist, had worked tirelessly to fight the Vail expansion through legal means. "There are lots of reasons to hate Vail," he said, "but not enough to justify arson."

So, why? Those who are directly involved in the cases—those who are under indictment or who have accepted plea bargains—won't talk about motives. Most of those who are closest to them won't say anything either. Government prosecutors have indicated that there may be more indictments, and many activists are afraid to talk openly about the actions and those who allegedly committed them.

It's hard, though, to escape the conclusion that the main motivation of the Eugene arsonists was sincere, passionate conviction.

"I believe these arsons were a result of total frustration," one Whiteaker activist who knows several of the defendants told me over coffee. "It's just very painful to witness, so clearly, the rape of the planet."

Consider the story of Bill Rodgers. He was forty at the time of his arrest, making him the oldest of those indicted in the Operation Backfire investigation. Authorities describe him as a ringleader in the group of arsonists—they say he served as a sort of mentor to Gerlach, for one. Police arrested him last December at the modest bookstore and community center he ran in Prescott, Arizona. Two weeks after his arrest, he put a plastic bag over his head and suffocated himself.

In a farewell letter, he wrote, "Certain human cultures have been waging war against the Earth for millennia. I chose to fight on the side of bears, mountain lions, skunks, bats, saguaros, cliff rose and all things wild. I am just the most recent casualty in that war. But tonight I have made a jail break—I am returning home, to the Earth, to the place of my origins."

Here's what activists like Rodgers believe: They believe we face a crisis of mass extinction, caused by civilization. They believe the atmosphere is being spoiled, the climate pitching on the verge of ruinous change, because of civilization. They believe our bodies are being poisoned and so are our spirits, by civilization.

They've considered the state of the planet and they've decided against some hopeful half critique. They've looked all the way down into the pit and, rightly or wrongly, come to the conclusion that the whole damn thing is undeniably, irretrievably messed up. The government is wrong, mainstream culture is wrong, the tokenist sellout environmental community is wrong, civilization itself is wrong.

The green anarchists are historical determinists, as are Marxists and Christian fundamentalists. Their worldview is based on more, though, than extrapolations of weighty political treatises or divinations of holy texts. It is based on the work of scientists such as E. O. Wilson and Jared Diamond and respected, peer-reviewed biologists and climatologists and ecologists the world over whose work suggests that human activity is having a calamitous effect on the Earth's natural systems.

Globalization. Capitalism. Greed. Civilization. Call it what you will. It will end, the green anarchists insist, whether by means of environmental collapse, violent revolution, or the collective enlightening of human consciousness.

"We are now witnessing the final days of Western Civilization," declared a recent posting on the Portland Independent Media Center website. "As this civilization decays around us—as the wars spread and the natural disasters increase in frequency—and as those trapped by western culture slowly break from their cognitive dissonance and open their hearts and minds, a new reality will begin to reveal itself. Our task is to let this transformation take its course, and to speed it along where we can."

History is littered with historical determinists who were convinced the revolution was just around the corner. A few were right, most were wrong. And history is full of social upheavals in which true believers decided the cause was so great that they would step beyond the boundaries of law. Some have been vindicated by history, some scorned.

When I consider the ELF arsonists, I find myself thinking of the militant nineteenth-century abolitionist John Brown. So appalled was Brown by the institution of slavery that he tried to spark a revolution. He thought all that was needed was a firm nudge and the whole South would erupt in a slave rebellion. He was wrong, and was caught. His actions enraged the southern populace, and the system against which he struggled prosecuted him, convicted him, and hanged him.

At the time he was viewed as a crazed visionary whose quixotic strivings had changed nothing. But as the forces of abolition gained strength—as the real revolution unfolded—he became something much more potent. He became a symbol. Over the course of decades, what was first considered lunacy and extremism came to be regarded as courage and righteousness.

Years from now, when we have a clearer understanding of the full damage we have done to the Earth, is it possible the ELF arsonists will be remembered in similar fashion?

From *Orion*, January/February 2007, pp. 60, 62–67. Copyright © 2007 by Matt Rasmussen. Reprinted by permission of the author.

Echoes of the Future

What the criminal complaint for the JFK terror plot suggests about shifting terrorist tactics.

DAVEED GARTENSTEIN-ROSS AND KYLE DABRUZZI

The face of terror is constantly evolving as terrorist tactics, and even the foot soldiers trying to attack America, change. When authorities announced last weekend that they had foiled a plot designed to blow up New York City's John F. Kennedy International Airport, its fuel tanks, and a jet fuel artery, the conspiracy, on the surface, seemed like more of the same. Although perhaps a bit more ambitious than the usual scheme, the JFK plot was consistent with past attempts in its targeting of a major economic artery and effort to attain maximum symbolic value. But a look at the details contained in the 33-page criminal complaint suggests a change in the modes of operation of America's enemies.

One significant aspect of the complaint is what it suggests about the threat of terrorist infiltration through our southern border. Within analytic circles there is a near consensus that America's northern border poses far more of a threat of terrorist infiltration than the southern border. This view is detailed at length in Richard Miniter's *Disinformation*, which explains that al Qaeda has had a long-term presence in Canada, and that attempted terrorist entry from the northern border will be aided by "a political climate far different from Mexico—one that actually defends accused terrorists."

In contrast, Miniter writes that "there are no known cases of al Qaeda terrorists sneaking across the Mexican border." As Miniter notes, a 2004 report by Robert S. Leiken of the Nixon Center examining how 212 "suspected or convicted" terrorists entered the United States finds that of all their means of entry, "terrorists stealing across the Mexican border comes last, virtually nil."

But the JFK criminal case may challenge these conclusions. All of the arrested plotters hail from South America and the Caribbean: Russell Defreitas is a U.S. citizen from Guyana; "Amir" Kareem Ibrahim is a citizen of Trinidad; and Abdul Kadir and Abdel Nur are citizens of Guyana. Seven unindicted coconspirators are also mentioned in the complaint, designated Individuals A through G. Six of these unindicted coconspirators are from Guyana; the seventh hails from Trinidad.

Besides the geographic origin of the plotters, their plan for moving terrorists into the United States is also significant. In paragraph 16 of the complaint, Individual A (whom some intelligence sources suspect may be Adnan El Shukrijumah) mentioned that in addition to plotting to strike the United States where it would do the most harm, he was working on a plan "to smuggle individuals, including mujahideen, from Asia into Guyana and then into the United States." The fact that he wanted to transport terrorists through Guyana into the U.S. may well cause analysts to rethink the terrorist threat emanating from the southern border.

It's unclear how Individual A intended to move terrorists into the United States. He could have planned a covert entry, either through the U.S.-Mexico border or the Florida Keys. Or he could have intended the would-be terrorists to come in through a traditional port of entry, perhaps disguising themselves as Latino so they wouldn't fit the typical terrorist profile. In late April, a British judge sentenced five men to life in prison for their roles in a plot to attack London targets with bombs made from a half-ton of fertilizer. One interesting fact revealed at trial was that one of the plotters, Rahman Adam, had legally changed his name to Anthony Garcia. The *Washington Post* noted that British investigators believed he did this "to conceal his Muslim and Arab background from police."

Besides the implications for border security, the geographic origins of the JFK plotters—and the connections they made use of along the way—may call into question analysts' assumptions about the strength of terrorist networks in Guyana and Trinidad.

One of the defendants, Abdul Kadir, had been a successful politician: he served in the Guyanese parliament and as the mayor of Linden, Guyana. Yet he had no compunction about getting involved in a terrorist plot against the United States. The criminal complaint details his involvement. He developed a codename system for the plot, calling it "the chicken hatchery" or "chicken farm." He walked two of the plotters through a mall in Georgetown, Guyana, explaining that he wanted people in

Georgetown to see them with him so anyone thinking of harming the plotters would "think twice." After examining video of the JFK airport taken by "mastermind" Russell Defreitas, Abdul Kadir said the video was insufficiently detailed for operational purposes, and suggested that the plotters use Google Earth software; he provided further technical advice on hiding the video from authorities. Abdul Kadir offered to help finance the plotters' return to New York, helped the plotters avoid Guyanese security's watchful eyes by meeting them at the airport, provided them with technical advice based on his background as an engineer, and set them up with contacts in Trinidad.

The Trinidad connection is likewise significant. The complaint explains that three plotters traveled to a compound of Jamaat al-Muslimeen (JAM), a terrorist group active in Trinidad and Tobago, where Abdel Nur allegedly met with the group's leader. According to the complaint, Abdel Nur presented details of the plan and arranged a later meeting to discuss JAM's possible support. Although this later meeting was aborted because of the plotters' safety concerns, JAM's clear interest in supporting a plot to strike a prominent U.S. target may cause a reevaluation of the group. Despite such high-profile activities as involvement in a 1990 coup attempt against Trinidad's government, a series of bomb attacks against Port of Spain and St. James in 2005, and the alleged murders of former JAM members, most analysts think of JAM as little more than a glorified criminal gang whose thuggish activities are overlaid with radical Islamic rhetoric. This common perception of JAM may no longer be accurate.

Finally, the details of the plot speak to the ongoing debate about the relevance of al Qaeda's central leadership. While the name "al Qaeda" is never mentioned in the complaint, a senior U.S. military intelligence officer says that "it's definitely there if you know what to look for." (Although two of the plotters, Ibrahim and Kadir, were Shia imams, the JAM group that they appealed to for assistance is Sunni—and some intelligence sources believe that their international terrorist connections might be affiliated with al Qaeda rather than Shia terror networks.)

The complaint outlines numerous international terrorist connections of two of the named defendants (Abdul Kadir and Ibrahim) as well as two of the unnamed coconspirators (Individuals A and E). The references to these international connections are significant. Moreover, as the plot moved past the discussion stage, Ibrahim planned to "present the plan to contacts overseas who may be interested in purchasing or funding it." This fits with al Qaeda's classic *modus operandi,* in which aspiring terrorists would propose attack plans to top al Qaeda leaders to solicit their blessing and support.

Some of the terrorist plots we have witnessed over the past few years that were initially thought to be the work of autonomous cells unconnected to the central al Qaeda network turned out to bear far more of the central leadership's imprimatur than was originally suspected. It increasingly seems that for catastrophic terror attacks—which the JFK plotters certainly saw their scheme as—localized terror cells consistently reach out to international terror networks for support, as opposed to going it alone.

While the joint efforts of the FBI and Trinidadian authorities are to be applauded, some of the tactics employed in this plot may be signs of what is yet to come. Officials must take notice of how terrorist networks are adapting and evolving if they are to keep future plots from coming to fruition.

DAVEED GARTENSTEIN-ROSS is a senior fellow at the Foundation for Defense of Democracies and the author of *My Year Inside Radical Islam.* **KYLE DABRUZZI** is a terrorism analyst at the Gartenstein-Ross Group.

From *The Weekly Standard,* by Daveed Gartenstein-Ross and Kyle Dabruzzi, June 7, 2007. Copyright © 2007 by Weekly Standard. Reprinted by permission.

Casting a Wider Net

The FBI goes global to find the source of a common type of anthrax used in domestic attacks

ALLAN LENGEL AND JOBY WARRICK

Five years after the anthrax attacks that killed five people, the FBI is now convinced that the lethal powder sent to the Senate was far less sophisticated than originally believed, widening the pool of possible suspects in a frustratingly slow investigation.

The finding, which resulted from countless scientific tests at numerous laboratories, appears to undermine the widely held belief that the attack was carried out by a government scientist or someone with access to a U.S. biodefense lab.

What was initially described as a near-military-grade biological weapon was ultimately found to have had a more ordinary pedigree, containing no additives and no signs of special processing to make the anthrax bacteria more deadly, law enforcement officials confirmed. In addition, the strain of anthrax used in the attacks has turned out to be more common than was initially believed, the officials say.

As a result, after a very public focus on government scientists as the likely source of the attacks, the FBI is today casting a far wider net, as investigators face the daunting prospect of an almost endless list of possible suspects in scores of countries around the globe.

"There is no significant signature in the powder that points to a domestic source," said one scientist who has extensively studied the tan, talc-like material that paralyzed much of Washington in the deadliest bioterrorism attack in U.S. history.

The FBI says it remains optimistic that it will find whoever killed five people—two of them from the Washington area—in a series of bioterrorism-by-mail attacks that rocked a nation still in shock from the Sept. 11 terrorist strikes. The bureau has assigned fresh leadership to the case—Special Agent Ed Montooth—and retains a full-time investigative force of 17 agents and 10 postal inspectors.

"There is confidence the case will be solved," said Joseph Persichini Jr., acting assistant director in charge of the FBI's Washington field office.

The prevailing views about the anthrax powder, meanwhile, have been coalescing among a small group of scientists and FBI officials over several years but rarely have been discussed publicly. In interviews and a recently published scientific article, law enforcement authorities have acknowledged that much of the conventional wisdom about the attacks turned out to be wrong.

Specifically, law enforcement authorities have refuted the widely reported claim that the anthrax spores had been "weaponized"—specially treated or processed to allow them to disperse more easily. They also have rejected reports that the powder was milled, or ground, to create finer particles that can penetrate deeply into the lungs. Such processing or additives might have suggested that the maker had access to the recipes of biological weapons made by the United States in the 1950s and 1960s.

In fact, the anthrax powder used in the 2001 attacks had no additives, writes Douglas J. Beecher, a scientist in the FBI laboratory's Hazardous Materials Response Unit, in an article in the science journal Applied and Environmental Microbiology.

"A widely circulated misconception is that the spores were produced using additives and sophisticated engineering supposedly akin to military weapons production," Beecher writes in the journal's August edition, in what is believed to be the most expansive public comment on the nature of the powder by any FBI official. "The idea is usually the basis for implying that the powders were inordinately dangerous compared to spores alone."

The FBI would not allow Beecher to be interviewed about his article. But other scientists familiar with the forensic investigation echoed his description. Whoever made the powder produced a deadly project of exceptional purity and quality—up to a trillion spores per gram—but used none of the tricks known to military bioweapons scientists to increase the lethality of the product. Officials stressed that the terrorist would have had to have considerable skills in microbiology and access to equipment.

"It wasn't weaponized. It was just nicely cleaned up," said one knowledgeable scientist who spoke on the condition he not be identified by name because the investigation is continuing. "Whoever did it was proud of their biology. They grew the spores, spun them down, cleaned up the debris. But there were no additives."

Moreover, scientists say, the particular strain of anthrax used in the attacks has turned to out to be a less significant clue than first believed. The highly virulent Ames strain was first isolated in the United States and was the basis for the anthrax weapons formerly created by the United States. The use of the Ames strain in the 2001 attack was initially seen as a strong clue linking the terrorist to the U.S. biodefense network.

> **Whoever made the powder produced a deadly project of exceptional purity and quality—up to a trillion spores per gram—but used none of the tricks known to military bioweapons scientists to increase the lethality of the product.**

But the more the FBI investigated, the more ubiquitous the Ames strain seemed, appearing in labs around the world including nations of the former Soviet Union.

"Ames was available in the Soviet Union," said former Soviet bioweapons scientist Sergei Popov, now a biodefense expert at George Mason University. "It could have come from anywhere in the world."

Many law enforcement officials believe that ever-improving technology eventually could lead to a break in the case. Ongoing tests could lead authorities to the lab where the anthrax originated—something authorities have said for years could help close the case.

More traditional tactics are still being used: The FBI has conducted 9,100 interviews and issued 6,000 subpoenas in one of the most exhaustive and expensive investigations in the bureau's history. Authorities say investigators continue to have a number of specific individuals in their sights, describing the suspect list as "fluid."

One prevailing theory among investigators is that the attacks came from within the United States rather than from an overseas terrorist organization.

However, a law enforcement official said, "we have not closed the door on any possibilities. There's a discrete number of individuals who continue to be investigated, both internationally and domestically."

Over the years, officials have publicly identified only one "person of interest," and that was more than four years ago. Steven J. Hatfill, a former Army scientist, has denied wrongdoing and has never been charged. He is suing the Justice Department, alleging that officials leaked false information about him that caused great harm.

Law enforcement officials won't talk about Hatfill.

Homeland Security Secretary Michael Chertoff, in a meeting this month with Washington Post reporters and editors, would not say whether any single individual continues to draw special attention as a "person of interest."

"I'm not telling you that right now the bureau is focused on someone or not focused on someone," Chertoff said. "There are in my experience a lot of instances where we might know or have a good reason to believe who committed a criminal act, but we may not be able to prove it. So when you say something is not solved, you should not assume from the fact that there is no criminal prosecution we don't have a good idea of what we think happened."

Persichini, of the FBI's Washington office, acknowledged frustrations but said that "no one in the FBI has for a moment stopped thinking about the innocent victims of these attacks, nor has the effort to solve this case in any way been slowed.

"While not well known to the public, the scientific advances gained from this investigation are unprecedented and have greatly strengthened the government's ability to prepare for—and prevent—biological attacks in the future," Persichini says.

Nonetheless, failure to solve the mystery has bred public skepticism.

"If the FBI's investigation has become a cold case, then it's time for [FBI Director Robert S. Mueller III] to acknowledge that and take steps to deal with it," said Sen. Charles E. Grassley (R-Iowa), a frequent critic of the FBI. "I'm concerned that the FBI may have spent too much time focusing [on] one theory of what happened and too little effort on the other possibilities."

Washington Post staff writer **SPENCER S. HSU** and staff researcher **MEG SMITH** contributed to this report.

From *The Washington Post,* by Allan Lengel and Joby Warrick, National Weekly Edition, October 2–8, 2006, p. 29. Copyright © 2006 by The Washington Post. Reprinted by permission.

Speaking for the Animals, or the Terrorists?

SCOTT SMALLWOOD

"History will be written about them. They will be defamed now, but they will be taught to children later. They will write storybooks about these people, like Harriet Tubman."
—Steven Best, an associate professor of philosophy at the U. of Texas at El Paso, speaking about animal-rights activists

The El Paso, Tex., suburbs stretch west, across the Rio Grande and into New Mexico. Just on the other side of the river lies this community of 2,500 people. In a gated housing development here, not far from a golf course and around the corner from a swimming pool, Steven Best lives alone—just him and his 10 cats.

He has turned one of his bedrooms into a home office. Tall bookshelves line three walls. Along another, near his computer, are posters of big cats, including a tiger and a mountain lion. Several cat beds sit on the desk.

None of this looks much like a press office for terrorists.

That is what Mr. Best has been accused of running. He is not a cat-loving professor of philosophy, some argue, but a mouthpiece for terrorists who attack university laboratories, factory farms, and pharmaceutical companies.

Mr. Best, an associate professor of philosophy at the University of Texas at El Paso, is one of the leading scholarly voices on animal rights. In the past year, though, he has taken on a role that, he believes, has gotten him into hot water in Washington and in his own department.

In December he co-founded the North American Animal Liberation Press Office, which answers questions and helps disseminate information about actions by the Animal Liberation Front. The animal-liberation group, along with another extremist group called the Earth Liberation Front, has been labeled by the Federal Bureau of Investigation as one of the most serious domestic-terrorism threats in the country.

While the groups have not killed anyone, since 1990 they have committed more than 1,200 attacks causing millions of dollars in damages, according to the FBI. Many of them have been attacks against university labs, including a raid on a Louisiana State University building in Baton Rouge in April.

The ALF has no real structure. A few people engage in a "direct action"—such as destroying computers, setting fire to a building, or "liberating" mink from fur farms—and then one or two days later they send a communiqué taking credit for the attack.

That's where Mr. Best comes in. The Animal Liberation Press Office has a fax machine in California ready to receive messages from ALF activists. After an attack, Mr. Best and three other press officers post the information on their Web site and answer reporters' questions. "We explain what the ALF is about," he says. "We interpret the nature of an action, and we explain why the action was taken."

Mr. Best balks at being labeled a "spokesman," however. That suggests a centralized organization and a hierarchy the ALF simply does not have, he says. He sees himself as a philosopher in action, a scholar who has the courage to put his theories into practice.

"I'm not in the ALF," he says, standing in his kitchen sipping coffee with soy milk. "If I were, I'd be wearing a mask, and you wouldn't know who I was. You're either above ground or you're underground, or you're a moron looking to get caught."

That may be true, says David Martosko, but it does not clear Mr. Best. Mr. Martosko, research director of the Center for Consumer Freedom, a Washington-based nonprofit organization that campaigns against the animal-rights movement, argues that groups like People for the Ethical Treatment of Animals and press officers like Mr. Best form an above-ground support system for the ALF. Mr. Martosko and other opponents maintain that Mr. Best is a spokesman for terrorists, who should not be able to use his faculty post to indoctrinate his students and offer violent extremists a dash of intellectual legitimacy.

"If a university professor were out there saying that abortion-clinic bombers had a good plan going," he says, "the university would sever the guy's tenure in a New York minute."

Friends and Enemies

In November members of the Animal Liberation Front broke into laboratories used by the University of Iowa's psychology department. They took 88 mice and 313 rats. They destroyed computers and poured acid on papers and equipment, causing about $450,000 worth of damage. In an anonymous message sent after the attacks, the perpetrators wrote: "Let this message be clear to all who victimize the innocent: We're watching. And by ax, drill, or crowbar—we're coming through your door."

The attacks sparked debate and outrage at Iowa, which was heightened two months later when a law-student group invited Mr. Best to speak at the university. Some psychology professors tried unsuccessfully to get the university's president to cancel the speech. Although the professors managed to retrieve much of their research data from the damaged computers, they were later hit with 400 unsolicited magazine subscriptions after their home addresses were posted by ALF activists.

At the Iowa speech, Mr. Best compared the Animal Liberation Front to 19th-century abolitionists, likening their "direct actions" to the Boston Tea Party. In a statement after the speech, he wrote: "Please, let's stop the hypocrisy and put our moral outrage in perspective. For every window or computer smashed in the name of animal liberation, a billion animals suffer horrendous torture and death at the hands of exploiters operating the fur farms, factory farms, slaughterhouses, rodeos, circuses, and laboratories."

In May Mr. Best's notoriety increased when he was invited to appear at a hearing of the U.S. Senate Committee on Environment and Public Works about animal- and eco-terrorism. Mr. Best declined, in part because he was scheduled to be out of the country.

But that did not keep his name from being tossed around on Capitol Hill. James M. Inhofe, a Republican from Oklahoma and chairman of the Senate committee, wondered why Mr. Best had been invited to speak at Iowa. "We cannot allow individuals and organizations to, in effect, aid and abet criminal behavior or provide comfort and support to them after the fact," he said at the hearing. "Just as we cannot allow individuals and organizations to surf in between the laws of permissible free speech and speech that incites violence when we know the goal is to inspire people to commit crimes of violence."

At the hearing, Mr. Martosko of the Center for Consumer Freedom urged Congress to investigate the ties between aboveground groups like PETA, and the ALF itself. The center, a nonprofit organization based in Washington, regularly battles animal-rights activists like PETA and gets its financial support mainly from food and restaurant companies, although it declines to identify them.

During his testimony, Mr. Martosko showed several photographs of Mr. Best. In one, the professor has his arm around Kevin Kjonaas, an activist who faces charges in New Jersey related to a campaign against a British drug-testing company. In another, Mr. Best stands next to Rodney Coronado and Gary Yourofsky, who both did time in prison for animal-liberation attacks.

"These are the guys, these are the ALF felons that Best hangs out with," says Mr. Martosko in a telephone interview. "This is his crowd."

The El Paso professor "may not have his fingerprints on a matchbook," Mr. Martosko continues, "but I think it's clear that he's trying to recruit young people." He points to an essay in which Mr. Best wrote that the movement needed to raise "an army of activists" and that the animal-liberation movement would benefit by "growing roots in academia."

Mr. Best fumes at those allegations. He calls Mr. Martosko a "vulgar McCarthy-ite" who is seeking to demonize the entire animal-rights movement. "I certainly do not recruit students into the ALF," he says. "I don't even know anyone in the ALF."

And he is proud to put his arm around men that some consider terrorists. "They are heroes of mine," he says. "History will be written about them. They will be defamed now, but they will be taught to children later. They will write storybooks about these people, like Harriet Tubman. And I respect them infinitely more than I respect a philosopher lost in abstraction."

No More Burgers

About 25 years ago, Mr. Best sat down in a White Castle restaurant in Chicago for his regular late-night fast-food fix. He had dropped out of high school a few years earlier and was working in factories and driving a truck while dreaming of a career as a jazz guitarist. At 22 he had scrapped the music fantasies and enrolled in a Chicago-area community college. After earning an associate degree in film and theater, he went south to the University of Illinois at Urbana-Champaign. On this night, at 2 A.M., he was a half-drunk undergraduate in philosophy, stopping for a double cheeseburger.

"I had an epiphany that what I was eating was the blood, the juices, the bones, the tendons, the muscles of an animal," he says. "It repulsed me, and I spit it out." Despite a few more attempts to eat fast-food burgers, he became a vegetarian and later a vegan, shunning all animal products.

At the time he was active in human-rights issues. He even sheltered illegal El Salvadoran refugees for a time. He went on to earn a master's degree in philosophy from the University of Chicago and a doctorate from the University of Texas at Austin in 1993. That year he started his first and only faculty job, at El Paso.

He has a mop of reddish-brown hair and dresses casually. At 49, he looks youthful despite the few spots of gray in his goatee. He describes himself as a philosophical bachelor who wants to preserve his autonomy by staying away from marriage. Maybe, he says, that's why he gets along with the cats: they all prefer a little isolation. All 10 of them were rescued by Mr. Best—some caught in alleys, some delivered as tiny kittens in a paper sack. That's how Shag and Willis arrived. They each fit into the palm of his hand and had to be bottle fed. Willis, with his "infinitely deep eyes," still sucks on Mr. Best's finger. Slim Shady, the newest addition, is young and aggressive. Chairman Meow, a longhaired Himalayan, is the loudest and the friendliest around strangers.

When talking about his cats, he does not look like the stubborn philosophy professor whom one colleague at El Paso describes as "very acerbic." Another calls him simply "angry." No one doubts his passion about animals, though.

For him, the campaign for animals' rights is the modern abolition movement. Expanding the notion of rights to include animals—just as it was expanded in centuries past to include women and blacks—is the next evolutionary step in man's moral progress, he says. And years from now, Mr. Best argues, people will look back on the way humans currently treat animals the way we now look at slavery.

Most of us focus on the differences between humans and animals, he says, but they are outweighed by the similarities. "We can say that we can build spaceships and they can't," he says. "We can write algebraic equations and they can't. Therefore, we must be better." But that doesn't make any sense to him.

"They know the difference between pleasure and pain," he says of animals. "They can experience a life of happiness and joy or a life of suffering and misery. If they can suffer like us, then they have a right to live a life free of suffering."

For him, and many in the animal-rights movement, the key is sentience. "That's why I'm not engaged in an act of cruelty right now," he says as he stands at his kitchen counter eating a pear. "That's why there is no Pear Liberation Front—because this does not have a brain, this does not have a nervous system. It cannot feel pain."

In El Paso Mr. Best has his own talk-radio show; he serves as vice president of a local vegetarian group; and he led a lobbying effort to get Sissy the elephant, who had been videotaped being beaten by an El Paso zookeeper, sent to a sanctuary in Tennessee. But Mr. Best staunchly maintains that he has never participated in any ALF action. He says he has never dressed up in black at night and broken into a mink farm or released animals from a university lab. That's not to say that he hasn't been arrested a few times.

In the 1990s, he participated in a PETA campaign against Wendy's restaurants. He walked through a waiting phalanx of police officers to the front of the restaurant, jumped on top of the counter, and loudly declared: "This store is closed for cruelty."

"The point," he says, "was not to have people right then and there stop eating their hamburgers. It was for them to think about the issues." He was taken down, handcuffed, and tossed into jail for the rest of the day. "For me this is philosophy in action. This is taking a stand for what you believe in."

Guilt by Association?

That's just what Rodney Coronado admires in Mr. Best. Mr. Coronado, one of the best-known ALF members, spent nearly five years in prison in the 1990s for an arson at a mink-research laboratory at Michigan State University. Now a regular on the animal-rights speaking circuit, Mr. Coronado says he is no longer a member of the animal-liberation group.

"Steve is true blue," he says. "A lot of professors are just chasing recognition and capitalizing on the latest social movement. He's not like that."

Mr. Best has always supported him and other animal-rights activists, Mr. Coronado says. "He kicks in $100 when we need it, and he always buys guys like me dinner because he knows we're broke."

But that should not make Mr. Best or other academics who support animal rights into de facto members of a terrorist organization, he says. "You can call me whatever you want, but these other people are professors," Mr. Coronado says. "That should be protected, sacred ground."

Nevertheless, having convicted arsonists as friends raises eyebrows. Brian O'Connor is a retired professor of anatomy and cell biology at the Indiana University School of Medicine. He worked with dogs in his research on the nervous system and always feared that he would be the victim of an ALF attack. That never came, but in his retirement he has become an expert on the movement and keeps tabs on developments through his blog, Animal Crackers. He says he agrees with the Center for Consumer Freedom that the best way to stop the ALF and people like Mr. Coronado and Mr. Best "is to attack them and reveal them for what they really are."

He is determined to expose what he believes is the incoherence of the animal-rights argument. Mr. Best is a "total ideologue," he says. "He's being very rational in living the AR philosophy." But that philosophy is flawed, Mr. O'Connor says. "If you honestly believe that each life is of equal value, then my dog's life has the same value as my wife's life."

That would mean, say opponents of Mr. Best like Mr. Martosko, that humans should stop using animals in medical research, a move that would have prevented the development of various lifesaving treatments, such as the polio vaccine.

"If you're talking about rights, then you have to be arbitrary about where you draw the line," says Mr. O'Connor. "Why sentience? Why not just being a human being?" Human beings are making that distinction, he says, and it can be pursued to strange extremes. "You can bestow rights to rocks. Or say that rivers have rights not to be desecrated. Why should we buy into their assumptions?"

Ousted

Since starting the animal-liberation press office and taking a higher profile role in defending the Animal Liberation Front, Mr. Best has lost his post as chairman of the philosophy department at El Paso. He maintains that the two things are inextricably linked. Others at the university, including Mr. Best's dean, say there is no connection.

This much is clear: The six other members of the philosophy department voted unanimously in March to recommend to their dean that Mr. Best be removed as chairman, a position he had held for four years.

Mr. Best calls that decision an ambush. He says that while he may not have been the perfect chairman, his colleagues never told him they had problems with him. After the vote, he says, students in the department told him that they heard other professors saying, "If we don't get rid of Best, we're going to have another Ward Churchill on our hands," referring to the controversial University of Colorado at Boulder professor.

But philosophy professors at El Paso say their decision had nothing to do with Mr. Best's activism. "We were extremely unsatisfied with his performance as chairman," says John Symons, an assistant professor. "From our perspective, this has nothing do with his politics. It was a matter of running the practical affairs of the department."

At the same time, Mr. Symons defends his colleague's activism. "Steve is a passionate defender of the Animal Liberation

Front," he says. "But he is by no means a recruiter for the Animal Liberation Front."

Howard C. Daudistel, dean of liberal arts at El Paso, says the change in leadership in the philosophy department was solely about administrative issues. "Our position is that Dr. Best, just as any faculty member, has a right to express his views and engage in a discourse off campus or in any setting, as long as he is not representing himself as speaking for the institution," he says.

The dean also says he spoke to Mr. Best about the charge that he was recruiting students to the ALF. "There's no evidence that he has used the classroom to recruit students to take part in any actions," Mr. Daudistel says.

Adrian Paredes, a student of Mr. Best's, says the entire notion is absurd. "The ALF isn't some big group," he says. "It's not an organization you could join. How could you even recruit for that? That's just crazy."

Mr. Best displays a dark sense of humor amid the criticism. As he sits in his living room, defending his activism and talking about his heroes within the animal-rights struggle, yet another cat—a slender black-and-white one named Gadget—strolls into the room.

"He's incredibly sweet," the professor says. "But he likes to start fights. He terrorizes the other cats." Gadget meows at the sliding-glass door, and Mr. Best lets him into the backyard. "That's why I call him Osama bin Gadget."

From *The Chronicle of Higher Education,* by Scott Smallwood, August 5, 2005. Copyright © 2005 by The Chronicle of Higher Education. Reproduced with permission. This article may not be published, reposted, or redistributed without the express permission of The Chronicle of Higher Education.

Article 21

José Padilla and the War on Rights

JENNY S. MARTINEZ

On June 9, 2002, an American citizen named José Padilla disappeared into a legal black hole. The government says he is a dangerous terrorist, but they have never charged him with a crime. For the nearly two years since he was arrested at Chicago O'Hare Airport, Mr. Padilla has been held without trial in solitary confinement in a military brig. Now the Supreme Court's decisions restricting the government's power to detain "enemy combatants" in the "war on terror" may finally have brought him back into the light. Mr. Padilla will get his day in court. But Mr. Padilla's saga remains a cautionary tale for all Americans concerned about preserving the liberty for which our ancestors fought and died, and which our troops overseas defend today.

I am one of Mr. Padilla's lawyers, but I have never met him. All I have seen of him is the same menacing picture that you have, the one that appears in every newspaper article about his case. I remember the first time I saw that picture, which was accompanied by a headline announcing that by arresting Mr. Padilla, the government had foiled a plot to set off a "dirty" radiological bomb, possibly in Washington, D.C. I was relieved to hear that this alleged plot had been thwarted. The Washington suburb of Arlington, Virginia, is my hometown, and I watched the smoking Pentagon from my office rooftop on the morning of September 11 and worried that my best friend's younger brother, a volunteer firefighter in Northern Virginia, might be in danger there. My mother was on an airplane to New York that morning, and until I got her cell phone call telling me she was safe, I was sick with fear. Even six months later, the threat of terrorism felt very personal to me.

I assumed that Mr. Padilla would be charged with a crime, that in the time-honored way he would be given his day in court, and that if the jury found him guilty, he would be locked up for a very, very long time. But that was not what happened.

Instead of charging Mr. Padilla with a crime, the president declared him an "enemy combatant." Some people think that Congress gave the president the power to imprison people as "enemy combatants" in the PATRIOT Act, but that law says nothing at all about such detentions. In fact, the term "enemy combatant" does not appear in any statute passed by Congress, nor in any regulation, nor in any international treaty. Searching for additional powers following September 11, the government plucked the term from *Ex parte Quirin,* a World War II–era Supreme Court decision upholding the government's right to put Nazi soldiers (whom the Court described as "enemy combatants") on trial in military commissions rather than in civilian courts. From this narrow decision, the government extrapolated that the president could hold anyone he decided was an "enemy combatant," without any real review by the courts, until the end of the "war on terror." This theory was novel, to say the least. While the government has captured and detained prisoners of war on the field of battle in many past wars, never before has it claimed the power to designate American citizens, arrested in civilian settings, as "enemies of the state" who can be held forever at the whim of the president.

It was only once the government took away all of Mr. Padilla's constitutional rights that I became involved in his case. For it seemed to me that if they could take away his rights, they could take away the rights of anyone. And that scared me more than the threat of another terrorist attack.

I am an international human rights lawyer. I do work in places like Bosnia and Rwanda, where tens or hundreds of thousands of people were killed because they were in the wrong ethnic group. I study countries like Chile, where thousands of people disappeared off the streets, never to be seen again, because they disagreed with the government. The reason I decided after law school to focus on international human rights rather than problems closer to home was that it seemed from where I stood that America was doing all right. We had some very ugly incidents in our past—slavery and segregation, the Japanese internment camps, and the displacement and slaughter of Native Americans for starters. Even today, not everyone in America is getting a fair shake. But we were founded on a set of ideals—liberty, equality and democracy— that ignited a fire of freedom worldwide. America was learning from its mistakes, and our current human rights problems seemed to pale in comparison to those in other countries.

I was shocked by the Padilla case. A system in which the government is allowed to lock up anyone it decides is an "enemy" without any trial or even the pretense of legal process seemed to me, frankly, like the kind of thing that happens in the messed-up third-world countries I spend most of my time thinking about, not what I expected out of America. And so, after following the case in the newspapers for a few months, I eventually volunteered to write an amicus, or "friend of the court," brief for the retired federal judges supporting Mr. Padilla's right to have his day in court. Amicus briefs are often filed by nonprofit activist groups like the ACLU, but it was highly unusual to have a distinguished group of retired judges (both Democrats and Republicans) weighing in with such a brief. As it turned out, they were not alone. By the time we got to the Supreme Court, there were dozens of briefs filed in Mr. Padilla's case and the cases of the other enemy combatants, by everyone from retired judges and law enforcement officials to former prisoners of war to Fred Korematsu, a Japanese American who was interned in World War II and whose name has become synonymous with the case he lost in the Supreme Court in 1944, one of the most disgraceful moments in the Supreme Court's history.

By the time I became involved in the case, Mr. Padilla had already been in jail for almost a year. He was initially arrested returning to the U.S. at Chicago O'Hare Airport on May 8, 2002, by civilian law enforcement agents. He was arrested pursuant to something called a material witness warrant, which allows an individual to be held so that he or she can give testimony in court or, in Mr. Padilla's case, before a grand jury. The warrant had been issued by a judge in the Southern District of New York, the federal court that sits in Lower Manhattan. Mr. Padilla was transported by the government from Chicago to New York. Upon his arrival, the court there appointed a lawyer to represent him in the material witness proceedings, Donna Newman. Ms. Newman is a criminal defense attorney in private practice, and it happened to be one of the few days a year she takes court-appointed indigent clients. Little did she know what she was getting into.

Ms. Newman met with Mr. Padilla several times at the Metropolitan Correctional Center, where he was being held, and filed papers with the court seeking his release. A hearing was scheduled for Tuesday, June 11, 2002. Two days before that hearing, Ms. Newman got a call from a young lawyer in the U.S. Attorney's office who was working on the case. He told her that the hearing was off. The president had declared her client an "enemy combatant" and the military had taken him away. At first, Ms. Newman thought the lawyer was joking with her. As the truth dawned on her, she was shocked.

At the time scheduled for the hearing, Ms. Newman appeared in court and filed a petition for a writ of habeas corpus, seeking Mr. Padilla's release. Ms. Newman sat alone at her table in the courtroom, without even a client next to her. She had heard on television that her client had been taken to a military brig in South Carolina. As she looked at the swarm of high-ranking government lawyers across the room, she realized she needed help. The judge quickly appointed as cocounsel Andrew Patel, another local defense attorney who had worked on some high-profile terrorism cases.

Ms. Newman and Mr. Patel quickly plunged into a world of arcane legal precedents. It seemed obvious to them from grade school civics class that in America, the government was not allowed to lock someone up forever without giving him a lawyer and a trial, but the government's case had a perverse, airtight logic to it: Mr. Padilla had no constitutional right to challenge his designation as a prisoner-of-war-like "enemy combatant" because enemy combatants have no constitutional rights. The government's argument was circular but maddeningly slippery. Newman and Patel found themselves reading cases about the writ of habeas corpus from England in the 1600s, cases from the 1800s involving swashbuckling seizures of ships as prizes of war on the high seas, and obscure treatises on the Geneva Conventions and other laws of war.

Throughout this time, the government refused to let Ms. Newman and Mr. Patel communicate with their client in any way. The government chillingly explained that allowing Mr. Padilla to learn that a court was hearing his case might give him hope that he would some day be released: "Only after such time as Padilla has perceived that help is not on the way can the United States reasonably expect to obtain all possible intelligence information from Padilla. . . . Providing him access to counsel now . . . would break—probably irreparably—the sense of dependency and trust that the interrogators are attempting to create." In court, the government claimed that they had the power to imprison Mr. Padilla until the "war on terror" was over, and the court had no power to intervene other than to make sure that there was "some evidence" to support the government's decision. The "some evidence" the government pointed to was a written affidavit from a midlevel Pentagon official, who recounted information reportedly given to the government by unnamed confidential sources. The affidavit alleged that Padilla was part of a plot to build and detonate a dirty bomb in the United States but acknowledged that the plot was "still in the initial planning stages" and "there was no specific time set for the operation to occur." (Deputy Secretary of Defense Paul Wolfowitz later stated publicly that "I don't think there was actually a plot beyond some fairly loose talk and his coming in here obviously to plan further deeds.")[1] The government admitted that the information provided by its confidential sources "may be part of an effort to mislead or confuse U.S. officials" and that one of the sources "recanted some of the information that he had provided." (Later press reports indicated that one of the confidential sources had given up Padilla's name while being subjected to "water-boarding," a form of torture in which the suspect is held down in a tub and made to think he will drown.) The government argued that the district court had no power to question the information in the affidavit and no authority to allow Mr. Padilla to come into the court to tell his side of the story. In effect, the government argued, the court's power was limited to rubber-stamping the government's decision to detain Padilla.

Rejecting the government's Orwellian logic, in December 2002, the district court held that even under the lax "some evidence" standard, Padilla was entitled to present his side of the case in court, and ordered that Padilla be allowed to meet with his lawyers. The district court agreed, however, that the government had the power to hold an American citizen arrested on American soil as an "enemy combatant." Seeking to avoid even the minimal challenge to its authority posed by the district court's ruling, the government took an immediate appeal to the federal circuit court in New York.

It was at this point that I became involved in the case, filing my brief on behalf of the retired federal judges. Although I started out as an amicus, as the case progressed, I began working more and more closely with Ms. Newman and Mr. Patel. Not only had I read all the same obscure cases and treatises they had, I had actually read even more because of my background working on war crimes issues for the United Nations International Criminal Tribunal for the Former Yugoslavia in the Hague. I had the distinction of actually having owned a copy of the Geneva Conventions prior to September 11, 2001, a rare thing among U.S. lawyers. By the time the U.S. Court of Appeals for the Second Circuit heard the case in November 2003, Ms. Newman and Mr. Patel decided to let me share some of the argument time as an amicus.

A month after the argument, the court issued a ruling in our favor. Going even further than the district court, the court of appeals held that the government lacked authority to hold a U.S. citizen seized in the U.S. as an "enemy combatant." Congress had not given the president such extraordinary power, and the president had no inherent power to deprive citizens of liberty in this way, the court held. The court rejected the government's reading of *Ex parte Quirin,* the lynchpin of its case, noting that it had involved the congressionally authorized trial by military commission (with lawyers and full opportunity for the defense to be heard) of admitted soldiers in the German army. The case provided no support for the unilateral presidential detention without trial of an individual who denied that he was a soldier at all. Mr. Padilla had to be charged with a crime or released in thirty days, the court ordered.

Again, the government quickly appealed. Once the case reached the Supreme Court, Ms. Newman and Mr. Patel (casting a wary eye at the ever-growing crowd of government lawyers across the courtroom) decided to ask me to stop being a mere friend of the court and join the core legal team for Mr. Padilla. I accepted. Jonathan Freiman, an appellate lawyer from Connecticut and part-time instructor at Yale who had written an amicus brief in the court of appeals for a broad spectrum of groups (including the conservative CATO and Rutherford Institutes), also came on board, as did David DeBruin, a top partner at Jenner & Block, a leading Supreme Court litigation firm in Washington, D.C.

Shortly before the first round of briefs were due in the Supreme Court, the government finally decided, out of the goodness of its heart and without acknowledging that he had any right to counsel, that Mr. Padilla could finally speak to his lawyers. Ms. Newman and Mr. Patel had put in for the necessary security clearances back in December 2002, when the district judge had ordered access. They were finally allowed to go visit him in March 2004, but under the strict rules imposed by the military, they were not allowed to say or ask much—and they were not allowed to tell the court or the rest of the legal team, let alone the rest of the world, what Mr. Padilla had said. All they could really tell us was that after two years of incommunicado interrogation, Mr. Padilla was apparently very glad to see them.

The case was argued before the Supreme Court on April 28, 2004, on the same day as the case of Yaser Hamdi, an American citizen seized in Afghanistan and also held as an "enemy combatant," and one week after the case concerning the Guantánamo detainees. Although any member of the team could have done the honors, in the end, I ended up making the oral presentation for Mr. Padilla to the high court.

The night after the case was argued in the Supreme Court, CBS broadcast the first photos of Abu Ghraib prison. That very morning, the government's lawyer had responded to questions from the justices about torture by explaining that our government didn't do that sort of thing. In the days that followed, more photos leaked, followed by memos justifying the potential abuse of detainees that were full of legal reasoning as contorted as the bodies in the photos.

After several weeks of this bad news, the government finally won more favorable headlines when the Justice Department held a press conference at which they finally revealed the "evidence" against Mr. Padilla—evidence that they had claimed for months would endanger national security if shared with a federal judge. Mr. Padilla, the government now claimed, had not really planned to set off a dirty bomb, but rather to blow up apartment buildings with natural gas. The government had his confession to this scheme now after months of interrogation,[2] and it was a good thing he had not been given his constitutional rights or he might have gotten off. The government was not trying to influence the Supreme Court, the government lawyers explained, but rather the court of public opinion. Mr. Padilla, still locked away in solitary, had no chance to hear about or respond to the only trial the government had seen fit to give him so far, this trial in the court of public opinion. A good friend of mine who lives in a high-rise in New York City told me at a picnic that she had supported my work on the case until she learned my client might have plotted to blow up apartment buildings like hers; that had hit a little too close to home, and she was no longer sure he ought to have constitutional rights. She was only partly joking.

Two months later, on June 28, 2002, the Supreme Court issued decisions in the three cases—the Guantánamo case (*Rasul v. Bush*), *Hamdi v. Rumsfeld,* and *Rumsfeld v. Padilla.* The Court ruled in favor of the detainees in *Rasul* and *Hamdi* but bounced *Padilla* on a technicality. In *Rasul,* the Court held by a vote of six to three that the U.S. federal courts have jurisdiction to entertain habeas petitions from prisoners at Guantánamo, sending the case back to the lower courts to determine what precisely the rights of the prisoners were.

The Court's decision in *Hamdi* was equally a defeat for the government but more confusing in the details. Only one member of the Court, Justice Thomas, agreed with the government's position. Four justices thought the government had no authority at all to hold a U.S. citizen, even one seized on an overseas battlefield, as an "enemy combatant." Leading the charge for this group was Justice Scalia, the Court's most conservative justice, who explained that the government's actions ran contrary to several hundred years of Anglo-American legal tradition beginning with the Magna Carta. Unless Congress suspended the writ of habeas corpus (a grave action the Constitution allows to be taken only in cases of "Rebellion" or "Invasion"), the government's only constitutional option was to charge Mr. Hamdi with a crime or release him. Justice Stevens, the Court's most liberal member, joined Justice Scalia. Justices Souter and Ginsburg reached the same conclusion about the government's lack of authority but relied mainly on a statute (passed in the 1970s to prevent recurrence of the Japanese internment camps) that provided that "[n]o citizen shall be imprisoned or otherwise detained by the United States except pursuant to an Act of Congress." Since no act of Congress expressly allowed the detention of U.S. citizens as enemy combatants, these justices reasoned, Mr. Hamdi could not be imprisoned without criminal charges.

The other four justices, in an opinion written by Justice O'Connor, found that the government had authority to hold people who were "part of or supporting forces hostile to the United States or coalition partners" in Afghanistan and "who engaged in an armed conflict against the United States there." But they also held that an individual like Mr. Hamdi—who, although he was apprehended in Afghanistan, claimed that he was not engaged in armed conflict against the U.S.—was entitled to access to counsel and a meaningful hearing at which he could present his side of the story and challenge the government's evidence.

Although the *Hamdi* decision set the floor in terms of the rights of U.S. citizens to have access to counsel and a fair hearing on their status, it left open the question whether the government had any authority at all to detain as "enemy combatants" citizens who were not captured on the battlefields of Afghanistan. Did the government have the authority to detain U.S. citizens arrested in the U.S. as "enemy combatants"? Justice O'Connor's opinion in *Hamdi* was careful not to say, noting that the Court's finding of authority to detain fighters in Afghanistan was premised on a reading of the law based on traditional warfare. "If the practical circumstances of a given conflict are entirely unlike those of the conflicts that informed the development of the law of war, that understanding may unravel." Detainees nabbed in the broader "war on terror"—a conflict that takes place everywhere, all the time, in which anyone walking down the street may be a combatant and which may last forever (in short, a conflict whose practical circumstances are entirely unlike traditional warfare)—were implicitly left for another day.

The Supreme Court dismissed the case presenting that very question—Mr. Padilla's case—on a technical issue of court procedure. The lower courts had all found that the case had been properly filed in New York—which was hardly surprising, given that the government had initially brought Mr. Padilla to New York and then whisked him away in the middle of the night just before his court hearing there. But the Supreme Court disagreed. The Court held that the only proper defendant for the suit was the commander of the brig where Mr. Padilla was currently imprisoned in South Carolina, rather than Secretary of Defense Donald Rumsfeld, to whose custody the presidential order had entrusted Padilla. Thus, the Court found, the suit could be brought only in South Carolina, and not in New York. After two years, Mr. Padilla must wait a little longer for his day in court. Four justices dissented, arguing that the Court should reach the merits as soon as possible, for "[a]t stake in this case is nothing less than the essence of a free society."

Within days, Mr. Padilla's petition was refiled in South Carolina. At a minimum, he will receive the hearing that the Supreme Court's decision in *Hamdi* guarantees. It is still possible—indeed probable—that the Supreme Court will rule that there is no authority to detain persons arrested in the U.S. as "enemy combatants." But the litigation will take several months more to reach the Supreme Court again, probably not until after this fall's election.

As for me, I still haven't met my client. Perhaps this delay will allow me time to get a security clearance so I can finally see him. As I have worked on this case, I have often thought of Attorney General John Ashcroft's menacing warning to civil libertarians: "To those who scare peace-loving people with phantoms of lost liberty, my message is this: Your tactics only aid terrorists, for they erode our national unity and diminish our resolve. They give ammunition to America's enemies and pause to America's friends."[3] I take that more or less personally.

To those like Mr. Ashcroft who would scare liberty-loving people with phantoms of lost security, *my* message is this: Your tactics only aid terrorists, for they erode our national unity and diminish our resolve. They give ammunition to America's enemies and pause to America's friends. No one who watched the attacks on September 11 can deny that terrorism represents a grave threat to American security, but winning the war on terror also requires that we remain true to our ideals. Guantánamo, the photos of Abu Ghraib, the image of America as a nation above the law—none of these things has helped us in the fight against terror. Moreover, the government's argument—that we must sacrifice human rights for security—presents a false choice. There is a balance to be struck, but it is far more nuanced than the current government recognizes.

Take the issue of detention. Many other democratic nations confronted with terrorist threats have enacted special measures for some kind of administrative detention of terrorists.[4] These nations include the U.K.,[5] Israel,[6] and Spain.[7] The administrative detention practices of many of these countries have been criticized by human rights activists, and many of these criticisms are legitimate, but it is notable that they all provide greater protection for human rights than does current U.S. practice with respect to so-called "enemy combatants." First, these other nations have passed actual legislation authorizing detention of suspected terrorists. By contrast, the U.S. has relied on presidential fiat. Second, the laws of our democratic allies provide for access to counsel and judicial review of detention within a matter of hours or days—not months or years. In the U.K., for example, terrorism detainees are entitled to counsel and judicial review as soon as "reasonably practicable," and in any event no later than 48 hours.[8] Detainees in Israel are entitled to see a judge within 48 hours.[9] In Spain, they are entitled to counsel and to be brought before a judge within 120 hours.[10] And so on. Third, most of these laws provide for time limits on detention. The U.K.'s 2000 and 2001 antiterrorism laws allow the government to hold citizen detainees in administrative detention for only 48 hours, with extension to seven days possible only with a judge's approval.[11] Spanish detainees must be charged within 72 hours, which can be extended by another 48 hours only by a judge.[12] Even where detention is indefinite, regular judicial review is required. Israel's 2002 Incarceration of Unlawful Combatants Law, for example, requires that a district court judge review the status of each detainee every six months to determine if the captive is still a threat to state security or if there are other circumstances that justify release.[13]

Moreover, overseas courts have stepped in to guarantee detainees' rights above and beyond those provided by legislation. In *Marab v. IDF Commander in the West Bank,* for example, the Israeli Supreme Court invalidated a military order that allowed investigative detention of Palestinians in the West Bank for 12 days without a judicial hearing. Rejecting the government's claim that security necessitated the delay, the Court held that "this approach is in conflict with the fundamentals of both international and Israeli law," which view "judicial review of detention proceedings essential for the protection of individual liberty."[14] Instead, the Court held, the detainee must be brought before a judge as promptly as possible.[15] Similarly, in invalidating Turkey's detention of suspected terrorists for more than 14 days without access to counsel or court, the European Court of Human Rights explained that although "the investigation of terrorist offences undoubtedly presents the authorities with special problems, it cannot accept that it is necessary to hold a suspect for fourteen days without judicial intervention."[16]

These examples show that detention of individuals for more than two years without access to counsel or a hearing before a neutral judge is well beyond the bounds of what civilized countries allow nowadays, even when fighting terrorism. Moreover, it is fundamentally contrary to American values. As the U.S. Supreme Court wrote in a case involving First Amendment rights during the Cold War,

> Implicit in the term "national defense" is the notion of defending those values and ideals which set this Nation apart.... It would indeed be ironic if, in the name of national defense, we would sanction the subversion of one of those liberties—the freedom of association—which makes the defense of the Nation worthwhile.[17]

The Israeli Supreme Court expressed a similar view in its decision banning torture and other cruel, inhuman, or degrading treatment in interrogation:

> This is the destiny of democracy, as not all means are acceptable to it, and not all practices employed by its enemies are open before it. Although a democracy must often fight with one hand tied behind its back, it nonetheless has the upper hand. Preserving the Rule of Law and recognition of an individual's liberty constitutes an important component in its understanding of security. At the end of the day, they strengthen its spirit and its strength and allow it to overcome its difficulties.[18]

The U.S. Supreme Court has come to the rescue of liberty for now, upholding the rule of law in the first round of "war on terror" cases, but in the end it is the American people that must defend our Constitution by making our views known. As Judge Learned Hand said, "Liberty lies in the hearts of men and women; when it dies there, no constitution, no law, no court can save it."[19] That perhaps is what democracy is all about. We alone can ensure that the "war on terror" does not become a "war on rights."

Notes

1. Http://usinfo.state.gov/topical/pol/terror/ 02061103.htm.
2. The government acknowledged in a footnote to its press release that Mr. Padilla continued to deny that he had actually planned to engage in any terrorist acts.
3. Testimony of Attorney General John Ashcroft before the Senate Judiciary Committee (Dec. 6, 2001).
4. Two excellent sources on comparative detention practices are Stephen J. Schulhofer, *Checks and Balances in Wartime,* 102 Mich. L. Rev. 1501 (forthcoming 2004), and *Brief Amicus Curiae of Comparative Law Scholars and Experts on the Laws of the United Kingdom and Israel in Support of Respondent, Rumsfeld v. Padilla,* No. 03-1027 (2004). This section draws particularly on the latter.
5. Terrorism Act, 2000, c.11, para. 41, sched. 8 (Eng.) and Anti-Terrorism, Crime and Security Act, 2001, c. 24, pt. 4 (Eng.) [hereinafter U.K. Act].
6. Emergency Powers (Detention) Law, 1979, 33 L.S. I. 89 (1978–79) (Isr.), and Incarceration of Unlawful Combatants Law, 2002 (Isr.), at www.Justice.gov.il/NR/rdonlyres/ 8459847C-84FD-956D-0F2CB10C948A/0/IncarcerationLaw L.438/01 [hereinafter Israeli Detention Law and Israeli Unlawful Combatants Law].
7. Spanish Constitution art. 17(2); L.E. Crim. Art. 496.
8. U.K. Act ¶ 7.
9. Israeli Detention Law § 4(a). Separate measures apply in the occupied territories.
10. Spain art. 17.
11. U.K. Act ¶ 436. U.K. law allows for indefinite detention of some aliens, however.
12. Spanish Constitution art. 17(2); L.E. Crim. Art. 496.
13. Israeli Unlawful Combatants Law § 5.
14. Marab v. IDF Commander in the West Bank.
15. ¶ 36.

16. Askoy v. Turkey, 23 Eur. H.R. Rep. 553 ¶ 78 (1996). *See also* Advisory Opinion OC-8/87, Habeas Corpus in Emergency Situations (arts. 27(2) and 7(6) of the American Convention on Human Rights), Inter-Am Ct. H.R. (Ser. A) No. 8 ¶ 12 (Jan. 30, 1987) ("[E]ven in emergency situations, the writ of habeas corpus may not be suspended or rendered ineffective.... To hold the contrary view—that is, that the executive branch is under no obligation to give reasons for a detention and may prolong such a detention indefinitely during states of emergency, without bringing the detainee before a judge... would... be equivalent to attributing uniquely judicial functions to the executive branch, which would violate the principle of separation of powers, a basic characteristic of the rule of law and of democratic systems.").

17. United States v. Robel, 389 U.S. at 264.

18. Supreme Court of Israel: Judgment Concerning the Legality of the General Security Service's Interrogation Methods, 38 I.L.M. 1471, 1488 (1999).

19. Learned Hand, *The Spirit of Liberty* 190 (1960).

From *Virginia Quarterly Review,* Fall 2004, pp. 56–67. Copyright © 2004 by Jenny S. Martinez. Reprinted by permission of the author.

UNIT 6
Terrorism and the Media

Unit Selections
22. **A Violent Episode in the Virtual World,** John Gray
23. **Terror's Server,** David Talbot
24. **The Globe of Villages,** Feisal Mohamed
25. **Congress and the "YouTube War",** Michael A. Cohen and Maria Figueroa Küpçü

Key Points to Consider
- How do media portrayals of terrorism affect public perception?
- Why is the Internet an ideal tool for terrorist organizations?
- Can regulation of the Internet help in the war on terror?

Student Web Site
www.mhcls.com/online

Internet References
Further information regarding these Web sites may be found in this book's preface or online.

Institute for Media, Peace and Security
http://www.mediapeace.org
Terrorism Files
http://www.terrorismfiles.org
The Middle East Media Research Institute
http://www.memri.org

Department of Defense photo by Tech. Sgt. Sean M. Worrell, U.S. Air Force

The media plays an important role in contemporary international terrorism. Terrorists use the media to transmit their message and to intimidate larger populations. Since the hijackings at Dawson's field in Jordan in 1970 and the massacre at the Munich Olympics in 1972, international terrorists have managed to exploit the media and have gained access to a global audience. The media provides terrorists with an inexpensive means of publicizing their cause and a forum to attract potential supporters. In the age of independent fund raising, terrorists have become increasingly dependent on accessible media coverage.

As media coverage has become more sophisticated, terrorist organizations have become increasingly conscious of in their interactions with the press. Managing public relations, drafting press releases, and arranging interviews have become important functions, often delegated to individuals or groups in the semi-legal periphery of the organization.

The impact of the increasingly symbiotic relationship between terrorists and media has been two-fold. On the one hand the media has provided terrorists with real-time coverage and immediate 24-hour access to a global public. As long as the explosion is big enough and the devastation horrific enough and there are cameras close by, media coverage of the incident is guaranteed. Holding true to the old axiom "if it bleeds, it leads," the media seems only willing to provide terrorists with free, unlimited, and at times indiscriminate coverage of their actions.

On the other hand, the media also provides terrorists with a means of ventilation, potentially reducing the number of violent incidents. This outlet subtly influences terrorists to function within certain, albeit extended, boundaries of social norms, as grave violations of these norms may elicit unintended or unwanted public backlash and a loss of support. In light of these contradictory tendencies, the debate about media censorship or self-censorship continues.

The Internet and new media have provided terrorists with instant unfiltered access to a new audience. Terrorists are becoming increasingly less dependent on traditional, or "big" media. As the "You Tube" generation engages in political discourse, the terrorists' use of this medium will continue to grow.

The articles in this unit explore the relationship between terrorism and the media. John Gray examines how media portrayals of terrorist acts can shape reality. He argues that through the media, each terrorist incident becomes a problem of the global community. David Talbot explores the extent to which tighter security and regulation of Internet content could aid the war on terror. Next, Feisal Mohamed discusses the role of the Internet in disseminating radical Islamic ideas. He argues that the medium of dissemination is as important as the content of the messages. Finally, Cohen and Küpçü argue that the rise of stateless enemies and Internet organization heralds a new type of war. They argue that the U.S. Congress needs to implement legislation to address this change in warfare.

A Violent Episode in the Virtual World

Terror and the UK—the media's globalisation of terror makes us feel part of a worldwide community facing a common problem, but this is a dangerous illusion.

JOHN GRAY

For those directly affected by them, the London bombings will always be an unalterable reality—an event, barely comprehensible in its pain and horror, with which they will struggle to come to terms for the remainder of their lives. For all the rest of us—the hundreds of millions or billions of people who watched the same images of bloodied commuters and cordoned-off Tube stations—the bombings are an episode in the virtual world that is being continuously manufactured by the media. In this simulated environment we can feel part of a global community facing a common problem. We are able to imagine that terror could be banished from our lives, as all the world's peoples and their leaders act in solidarity against a universal evil.

These sentiments are humane and generous, but they can easily turn into a sort of moral narcissism that willingly colludes in the deceptions of our leaders. The politicians who gathered at Gleneagles spoke as if the world could be reshaped by their good intentions. The truth is that they were deeply divided in what they wanted, and the world is not so simple or so malleable. Like almost every gathering of global leaders at the present time, Gleneagles was a media event before it was anything else.

The trouble with the omnipresence of the media in politics is that it tends to blur the distinction between reality and appearance. The causes of human action are obscure, and the course of events at times indecipherable; a central task of the media is to contrive a coherent narrative from this chaos. In doing so, they can end up shaping reality—but not in a manner that anyone intended or predicted. For example, there may no longer be anything resembling a globally organised terrorist network, but by instantaneously disseminating the same images of carnage and panic throughout the world, the media have globalised our perception of terror. Governments behave as if this media apparition were an actual entity, with the result that the policies that are adopted in order to resist terrorism are ineffective and sometimes disastrously counter-productive.

Western military intervention in Afghanistan practically destroyed al-Qaeda as an effective force. With its training camps in ruins and its leadership in hiding, the structure of the network fragmented and its capacity for action was correspondingly diminished. The effect of the war in Iraq has been to revivify al-Qaeda, but in a new and possibly more dangerous form. It has become an idea or a cause that can be taken up by anyone, and if the fluid and shifting groups of which it is at present composed appear to act in a concerted fashion, it may be by responding to media reports of each other's activities rather than by any kind of direct, systematic co-ordination. Their goal is to shift the public mood, and they attempt to do this by acts of spectacular violence that are transmitted worldwide via television. The type of terrorism that London suffered on 7 July may well have evolved as a by-product of the global media.

The development of terrorism illustrates a complex feedback Between the virtual world constructed by the media and the actual course of history. Al-Qaeda is now very largely an artefact of the communication industry—but it is also real, with a demonstrated capacity for mass murder. This is a development that exemplifies both the power of the media and the fragility of that power. The war in Iraq was launched on the basis of deceptive claims about Saddam Hussein's links with the attacks of 11 September 2001, and the self-deluding belief that the US would be accepted as a liberator of the Iraqi people. These fantasies have been demolished by events, and no amount of news management has been able to mask the scale and ferocity of the insurgency against the occupying forces. There are well-founded reports that US forces have been in talks with rebel commanders, and leaks from British sources suggesting that troop withdrawal is now on the agenda. Reality has smashed through the media constructions. At the same time, Tony Blair and George W Bush continue to try to use media jamborees such as the G8 meeting to demonstrate a solidarity in the face of terror that masks profound disagreement between the US administration and the governments of nearly every other country about how best to respond to it.

There is a tendency among some media analysts to talk as if the global communications industry actually moulds the pattern of events. For them the world is what appears in the media, and there is no difference between perception and reality. Certainly many politicians have come to subscribe to a version of this postmodern philosophy—Blair foremost among them. Yet the world is not in the end a human construction, and this is nowhere clearer than in regard to the issue on which the Gleneagles meeting failed most miserably. Climate change is a physical process that goes on entirely independently of human consciousness. Whatever politicians, opinion-formers or humanity at large may think or feel, a shift in the planetary environment is taking place that will alter irreversibly the way everyone lives in future. The basis for this belief is scientific observation of measurable changes in the material world: human emotions and perceptions are irrelevant. The mix of cynical news management and moral narcissism that is the core of contemporary politics serves only to postpone a brutal encounter with reality.

However, terrorism and climate change have a common feature that helps to explain the way they are treated in the media and by politicians. Both are not wholly soluble problems. Terrorism has been greatly boosted by the Iraq war; it is as true today as it was before London was bombed that the prudent and honourable course of action for Britain is to sever its connection with the Bush administration's folly and withdraw its troops as quickly and as completely as possible. Yet while withdrawal may diminish the terrorist threat to Britain, it will not remove it—there is too much hatred loose in the world, and terrorists are not always motivated by clear strategic goals. We will always be at risk, whatever we do.

The situation is even starker with regard to climate change. The scientific consensus is that there is a great deal of global warming in the pipeline, which even the wholesale abandonment of fossil fuels—if that were possible—would not much reduce. We no longer have the option of forestalling climate change; we can only adjust to it. Adjustment may prove extremely difficult, however, and will necessarily involve alterations in our current way of life. Sensing this, politicians and the public prefer to continue the ritual of announcing targets that will not be reached and which, even if they were met, would not make much difference.

Thinkers of the left often berate the media for skirting round the truth, and some write as if there were a conspiracy to deny the facts of power and oppression. It would be more accurate to say that the media insulate the public from realities it cannot tolerate. We seem to have lost the art of living in an intractable world, so we contrive an alternate reality in which insoluble problems can be conjured away by displays of goodwill. But the problems never really go away, and we would be better off trying to think about them clearly than seeking false security in a collective dream.

JOHN GRAY is the author of *Al-Qaeda and What It Means To Be Modern* (Faber & Faber.)

From *New Statesman*, July 18, 2005. Copyright © 2005 by New Statesman, Ltd. Reprinted by permission.

Article 23

Terror's Server

**Fraud, gruesome propaganda, terror planning:
The Net enables it all. The online industry can help fix it.**

DAVID TALBOT

Two hundred two people died in the Bali, Indonesia, disco bombing of October 12, 2002, when a suicide bomber blew himself up on a tourist-bar dance floor, and then, moments later, a second bomber detonated an explosives-filled Mitsubishi van parked outside. Now, the mastermind of the attacks—Imam Samudra, a 35-year-old Islamist militant with links to al-Qaeda—has written a jailhouse memoir that offers a primer on the more sophisticated crime of online credit card fraud, which it promotes as a way for Muslim radicals to fund their activities.

Law enforcement authorities say evidence collected from Samudra's laptop computer shows he tried to finance the Bali bombing by committing acts of fraud over the Internet. And his new writings suggest that online fraud—which in 2003 cost credit card companies and banks $1.2 billion in the United States alone—might become a key weapon in terrorist arsenals, if it's not already. "We know that terrorist groups throughout the world have financed themselves through crime," says Richard Clarke, the former U.S. counterterrorism czar for President Bush and President Clinton. "There is beginning to be a reason to conclude that one of the ways they are financing themselves is through cyber-crime."

Online fraud would thereby join the other major ways in which terrorist groups exploit the Internet. The September 11 plotters are known to have used the Internet for international communications and information gathering. Hundreds of jihadist websites are used for propaganda and fund-raising purposes and are as easily accessible as the mainstream websites of major news organizations. And in 2004, the Web was awash with raw video of hostage beheadings perpetrated by followers of Abu Musabal-Zarqawi, the Jordanian-born terror leader operating in Iraq. This was no fringe phenomenon. Tens of millions of people downloaded the video files, a kind of vast medieval spectacle enabled by numberless Web hosting companies and Internet service providers, or ISPs. "I don't know where the line is. But certainly, we have passed it in the abuse of the Internet," says Gabriel Weimann, a professor of communications at the University of Haifa, who tracks use of the Internet by terrorist groups.

Meeting these myriad challenges will require new technology and, some say, stronger self-regulation by the online industry, if only to ward off the more onerous changes or restrictions that might someday be mandated by legal authorities or by the security demands of business interests. According to Vinton Cerf, a founding father of the Internet who codesigned its protocols, extreme violent content on the Net is "a terribly difficult conundrum to try and resolve in a way that is constructive." But, he adds, "it does not mean we shouldn't do anything. The industry has a fair amount of potential input, if it is to try to figure out how on earth to discipline itself. The question is, which parts of the industry can do it?" The roadblocks are myriad, he notes: information can literally come from anywhere, and even if major industry players agree to restrictions, Internet users themselves could obviously go on sharing content. "As always, the difficult question will be, Who decides what is acceptable content and on what basis?"

Some work is already going on in the broader battle against terrorist use of the Internet. Research labs are developing new algorithms aimed at making it easier for investigators to comb through e-mails and chat-room dialogue to uncover criminal plots. Meanwhile, the industry's anti-spam efforts are providing new tools for authenticating e-mail senders using cryptography and other methods, which will also help to thwart fraud; clearly, terrorist exploitation of the Internet adds a national-security dimension to these efforts. The question going forward is whether the terrorist use of the medium, and the emerging responses, will help usher in an era in which the distribution of online content is more tightly controlled and tracked, for better or worse.

The Rise of Internet Terror

Today, most experts agree that the Internet is not just a tool of terrorist organizations, but is central to their operations*. Some say that al-Qaeda's online presence has become more potent and pertinent than its actual physical presence since the September 11 attacks. "When we say al-Qaeda is a global ideology, this is where it exists on the Internet," says Michael Doran, a Near East scholar and terrorism expert at Princeton University. "That, in itself, I find absolutely amazing. Just a few years ago, an organization like this would have been more cultlike in nature. It wouldn't be able to spread around the world the way it does with the Internet."

The universe of terror-related websites extends far beyond al-Qaeda, of course. According to Weimann, the number of such websites has leapt from only 12 in 1997 to around 4,300 today. (This includes sites operated by groups like Hamas and Hezbollah, and others in South America and other parts of the world.) "In seven years it has exploded, and I am quite sure the number will grow next week and the week after," says Weimann, who described the trend in his report "How Modern Terrorism Uses the Internet," published by the United States Institute of Peace, and who is now at work on a book, *Terrorism and the Internet,* due out later this year.

These sites serve as a means to recruit members, solicit funds, and promote and spread ideology. "While the [common] perception is that [terrorists] are not well educated or very sophisticated about telecommunications or the Internet, we know that that isn't true," says Ronald Dick, a former FBI deputy assistant director who headed the FBI's National Infrastructure Protection Center. "The individuals that the FBI and other law enforcement agencies have arrested have engineering and telecommunications backgrounds; they have been trained in academic institutes as to what these capabilities are." (Militant Islam, despite its roots in puritanical Wahhabism, taps the well of Western liberal education: Khalid Sheikh Mohammed, the principal September 11 mastermind, was educated in the U.S. in mechanical engineering; Osama bin Laden's deputy Ayman al-Zawahiri was trained in Egypt as a surgeon.)

The Web gives jihad a public face. But on a less visible level, the Internet provides the means for extremist groups to surreptitiously organize attacks and gather information. The September 11 hijackers used conventional tools like chat rooms and e-mail to communicate and used the Web to gather basic information on targets, says Philip Zelikow, a historian at the University of Virginia and the former executive director of the 9/11 Commission. "The conspirators used the Internet, usually with coded messages, as an important medium for international communication," he says. (Some aspects of the terrorists' Internet use remain classified; for example, when asked whether the Internet played a role in recruitment of the hijackers, Zelikow said he could not comment.)

Finally, terrorists are learning that they can distribute images of atrocities with the help of the Web. In 2002, the Web facilitated wide dissemination of videos showing the beheading of *Wall Street Journal* reporter Daniel Pearl, despite FBI requests that websites not post them. Then, in 2004, Zarqawi made the gruesome tactic a cornerstone of his terror strategy, starting with the murder of the American civilian contractor Nicholas Berg—which law enforcement agents believe was carried out by Zarqawi himself. From Zarqawi's perspective, the campaign was a rousing success. Images of orange-clad hostages became a headline-news staple around the world— and the full, raw videos of their murders spread rapidly around the Web. "The Internet allows a small group to publicize such horrific and gruesome acts in seconds, for very little or no cost, worldwide, to huge audiences, in the most powerful way," says Weimann.

And there's a large market for such material. According to Dan Klinker, webmaster of a leading online gore site, Ogrish.com, consumption of such material is brisk. Klinker, who says he operates from offices in Western and Eastern Europe and New York City, says his aim is to "open people's eyes and make them aware of reality." It's clear that many eyes have taken in these images thanks to sites like his. Each beheading video has been downloaded from Klinker's site several million times, he says, and the Berg video tops the list at 15 million. "During certain events (beheadings, etc.) the servers can barely handle the insane bandwidths—sometimes 50,000 to 60,000 visitors an hour," Klinker says.

Avoiding the Slippery Slope

To be sure, Internet users who want to block objectionable content can purchase a variety of filtering-software products that attempt to block sexual or violent content. But they are far from perfect. And though a hodgepodge of Web page rating schemes are in various stages of implementation, no universal rating system is in effect—and none is mandated—that would make filters chosen by consumers more effective.

But passing laws aimed at allowing tighter filtering—to say nothing of actually mandating filtering—is problematical. Laws aimed at blocking minors access to pornography, like the Communications Decency Act and Childrens Online Protection Act, have been struck down in the courts on First Amendment grounds, and the same fate has befallen some state laws, often for good reason: the filtering tools sometimes throw out the good with the bad. "For better or worse, the courts are more concerned about protecting the First Amendment rights of adults than protecting children from harmful material," says Ian Ballon, an expert on cyberspace law and a partner at Manatt, Phelps, and Phillips in Palo Alto, CA. Pornography access, he says, "is something the courts have been more comfortable regulating in the physical world than on the Internet." The same challenges pertain to images of extreme violence, he adds.

The Federal Communications Commission enforces "decency" on the nation's airwaves as part of its decades-old mission of licensing and regulating television and radio stations. Internet content, by contrast, is essentially unregulated. And so, in 2004, as millions of people watched video of beheadings on their computers, the FCC fined CBS $550,000 for broadcasting the exposure of singer Janet Jacksons breast during the Super Bowl halftime show on television.

"While not flatly impossible, [Internet content] regulation is hampered by the variety of places around the world at which it can be hosted," says Jonathan Zittrain, codirector of the Berkman Center for Internet and Society at Harvard Law School—and thats to say nothing of First Amendment concerns. As Zittrain sees it, "its a gift that the sites are up there, because it gives us an opportunity for counterintelligence."

Industry adoption of tighter editorial controls would be a matter of good taste and of supporting the war on terror, says Richard Clarke.

As a deterrent, criminal prosecution has also had limited success. Even when those suspected of providing Internet-based assistance to terror cells are in the United States, obtaining convictions can be difficult. Early last year, under provisions of the Patriot Act, the U.S. Department of Justice charged Sami Omar al-Hussayen, a student at the University of Idaho, with using the Internet to aid terrorists. The government alleged that al-Hussayen maintained websites that promoted jihadist-related activities, including funding terrorists. But his defense argued that he was simply using his skills to promote Islam and wasn't responsible for the sites radical content. The judge reminded the jury that, in any case, the Constitution protects most speech. The jury cleared al-Hussayen on the terrorism charges but deadlocked on visa-related charges; al-Hussayen agreed to return home to his native Saudi Arabia rather than face a retrial on the visa counts.

Technology and ISPs

But the government and private-sector strategy for combatting terrorist use of the Internet has several facets. Certainly, agencies like the FBI and the National Security Agency—and a variety of watchdog groups, such as the Site Institute, a nonprofit organization based in an East Coast location that it asked not be publicized—closely monitor jihadist and other terrorist sites to keep abreast of their public statements and internal communications, to the extent possible.

It's a massive, needle-in-a-haystack job, but it can yield a steady stream of intelligence tidbits and warnings. For example, the Site Institute recently discovered, on a forum called the Jihadi Message Board, an Arabic translation of a U.S. Air Force Web page that mentioned an American airman of Lebanese descent. According to Rita Katz, executive director of the Site Institute, the jihadist page added, in Arabic, "This hypocrite will be going to Iraq in September of this year [2004]—I pray to Allah that his cunning leads to his slaughter. I hope that he will be slaughtered the Zarqawi's way, and then [go from there] to the lowest point in Hell." The Site Institute alerted the military. Today, on one if its office walls hangs a plaque offering the thanks of the Air Force Office of Special Investigations.

New technology may also give intelligence agencies the tools to sift through online communications and discover terrorist plots. For example, research suggests that people with nefarious intent tend to exhibit distinct patterns in their use of e-mails or online forums like chat rooms. Whereas most people establish a wide variety of contacts over time, those engaged in plotting a crime tend to keep in touch only with a very tight circle of people, says William Wallace, an operations researcher at Rensselaer Polytechnic Institute.

This phenomenon is quite predictable. "Very few groups of people communicate repeatedly only among themselves," says Wallace. "It's very rare; they don't trust people outside the group to communicate. When 80 percent of communications is within a regular group, this is where we think we will find the groups who are planning activities that are malicious." Of course, not all such groups will prove to be malicious; the odd high-school reunion will crop up. But Wallaces group is developing an algorithm that will narrow down the field of so-called social networks to those that warrant the scrutiny of intelligence officials. The algorithm is scheduled for completion and delivery to intelligence agencies this summer.

And of course, the wider fight against spam and online fraud continues apace. One of the greatest challenges facing anti-fraud forces is the ease with which con artists can doctor their e-mails so that they appear to come from known and trusted sources, such as colleagues or banks. In a scam known as "phishing," this tactic can trick recipients into revealing bank account numbers and passwords. Preventing such scams, according to Clarke, "is relevant to counterterrorism because it would prevent a lot of cyber-crime, which may be how [terrorists] are funding themselves. It may also make it difficult to assume identities for one-time-use communications."

New e-mail authentication methods may offer a line of defense. Last fall, AOL endorsed a Microsoft-designed system called Sender ID that closes certain security loopholes and matches the IP (Internet Protocol) address of the server sending

A Window on Online Fraud

In 2003, 124,509 complaints of Internet fraud and crime were made to the U.S. Internet Crime Complaint Center, an offshoot of the FBI that takes complaints largely from the United States. The perpetrators' reported home countries broke down as follows:

Rank	Country	Reports
1	United States	76.4%
2	Canada	3.3%
3	Nigeria	2.9%
4	Italy	2.5%
5	Spain	2.4%
6	Romania	1.5%
7	Germany	1.3%
8	United Kingdom	1.3%
9	South Africa	1.1%
10	Netherlands	0.9%

Source: National White Collar Crime Center and the FBI.

an inbound e-mail against a list of servers authorized to send mail from the message's purported source. Yahoo, the world's largest e-mail provider with some 40 million accounts, is now rolling out its own system, called Domain Keys, which tags each outgoing e-mail message with an encrypted signature that can be used by the recipient to verify that the message came from the purported domain. Google is using the technology with its Gmail accounts, and other big ISPs, including Earthlink, are following suit.

Finally, the bigger ISPs are stepping in with their own reactive efforts. Their "terms of service" are usually broad enough to allow them the latitude to pull down objectionable sites when asked to do so. "When you are talking about an online community, the power comes from the individual," says Mary Osako, Yahoo's director of communications. "We encourage our users to send [any concerns about questionable] content to us—and we take action on every report."

Too Little, or Too Much

But most legal, policy, and security experts agree that these efforts, taken together, still don't amount to a real solution. The new anti-spam initiatives represent only the latest phase of an ongoing battle. "The first step is, the industry has to realize there is a problem that is bigger than they want to admit," says Peter Neumann, a computer scientist at SRI International, a nonprofit research institute in Menlo Park, CA. "There's a huge culture change that's needed here to create trustworthy systems. At the moment we dont have anything I would call a trustworthy system." Even efforts to use cryptography to confirm the authenticity of e-mail senders, he says, are a mere palliative. There are still lots of problems with online security, says Neumann. "Look at it as a very large iceberg. This shaves off one-fourth of a percent, maybe 2 percent—but its a little bit off the top."

But if it's true that existing responses are insufficient to address the problem, it may also be true that we're at risk of an overreaction. If concrete links between online fraud and terrorist attacks begin emerging, governments could decide that the Internet needs more oversight and create new regulatory structures. "The ISPs could solve most of the spam and phishing problems if made to do so by the FCC," notes Clarke. Even if the Bali bombers writings don't create such a reaction, something else might. If no discovery of a strong connection between online fraud and terrorism is made, another trigger could be an actual act of "cyberterrorism"—the long-feared use of the Internet to wage digital attacks against targets like city power grids and air traffic control or communications systems. It could be some online display of homicide so appalling that it spawns a new drive for online decency, one countenanced by a newly conservative Supreme Court. Terrorism aside, the trigger could be a pure business decision, one aimed at making the Internet more transparent and more secure.

Zittrain concurs with Neumann but also predicts an impending overreaction. Terrorism or no terrorism, he sees a convergence of security, legal, and business trends that will force the Internet to change, and not necessarily for the better. "Collectively speaking, there are going to be technological changes to how the Internet functions—driven either by the law or by collective action. If you look at what they are doing about spam, it has this shape to it," Zittrain says. And while technological change might improve online security, he says, "it will make the Internet less flexible. If its no longer possible for two guys in a garage to write and distribute killer-app code without clearing it first with entrenched interests, we stand to lose the very processes that gave us the Web browser, instant messaging, Linux, and e-mail."

> **The first needed step: a culture change in the industry, to acknowledge a problem bigger than they want to admit, says Peter Neumann.**

A concerted push toward tighter controls is not yet evident. But if extremely violent content or terrorist use of the Internet might someday spur such a push, a chance for preemptive action may lie with ISPs and Web hosting companies. Their efforts need not be limited to fighting spam and fraud. With respect to the content they publish, Web hosting companies could act more like their older cousins, the television broadcasters and newspaper and magazine editors, and exercise a little editorial judgment, simply by enforcing existing terms of service.

Is Web content already subject to any such editorial judgment? Generally not, but sometimes, the hopeful eye can discern what appear to be its consequences. Consider the mysterious inconsistency among the results returned when you enter the word "beheading" into the major search engines. On Google and MSN, the top returns are a mixed bag of links to responsible news accounts, historical information, and ghoulish sites that offer raw video with teasers like "World of Death, Iraq beheading videos, death photos, suicides and crime scenes." Clearly, such results are the product of algorithms geared to finding the most popular, relevant, and well-linked sites.

But enter the same search term at Yahoo, and the top returns are profiles of the U.S. and British victims of beheading in Iraq. The first 10 results include links to biographies of Eugene Armstrong, Jack Hensley, Kenneth Bigley, Nicholas Berg, Paul Johnson, and Daniel Pearl, as well as to memorial websites. You have to load the second page of search results to find a link to Ogrish.com. Is this oddly tactful ordering the aberrant result of an algorithm as pitiless as the ones that churn up gore links elsewhere? Or is Yahoo, perhaps in a nod to the victims' memories and their families' feelings, making an exception of the words "behead" and "beheading," treating them differently than it does thematically comparable words like "killing" and "stabbing?"

Yahoo's Osako did not reply to questions about this search-return oddity; certainly, a technological explanation cannot be excluded. But it's clear that such questions are very sensitive for an industry that has, to date, enjoyed little intervention or regulation. In its response to complaints, says Richard Clarke, "the industry is very willing to cooperate and be good citizens in order to stave off regulation." Whether it goes further and adopts a stricter editorial posture, he adds, "is a decision for the ISP [and Web hosting company] to make as a matter of good taste and as a matter of supporting the U.S. in the global war on terror." If such decisions evolve into the industrywide assumption of a more journalistic role, they could, in the end, be the surest route to a more responsible medium—one that is less easy to exploit and not so vulnerable to a clampdown.

DAVID TALBOT is *Technology Review's* chief correspondent.

The Globe of Villages
Digital Media and the Rise of Homegrown Terrorism

FEISAL G. MOHAMED

We have been told that the August 2006 plot to attack several U.S.-bound flights departing from London's Heathrow Airport was hatched largely by Muslim Britons. This is becoming a familiar story. Earlier this summer, the Royal Canadian Mounted Police foiled a homegrown Toronto cell in its attempt to blow up Parliament with a fertilizer bomb similar to that used by Timothy McVeigh in the Oklahoma City bombing. The July 7, 2005, attacks on London buses and subways were carried out largely by British citizens, and this was not the first such occurrence: two Britons traveled to Tel Aviv in 2003 to conduct a suicide bombing of a nightclub that killed three and wounded sixty.

This country too has produced its share of accused or convicted jihadists. The "Lackawanna Six," all American citizens of Yemeni heritage, were arrested in 2002 for attending an al-Qaeda camp in Afghanistan—much like Hamid Hayat, a second-generation Pakistani-American, who was convicted last year, albeit on dubious evidence, for receiving jihadist training in Pakistan. Iyman Faris, an American citizen born in Kashmir, was sentenced to twenty years in prison in 2005 for participating in a plan to attack the Brooklyn Bridge. These men are joined by several other Americans who have been found guilty of providing material or logistic support to Islamist terrorists: Marwan Othman el-Hindi, Uzair Paracha, Junaid Babar, and Ali al-Timimi and his "Virginia jihadists." I say nothing of the Miami "cell" arrested in June 2006 for conspiring with al-Qaeda, whose members seemed more interested in using terrorist funds to buy a new wardrobe than in waging holy war; or of Naveed Haq, whose attack on a Jewish community center in Seattle this August killed one and injured five (it has been suggested that he acted entirely on his own and has a history of mental illness); nor am I concerned with such converts as José Padilla, Richard Reid, and the three recently arrested in connection with the attempt to explode passenger jets over the Atlantic: Don Stewart-Whyte, Brian Young, and Oliver Savant. (One wonders if these men turned to violence after converting to Islam or if they converted to Islam so that they might engage in spectacular anti-Western violence.)

As yet we have not been offered a satisfactory explanation of this political or religious zealotry. The terms by which foreign terrorism is made scrutable are quite familiar by now: faced with a lack of opportunity in the Arab world and the humiliations—real and imagined—dealt to one's coreligionists, desperate youth come to see themselves as engaged in cosmic warfare against iniquity and turn to violence. In this vein, Mohammed Atta, the ring-leader of the September 11 attacks, is held up as the paradigmatic modern terrorist. Despite his education and residence in Germany, he became hostile toward the West upon return to his native Egypt, where his world-class training as an engineer fitted him only for unemployment, and where he saw the birthplace of one of the world's great civilizations reduced to a satrapy prostrating itself before the Western tourist dollar. Such a narrative of the development of a terrorist has provided comfort in the West across the political spectrum. The conservative finds in it an irreconcilable clash of civilizations: no matter how much we give to these people they still hate us; best to have a firm hand. The liberal finds in it evidence of universal outrage over the evils of global capitalism and American foreign policy: if Western industry, and particularly big oil, had a shred of regard for the prosperity of the Arab majority, if the United States did not prop up Arab tyrants and simultaneously inflict suffering on the Palestinians and Iraqis, there would be no terrorists.

But the phenomenon of Western jihadists is harder to explain than this suggests. If religion is the explanation for terrorism—if we argue that Iran and Saudi Arabia have used their oil wealth to assure the global spread of retrograde ideas in both of Islam's major sects, so that each one now strives to outdo the other in paranoia—we still cannot entirely explain why lunatic Muslim clerics have found an audience among young men born into liberal societies. And if politics and economics are the explanation for terrorism, why is it that those who are stakeholders in affluent Western democracies feel directly involved in political struggles taking place on the other side of the planet?

The real question is, what makes the religion and politics of radical Islam seem to apply to the situation of a Muslim in London, Toronto, or Brooklyn? This is not the same as the question that is often identified as pressing: whether Muslim immigrants in the West are assimilating into the host culture.

Many immigrant communities show little regard for assimilation. Any walk through a self-respecting Chinatown, for example, will reveal a significant number of individuals making a life in the West that is culturally closer to the motherland than to their adopted home. Those who clamor for fuller assimilation of Muslims reveal their discomfort with the increasingly multicultural complexion of the West in a way only tangentially related to this particular minority group; they use terrorism as a cover for their dislike of foreign dress, beliefs, and manners. Nor can the isolation of the Muslim community—imposed from within and without—be regarded as the key motivation for violence. Isolation has always been, and ever will be, a condition of immigrant life, and there are many fewer obstacles faced by Muslims today than have been peacefully overcome by the Asian, Jewish, Irish, Italian, Mexican, Native, and African Americans who have suffered most in the long and continuing struggle to broaden this country's promise of dignity and prosperity.

Present-day conditions of immigration do seem, however, to foster an especially keen sense of unity between diaspora and kin country. The first such condition is the mobility of the modern world, which produces a constant state of traffic between East and West. Rather than arrival en masse and slow adaptation, the modern immigrant community is in a state of constant exchange with the mother country. Those who immigrate will travel home regularly; many who reside in the West will do so temporarily; this allows cultural and emotional bonds with non-Western society to remain firmly intact.

The exchange of people across East and West, however, may not be as important as it seems at first glance. Even the influence of itinerant Muslim preachers may not be as decisive as it looks. A good deal has been done, in England especially, to crack down on radical clerics; perhaps that country has learned the lesson of its seventeenth-century civil wars, fired as they were from the Puritan pulpit. But a recent survey by the Federation of Student Islamic Societies suggests that the vast majority of young British Muslims get their ideas outside of the mosque. The underground meeting and the Web site are the crucial milieus of the radical subculture.

It is the means by which ideas, rather than people, are exchanged that is the real issue, and especially the way in which modern communications make it possible to identify exclusively with one's kin country while living elsewhere.

One of the consequences of the Internet is its generation of communities of readers without geographical association. As a technology bound to the distribution of physical objects, the printed page necessarily reflects the values of a given locale. If we were still shackled to print—and I mean the cast-metal-striking-paper kind, not the ink or laser jet variety—the cost of delivering al-Qaeda propaganda to East London would be prohibitive; the lack of broad demand would make it a hopeless venture. The dissemination of ideas on the Web is not married to the local market; once one has a functioning computer and an active Internet connection, it is just as easy to access al-Jazeera as it is FoxNews. The market forces governing such access have shifted profoundly, so that where one lives is no longer an index of what one reads or thinks. This may be why a recent Pew study found that many of the most obnoxious ideas of the Arab world are alive and well in Europe: for example, 56 percent of the British Muslims surveyed claimed that Arabs did not carry out the September 11 attacks, as compared to 53 percent in Jordan, 41 percent in Pakistan, and 47 percent in Nigeria. This may also be why many young Muslims born and raised in the West are more radical in their religious views than their parents are. Greater technological savvy seems to foster, rather than to diminish, the influence of Eastern delusion.

What I am suggesting here goes beyond the now-redundant claim that the Internet has been an important means by which Islamism organizes itself. As the *Washington Post* observed in August 2005, attacks on al-Qaeda camps in Afghanistan have led to the creation of virtual training facilities. "To join the great training camps you don't have to travel to other lands," one Saudi magazine claims, "alone, in your home or with a group of your brothers, you too can begin to execute the training program." Michael Dartnell's recent book *Insurgency Online* shows how the Internet has allowed non-state actors to achieve new levels of organization and thus to exert previously unimaginable political influence. Even Michael Chertoff has emerged from the Department of Homeland Security's thick cloud of bureaucracy to shed some light on this front, claiming in a recent issue of the *Atlantic Monthly*, that "we have to look at the onset of virtual terrorism—virtual jihad—where groups radicalize themselves over the Internet."

The shortcoming of such commentary is that it commits what Marshall McLuhan described as the cardinal sin of media studies: it focuses on content rather than on the medium itself. We miss the point in claiming that the jihadists are visiting the wrong Web sites. What is really significant is that the Internet has made it possible for new human relationships to emerge. "The medium is the message," in McLuhan's famous phrase, "because it is the medium that shapes and controls the scale and form of human association and action."

It is a commonplace of cultural history to say that vernacular print and its reading public helped to create the idea of the modern nation-state. Electronic communications are causing this idea to dissolve. Individuals are led into a mystique of participation in affairs across the globe, from one laptop in East London to another in the mountains outside of Jalalabad. And in electronic media this mystique of participation is the end itself, rather than argument and explanation. No longer is society bound by the rational interpretation of the physical and social world that print generates—the anvil on which the liberal tradition was forged. Instead it is being rent asunder as various groups are drawn to the visceral totems of image-based media. Though McLuhan thought that the sense of universal participation generated by electronic media would put an end to parochialism, quite the opposite has occurred. Rather than his global village, we have become a globe of villages; we live in a cacophony of hidebound parochialisms where individuals seek association only with those to whom they relate by way of primordial intuition.

McLuhan may have been correct to say that the most "backward," the least literate parts of the world would take up the new media most eagerly, but he did not foresee the conflicts that the new media might create within a multicultural West. The liberal state, with its dependence on rational association, is dissolving into a collection of masses united by the parochialisms of "religion" and "culture," a phenomenon to be observed among Muslims and non-Muslims alike.

Can a little Internet surfing really do all that? Yes, and to illustrate why it is so, allow me a moment of autobiography. I was once reading a Philip Roth novel and came across the phrase, "Newark was all of Jewry to me"—I can't remember which one it was; it could have been any of Roth's works. This single statement made me realize more about my own ethnicity than any other I have encountered before or since. As with Roth, everything I had grown up recognizing as a part of my ethnic heritage—Egyptians don't play sports, drink, or curse; they wear their religion lightly, laugh from the soul, and are moved to outrage only when their children underachieve at school—had been learned from the hundred or so households of Egyptian emigrés in my home-town of Edmonton, Canada, nearly all of whom, men and women, I proudly stress, were university-educated professionals. Only after reading Roth's statement did it occur to me that though I had always identified myself as Egyptian-Canadian, my sense of what was Egyptian had little connection to the seventy-two million individuals living a world away in Egypt, most of whom eke out a subsistence living using agricultural techniques that have not changed in the past millennium.

At the same moment, I saw that my sense of identity was very much like that of an author with whom it should be doubly antithetical: he being a Jewish American and I a Muslim Canadian. And recognizing this unexpected proximity made me realize that a minority experience much like my own had found its way into the mainstream of North American life. This led me along a chain of ideas to the point with which I began this essay: that isolation has always been, and always will be, a condition of immigrant life.

But had I grown up in the age of the blogosphere, I might have found a radically different narrative by which to explain my minority experience. If I had spent my time surfing the Net rather than reading novels, I might have been more prone to isolate myself with my coreligionists rather than to see myself as having a specifically Western experience of the world. This is also the great irony that home-grown jihadists fail to see: though they may feel a mystique of participation with the plight of Muslims on the other side of the planet, it is only a mystique. Looking at their blogs shows just how thoroughly their lives and hopes partake in the Western version of self-indulgent, egocentric adolescence. Toronto's *Globe and Mail* has provided a look at the blog of Zakaria Amara, leader of that city's homegrown jihadists, which reveals this sensibility: underneath the Islamist rhetoric one finds a teenager confused by his raging hormones, convinced that the older generation has accepted a corrupt world and fallen into lethargic inaction—and anxious over college applications. Had he been reading Roth rather than the ravings of zealots to which the Internet provides too-ready access, he might have found quite a different sympathetic voice to help him make sense of himself and the world around him.

This is not to say that current efforts to crack down on radical Islam are entirely misguided. No civil society should tolerate a cleric who advocates its destruction and incites his listeners to do the necessary work. The move in Britain to observe mosques and to expel radical imams is entirely appropriate. But if Western Muslims are to carve out their own identity as other minorities have done—neither "assimilated" nor clinging to the bigotries of the motherland—the brand of identity to which electronic media contribute must also be addressed. A robust censorship of radical Web sites would only address content; we also need to promote real literacy and the concomitant primacy of reason. If the new vogue for religion-based schooling is allowed to flourish, it must force students to become "people of the book," to use the Prophet Muhammad's phrase. Emphasizing only science and religion, with little regard for a humanities curriculum of literature and history, creates an intellectual environment where parochialism flourishes.

It is through literacy that we become rational observers of both West and East, and it is through literacy that Muslims can reclaim the long intellectual and artistic traditions that have been occluded by the rise in the twentieth century of Saudi Wahhabism, Iranian radical Shiism, and the Arab world's histrionic opposition to the state of Israel. Only then will Muslims themselves tear the veil of false holiness off a radical Islam that is itself a cover for the political tyrannies of today's Middle East.

FEISAL G. MOHAMED is assistant professor of English at Texas Tech University and a Milton scholar.

Congress and the "YouTube War"

MICHAEL A. COHEN AND MARIA FIGUEROA KÜPÇÜ

The United States is "fighting a different kind of enemy" in its War on Terror, or so says President Bush. He's right. For the first time since the days of the Barbary pirates, America is doing active battle not with a rival nation, but with a non-state actor (al Qaeda) that lacks a geographical home, is motivated by ideology more than territorial ambition, and whose victories are defined in non-military terms. It is an enemy that uses communication technology, public opinion, and the global 24-hour news cycle to wage its battles. It is, in a very real sense, the first "YouTube War" of the twenty-first century.

The rise of al Qaeda is a sign of the era in which we live. With the spread of economic and political liberalization, with the advent of new communication technology, and with the gradual erosion of state power and influence, individuals, organizations, and institutions are enjoying an unprecedented opportunity to affect international events. The rise of the non-state actor stands to become the most resonant characteristic of global affairs at the dawn of the twenty-first century.

Yet the stateless nature of this different kind of enemy is not being reflected in America's current anti-terrorism strategy. In fact, the United States is wielding a military approach against its jihadist foes that is straight out of a twentieth-century playbook. President Bush has chosen to wage this "different kind of war" in Iraq, in a manner reminiscent of the Balkan wars, the conflict in Rwanda, and even the Vietnam War—a territorial, resource-based conflict between rival ethnic and religious groups competing for the spoils of political power.

The New Global Environment

Five years after the attacks of September 11, it is long overdue for the United States to factor this new global environment into its approach for fighting the War on Terror. For five years, Congress has followed the White House's lead in fighting terrorism, with rather uncertain results. In recent congressional elections, the manner in which America is fighting the War on Terror was rarely debated. But, as the 110th Congress implements a legislative agenda for the next two years, it is of critical importance that it do more than simply articulate the fact that America is fighting a "different kind of war"—and instead ensure that the United States fight that war differently.

To be sure, broader American success in the War on Terror can only come when the albatross of U.S. involvement in Iraq comes to an end. It has been, and will continue to be, near impossible to wage an effective war against a non-state actor so long as America is mired in a state-based civil war that is weakening its global credibility and diverting its attention and resources. The drawdown of American troops in Iraq would help to refocus America's antiterrorism agenda on al Qaeda and remove from its jihadist enemies the rallying cry of opposition to the continued occupation. The president's recent protestations notwithstanding, Iraq is not where the War on Terror will be won or lost. What happens in Iraq will not stop the jihadists from waging their civilizational struggle against the United States.

America is mired in a generation-long battle and what is needed today is a comprehensive antiterror strategy that takes into full account the attributes and characteristics of the enemy that America is facing. In the immediate term, that means recalibrating the efficacy of military power in a war against non-state actors, focusing on the tools of public perception to win the war of ideas, and above all, utilizing the capabilities, knowledge, and resources of constructive non-state actors on behalf of U.S. foreign policy goals.

The Trap Called Iraq

There is probably no more venerated—and well-funded—public institution in American society than the U.S. military. Few in Congress have openly questioned the effectiveness of the military as a tool for fighting terrorism. But America's military has significant limitations when it comes to defeating a non-state actor enemy such as al Qaeda. In the wake of September 11, the Bush administration (understandably) made military power the tip of the sword in America's response and the U.S. military effort in Afghanistan remains the most effective tactic that has been employed against al Qaeda: removing the terrorists' home base, dispersing their leaders, and severely degrading the group's ability to wage attacks against America.

The war in Iraq, on the other hand, has tragically laid bare the limitations of using military force when fighting a non-state actor. Prior to September 11, Osama bin Laden and his top cohorts expressed a willingness, even desire, for the United States to invade and occupy a Muslim country. They saw the benefits of a long, protracted struggle between the United States and an Islamic enemy—and they have reaped great rewards from the U.S. war in Iraq. Instead of focusing U.S. political, military, and economic power on fighting terrorism, preventing Afghanistan from again becoming a base of operations for al Qaeda, and organizing an antiterror coalition of like-minded nations, Washington has mired the nation in an internecine, sectarian conflict. Above all, the war in Iraq has shown the limitations of U.S. political will and military might. No longer is America perceived as the invincible, benevolent power that it was before it invaded Iraq. As a result, America's deterrent power has been significantly and fundamentally eroded.

It may be the ultimate irony of America's post-9/11 warrior ethic that the law enforcement officials who prevented the bombing of trans-Atlantic flights to the United States last summer have done as much or more to directly protect the American people than the troops who have rotated through Iraq. This, of course, is not to impugn the soldiers who are fighting and dying in Iraq, but instead the leaders who sent them there. During the 2004 presidential campaign, Senator John Kerry was excoriated by the Bush camp for intimating that the War on Terror could be treated as a law enforcement matter. When one considers how easily the 9/11 attacks could have been prevented by effective coordination among America's law enforcement agencies, one can't help but wonder whether the senator was on to something. The reality is that, in an era of asymmetric threats and non-state actors, the sledgehammer of American military force is not necessarily the best means of protecting America's interests—sometimes, it's just old-fashioned police work.

Winning the War of Ideas

In April 2003, it seemed for a moment that the dominant image of the Iraq war would be the toppling of the Saddam Hussein statue in Baghdad's Republic Square. Instead, it is likely to be the pathetic, hooded, and tortured Iraqis at Abu Ghraib prison, the Internet videos of Iraqi insurgents attacking American troops, or a defiant Saddam at the gallows.

In the era of the non-state actor, public perception is crucial, but soldiers don't do public relations. They fight wars and they kill their enemies—and few have been more effective at this essential skill than the U.S. military. But few armies have been more unprepared for the public relations element of twenty-first century conflict. As Thomas Ricks' recent book, *Fiasco*, makes clear, the U.S. military is unsuited for fighting counter-insurgencies. The rampant disclosures of abuse, which culminated in the Abu Ghraib scandal, were largely the result of sending well-trained military units into a guerrilla conflict in a strange land, where years of military training provided little preparation for the daily challenge of armed occupation. The result was a precipitous decline in America's standing around the world, even among its allies. Recent polling data shows that strong majorities in Germany (78 percent) and Great Britain (56 percent) agreed that the United States was doing a "bad job" of promoting human rights. In a similar poll taken in 1998, fewer than one in four Germans (24 percent) and Britons (22 percent) held that view.[1]

The importance of public perceptions was not lost on America's enemy. As former Central Intelligence Agency (CIA) deputy director John E. McLaughlin has noted, al Qaeda today is driven primarily by "ideology and the Internet." Right now, the morbidly curious can log onto YouTube.com and other viral video sites that popularize free content through the Internet or any number of jihadist websites to see videos of the killing of American soldiers and Improvised Explosive Device (IED) attacks against coalition troops. As disturbing as these images are, they provide graphic evidence of al Qaeda's success in using Iraq to create a prime recruiting tool for the terrorists of tomorrow. As a recent memo by the director of strategic communications at the U.S. embassy in Baghdad points out, "Insurgents, sectarian elements, and others are taking control of the message at the public level." The level of sophistication from insurgent forces is extraordinary, attacks on U.S. forces are filmed from multiple angles with high-resolution optics. Footage is actually edited and soundtracks feature religious statements. According to a recent *Newsweek* article, "U.S. officials believe insurgents attack American forces primarily to generate fresh footage." This contrasts greatly with the normal U.S. response to military actions taken in Iraq—a press release.[2]

However, the White House continues to blame public relations failures for undermining U.S. effectiveness in the War on Terror. In a *Los Angeles Times* op-ed in early 2006, former secretary of defense Donald Rumsfeld bragged about the new "strategic communications framework" put forward by the Pentagon to get out America's story. This past October, word leaked that the Pentagon plans to ramp up its communications effort by creating a rapid response media unit. But even the best communications plan is mere window dressing if you don't have a good story to tell. A November 2006 *Atlantic Monthly* profile of Karen Hughes was illuminating in this regard. The top U.S. public diplomat noted how hard it was for her to "sell" America in the Arab world because of the conflict in Iraq.

Iraq notwithstanding, recalibrating the public perception of U.S. foreign policy must be front and center in the minds of the new Congress. It is a great irony of the War on Terror that, while sizable percentages of Muslims are rejecting violence and, in particular, suicide bombings, this has not translated into a more positive view of the United States and its foreign policy objectives. In the five most predominately Muslim countries, sizable majorities continue to express markedly negative views of America and, in particular, the War on Terror.

Yet Washington's public diplomacy efforts have sputtered. Since 2003, the State Department has been justly faulted for its lack of an overall strategy, qualified staff, and culturally sophisticated approach to public diplomacy—and for not utilizing the lessons of private-sector campaigns more effectively.[3] Reinvigorating the effort will require not only presidential involvement, but also genuine public measures to improve America's image overseas.

These can run the gamut from small but meaningful initiatives such as the opening (rather than the closing) of American libraries in foreign locales, increased student exchange programs, foreign scholarships, and wide-ranging public health initiatives to the more vigorous engagement of American business, non-profits, and even public relations firms in changing perceptions of the United States around the world. When fighting an enemy as media savvy as al Qaeda, Washington needs to take far more seriously the crucial importance of public perception in the YouTube era.

Utilizing Non-State Actors

The universal recognition of organizations like al Qaeda is a clear example of the success of non-state actors in placing themselves on the world's radar screens. But just as terrorist groups have been able to project themselves, so too have individuals, organizations, and corporations shown the ways in which altruistically minded non-state actors can change the world for the better. In an era of growing privatization in foreign affairs, the United States needs to do more to use these influential non-state actors to further foreign policy objectives.

Take the example of Rita Katz, a freelance intelligence gatherer, whose company, the Search for International Terrorist Entities Institute (SITE), provides some of the most up-to-date intelligence about terrorist organizations. Katz and others in the freelance intelligence field have been extraordinarily effective at ferreting out time-sensitive and actionable intelligence resources. At a time when only several dozen people in the FBI have proficiency in Arabic, policymakers should look more closely at individuals like Katz for clues that will uncover a terrorist attack before it occurs. Moreover, groups like SITE or the Investigative Project, headed by Steve Emerson, have shown an ability to harvest public sources of information in areas that traditional intelligence-gatherers eschew.

As Emerson notes, America's intelligence agencies are hindered by a bureaucratic culture that is overly compartmentalized, resists information-sharing, and has an innate distrust of open source information, which is why outside groups "can do a lot more."[4] But private intelligence is but one piece of the puzzle. There are numerous other examples of non-state actors furthering national security by drawing on the work of political consultants who advise opposition movements in former Yugoslavia, Georgia, and Ukraine; of trial lawyers who seek to hold state sponsors of terrorists legally responsible; and military contractors who train modern armed forces.

The Bush administration has used some of these groups in isolated circumstances, but the practice of actively drawing on the know-how of non-state actors should become a fundamental element of foreign policy. With Congress' urging, government agencies should be creating departmental liaisons specifically geared toward reaching non-state actors and utilizing their discrete expertise.

Regulating Military Contractors

Above all, Congress must draft commonsense guidelines for non-state actors to develop relationships that are based on transparency, accountability, and oversight. Consider the case of military contractors. In Bosnia, these groups provided essential security support for U.S. peacekeeping troops. In Afghanistan, private military contractors (PMCs) helped U.S. forces attack al Qaeda leaders and recruit proxy Afghan armies. In Iraq, PMCs are the backbone of the U.S. occupation, providing essential administrative and security services. According to recent Pentagon estimates, there are currently 25,000 private security contractors (PSCs) engaged in Iraq. This private army of contractors represents the second-largest contingent of armed personnel serving in Iraq who provide essential support to America's overburdened military. Since April 2003, the Labor Department estimates that more than 670 contractors have been killed—a total greater than all non-U.S. coalition fatalities combined.[5]

Yet few are asking the difficult questions about their responsibilities. Many firms operate in a gray zone beyond congressional oversight, military codes of conduct, and even international law. For example, in the United States, only recently have legislative changes made it possible for PSCs to be held accountable under the Uniform Code of Military Justice, the legal code that applies to U.S. military personnel. This attempt at enhancing accountability on the battlefield is a step in the right direction, though it remains to be seen if it is actually implementable. While certain international conventions apply to armed civilians, enforcement of these rules is discretionary and has been generally non-existent. In Iraq, if a contractor kills an Iraqi civilian, there is virtually no legal recourse for the victim's family. The involvement of civilian contractors in military roles also creates operational challenges. Private security contractors are outside the official chain of command and control. But, to the average Iraqi citizen, the actions of contractors are indistinguishable from those of soldiers. They are just more Americans carrying guns—uniform or no uniform. As a result, illegal actions by PSCs reflect directly—often negatively—on their home country.

Clearly, America's reliance on PSCs is growing faster than Washington's ability or inclination to regulate them. Congressional action is long overdue.

Supporting Those "Supporting Democracy"

In addition, Congress and the Bush administration need to do a better job of standing up for individuals and organizations that work to promote democracy overseas. For more than a decade, foreign funds, not only from sympathetic foreign governments, but from a number of non-state actors, non-governmental organizations (NGOS), and wealthy individuals, have flowed freely into nascent democracies. This seed capital has paid for political expertise, civic organizing, and public relations programs that have helped propel democratic movements.

But in January 2006, Russian president Vladimir Putin signed legislation oppressively regulating non-governmental organizations in Russia. The bill created a government agency with a mandate to monitor more than 400,000 civil society groups now in existence and shut down those whose activities "contradict the constitution or the laws of the Russian Federation." This effort was widely perceived as a direct attack on a fledgling Russian democracy.

Yet while the Bush administration protested, the complaints were half-hearted and lacking true diplomatic muscle. Restricting the work of NGOS is a shot across the bow to the administration's stated policy of encouraging the spread of democracy. Moreover, when U.S. international credibility is in decline, NGOS and advocacy groups can play a unique role in circumventing diplomatic channels and promoting objectives fundamental to national interests. But they need diplomatic support. The success of President Vladimir Putin's efforts at stifling democracy advocates may encourage emulation otherwise. Congress should take up the issue of NGOS operating freely in Russia today as it did the issue of Jewish *refuseniks* in the past.

Engaging the Business Community

Last November, a G-8 sponsored conference of global business leaders debated how they might help in the fight against terrorism.[6] The results were achievable ideas for cross-border collaboration: improved monitoring of terrorist activity in the financial, telecommunications, and Internet sectors, and agreement to prioritize sectors that were potential targets of a terrorist attack, such as infrastructure, international trade supply chains, and centers of tourism. Heads of international transport unions, banks, agricultural and industry conglomerates, and even the World Diamond Council offered models of how new standards and information-sharing could help to expose havens of criminal activity. Above all, business leaders acknowledged that thus far their efforts have been reactive—protecting employees and assets—but precious little effort has been put toward proactively countering terrorist operations.

Initiatives to harness the resources and innovation of the private sector are encouraging. Collaboration between business and government to fight terrorism can be especially effective when implemented at the local and regional level. But this is no easy task. Government officials are often unable to speak the language of non-state actors and the communication gap has frustrated a number of well-intentioned proposals. Congress must ultimately ensure that the engagement of the private sector is abetted with incentives and leadership, so that segmented actions become a sum greater than their parts.

Congress, in short, has an opportunity to change the course of the War on Terror and ensure that America is fighting this "different kind of enemy" in a different and effective manner. To do so, Washington must recognize the changing nature of global relations, which offers greater opportunities for non-state actors, but also demands of them greater responsibilities. Doing so is a complicated endeavor, but it must become a defining feature of U.S. foreign policy. To successfully wage the War on Terror requires more than tough talk and the sword of military tactics—it requires a fundamental rethinking of the forces driving global affairs in the twenty-first century.

Notes

1. "American and International Opinion on the Rights of Terrorism Suspects," Program on International Policy Attitudes, University of Maryland, July 17, 2006, at www.worldpublicopinion.org.
2. Scott Johnson, "We're Losing the Info War," Newsweek, January 15, 2007.
3. "U.S. Public Diplomacy: State Department Efforts Lack Certain Communication Elements and Face Persistent Elements," Government Accountability Office report, May 2006.
4. Michael Isikoff and Mark Hosenball, "How Clarke Outsourced Terror Intel," Newsweek, March 31, 2004.
5. See www.globalsecurity.org, updated August 2006.
6. Global Forum for Partnerships between States and Businesses to Counter Terrorism, Moscow, November 30, 2006.

MICHAEL A. COHEN AND MARIA FIGUEROA KÜPÇÜ are co-directors of the Privatization of Foreign Policy Initiative at the New America Foundation.

UNIT 7
Terrorism and Religion

Unit Selections
26. **Qutbism: An Ideology of Islamic-Fascism,** Dale Eikmeier
27. **The Madrassa Scapegoat,** Peter Bergen and Swati Pandey
28. **Holy Orders,** Mark Juergensmeyer

Key Points to Consider
- Why is it important to understand terrorist ideologies?
- What are the implications of the emergence of a 'Talibanistan'?
- Do Islamic schools contribute to the problem of terrorism?
- Was the conflict in Northern Ireland religious?

Student Web Site
www.mhcls.com/online

Internet References
Further information regarding these Web sites may be found in this book's preface or online.

FACSNET: "Understanding Faith and Terrorism"
http://www.facsnet.org/issues/faith/terrorism.php3#

Islam Denounces Terrorism
http://www.islamdenouncesterrorism.com

Religious Tolerance Organization
http://www.religioustolerance.org/curr_war.htm

SITE Institute
http://www.siteinstitute.org/

Over the past decade, the topic of religion has played an increasingly prominent role in discussions of international terrorism. Fears of what some have called the resurgence of fundamentalist Islam have spawned visions of inevitable clashes of civilizations. Even before the events of September 11th, the term religious terrorism had become a staple in the vocabulary of many U.S. policymakers.

While there is currently no commonly accepted definition of religious terrorism, one should note that in the popular press the term religious terrorism is often used as a euphemism for political violence committed by Muslims. It is naïve to presume that all political violence committed by members of a particular religious group is necessarily religious violence. The relationship between religion and political violence is much more complex.

Experts have noted that many of today's religious terrorists were nationalists yesterday and Marxists the day before. Unlike their historical predecessors like the *Thugs* in India who killed to sacrifice the blood of their victims to the Goddess *Kali,* today's religious terrorists see violence as a means of achieving political, economic, and social objectives. Religion is often seen a means, rather than an end in itself. In many cases religious ideologies have taken over where other ideologies have failed.

Ideologies are systems of belief that justify behavior. They serve three primary functions: (1) They polarize and mobilize populations toward common objectives; (2) They create a sense of security by providing a system of norms and values; and (3) They provide the basis for the justification and rationalization of human behavior. Ideologies do not necessarily cause violence. They do, however, provide an effective means polarizing populations and organizing political dissent.

While the emergence of religious ideologies signals an important shift in international terrorism, the role of religion in international terrorism is often exaggerated or misunderstood. Religion is not the cause of contemporary political violence. It does, however, provide an effective means for organizing political dissent. In some parts of the world political extremists have infiltrated the mosques, temples and churches and have managed to hijack and pervert religious doctrine, superimposing their own views of the world and encouraging the use of violence.

The three articles in this unit provide an overview of the relationship between religion and terrorism. In the first selection, Dale

Department of Defense photo by LCPL J.A Chaverri, USMC

Eikmeier highlights the basic tenets of Qutbism. He argues that an understanding of the enemy's ideology is crucial to long-term success against terrorism. The second article examines the role of Islamic schools in terrorist training. It argues that highly educated individuals are more likely to be involved in major attacks than those who attended religious schools. The last selection argues that religion is a tool of the powerless fighting against the perceived moral corruption of Western secular society.

Qutbism: An Ideology of Islamic-Fascism

DALE C. EIKMEIER

The recently published *National Military Strategic Plan for the War on Terrorism* (NMSP-WOT) is to be commended for identifying "ideology" as al Qaeda's center of gravity.[1] The identification of an ideology as the center of gravity rather than an individual or group is a significant shift from a "capture and kill" philosophy to a strategy focused on defeating the root cause of Islamic terrorism. Accordingly, the plan's principal focus is on attacking and countering an ideology that fuels Islamic terrorism. Unfortunately, the NMSP-WOT fails to identify the ideology or suggest ways to counter it. The plan merely describes the ideology as "extremist." This description contributes little to the public's understanding of the threat or to the capabilities of the strategist who ultimately must attack and defeat it. The intent of this article is to identify the ideology of the Islamic terrorists and recommend how to successfully counter it.

Sun Tzu wisely said, "Know the enemy and know yourself; in a hundred battles you will never be in peril."[2] Our success in the War on Terrorism depends on knowing who the enemy is and understanding his ideology. While characterizing and labeling an enemy may serve such a purpose, it is only useful if the labels are clearly defined and understood. Otherwise, overly broad characterizations obscure our ability to truly "know the enemy," they diffuse efforts, and place potential allies and neutrals in the enemy's camp. Unfortunately, the War on Terrorism's use of labels contributes a great deal to the misunderstandings associated with the latter. The fact is, five years after 9/11 the NMSP-WOT provides little specific guidance, other than labeling the enemy as extremist.[3] This inability to focus on the specific threat and its supporting philosophy reflects our own rigid adherence to political correctness and is being exploited by militant Islamists portraying these overly broad descriptions as a war against Islam. As David F. Forte states "We must not fail . . . to distinguish between the homicidal revolutionaries like bin Laden and mainstream Muslim believers."[4]

Knowing the enemy requires an understanding of militant Islam's ideology and recognizing that it is the militants' "center of gravity."[5] Their extremist ideology has been called many things, "Militant Islam," "Salafism," "Islamism," "Wahhabism," "Qutbism," "Jihadism," and even "Islam."[6] Since most ideologies reflect the integration of various related concepts, theories, and aims that have evolved over time into a broader body of thought, no label is entirely perfect and all are subject to critique. However, it appears that President Bush has ended the debate and accepted "Islamic-Fascism" as the ideological label.[7] While Islamic-Fascism immediately conjures up images of an evil to be resisted and is therefore useful as a public relations term, intellectually it does little for the serious students of Islam or the strategic planners charged with its defeat.

So what is this ideology we label Islamic-Fascism? What are its sources, theories, aims, and who are its proponents? The answers to many of these questions can be found in a collection of violent Islamic thought called Qutbism.[8] Qutbism refers to the writings of Sayyid Qutb and other Islamic theoreticians, e.g., Abul Ala Maududi and Hassan al Banna, that provide the intellectual rationale underpinning Islamic-Fascism. Qutbism is not a structured body of thought from any single person (despite its name), source, time, or sect; rather it is a fusion of puritanical and intolerant Islamic orientations that include elements from both the Sunni and Shia sects of Islam that have been combined with broader Islamist goals and methodologies. Qutbism integrates the Islamist teachings of Maududi and al Banna with the arguments of Sayyid Qutb to justify armed jihad in the advance of Islam, and other violent methods utilized by twentieth century militants. Qutbism advocates violence and justifies terrorism against non-Muslims and apostates in an effort to bring about the reign of God. Others, i.e., Ayman Al-Zawahiri, Abdullah Azzam, and Osama bin Laden built terrorist organizations based on the principles of Qutbism and turned the ideology of Islamic-Fascism into a global action plan.

The Foundation: Puritan Islam

Qutbism is structured on a common foundation of puritan Islamist orientations such as Wahabbi, Salafi, and Deobandi.[9] These orientations share several traits and beliefs:

- A belief that Muslims have deviated from true Islam and must return to "pure Islam" as originally practiced during the time of the Prophet.[10]
- The path to "pure Islam" is only through a literal and strict interpretation of the Quran and Hadith, along with implementation of the Prophet's commands.[11]
- Muslims should individually interpret the original sources without being slavishly bound to the interpretations of Islamic scholars.[12]
- That any interpretation of the Quran from a historical, contextual perspective is a corruption, and that the majority of Islamic history and the classical jurisprudential tradition is mere sophistry.[13]

The Architects: Islamist Theoreticians

While puritan Islamic orientations set the foundation, it was Islamist theoreticians who built Qutbism's intellectual framework. One of the founding fathers of modern Islamist thought is Abul Ala Maududi

Article 26. Qutbism: An Ideology of Islamic-Fascism

(1903–1979), a Deobandi alumni.[14] Maududi believed the Muslim community's decline resulted from practicing a corrupted form of Islam contaminated by non-Islamic ideas and culture. Maududi reminded Muslims that Islam is more than a religion; it is a complete social system that guides and controls every aspect of life including government.[15] He believed tolerance of non-Muslim rule and non-Islamic concepts and systems was an insult to God. Therefore, the only way Muslims might practice pure Islam and assume their rightful place in the world is through the establishment of Islamic states, where Islam rules independent of non-Islamic influences. These Islamic states would eventually spread Islam across the globe and establish God's reign. Maududi argued the only practical way to accomplish Islamic rule is through jihad.

Maududi explained his concepts in *Jihad in Islam*.

> In reality Islam is a militant ideology and programme which seeks to alter the social order of the whole world and rebuild it in conformity with its own tenets and ideals. "Muslim" is the title of that International Militant Party organized by Islam to carry into effect its militant programme. And "Jihad" refers to that militant struggle and utmost exertion which the Islamic Party brings into play to achieve this objective.
>
> Islam wishes to destroy all States and Governments anywhere on the face of the earth which are opposed to the ideology and programme of Islam regardless of the country or the Nation which rules it.
>
> It must be evident to you from this discussion that the objective of Islamic "Jihad" is to eliminate the rule of an un-Islamic system and establish in its stead an Islamic system of State rule. Islam does not intend to confine this revolution to a single State or a few countries; the aim of Islam is to bring about a universal revolution.[16]

Maududi's *Jihad in Islam* articulated the goals of an evolving Islamist ideology by reiterating the strategic objective of global Islamic rule and designating jihad as the way to achieve it. Thinkers like Hassan al Banna, in *Jihad,* Muhammad Adb al Salam Faraj, *The Neglected Duty,* and Sayyid Qutb, *In the Shade of the Quran* and *Milestones* espoused similar ideas and attempted to put them into practice.[17]

Hassan al Banna (1905–1949), founder of the al-Ikhwan al-Muslimun (Muslim Brotherhood), believed, like Maududi, that a revival of "pure Islam" was the antidote to Western domination and a cure for the malady infecting the Muslim world.[18] A charismatic leader and organizer, al Banna implemented the Islamist vision by organizing the Muslim Brotherhood in 1928 with the objective of establishing government rule on the basis of Islamic values.[19] His approach was gradualist rather than revolutionary. By providing basic services to the community including schools, mosques, and factories he sought popular support for Islamist goals through persuasion.[20] However, despite this, al Banna never articulated a practical method for taking power.[21] Additionally, al Banna's domineering personality and micro-managerial leadership style created a fragile organization that fragmented following his death in 1949.

Hassan al Banna's lasting legacy was reminding Muslims that the Quran says jihad against un-believers is an obligation of all Muslims. He also argued that jihad was not just the defense of Muslim lands but a means "to safeguard the mission of spreading Islam."[22] The idea of jihad to spread Islam and to establish the Islamic state was then expanded by his contemporary Sayyid Qutb.

Sayyid Qutb (1906–1966) is regarded by some as the founding father and leading theoretician of the contemporary extremist movement.[23] According to William McCants of the US Military Academy's Combating Terrorism Center, our jihadi enemies "cite Sayyid Qutb repeatedly and consider themselves his intellectual descendants."[24] Qutb became one of the leading spokesmen and thinkers of the Muslim Brotherhood, persuasively advocating the use of violence to establish Islamic rule and like Maududi inspired thousands to take up the cause of "establishing God's rule on earth."[25] Unlike al Banna who tried to build an Islamic society from the bottom up, Qutb changed the strategy by developing a top-down approach that focused on removing non-Islamic rulers and governments.

Qutb argued that the entire world, including the Muslim, was in a state of *jahiliyah,* or ignorance where man's way had replaced God's way.[26] According to Qutb, since jahiliyah and Islam cannot co-exist, offensive jihad was necessary to destroy jahiliyah society and bring the entire world to Islam.[27] Until jahiliyah is defeated, all true Muslims have a personal obligation to wage offensive jihad. When Qutb added offensive jihad to the widely accepted concept of defensive jihad, Qutb broke with mainstream Islam and ridiculed Muslim scholars:

> Those who say that Islamic Jihad was merely for the defense of the "home land of Islam" diminish the greatness of the Islamic way of life and consider it less important [than] their "homeland." . . . However, [Islamic community] defense is not the ultimate objective of the Islamic movement of jihad but it is a mean of establishing the Divine authority within it so that it becomes the headquarters for the movement of Islam, which is then to be carried throughout the earth to the whole of mankind. . . .[28]

Thus offensive jihad against non-Muslims in the cause of spreading Islam and the rule of God was not only justified, it was glorious.

In addition to offensive jihad Sayyid Qutb used the Islamic concept of "takfir" or excommunication of apostates.[29] Declaring someone takfir provided a legal loophole around the prohibition of killing another Muslim and in fact made it a religious obligation to execute the apostate. The obvious use of this concept was to declare secular rulers, officials or organizations, or any Muslims that opposed the Islamist agenda a takfir thereby justifying assassinations and attacks against them. Sheikh Omar Abdel Rahman, who was later convicted in the 1993 World Trade Center attack, invoked Qutb's takfirist writings during his trial for the assassination of President Anwar Sadat.[30] The takfir concept along with "offensive jihad" became a blank check for any Islamic extremist to justify attacks against anyone.

Fawaz A. Gerges, who claims to have interviewed Islamic terrorists in several countries, states "Qutb showed them the way forward and . . . they referred to [him] as a *shadhid,* or martyr." He describes how "jihadis look up to Qutb as a founding spiritual father, if not the mufti, or theoretician of their contemporary movement."[31] Ayman al-Zawahiri credits Qutb's execution in 1966 for lighting the jihadist fire. Al-Zawahiri claims Qutb dramatically altered the direction of the Islamist movement by forcefully driving the idea of "the urgent need to attack the near enemy" (rulers and secular governments in Muslim countries).[32]

Qutb's theory of unrestricted jihad ". . . against every obstacle that comes into the way of worshiping God and the implementation of the divine authority on earth . . . " is the intellectual basis behind the exhortations of Abdullah Azzam and Ayman al-Zawahiri and ultimately the establishment of Osama bin Laden's al Qaeda.[33]

The Contractors

Qutb's disciples, Abdullah Azzam and Ayman al-Zawahiri, introduced Osama bin Laden to Qutb's ideology. Azzam first met bin Laden when he lectured at King Adbul Aziz University in Jeddah, Saudi Arabia, where bin Laden was studying under Mohammad Qutb, Sayyid's brother.[34] In response to the Soviet invasion of Afghanistan, Azzam left Saudi Arabia and established the *Maktab al-Khadamat* or "Services Offices" in Pakistan to organize, train, and support international mujahideen fighting in Afghanistan. Bin Laden joined Azzam in 1984 and supported the mujahideen effort through his *Bait ul-Ansar* or "House of Helpers." Azzam's mentorship provided the young bin Laden the practical experience to develop the logistical and organizational skills necessary for recruiting, training, and funding a jihadi network with global reach. After the Soviet withdrawal from Afghanistan, Azzam attempted to shift the jihadi effort to Palestine. This shift created a rift with bin Laden—who was under the ideological mentorship of Ayman al-Zawahiri—over the direction of the organization. Conveniently for bin Laden, Azzam was killed in Peshawar by assassins in November 1989 and bin Laden assumed full control of the Maktab.[35]

Ayman al-Zawahiri, a prolific writer on Qutb's ideas, met Osama bin Laden during the Afghan war. Their close relationship resulted in the 1989 merger of the Maktab and Egyptian Jihad that formed al Qaeda. Al-Zawahiri served as the organization's ideologist while bin Laden was the organizer and leader.[36] Al-Zawahiri authored al Qaeda's manifesto *Knights Under the Prophet's Banner* which clearly links the Islamist's goal with Qutb's strategy of unrestricted jihad.[37] Significantly, it explains al Qaeda's rational for attacking the "far enemy" (the US, Israel, and other non-Muslim powers) first.[38]

The "far enemy first" strategy was revolutionary as it overthrew the accepted "near enemy strategy" of al Banna, Qutb, Azzam, and Faraj.[39] This shift was the result of careful strategic decisionmaking by al-Zawahiri and bin Laden. It is only natural to assume that the two compared the failures of the Muslim Brotherhood, al-Jamaa al-Islamiya, Egyptian Jihad, and other organizations to prevail over the "near enemy," to the successes of the Afghan mujahideen in their victory over the Soviets. They reasonably concluded that the "far enemy" strategy was the wiser course of action.[40]

- Advantages of Jihad against the infidel "far enemy."
  - Unifies and rallies international Muslim support.
  - Allows greater sanctuary in supportive states.
  - Is easier to portray as the defense of Islam and a religious obligation.
  - Attacks the source of power behind "apostate regimes."
  - Is easier because infidel countermeasures are limited and less effective.
- Disadvantages of Jihad against the "near enemy."
  - Splits Muslims and localizes support.
  - Subjects the organization to more effective state security organs.
  - Geography and political factors limit internal sanctuary.
  - Local politics versus religious issues confuse the members and the people, weakening their resolve.
  - Western support to apostate regimes not affected.

For these reasons al Qaeda in the 1990s focused its efforts on the "far enemy" and the United States in particular. Zawahiri and bin Laden pushed a shift from small isolated extremists attacking local apostate regimes to clear-cut and unified jihad against infidels. The intent was not so much as to destroy the West, but rather to unify Muslim masses behind al Qaeda's goals.[41] The intent of progressively spectacular attacks against US and Western interests was to drive the United States from the Middle East, thus weakening apostate Muslim regimes and increasing al Qaeda's prestige. They intended the attacks of 9/11 to provoke an inevitable infidel retaliation that would rally ordinary Muslims to global jihad in defense of Islam. Al-Zawahiri and bin Laden thought that by changing the target of the Qutbist strategy, they could turn the struggle into a war between Islam and the West. Naturally, pro-western secular regimes in Muslim lands would be the first casualties of this war. As these regimes fell they would be replaced by Islamic rule; thus setting the initial stage for further Islamic conquests.

Osama bin Laden's chief contribution to Qutbism may be his management and organizational skills. The Muslim Brotherhood's collapse after al Banna's death demonstrated the fragility of hierarchical organizations dependent on a single leader. It can be assumed that bin Laden as a business management student and protégé of Azzam learned from al Banna's mistakes and designed al Qaeda as a networked organization of franchises rather than a conventional hierarchical organization. His organizational design facilitated the rapid globalization of Qutbism and distribution of resources, while building durability and protective firewalls between cells.

Whether al Qaeda's leadership is the central planning and controlling hub or only the ideological center of loosely affiliated groups is debatable.[42] What is clear is that al Qaeda cells share Qutbist ideology and goals. This is why it is essential that the *National Military Strategic Plan for the War on Terrorism* correctly identifies ideology, not the leadership or organization of a particular group, as the center of gravity. The question then becomes how best to attack it.

Attacking the Center of Gravity

There are five "lines of operations" to be utilized in the attack on Qutbism, the ideological center of gravity for the Islamic-Fascist movement. Four of these lines are entirely the responsibility of the Muslim world: The message, the messenger(s), the ideology's supporting institutions, and the institutions of the counter-ideology. A fifth line lies in both the Muslim and non-Muslim worlds and is the defense of the universally accepted values, norms, and principles of modern civilization. Any successful strategy for the War on Terrorism requires synchronized efforts along all five lines to pressure and eventually collapse the ideological center of gravity. In theory this would strip al Qaeda and its affiliates of their source of power and bring victory in the war against the jihadi.

First Line of Operation: Attack the Message

The first and most important line of operation is attacking the Qutbist message. While the West has a supporting role, it is ultimately the responsibility of the Islamic world to lead this effort.[43] Obviously, only moderate Islam can undermine Qutbism's theological foundations. The most credible weapons in this attack are the voices of mainstream Muslims and scholars. Abdal-Hakim Murad, a British Muslim, explains:

> Certainly, neither bin-Laden nor his principal associate, Ayman al-Zawahiri, are graduates of Islamic universities. And so their proclamations ignore 14 centuries of Muslim scholarship, and

instead take the form of lists of anti-American grievances and of Koranic quotations referring to early Muslim wars against Arab idolaters. These are followed by the conclusion that all Americans, civilian and military, are to be wiped off the face of the Earth. All this amounts to an odd and extreme violation of the normal methods of Islamic scholarship. Had the authors of such fatwas followed the norms of their religion, they would have had to acknowledge that no school of mainstream Islam allows the targeting of civilians. An insurrectionist who kills non-combatants is guilty of *baghy,* "armed aggression," a capital offense in Islamic law.[44]

Moderate Islam's faithful should be given the encouragement and tools required to make their voices heard, so they might direct fellow Muslims who have let anger mislead them to a more radical ideology.

> "Creditability of a message relies not only on logic and reasoning but also on the credentials of the messenger."

One method of rescuing the jihadi from Qutbism is "hujjat" or proof. Yemeni Judge Hamoud Al-Hitar believes that terrorism has an intellectual base and it can be defeated intellectually.[45] He uses hujjat in theological dialogues that challenge and then correct the wayward beliefs of the jihadi. Hitar believes that moderate Islam can rescue the jihadi whom he believes are ordinary people that have been led astray by al Qaeda propaganda. His successful record of rehabilitation has piqued the interest of several countries that see his methodology as a powerful anti-terrorism technique.[46]

Mohammed VI, the King of Morocco, in response to the 2003 Casablanca bombings, took a number of steps to attack the extremist's message and recapture a large segment of Moroccan society (disillusioned youth) that had fallen under the influence of radical imams. He established special training programs for imams and a unique program to train female religious guides. The King's establishment of the Council of Religious Scholars, a group responsible for issuing religious edicts, was well received by Muslims.[47]

Respected Islamic leaders increasingly are speaking out against Islamic-Fascism. Sheikh-ul-Islam, Talghat Tajuddin, the Supreme Mufti of the Commonwealth of Independent States, recently challenged all Muslims to resist extremism and defend Islam:

> Violent, extremist Islamists invoke on their own head the true jihad. Challenging all the peoples of the Earth, and first of all mainstream Islam, professed by the overwhelming majority of the Islamic world, these forces put themselves in opposition to Islam. And reacting against them is a religious, moral, social, and political duty of each Muslim.[48]

Attacking the message also requires a paradigm shift for moderate Muslim spokesmen. Defending Islam as a religion of peace and tolerance with the subliminal objective of blunting Western criticism of Islamic extremism does little to help in defeating the terrorist or saving Islam. These spokesmen need to shift to the offensive, targeting their rhetoric and philosophy against their own disillusioned people in an effort to expose Islamic-Fascism for the evil it is. This is probably the only way they will extract themselves and their followers from the catastrophic plague infecting Muslim culture and threatening world peace. Failure to actively pursue such a strategy might suggest that the problem is not with extremism but with the basic tenets of Islam.

Second Line of Operation: Attack the Messenger

Creditability of a message relies not only on logic and reasoning but also on the credentials of the messenger. Many of Qutbism's proponents are individuals with questionable religious credentials, yet they claim religious authority. These misrepresentations can be their achilles heel and the means to discredit them and their message. With the exception of Abul Ala Maududi and Abdullah Azzam, none of Qutbism's main theoreticians trained at Islam's recognized centers of learning. Although a devout Muslim, Hassan al Banna was a teacher and community activist. Sayyid Qutb was a literary critic. Muhammad Abd al-Salam Faraj was an electrician. Ayman al-Zawahiri is a physician. Osama bin Laden trained to be a businessman. As Muslims, al Banna, Qutb, Faraj, al-Zawahiri, and bin Laden may have the right to claim a singular understanding of God's will, the intent of the Prophet, and how Muslims should live. However, the more formally and rigorously trained, moderate Islamic scholars exercising the collective wisdom of 14 centuries of Islamic theology should be able to challenge and refute their extreme Qutbism positions.

Third and Fourth Lines of Operation: Attack Islamic-Fascism's Supporting Institutions and Support Mainstream Islamic Institutions

The third and fourth lines of operation are mirror images, one being the negative image of a positive. Moderate Islam and Islamic-Fascism essentially have the same institutional support structures which fall into three categories; educational, financial, and informational. Educational institutions include schools, universities, mosques, and centers. Funding for these institutions include private donations, charities, endowments, and state sponsorship. Informational institutions include centers, dedicated media, independent media, state controlled media, and organizational outreach. The tactic that moderate Muslims and those fighting against extremism should use is to restrict and close those institutions advocating Qutbism while promoting others that offer positive alternatives. Actions along these two lines complement one another and should be synchronized to obtain the most effective synergistic results.

Societies not only have the right to self-defense, but an obligation to protect themselves against Islamic-Fascism's use of unrestricted jihad. A claim of religious obligation or freedom does not supplant the right to self-defense. Simply put, the murder of non-Muslims cannot be protected under the guise of Islamic religious or cultural freedom. Therefore, any religious or secular institution supporting Qutbism should be restricted or closed. There are recognized governmental and religious authorities with the ability to enact the appropriate legislation that would facilitate restrictions on or the closing of Qutbist institutions. Conversely, institutions that provide alternatives to Qutbism or support moderate Islam need to be recognized and supported. The measures taken by the King of Morocco and others are clear examples of what can be done. Only by enabling advocates and disciples of moderate Islam can we expect to counter the siren-call of Qutbism and its associated terrorism.

Fifth Line of Operation: Inoculation

While the Muslim world wrestles with the future of Islam the rest of the world must inoculate itself against the ideology of Islamic-Fascism. Inoculation not only enables continued resistance to the spread of Islamic-Fascism but sets the stage for its eventual elimination. Inoculation comes in two ways. The first is the answer to the wartime question, what are we fighting against. The second form of inoculation answers the question, what are we fighting for. The answer to these two questions serves to immunize the societal body against the corrupting message of Islamic-Fascism. It has the associated benefit of strengthening society to fight for the elimination of such a message or philosophy.

Inoculation requires information campaigns and the education of individuals regarding the anti-human rights and religiously intolerant agenda of the Qutbists. The most effective weapon we might utilize in this campaign is the Qutbists' own words and writings. Exposing the greater society to writings promoting world conquest, the murder of non-Muslims, and total submission to a particular view of what the world should be would go a long way in alerting nations to the threat they need to be prepared to resist.

The second half of the inoculation explains to the various societies what they must protect and promote. Towards this end an information campaign is required in an effort to promote a vigorous defense of what many nations term "universally accepted values." These universal values are perhaps best summarized in the United Nations' Universal Declaration of Human Rights and the United States Bill of Rights. Treaties, conventions, constitutions, courts, and tradition have further defined these values, the result being an established and widely accepted body of norms and goals for civilized behavior. The objective in this part of the inoculation is to promote the superiority of values and principles so that societies worldwide might enthusiastically defend them against the threat posed by the Islamic-Fascists.

Conclusion

The 9/11 hijackers and London's 7/7 bombers were not poor, uneducated, and hopeless men without futures. They had futures, but were seduced by an extremist ideology disguised as an obligation to God. The *National Military Strategic Plan for the War on Terrorism* correctly identifies ideology as the center of gravity. It recognizes that this is a war of ideas between competing social and religious systems, one offering the promise of individual liberty and the other, Islamic-Fascism. To successfully defend freedom against the threat poised by Islamic-Fascism, global leaders and individuals must understand the foundation of Qutbism as primarily derived from Sayyid Qutb. Understanding Qutbism, exposing and discrediting it as an extremist theology and strategy is the most direct course to the defeat of the Islamic-Fascist movement's center of gravity and victory in the War on Terrorism.

Notes

1. *Center of Gravity,* Primary Sources of Moral or Physical Strength, Power, and Resistance; Joe Strange, *Centers of Gravity & Critical Vulnerabilities* (Quantico, Va.: Marine Corps Univ. Foundation, 1996), p. ix.
2. Sun Tzu, *The Art of War* (London, Eng.: Oxford Univ. Press, 1963), p. 84.
3. Chairman of the Joint Chiefs of Staff, *National Military Strategic Plan for the War on Terrorism* (Washington, 1 February 2006), http://www.defenselink.mil/qdr/docs/2005-01-25-Strategic-Plan.pdf, p. 3.
4. David F. Forte, *Religion is Not the Enemy,* http://www.nationalreview.com/comment/comment-forte101901.shtml.
5. *Center of Gravity,* Strange, p. ix.
6. Personal interview with Dr. Sherifa Zuhur, 31 July 2006; Email exchange with William McCants, 6 August 2006; Email exchanges with Dr. Andrew Bostom, July-August 2006.
7. "Bush: U.S. at War with 'Islamic Fascists,'" *CNN.com,* 10 August 2006, http://www.cnn.com/2006/POLITICS/08/10/washington.terror.plot/index.html.
8. William McCants, *Problems with the Arabic Name Game,* http://www.ctc.usma.edu/research/Problems%20with%20the%20Arabic%20Name%20Game.pdf, see also, Thomas O'Connor, *Islamist Extremism: Jihadism, Qutbism, and Wahhabism,* http://faculty.ncwc.edu/toconnor/429/429lect14.htm.
9. Islamism and Islamist are terms describing the worldwide puritanical Islamic revival movement that seeks to replace secular governments with Shari'a law and establish theocracies throughout the world. See O'Connor.
10. Khaled Abou El Fadl, *Islam and the Theology of Power,* http://www.islamfortoday.com/elfadl01.htm.
11. Ibid.
12. Ibid.
13. Ibid.
14. Abdul-Majid Jaffry, *Maulana Maududi's Two-Nation Theory,* http://www.witness-pioneer.org/vil/Articles/politics/mawdudi2.html. *Who was Abu Alaa Maududi?* http://www.thewahhabimyth.com/mawdudi.htm.
15. Abu al-Ala Mawdudi, *Human Rights, the West and Islam,* http://www.jamaat.org/islam/Human-RightsPolitical.html#Human; Abdul-Majid Jaffry; G. F. Haddad, *A Word About Mawdudi's Ideas,* http:// www.sunnah.org/history/Innovators/mawdudi2.htm; Abdul-Majid Jaffry.
16. Sayyeed Abdul-Ala Maududi, *Jihad in Islam* (Lahore, Pakistan: Islamic Publications), pp. 8, 9, and 24, http://www.islamistwatch.org/texts/maududi/maududi.html.
17. Online library, preface by Dr. A. M. A. Fahmy of the International Islamic forum, http://www.youngmuslims.ca/online_library/books/jihad/. Muhammad Adb al Salam Faraj, *The Neglected Duty,* trans., Johannes Jansen (New York: MacMillian Publishing, November 1986). Syed Qutb, *In the Shade of the Quran,* trans. by A. A. Shamis (Riyadh, Saudi Arabia: WAMY International, June 1995), [World Assembly of Muslim Youth is a Saudi nongovernmental organization that promotes Wahhabism.], http://www.youngmuslims.ca/online_library/tafsir/syed_qutb/; Syed Qutb, *Milestones* (American Trust Publications, December 1991), http://www.youngmuslims.ca/online_library/books/milestones/hold/index_2.asp.
18. Trevor Stanley, "Hassan al-Banna: Founder of the Muslim Brotherhood, Ikhwan al-Muslimum," *Perspectives on World History and Current Events,* 2005, http://www.pwhce.org/banna.html.
19. Yasser Khalil, *Hassan al-Banna–A Great Muslim and Teacher of Da'wa,* http://www.jannah.org/articles/hassan.html.

20. Ibid.
21. Stanley.
22. Hassan al-Banna, "Why Do the Muslims Fight," contained in *Jihad in Modern Islamic Thought A Collection,* ed., Sheikh Abdullah Bin Muhammad Bin Humaid, http://www.majalla.org/.
23. Fawaz A. Gerges, *The Far Enemy: Why Jihad Went Global* (Bronxville, N.Y.: Sarah Lawrence College) prologue, http://www.cambridge.org/us/catalogue/catalogue.asp?isbn=9780521791403.
24. McCants.
25. Sayyid Qutb, "The Right to Judge," contained in *Jihad in Modern Islamic Thought A Collection; Who was Sayyid Qutb,* http://www.thewahhabimyth.com/qutb.htm.
26. Jahiliyah, literally "ignorance," is a concise expression for the pagan practice of the days before the advent of the Prophet Muhammad (S. A. W.). Jahiliyah denotes all those world-views and ways of life which are based on rejection or disregard of heavenly guidance communicated to mankind through the Prophets and Messengers of God; the attitude of treating human life—either wholly or partly—as independent of the directives of God. http://www.islam101.com/selections/glossaryJ.html. See also, Sayyid Qutb, "The Right to Judge."
27. Qutb, "The Right to Judge."
28. Sayyid Qutb, "On Jihad," in *Jihad in Modern Islamic Thought A Collection.*
29. Takfir or takfeer. The term refers to the practice of excommunication or declaring that a Muslim individual or a Muslim group is apostate or non-believers. Some consider the punishment for being a Takfir death, http://atheism.about.com/library/glossary/islam/bldef_takfir.htm, http://www.pwhce.org/takfiri.html.
30. Gerges.
31. Ibid.
32. Ibid.
33. Ibid.
34. Kenneth Katzman, *Al Qaeda: Profile and Threat Assessment,* Congressional Research Service Report for Congress, the Library of Congress, 17 August 2005, http://www.fas.org/sgp/crs/terror/RL33038.pdf.
35. Ibid.
36. Christopher Henzel, "The Origins of al Qaeda's Ideology: Implications for US Strategy," *Parameters,* 35 (Spring 2005), http://www.carlisle.army.mil/usawc/Parameters/05spring/henzel.htm.
37. Youssef H. Aboul-Enein, "Ayman Al-Zawahiri's Knights under the Prophet's Banner: The al-Qaeda Manifesto," *Military Review* 85 (January–February 2005), http://usacac.army.mil/CAC/milreview/English/JanFeb05/JanFeb05/Bbobjan.pdf; Michael G. Knapp, "Distortion of Islam by Muslim Extremists," *Military Intelligence Professional Bulletin* (July–September 2002), 37–42; Nimrod Raphaeli, *Ayman Muhammad Rabi' Al-Zawahiri: The Making of an Arch Terrorist,* http://www.jewishvirtuallibrary.org/jsource/biography/Zawahiri.html; Henzel.
38. Henzel.
39. Abd al-Salam Faraj, author of *The Neglected Duty,* was a Qutbist who lead the assassination conspiracy against Anwar Sadat. He was a forceful voice that advocated attacks against the "near enemy," apostate Muslim regimes.
40. For a similar conclusion, see Giles Kepel, *The War for Muslim Minds: Islam and the West,* trans., Pascale Ghazaleh (Cambridge, Mass.: Belknap Press, 2004), pp. 1–2.
41. Henzel.
42. Katzman.
43. See Sami G. Hajjar, "Avoiding Holy War: Ensuring That the War on Terrorism is Not Perceived as a War on Islam," in *Defeating Terrorism: Strategic Issues Analysis,* ed., John Martin (Carlisle, Pa.: US Army War College, Strategic Studies Institute, January 2002), p. 17, http://www.strategicstudiesinstitute.army.mil/pubs/display.cfm?PubID=273.
44. Abdal-Hakim Murad, *Bin Laden's Violence is a Heresy Against Islam,* http://www.islamfortoday.com/murad04.htm.
45. James Brandon, "Koranic Duels Ease Terror," *The Christian Science Monitor,* 4 February 2005, p. 1, http://www.csmonitor.com/2005/0204/p01s04-wome.html.
46. Peter Willems, "The Dialogue Committee is Known Internationally," *Yemen Times,* http://www.yementimes.com/article.shtml?i=799&p=community&a=2.
47. Scheherezade Faramarzi, "Female Preachers Graduate," *Associated Press,* 4 May 2006.
48. Sheikh-ul-Islam, Talghat Tajuddin in a speech "The Threat of Islam or the Threat to Islam," Moscow, 28 June 2001, trans., M. Conserva, http://www.islamfortoday.com/tajuddin01.htm.

COLONEL DALE C. EIKMEIER is a strategic planner at the US Army War College's Center for Strategic Leadership. He has held a variety of command and staff assignments in CONUS, Europe, the Middle East, and Asia. He recently served as a strategist with the Multinational Forces-Iraq where he worked with the Iraqi National Security Advisor's staff. He also served as a staff augmentee planner with the J3, US Central Command, Forward, in support of Operation Enduring Freedom.

The Madrassa Scapegoat

PETER BERGEN AND SWATI PANDEY

Madrassas have become a potent symbol as terrorist factories since the September 11 attacks, evoking condemnation and fear among Western countries. The word first entered the political lexicon when the largely madrassa-educated Taliban in Afghanistan became the target of a U.S.-led strike in late 2001. Although none of the September 11 terrorists were members of the Taliban, madrassas became linked with terrorism in the months that followed, and the association stuck. For Western politicians, a certain type of education, such as the exclusive and rote learning of the Qur'an that some madrassas offer, seemed to be the only explanation for the inculcation of hate and irrationality in Islamist terrorists.

In October 2003, for example, Secretary of Defense Donald H. Rumsfeld wondered, "Are we capturing, killing or deterring and dissuading more terrorists every day than the madrassas and the radical clerics are recruiting, training and deploying against us?"[1] In the July 2004 report of the National Commission on Terrorist Attacks Upon the United States, commonly known as the 9-11 Commission, madrassas were described as "incubators of violent extremism," despite the fact that the report did not mention whether any of the 19 hijackers had attended a madrassa.[2] In the summer of 2005, Rumsfeld still worried about madrassas that "train people to be suicide killers and extremists, violent extremists."[3] As the United States marked the fourth anniversary of the September 11 attacks in the autumn of 2005, several U.S. publications continued to claim that madrassas produce terrorists, describing them as "hate factories."[4]

Yet, careful examination of the 79 terrorists responsible for five of the worst anti-Western terrorist attacks in recent memory—the World Trade Center bombing in 1993, the Africa embassy bombings in 1998, the September 11 attacks, the Bali nightclub bombings in 2002, and the London bombings on July 7, 2005—reveals that only in rare cases were madrassa graduates involved. All of those credited with masterminding the five terrorist attacks had university degrees, and none of them had attended a madrassa. Within our entire sample, only 11 percent of the terrorists had attended madrassas. (For about one-fifth of the terrorists, educational background could not be determined by examining the public record.) Yet, more than half of the group we assessed attended a university, making them as well educated as the average American: whereas 54 percent of the terrorists were found to have had some college education or to have graduated from university, only 52 percent of Americans can claim similar academic credentials. Two of our sample had doctoral degrees, and two others had begun working toward their doctorates. Significantly, we found that, of those who did attend college and/or graduate school, 48 percent attended schools in the West, and 58 percent attained scientific or technical degrees. Engineering was the most popular subject studied by the terrorists in our sample, followed by medicine.

None of the apparent masterminds of the five terrorist attacks had attended a madrassa.

The data raise questions about what type of education, if any, is actually more likely to contribute to the motivation or skills required to execute a terrorist attack. Researchers such as Dr. Marc Sageman have argued that madrassas are less closely correlated with producing terrorists than are Western colleges, where students from abroad may feel alienated or oppressed and may turn toward militant Islam.[5] Given that 27 percent of the group attended Western schools, nearly three times as many as attended madrassas, our sample seems to confirm this trend. The data also show a strong correlation between technical education and terrorism, suggesting that perpetrating large-scale attacks requires not only a college education but also a facility with technology. This type of education is simply not available at the vast majority of madrassas.

These findings suggest that madrassas should not be a national security concern for Western countries because they do not provide potential terrorists with the language and technical skills necessary to attack Western targets. This is not to say that madrassas do not still pose problems. To the extent that they hinder development by failing properly to educate students in Asian, Arab, and African countries and that they create sectarian violence, particularly in Pakistan, madrassas should remain on policymakers' minds as a regional concern.[6] A national security policy focused on madrassas as a principal source of terrorism, however, is misguided.

The Truth about Terrorist Education

"Madrassa" is a widely used and misused term. In Arabic, the word means simply "school."[7] Madrassas vary from country to country or even from town to town. They can be a day or boarding school, a school with a general curriculum, or a purely religious school attached to a mosque.[8] For the purposes of our study, "madrassa" refers to a school providing a secondary-level education in Islamic religious subjects.[9] We examined information available in U.S., European, Asian, and Middle Eastern newspapers; U.S. government reports; and books about terrorism to determine which of the 79 terrorists responsible for the five major attacks attended such madrassas. In the one instance when a terrorist was found to have attended a madrassa and later a university, we classified him as a graduate of both types of schools. Attacks in which information about the terrorists' education was scant, such as the 2000 attack on the USS *Cole* and the 2004 Madrid train bombings, were excluded from the study.

The 1993 World Trade Center Bombing

On February 26, 1993, a truck bomb exploded in the parking garage beneath the twin towers of the World Trade Center, killing six people and injuring more than 1,000. Ringleader Ramzi Yousef had hoped the bomb would kill tens of thousands by making one tower collapse onto the other. The 12 men, including Yousef, responsible for this first World Trade Center bombing were the best educated of any group we studied. All of them had some college education, with most having studied in universities in the Middle East and North Africa, and two having graduated from Western colleges. The spiritual guide of this terrorist cell, the Egyptian cleric Sheik Omar Abdel Rahman, had a master's degree and had started on his doctoral dissertation at Al Azhar University in Cairo—the Oxford of the Islamic world. Yousef, the mastermind of the plot and the nephew of the operational commander of the September 11 attacks, obtained a degree in engineering from a college in Wales. None of the attackers appeared to have attended a madrassa.

The 1998 Africa Embassy Bombings

On August 7, 1998, nearly simultaneous bombings at the U.S. embassies in Tanzania and Kenya killed 224 people. The attacks were the largest perpetrated by Al Qaeda at the time and catapulted the group and its leader, Osama bin Laden, into the public eye. The 16 attackers who orchestrated the bombings were found largely to be part of a local Al Qaeda cell. This group of men had one Western-born member, Rashed Daoud al-Owhali, who hailed from Liverpool and claimed to have been indoctrinated not at a madrassa but by audio tapes about the Afghan jihad. Recent attacks in Madrid and London have shown that immigrants and the children of immigrants living in Europe may be more dangerous than far-flung madrassa graduates. Sageman, along with scholars such as Olivier Roy and Robert S. Leiken, have noted that living in the West alienates many immigrants and has a strong correlation to Western-based terrorist activity.[10] The Africa group demonstrates another trend that later reappeared in the 2004 Madrid bombings: the formation of ties between the undereducated (and easily influenced or even criminal) and the well educated. Seven of the 16 plotters in the Africa group attended college, with two, Wadih El-Hage and Ali Mohamed, attending Western schools.

The September 11 Attacks

In the most devastating terrorist attack to date, 19 hijackers crashed three planes into the World Trade Center and the Pentagon, with a fourth plane crashing in rural Pennsylvania; nearly 3,000 people were killed. The four pilots who led the September 11 attacks all spent time at universities outside of their home countries, three of them in Germany. As the 9-11 Commission detailed, the plot took shape in Germany as they were completing their degrees.[11] The lead hijacker, Muhammad Atta, had a doctorate in urban preservation and planning from the University of Hamburg-Harburg in Germany. The 15 "muscle hijackers" vary in educational background. Little is known about some of them, including Khalid al-Mihdhar, who met the pilot, Nawaf al Hazmi, while fighting in Bosnia. Indeed, several of the terrorists we studied, if they were not well educated, were so-called career jihadists with experience fighting in regions such as Bosnia and Afghanistan. Still, even of the muscle group, six of the 15 had completed some university studies. Finally, we also examined the so-called secondary planners, who had overall control of the operation, many of whom were longtime Al Qaeda operatives, and found that all of them had attended college in Europe or the United States. Khalid Sheikh Muhammad, the operational commander of the September 11 attacks, had obtained a degree in engineering from a college in North Carolina.

Despite the fact that much of the information about the educational backgrounds of the September 11 planners and pilots has been widely reported, otherwise sophisticated analysts persist in believing that they were the products of madrassas. In his 2005 book *Future Jihad,* Walid Phares, a professor of Middle Eastern studies at Florida Atlantic University and a frequent commentator on U.S. television, explained that Wahhabism "produced the religious schools; the religious schools produced the jihadists. Among them [were] Osama bin Laden and the nineteen perpetrators of September 11."[12] In fact, bin Laden did not attend a religious school when he was growing up in Jeddah, Saudi Arabia, studying instead at the relatively progressive, European-influenced Al Thagr High School and later at King Abdul Aziz University, where he focused on economics.[13] From what is available on the public record, it seems that none of the 19 hijackers attended madrassas.

Madrassas should not be a national security concern for Western countries.

The 2002 Bali Nightclubs Bombing

Islamist terrorists attacked two tourist hotspots in Bali in October 2002, killing more than 200. As was the case with the Africa embassy bombings, the Bali attack was aimed at Western targets, in this case tourists, in a non-Western country. Yet, unlike the previous examples, Bali is the only terrorist attack to have been perpetrated in part by terrorists who attended madrassas. Nine of the 22 perpetrators attended the Al Mukmin, Al Tarbiyah Luqmanul Hakiern, and SMP Pemalang pesantran—Islamic schools of a kind particular to Indonesia.

Most Indonesian madrassas are part of the state school system and teach a broad range of subjects. Pesantren, however, such as Al Mukmin, operate outside of this system and are generally boarding schools. The curriculum at pesantren usually focuses on religion and often offers practical courses in farming or small industry.[14] This constellation of schools, particularly Al Mukmin, provided many recruits to Jemaah Islamiyah, the militant Islamist group that seeks to create fundamentalist theocracies in countries across Southeast Asia.

Even in the Bali attacks, however, five of the 22 members of the group had college degrees, particularly the key planners. The mastermind of the Bali plot, Dr. Azahari Husin, who was killed in a shootout with Indonesian police in November 2005, obtained his doctorate from the University of Reading in the United Kingdom prior to becoming a lecturer at a Malaysian university.[15] Noordin Muhammad Top attended the same Malaysian school. The third mastermind, Zulkarnaen, also known as Daud, studied biology at an Indonesian college. Azahari and Top are also suspected of involvement in the 2005 Bali bombings that killed 22 people.

The July 7, 2005, London Bombings

The July 7, 2005, bombings of three subway stations and a bus in London killed 56 people, including the suicide bombers, and were the work of homegrown British terrorists with suspected Al Qaeda ties.[16] The initial news coverage of the attack featured hyperventilating reports that the four men responsible had attended madrassas. One such piece in the *Evening Standard* stated that three of the bombers attended madrassas, which it termed "haven[s] for so-called Islamic warriors."[17] In fact, three of the four suicide attackers had some college education, and none attended a madrassa until adulthood, when their attendance consisted of brief visits lasting for periods from a few weeks to a few months. The suicide bombers made a conscious decision to travel halfway around the globe to attend radical Pakistani madrassas after they had already been radicalized in their hometown of Leeds in the United Kingdom.

Of the four suicide attackers, Hasib Hussain, a man of Pakistani descent, attended Ingram Road Primary School in Holbeck and began his secondary education at South Leeds High School. Although he did not take his postsecondary school subject exams, he held a GNVQ, or vocational degree, in business studies. He visited Pakistan in 2003, when he was likely 16 or 17, after making a pilgrimage to Mecca. It was around this time that, back in England, he began socializing with two of the other bombers, Shehzad Tanweer and Muhammad Sidique Khan, with whom he frequented the Stratford Street mosque and the Hamara Youth Access Point, a teenage center in Leeds. Khan and Tanweer have similar backgrounds of elementary and secondary education in the United Kingdom. Khan later studied child care at Dewsbury College, and Tanweer studied sports science at Leeds Metropolitan University. Similar to Hussain, Tanweer traveled to Pakistan to study briefly at a madrassa in 2004, at the age of 21. The fourth bomber, Jamaican-born Germaine Lindsay, attended Rawthorpe High School in Huddersfield in the United Kingdom and converted to Islam at the age of 15.[18] Local influences appeared to play a far greater role in the radicalization of these young men than did their brief trips to Pakistani madrassas.

Where Are Terrorists Really Educated?

History has taught that terrorism has been a largely bourgeois endeavor, from the Russian anarchists of the late nineteenth century to the German Marxists of the Bader-Meinhof gang of the 1970s to the apocalyptic Japanese terror cult Aum Shinrikyo of the 1990s. Islamist terrorists turn out to be no different. It thus comes as no surprise that missions undertaken by Al Qaeda and its affiliated groups are not the work of impoverished, undereducated madrassa graduates, but rather of relatively prosperous university graduates with technical degrees that were often attained in the West.

Bin Laden, Al Qaeda's leader, is the college-educated son of a billionaire; his deputy, Dr. Ayman al-Zawahiri, is a surgeon from a distinguished Egyptian family. Ali Mohamed, Al Qaeda's longtime military trainer, is a former Egyptian army major with a degree in psychology who started work on a doctorate in Islamic history when he moved to the United States in the mid-1980s. Other Al Qaeda leaders worked in white collar professions such as accounting, the vocation of Rifa'i Taha, a leader of the Egyptian terrorist organization known as the Islamic Group, who signed on to Al Qaeda's declaration of war against the United States in 1998.

Immigrants and their children in Europe may be more dangerous than madrassa grads.

Our findings suggest that policymakers' concerns regarding madrassas are overwrought. More than half of the terrorists that we studied took university-level courses, and nearly half of this group attended Western schools. The majority of the college-educated group had technical degrees, which sometimes provided skills for their later careers as terrorists. Yousef's degree in electrical engineering, for example, served him well when he built the bomb that was detonated underneath the World Trade Center in 1993. It was the rare terrorist who studied exclusively at a madrassa, and only one terrorist managed to transition from madrassa to university, suggesting that madrassas simply should not be part of the profile of a terrorist capable of launching a significant anti-Western attack. Only in Southeast Asia, as seen in the Bali attack in 2002, did madrassas play a role in the terrorists' education. Yet, even in this example, the madrassa graduates paired up with better-educated counterparts to execute the attacks. Masterminding a large-scale attack thus requires technical skills beyond those provided by a madrassa education.

Because madrassas generally cannot produce the skilled terrorists capable of committing or organizing attacks in Western countries, they should not be a national security concern. Conceiving of them as such will lead to ineffective policies, and cracking down on madrassas may even harm the allies that Washington attempts to help. In countries such as Pakistan, where madrassas play a significant role in education, particularly in rural areas, the wholesale closure of madrassas may only damage the educational system and further increase regional tensions. One of Gen. President Pervez Musharraf's plans to reduce extremism, expelling foreign students and dual citizens, may be effective in reducing the number of militant Arabs studying in Pakistan but may also harm neighboring countries such as Afghanistan, which rely on Pakistani madrassas, by leaving thousands of poor Afghans without any education.[19]

> **Cracking down on madrassas may even harm the allies that Washington attempts to help.**

This is not to suggest that Western countries should ignore madrassas entirely. To the extent that they remain a domestic problem because they undermine educational development and spawn sectarian violence, particularly in Pakistan, Western policymakers should remain vigilant about working with local governments to improve madrassas, as well as state schools. Efforts at observation and regulation might be more usefully directed toward European Islamic centers such as the Hamara Youth Access Point, where the London bombers gathered. Armed with a more realistic understanding of religious schools, particularly the differences in the curricula they provide across countries and regions, policymakers can hone their strategy with respect to madrassas. Only by eliminating the assumption that madrassas produce terrorists capable of carrying out major attacks can Western countries shape more effective policies to ensure national security.

Notes

1. "Rumsfeld's War-on-Terror Memo," May 20, 2005, http://www.usatoday.com/news/washington/executive/rumsfeld-memo.htm (reproducing memo titled "Global War on Terrorism" to Gen. Dick Myers, Paul Wolfowitz, Gen. Pete Pace, and Doug Feith, dated October 26, 2003).
2. *The 9/11 Commission Report: The Final Report of the National Commission on Terrorist Attacks Upon the United States* (New York: W.W. Norton, 2004), p. 367.
3. Donald Rumsfeld, interview by Charlie Rose, *Charlie Rose Show*, PBS, August 20, 2005.
4. Alex Alexiev, "If We Are to Win the War on Terror, We Must Do Far More," *National Review*, November 7, 2005; Nicholas D. Kristof, "Schoolyard Bully Diplomacy," *New York Times*, October 16, 2005, sec. 4, p. 13.
5. See Marc Sageman, *Understanding Terrorist Networks* (Philadelphia: University of Pennsylvania Press, 2004).
6. For a detailed study of the relationship between madrassas and violence in Pakistan, see Saleem H. Ali, "Islamic Education and Conflict: Understanding the Madrassahs of Pakistan" (draft report, United States Institute of Peace, July 1, 2005).
7. Febe Armanios, "Islamic Religious Schools, *Madrasas*: Background," *CRS Report for Congress*, RS21654 (October 29, 2003), p. 1, http://fpc.state.gov/documents/organization/26014.pdf.
8. Ibid., pp. 1–2.
9. Ibid., p. 2.
10. See generally Olivier Roy, *Globalized Islam: The Search for a New Umma* (New York: Columbia University Press, 2004); Robert S. Leiken, "Europe's Angry Muslims," *Foreign Affairs* 84, no. 4 (July/August 2005): 120–135.
11. *9/11 Commission Report*, pp. 160–169.
12. Walid Phares, *Future Jihad: Terrorist Strategies Against America* (New York: Palgrave Macmillan, 2005), p. 63.
13. Peter Bergen, *The Osama bin Laden I Know: An Oral History of Al Qaeda's Leader* (New York: Free Press, 2006), chap. 1.
14. Uzma Anzar, "Islamic Education: A Brief History of Madrassas With Comments on Curricula and Current Pedagogical Practices" (draft report, March 2003).
15. Richard C. Paddok, "Terrorism Suspect Dies in Standoff," *Los Angeles Times*, November 10, 2005, p. A4.
16. See Peter Bergen and Paul Cruickshank, "Clerical Error: The Dangers of Tolerance," *New Republic*, August 8, 2005, pp. 10–12.
17. Richard Edwards, "On Their Way to Terror School," *Evening Standard*, July 18, 2005, p. C1.
18. Ian Herbert, "Portrait of Bomber as a Dupe Fails to Convince Bereaved," *Independent*, September 24, 2005, p. 16.
19. Naveed Ahmad, "Pakistani Madrassas Under Attack," *Security Watch*, October 8, 2005, http://www.isn.ethz.ch/news/sw/details.cfm?ID=12418.

PETER BERGEN is a Schwartz fellow at the New America Foundation and an adjunct professor at the School of Advanced International Studies at Johns Hopkins University. **SWATI PANDEY** is a researcher and writer at the Los Angeles Times.

Holy Orders
Religious Opposition to Modern States

MARK JUERGENSMEYER

No one who watched in horror as the towers of the World Trade Center crumbled into dust on September 11, 2001, could doubt that the real target of the terrorist assault was US global power. Those involved in similar attacks and in similar groups have said as much. Mahmood Abouhalima, one of the Al Qaeda-linked activists convicted for his role in the 1993 attack on the World Trade Center, told me in a prison interview that buildings such as these were chosen to dramatically demonstrate that "the government is the enemy."

While the US government and its allies have been frequent targets of recent terrorist acts, religious leaders and groups are seldom targeted. An anomaly in this regard was the assault on the Shi'a shrine in the Iraqi city of Najaf on August 29, 2003, which killed more than 80 people including the venerable Ayatollah Mohammad Baqir al Hakim. The Al Qaeda activists who allegedly perpetrated this act were likely more incensed over the Ayatollah's implicit support for the US-backed Iraqi Governing Council than they were jealous of his popularity with Shi'a Muslims. Since the United Nations has also indirectly supported the US occupation of Iraq and Afghanistan, it too has been subject to Osama bin Laden's rage. This may well be the reason why the UN office in Baghdad was the target of the devastating assault on August 19, 2003, which killed the distinguished UN envoy Sergio Vieira de Mello. Despite the seeming diversity of the targets, the object of most recent acts of religious terror is an old foe of religion: the secular state.

Secular governments have been the objects of terrorism in virtually every religious tradition—not just Islam. A Christian terrorist, Timothy McVeigh, bombed the Oklahoma City Federal Building on April 19, 1995. A Jewish activist, Yigal Amir, assassinated Israel's Prime Minister Yitzhak Rabin. A Buddhist follower, Shoko Asahara, orchestrated the nerve gas attacks in the Tokyo subways near the Japanese parliament buildings. Hindu and Sikh militants have targeted government offices and political leaders in India. In addition to government offices and leaders, symbols of decadent secular life have also been targets of religious terror. In August 2003, the Marriott Hotel in Jakarta, frequented by Westerners and Westernized Indonesians, was struck by a car bomb. The event resembled the December 2002 attacks on Bali nightclubs, whose main patrons were college-age Australians. In the United States, abortion clinics and gay bars have been targeted. The 2003 bombings in Morocco were aimed at clubs popular with tourists from Spain, Belgium, and Israel. Two questions arise regarding this spate of vicious religious assaults on secular government and secular life around the world. Why is religion the basis for opposition to the state? And why is this happening now?

Why Religion?

Religious activists are puzzling anomalies in the secular world. Most religious people and their organizations either firmly support the secular state or quiescently tolerate it. Bin Laden's Al Qaeda, like most of the new religious activist groups, is a small group at the extreme end of a hostile subculture that is itself a small minority within the larger Muslim world. Bin Laden is no more representative of Islam than McVeigh is of Christianity or Asahara of Buddhism.

Still, it is undeniable that the ideals of activists like bin Laden are authentically and thoroughly religious. Moreover, even though their network consists of only a few thousand members, they have enjoyed an increase in popularity in the Muslim world after September 11, 2001, especially after the US-led occupations of Afghanistan and Iraq. The authority of religion has given bin Laden's cadres the moral legitimacy to employ violence in assaulting symbols of global economic and political power. Religion has also provided them the metaphor of cosmic war, an image of spiritual struggle that every religion contains within its repository of symbols, seen as the fight between good and bad, truth and evil. In this sense, attacks such as those on the World Trade Center and UN headquarters in Baghdad were very religious. They were meant to be catastrophic acts of biblical proportions.

From Worldly Struggles to Sacred Battles

Although recent acts of religious terrorism such as the attacks on the World Trade Center and United Nations had no obvious military goal, they were intended to make an impact on the public consciousness. They are a kind of perverse performance of power meant to ennoble the perpetrators' views of the world while drawing viewers into their notions of cosmic war. In my 2003 study of the global rise of religious violence, *Terror in the Mind of God,* I found a strikingly familiar pattern. In almost every recent case of religious violence, concepts of cosmic war have been accompanied by claims of moral justification. It is not so much that religion has become politicized but that politics has become religionized. Through enduring absolutism, worldly struggles have been lifted into the high proscenium of sacred battle.

This is what makes religious warfare so difficult to address. Enemies become satanized, and thus compromise and negotiation become difficult. The rewards for those who fight for the cause are trans-temporal, and the timelines of their struggles are vast. Most social and political struggles look for conclusions within the lifetimes of their participants, but religious struggles can take generations to succeed.

I once had the opportunity to point out the futility—in secular military terms—of the radical Islamic struggle in Palestine to Dr. Abdul Aziz Rantisi, the head of the political wing of the Hamas movement. It seemed to me that Israel's military force was strong enough that a Palestinian military effort could never succeed. Dr. Rantisi assured me that "Palestine was occupied before, for two hundred years." He explained that he and his Palestinian comrades "can wait again—at least that long." In his calculation, the struggles of God can endure for eons before their ultimate victory.

Insofar as the US public and its leaders embraced the image of war following the September 11 attacks, the US view of the war was also prone to religionization. "God Bless America" became the country's unofficial national anthem. US President George Bush spoke of defending America's "righteous cause" and of the "absolute evil" of its enemies. However, the US military engagement in the months following September 11 was primarily a secular commitment to a definable goal and largely restricted to objectives in which civil liberties and moral rules of engagement still applied.

In purely religious battles waged in divine time and with heavenly rewards, there is no need to compromise goals. There is also no need to contend with society's laws and limitations when one is obeying a higher authority. In spiritualizing violence, religion gives the act of violence remarkable power.

Ironically, the reverse is also true: terrorism can empower religion. Although sporadic acts of terrorism do not lead to the establishment of new religious states, they make the political potency of religious ideology impossible to ignore. The first wave of religious activism, from the Islamic revolution in Iran in 1978 to the emergence of Hamas during the Palestinian *intifada* in the early 1990s, focused on religious nationalism and the vision of individual religious states. Now religious activism has an increasingly global vision. The Christian militia, the Japanese Aum Shinrikyo, and the Al Qaeda network all target what they regard as a repressive and secular form of global culture and control.

Part of the attraction of religious ideologies is that they are so personal. They impart a sense of redemption and dignity to those who uphold them, often men who feel marginalized from public life. One can view their efforts to demonize their enemies and embrace ideas of cosmic war as attempts at ennoblement and empowerment. Such efforts would be poignant if they were not so horribly destructive.

Yet they are not just personal acts. These violent efforts of symbolic empowerment have an effect beyond whatever personal satisfaction and feelings of potency they impart to those who support and conduct them. The very act of killing on behalf of a moral code is a political statement. Such acts break the state's monopoly on morally sanctioned killing. By putting the right to take life in their own hands, the perpetrators of religious violence make a daring claim of power on behalf of the powerless—a basis of legitimacy for public order other than that on which the secular state relies.

Coincidence of Globalization and Modernization

These recent acts of religious violence are occurring in a way different from the various forms of holy warfare that have occurred throughout history. They are responses to a contemporary theme in the world's political and social life: globalization. The World Trade Center symbolized bin Laden's hatred of two aspects of secular government—a certain kind of modernization and a certain kind of globalization— even though the Al Qaeda network was itself both modern and transnational. Its members were often highly sophisticated and technically skilled professionals, and its organization was composed of followers of various nationalities who moved effortlessly from place to place with no obvious nationalist agenda or allegiance. In a sense, they were not opposed to modernity and globalization, so long as it fit their own design. But they loathed the Western-style modernity that they perceived secular globalization was forcing upon them.

Some 23 years earlier, during the Islamic revolution in Iran, Ayatollah Khomeini rallied the masses with the similar notion that the United States was forcing its economic exploitation, political institutions, and secular culture on an unknowing Islamic society. The Ayatollah accused urban Iranians of having succumbed to "Westoxification"—an inebriation with Western culture and ideas. The many strident movements of religious nationalism that have erupted around the world in the more than two decades following the Iranian revolution have echoed this cry. This anti-Westernism has at heart an opposition to a certain kind of modernism that is secular, individualistic, and skeptical. Yet, in a curious way, by accepting the modern notion of the nation-state and adopting the technological and financial instruments of modern society, many of these movements of religious nationalism have claimed a kind of modernity on their own behalf.

Religious politics could be regarded as an opportunistic infection that has set in at the present weakened stage of the secular nation-state. Globalization has crippled secular nationalism and the nation-state in several ways. It has weakened them economically, not only through the global reach of transnational businesses, but also by the transnational nature of their labor supply, currency, and financial instruments. Globalization

> ## Re-Evaluating Religion
>
> In an age of globalization, pre-modernists, modernists, and post-modernists offer contrasting perspectives on the role of religion.
>
> ### Pre-Modernist Perspective
> - Views religious organizations as essential to effective opposition of communist and authoritarian regimes
> - Relies on past historical experience
> - Thinks that the spread of secularization by means of globalization will cause only negative effects by destroying the power of religious organizations to check the power of government
>
> ### Modernist Perspective
> - Believes globalization is a drive force in the secularization of society and slow disappearance of religious groups throughout the world
> - Argues that religions that abide in the modern age exist as marginal communities that sometimes initiate conflict against secularization
> - Holds that religious organizations can play the positive role of correcting accidental distortions or perversions of the generally beneficial course of modernization
>
> ### Post-Modernist Perspective
> - Rejects traditional, pre-modern religions
> - Allows for "spiritual experiences" to occur without religious constraints
> - Considers expressive individualism to be a core value. Globalization brings about the success of expressive individualism breaking up all traditional, local, and governmental structures.
>
> —Foreign Policy Research Institute

has eroded their sense of national identity and unity through the expansion of media and communications, technology, and popular culture, and through the unchallenged military power of the United States. Some of the most intense movements for ethnic and religious nationalism have arisen in states where local leaders have felt exploited by the global economy, unable to gain military leverage against what they regard as corrupt leaders promoted by the United States, and invaded by images of US popular culture on television, the Internet, and motion pictures.

Other aspects of globalization—the emergence of multicultural societies through global diasporas of peoples and cultures and the suggestion that global military and political control might fashion a "new world order"—has also elicited fear. Bin Laden and other Islamic activists have exploited this specter, and it has caused many concerned citizens in the Islamic world to see the US military response to the September 11 attacks as an imperialistic venture and a bully's crusade, rather than the righteous wrath of an injured victim. When US leaders included the invasion and occupation of Iraq as part of its "war against terror," the operation was commonly portrayed in the Muslim world as a ploy for the United States to expand its global reach.

> "By adopting the... instruments of modern society, many of these movements of religious nationalism have claimed a kind of modernity on their own behalf.

This image of a sinister US role in creating a new world order of globalization is also feared in some quarters of the West. Within the United States, for example, the Christian Identity movement and Christian militia organizations have been alarmed over what they imagine to be a massive global conspiracy of liberal US politicians and the United Nations to control the world. Timothy McVeigh's favorite book, *The Turner Diaries,* is based on the premise that the United States has already unwittingly succumbed to a conspiracy of global control from which it needs to be liberated through terrorist actions and guerilla bands. In Japan, a similar conspiracy theory motivated leaders of the Aum Shinrikyo religious movement to predict a catastrophic World War III, and attempted to simulate Armageddon with their 1995 nerve gas attack in a Tokyo subway train.

Identity and Control

As far-fetched as the idea of a "new world order" of global control may be, there is some truth to the notion that the integration of societies and the globalization of culture have brought the world closer together. Although it is unlikely that a cartel of malicious schemers designed this global trend, the effect of globalization on local societies and national identities has nonetheless been profound. It has undermined the modern idea of the state by providing non-national and transnational forms of economic, social, and cultural interaction. The global economic and social ties of the inhabitants of contemporary global cities are intertwined in a way that supercedes the idea of a national social contract—the Enlightenment notion that peoples in particular regions are naturally linked together in a specific country. In a global world, it is hard to say where particular regions begin and end. For that matter, in multicultural societies, it is hard to say how the "people" of a particular nation should be defined.

This is where religion and ethnicity step in to redefine public communities. The decay of the nation-state and disillusionment with old forms of secular nationalism have produced both the opportunity and the need for nationalisms. The opportunity has arisen because the old orders seem so weak, yet the need for national identity persists because no single alternative form of social cohesion and affiliation has yet appeared to dominate public life the way the nation-state did in the 20th century. In a curious way, traditional forms of social identity have helped to rescue one of Western modernity's central themes: the idea of nationhood. In the increasing absence of any other demarcation of national loyalty and commitment, these old staples—religion, ethnicity, and traditional culture—have become resources for national identification.

Consequently, religious and ethnic nationalism has provided a solution in the contemporary political climate to the perceived insufficiencies of Western-style secular politics. As secular ties have begun to unravel in the post-Soviet and postcolonial era, local leaders have searched for new anchors with which to ground their social identities and political loyalties. What is significant about these ethno-religious movements is their creativity—not just their use of technology and mass media, but also their appropriation of national and global networks. Although many of the framers of the new nationalisms have reached back into history for ancient images and concepts that will give them credibility, theirs are not simply efforts to resuscitate old ideas from the past. These are contemporary ideologies that meet present-day social and political needs.

In the context of Western modernism, the notion that indigenous culture can provide the basis for new political institutions, including resuscitated forms of the nation-state, is revolutionary. Movements that support ethno-religious nationalism are therefore often confrontational and sometimes violent. They reject the intervention of outsiders and their ideologies and, at the risk of being intolerant, pander to their indigenous cultural bases and enforce traditional social boundaries. It is thus no surprise that they clash with each other and with defenders of the secular state. Yet even such conflicts serve a purpose for the movements: they help define who they are as a people and who they are not. They are not, for instance, secular modernists.

Understandably, then, these movements of anti-Western modernism are ambivalent about modernity, unsure whether it is necessarily Western and always evil. They are also ambivalent about globalization, the most recent stage of modernity. On one hand, these political movements of anti-modernity are reactions to the globalization of Western culture. They are responses to the insufficiencies of what is often touted as the world's global standard: the elements of secular, Westernized urban society that are found not only in the West but in many parts of the former Third World, seen by their detractors as vestiges of colonialism. On the other hand, these new ethno-religious identities are alternative modernities with international and supernational aspects of their own. This means that in the future, some forms of anti-modernism will be global, some will be virulently antiglobal, and yet others will be content with creating their own alternative modernities in ethno-religious nation-states.

Each of these forms of religious anti-modernism contains a paradoxical relationship between forms of globalization and emerging religious and ethnic nationalisms. One of history's ironies is that the globalism of culture and the emergence of transnational political and economic institutions enhance the need for local identities. They also promote a more localized form of authority and social accountability.

The crucial problems in an era of globalization are identity and control. The two are linked in that a loss of a sense of belonging leads to a feeling of powerlessness. At the same time, what has been perceived as a loss of faith in secular nationalism is experienced as a loss of agency as well as selfhood. For these reasons, the assertion of traditional forms of religious identities are linked to attempts to reclaim personal and cultural power. The vicious outbreaks of antimodernist religious terrorism in the first few years of the 21st century can be seen as tragic attempts to regain social control through acts of violence. Until there is a surer sense of citizenship in a global order, religious visions of moral order will continue to appear as attractive, though often disruptive, solutions to the problems of authority, identity, and belonging in a globalized world.

MARK JUERGENSMEYER is Professor of Sociology and Director of Global and International Studies at the University of California, Santa Barbara.

From *Harvard International Review*, Winter 2004, pp. 34–38. Copyright © 2004 by the President of Harvard College. Reprinted by permission.

UNIT 8
Women and Terrorism

Unit Selections
29. **Female Suicide Bombers: A Global Trend,** Mia Bloom
30. **Cross-Regional Trends in Female Terrorism,** Karla J. Cunningham
31. **Explosive Baggage: Female Palestinian Suicide Bombers and the Rhetoric of Emotion,** Terri Toles Patkin
32. **The Bomb Under the Abaya,** Judith Miller
33. **Picked Last: Women and Terrorism,** Alisa Stack-O'Connor

Key Points to Consider
- Why are the experiences of women often misunderstood?
- Why do terrorist organizations recruit women?
- Should female terrorists be viewed as "portents of gender equality"?
- How should governments respond to the threat of female terrorists?

Student Web Site
www.mhcls.com/online

Internet References
Further information regarding these Web sites may be found in this book's preface or online.

Free Muslims Against Terrorism Jihad
http://www.freemuslims.org/news/articles.php?article=140
Foreign Policy Association—Terrorism
http://www.fpa.org/newsletter_info2478/newsletter_info.htm
Israel Ministry of Foreign Affairs—The Exploitation of Palestinian Women for Terrorism
http://www.mfa.gov.il/mfa/go.asp?MFA0//10
Women, Militarism, and Violence
http://www.iwpr.org/pdf/terorrism.pdf

Department of Defense photo by MC3 William S. Parker

Women are often portrayed as victims of political violence. But the fact that women have played a critical role in the evolution of contemporary international terrorism is too frequently ignored. In the 1970s women like Ulrike Meinhof and Gudrun Ensslin of the German Baader-Meinhof Gang, Mara Cagol of the Red Brigades in Italy, Fusako Shigenobu of the Japanese Red Army, and Leila Khaled of the Palestine Liberation Organization held key roles in their organizations and significantly influenced the development of modern terrorism.

Today, while often less visible than their male counterparts, women are once again actively involved in international terrorism, with their involvement seen to be on the rise. Women like American Lori Berenson, a former anthropology student at MIT, who became involved with the Tupac Amaru Revolutionary Movement (MRTA) and Shinaz Amuri (AKA Wafa Idris), a 28-year-old volunteer medic who became a young Palestinian heroine after she killed herself in a suicide bombing, are the role models for a new generation of women bent on creating terror.

In the first article, Mia Bloom examines the motives of women who choose to become suicide bombers and discusses potential reasons for recruitment of women by terrorist organizations. She concludes that despite their increased involvement that these women are not likely to become "portents of gender equality." In the second article, Karla Cunningham examines the roles of female terrorists in various regions of the world, focusing on why they engage in political violence. She also discusses the future role of women in international terrorism. Next, Terri Toles Patkin looks at the role of women in a culture of violence. She argues that a lack of opportunities and a culture of martyrdom motivate young Palestinina women to become suicide bombers. She provides a series of short biographical profiles of what some believe to be a new generation of suicide bombers. In the fourth article, Judith Miller interviews two would-be women suicide bombers in Israel's Hasharon prison. Based on her interviews and a review of the expert literature on the subject, she explores how governments can best respond to this threat. Finally, Alisa Stack-O'Connor examines how and why terrorist organizations use women in their attacks. Focusing on their propaganda value, the obstacles they face, and the tactical advantage they provide, she emphasizes the importance of women's role in terrorist organizations.

Female Suicide Bombers
A Global Trend

MIA BLOOM

Ever since Muriel Degauque, a Belgian convert to radical Islam, blew herself up in Iraq last November, questions have surfaced about the growing role of women in terrorism. Degauque's attack occurred on the same day that Sajida Atrous al-Rishawi's improvised explosive device (IED) failed to detonate at a wedding in Amman. This apparent growing trend of women bombers has the general public and counterterrorism specialists concerned because of its implication that women will be key players in future terrorist attacks.

Yet the recent focus on female suicide bombers neglects the long history of female involvement in political violence. In reality women have participated in insurgency, revolution, and war for a long time. Women have played prominent roles in the Russian Narodnaya Volya in the nineteenth century, the Irish Republican Army, the Baader-Meinhof organization in Germany, the Italian Red Brigades, and the Popular Front for the Liberation of Palestine. Historically, however, women have mostly played supporting roles. "Society, through its body of rules and its numerous institutions, has conventionally dictated [women's] roles within the boundaries of militancy. Assisting in subordinate roles is welcomed and encouraged. Actually fighting in the war is not."[1] Most often, the primary contribution expected of women has been to sustain an insurgency by giving birth to many fighters and raising them in a revolutionary environment.

Women are now taking a leading role in conflicts by becoming suicide bombers—using their bodies as human detonators for the explosive material strapped around their waists. The first female suicide bomber, a seventeen-year-old Lebanese girl named Sana'a Mehaydali, was sent by the Syrian Socialist National Party (SSNP/PPS), a secular, pro-Syrian Lebanese organization, to blow herself up near an Israeli convoy in Lebanon in 1985, killing five Israeli soldiers. Of the twelve suicide attacks conducted by the SSNP, women took part in six of them. From Lebanon, the incidence of female bombers spread to other countries—Sri Lanka, Turkey, Chechnya, Israel, and now Iraq. Out of the approximately seventeen groups that have started using the tactical innovation of suicide bombing, women have been operatives in more than half of them.[2] Between 1985 and 2006, there have been in excess of 220 women suicide bombers, representing about 15 percent of the total.[3] Moreover, the upsurge in the number of female bombers has come from both secular and religious organizations, even though religious groups initially resisted using women.

Their participation in suicide bombings starkly contradicts the theory that women are more likely to choose peaceful mechanisms for conflict resolution than men are—that women are inherently more disposed toward moderation, compromise, and tolerance in their attitudes toward international conflict.[4] (In fact, most existing notions of women in the midst of conflict portray them as *victims* of war rather than as perpetrators.) Complicating these notions of femininity further is the fact that the IED is often disguised under a woman's clothing to make her appear pregnant, and so beyond suspicion or reproach. On April 25, 2006, Kanapathipillai Manjula Devi, used such a tactic to penetrate a military hospital in Colombo, Sri Lanka. Posing as the wife of a soldier on her way to the maternity clinic, she gained access to the high-security facility.[5] She had even visited the maternity clinic for several weeks prior to her attack to maintain her cover.[6] The advent of women suicide bombers has thus transformed the revolutionary womb into an exploding one.

Why do women become suicide bombers? Motives vary: to avenge a personal loss, to redeem the family name, to escape a life of sheltered monotony and achieve fame, or to equalize the patriarchal societies in which they live.

In many instances, the women are seeking revenge. Consider, for example, the women who join the Liberation Tigers of Tamil Eelam (LTTE), which is based in the Tamil areas, in the northern and eastern provinces, of Sri Lanka.[7] According to anthropologist Darini Rajasingham-Senanayake, the government has committed organized violence against the Tamils through a systematic campaign of disappearances, rape, checkpoint searches, and torture—as well as the elimination of whole villages in remote areas.[8] Moreover, in the midst of conflict, the government forces have not been mindful to differentiate civilians from combatants and militants.

These oppressive tactics, along with civilian deaths, have soured the Tamil population on the government's assurances of devolution and equal rights, which in turn has emboldened the LTTE and solidified their control of Jaffna.[9] Rajasingham-Senanayake explains, "In this context militant groups who infiltrate camps have little difficulty in recruiting new cadres from deeply frustrated and resentful youth, men and women, girls and boys."[10] In fact, the atrocities need not even hurt a Tamil woman directly for her to join the LTTE, as long as they affect the Tamil community as a whole:

> Witnessing rape . . . hearing about rape from other villagers and the Army's killing of Tamil youth (girls and boys arrested by the Sri Lankan Army) . . . and the feeling of helplessness in not being able to defend against the Sri Lankan Army are the main reasons for the girls joining the LTTE.[11]

As the example of the Tamil women demonstrates, women generally become involved, at least initially, for personal, rather than ideological, reasons. In Chechnya, to give another example, the female operatives are called 'Black Widows,' because many were the sisters, mothers, or wives of Chechen men killed in battles with federal troops.[12]

Zarema Muzhikhoyeva was one such widow. On July 10, 2003, she was arrested carrying a homemade bomb on Tverskaya-Yamskaya Ulitsa.

> Muzhikhoyeva [admitted to having been] recruited by Chechen rebels as a suicide bomber, in exchange for $1,000 in compensation to her relatives to repay for jewelry she had stolen from them. . . . When the rebels sent her to Moscow to carry out her mission, she changed her mind and got herself arrested by police.[13]

Muzhikhoyeva was the first bomber to be captured alive. When the court sentenced her to the maximum of twenty years despite the fact that she had opted not to explode her cargo, Muzhikhoyeva shouted, "Now I know why everyone hates the Russians!"—adding that she would return and "blow you all up."[14] This powerful image resonated throughout the Chechen community. Even though Muzhikhoyeva had done the right thing, the Russian court had not granted her any leniency, radicalizing her even more in the process.

However, while women usually become suicide bombers in response to a personal tragedy, some may also believe they can change their society's gender norms through militant involvement. According to Clara Beyler, a counterterrorism analyst in Washington, D.C., and formerly a researcher for the International Policy Institute for Counterterrorism in Herzliya, Israel,

> There is a difference between men and women suicide attackers: women consider combat as a way to escape the predestined life that is expected of them. When women become human bombs, their intent is to make a statement not only in the name of a country, a religion, a leader, but also in the name of their gender.[15]

Again, the Chechen Black Widows provide strong support for this idea. Historically, a woman's most relevant role in Chechen society was to raise children, form their characters, and make them strong so that they became warriors for the Islamic faith (*mujahideen*) when they grew up. Even after they were allowed to be a part of battles, female insurgents were initially used merely to supply medical aid, food, and water to the men; they also carried weapons and ammunition across enemy territory and maintained the guerrillas' morale. At the Dubrovka theater siege, for example, the men took care of the explosives and intimidation, while the women distributed medical supplies, blankets, water, chewing gum, and chocolate. Though the women allegedly toyed threateningly with their two-kilo bomb belts, they did not control the detonators—the men retained control of the remotes.[16]

The Black Widows, on the other hand,

> choose to die as a bomber in order to show the strength of the resistance. They can wear kamikaze bomb-belts, or drive a truck that is full of explosives. Chechen guerrillas are inspired with the image of Khava Barayeva—the first to walk the way of martyrdom. Chechen rebels . . . write poems and songs about her.[17]

The use of female operatives, especially by a religious militant organization like the Chechen Al Ansar al-Mujahideen, is significant. Until recently, a female bomber was almost certainly sent by a secular organization. In effect,

> [t]he growth in the number of Chechen female suicide bombers signaled the beginning of a change in the position of fundamentalist Islamic organizations regarding the involvement of women in suicide attacks—a change that [has since] become devastatingly apparent.[18]

The idea of violence empowering women had already spread through the West Bank and the Gaza Strip. On January 27, 2002, Wafa Idris became the first Palestinian woman to perpetrate an act of suicide terror. A twenty-seven-year-old aid worker for the Palestinian Red Crescent Society from the Al-Am'ari refugee camp near Ramallah, she was carrying a backpack with explosives:

> The bomb in her rucksack was made with TNT packed into pipes. Triacetone triperoxide, made by mixing acetone with phosphate, is ground to a powder. In a grotesque parody of the domestic female stereotype, it is usually ground in a food mixer, before being fed into metal tubes.[19]

On the way to delivering it to someone else, she got stuck in a revolving door, detonating the explosives.[20] She killed one Israeli civilian and wounded 140 others.

Though her death was allegedly accidental, it instantly transformed her into a cult heroine throughout the Arab world. The military wing of Fatah, the Al-Aqsa Martyrs Brigades, took responsibility for the attack three days later. Birzeit students appealed for more women to emulate Idris. Commenting on Idris's death, female students stated, "The struggle is not limited strictly to men. . . . It's unusual [for a Palestinian woman to martyr herself], but I support it. . . . Society does not accept this idea because it is relatively new, but after it happens again, it will become routine."[21] And in an editorial entitled, "It's a Woman!" *Al-Sha'ab* proclaimed:

It is a woman who teaches you today a lesson in heroism, who teaches you the meaning of Jihad, and the way to die a martyr's death. It is a woman who has shocked the enemy, with her thin, meager, and weak body. . . . It is a woman who blew herself up, and with her exploded all the myths about women's weakness, submissiveness, and enslavement. . . . It is a woman who has now proven that the meaning of [women's] liberation is the liberation of the body from the trials and tribulations of this world . . . and the acceptance of death with a powerful, courageous embrace.[22]

The Al-Aqsa Martyrs Brigade even set up a special unit to train female suicide bombers and named it after Wafa Idris.[23] "We have 200 young women from the Bethlehem area alone ready to sacrifice themselves for the homeland," bragged one Al-Aqsa leader.[24] Matti Steinberg, a former special advisor on Arab affairs to the Israeli government, described how a Hamas bimonthly publication—dedicated to women—was replete with letters to the editor from Palestinian women asking for permission to participate directly in the conflict and asserting their right to be martyrs.[25]

Palestinian women have torn the gender classification out of their birth certificates, declaring that sacrifice for the Palestinian homeland would not be for men alone; on the contrary, all Palestinian women will write the history of the liberation with their blood, and will become time bombs in the face of the Israeli enemy. They will not settle for being mothers of martyrs.[26]

This participation of Palestinian women in violence had global reverberations. In 2002, Indian security forces twice went on high alert, in January and again in August, to guard against possible attacks by female suicide bombers. The suspects sprang from two Pakistan-based Islamic organizations, Jaish-e-Mohammed and Lashkar-e-Taiba, both associated with Al Qaeda. In March 2003, *Asharq Al-Awsat* published an interview with a woman calling herself 'Um Osama,' the alleged leader of the women *mujahideen* of Al Qaeda. The Al Qaeda network claimed to have set up squads of female suicide bombers—purportedly including Afghans, Arabs, Chechens, and other nationalities—under orders from bin Laden to attack the United States:

We are preparing for the new strike announced by our leaders, and I declare that it will make America forget . . . the September 11 attacks. The idea came from the success of martyr operations carried out by young Palestinian women in the occupied territories. Our organization is open to all Muslim women wanting to serve the (Islamic) nation. . . .[27]

The involvement of Palestinian women in suicide bombings has also had an extreme impact on the cultural norms of Palestinian society. Palestinians have long had a set of rules that describe and limit gender roles (although Palestinian women have been mobilized politically since the 1960s). These rules have dictated the separation of the sexes and restricted women to the private sphere—particularly in rural areas. Through violence, women have placed themselves on the frontlines, in public, alongside men to whom they are not related. This has resulted in a double trajectory for militant Palestinian women—convincing society of their valid contributions while at the same time reconstructing the normative ideals of the society.[28]

At the same time, it is difficult to ascertain whether terrorist organizations are actually employing women out of a heightened sense of gender equality. According to Farhana Ali, an international policy analyst at the RAND Corporation:

The liberal door that now permits women to participate in operations will likely close once male jihadists gain new recruits and score a few successes in the war on terrorism. At the same time that a Muslim woman is indispensable to male-dominated terrorist groups and the war effort, she also is expendable. The sudden increase in female bombers over the past year may represent nothing more than a riding wave of al-Qaeda's success rather than a lasting effort in the global jihad. . . . [T]here is no indication that these men would allow the mujahidaat to prevail authority and replace images of the male folk-hero.[29]

Indeed, the drive to recruit women as suicide bombers may actually be little more than a tactical response to the need for more manpower. Besides adding women to their numbers, insurgent organizations can shame the men into participating, in the style of right-wing Hindu women who goad men into action by saying, "Don't be a bunch of eunuchs."[30] This point is underscored by the bombers themselves. A propaganda slogan in Chechnya reads: "Women's courage is a disgrace to that of modern men."[31] And in the martyrdom video Ayat Akras—an eighteen-year-old Palestinian woman who set off a bomb in the Supersol supermarket in Jerusalem—taped before she blew herself up, she stated, "*I am going to fight* [emphasis added] instead of the sleeping Arab armies who are watching Palestinian girls fighting alone"—an apparent jab at Arab leaders for not being sufficiently proactive or manly.[32]

It appears that insurgent organizations in Iraq are similarly inspired. Although women form a very small number of the bombers in Iraq, the message is that men should not let women do their fighting for them. On March 29, 2003, within weeks of the U.S. invasion of Iraq, two women (one of whom was pregnant) perpetrated suicide attacks against the Coalition forces. Then, on April 4, 2003, Al-Jazeera television played a video of two Iraqi women vowing to commit suicide attacks: "We say to our leader and holy war comrade, the hero commander Saddam Hussein, that you have sisters that you and history will boast about." In a separate video, another woman, identified as Wadad Jamil Jassem, assumed a similar position: "I have devoted myself [to] Jihad for the sake of God and against the American, British, and Israeli infidels and to defend the soil of our precious and dear country."[33]

Terrorist groups may also find women useful as suicide bombers because of the widespread assumption that women are inherently nonviolent. Women can bypass, for example, Israel's restrictive checkpoints and border policy, which has proven fairly effective against Palestinian insurgent organizations inside the occupied territories. Since the mid-1990s, it has been almost impossible for unmarried men under the age of forty to get permits to cross the border into Israel. Women don't arouse suspicion like men and blend in more effectively with Israeli civilians: "Attacks perpetrated by women have tended to be those where the terrorist planners needed the perpetrator to blend in on the Israeli 'street.' These female terrorists . . . westernize their appearance, adopting modern hairstyles and short skirts."[34] This is reminiscent of the ways in which women in Algeria transformed their appearance to participate in the FLN revolution against the French occupation during the Battle of Algiers in the early 1960s. The use of the least likely suspect is the most likely tactical adaptation for a terrorist group under scrutiny. Terrorist groups have therefore looked further afield for volunteers, to women and children.

A growing number of insurgent organizations are also taking advantage of the fact that suicide bombing, especially when perpetrated by women and young girls, garners a lot of media attention, both in the West and in the Middle East. Attacks by women receive eight times the media coverage as attacks by men, again largely because of the expectation that women are not violent. Realizing this, the Al-Aqsa Martyrs Brigades have drawn propaganda mileage from their female bombers.[35] The image of women defying tradition to sacrifice their lives for the Palestinian cause has drawn more attention to the despair of the Palestinian people. "Suicide attacks are done for effect, and the more dramatic the effect, the stronger the message; thus a potential interest on the part of some groups in recruiting women." [36]

This tactic also makes the terrorists appear more threatening by erasing the imagined barriers between combatants and noncombatants, terrorists and innocent civilians. This is the underlying message conveyed by female bombers: terrorism has moved beyond a fringe phenomenon; insurgents are all around you. For secular militant Palestinian groups at least, Akras's death demonstrated that they are not all religious fanatics who believe that God will grant them entrance to Paradise or reward them with seventy-two virgins (*houris*). Nor are the leaders all gripped by a burning desire to see all females locked behind black veils. For them, the involvement of women is meant to signal that they are waging a political war, not a religious one—and the suicide bombings are a carefully planned and executed part of a precise political strategy.[37]

Degauque's attack raises an added element of female converts, of which there are thousands in Europe, married to Muslim men and willing to make the sacrifice. Increasingly, bombers in Iraq have been female converts to Islam and not Arab women. On June 2, 2006, a woman known only as Sonja B, a German convert to Islam, was seized in Germany, foiling her planned attack in Iraq. After his arrest last November in Morocco with sixteen other militants suspected of terrorist activities, Mohamed Reha, a Moroccan Belgian affiliated with the Moroccan Islamic Combat Group (GICM), claimed, "The partners of several suspected terrorists being detained in Belgium are ready to carry out suicide attacks in Morocco."[38] He continued: "Many Muslim women whose husbands were arrested in Belgium would like to become involved in Jihad, the holy war. [I was asked] to help them by finding someone to train them and supply them with explosives." According to Belgian sources, an Algerian named Khalid Abou Bassir, who claims to be the coordinator for Al Qaeda in Europe, was designated to lead a team of female suicide bombers.[39]

Converts are a particularly dangerous group, not only because they can evade most profiles, but also because they carry European passports. Also, like in most faiths, converts may feel the need to prove themselves and can be more radical in their views than are people born into the faith—thus making them more susceptible to extremist interpretations of Islam. Converts, male as well as female, may very well be a key resource in the future for terrorist organizations. Pascal Cruypennick was arrested in Belgium for sending suicide bombers to Iraq; other converts, like Richard Reid and Jose Padilla, are also in custody. In Belgium, as in many other countries in Europe, it appears converts are leading the charge to jihad in Iraq.

Are women suicide bombers portents of gender equality in their societies?

Unlikely. Fanaticism and death cults generally do not lead to liberation politics for women. Women may exhibit courage and steely resolve as terrorists, but if they are part of a system that affords them unequal status, then feminism doesn't apply.[40] It is telling that the women who participate in suicide bombings are usually among the most socially vulnerable: widows and rape victims. In fact, in several instances, the women were raped or sexually abused not by representatives of the state but by the insurgents themselves. As such they are stigmatized, and thus easily recruited and exploited.

> Those who send these women do not really care for women's rights; they are exploiting the personal frustrations . . . of these women for their own political goals, while they continue to limit the role of women in other aspects of life.[41]

The evidence that males in terrorist organizations exercise control over the women is also strong. Palestinian female cadres are not welcomed into the paramilitary terrorist factions, which remain dominated by men. Even in the Al-Aqsa Martyrs Brigades, women are not welcomed by the ranks of the male fighters. And in Sri Lanka, where women constitute 30 percent of the suicide attackers and form crucial conventional fighting units, few women are among the top leadership. Beyler remarks:

> It is mostly men who govern this infrastructure. . . . Women are rarely involved in the higher echelons of the decision-making process of these groups. Women may volunteer, or . . . be coerced to conduct a murderous strike, but the woman's role is ultimately dictated by the patriarchal hierarchy that rules Palestinian society and its terrorist groups.[42]

In fact, the LTTE has attempted to compel married Tamil women, including retired female cadres, to adopt more traditional and conservative forms of dress (the sari and head coverings) and not wear trousers in LTTE-controlled areas.

However, some may argue that there is a difference between the lower-ranking female operatives in terrorist groups and the women who are planners and leaders, such as Ulrike Meinhof, who provided the intellectual backbone of the Baader-Meinhof organization. The assassination of Czar Alexander II in 1881 was also organized by a woman, and many other nineteenth-century revolutionaries were female. Nevertheless, in many cases, women's participation in violence did not lead to their equal status in the societies that formed subsequent to the revolutions. It is interesting to note that the women who played violent roles in revolutionary movements in Iran, Palestine, and Algeria were not included in the leadership of the successor regimes.

The problem lies in the fact that these women, rather than confronting archaic patriarchal notions of women and exploding these myths from within, are actually operating under them. These include a well-scripted set of rules in which women sacrifice themselves; the patriarchal conception of motherhood, for example, is one of self-denial and self-effacement. In a sense, martyrdom is the ultimate and twisted fulfillment of these ideals. So, the spectacle of female suicide bombers doesn't challenge the patriarchy as much as provide evidence of its power. The message female suicide bombers send is that they are more valuable to their societies dead than they ever could have been alive.

Notes

1. Lucy Frazier, "Abandon Weeping for Weapons: Palestinian Women Suicide Bombers," http://www.nyu.edu/classes/keefer/joe/frazier.html (accessed November 21, 2003).
2. "From Jerusalem to Jakarta and from Bali to Baghdad, the suicide bomber is clearly the weapon of choice for international terrorists." Quoting Don Van Natta, Jr., "Big Bang Theory: The Terror Industry Fields its Ultimate Weapon," *New York Times*, August 24, 2003, sec. 4, 1.
3. Yoram Schweitzer, ed., *Female Suicide Bombers: Dying for Equality?* Jaffee Center for Strategic Studies, Memorandum 84, August 2006, 8.
4. Emile Sahliyeh and Zixian Deng, "The Determinants of Palestinians' Attitude Toward Peace with Israel," *International Studies Quarterly* 47 (4) (December 2003): 701.
5. Arjuna Guwardena, "Female Black Tigers: A Different Breed of Cat," in Schweitzer, ed., *Female Suicide Bombers*, 87.
6. Tamil sources, interview by Mia Bloom, July 2006.
7. In July 1997 three national human rights commissions established in 1994 found that there had been 16,742 disappearances since July 1988.
8. Darini Rajasingham-Senanayake, interview by Mia Bloom, Colombo, Sri Lanka, October 25, 2002.
9. Robert I. Rotberg, ed., *Creating Peace in Sri Lanka: Civil War and Reconciliation* (Cambridge, Mass.: World Peace Foundation and the Belfer Center for Science and International Affairs, 1999), 9.
10. Rajasingham-Senanayake in ibid., 62.
11. Tamil sources, personal correspondence with the author, November 26, 2003.
12. There is some dispute about whether the Black Widows are in fact widows. Irina Bazarya argues that many are not widows but have been a product of societal forces predisposing and molding them to become militants as an expression of Ayat, traditional Chechen mores (Ph.D. thesis, University of Cincinnati, forthcoming).
13. Anatoly Medetsky, "Court Tries Alleged Tverskaya Bomber," *St. Petersburg Times*, March 30, 2004.
14. Steven Lee Meyers, "From Dismal Chechnya, Women Turn to Bombs," *New York Times*, September 10, 2004.
15. Clara Beyler, "Messengers of Death: Female Suicide Bombers," http://www.ict.org.il/articles/articledet.cfm?articleid=470.
16. Anne Speckhard and Khapta Akhmedova, "Black Widows: The Chechen Female Suicide Terrorists," in Schweitzer, *Female Suicide Bombers*, 63–90.
17. Ibid.
18. Yoram Schweitzer, "A Fundamental Change in Tactics," *Washington Post*, October 19, 2003, B03.
19. Giles Foden, "Death and the Maidens," *The Guardian*, July 18, 2003.
20. *Agence France Presse*, April 12, 2002.
21. *Kul al-Arab* (Israel), February 1, 2002.
22. *Al-Sha'ab* (Egypt), February 1, 2002.
23. Sophie Claudet, "More Palestinian Women Suicide Bombers Could Be On The Way: Analysts," *Middle East Times*, March 1, 2002.
24. Graham Usher, "At 18, Bomber Became Martyr and Murderer," *The Guardian*, March 30, 2002.
25. Matti Steinberg, interview by Mia Bloom, September 2002.
26. According to Dr. Samiya Sa'ad Al-Din, *Al-Akhbar* (Egypt), February 1, 2002.
27. "Bin Laden Has Set Up Female Suicide Squads: Report," *Arab News*, Dubai, March 13, 2003.
28. Frazier, "Abandon Weeping for Weapons."
29. Farhana Ali, "Muslim Female Fighters: An Emerging Trend," *Terrorism Monitor* 3 (21) (November 3, 2005).
30. Amrita Basu, "Hindu Women's Activism and the Questions it Raises," in Patricia Jeffrey and Amrita Basu, eds., *Appropriating Gender: Women's Activism and Politicized Religion in South Asia* (London: Routledge, 1998).
31. Dimitri Sudakov, "Shamil Besaev Trains Female Suicide Bombers," *Pravda*, May 15, 2003.
32. Libby Copeland, "Female Suicide Bombers: The New Factor in Mideast's Deadly Equation," *Washington Post*, April 27, 2002, C1.
33. Cited by Roman Kupchinsky in "'Smart Bombs' with Souls," *Organized Crime and Terrorism Watch* 3 (13) (April 17, 2003).
34. Yoni Fighel, "Palestinian Islamic Jihad and Female Suicide Bombers," October 6, 2003, www.ict.org.
35. Scott Atran argues that as a result of Akras's martyrdom, Saudi Arabia sent 100 million dollars to fund the Al-Aqsa Intifada.
36. Claudet, "More Palestinian Women Suicide Bombers Could Be On The Way."
37. Usher, "At 18, Bomber Became Martyr and Murderer."
38. AFP report, cited by *De Standaard*.
39. The use of women remains a point of contestation among different streams of Salafism in Al Qaeda Central. The

recently killed Abu Musab al-Zarqawi certainly had no qualms about using women in Iraq or Jordan, but other militants, like Samir Azzouz, have thus far refused. As long as the majority of suicide bombers in Iraq come from the Gulf, the numbers of women will remain low since neither the Saudis nor other more conservative Wahhabis will permit women to go on jihad.

40. Foden, "Death and the Maidens."
41. Ibid.
42. Clara Beyler, "Using Palestinian Women as Bombs," *New York Sun,* November 15, 2006.

MIA BLOOM is assistant professor of international affairs at the University of Georgia. She is the author of *"Dying to Kill: The Allure of Suicide Terror"* (2005).

Article 30

Cross-Regional Trends in Female Terrorism

> Worldwide, women have historically participated in terrorist groups but their low numbers and seemingly passive roles have undermined their credibility as terrorist actors for many observers. This analysis contends that female involvement with terrorist activity is widening ideologically, logistically, and regionally for several reasons: increasing contextual pressures (e.g., domestic/international enforcement, conflict, social dislocation) create a mutually reinforcing process driving terrorist organizations to recruit women at the same time women's motivations to join these groups increases; contextual pressures impact societal controls over women that may facilitate, if not necessitate, more overt political participation up to, and including, political violence; and operational imperatives often make female members highly effective actors for their organizations, inducing leaders toward "actor innovation" to gain strategic advantage against their adversary.

KARLA J. CUNNINGHAM
Department of Political Science, SUNY Geneseo, Geneseo, New York, USA

Although women have historically been participants in terrorist groups[1] in Sri Lanka, Iran, West Germany, Italy, and Japan, to name a few cases, very little scholarly attention has been directed toward the following questions: first, why women join these groups and the types of roles they play; and second, why terrorist organizations recruit and operationalize women and how this process proceeds within societies that are usually highly restrictive of women's public roles. Answering these questions may facilitate the creation of a comprehensive strategy for combating terrorism and limiting political violence. Regardless of region, women's involvement with politically violent organizations and movements highlights several generalizable themes. First, there is a general assumption that most women who become involved with terrorist organizations do so for personal reasons, whether a personal relationship with a man or because of a personal tragedy (e.g., death of a family member, rape). This assumption mirrors theories about female criminal activity in the domestic realm, as well as legitimate political activity by women,[2] and diminishes women's credibility and influence both within and outside organizations.

Second, because women are not considered credible or likely perpetrators of terrorist violence, they can more easily carry out attacks and assist their organizations. Women are able to use their gender to avoid detection on several fronts: first, their "non-threatening" nature may prevent in-depth scrutiny at the most basic level as they are simply not considered important enough to warrant investigation; second, sensitivities regarding more thorough searches, particularly of women's bodies, may hamper stricter scrutiny; and third, a woman's ability to get pregnant and the attendant changes to her body facilitate concealment of weapons and bombs using maternity clothing, as well as further impeding inspection because of impropriety issues. Finally, popular opinion typically considers women as victims of violence, including terrorism, rather than perpetrators, a perspective that is even more entrenched when considering women from states and societies that are believed to be extremely "oppressed" such as those in the Middle East and North Africa (MENA). Such a perspective is frequently translated into official and operational policy, wherein women are not seriously scrutinized as operational elements within terrorist and guerilla organizations because of limited resources and threat perception.

This analysis contends that female involvement with terrorist activity is widening ideologically, logistically, and regionally for several reasons: first, increasing contextual pressures (e.g., domestic/international enforcement, conflict, social dislocation) creates a mutually reinforcing process driving terrorist organizations to recruit women at the same time women's motivations to join these groups increases; contextual pressures impact societal controls over women thereby facilitating, if not necessitating, more overt political participation up to, and including, political violence; and operational imperatives often make female members highly effective actors for their organizations, inducing leaders toward "actor innovation" to gain strategic advantage against their adversary.[3]

Contextual Pressures and Innovation

Since 11 September 2001 United States law enforcement and national security efforts have been aggressively targeted at identifying current and potential terrorist actors who threaten the country's interests. This activity has largely centered on Muslim males because of the types of terrorist attacks that have threatened the United States over the past decade (e.g., the World Trade Center (1993), the African Embassy bombings (1998), and the USS *Cole* bombing (2000) to name a few). All of the incidents were planned and implemented by Muslim, and predominantly Arab, males residing within the United States or abroad.

Terrorist organizations tend to be highly adaptive and although there are fundamental differences among terrorist groups along ideological lines (e.g., ethnonationalist, religious, MarxistLeninist) that influence the types of ends these organizations seek, they are typically unified in terms of the means (e.g., political violence) they are willing to employ to achieve their goals. The means/goals dichotomy is reflected by the absence of a single definition of terrorism with which all can agree.[4] Nevertheless, an ancient Chinese proverb quickly gets to the heart of terrorism noting that its purpose is "to kill one and frighten 10,000 others."[5]

Problematic, and evidenced by the evolving nature of campaigns in Sri Lanka and Israel/Palestine, as well as historical examples from Ireland and Lebanon, is that terrorist organizations tend to adapt to high levels of external pressure by altering their techniques and targets. Terrorist organizations learn from each other and "[t]he history of terrorism reveals a series of innovations, as terrorists deliberately selected targets considered taboo and locales where violence was unexpected. These innovations were then rapidly diffused, especially in the modem era of instantaneous and global communications."[6] Corresponding to existing terrorism theory, the use of suicide campaigns is an example of one type of tactical adaptation utilized by terrorist organizations, especially in the Arab–Israeli conflict and Sri Lanka, and both cases have also witnessed an evolution in targets (e.g., combatant to civilian).

This analysis suggests that terrorist organizations "innovate" on an additional level, particularly under heavy government pressure or to exploit external conditions, to include new actors or perpetrators.[7] In both Sri Lanka[8] and Palestine, female participation within politically violent organizations has increased and women's roles have expanded to include suicide terrorism. Sri Lanka's "Black Tigers," composed of roughly 50 percent women, is symbolic of this adaptation. In 2002, the Al-Aqsa Martyrs Brigade in the Occupied Territories began actively recruiting women to act as suicide bombers in its campaign against Israeli targets. Other organizations have demonstrated efforts to recruit and employ wo men. For example, the Algerian-based Islamic Action Group (GIA) operation planned for the Millennium celebration in 1999 reportedly had a woman, Lucia Garofalo, as a central character. The Revolutionary Armed Forces of Colombia (FARC) and Peru's Shining Path have growing levels of female operatives, and even right-wing extremist groups in the United States, such as the World Church of the Creator (WCOTC), are reportedly witnessing high female recruitment levels and one woman associated with the rightist movement, Erica Chase, went on trial in summer 2002 with her boyfriend in an alleged plot to bomb symbolic African-American and Jewish targets.

Women's Political Violence and the Role of Society: The Case of Algeria

Almost universally women have been considered peripheral players by both observers and many terrorist organizations, typically relegated to support functions such as providing safe houses or gathering intelligence. However, women have been central members of some organizations, such as Shigenobu Fusako, founder and leader of the Japanese Red Army (JRA), and Ulrike Meinhof, an influential member of the West German Baader-Meinhof Gang. In Iran, Ashraf Rabi was arrested in 1974 by the SAVAK, the country's secret police, after a bomb accidentally detonated in her headquarters. In Sri Lanka, women have been effective suicide bombers for the Liberation Tigers for Tamil Eelam (LTTE) and interestingly, their role is modeled after women's participation in the Indian National Army (INA) during the 1940s war with Britain, which included female suicide bombers.[9] Women have also historically been active, albeit less visible members, of a range of right-wing organizations including the Ku Klux Klan (KKK)[10] and the Third Reich.[11] If women's involvement with political violence is interpreted more broadly to include revolutionary movements, then scholarly discourse clearly demonstrates the importance of women like Joan of Arc and women during the Russian Revolution.[12]

Thus, even a cursory look at history provides numerous examples of a diverse array of cases and roles of women's involvement with political violence. Despite historical evidence though, most observers remain surprised and baffled by women's willingness to engage in political violence, especially within the context of terrorism. Importantly, the "invisibility" of women both within terrorist organizations, and particularly their assumed invisibility within many of the societies that experience terrorism, makes women an attractive actor for these organizations, an advantage that female members also acknowledge. This invisibility also makes scholarly inquiry of the phenomenon more difficult and may lull observers into the false assumption that women are insignificant actors within terrorist organizations.

An analysis of the role of "veiled" and "unveiled" women during the 1950s Algerian resistance against the French provides insights into the process by which women were consciously mobilized into "terrorist" roles within a MENA case by both politically violent organizations and the women who chose to join these organizations. Significantly, "[t]he Algerian woman's entrance into the Revolution as political agent was simultaneous with the deployment of the necessarily violent 'technique of terrorism,'" and the veil became "both a dress and a mask," facilitating women's operational utility during the Revolution.[13]

Mirroring scholarly discourse on the "popular upsurge" in transitions against authoritarian rule in which civil society "surges" and then retreats, women's incorporation into the Algerian resistance movement emerged within a process of resistance to international oppression, suggesting that the societal sector may have been momentarily, albeit effectively, mobilized to include women.[14]

The phased mobilization of women into the Algerian resistance movement, and the societal environment that facilitated it, is argued to have had three distinct junctures. Prior to 1956, Algerian resistance led to the "cult of the veil" and women's decisions to veil were an active response to colonial attempts to unveil them and thereby dominate society even further. Only men were involved in armed struggle during this period but French adaptation to resistance tactics prompted male leaders to hesitantly transform their strategy and include women in the "public struggle." This initiated the second phase of women's mobilization, wherein "terrorist tactics are first fully utilized" and the conflict moved to urban areas and women unveiled in order to exploit their opponent. The final phase occurred when "woman ... was transformed into a 'woman-arsenal': Carrying revolvers, grenades, hundreds of false identity cards or bombs, the unveiled Algerian woman move[d] like a fish in the Western waters."[15] "By 1957, the veil reappeared because everyone was a suspected terrorist and the veil facilitated the concealment of weapons." Further, "[r]esistance [wa]s generated through the manipulation, transformation, and reappropriation of the traditional Arab woman's veil into a 'technique of camouflage' for guerilla warfare."[16]

The societal process(es) that facilitated the coalescence of organizational and individualist interests in Algeria is significant. There occurred "[a] transformation of the Muslim notion of femininity, even if only momentarily during decolonization, [which] is central to theorizing the general range of *possibilities* for Algerian women's subjectivity and agency."[17] Significantly, this same type of process has been visible within the Palestinian context for at least three decades. Although women were not actively visible in the earlier periods of the Arab–Israeli conflict, with the creation of the General Union of Palestinian Women (1969) and the spread of education, there was a growing idea among Palestinian leaders "that women constitute half the available manpower resource, one that a small, embattled nation cannot afford to waste. Women began to participate, publicly, in every crisis, from Wahdat camp in the 1970 Amman battles to the latest Israeli invasion in South Lebanon." Although women were willing to participate, and Palestinian leaders were clearly willing to rely on them, Arafat's conception of their role conflicted with societal conceptions of women's roles, thereby making it difficult for women to fully participate in the conflict.[18]

The Algerian case is illustrative of a number of themes that will be developed in this article. First, there was a mutually reinforcing process driving both women and organizations using political violence together. The revolutionary features of Algerian resistance against external, colonial control led to broad political mobilization that included women, a process engendered not only by the promise of socialist "equality" but also by the colonial state's efforts to regulate the veil. Furthermore, the entrenched features of a war for independence inextricably involves virtually every societal segment and ensures that the conflict extends to the household level. Second, the deepening sociopolitical process of the resistance increasingly overlapped with operational imperatives within the all-male resistance movement that indicated the utility of using women against the French.

Third, Algerian men and women generally shared the same political objective—freedom from French colonial domination. Equally significant, however, is that women and men held a secondary, albeit divergent, goal regarding social change; women clearly wished for greater equality, albeit not in the Western feminist sense, whereas men saw social change as asserting more authentic cultural forms (e.g., Islam). The articulation of the latter's vision of social change is captured in *La Charte d'Alger* (1964) wherein women's inferiority under colonialism resulted from poor interpretations of Islam to which women "naturally" reacted. As a result, "[t]he war of liberation enabled the Algerian woman to assert herself by carrying out responsibilities *side by side* with man and taking part in the struggle.... In this sense the charter reveals its unwillingness discursively to allow women's participation in the war to be the product of their chosen activity. Women's historical action is legitimized by their proximity to men ... not by their agency."[19]

This process led to two outcomes that are visible in other cases. First, upon achieving the group's ends, women's participation therein is reinterpreted or reframed as less authentic, which allows women to be legitimately politically peripheralized (i.e., because they were not full and "authentic" participants) and their objectives, particularly with respect to social change, to be dismissed. Second, women's participation is not individually chosen; rather, it is facilitated by relationships with others or structural factors (e.g., poverty) that distance women from the violence they participated in, allowing society (and emergent political leaders) to not only separate women from the citizenship rights inherent in military-type service but also placing women's violence within a more palatable context. Importantly, this process mirrors women's participation in war and even instances of political mobilization within more limited (i.e., less violent) environments of political change, suggesting that it is not unique to terrorist or revolutionary structures and rather reflects more embedded features of female citizenship and political participation.

Patterns of Operational Female Terrorism

Not only have women historically been active in politically violent organizations, the regional and ideological scope of this activity has been equally broad. Women have been operational (e.g., regulars) in virtually every region and there are clear trends toward women becoming more fully incorporated into numerous terrorist organizations. Cases from Colombia, Italy, Sri Lanka, Pakistan, Turkey, Iran, Norway, and the United States suggest that women have not only functioned in support capacities, but have also been leaders in organization, recruitment, and fund-raising, as well as tasked with carrying out the most deadly missions undertaken by terrorist organizations—suicide bombings. Regardless of the region, it is clear that women are choosing to participate in politically violent organizations irrespective of their respective organizational leaders' motives for recruiting them.[20]

European Female Terrorism

European terrorist organizations are among the oldest groups to examine and offer the first insights into women's roles in these organizations. Women have been drawn to leftist and rightist organizations in Europe, and have thus been involved in groups with goals ranging from separatism to Marxist-Leninism. Women have been, and in certain cases continue to be, active members of several terrorist organizations within Europe including the Euskadi Ta Askatasuna (ETA, Basque Homeland and Unity), the Irish Republican Army (IRA), and the Italian Red Brigades (RD), to name a few. Mirroring the Palestinian conflict, which will be discussed later, Irish women, particularly mothers, have been widely active in their conflict with the British, which was waged close to home in their neighborhoods and communities.

One examination of the operational role of women in Italy's various terrorist factions during the 1960s and 1970s identifies several important tendencies. Although women generally accounted for no more than 20 percent of terrorist membership during this period, Italian women who participated in terrorist organizations were overwhelmingly drawn to leftist and nationalist organizations. This corresponded to a general period of social change, evidenced by movement in areas such as divorce, abortion, education, and employment, which allowed the Italian left to recruit and mobilize the country's women.[21] Women within the Italian left had a good chance of functioning as "regulars" and occasionally in leadership roles, particularly during the later stages of the organization's operations.[22]

The Italian experience correlates with a general trend[23] in which leftist organizations tend to attract more female recruits not only because their ideological message for political and social change (e.g., equality) resonates with women, but also because those ideas influence leadership structures within the groups. As a result, "[w]omen tend to be over-represented in positions of leadership in left-wing groups and to be underrepresented in right-wing groups."[24] Conversely, rightist organizations have more limited recruitment of women and they have historically been characterized by an almost uniform absence of female leaders. In Norway, male domination of rightist organizations, and the inability of women to obtain leadership positions, prompted the creation of Valkyria, an all-women rightist organization that allowed members to develop leadership skills and opinions.[25]

North American Female Terrorism

Women's roles North American-based terrorist organizations mirrors the variability of Europe but includes an international element that is distinguishing, at least at this juncture. First, there is an important division between women based on "origination," for lack of a better word. One group of women involved in alleged terrorist organizations are members of, or closely tied with, an expatriate or immigrant community that has links to international terrorism. The other group of women has links to domestic terrorist organizations,[26] and within this category there are three subsets: those belonging to right-wing organizations that include the WCOTC[27] and the Aryan Nation, as well as militia movements and "patriot" organizations; those belonging to "leftist" groups typically linked to Puerto Rican nationalism;[28] and those belonging to "special interest" terrorist groups that range from leftist to rightist including the Animal Liberation Front (ALF), the Earth Liberation Front (ELF), and anti-abortion activists.[29] Second, women's roles in North American terrorist organizations are highly influenced by their organization's target. For most international terrorist organizations, North America is less a theater of operation than an extremely important locus of financial, logistical, and ideological support for operations in other parts of the world. Obviously, for domestic terrorist organizations this is not a limiting factor. Third, readily available social and political freedoms in the region facilitate travel, communication, and organizational advancement that may be unattainable in other states. Finally, most connections involve both Canada and the United States, particularly with respect to legal entry and residency status for international terrorist groups.

Both the Mujahadeen-e-Khalq (MEK) and the Kurdistan Workers' Party (PKK) have attracted official attention in both the United States and Canada since 2000 for incidents involving female members. Mahnaz Samadi became a member of the MEK in 1980 and was an active fighter for the organization against Iranian targets in the 1980s, including alleged terrorist attacks in Tehran in 1982. After becoming leader of the National Liberation Army and the National Council of Resistance (NCR), a MEK civilian front, she replaced Robab Farahi-Mahdavieh in 1993 to head NCR fundraising in North America. Mahdavieh is alleged to have been involved with the 1992 attack against the Iranian embassy in Ottawa, leading to her deportation from Canada in 1993. Samadi was arrested in 2000 by Canadian officials and was deported to the United States where senior officials became involved to prevent her deportation to Iran.[30] A similar fund-raising role was allegedly carried out by Zehra Saygili (a.k.a. Aynur Saygili, Beser Gezer)[31] and Hanan Ahmed Osman (a.k.a. Helin Baran)[32] both with the PKK. Osman allegedly entered Canada in 1984 and was granted refugee status. She then turned to recruiting, fund-raising, and propaganda activities on behalf of the PKK. Saygili arrived in Canada in 1996 and allegedly became active with the Kurdish Cultural Association in Montreal to raise money and support for the PKK.[33]

Another woman suspected of having ties with terrorist networks, but later cleared by the U.S. government under somewhat vague circumstances, was a Montreal woman born in Italy, Lucia Garofalo. Garofalo was allegedly linked to Ahmed Ressam, who was found guilty in U.S. federal court of plotting a terrorist attack within the United States around the Millennium celebrations. Garofalo pled guilty to two counts of illegally transporting individuals into the United States, including her attempt to smuggle Bouabide Chamchi through an unstaffed border crossing in Vermont. She also admitted to providing him with a stolen French passport. Garofalo and Chamchi were arrested after explosive-sniffing dogs positively indicated on the vehicle she was driving. One week before attempting to transport Chamchi into the United States, Garofalo reportedly successfully transported a Pakistani man into the country, raising speculation at the time that she was transporting aliens into the United States. Phone records linking Garofalo with Ressam and other members of the conspiracy, vehicle ownership by a reported member of the Algerian Islamic League, travel records showing numerous trips to Europe, Morocco, and Libya without apparent funding to support such travel, and personal ties linked Garofalo to several individuals indicted in the Millennium operation.[34] Because terrorist charges have been dropped against Ms. Garofalo, her overall role in the Millennium plot is unknown and likely minimal; however, she is reported to have had contact with a large number of individuals linked to the plot and is married to Yamin Rachek who was deported from Canada and has been wanted by both German and British officials for theft and passport fraud. In an effort to secure counsel for her husband, Garofalo allegedly was in contact with one of the individuals linked to the Millennium plot.

Both the Anti-Defamation League (ADL)[35] and the Southern Poverty Law Center (SPLC) have noted an emerging trend in U.S. right-wing movements involving the growing mobilization of female members, particularly on the Internet. According to the SPLC, women now make up 25 percent of right-wing groups in the United States and as much as 50 percent of new recruits, and these young women want a greater role in their organizations, including leadership, than their predecessors have demanded.[36] Considering that domestic terrorism remains the most likely source of terrorist activity in the United States, according to the Federal Bureau of Investigation (FBI), and that right-wing terrorist groups are among the most active domestic terrorists in the country, this trend is noteworthy.

Lisa Turner, founder of the "Women's Frontier" of the WCOTC, provides insights into the perceived role of women for this and other White supremacist organizations.[37] Although acknowledging the role of women in combat and as martyrs for the organization (particularly Vicki Weaver and Kathy Ainsworth[38]), Turner states that "most women are not 'Shining Path' guerilla fighters." She rejects the use of women as suicide bombers ("cannon fodder") by the LTTE not on the basis that such a role is beyond women, but that it emanates from male exploitation of women that appears conjoined with their "non-White" status. Turner concentrates on avoiding a generalized understanding of what is, or is not, a revolutionary and from this argument she asserts that women's roles within the organization should be a function of their unique talents and abilities. This includes leadership positions and she notes that women can become Reverends within the organization as well as Hasta Primus, the second highest position within the organization and the main assistant to the group's leader, the Pontifex Maximus.[39] Female leadership within right-wing groups is not isolated to the WCOTC; Rachel Pendergraft is reportedly a lieutenant in the Ku Klux Klan, an organization that has clearly targeted potential and current members with a women's website.[40] Women have also been associated with potentially more violent activities, such as Erica Chase, who went on trial in summer 2002 for an alleged plot to bomb prominent African-American and Jewish targets.

Women have played a central and important role in the Puerto Rican nationalist movement, particularly the Puerto Rican Armed Forces of National Liberation (FLAN) and *Los Macheteros* (The Machete Wielders or the Puerto Rican Peoples' Army), both designated as terrorist organizations by the FBI. Women such as Blanca Canales and Adelfa Vera were significant leaders in the early nationalist movement and women are significantly represented in nonterrorist, but "supportive" entities like the Puerto Rican New Independence Movement (NMIP) and various demonstrations surrounding U.S. military exercises on Vieques. Additionally, women have been tried and incarcerated in the United States for their affiliation and actions with Puerto Rican nationalist movements. For example, 5 of 15 individuals arrested and tried by the United States between 1980 and 1985 for sedition, conspiracy, and illegal weapons possession were women (Dylcia Pagan, Alejandrina Torres, Carmen Valentin, and Alicia and Ida Luz Rodriguez) with Pagan (a.k.a. Dylcia Pagan Morales) considered the leader of the group by the government.[41]

For both the ALF and ELF, the most visible members are male, as evidenced by spokespeople (e.g., Craig Rosebraugh of the ELF) and arrests. However, this surface impression is likely not indicative of the actual rosters of these organizations and the individuals who take part in their operations. According to the FBI, the ELF and ALF have committed 600 criminal acts since 1996 amounting to more than US$42 million in damages.[42] Neither the ALF nor ELF disseminate lists of their members and members' names tend to only come to the surface based on arrest records.[43] In a report documenting actions undertaken by the ELF and ALF in 2001, of the 23 individuals associated with various legal actions ranging from arrest, imprisonment, and subpoenas only 3 were women.[44] However, this should not be construed as totally representative of female participation rates within these organizations, based upon historical trends that clearly demonstrate higher female participation rates within leftist organizations.

To date women affiliated with designated terrorist organizations in North America, both international and domestic, have played mixed roles in their respective organizations. International organizations appear to have incorporated women into more important structures, particularly those associated with fund-raising and recruitment, although cases remain few and far between. Domestic terrorist groups are increasingly targeting females for recruitment, and are attracting a diverse occupational and generational group of women. However, their roles within the leadership structures of their respective organizations is either minimal (right wing) or unknown (special interest). Leftist organizations have traditionally centered on Puerto Rican independence and have frequently involved women in a variety of capacities, including leadership positions, mirroring trends visible in Latin America and other "nationalist" settings.

Latin American Female Terrorism

Women have historically been involved in numerous revolutionary movements in Latin America (e.g., Cuba, El Salvador,

Nicaragua, Mexico) so their more visible role in groups like the FARC and Shining Path is not surprising.[45] Within Latin America, two of the most notable terrorist organizations designated by the U.S. Department of State, Colombia's FARC and the Shining Path of Peru, have increasingly incorporated women into their organizations. Figures on total female membership within the FARC vary from 20 to 40 percent, with a general average of 30 percent.[46] Although the FARC's senior leadership structure, particularly the Secretariat, remains all male, women have been ascending throughout the group's ranks, with women now reportedly bearing the title "Commandante." Like Shining Path, the FARC has recruited and retained women for more than a dozen years. Unlike the FARC, the Shining Path's senior leadership structure, the Central Committee, is composed of 8 women (out of 19).[47] The Latin American phenomenon of "machismo" is noted as responsible for the continuation of senior male leadership for the FARC and the "cult of personality" that is said to surround the Shining Path's former leader, Abimael Guzman. As with the LTTE, women of both groups experience the same types of training and expectations as their male counterparts and women have been increasingly used in intelligence roles by the FARC.[48]

In Latin America, female activism in politically violent organizations remains concentrated within leftist movements, corresponding to themes seen in Europe and North America. In both Colombia and Peru, the revolutionary features of the respective movements is significant, mirroring processes in Palestine and Sri Lanka, as well as Iran, South Africa, and Eritrea. For the most part, women join the FARC and Shining Path while young, engage in all facets of the organization, and often remain members for life, although activism rates may alter with age, as is true with their male counterparts. Also noteworthy is that cases drawn from three regions (South Asia, Middle East, Latin America) confront more generalized poverty and "youth bulges" than is true of North America and Europe. Between 1983 and 2000, the percentage of the population living on less than US$2 per day was 45.4 for Sri Lanka, 36 for Colombia, and 41.4 for Peru. Data released by the Palestinian Central Bureau of Statistics in early 2002 showed that 57.8 percent of those living in the West Bank and 84.6 percent of those living in the Gaza Strip were living below the poverty line. In addition to poverty, each of these states is confronting some form of "youth bulge" evidenced by the percentage of their populations between 0 and 14 as reported in 2001. These figures ranged from 25.9 percent in Sri Lanka, 31.88 percent in Colombia, 34.41 percent in Peru, 49.89 percent in the Gaza Strip, and 44.61 percent in the West Bank.[49] Thus, the fact that poor, young individuals are frequently drawn to terrorist organizations and politically violent groups is neither regionally limited nor gendered.

South Asian Female Terrorism

The Sri Lankan case shares some parallels with MENA terrorist organizations, including the structural imperatives that favor the use of women as suicide bombers, the intersection of political and sociocultural goals of liberation, and sociocultural norms that idealize sacrifice.[50] As of 2000, roughly half of the LTTE's membership[51] were females, who are frequently recruited as children into the Black Tigers, an elite bomb squad composed of women and men.[52] Women enjoy equivalent training and combat experience with their male counterparts and are fully incorporated into the extant structure of the LTTE. Women's utility as suicide bombers derives from their general exclusion from the established "profile" of such actors employed by many police and security forces (e.g., young males), allowing them to better avoid scrutiny and reach their targets. The 1991 assassination of Rajiv Gandhi, then leader of India, by a young Tamil woman who garlanded him, bowed at his feet, and then detonated a bomb that killed them both, provides proof of the power of this terrorist weapon. However, that woman, identified as Dhanu (a.k.a. Tanu), suggests some of the contradictory themes that arise when considering women's roles in the LTTE.

Reportedly prompted to join the LTTE because she was gang-raped by Indian peacekeeping forces who also killed her brothers,[53] Dhanu has become an important mythical force utilized for further recruitment as rape has been identified as one of the primary reasons motivating young women to join the LTTE. The goal of *eelam* (freedom) pursued by the LTTE is said to be conjoined with the pursuit of similar personal, and perhaps even societal, freedom for female recruits as "[f]ighting for Tamil freedom is often the only way a woman has to redeem herself."[54] Also inherent in the struggle is the idea(l) of sacrifice, particularly for Tamil rape victims who are said to be socially prohibited from marriage and childbearing. Equating the sacrifice of the female bomber as an extension of motherhood, suicide bombings become an acceptable "offering" for women who can never be mothers, a process that is reportedly encouraged by their families.[55] "As a rule, women are represented as the core symbols of the nation's identity" and the "Tamil political movements have used women's identity as a core element in their nationalism."[56]

According to *Jane's Intelligence Review,* "suicide terrorism is the readiness to sacrifice one's life in the process of destroying or attempting to destroy a target to advance a political goal. The aim of the psychologically and physically war-trained terrorist is to die while destroying the enemy target.[57] It is also on the increase. Aside from the LTTE, the main groups that employ suicide terrorism in pursuit of their objectives are located in, or linked to, the Middle East, such as Hamas, Hizballah, and Islamic Jihad. The LTTE is the only current example of a terrorist organization that has permanently adopted "suicide terrorism as a legitimate and permanent strategy."[58] Suicide terrorism in this context is the result of a "cult of personality" rather than a religious cult, demonstrating that "under certain extreme political and psychological circumstances secular volunteers are fully capable of martyrdom."[59]

Sri Lanka is not the only place in South Asia, however, where women are, or have been, allegedly involved with terrorism. Among Sikh militants, women have participated in an array of roles including armed combat. Importantly, Sikhism does not distinguish between male and female equality forming a religio-societal grounding that neither precludes female combat nor categorizes that role as uniquely masculine (or "unfeminine"). Rather, societal resistance to female combat roles is fostered by well-founded fears of sexual abuse, rape, and sexual torture of women if captured. Within the Sikh case, women's "support" roles are not viewed as peripheralized or indicative of women's marginalization within the political sphere. Instead, women's support of their husbands and sons is seen to critically enable their ability to fight and die for the nation, and women's roles as mothers producing future fighters for that nation is also recognized. As a result, "[w]hile it is obvious that the celebrated virtues of courage, bold action, and strong speech are consonant with masculinity as understood in the West, among Sikhs these qualities are treated as neither masculine nor feminine, but simply as Sikh, values. Women may be bound to the kitchen and may have babies in their arms, but they are still fully *expected* to behave as soldiers, if necessary."[60]

Additional examples of women's participation with politically violent organizations relate to the Indian–Pakistan confrontation over Kashmir. According to Indian sources, Shamshad Begum was arrested by Indian security forces in October 2001 for allegedly acting as a guide responsible for identifying safe travel routes for members of Hizbul Mujahadeen.[61] Another female member of the same organization was reportedly killed by Lashker-e-Taiyaba members. Indian sources claim that women are drawn to the organization for financial motives, and women's roles as couriers have been improved by a "requirement" to wear a *burqa*.[62] Reports of female involvement in terrorist groups expanded by December 2001 as the Indian press reported female bomb squads were being prepared by Pakistan-supported groups in Kashmir for attacks against senior officials during the Republic Day Parade.[63]

Several themes arise from the South Asian context that provide additional insight into female terrorists, particularly suicide terrorism. First, personal motives (e.g., family, rape, financial) are argued to greatly influence women to join organizations like the LTTE and, even more importantly, into becoming suicide bombers (e.g., rape). Second, freedom and liberation are key themes at both the collective and individualistic levels. Collectively, freedom and liberation capture the legitimating ideology of the LTTE vis-á-vis the Sinhalese and the Indian governments, the mujahadeen in Kashmir vis-á-vis India, and the Sikhs vis-á-vis India for Khalistan. Liberation also appears to be conceptualized individualistically as, according to one Tamil Tiger, "the use of women in war is part of a larger vision of the guerrilla leadership to liberate Tamil women from the bonds of tradition."[64] However, this has led to accusations that women are less committed to *eelam* as their primary motivation for participating in the LTTE, joining instead for personal vengeance.[65] The idea of sacrifice as an ideal is the third theme and it centers both on the role of women within society as a whole (e.g., motherhood) as well as for suicide bombers more particularly. Female sacrifice for her family, and particularly for her male children, is seen as a generalized cultural norm that is usefully extended to female self-sacrifice for her community and family, particularly if she is unable (e.g., because of rape), to undertake her role as wife and mother within the society. In both the Sikh and Sri Lankan examples, female martyrdom is viewed as necessary to overcome the individual and—more importantly—collective shame of dishonor caused by rape. Fourth, the personalism of women's motives that arguably drive them to join organizations like the LTTE is both responsible for somehow diminishing the overall "authenticness" of women's roles in these organizations, particularly for outside observers, and allowing for charges of LTTE exploitation of its female cadre who are used as "throw-aways" or "as artillery."[66]

Middle East and North African Female Terrorism

From the earliest days of the Palestinian resistance, women have been involved in both the leftist and rightist sides of the Palestinian struggle against Israel.[67] The events of 2002 suggest that this pattern remains intact. Through April 2002 four Palestinian women have become suicide bombers on behalf of the Al-Aqsa Martyrs Brigade, an offshoot of Fatah, prompting, in part, a major Israeli military offensive against the Palestinians begun in March 2002. However, although these attacks have shocked Israeli security analysts, there is a sustained, and varied, history of Palestinian women who have been involved with terrorist organizations, particularly since the nationalist-based movements began to increasingly carry out violent activities in the 1960s. One of the most well-known female terrorists is Leila Khaled, affiliated with the Popular Front for the Liberation of Palestine (PFLP), who hijacked a plane in 1969. Another woman convicted of planting a bomb in a Jerusalem supermarket during 1969, Randa Nabulsi, was sentenced to 10 years imprisonment.[68] Although there has been a low probability that women will be used by Islamist terrorist groups, continuing the trend of lower female representation among rightist organizations, there is precedent for such inclusion in Palestine. Etaf Aliyan, a Palestinian woman who is also a member of Islamic Jihad, was scheduled to drive a car loaded with explosives into a Jerusalem police station in 1987 but was apprehended before the attack could take place. If the attack had occurred, it would have represented "the first suicide vehicle bombing in Israel"[69] and significantly, it would have been implemented by a woman.

Women's roles were increasing among secular and Islamist Palestinian organizations before 2002, suggesting a warning sign of the impending escalation of Palestinian violence against Israeli targets. In particular, there was an apparent trend in women's growing roles within the Palestinian resistance that was initiated with examples of male/female collaboration (e.g., suggesting female training by more experienced males), followed by individual women planting explosive devices but not detonating them, to the culmination wherein women were tasked with actually detonating bombs on their own persons. Thus, in hindsight suicide bombing by women appeared to be a logical progression in women's operations within various organizations, and suggests that women may be tasked with tandem suicide bombing and other operations in the future.

For example, Ahlam Al-Tamimi was arrested by Israel's Shabak in 2001, charged with extending logistical support to the Hamas cell that attacked the Sbarro pizzeria in West Jerusalem. She reportedly worked with Mohamed Daghles, a member of the Palestinian Authority security body. The two are linked to at least two incidents in summer 2001. In July, Al-Tamimi reportedly carried a bomb disguised as a beer can into a West

Jerusalem supermarket that detonated but did not injure anyone. In August, Al-Tamimi was linked to a Hamas bomber who carried a bomb in a guitar case into a Sbarro pizzeria that killed the bomber and 15 others.[70] In another instance, on 3 August 2001, Ayman Razawi (a.k.a. Imman Ghazawi, Iman Ghazawi, Immam Ghazawi), 23,[71] a mother of 2, was caught before she could plant an 11-pound bomb packed with nails and screws hidden in a laundry detergent box in a Tel Aviv bus station. However, despite the escalating role of women in the *intifada,* the prospect of a female suicide bomber remained remote through the first weeks of 2002 because "[t]here have been very few cases of Arab women found infiltrating Israel on a mission to murder civilians."[72]

That perception changed dramatically in the wake of 28 January 2002 when Wafa Idris (a.k.a. Wafa Idrees, Shahanaz Al Amouri),[73] 28, detonated a 22-pound bomb in Jerusalem that killed her, an 81-year-old Israeli man, and injured more than 100 others. Confusion punctuated the immediate aftermath of the attack given that heretofore women had only helped plant bombs and it was not clear whether Idris had intended to detonate the explosive or whether the explosion was accidental. Equally unclear was whether she was acting on behalf of some group or how she had obtained the explosives. This confusion made the Israelis reticent to confirm that the attack constituted the first "official" case of a female suicide bomber related to the Arab–Israeli conflict and, therefore, a significant shift in the security framework within which the Israelis would have to operate. As Steve Emerson is quoted as stating in the wake of Idris's attack, if true the bombing "opens a whole new demographic pool of potential bombers."[74] By early February the Israelis declared that Wafa Idris was a suicide bomber[75]—a first. The Fatah-linked Al-Aqsa Martyrs Brigade (a.k.a. Al Aqsa Brigades) claimed responsibility for her attack and described Idris as a "martyr."

Idris's motivation to commit a suicide operation was arguably prompted by a sense of hopelessness under occupation and rage, not heaven as promised to her male counterparts.[76] As a result, her action is seen "to have been motivated more by nationalist than religious fervor,"[77] a motivation that is frequently attributed to her male counterparts. In addition to not being a "known" member of a terrorist organization, and therefore more likely to be identified as a potential suicide bomber, Idris did not carry out the attack in the "normal" fashion. She carried the bomb in a backpack, rather than strapped to her waist, raising widespread speculation that she did not intend to detonate the bomb and the explosion was accidental.[78] Another cause for skepticism about Idris's role in the attack arose from the lack of a note and martyr's video, which are typically left behind by one engaging in a "martyr's operation."

The response by secular and Islamist Palestinian leaders to the attack is important. Although the Al-Aqsa Martyrs Brigade claimed responsibility for the attack, it did not do so immediately. The strong reaction by the "Arab street" to the attack, and the heightened sense of insecurity noted by Israeli officials, provide two excellent reasons why women's operational utility increased for Al-Aqsa's leaders. First, Idris's action resonated strongly throughout the Arab world. Egypt's weekly *Al-Sha'ab* published an editorial on 1 February 2002 entitled "It's a Woman!" that is reflective of the general tone that emanated throughout the Arab press regarding the attack. The editorial stated, in part, "It is a woman who teaches you today a lesson in heroism, who teaches you the meaning of Jihad, and the way to die a martyr's death. . . . It is a woman who has shocked the enemy, with her thin, meager, and weak body. . . . It is a woman who blew herself up, and with her exploded all the myths about women's weakness, submissiveness, and enslavement."[79]

The profound reaction to her attack by the masses both within and outside Palestine created a turning point for the Al-Aqsa Martyrs Brigade that had two effects: first, a willingness to use both men and women in terrorist attacks and second, an acknowledgment of the utility of using suicide bombers against civilian targets within Israel to undermine Israeli security and force Israel to negotiate from a position of weakness. Within days of the attack, Abu-Ahman, founder and leader of Al-Aqsa, showed signs of a tactical shift, asserting that there would be a "qualitative military operation by Al-Aqsa Battalions (*sic*) against Israeli targets," within a short period of time[80] that was clearly designed to take advantage of the psychological and tactical significance of female members of the organization. By the end of February, the Al-Aqsa Martyrs Brigade reportedly confirmed it had created a "special women's unit" named after Wafa Idris[81] to carry out attacks. Subsequent attacks by female suicide bombers over the next three months did not confirm the existence of a "special unit," but it did signify the group's willingness to utilize female members for suicide operations was not a fluke.

Reactions by Islamists were more mixed and muted, but not rejective in the immediate aftermath of the attack. Sheikh Ahmad Yassin, spiritual leader of Hamas, initially opposed Idris's action citing personnel imperatives, stating that "in this phase (of the uprising), the participation of women is not needed in martyr operations, like men." He went on to note that "[w]e can't meet the growing demands of young men who wish to carry out martyr operations," and "women form the second line of defence (*sic*) in the resistance to the occupation." However, he later qualified his objection when he added that if a Hamas woman wanted to carry out a "martyr operation," she should be accompanied by a man if the operation required her to be away more than a day and a night. Hamas leaders Sheikh Hassan Yusef and Isma'eel Abu Shanab noted that there was no *fatwa* (religious decree) that prevented a woman from being a martyr, ostensibly against Israeli occupation in the Palestinian territories.[82] Sheikh Abdullah Nimr Darwish, spiritual leader of Arabs in Israel, was more forceful in advocating the new role for women, driven in large part by the extension of the occupation to the home. He stated "the women will fight. Now the Palestinians prefer to be killed at the front rather than wait and be killed at home. . . . Israel has the Dimona nuclear plant, but we Palestinians have a stronger Dimona—the suiciders. We can use them on a daily basis. He also pointed, with pride, at the sight of Palestinian women in white shrouds at funerals—a sign of their readiness to become shuhada, or martyr." Further, women lined up to become martyrs, shouting "make a bomb of me, please!"[83] All of these reactions were in keeping with the August 2001 *fatwa* issued by the High Islamic Council in Saudi Arabia urging women to join the fight against Israel as martyrs.

Despite Israeli assertions that Idris's attack was a planned suicide bombing, significant uncertainty surrounds the authenticity of this attack as an Al-Aqsa Martyrs Brigade—planned suicide attack. More likely is that Idris was to plant the bomb as Al-Tamimi and Razawi were to have done in 2001. Nevertheless, Al-Aqsa learned an important lesson about the utility of female suicide bombers, and the uncertainties of the Idris case were addressed in subsequent attacks by female martyrs: Darin Abu Aysheh (a.k.a. Dareen Abu Ashai, dareen Abu Eishi), 21, detonated an explosive device on 27 February 2002 at an Israeli checkpoint in the West Bank;[84] Ayat Akhras, 18, blew herself up on 29 March 2002 at a Jerusalem neighborhood grocery store in a wave of Passover attacks that followed Israeli attacks against Arafat's headquarters;[85] and Andalib Takafka blew herself up in a crowded Jerusalem market, killing 6 and wounding more than 50 people on 12 April 2002, undermining efforts by the U.S. Secretary of State Colin Powell to move ahead with peace talks.[86]

Historical and recent cases of female Palestinian terrorism suggest several trends. First, female activism has tended to be more active within the secularist context (e.g., leftist) rather than among Islamists (e.g., rightist), reflecting a general global trend. However, although women have been more active with the nationalist/secular side of the Palestinian movement, women have been linked to Islamist groups either directly or in terms of their overall support. Second, as the conflict with Israel deepened, the scope of activism widened to include women in an increasing array of activities, up to and including suicide bombing, and women pushed for these expanded roles. Third, women activists have tended to be young, with one or more politically active family members (male), and exposed to some form of loss (e.g., within their family or immediate community) that arguably contributed to their mobilization. Importantly, marital, educational, and maternal status were not uniform factors. Also, these factors are not radically divergent from males who undertake suicide operations within this context. Fourth, Palestinian secular leaders' willingness to include women in martyr operations was influenced by security assessments (e.g., an ability to evade security scrutiny and travel more deeply into Israel), operational constraints (e.g., growing Israeli pressure on male operatives), and publicity. Female suicide bombers represent one way to overcome Israeli security pressures, heighten Israeli insecurity, and exhaust Israeli security resources by significantly increasing the operational range and available pool for suicide operations. Akhras is an exemplary case as witnesses noted she looked "European," and dressed like any Israeli schoolgirl.[87] Trying to protect against that type of terrorist represents a fundamental challenge for any security apparatus.

Conclusion: Preliminary Trends and Themes

Although there is a tendency to dismiss the overall threat of women suicide bombers, or female terrorists more broadly, because they have historically engaged in such a small percentage of terrorist activities, contextual pressures are creating a convergence between individual women, terrorist organization leaders, and society that is not only increasing the rate of female activity within terrorist and politically violent organizations, but is also expanding their operational range. The tactical advantage of this convergence is apparent particularly with respect to female suicide bombers, a tactic designed to attract attention and instill widespread fear in the target audience, because as one observer noted in the wake of Idris's attack, "it's the women we remember."[88] Because suicide terrorism is designed to attract attention and precipitate fear, in an increasingly charged atmosphere it takes more and more to attract attention, increasing the utility of female suicide bombers. Female suicide bombers also fundamentally challenge existing security assessments and socially derived norms regarding women's behavior, heightening the fear factor. Finally, and more significantly, the small number of women who have, to date, been used in such operations suggests that they will be able to better evade detection than their male counterparts.

Leftist organizations may be more likely to initially recruit or attract women because their goals tend to conform more easily to general processes of social change in society. Nevertheless, security, operational, and publicity assessments inducing secular organizations to recruit and operationalize women in a variety of roles, including as suicide bombers, may spread to rightist organizations including Islamist groups and right-wing organizations. This process may first be visible in Palestine if violence is prolonged or deepens for four reasons: first, women are operationally significant to achieve the over-all goals of the *intifada* in a manner that at least immediately overrides potential social costs of their mobilization; second, given the nascent "public" political roles of women in the region, and sociocultural factors that facilitate this role, women could very well be "demobilized" back into the private realm with little effort; third, nothing in Islam precludes women from serving in this function; and fourth, as the conflict has progressed the lines between the secular/nationalists (e.g., Fatah) and the Islamists (e.g., Hamas) has blurred.[89] Furthermore, it is also possible that groups like Al Qaeda may see women as operationally useful, as enabling conditions abound, including: the horizontal structure and loose affiliations of these organizations, the "war on terrorism" and its escalating enforcement efforts, and no overt religious prohibition against women's activity.

There is a real fascination for many observers with why women join and participate in groups like the FARC, Shining Path, the LTTE, and even the Palestinian groups, perhaps in part because this membership is fairly visible and sizable within their respective organizations. This focus is not overly surprising "[b]ecause politics, and especially revolutionary politics, has traditionally been regarded as a male affair . . . [and as a result] the historian has never really had to 'explain' why an individual man chose to enter political activity."[90] Ergo, trying to "explain" why an individual woman engages in not just political activity but violent political activity becomes quite necessary because there is something not quite "natural" about it.

Both women and men join politically violent organizations, and engage in an array of activities within those organizations, for similar reasons. Most frequently, individuals want to achieve some form of political change, whether revolutionary or more limited in nature. At the most basic level, groups that use political violence as a tactic have as their end-goal a right to draw up and implement new rules of the political game. In revolutionary or nationalist contexts like Palestine, Colombia, and Sri Lanka, the potential political change is far-reaching and typically involves replacing some form of external (or externally linked) leadership. However, political institutions do not arise in a cultural vacuum and often necessitate some form of social change.

Typically women are said to have engaged in political violence for personal (private) reasons, whether because of a male family member, poverty, rape, or similar factors. Importantly, this argument suggests women do not choose their participation consciously, but are rather drawn in as reluctant, if not victimized, participants. Even women who join for ideological (public) reasons are suspect, especially in revolutionary contexts. Here, women's motivations for "freedom" are viewed dualistically as both collective (e.g., independence) and individualistic (e.g., equality) or their ideological motivations are not fully developed, making them "helpers" to men rather than ideologues in their own right. The Algerian case suggests dualistic goals for both men and women, differing only with respect to their conceptualization of social change, the secondary goal, not political change, the primary goal. Nevertheless, there remains an entrenched belief that women's motives are more personal (and private), leaving behind an impression of insincerity and shallowness that prevents women from having any fundamental voice in creating new structures.

In addition to determining why women join organizations there is an equal effort to untangle what women do once they join. Although women have historically been involved with politically violent organizations, most of their activities have been in "support" capacities; thus, their presence has been seen as passive. Usually, this support has come from mothers, who have moral authority, a certain degree of safety vis-á-vis the adversary, and fairly clear boundaries within which they operate (both with respect to their own societies and the adversary).[91] Such action is typically viewed as initiated by the women themselves, and while resistance or terrorist leaders may exploit this activity through propaganda, the role is so natural, if not expected in a highly conflictual context, that very few find this type of activity threatening (e.g., Ireland, Sri Lanka, and Palestine).

This is not true of the "warrior" women. Even a cursory review of interviews with these women demonstrates that women are pushing for expanded roles within their respective organizations, from leadership to combat, and that a growing number of younger women are joining organizations and staying. However, what is equally clear is that for most observers (e.g., academic, journalistic, policymakers) this choice seems so foreign and unnatural to women that there must be an explanation beyond simply that women want to fight for their respective causes.[92] As a result, women are duped into being "cannon fodder" as they are tasked with the most dangerous missions because they are expendable to their leaders. Additionally, history is replete with cases where women's support and service have not produced extended political freedom. But here is the rub, and the significance of the expanding roles of women in various organizations on both the left and right. As female "warriors," women are able to carve out roles themselves both within their respective organizations and with the hope of doing so in the structures that result from the struggle. Significantly, the women who are being drawn to these movements may be attracted by political opportunities implied by combatant (public) roles regarding citizenship that were denied their mothers who remained altogether private during earlier conflicts. Although it is safer and easier to simply dismiss "warrior" women as pawns of male leaders, as "dupes," and as misguided women who have lost sight of their femininity, this obscures the more interesting issue of why and how women have concluded that political violence will help them achieve desired political (and perhaps social) ends.

In evaluating the roles of women in terrorist and politically violent organizations, it remains prudent to be cognizant of the following: first, the implications of limited data; second, the possibility of denial and deception; third, that invisibility does not necessarily equate with passivity or powerlessness; and fourth, organizational versus societal imperatives. The secretiveness of many of the groups addressed in this study underscores the difficulties with obtaining reliable information related to both male and female recruitment, leadership, and operational roles. Furthermore, group leaders may mislead observers regarding the depth and breadth of female participation in their groups, either through inflation or under-inflation, to gain strategic advantages vis-á-vis their adversaries. Relatedly, just because women are not necessarily visible participants within organizations does not correlate with their absence or passivity within said organizations. Women's operational strengths and tactical advantages may induce leaders to keep female participants well-hidden until contextual pressures necessitate the group show its hand. Finally, it should not be immediately concluded that societal structures that traditionally limit female public roles will hold under tremendous conflict, nor that such structures will necessarily dictate women's roles once within politically violent organizations.

As a result, academic and policy observers must be extremely cautious in how they approach and frame female activism within terrorist or politically violent organizations. Women have been, and will continue to be, willing to serve in a variety of groups, including right wing/religious and, significantly, they may very well be tasked in combatant roles. Terrorist or politically violent organizations are extremely aware of the potential utility of female members because this actor allows them to play on established biases and assumptions in their adversary. Terrorist organizations engage in "actor innovation" because women are able to penetrate more deeply into their targets to gather intelligence or carry out violent operations than many of their male counterparts. These organizations are interested in immediate results; the system that results will be dealt with later. This same imperative drives both female members of these organizations and the societies within which this process occurs. Societies that are under extreme strain due to occupation or conflict will often loosen their constraints on women to facilitate the convergence of individual and terrorist organizational interests.

The aftermath of this process remains generally uncertain, as many of the cases discussed herein remain unresolved.

Notes

1. Organizations labeled as "terrorist" are derived from the United States Department of State listing of designated terrorist organizations through either support or operational activities (see *Patterns of Global Terrorism 2000,* available at (http://www.state.gov/s/ct/rls/pgtrpt/2000/2450.htm). This analysis will utilize this designation for the sake of simplicity.

2. Because a woman's place is "naturally" private her motivation to become "public" would have to be personal. This suggests as well that once this personal reason has been resolved she will willingly and naturally return to her normal, private, role.

3. The common belief that women's participation in political violence is quite limited is not supported by even a cursory examination of history. However, what is clear from that cursory look is that women's experiences with political violence have not received sustained attention, and what examination has occurred has often been heavily influenced by established Western norms of appropriate female behavior. Given the constraints of any article-length analysis, certain limitations were necessary in approaching the subject matter. As a result, this work should not be construed as an exhaustive inventory of women's participation in politically violent or terrorist organizations, past or present, but rather a selective examination of primarily current critical cases.

4. Several of the most oft-quoted terrorism definitions include those used by the United States Federal Bureau of Investigation (FBI), the United States Department of State, and the United States Department of Defense (DoD). The FBI defines terrorism as "the unlawful use of force and violence against persons or property to intimidate or coerce a government, the civilian population, or any segment thereof, in furtherance of political or social objectives" (28 Code of Federal Regulations Section 0.85). The State Department defines terrorism as "premeditated, politically motivated violence perpetrated against noncombatant targets by subnational groups or clandestine agents, usually intended to influence an audience" (United States Department of State, *Patterns of Global Terrorism 2000,* available at (http://www.state.gov/s/ct/rls/pgtrpt/2000/). 13 April 2001). Problematic with both definitions, however, is that they fail to capture organizations motivated by religious or economic motives, such as Islamist organizations in the Middle East and North Africa (MENA) or narcoterrorist organizations such as the Revolutionary Armed Forces of Columbia (FARC) and National Liberation Army (ELN) in Colombia. The DoD partially overcomes this deficiency by widening the goal orientation of terrorist organizations as it defines terrorism as "the calculated use of violence or the threat of violence to inculcate fear; intended to coerce or to intimidate governments or societies in the pursuit of goals that are generally political, religious, or ideological" (Department of Defense, "DoD Combating Terrorism Program," Directive Number 2000.12, available at (http://www.defenselink. mil/pubs/downing_rpt/annx_e.html), 15 September 1996).

5. Jamie L. Rhee, "Comment: Rational and Constitutional Approaches to Airline Safety in the Face of Terrorist Threats," *DePaul Law Review* 49(847) Lexis/Nexis (Spring 2000).

6. Martha Crenshaw, "The Logic of Terrorism: Terrorist Behavior as a Product of Strategic Choice," in Walter Reich, ed., *Origins of Terrorism: Psychologies, Ideologies, Theologies, States of Mind* (Washington, DC: Woodrow Wilson Center Press, 1998), p. 15.

7. If we examine state behavior with respect to military recruitment, we see a similar process. Samarasinghe notes "most nations have increased women's military roles only when there has been a shortage of qualified men and a pressing need for more warriors. . . . The decision to permit women into combat is made by men. . . . [And] the allowable space within which women could operate in military units is also determined by them." (Vidyamali Samarasinghe, "Soldiers, Housewives and Peace Makers: Ethnic Conflict and Gender in Sri Lanka," *Ethnic Studies Report* XIV(2) (July 1996), p. 213).

8. As of early 2002, a cease-fire deal was secured between the Tamil Tigers and the government of Sri Lanka, halting the type of violence that will be discussed in this article. However, even if this activity is now a matter of historical record, rather than a current phenomenon, it offers important insights into how women were (are) mobilized into a politically violent movement.

9. Peter Schalk, "Women Fighters of the Liberation Tigers in Tamil Ilam. The Martial Feminism of Atel Palacinkam," *South Asia Research* 14(2) (Autumn 1994), pp. 174–175.

10. See Kathleen M. Blee's *Women of the Klan: Racism and Gender in the 1920s* (Berkeley: University of California Press, 1991) for an interesting study of this widely overlooked phenomenon.

11. See Claudia Koonz, "Women in Nazi Germany," in Renate Bridenthal and Claudia Koonz, eds., *Becoming Visible, Women in European History* (Boston: Houghton Mifflin, 1977).

12. Marie Marmo Mullaney, "Women and the Theory of the 'Revolutionary Personality': Comments, Criticisms, and Suggestions for Further Study," *The Social Science Journal* 21(2) (April 1984), pp. 49–70.

13. Jeffrey Louis Decker, "Terrorism (Un)Veiled: Frantz Fanon and the Women of Algiers," *Cultural Critique* 17 (Winter 1990), pp. 180–181.

14. Although O'Donnell and Schmitter's argument centers around mobilization against domestic authoritarian rule, there are parallels in the decolonization process that makes this comparison useful. See Guillermo O'Donnell and Philippe C. Schmitter, *Transitions from Authoritarian Rule: Tentative Conclusions About Uncertain Democracies* (Baltimore, MD: The Johns Hopkins University Press, 1986). With respect to civil society, O'Donnell and Schmitter argue that "private" civil society mobilizes only temporarily to become "public" to achieve its goal (transition from authoritarianism). Once that goal is achieved, civil society willingly returns to its "natural" private sphere. This conceptualization bears striking parallels to the role of women wherein Algeria's "private" women (a role physically visible through the veil) are temporarily mobilized into "public" action to achieve independence. However, once the aim of the mobilization is completed (e.g., independence) they are assumed to willingly and naturally return to their private role. However, not all scholars (Karla J. Cunningham, "Regime and Society in Jordan: An Analysis of Jordanian Liberalization," Dissertation, University at Buffalo, 1997; Peter P. Ekeh, "Historical and Cross-Cultural Contexts of Civil Society in Africa," Paper presented at the United States Agency

15. The account of these phases are taken from Decker, "Terrorism (Un)Veiled," pp. 190–192. The first quotation is located on p. 191, the second is on p. 192.
16. Ibid., p. 193.
17. Ibid., p. 183, emphasis in original.
18. This account of the conflicting interests of Palestinian women, leaders, and society was discussed by Soraya Antonius, "Fighting on Two Fronts: Conversations with Palestinian Women," *Journal of Palestine Studies* 5 (October 1979), pp. 28–30.
19. Marnia Lazreg, "Citizenship and Gender in Algeria," in Saud Joseph, ed., *Gender and Citizenship in the Middle East* (Syracuse, NY: Syracuse University Press, 2000), p. 62, emphasis in original.
20. The regional cases that are discussed later are utilized to demonstrate these developments given the constraints of an article. However, it should be understood that this is not, and is not intended to be, an exhaustive inventory of cases in which women have engaged in political violence or terrorism. Cases from Africa (Eritrea, South Africa) and East Asia (Japan, Korea, Vietnam) are also worth investigating.
21. Leonard Weinberg and William Lee Eubank, "Italian Women Terrorists," *Terrorism: An International Journal* 9(3) (1987), p. 247.
22. Weinberg and Eubank, 1987, pp. 250–252. The authors' conclusions are based on biographical reviews of female terrorists reported in two major Italian newspapers. Concentrating on individuals identified and arrested by the Italian government, the authors admit that their information "does not represent a sample of terrorists" (Ibid., p. 248). A point to consider is that women's roles and representation may remain somewhat skewed, even in this worthwhile study, because one of the apparent operational advantages of female members to terrorist organizations, at least in other contexts, is that they tend to go unnoticed by officials. As a result, relying on official recognition of key women may not provide the fullest picture of women's roles in varying terrorist organizations.
23. For a good analysis of female participation in left- and right-wing organizations within the United States during the 1960s and 1970s please see Jeffrey S. Handler, "Socioeconomic Profile of an American Terrorist: 1960s and 1970s," *Terrorism* 13(3) (May–June 1990), pp. 195–213.
24. Ibid., 1990, p. 204.
25. Katrine Fangen, "Separate or Equal? The Emergence of an All-Female Group in Norway's Rightist Underground," *Terrorism and Political Violence* 9(3) (Autumn 1997), pp. 122–164. In contrast, leftist women tend to organize their own organizations to pursue a particular objective (Ibid., p. 122).
26. According to the FBI, domestic terrorism is "the unlawful use, or threatened use, of force or violence by a group or individual based and operating entirely within the United States or Puerto Rico without foreign direction committed against persons or property to intimidate or coerce a government, the civilian population, or any segment thereof in furtherance of political or social objections" (United States Department of Justice Federal Bureau of Investigation, Terrorism in the United States 1999, Counterterrorism Threat Assessment and Warning Unit, Counterterrorism Division, available at http://www.fbi.gov/publications/terror/terror99.pdf,1999). For the purposes of this study, FBI official designations of domestic terrorist status will be utilized in characterizing a group as terrorist. Between 1980–1999 there were 327 incidents or suspected incidents of terrorism within the United States, of which 239 were attributed to domestic terrorism (Ibid.). The analysis of domestic terrorism offered in this article is focused on groups or categories the FBI deems as generally active. As a result, historical examples of female participation may not be included, particularly if the group is no longer actively identified by the FBI as a terrorist threat.
27. According to the FBI, the WCOTC has been linked to acts of domestic terrorism including the July 1999 shootings of several racial minorities by Benjamin Nathaniel Smith in Illinois and Indiana (United States Department of Justice Federal Bureau of Investigation, 1999).
28. Women's participation with left-wing movements is long-standing, with prominent examples from the 1960s and 1970s including the Weathermen, the Black Panthers, and the Symbionese Liberation Army. The discussion of left-wing terrorism in this article does not focus on these examples because they have diminished or disappeared, at least with respect to FBI reporting of left-wing terrorism.
29. Please note that these three generalized categorizes have been created to facilitate discussion within the limited confines of this article. There is tremendous variation within the three categories that such grouping tends to obscure.
30. Background on Samadi and Mahdavieh were drawn from: Aaron Sands, "Secret Arrest of Saddam Ally," *Ottawa Citizen* 1 February 2000, Lexis/Nexis, 3 March 2002; Moira Farrow, "Woman Ordered Deported Not a Terrorist Lawyer Says," *The Vancouver Sun,* 8 April 1993 Lexis/Nexis, 3 March 2002.
31. See *Zehra Saygili v. The Minister of Citizenship & Immigration and Solicitor General for Canada,* Court No. DES-6-96, available at (http://decisions.fct-cf.gc.ca/cf/1997/des-6-96.html).
32. Tom Godfrey, "Lax Security Screening Has Allowed 'Sleeper' Terrorists to Infiltrate Canada for Years," *Toronto Sun,* 7 October 2001, available at (http://www.canoe.ca/TorontoNews/04n1.html).
33. The PKK reportedly used women as suicide bombers in Turkey during 1998, but ended the tactic thereafter, suggesting that suicide terrorism was used temporarily to achieve a specific objective (Ehud Sprinzak, "Rational Fanatics," *Foreign Policy* 120 (September/October 2000), ProQuest, 25 March 2002, pp. 4–5). For more information on the PKK's use of suicide bombing during 1998 please see "Female Separatist Rebel Captured in Southeastern Turkey," *BBC Worldwide Monitoring,* 15 August 1998, Lexis/Nexis, 31 January 2002; "Female 'Terrorist' Reportedly Carries Out Suicide Bombing," *BBC Worldwide Monitoring,* 24 December 1998, Lexis/Nexis, 31 January 2002; and "Child Wounded in Female Suicide Bombers' Attack in Southeastern Turkey," *BBC Worldwide Monitoring,* 17 November 1998, Lexis/Nexis, 31 January 2002.
34. For the ups and downs of this particular case see Neil MacFarquhar, "Woman Freed After Pleading in Border Case," *The New York Times,* 16 February 2000, Lexis/Nexis, 25

March 2002; Michael G. Crawford, "MILNET: The Algerian Y2K Bomb Case," 2001, available at (http://www.milnet.com/milnet/y2kbomb/y2kbomb.htm), 7 March 2002; Cindy Rodriguez, "Stress Line US Tries to Tighten Security on Canadian Border," *The Boston Globe,* 7 November 2001, Lexis/Nexis, 6 March 2002; Lloyd Robertson, "Lucia Garofalo Pleaded Guilty to Immigration Charges Today But Was Cleared of Terrorism Charges," *CTV Television, Inc.,* 15 February 2000, Lexis/Nexis, 6 March 2002; David Arnold, "Garofalo Might Go Free: U.S. to Recommend Release of Montrealer Suspected of Terrorism Link," *The Gazette* (Montreal), 15 February 2000, Lexis/Nexis, 6 March 2002; "Special Report: The Future of Terror: On Guard: America is the Dominant Nation Entering the New Century—and the Top Target for Extremists," *Newsweek International,* 10 January 2000, Lexis/Nexis, 6 March 2002; "Canadian Police Search Apartment of Accomplice of Terrorism Suspect," *Agence France Presse,* 24 December 1999, Lexis/Nexis, 6 March 2002; Butler T. Gray, "U.S. Prosecutors Link Arrests in Vermont and Washington State," *Washington File, United States Department of State International Information Programs,* 1999, available at (http://usinfo.state.gov/topical/pol/terror/99123004.htm), 15 March 2002; and "Canadian Woman Has Ties to Washington Bomb Suspect, 2 Algerian Terrorist Groups," *CNN.com,* 30 December 1999, available at (http://www.cnn.com/2000/US/01/12/border.arrest.02), 15 March 2002.

35. "Feminism Perverted: Extremist Women on the World Wide Web," Anti-Defamation League, 2000, available at (http://www.adl.org/special_reports/extremist_women_on_web/print.html), 18 February 2002.

36. "All in the Family," Southern Poverty Law Center, n.d., available at (http://www.splcenter.org/intelligenceproject/ip-4k2.html), 28 March 2002. Also see Jim Nesbitt, "The American Scene: White Supremacist Women Push for Greater Role in Movement," Newhouse News Service, 1999, available at (http://www.newhousenews.com/archive/story1a1022.html) accessed 24 July 2002.

37. Turner's efforts to create a women's organization within the larger movement is noteworthy and parallels Norwegian experiences (see Fangen, "Separate or Equal?," especially pp. 124–127, 128–140, 144–155).

38. Vicki Weaver, wife of Randy Weaver, was shot by an FBI sniper in August 1992. Randy Weaver, a white separatist, was accused by the government of illegal weapons sales. Kathy Ainsworth was killed by the FBI in 1968 when she and another man tried to plant a bomb at the house of an ADL leader in Mississippi, allegedly on behalf of the Ku Klux Klan. She is one of the only known women affiliated with the white supremacy movement in the United States to be tasked with this type of mission. Interestingly, an additional woman often noted as a "martyr" is Hanna Reitsch who was reportedly a leading proponent of suicide plane missions on behalf of the Nazis during World War II (see http://www.sigrdrifa.com/sigrdrifa/67hanna.html for a sample biography). For additional information on "martyrs" identified by the white supremacist movement (see http://www.volksfrontusa.org/martyrs.shtml).

39. Turner's argument regarding women's roles in the WCOTC were taken from Sister Lisa Turner, "The Women of the Creativity Revolution," ChurchFliers.com, n.d., available at (http://www.churchfliers.com/sub_articles/women.html).

2 April 2002. In looking at the WCOTC site over a period of several months, there have been clear changes in the positioning of women's sites. In April 2002, women's issues were clearly not a priority but there was a direct link on the main page directing women to four white women's movement sites: Elisha Strom: A Woman's Voice, available at (http://www.elishastrom.com), Free Our Women Campaign (FOW), available at (http://www.midhnottsol.org/fow/index.html). Mothers of the Movement (MOTM), available at (http://www.sigrdrifa.com/motm), and Sigrdrifa.com—Premier Voice of the Proud White Women, available at (http://www.sigrdrifa.com). Sigrdrifa publishes a journal that addresses a wide range of issues important to women in the movement including feminism, women's roles in the organizations, recruitment, and prison outreach. Elisha Strom's "Angry White Woman" site covers an array of issues clearly central to women in the movement, including debates over feminism and the importance of motherhood. She is also extremely critical of Kathleen M. Blee's works on the white power movement (see Blee, Women of the Clan, 1991 and *Inside Organized Racism: Women in the Hate Movement,* Berkeley: University of California Press, 2002). The WCOTC links, however, are not fully representative of the websites oriented toward women in the white power movement. Stormfront has a women's page as well which links into a variety of profiles of women who have joined the white power movement (see http://www.stormfront.org). Through their links page Women for Aryan Unity can be assessed at (http://www.wau14.cjb.net/), which features a picture of a white woman holding her baby that acts as the site's gateway to a site dedicated to the more pagan side of the white power movement, pictures of the Aryan sisterhood including tatoos, childrearing tips, and similar features. By July 2002, the WCOTC had removed the linkage to women's sites from their main page for unknown reasons, although this author speculates that the growing outside scholarly and activist scrutiny of these women is unwelcome by the organization for various reasons, including operational. Attempts to find the Women's Frontier using the WCOTC search engine as of July 2002 were ineffectual, bringing up only four articles apparently targeted to women, including the aforementioned article, none of which was accessible.

40. See (http://www.kukluxklan.org/lady4.htm) for the KKK's "Woman to Woman" website, which covers a range of issues including children, attacks against the feminist movement, and even women's roles in combat.

41. In 1999 President Clinton offered the individuals arrested and convicted during this time, known by many Puerto Rican activists as the "independentistas," clemency. All but two accepted the offer.

42. Dale L. Watson, "The Terrorist Threat Confronting the United States," Statement before the Senate Select Committee on Intelligence, Washington, D.C., 6 February 2002, available at (http://www.fbi.gov/congress/congress02/watson020602.htm). 18 February 2002.

43. See "What is the Earth Liberation Front (ELF)?" available at (http://www.animalliberation.net/library/facts/elf.html) for details on organizational features of the group.

44. "2001 Year End Direct Action Report Released by ALF Press Office," 2001, available at (http://www.earthliberationfront.com/library/2001DirectActions.pdf), 30 March 2002.

45. For a useful examination of women's roles in Latin American guerilla movements please see Linda M. Lobao, "Women in Revolutionary Movements: Changing Patterns of Latin American Guerilla Struggle," *Dialectical Anthropology* 15 (1999), pp. 211–232.

46. For varying figures see Jeremy McDermott, "Girl Guerillas Fight Their Way to the Top of Revolutionary Ranks," *Scotland on Sunday,* 23 December 2001, Lexis/Nexis, 2 April 2002; Karl Penhaul, "Battle of the Sexes: Female Rebels Battle Colombian Troops in the Field and Machismo in Guerilla Ranks," *San Francisco Chronicle* 11 January 2001, Lexis/Nexis, 2 April 2002; and Martin Hodgson, "Girls Swap Diapers for Rebel Life," The Christian Science Monitor, 6 October 2000, available at (http://www.csmonitor.com/durable/2000/10/06/p6s1.htm). 2 April 2002. Aside from a fascination with the makeup habits of the female FARC members, these articles offer some insights into the motivations driving women into the FARC's ranks.

47. M. Elaine Mar, "Shining Path Women," n.d., *Harvard Magazine,* available at (http://www.harvardmagazine.com/issues/mj96/right.violence.html). 2 April 2002. During the late 1980s, "approximately 35 percent of the military leaders of . . . [the Shining Path], primarily at the level of underground cells . . . [were] also women" (Juan Lazaro, "Women and Political Violence in Contemporary Peru," *Dialectical Anthropology* 15(2–3) (1990), p. 234). Additionally, by 1987 roughly 1,000 women had been arrested on suspicion of terrorism in Peru including four senior Shining Path female leaders: Laura Zambrano ("Camarada Meche"), Fiorella Montano ("Lucia"), Margie Clavo Peralta, and Edith Lagos (Ibid., p. 243).

48. This position is advanced by McDermott, "Girl Guerillas Fight Their Way to the Top."

49. This data was drawn from several sources. Poverty rates for Colombia, Peru, and Sri Lanka were taken from the United Nations Development Programme, *Human Development Report 2002,* available at (http://www.undp.org/hdr2002/) whereas the data for the Gaza Strip and the West Bank were found in "More Than Two Thirds of Palestinian Children Living on Less than US$1.90/day," 21 May 2002, available at (http://www.iap.org/newsmay213.htm). The demographic data can be found in the Central Intelligence Agency's *The World Factbook 2001,* available at (http://www.cia.gov/cia/publications/factbook/index.html).

50. Interestingly, the LTTE's creation of an organized squad of female suicide bombers is said to be mirrored after the Indian National Army's (INA) activities against the British during the early to mid-1940s (see Schalk, "Women Fighters of the Liberation," p. 174).

51. United States Department of State, *Patterns of Global Terrorism 2000,* "Asia Overview," 30 April 2001, available at (http://www.state.gov/s/ct/rls/pgtrpt/2000/2432.htm). 2 April 2002.

52. Some observers further identify the female cadre of the Black Tigers as the "Birds of Freedom." See, for example, Charu Lata Joshi, "Sri Lanka: Suicide Bombers," *Far Eastern Economic Review,* 1 June 2000, available at (http://www.feer.com/_0006_0l/p64currents.html), 11 March 2002. The idea of a bird carrying the soul of the martyr to paradise is a theme seen in Islamist discourse on martyr operations.

53. Ana Cutter, "Tamil Tigresses: Hindu Martyrs," n.d., available at (http://www.columbia.edu/cu/sipa/PUBS/SLANT/SPRING98/article5.html), 11 March 2002. Also see Frederica Jansz, "Why Do They Blow Themselves Up?" *The Sunday Times,* 15 March 1998, available at (http://www.1acnet.org/suntimes/980315/plus4.html), 3 April 2002.

54. Cutter, "Tamil Tigresses."

55. Ibid.

56. Joke Schrijvers, "Fighters, Victims and Survivors: Constructions of Ethnicity, Gender and Refugeeness among Tamils in Sri Lanka," *Journal of Refugee Studies* 12 (3 September 1999). The quotation on women as core national symbols is on p. 308; the quote on Tamil use of women's identity is on p. 311; and the quote on purity and suicide bombing is on p. 319 with emphasis in the original.

57. "Suicide Terrorism: A Global Threat," *Jane's Intelligence Review,* 20 October 2000, available at (http://www.janes.com/security/regional_security/news/usscole/jir001020_1_n.shtml), 11 November 2001.

58. Sprinzak, "Rational Fanatics," p. 6.

59. Ibid.

60. The discussion of the role of Sikh women was drawn from Cynthia Keppley Mahmood, *Fighting for Faith and Nation: Dialogues with Sikh Militants* (Philadelphia: University of Pennsylvania Press, 1996), pp. 213–234. The quotation is located on pp. 230–231, emphasis added.

61. "Veiled Women Show the Way to Terrorists in the Kashmir," *The Statesman* (India), 20 October 2001, Lexis/Nexis, 31 January 2002.

62. Ibid. This line of reasoning is very reminiscent of Decker's discussion of Algerian women during the Resistance.

63. For example see "Indian Intelligence Agencies Warn of Possible Female Suicide Squad Attacks," *BBC Worldwide Monitoring,* (originally published in *The Asian Age,* Delhi), 14 December 2001, Lexis/Nexis, 31 January 2002. Although no attacks occurred during the 26 January 2002 festivities, security was reportedly tight.

64. "Female Fighters Push on for Tamil Victory," *Michigan Daily.com* CX (93) 10 March 2000, available at (http://www.pub.umich.edu/daily/2000/mar/03-10-2000/news/09.html), 2 April 2002.

65. Jansz, "Why Do They Blow Themselves Up?"

66. The artillery reference was reportedly made by a Sri Lankan military source ("Female Fighters Push on for Tamil Victory").

67. For two good studies on the role of women in Palestinian resistance both before and during the first *intifada* see Antonius, "Fighting on Two Fronts," pp. 26–45 and Graham Usher, "Palestinian Women, the Intifada and the State of Independence," *Race & Class* 34(3) (January–March 1993), pp. 31–43.

68. Majeda Al-Batsh, "Mystery Surrounds Palestinian Woman Suicide Bomber,"*Agence France Presse,* 28 January 2002, Lexis/Nexis, 6 February 2002.

69. David Sharrock, "Women: The Suicide Bomber's Story," *The Guardian,* 5 May 1998, Lexis/Nexis, 30 March 2002.

70. For more information on Al-Tamimi and the Summer 2001 incidents that appear linked to her see Wafa Amr, "Palestinian Women Play Role in Fighting Occupation," *Jordan Times,* 29 January 2002, available at (http://www.jordantimes.com/tue/news/news6.htm). 3 February 2002; also see "Shabak Accuses Young Palestinian Woman of Assisting Hamas Cell," The

Palestinian Information Center, 17 September 2001, available at (http://www.palestineinfo.com/daily_news/prev_editions/2001/ep01/17sep01.htm), 3 February 2002. As of 12 February 2002, Al-Tamimi remains in Israeli custody awaiting trial (see http://www.palestinemirror.org/Other%20Updates/palestinian_women_political_prisoners.htm).

71. Ghazawi's age has been quoted as either 23 or 24 (see Majeda Al-Batsh, "Palestinian Mother, 24, Is Among Loners Mounting Attacks On Israel," *Agence France Presse,* 6 September 2001, Lexis/Nexis, 30 March 2002; David Rudge, "Alert Security Guard Foils TA Bombing," *The Jerusalem Post,* 5 August 2001, Lexis/Nexis, 30 March 2002; "Palestinians' New Weapon: Women Suicide Bombers," *The Straits Times (Singapore),* 6 August 2001, Lexis/Nexis, 30 March 2002; Uzi Mahnaimi, "Israeli Fear As Women Join Suicide Squad," *Sunday Times (London),* 5 August 2001, Lexis/Nexis, 30 March 2002; and Douglas Davis, "Women Warriors," *Jewish World Review,* 9 August 2001, available at (http://www.jewishworldreview.com/080l/women.warriors.asp), 30 March 2002).

72. Phil Reeves, "The Paramedic Who Became Another 'Martyr' for Palestine," *The Independent,* 31 January 2002, available at (http://www.ccmep.org/hotnews/parameic013102.html), 6 March 2002.

73. Hizbollah television identified the bomber as Shahanaz Al Amouri following the attack. See Imigo Gilmore, "Woman Suicide Bomber Shakes Israelis," *The Daily Telegraph* (London), 28 January 2002, Lexis/Nexis, 6 March 2002.

74. William Neuman, "Femmes Fatales Herald New Terror Era," *The New York Post,* 28 January 2002, Lexis/Nexis, 11 March 2002.

75. James Bennet, "Israelis Declare Arab Woman Was In Fact a Suicide Bomber," *The New York Times,* 9 February 2002, Lexis/Nexis, 11 March 2002.

76. Larnis Andoni, "Wafa Idrees: A Symbol of a Generation," *Arabic Media Internet Network* (AMIN), 23 February 2002, available at (http://www.amin.org/eng/uncat/2002/feb/feb23.html), 6 March 2002.

77. Reeves, "The Paramedic Who Became Another 'Martyr' "; James Bennet, "Filling in the Blanks on Palestinian Bomber," *The New York Times,* 31 January 2002, Lexis/Nexis, 6 March 2002; and Wafa Amr, "Palestinian Woman Bomber Yearned for Martyrdom," *The Jordan Times,* 31 January 2002, available at (http://www.jordantimes.com). 31 January 2002.

78. Peter Beaumont, "From an Angel of Mercy to Angel of Death," *The Guardian,* 31 January 2002, available at (http://www.guardian.co.uk/Print/0,3858,4346503,00.html). 6 March 2002.

79. Quoted in "Inquiry and Analysis No. 84: Jihad and Terrorism Studies Wafa Idris: The Celebration of the First Female Palestinian Suicide Bomber—Part II," *The Middle East Media and Research Institute,* 13 February 2002, available at (http://www.memri.org). 6 March 2002. Also see James Bennet, "Arab Press Glorifies Bomber as Heroine," *The New York Times,* 11 February 2002, Lexis/Nexis, 6 March 2002.

80. "Militant Palestinian Leader on Imminent Operations with 15-km Rockets," *BBC Monitoring Middle East,* 4 February 2002, Lexis/Nexis, 4 March 2002.

81. Sophie Claudet, "More Palestinian Women Suicide Bombers Could Be On the Way: Analysts," *Agence France Presse,* 28 February 2002, Lexis/Nexis, 16 March 2002.

82. Yassin and Yusef's points were taken from "We Don't Need Women Suicide Bombers: Hamas Spiritual Leader," *Agence France Presse,* 2 February 2002, Lexis/Nexis, 6 March 2002; "Islam Not (sic) Forbid Women From Carrying Out Suicide Attack," *Xinhua,* 28 February 2002, Lexis/Nexis, 31 January 2002. For further accounts of the range of religious responses to Idris' action please see "Inquiry and Analysis No. 83: Jihad and Terrorism Studies—Wafa Idris: The Celebration of the First Female Palestinian Suicide Bomber—Part I," *The Middle East Media and Research Institute,* 12 February 2002, available at (http://www.memri.org), 6 March 2002.

83. Darwish's statements were taken from "Palestinians' New Weapon: Women Suicide Bombers," *The Straits Times (Singapore),* 6 August 2001, Lexis/Nexis, 31 January 2002.

84. Mohammed Daraghmeh, "Woman Suicide Bomber Rejected by Hamas," *The Independent,* 1 March 2002, Lexis/Nexis, 6 March 2002; Mohammad Daraghmeh, "Woman Bomber Wanted to Carry Out Sbarro-Like Attack," *The Jerusalem Post,* 1 March 2002, Lexis/Nexis, 6 March 2002; "Woman Suicide Bomber was 21-Year Old Palestinian Student," *Agence France Presse,* 28 February 2002, Lexis/Nexis, 6 March 2002; Sandro Contenta, "Student 'Had a Wish to Become a Martyr,' " *Toronto Star,* 1 March 2002, Lexis/Nexis, 13 March 2002; Stephen Farrell, "Daughter's Dedication Was Beyond Doubt," *The Times* (London), 1 March 2002, Lexis/Nexis, 13 March 2002.

85. See "Deadly Secret of Quiet High School Girl Who Became a Suicide Bomber," *The Herald* (Glasgow) 30 March 2002, Lexis/Nexis, 1 April 2002; Anton La Guardia, "The Girl Who Brought Terror to the Supermarket," *The Daily Telegraph* (London), 30 March 2002, Lexis/Nexis, 1 April 2002; and Cameron W. Barr, "Why a Palestinian Girl Now Wants to Be a Suicide Bomber," *The Christian Science Monitor,* 1 April 2002, Lexis/Nexis, 1 April 2002; Eric Silver, "Middle East Crisis: Schoolgirl Suicide Bomber Kills Two in Supermarket," *The Independent* (London), 30 March 2002, 1 April 2002; Philip Jacobson, "Terror of the Girl Martyrs," *Sunday Mirror,* 31 March 2002, Lexis/Nexis, 1 April 2002. The reference to the militia linked to Arafat is a thinly disguised reference to the Al-Aqsa Martyrs Brigade.

86. David Lamb, "The World; Gruesome Change from the Ordinary; Conflict: A Quiet, Young Seamstress Further Widened the Mideast Breach When She Joined the Ranks of Palestinian Suicide Bombers," *The Los Angeles Times,* 14 April 2002, ProQuest, 3 June 2002;

"Jerusalem Shocked by Suicide Bomb; Woman Bomber Kills Six in Attempt to Derail Powell Peace Talks," Belfast News Letter, 13 April 2002, Lexis/Nexis, 3 June 2002.

87. Jacobson, "Terror of the Girl Martyrs."

88. Melanie Reid, "Myth That Women Are the Most Deadly Killers of All," *The Herald (Glasgow)* 29 January 2002, Lexis/Nexis, 6 February 2002.

89. This last point is reinforced by reports emanating from the territories that suggest at least a temporary "alignment" between the two sides. For example, in Jenin Hamas and Fatah reportedly joined together to distribute "explosive belts" and hand grenades to individuals in the camp for self defense. A woman, Ilham Dosuki, reportedly blew herself up on 6 April 2002 as soldiers approached the door to her home ("Fierce Battles in Jenin, Nablus: Unconfirmed Reports: Scores of

Palestinians Killed and Injured in Jenin Refugee Camp," 2002, *Al-Bawaba,* 6 April 2002, available at (http://www.albawaba.com/). 6 April 2002.

90. Mullaney, "Women and the Theory of the 'Revolutionary Personality'," p. 54.

91. See Antonius, "Fighting on Two Fronts," pp. 26–45 and Juliane Hammer, "Prayer, *Hijab* and the *Intifada:* The Influence of the Islamic Movement on Palestinian Women," *Islam and Christian-Muslim Relations* 11(3) (October 2000), pp. 299–320 for additional information on the role of mothers in the Palestinian resistance to Israeli occupation.

92. This argumentation is directed from a number of sources, including feminist scholars who view violent women as "unnatural" because women are naturally peaceful, a feminine attribute that is superior and morally virtuous. Thus, violent women are either duped by male leaders or have internalized masculine (violent) traits in lieu of female traits (nonviolence). This reasoning is shared, interestingly enough, by many conservative thinkers.

Address correspondence to **KARLA J. CUNNINGHAM,** PhD, Department of Political Science, SUNY Geneseo, 1 College Circle, Geneseo, NY 14454, USA. Email: cunningh@geneseo.edu

Article 31

Explosive Baggage: Female Palestinian Suicide Bombers and the Rhetoric of Emotion

This paper examines the rhetoric of emotion surrounding the first female Palestinian suicide bombers. The influence of gender in recruitment, training and compensation by the terrorist organization are considered within the context of the tension between gender equality and tradition in Palestinian culture. The carefully-edited discourse of the bombers themselves is juxtaposed with the discounting of those statements by friends, family and the media in an attempt to understand the motivations for engaging in terror. Media coverage, particularly in the West, appears to actively search for alternate explanations behind women's participation in terror in a way that does not seem paralleled in the coverage of male suicide bombers, whose official ideological statements appear to be taken at face value.

TERRI TOLES PATKIN

There is a powerful psychological effect associated with being prepared to die for a cause. A *suicide bombing* is a bomb attack on people or property, delivered by a person who knows the explosion will cause his or her own death. Although the concept predates the label (suicide attacks occurred in the ancient world, kamikaze pilots in World War II chose to die for their country), the term became popularized in 1983 after an explosives-laden pickup track crashed into a Beirut, Lebanon, facility housing U.S. Marines. However, the use of suicide operatives in nationalist terror organizations in recent decades marks a change from the 1960s and 1970s practice of conserving manpower by carrying out attacks while keeping operatives at a safe distance (Lewis, 2003). Suicide bombings—inexpensive, effective, media-friendly and with a built-in intelligent guidance and delivery system—are chillingly effective as psychological warfare (Hoffman, 2003). Suicide bombing redefines basic cultural relationships and merges private, psychological motivations with public, ideologically-charged actions. Killing oneself is no longer an act of self-destruction (*intihar*), but rather divinely commanded martyrdom (*istishad*) in defense of the faith (Stern, 2003).

Today, the Arab press generally refer to a suicide bomber as a *human bomb*. The Bush administration briefly tried to get journalists to use the term *homicide bombing,* but it did not gain currency (Suicide Bomber, 2003; Suicide Bombing, 2003). Suicide bombers are not suffering from clinical depression or emotional difficulties; they perceive themselves as fulfilling a holy mission that will make them martyrs. The action is not "suicide" but rather "martyrdom" and thus does not violate religious prohibitions against killing oneself (Atran, 2003; Lewis, 2003; Reuter, 2004; Schweitzer, 2000).

The tactic was introduced into Palestinian areas gradually starting in the late 1980s. Hezbollah pioneered the use of suicide bombing, claiming responsibility for attacks on the U.S. Marine barracks in Beirut (1983), the hijacking of TWA flight 847 (1985) and a series of lethal attacks on Israeli targets. Like many other Islamist organizations, Hezbollah engages in both guerrilla warfare against Israeli military targets and terrorism targeting the civilian population, as well as sponsoring social programs for the Palestinian population (Byman, 2003).

By the mid-1990s, Hamas, Islamic Jihad, and Hezbollah had all used suicide bombings as a means to derail the Oslo peace process. Palestinian terrorist groups in Israel during this period also included Palestinian Islamic Jihad, Islamic Resistance Movement (Hamas), Umar al-Mukhtar Forces, Al-Aqsa Martyrs Brigade, and Salah al-Din Battalions (Office of the Coordinator for Counterterrorism, 2000). The Islamist agenda shared by many of these organizations has led to the "second intifada," during which suicide bombings have escalated. There have been more volunteers for suicide attacks (including women) and planning for each attack has been less rigorous than in the past (Atran, 2003).

As the Palestinian point of view shifted from negotiation about specific tracts of land to a no-compromise drive toward a final victory, the psychology of terrorism shifted from martyrdom as a means to martyrdom as an end (Brooks, 2002). The Palestine Liberation Organization's (PLO) goal is the creation of a secular state; Hamas and similar organizations merge religion with political and social activism and add terrorist activities to the mix (Reuter, 2004). For example, "Hamas calls all Muslims to give up their secular culture and lifestyles and return to religious observance: prayer, fasting, Islamic dress, moral and social values to re-create a proper Islamic society so that Muslim society can again become strong and wage a successful jihad to liberate Palestine from Israeli control" (Esposito, 2002: 95–96).

Terrorist activity in Israel is organized; suicide bombings do not represent the actions of lone, crazed individuals. Suicide terrorism is perceived by the sponsoring organizations as most painful way to inflict damage on the Israeli occupation forces, and a way to make the cost of the conflict unbearable. The movement recognizes that it does not have a nuclear arsenal, tanks or rockets, but says that its "exploding Islamic human bombs" are far superior (Hassan, 2001). Two-thirds of all suicide bombings in Israel have occurred in the past three years (Burns, 2003; Hoffman, 2003; IDF Spokesperson, 2002). The attacks take place in shopping malls, on buses, in supermarkets, in restaurants and cafes, on street corners—places where the fabric of everyday life is suddenly rent by an explosion, blood and terror.

What Makes Terrorists Tick: Motivations Sacred and Secular

The dynamics of the terrorist group shape individual behavior, giving many members a strong sense of belonging, of importance, and of personal significance (Post, 1990). Suicide bombers often articulate a sense of personal, sacred mission. When Hezbollah introduced suicide bombing as a tactic in the mid-1980s, it soon became clear that the religious fervor of the bombers could help the organization compensate for its small numbers and inadequate military capabilities (Kramer, 1990).

Resentment and self-righteousness are often considered to be the underlying motivators for engaging in terrorism. Perceiving themselves as victims, the terrorists hone a hypersensitive awareness of slights and humiliations inflicted upon themselves or their particular group, and picture themselves as part of an elite heroically struggling to right the injustices of an unfair world. Terrorists share several characteristics: "oversimplification of issues, frustration about an inability to change society, a sense of self-righteousness, a utopian belief in the world, a feeling of social isolation, a need to assert his own existence, and a cold-blooded willingness to kill" (Davis, 2001: n.pag.). According to the Palestinian Authority, the typical suicide bomber (prior to the Second Intifada and the September 11 attacks) fit a standard profile: young, male, unemployed, with few prospects economically or socially, mildly religious. He is persuaded to join the movement because of both pragmatic and ideological reasons; the allure of martyrdom may in fact take second place to the very tangible economic and social benefits his family will receive after his action (Reuter, 2004; Stern, 2003). Post September 11, the profile has become less clear, with men, women and even children being included. All strata of society are represented, all marital statuses, all educational levels (Hoffman, 2003).

The myth that suicide bombers are driven to their actions by the frustration stemming from poverty and ignorance is exploded by the actuality that today's Palestinian bombers tend to be well educated and relatively economically stable (Atran, 2003; Brooks, 2002; Hassan, 2001; Stern, 2003). While cash payments from abroad to families of suicide bombers continue, now all levels of the economic and educational spectrum are represented (Stern, 2003; Tierney, 2002). Despite well-publicized photos of families holding checks for as much as $25,000, the bomber's family may receive little direct financial incentive (Reuter, 2004). Often, the bomber has a close friend or family member who has been killed by Israeli soldiers or has spent time in Israeli custody, but the most crucial factor appears to be loyalty to the terrorist organization, about which members speak in family metaphors (Atran, 2003; Brooks, 2002; Hassan, 2001; Stern, 2003).

Religious terrorists believe their goals and activities are sanctioned by divine authority. Martyrdom, the voluntary acceptance of death as a demonstration of religious truth, is a concept central to Islam. Suicide bombers view themselves as martyrs fighting a *jihad* against their heretic, apostate opponents (Rapoport, 1990). Transforming oneself into a living bomb is perceived as the equivalent of using a gun against one's enemies. The struggle is much the same, the only difference being one of chronology: the bomber dies *while* killing several enemies rather than *after* doing so (Kramer, 1990). Being "ready to die" is not the same as "seeking to die." Further, some whose death is interpreted as suicide may have been tricked into the action by those controlling their activities ("remote-control martyrs") (Esposito, 2002; Lewis, 2003; Merari, 1990).

Suicide bombing to date always occurs within the context of a terrorist organization; bombers do not act individually (Hassan, 2001; Hoffman, 2003). Personal revenge is not the primary motivator for Palestinian suicide bombers, and such an impetus in fact would negate the promise of martyrdom. There is not one instance of a lone, crazed Palestinian who has gotten hold of a bomb and set off to kill Israelis or even of an independent suicide bomber acting without the support of an established organization (Atran, 2003; Brooks, 2002; Victor, 2003).

It is, of course, difficult to ascertain what terrorists are "really" thinking or what "really" motivates them, especially considering the tendency of terror organizations to maintain high levels of secrecy and the contextual situation of long-standing sociocultural conflicts (Hassan, 2001). Similarly, it is easy to misinterpret the happy expressions often seen on the faces of suicide bombers. A smile may mean contemplation of eternal paradise or it may represent satisfaction that the individual has helped the organization advance their goals one step forward (Kramer, 1990). Of necessity, this analysis relies on secondary sources. It is important to note that, with few exceptions, we do not hear the voices of the women involved in terrorist organizations themselves, except in the officially sponsored and edited video testaments that the martyrs leave behind. Perhaps inevitably, we cannot know with certainty the extent of their ideological fervor, nor can we pinpoint their emotional and cognitive responses to engaging in terror. We are left only with observations of behavior in public, i.e. the actual suicide bombing or attempt, and the post-detonation interpretations of family and friends, and so must extrapolate all manner of important background as we reconstruct the influences leading up to the terrorist act.

The Care and Feeding of Terrorist Trainees

The terrorist recruitment process is complex. Hamas and Islamic Jihad do not accept all the volunteers for martyrdom who approach them; in fact, leaders call fending off the crowds insisting on retaliatory human bombing missions their biggest problem lately (Hassan, 2001). Until recently, all recruits have been male. The sponsoring organizations usually (but not always) reject those under 18, and those who are married or the sole wage earners in their families. Siblings are not accepted together. Pious youths who can be discreet among friends and family are preferred as are those who could "pass" as an Israeli Jew for long enough to infiltrate into the targeted area.

Training for *jihad* includes instruction in small arms practice, cartography, targeting, mines, and demolitions and poisons, as well as religious instruction and prepackaged justifications for killing Americans and Jews (Olcott and Babajanov, 2003). New recruits are asked to provide their reasons for volunteering and assure the trainer of the seriousness of their intentions. At the same time, the organization interviews the recruit's friends and family members in order to ensure that the newcomer is not an Israeli spy (Victor, 2003). Appropriate disguise and demeanor are discussed and practiced during training sessions (Reuter, 2004) and recruits are sometimes placed in situations where their lives are in danger in order to assess their responses (Victor, 2003).

Recruits view suicide missions as the shortest path to heaven. If their joy at attaining paradise ever falters, the "assistants" who constantly accompany the trainees remind them of the pain associated with sickness and old age, encourage them to re-enact previous terror operations, and assure them that death will be swift and painless and that the doors to paradise beckon. In actuality, fear of impending death is not an issue for recruits as much as awe: the prospective martyr expects to attain paradise imminently and is anxious that something might go wrong and keep him from the presence of Allah (Brooks, 2002; Hassan, 2001).

Heaven is conceptualized as a place of perfection, a lovely garden containing trees, fruit orchards, animals, exquisite foods, beverages, clothing and scenery (Stern, 2003). One lives in a beautiful home with a pleasant smell of perfume, with servants attending to one's every need, and family members from this life and the next close at hand (Rewards Promised to Suicide Bombers in Paradise, 2002). The martyr achieves atonement for all of his sins with the first drop of blood shed, and ten minutes after martyrdom weds 72 beautiful dark-eyed virgins whose home is in heaven. The 72 virgins are actually the reward for every believer admitted to paradise, according to mainstream Islamic theology, and the pleasures they offer are not sensual. But that doesn't make the prospect any less appealing to teenage boys. Indeed, the "Israeli Defense Forces report that one of the suicide bombers whose attack they managed to prevent had wrapped toilet paper around his genitals, apparently to protect them for later use in paradise" (Stern, 2003: 55). (As it turns out (Stern, 2003), the promise of 72 virgins (*houri*) may result from a mistranslation of the word *hur* (white raisins, an ancient regional delicacy).

Trainees pray and read sections of the Koran dealing with themes of jihad, war, Allah's favors and the importance of faith. They attend religious lectures for two to four hours a day, fast, pay off their debts, and ask for forgiveness for actual or perceived offenses. After studying for many months, the candidate is titled *al shaheed al hayy*, the "living martyr" or "one who is waiting for martyrdom." In the days preceding an operation, the candidate prepares a will (on paper, audiotape or video), emphasizing the voluntary nature of the mission and exhorting others to imitate him. He repeatedly watches his own video as well as those of others, growing more comfortable with the idea of death (Hoffman, 2003). He may also view videos showing Israeli attacks on Palestinians to bolster his resolve (Victor, 2003).

On the designated day, he completes a ritual bath, puts on clean clothes and tucks a Koran in the left breast pocket above the heart, prays, and straps on the explosives or picks up the briefcase or bag containing the bomb. The trainer wishes him success so that he will attain paradise and the trainee responds that they will meet in paradise. As he pushes the detonator, he says "*Allahu akbar*" ("Allah is great. All praise to him.") (Hassan, 2001). Afterwards, the sponsoring organization pays for the *shaheed*'s (martyr) memorial service and burial as well as making financial contributions to the bomber's family (Reuter, 2004).

The Changing Role of Female Recruits in Terrorist Organizations

Women have participated in terrorist groups worldwide, but their relatively low numbers and roles often centering on support of their male colleagues have diminished onlooker perceptions of their importance. Women tend to be more actively involved in nationalist/secular terror organizations rather than Islamist/religious groups. Women in Palestinian groups are often enthusiastic about their increased roles, especially as the conflict with Israel deepens (Cunningham, 2003).

The arguments for women to join armed forces have been well-developed: the defense of one's country is the duty and right of all citizens, women need to participate in the military if they are to have real equality with men, it will give women more self-confidence and might benefit the armed forces. The counter-arguments have been equally well-developed: engaging in violence does not serve women's (or anyone else's) ultimate interests, women have too many other burdens (such as childcare) in society, women as givers of life should not be involved in taking life (Brock-Utne, 1985). Female involvement in historical terrorist or revolutionary uprisings has also been well documented (Schweitzer, 2000). Women have been responsible for significant numbers of the suicide bombings carried out by the Liberation Tigers of Tamil Eelam in Sri Lanka and the Kurdish Workers' Party PKK. In some cases, women accounted for as many as 66% of the suicide bombings completed by the organization (Stern, 2003).

Still, most terrorist organizations are androcentric, and many are rooted in fundamentalist religious ideologies which require the exclusion of women from public life, especially in Islamic contexts. Although women are often motivated to join terrorist movements by the same political and economic concerns as men, they also join or are encouraged to join revolutionary struggles on behalf of their practical and strategic gender interests (Peterson and Sisson, 1999). Women may also play a supporting role in terrorism in their traditional roles as wives and mothers by nurturing families committed to terrorist causes, willingly sacrificing their children to militarist actions and engaging in peripheral activities such as carrying supplies or messages for terrorist groups. While men may support terrorism from a desire to bring about social justice, women are more often found to articulate "private" concerns such as using terrorism as a means to protect their families, homes and communities (Caiazza, 2001). Although patriarchal norms often preclude women from militaristic actions and limit their public roles, some women have taken part in terrorism when there are few perceived outlets for gender equality (Caiazza, 2001; Elshtain, 2003). Indeed, the rationale offered for engaging in terrorism may center on defending the "purity" of women in traditional roles. However, there is increasing evidence that women in terrorist organizations are moving away from the traditional "support" role (FBI Warns of Female Terror Recruits, 2003; Lewis, 2003).

Women who join terrorist groups tend to be older and better educated than their male counterparts. And yet, perceptions of women's motivations for terrorism continue to be colored by the notion that women are emotional and irrational, perhaps even driven by hormonal imbalances; rarely have their actions been interpreted as intelligent, rational decisions. "The average depiction of women terrorists draws on notions that they are (a) extremist feminists; (b) only bound into terrorism via a relationship with a man; (c) only acting in supporting roles within terrorist organizations; (d) mentally inept; (e) unfeminine in some way; or any combination of the above. . . . She is seldom the highly reasoned, non-emotive, political animal that is the picture of her male counterpart; in short, she rarely escapes her sex" (Talbot, 2001: n.pag.). But when one asks women themselves about their terrorist activity, they do not perceive their involvement as passive; they regard themselves as empowered political actors, not as auxiliaries to their more self-aware male counterparts (Talbot, 2001).

Al-Qaeda is reported to have begun recruiting women for terrorist attacks following successful Chechen and Palestinian operations (FBI Warns of Female Terror Recruits, 2003). This would, of course, expand their personnel, but the concept is ironic, given Al-Qaeda's historical link with the socially repressive policies towards women enacted by the Taliban in Afghanistan. Women drawn to terrorist organizations for support of societal and ideological change may also hold a parallel desire for change in private role behaviors. Political changes on the societal level are often reflected in the home. Men in terrorist groups often report a desire to return to "authentic" traditional role relationships where women have a stronger interest in attaining social equality (Cunningham, 2003). The emotional baggage surrounding cultural gender roles cannot be jettisoned as easily as a bomb-filled suitcase on a crowded city bus.

Although women have been involved since the beginning of the struggle between the Israelis and the Palestinians (in 1960, one woman hijacked a plane, others have successfully planted bombs in various locations), recently women's roles have escalated. Suicide bombing represents the next step after completing assignments to plant and detonate bombs without injuring oneself (Cunningham, 2003). Until recently, female suicide bombers were extremely rare among Muslims, and some fundamentalist Islamic terror groups do not even now permit women to take part in terrorist activities, particularly not suicide operations. Historically, Hamas and Islamic Jihad were adamant that women should not participate in violent demonstrations but rather remain at home in their established roles as mothers and homemakers, donning traditional dress and head coverings (Victor, 2003).

But in 2002, Yasser Arafat gave his "army of roses" speech in which he called upon women to join as equals in the struggle against Israel, coining the term *shaheeda,* the feminine of the Arabic word for martyr (Victor, 2003). That same afternoon, Wafa Idris became the first female Palestinian suicide bomber (Reynolds, 2002; Tierney, 2002). Soon afterward, Al-Aqsa Brigades actively began recruiting women as suicide bombers, opening a woman's suicide unit in Idris' honor (Victor, 2003). Palestinian women are recruited by men (brothers, uncles, teachers or religious leaders), not by other women, although young girls now look to the mediated images of the first female suicide bombers as role models (Victor, 2003). The men persuade the female recruits that the most valuable thing they can do with their life is to end it; a suicide bombing often provides a dual function as an attack against Israel and a redemption of personal or family honor, a highly salient value in Palestinian culture (Victor, 2003).

If anything, women may be seen as holding a deeper commitment to the "cause" than men, due to the emotive soul-searching that shapes their decision to participate. While not all women who apply are accepted, those who are believe it is their duty to volunteer for their country. "I could die at any time, so I will die for my people" one trainee says (Tierney, 2002: n.pag.). Women terrorists are likened to a lioness protecting her cubs; it is said that the woman views her cause as a surrogate child. Indeed the presence of women as terrorist actors may play on cultural images of victimization just as much as retaliatory strikes do (Talbot, 2001).

Ironically, the perception of female weakness can increase a woman's effectiveness in terror operations. Many female terrorists have exploited male assumptions about the "innocent woman" as a way to evade search and detection by predominantly male military forces, sometimes reverting to voluminous traditional dress, other times using fictive pregnancy or even real infants to hide explosive equipment. Other stereotypes, such as age, are also utilized. Soldiers may ignore an old woman egging on stone throwers, feeling it more important to capture the young boys following her instructions (Talbot, 2001). Israeli Security Sources admit (2002, 2003b) that, especially when dressed in Western clothes with modern hairstyles or maternity clothes, women can exploit the presumption of innocence, and soldiers may be hesitant to perform thorough body searches of women passing through checkpoints.

However, this strategy can also backfire for the sponsoring terrorist organization. For example, Thawiya Hamour, 26, decided to abort her suicide mission at the last moment, "claiming her operators directed her to dress provocatively like an Israeli woman, such as wearing her hair down, using heavy makeup, and donning tight pants. During media interviews Hamour stated, 'I wasn't afraid. I'm not afraid to die. I went for personal reasons. However, I did not want to arrive 'upstairs' for impure reasons. I did not want to dress that way, because it is against my religion." (Israeli Security Sources, 2003b: n.pag.). Not surprisingly, checkpoint security guidelines have evolved in response to terrorists' use of gender expectations (Victor, 2003).

Media Images and the Rhetoric of Domesticity

Communication serves as a dynamic foundation for interaction among individuals, a systemic process through which meanings are created and relationships formed. The connection between gender roles and the structures, vocabularies and styles of using language has been well documented. Women are more concerned with inner feelings, relational issues, nurturance and emotional support; men are more concerned with sharing activities than sharing feelings. Women's relational perspective contrasts with men's contextual perspective (Gilligan, 1982; Lakoff, 1976; McConnell-Ginet, 1980; O'Barr and Atkins, 1980; Tannen, 1990; Wardhaugh, 1986: Wood, 1994). This difference is intuitively exploited in media reports about terrorist motivations.

Terrorist organizations typically plan their activities to achieve the greatest media coverage and most positive spin for their story. The rhetoric surrounding suicide bombers makes good use of the metaphors of domesticity. Small training cells operate in isolation from one another (Reuter, 2004), and one's training cell of three to eight other terrorists becomes a "family of fictive kin for whom they are willing to die as a mother for her child or a soldier for his buddies" (Atran, 2003: 11). Indeed, the very point of suicide terrorism is an attack on the opposition's comfortable domesticity; the killer's goal is to disrupt everyday life to the greatest degree possible. The warm image of family distracts from the cold reality of carefully premeditated mass murder.

Following a bombing, even in the midst of personal grief, the terrorist's "family and sponsoring organization celebrate his martyrdom with festivities, as if it were a wedding. Hundreds of guests congregate at the house to offer congratulations. The hosts serve the juices and sweets that the young man specified in his will. Often, the mother will ululate in joy over the honor that Allah has bestowed upon her family" (Hassan, 2001, n.pag.). After a "successful" suicide bombing, the bomber's parents and family members are often interviewed on television, proudly expressing their joy at their child's martyrdom and even their readiness to send another child off to the afterlife should the opportunity present itself. Parents may distribute candy to neighborhood children in celebration of their child's martyrdom (Victor, 2003). "We are receiving congratulations from people.... Why should we cry? It is like her wedding today, the happiest day for her," (Murphy, 2003: n.pag.) said a brother following Hanadi Tayseer Jaradat's death.

The image is of parents so wronged and humiliated by the Israelis that they would rather sacrifice their children than continue to endure. Both mothers and fathers present this public face, downplaying the material and status benefits associated with having a martyr in the family and utilizing their personal tragedy as an illustration of the organization's ideological stance. While some parents assure the Western media that they would have stopped their child from committing suicide if they have known of the child's plan, they simultaneously express pride in the child's final act (Copeland, 2002). However, there is some evidence that parents, especially mothers, recognize this dissonance and experience a delayed grief reaction that must of necessity be masked from the Palestinian media (Victor, 2003). Privately, some parents will admit that they had "other plans" for their child than martyrdom (Reuter, 2004). These "other plans" may reflect traditional values: one mother, whose daughter did not complete her mission, expresses relief: she would have been "proud" of a son who martyred himself, because that is "normal," but her unmarried daughter should aspire to marriage and children, not martyrdom (Victor, 2003).

Following the attack, the organization distributes copies of the martyr's audio or video testament to the media and to local organizations in addition to the posed photographs, often posted on billboards, that the terrorist organizations use for recruiting purposes. "The video testaments, which are shot against a background of the sponsoring organization's banner and slogans, show the living martyr reciting the Koran, posing with guns and bombs, exhorting his comrades to follow his example, and extolling the virtues of jihad" (Hassan, 2001, n.pag.). These, of course, also make it that much more difficult for the "living martyr" to back out of his commitment to be used by the organization in a "sacred explosion" (Brooks, 2002; Hoffman, 2003; Stern, 2003).

The videos follow a standard format, although the *shaheed* or *shaheeda* is permitted to choose from a variety of common backdrops such as a plaster model of the Al-Aqsa mosque, various organizational flags, weapons and the like. Typically, the bomber stands before a flag, holding a Koran and an automatic weapon, and reads a script that may have been written by the bomber or by the handler. The speech discusses motivations for the bombing and leaves messages of hope and inspiration for surviving family members (Reuter, 2004; Victor, 2003). There may also be a private testament left for family only, and while this appears to reflect a more authentic view of the individual's motivations, the private testaments are for obvious reasons more difficult to obtain for analysis (Reuter, 2004).

Posters and calendars glorifying the "martyr of the month" reinforce the culture of martyrdom along with chants, slogans, graffitti and victory gestures. These not only legitimate the organization's success in the specific attack, but provide encouragement to other young people, background for sermons in mosques, and material for posters, videos and demonstrations (Brooks, 2002). Suicide bombing is particularly well-suited to the television age—from the compelling footage of the bomber's

Article 31. Explosive Baggage: Female Palestinian Suicide Bombers and the Rhetoric of Emotion

last farewells to the graphic images of death and destruction to the marches and celebrations after the attacks, from the newspaper announcements of the weddings between bombers and the dark-eyed virgins in paradise to the displays of material wealth the family acquires from the cash awards, a suicide bombing makes for gripping media drama (Dickey, 2002; Hassan, 2001). Names of terrorists may even appear in crossword puzzles as answers to clues such as "famous Palestinian martyr" (Marcus, 2002). Martyrdom is emerging as the short road to celebrity for impoverished teens with few prospects.

For instance, the Palestinian Authority immediately turned Wafa Idris, the first female suicide bomber, into a heroine, holding a demonstration in her honor with young girls carrying posters illustrated with her picture and eulogizing her with "great pride" (Marcus, 2003). Music videos morphed images of a woman singing into a uniformed female warrior proclaiming her willingness to die as a martyr, a concert honoring Idris has been broadcast repeatedly, and summer camps for Palestinian girls were named to honor Idris and other female suicide bombers (Marcus, 2003).

To the terrorist, the identity of the victims is incidental to the larger purpose of gaining publicity for the terrorist agenda and instilling fear in the public at large. Moral justification can be offered through theological gymnastics that diffuse and displace responsibility for murder, minimizing the consequences and dehumanizing the victims. One such psychosocial strategy centers on the use of euphemistic labeling: terrorists become "freedom fighters" engaging in "operations" that cause "collateral damage" to an "occupying force." Such sanitizing language cleans up audience evaluations of the terrorists' actions (Bandura, 1990). Sanitized language allows participants to divorce themselves from accountability and perhaps to tame the uncontrollable forces associated with dangerous technologies. Just as imagery that domesticates and humanizes weapons make it possible for use to think about the unthinkable precisely because that language makes domesticity, the warm and playful, even sexuality, part of the technological world (Cohn, 1987a; Cohn, 1987b; Cohn, 1990), so too can terrorism be presented in a positive light.

Potential bombers who complete the training but have a change of heart before the final operation appear to take a broader view of the consequences and implications of the act. Tauriya Hamamra, who rejected her orders to dress in modern clothing, said "I began to think about killing people—babies, women, sick people, and to imagine my family sitting in a restaurant and someone coming in and blowing them up . . . God would not see it as a good reason for committing suicide and therefore would not accept me as a *shaheed*" (Shin Bet, 2004: n.pag.). Hamamra accused her operators of "making a business out of the blood of *shaheeds*" (International Christian Embassy Jerusalem, 2002: n.pag.). Similarly, Arin Ahmed decided not to follow through on a bombing when she was unable to depersonalize her victims, but instead began to see them as people who looked like a friend, an aging grandmother, etc. "I suddenly understood what I was about to do and I said to myself, 'How can I do such a thing?" (Fields, 2002: n.pag.).

How *can* suicide bombers do such a thing? How does "Suha" come to the conclusion that "you don't think about the explosive belt or about your body being ripped into pieces. We are suffering. We are dying while we are still alive . . . I am prepared to sacrifice my life for the cause" (Zoroya, 2002: n. pag.), while others pull back from the brink of self- and other-destruction?

What little we know of the motivations of female Palestinian suicide bombers emerges from the juxtaposition of the carefully edited video testaments with their practiced statements and the public interpretations of the bombers' motives offered by family and friends to reporters. We are left with a jarring disconnect between the discourse of the bombers themselves and the discounting of those statements by friends, family and the media as we attempt to understand the action. Chesler (2004) asks whether Palestinian female suicide bombers are willing participants in terror or victims of indoctrination, force or clinical depression. Are they victims of honor killings, atoning for cheating on their husbands or becoming pregnant or being raped? While the male terrorist is pictured as a "living weapon" the ultimate in macho potency (Morgan, 2002), the female terrorist is often suspected of joining the movement for emotional or social reasons.

Palestinian women have historically been among the least bound by traditional roles in Arab society, and some may see martyrdom as a way to achieve equality and fight powerlessness (Copeland, 2002). However, women in Palestinian culture embody the honor of their family, and any hint of impropriety may have serious consequences (Elshtain, 2003; Hassan, 2001). "The unmarried Palestinian woman today lives under a stringent set of social and religious rules: if she is too educated, she is considered abnormal; if she looks at a man, she risks exclusion; if she sleeps with a man, and especially if she gets pregnant, she disgraces the family and risks death at the hands of her male relatives" (Victor, 2003: 193). Terrorism may be a means of rehabilitating one's personal or family status (Israeli Security Sources, 2003b). Palestinian women voluntarily engaging in terrorism are described in media accounts as having a large amount of "personal baggage." They are portrayed as divorced, barren, influenced by brothers, uncles or other male family members, grief-stricken from the death of a friend or relative, wanting to clear the family's name following a drop in status (either personal or that of a family member), romantically attached to other terrorists, or suicidal following a broken love affair and exploited by the organization (Israeli Security Sources, 2003b). While there are individual differences, the attribution of personal and social motives appears to dominate.

While each of the female Palestinian suicide bombers to date arrived at the decision to self-detonate by a unique path, their official statements share the same general tone as the officially-sponsored discourse as their male counterparts. Media coverage, particularly in the West, appears to actively search for alternate explanations behind women's participation in terror in a way that does not seem paralleled in the coverage of male suicide bombers, whose official ideological statements appear to be taken at face value. In the case of the relatively few female terrorists, media coverage profoundly emphasizes the emotional over the ideological in an effort to provide comprehensible explanations.

For example, media coverage of trend-setting female suicide bomber Wafa Idris (detonation 1/27/02) focused on her roles as a good friend and a loving daughter who volunteered with the Palestinian Red Crescent and had twice been hit by plastic-coated bullets in the line of duty. Friends say she was haunted by the terrible things she'd seen, but still wondered if she chose to die because her marriage had broken up (Beaumont, 2002). Although her sister reported that Idris used to say that she wanted to die as a martyr, her family expressed surprise at learning of her terrorist links. They said she was a cheerful if sometimes hot-tempered young woman. She and her husband had divorced when it became clear she could not have children after a miscarriage (Victor, 2003). Idris may have been depressed, stating (Victor, 2003: 196): "I have become a burden on my family. They tell me they love me and want me, but I know from their gestures and expressions that they wish I didn't exist."

Rather than exploring her ideological motivations, however, reporters struggled to uncover a domestic explanation for her actions: "She moved back to the family home, where her corner of one room was dark and simple—a battered teddy bear sat on a table. On another sat a can of hair foam and a brush" (Female Suicide Bomber Wanted to the a Martyr, 2002: n.pag.). Her attack resonated throughout the Arab world, sparking editorials celebrating her heroism and saying she also exploded myths about women's weakness. Even though there was some ambiguity about whether Idris was meant to merely plant the bomb or perform a suicide mission—she never made the customary suicide video but a video with very poor production values featuring a fully-veiled women speaking in a muffled voice has been attributed to her (Victor, 2003)—Al-Aqsa quickly realized the efficacy of using women as suicide bombers (Cunningham, 2003).

The second female suicide bomber, Dareen Abu Aysheh, 21 (detonation 2/27/02), was a student who highlighted the role of women in the struggle against the Israelis in her video (Palestinian Women Martyrs Against the Israeli Occupation, 2004). An independent-minded scholar and a feminist who planned to become a university professor of English literature, she had been resisting strong family pressure to marry and bear children for some time. During a humiliating encounter at an Israeli checkpoint, her honor was stained when she was forced by soldiers to kiss a male cousin in order to save a baby's life. However, she rejected the cousin's later offer of marriage in order to preserve her reputation. The event seems to have crystallized her rage at the occupation, and she accepted the cousin's offer of an alternative plan to avoid family disgrace, i.e. becoming a *shaheeda* (Victor, 2003). Dareen Abu Aysheh said in her suicide video, "Let Sharon [the Israeli Prime Minister] the coward know that every Palestinian woman will give birth to an army of martyrs, and her role will not only be confined to weeping over a son, brother or husband instead (sic), she will become a martyr herself" (Palestinian Women Martyrs Against the Israeli Occupation, 2004).

Ayat Akhras, 18 (detonation 3/29/02), the youngest female suicide bomber to date, had the previous day sat with her fiancé and talked about getting married after graduating from high school (Palestinian Women Martyrs Against the Israeli Occupation, 2004). In her video, Akhras stated "I am going to fight instead of the sleeping Arab armies who are watching Palestinian girls fighting alone" (Copeland, 2002: C01). Although she was known for her intense interest in political matters, observers indicate that she may have been motivated in large part by the disgrace her family had faced in the Palestinian community when her father refused to quit his job working for Israelis (Victor, 2003). Again the words of the bomber herself are discounted by observers in favor of an emotion-based interpretation.

Andaleeb Takafka, 20 (detonation 4/12/02), was concerned with the suffering of the Palestinian people (Palestinian Women Martyrs Against the Israeli Occupation, 2004). Her latent motives have been identified as apolitical, however. She had long collected movie magazines and posters of celebrities, but in the months before her bombing she replaced those with posters of martyrs, especially Wafa Idris. Takatka indicated to her handlers that she viewed martyrdom as a road to celebrity (Victor, 2003).

Hiba Daraghmah, 19 (detonation 5/19/03), was a student of English literature who showed the world her unveiled face for the first time on the Islamic Jihad poster released after her death (Palestinian Women Martyrs Against the Israeli Occupation, 2004). She became very religious and began wearing traditional dress after being raped by an uncle at the age of fourteen, and her decision to kill herself may have resulted from long-term psychological trauma from the episode (Victor, 2003).

Hanadi Tayseer Jaradat, 29 (detonation 10/4/03), was an attorney who may have been motivated by revenge for the killing of her younger brother and cousin by Israeli forces in the raid on Jenin (Palestinian Women Martyrs Against the Israeli Occupation, 2004). "By the will of God I decided to be the sixth martyr who makes her body full with splinters in order to enter every Zionist heart who occupied our country. We are not the only ones who will taste death from their occupation. As they sow so will they reap," she said in her video (Toolis, 2003: n.pag.). Her family reports that Jaradat was "inconsolable" following her brother's death and that her religiosity had strengthened in recent weeks (Murphy, 2003). The only way to release her emotions was, apparently, to become a suicide bomber.

Reem Salih al-Rayasha, 21 (detonation 1/14/04), was a university student from a wealthy family who was said to love her two children dearly (Palestinian Women Martyrs Against the Israeli Occupation, 2004). She was photographed with her two small children prior to her attack but noted that motherhood does not compare to the ability to "turn my body into deadly shrapnel against the Zionists and to knock on the doors of heaven with the skulls of Zionists" (Myre, 2004: n.pag.). She said she always wanted "to carry out a martyr attack, where parts of my body can fly all over" (Suicide bombing kills 4 Israelis, 2004: n.pag.) and continues (Myre, 2004: n.pag.), "God gave me the ability to be a mother of two children who I love so. But my wish to meet God in paradise is greater, so I decided to be a martyr for the sake of my people. I am convinced God will help and take care of my children." Observers struggled to find a motive behind al-Rayasha's attack: she was a wealthy woman, married with children, and had no close friends or family members to avenge (El-Haddad, 2004).

However, a number of press reports indicated that she may have carried out the attack in order to atone for an affair she was having with a married man (O'Loughlin, 2004).

Women's Role in the Culture of Martyrdom

To some extent, it does not matter whether these seven women decided to commit acts of terror because of external social pressures or internal ideology, or whether the media spin simply reflects the outsider's need to make sense of the apparent contradiction between "nurturing female" and "calculating killer". In either case, the point remains: the women believe. This belief may uphold the rhetoric of martyrdom or it may sustain the cultural values that encourage individuals to sacrifice themselves for personal or family honor. But in either case, the decision to become a suicide bomber reflects a lifetime of immersion in a culture that regards terrorism as an acceptable behavioral choice, and is as voluntary as any culturally-influenced choice may be.

Today's Palestinian children experience anticipatory socialization into terror from early childhood; infants have even been proudly dressed as mini-bombers by their parents (Atran, 2003). The innocent look of these young people combined with their susceptibility to persuasion makes them a likely target for terrorist influence. Recruitment of young people in schools, camps and through pervasive cultural support has grown stronger over time (Israeli Security Sources, 2003a). Polls show that 70 to 80 percent of Palestinians now support this postmodern culture of terror—far more than ever supported the peace process (Brooks, 2002; Stern, 2003). Young girls join boys at playing at suicide missions, and an eight-year-old girl may calmly sit at the dinner table and announce her intention to become a *shaheeda* (Reuter, 2004). Six year old girls in class offer their reasons for wanting to become martyrs: "to have everything in Paradise . . . to kill the Jewish . . . to live near our God . . . we never die" (Victor, 2003: 185).

Twelve year old girls are even more articulate. They hope to become martyrs in order "to follow my brother . . . to my country everything I can . . . to free my people from occupation . . . there is no hope for peace" (Victor, 2003: 188–189). A "good" Palestinian girl may ask for an automatic rifle as a wedding gift, as did Jasmeen, who said, "I do not want gold, or a diamond ring, or jewelry, but rather a M-16, and if only I can acquire this I will wish for no more to be paid by my fiancé" (Marcus, 2002: n.pag.). But it is not clear that young children really understand the meaning behind the rhetoric about "travelling to Paradise." Shireen Rabiya, 15, who was captured by the Israelis before she could complete her suicide mission, says "It sounded like fun. It sounded exciting and so many others had done it or tried that I thought, why not me?" (Victor, 2003: 261).

To some extent, all suicide operatives are victims, not only of the terrorist organizations, but of the cultural conditioning that lures them into believing that their ultimate life purpose lies in an untimely death. Military commanders for Hamas and Islamic Jihad see the human bomb—male or female—as an inexpensive, easily targetable weapon that is uniquely capable of striking fear in Israeli hearts. "The more training a soldier receives, the more skilled he is at avoiding death, whereas the opposite is true for a suicide bomber" (Stern, 2003: 52). The routinization of suicide means that operational planning has become less intensive in recent months as the numbers of volunteers increase (Reuter, 2004). The only needed supplies are readily available and inexpensive: gunpowder, nails, a light switch, a battery, mercury, acetone, a wide belt, and transportation to the target site (Reuter, 2004; Victor, 2003). Another cost-effective reason for scheduling suicide bombings is that they eliminate the need to arrange an escape plan—often the most challenging part of a terrorist operation (Hoffman, 2003). The total cost of a suicide operation is approximately $150—and the bomber's life (Atran, 2003; Hassan, 2001). The bombings are simultaneously simple and sophisticated, the ultimate poor person's smart bomb.

From an economic point of view, the female suicide bomber is a much better investment than even her male counterpart. A volunteer female suicide bomber typically trains for a period of only two to eight weeks, depending on the woman involved, far less than the months-long male course (Cunningham, 2003). Women require less persuasion (they are considerably less inclined to be swayed by promises of virgins in paradise) and the simplicity of their missions demands little technical expertise (Tierney, 2002). Women have already made a long ideological journey before they set foot in the door of the terrorist organization; they arrive ready to take that final step. They are paid less, too: the organization that takes responsibility for the suicide attack typically gives a lifetime stipend to the family of $400 a month for male suicide bombers but only $200 a month for females (Victor, 2003).

In radical Islam, women's status as subordinate is fundamental: women are considered unclean, they must be kept hidden and their bodies covered, they must be made subordinate to men (Elshtain, 2003). Just as lower status laborers do the menial work of society—cleaning, taking out the garbage—so too can they be expended in the task of removing the enemy a few at a time. "Indeed, up till now, the children of leaders have not been involved in suicide missions, but are usually sent off to Amman, Europe or the United States to study, far from the trauma and danger of the Intifada" (Victor, 2003:114–115).

The female suicide bomber turns into a victim in the midst of what she may consider the most empowered act of her life. Her complex mix of ideological, psychological and sociological motivations is reduced by the media to a poignant struggle with her feelings as an outsider in a warm, traditional community. And if the terrorist organizations can convince women that killing themselves for the "cause" not only incorporates political and religious benefits but also serves as a way to bring personal honor to themselves and their families, they manage to isolate and eliminate the most dangerous women of all in a traditional society—those courageous enough to independently take on a previously male role and perform an ideological act in a public setting.

Understanding female terrorists as socially vulnerable victims of calculated emotional blackmail by male-dominated terrorist organizations is obvious sexism. But the refusal to admit that both men and women absorb the lessons of the Palestinian culture of martyrdom is equally limiting. In a society with restricted options and opportunities, especially for women, where children are socialized into terror from their earliest years and where martyrs attain the status of celebrities, where daily life provides endless examples of humiliation and deprivation in a culture where honor has historically been among the most salient values, where religious leaders provide elaborate theological justifications for martyrdom, is it any surprise that young people, female and male, eagerly line up for a one-way ticket to Paradise?

References

Atran, S. (2003). *Genesis and Future of Suicide Terrorism.* Retrieved 9/29/03 from www.interdisciplines.org/terrorism/papers/1/12/printable/paper

Bandura, A. (1990). Mechanisms of Moral Disengagement. In W. Reich (Ed.), *Origins of Terrorism: Psychologies, ideologies, theologies, states of mind* (pp. 161–191). Cambridge: Cambridge University Press.

Beaumont, P. (2002). Suicide Notes. *The Observer.* Retrieved 3/28/04 from http://observer.guardian.co.uk/2002review/story/0,12715,862850,00.html.

Brock-Utne, B.(1985). *Educating for Peace: A Feminist Perspective.* New York: Pergamon Press.

Brooks, D. (2002). The Culture of Martyrdom. *Atlantic Monthly,* 289(6): 18–24.

Burns, J.F. (2003, October 7). Bomber Left Her Family With a Smile and a Life. *The New York Times,* p. A13.

Byman, D. (2003). Should Hezbollah Be Next? *Foreign Affairs* 82(6):54–67.

Caiazza, A. (2001). *Why Gender Matters in Understanding September 11: Women, Militarism, and Violence.* Washington, D.C.: Institute for Women's Policy Research.

Chesler, P. (2004, January 22). Forced Female Suicide. FrontPageMagazine.com. Retrieved 6/29/04 from www.frontpagemag.com/Articles/Printable.asp?ID=11855

Cohn, C. (1987a). Sex and Death in the Rational World of Defense Intellectuals. Signs: *Journal of Women in Culture and Society* 12(4): 687–718.

Cohn, C. (1987b). Slick'ems, Glick'ems, Christmas Trees, and Cookie Cutters: Nuclear Language and how we learned to pat the bomb. *Bulletin of the Atomic Scientists* 43(5): 17–24.

Cohn, C. (1990). "Clean Bombs" and Clean Language. In J.B. Elshtain and S. Tobias (Eds.), *Women, Militarism & War: Essays in History, Politics and Social Theory* (pp. 33–55). Savage, MD: Rowman and Littlefield.

Copeland, L. (2002, April 27). Female Suicide Bombers: The New Factor in Mideast's Deadly Equation. *Washington Post:* C01.

Cunningham, K.J. (2003). Cross-Regional Trends in Female Terrorism. *Studies in Conflict & Terrorism* 26:171–195.

Davis, P.B. (2001). The Terrorist Mentality. *Cerebrum: The Dana Forum on Brain Science* 3(3). Retrieved 10/4/03 from www.dushkin.com/powerweb/0072551054/article.mhtml?Article=30849

Dickey, C. (2002, April 15). Inside Suicide, Inc. *Newsweek,* pp. 26–32.

El-Haddad, L. (2004, January 23). A Palestinian mother becomes a human bomb. Retrieved 7/8/04 from http://english.aljazeera.net/NR/exeres/554FAF3A-B267-427A-B9EC-54881BDE0A2E.htm

Elshtain, J.B. (2003). *Just War Against Terror.* New York: Basic Books.

Esposito, J.L. (2002). *Unholy War: Terror in the Name of Islam.* New York: Oxford University Press.

FBI Warns of Female Terror Recruits. (2003, April 1). Retrieved 3/28/04 from www.girlswithguns.org/news/news0005.htm

Female suicide bomber wanted to die a martyr. (2002, January 31). *Irish Examiner.* Retrieved 9/29/03 from http://archives.tcm.ie/irishexaminer/2002/01/31/

Fields, S. (2002, July 1). When a suicide bomber fails. *Jewish World Review.* Retrieved 6/29/04 from www.jewishworkreview.com/cols/fields070102.asia

Gilligan, C. (1982). *In A Different Voice.* Cambridge: Harvard University Press.

Hassan, N. (2001, November 19). An Arsenal of Believers. *The New Yorker.* Retrieved 11/11/03 from www.newyorker.com/printable/?fact/011119fa_FACT1

Hoffman, B. (2003, June). The Logic of Suicide Terrorism. *Atlantic Monthly.* Retrieved 9/29/03 from http://www.theatlantic.com/issues/2003/06/hoffman.htm

IDF Spokesperson. (2002). Suicide Terror: Its use and rationalization. Retrieved 9/29/03 from www.mfa.gov.il/mfa.go.asp?MFAH0m6k0

International Christian Embassy Jerusalem. (2002, May 31). Female Bomber Disgusted By Fatah Handlers. Retrieved 6/29/04 from http://truthnews.com/world/2002060103.htm

Israeli Security Sources. (2002). Blackmailing Young Women into Suicide Terrorism. Retrieved 9/29/03 from www.mfa.gov.il/mfa.go.asp?MFAH0n2a0

Israeli Security Sources. (2003a). Participation of Children and Teenagers in Terrorist Activity during the "Al-Aqsa" Intifada. Retrieved 9/29/03 from www.mfa.gov.il/mfa.go.asp?MFAH0n100

Israeli Security Sources. (2003b). The Role of Palestinian Women in Suicide Terrorism. Retrieved 9/29/03 from www.mfa.gov.il/mfa.go.asp?MFAH0n210

Kramer, M. (1990). The Moral Logic of Hizballah. In W. Reich (Ed.), *Origins of Terrorism: Psychologies, ideologies, theologies, states of mind* (pp. 131–157). Cambridge: Cambridge University Press, pp. 131–157.

Lakoff, R. (1976). *Language and Women's Place.* New York: Octagon Books.

Lewis, B. (2003). *The Crisis of Islam: Holy War and Unholy Terror.* New York: Modern Library.

Marcus, I. (2002, March 12). Encouraging Women Terrorists. *Palestinian Media Watch Bulletin.* Retrieved 6/29/04 from www.science.co.il/Arab-Israeli-conflict/Articles/Marcus-2002-03-12.asp

Marcus, I. (2003, October 9). Promoting Women Terrorists. *Palestinian Media Watch Bulletin.* Retrieved 6/29/04 from www.israel-wat.com/idris_eng2.htm

McConnell-Ginet, S. (1980). Linguistics and the Feminist Challenge. In S. McConnell-Ginet, R. Borker and N. Furman (Eds.), *Women and Language in Literature and Society* (pp. 3–25). New York: Praeger Publishers.

Merari, A. (1990). The readiness to kill and die: Suicidal terrorism in the Middle East. In W. Reich (Ed.), *Origins of Terrorism: Psychologies, ideologies, theologies, states of mind* (pp. 192–207). Cambridge: Cambridge University Press.

Morgan, R. (2002). Demon Lover. Ms (Dec.2001–Jan.2002). Retrieved 10/4/03 from www.dushkin.com/powerweb/0072551054/article.mhtml?article=34717

Murphy, V. (2003, October 15). Mid-East cycle of vengeance. BBC News Online. Retrieved 7/8/04 from http://news.bbc.co.uk/2/hi/middleeast/3165604.stm

Myre, G. (2004, January 15). Gaza Mother, 22, Kills Four Israelis in Suicide Bombing. *New York Times.* Retrieved 6/29/04 from www.nytimes.com/2004/01/15/international/middleeast/15MIDE.html

O'Barr, W.M. and Atkins, B.K. (1980). "Women's Language" or "Powerless Language"? In S. McConnell-Ginet, R. Borker and N. Furman (Eds.), *Women and Language in Literature and Society* (pp. 93–110). New York: Praeger Publishers.

Office of the Coordinator for Counterterrorism, U.S. Department of State. (2001, April 30). Background Information on Terrorist Groups. Retrieved 9/29/03 from http://www.state.gov/s/ct/rls/pgtrpt/2000/2450.htm

Olcott, M.B. and Babajanov, B. (2003). The Terrorist Notebooks. *Foreign Policy* (March/April): 30–40.

O'Loughlin, E. (2004, January 27). As deadly as the male. *Sydney Morning Herald.* Retrieved 7/8/04 from www.smh.com.au/articles/2004/01/26/1075087955902.html?from=storyrhs

Palestinian Women Martyrs Against the Israeli Occupation. (2004). Retrieved 6/29/04 from www.91lreview.org/Wget/aztlan.net/women_martyrs.htm

Peterson, V. S. and Runyan, A.S. (1999). The Politics of Resistance: Women as Nonstate, Antistate, and Transstate Actors. In V.S. Peterson and A.S. Runyan (Eds.), *Global Gender Issues* (pp. 163–211). Boulder, CO: Westview Press.

Post, J.M. (1990). Terrorist psycho-logic: Terrorist behavior as a product of psychological forces. In W. Reich (Ed.), *Origins of Terrorism." Psychologies, ideologies, theologies, states of mind* (pp. 25–40). Cambridge: Cambridge University Press.

Rapoport, D.C. (1990). Sacred Terror: A contemporary example from Islam. In W. Reich (Ed.), *Origins of Terrorism: Psychologies, ideologies, theologies, states of mind* (pp. 103–130). Cambridge: Cambridge University Press.

Reuter, C. (2004). *My Life Is A Weapon: A Modern History of Suicide Bombing.* Princeton: Princeton University Press.

Rewards Promised to Suicide Bombers in Heaven. (2002) Retrieved 10/1/03 from www.idf.il/newsite/english/1201-3.stm

Reynolds, J. (2002). Mystery over female 'suicide bomber.' Retrieved 9/29/03 from http://news.bbc.co.uk/l/hi/world/middle_east/1788694.stm

Schweitzer, Y. (2000). *Suicide Terrorism: Development and Characteristics.* Herzliya, Israel: International Policy Institute for Counter-Terrorism.

Shin Bet, IDF nab reluctant female suicide bombers. (2004, June 29). *Ha'aretz.* Retrieved 6/29/04 from www.haaretzdaily.com/hasen/pages/ShArt.jhtml?itemNo=170364

Stern, J. (2003). *Terror in the Name of God: Why Religious Militants Kill.* New York: HarperCollins.

Suicide Bomber. (2003). Retrieved 9/29/03 from www.wordspy.com/words/suicidebomber.asp

Suicide Bombing. (2003). Retrieved 9/29/03 from www.wikipedia.org/w/wiki/phtml?Title=Suicide_bombing

Suicide bombing kills 4 Israelis. (2004, January 14). Retrieved 6/29/04 from www.cbc.ca/storyview/MSN/2004/01/14/israelbomb040114

Talbot, R. (2001). Myths in the Representation of Women Terrorists. *Eire-Ireland.* Retrieved 10/4/03 from www.dushkin.com/powerweb/0072551054/article.mhtml?article=31680

Tannen, D. (1990). *You Just Don't Understand. Women and Men in Conversation.* New York: Ballantine Books.

Tierney, M. (2002, August 2). Young, Gifted, and Ready to Kill. *The Glasgow Herald.* Retrieved 10/4/03 from www.dushkin.com/powerweb/0072551054/article.mhtml?artiele=34716

Toolis, K. (2003, October 12). Why Women Turn To Suicide Bombing. *The Observer.* Retrieved 6/29/04 from www.countercurrents.org/pa-toolis121003.htm

Victor, B. (2003). *Army of Roses: Inside the Worm of Palestinian Women Suicide Bombers.* New York: St. Martin's Press.

Wardhaugh, R. (1986). *An Introduction to Sociolinguistics.* Oxford: Basil Blackwell. Wood, J.T. (1994). *Gendered Lives: Communication, Gender and Culture.* Belmont, CA: Wadsworth Publishing Company.

Zoroya, G. (2002, April 22). Woman described the mentality of a suicide bomber. *USA Today.* Retrieved 6/29/04 from www.usatoday.com/news/world/2002/04/22/cover.htm

---

TERRI TOLES PATKIN is Professor of Communication at Eastern Connecticut State University. Her research interests include the intersection between mass and interpersonal communication, the influence of communication on culture, organizational communication, and persuasion. Please direct all correspondence to patkin@easternct.edu.

The Bomb Under the Abaya

JUDITH MILLER

The suicide vest, stuffed with explosives, nails, ball bearings and various metal fragments, weighed close to 40 pounds. But it felt "like roses on my shoulders," Shefa'a al-Qudsi told me when I interviewed her this spring in an Israeli security prison near Tel Aviv. "I was even more eager to do it after I put the vest on," said the now 31-year-old Palestinian from Tulkarem. "Many would have died. No fence in the world would have stopped me."

Wafa al-Biss, who is now 23, had the opposite reaction when she tried on the explosive pants she had been given for her mission. "I told them the pants were too tight and too heavy," she said, tugging at her headscarf with her scarred fingertips as she recounted her conversation with the men who were sending her to kill and die. "They said: 'Don't worry. We have a bigger size for you!' I looked in the mirror and didn't recognize myself," al-Biss told me, her eyes welling with tears. "And I thought: What am I doing here?"

The two women with their opposite reactions to the prospect of becoming human bombs had been brought together by Israeli counterterrorism officials in Ward 12 of Hasharon Security Prison, an austere facility a half-hour drive north of Tel Aviv. The sprawling, multi-story concrete structure, surrounded by concertina wire and florescent-lit guard towers, is located in the Plain of Sharon where lush citrus groves embrace the prison in a sea of green. Clearly visible from a major highway, tens of thousands of Israeli commuters pass the unmarked facility each day en route to Tel Aviv.

Wafa al-Biss and Shefa'a al-Qudsi live among more than 60 other Palestinian women involved in terrorism—would-be bombers, spotters, supporters of and counselors to future *shaheeds* and *shaheedas,* male and female martyrs, as Palestinians call them. Twelve of some 22 women who have participated since 2002 in such suicide missions survived and are now confined here and in similar prisons, where Israeli intelligence officials have been studying them intensively. Cynics may say that these women prisoners were the beneficiaries of second thoughts, but Israeli officials assert that most of them, including Shefa'a al-Qudsi, were either apprehended before they could reach their targets, or, as in the case of Wafa al-Biss, discovered too late that the devices they were wearing were faulty.

What Israeli officials have more difficulty explaining is why they chose to sacrifice themselves to kill Israelis. Why are so many so eager to do something so profoundly contrary to the human instinct for survival?

Because I found conflicting and only partial answers in the many books that have already been written on suicide attacks, I went to the gates of Hasharon prison to talk to the women themselves. Since Israel has in detention among the largest number of people who have tried and failed to carry out *istishhad,* or religiously blessed self-sacrifice—nearly half of the 380 aspiring suicide bombers since 2002 have failed or were stopped before carrying out their missions—it seemed a natural place to start.

What led Palestinians to this deadly choice? Were the motives similar to those of the seemingly endless reservoir of suicide bombers who have killed so many Iraqis and Americans in Iraq? Are the motives similar to those of suicide bombers in Afghanistan, where U.S. soldiers and Afghan civilians alike now face growing peril? Are New Yorkers and other Americans likely to confront suicide attacks like those that Israelis, Sri Lankans, Turks and others have endured?

The prison holding more than 60 Palestinian women was clean but icy cold on the spring morning that my translator and I arrived. Escorted by male and female prison guards armed with mace and revolvers, we were guided through a labyrinth of wire and steel, along long, narrow corridors separated by several thick steel doors and gates to Wards 11 and 12, where veterans of failed suicide missions and other serious security crimes are held.

Each ward has two tiers of cells, which vary in size, holding one to 10 prisoners. They surround a small open-air courtyard where the women eat in good weather, talk, read, play cards, and exercise. On the day of my visit, several were walking there, arm-in-arm. Others were sweeping the courtyard or wiping the narrow windows of the thick doors of the cells that confine them at night and during the day unless they are eating, praying, exercising, or studying Hebrew or other courses the prison offers. Shefa'a al-Qudsi, unusual among Palestinian women suicide bombers, who tend to be better educated than their male counterparts, earned her high school diploma here.

Most of the women in Ward 12 are members of Hamas, the militant Islamic group that wants to create an Islamic Palestinian state in all of Israel and refuses to recognize the existence of the Jewish state. Almost all wore headscarves.

Why are so many so eager to do something so profoundly contrary to the human instinct for survival?

Soon after we entered the ward, a tall, stern-looking young prisoner—the unit's designated political leader in *hijab* and *jilbab,* a full-length traditional dress—approached my male translator and me. She was all business: Who were we? she asked, her eyes narrowing. What did we want?

We were journalists, I replied—from America, in my case.

"We don't like America because of the war in Iraq and your support for the Zionists and Jews," she declared abruptly and turned away.

The other women watched her carefully. As the ward's spokesperson, she defined what the women could say. This was the party line, and I sensed I would soon hear it again from the women who had agreed to meet me separately.

Ward 11 had four such "leaders"—one from each of the factions represented here, the Palestine Liberation Organization's Fatah, the two leading militant Islamic groups—Hamas and Islamic Jihad—and the leftist, secular Popular Front for the Liberation of Palestine. The women, permitted to wear their own clothes, buy and cook their own food if they can afford it, are also allowed to celebrate holidays and visit with their families—if only through glass partitions and monitored telephones. Also in contrast to American jails where personal items are severely restricted, several of the women had numerous photographs and personal memorabilia in their cells, along with television sets. They watch what they want, the women told me, which in these wards were mostly soap operas and Al Jazeera, the Qatari-owned satellite news station that champions Arab causes and praises suicide bombers in Palestine and Iraq as "martyrs."

I was unprepared for the children. When I entered Ward 12, one of the ward's two infants was being fed by her mother and fussed over by other inmates. Israel, I was told, lets babies remain with their mothers until they are two years old. Some of these women decided to become suicide bombers or support terrorism when, or perhaps because they were pregnant, or like Shefa'a, had an infant at home.

"We try to live our lives," Shefa'a al-Qudsi told me. "But prison is a graveyard for the living."

Shefa'a al-Qudsi had been in prison for five years, since she was 26. Her daughter, Diana, was a year old when the police arrested her at her parents' house hours before she was supposed to carry out her suicide attack at a hotel disco in Netanya, a beach town north of Tel Aviv. Now her daughter, whom she has rarely seen in prison, is six. Eager to be reunited with her, she is scheduled to be released in October.

"Although I've spent the best years of my life in here," she said. "I regret nothing. What I did was not wrong."

Shefa'a al-Qudsi is one of 10 children. She says she had a "good and comfortable life, everything I needed" before deciding to sacrifice herself for Palestine. A younger brother was also arrested en route to his own suicide attack in February 2002, two months before she was picked up. Shefa'a is also rare in having actively sought recruitment and planning her own attack.

"The guys wanted me to do the operation in Hadera," she said, referring to another neighboring seaside Israeli town. "But I had worked for eight years as a hair dresser, often in Israel. I had some Israeli clients and knew Netanya like the back of my hand. There was a hotel there with a dancing hall, a beautiful place by the sea. A lot of Orthodox Jews live nearby; it was usually crowded. Because the Israelis demolished everything beautiful in our lives, I wanted to do the same to them.

"I chose Netanya," she said proudly. "I told the guys: bring me the explosives; I'll do the rest." She also decided to disguise herself as a pregnant woman to avoid suspicion.

Several things led her to act, she told me. First was Israel's occupation. Life had become intolerable since the onset of the second Intifada in September 2000, the Palestinian uprising that followed the collapse of peace talks between Palestinians and Israelis which had limped along since the 1993 Oslo peace accords, a period of great hope turned sour. While young Palestinians threw stones during the first Intifada, between 1987 and 1993, they discovered a more devastating weapon in round two. Suicide bombings soared after September 2000, with the visit of Israeli Prime Minister Ariel Sharon to Jerusalem's Temple Mount, sacred to Jews, and also the site of the Al Aqsa mosque, which Muslims revere. His visit was the flashpoint for the second, so-called "Al Aqsa" intifada. In January, 2002, a young Palestinian woman named Wafa Idris was catapulted into Palestinian celebrity by becoming the forty-seventh Palestinian suicide bomber—but the first woman to kill herself while murdering Israelis. Her picture was everywhere in the West Bank and Gaza—on Palestinian TV, on posters. Poets wrote songs in her honor. Women named daughters after her.

Shefa'a told me that Idris's example had inspired her. "She opened the door for women to do something important in our struggle," she said. "Til Wafa, women had just helped jihad by making food. I thought: We can do more."

Living conditions on the occupied West Bank and Gaza deteriorated as the second Intifada dragged on. "Two of my cousins were killed, my brother was jailed. The army invaded our city and demolished houses. A war raged inside me: Should I, or should I not do something? The Israelis were killing us like rats and nobody was doing anything, not the Arabs, nobody. And I thought: No one will help us. I must make these dogs know how we feel. Even bullets that miss make noise."

Then her youngest brother was arrested. "Mahmoud was only 15 but prepared to be a martyr" she said. He is now serving an 18-year sentence in another security prison. "My family and I were shocked. But I was ashamed to be doing nothing."

Though not politically active, she persuaded them at a local mosque to help her become a suicide bomber.

Through a cousin, she contacted the *shabbab*—"the guys" from the Al Aqsa Martyrs Brigade, sponsored by the late Yasir Arafat's secular Al-Fatah. Though she had not been politically active, she persuaded them at a local mosque to help her become a suicide bomber. They initially hesitated, she recalled, asking about her daughter.

"I told them that my body would be a bridge to a better future that my daughter would walk over," she said. "Yes, I would die, but I would help give her a better life, a future without occupation. I was placing her fate in Allah's hands."

In the days before her attack, she kept her daughter close by as she read the Koran and prayed. While her family suspected something was wrong, since she was not normally religious, they said nothing. The plot was foiled only after an informant disclosed her plans to the Israelis, she complained bitterly. She was arrested the night before she was to receive a coded cell-phone message signaling the start of the operation: "The wedding has begun."

I sensed that al-Qudsi's motives *were* more complex, and as we talked, this seemingly determined young woman's confidence flagged as she recounted her failed marriage and the other disappointments that made martyrdom so attractive. While all of her siblings had finished college, she had dropped out of high school at 16 "to marry the man I loved," her first cousin. But Essam had humiliated her by marrying a Romanian while working in Europe and asking her for a divorce. At 19, she returned to her parents' home, rejected, a single mother with dubious remarriage prospects. Essam eventually asked her to remarry him after his second wife left him and their two children to return to Romania, she said. But she refused, "as a matter of dignity."

Al-Qudsi now claims to be optimistic about the future. Given her sacrifice, she says, "many jobs will be waiting for me." She may work in the part of the Palestinian Authority still run by Yasir Arafat's Fatah, or at the "prisoners club," which has paid her family 1000 shekels a month since her incarceration—about $350 a month, not an insignificant sum in economically hard-pressed Palestine whose average per capita annual income is under $1,000. Her father has opened a new cafe in Tulkarem. With her enhanced social status as a would-be *shaheeda,* she looks forward to working with men now, she said. "I've had more than enough of women in jail," she laughed. But she does not want to remarry, to go "from one prison to another."

She has become "more political" and "closer to God" in prison, she says. She has also perfected her Hebrew. "We need to know the language of our enemy to better confront him, she said, a giggle softening the threat she is still determined to convey.

Would she discourage her daughter Diana from emulating her path towards martyrdom? I asked her. "I will teach her that education is the most important thing in life," she replied. "But our children can be shot coming home from school. The best of our children become martyrs, whether or not they want to be. So if she wanted to do this, I wouldn't try to stop her."

If Shefa'a al-Qudsi was a willing human weapon in her people's asymmetric war against an overwhelmingly powerful enemy, Wafa al-Biss, 23, is her opposite—the quintessential victim.

Now in the second year of a 12-year sentence, she was deeply distraught on the day she agreed to speak to me. She had never really wanted to become a suicide bomber, she told me tearfully. Life and bad luck had given her no choice. Born into wretched poverty in Jabalya refugee camp in Gaza, one of 12 children, she said that much of her body and fingertips had been burned in a freak cooking accident at home the year before her failed mission. She had been coaxed, no, coerced into becoming a martyr by "Abul Khair," an older man from the Al-Aqsa Martyr's Brigade. "I wish I had never met him," she said bitterly.

With her lovely face and soft voice, Wafa al-Biss was not at all what I expected from what I had read about her and seen on videotape. Hours after her arrest on June 6, 2005 at the Erez crossing, the main transit point between Israel and Gaza, Israeli intelligence had hauled her before reporters to discuss her failed mission. Her neck and hands were still covered with scars and bandages from the kitchen gas explosion in her home months earlier.

At the press conference, according to several articles, Wafa al-Biss was a study in defiance—the model would-be martyr. Her greatest wish, her "dream" since childhood, she declared, was martyrdom. "I believe in death," she told reporters. Her target was an Israeli hospital, perhaps even Soroka Hospital in Beersheba, where she had been treated for her burns, which had probably saved her life. "I wanted to kill 20, 50 Jews. Yes!" she exclaimed, "even babies. You kill our babies!"

She might have succeeded had the Shin Bet, Israel's domestic security service, not warned checkpoints to be on the lookout for a female suicide bomber from Gaza. When a soldier noticed something odd in the young woman's gait as she entered the transit hall, she was ordered to stop and remove her long, dark cloak. Stranded between a metal turnstile behind her and an iron gate in front of her, Wafa al-Biss found herself alone in the evacuated hall. As military surveillance cameras recorded her every move, a solider ordered her again to disrobe and drop her bomb.

She had never really wanted to become a suicide bomber. She had been coerced by an older man.

Panicked and frustrated, Wafa al-Biss decided to kill herself anyway. Security camera video shows her reaching into her right pocket to pull the detonator string. But instead of exploding in a lethal mass of fire, smoke, and metal shards, the string came out in her hand. Again and again she thrust her hand into her pocket, pushing the detonator. The cameras dispassionately record her failed mission's final moments—Wafa al-Biss, alone in the hall, screaming and crying, clawing at her face—condemned to live.

"I don't care about Jews and Arabs," she told me in the prison; she had never been political. Israelis at Soroka, where she had spent three months with her burns, treated her with "respect and dignity," she said. "They had been very kind," she said. "But I still wanted to kill myself."

She had tried to do so even before the gas accident, on her birthday in November 2004, that had scarred her body, deformed the fifth digits of both hands, and left her fingertips and chin discolored. Long before that, she told me, she had been in despair. She had grown up desperately poor. Her father was "primitive." He rarely let her go out except to school or the mosque. He and her brothers beat her. She tried to throw herself out a window at age 18, but courage failed her. "Islam says you can't kill yourself. I was afraid of the shame for my family," she said.

"If my family had been normal, if I could have afforded to have been treated in America, if I could wear my hair and live my life like yours," she said, "I would never have thought about killing myself."

Instead, she said, she approached a group known to be associated with the "Resistance." Would they accept her as a martyr?

At first, the man she came to know only as Abul Khair, whom she met secretly at Al Shifa Hospital in Gaza, urged her to think it over. Despite the reverence that fellow Gazans showed martyrs and their families, she hesitated. She called him a week later to say she had changed her mind.

"But they hunted me like prey," she recalled. "Abul Khair kept calling," she said. "He told me a guy they were counting on had backed out of an operation; they needed me. 'Look at your future,' they told me. 'No one will ever marry you.' I knew it was true. I was not good at school. I had no future."

She agreed to meet him again, this time at the Haifa mosque. Would God grant her anything she wanted in paradise? she asked him. "Would he give me new skin?"

Yes, he told her.

"What did death feel like?" she pressed him.

She wouldn't feel anything, she quoted him as saying. "It's like a pin prick."

"I wanted to believe him," she told me. "He looked religious, like someone you could trust. He told me I was very brave. He made me feel important." She agreed to become a shaheeda.

> **" 'Look at your future,' they told me. 'No one will ever marry you.' I knew it was true. I had no future."**

When she returned home, upset and crying, her mother sensed something was wrong. "I lied and told her that my finger hurt. Her mother made her some food and told her it would be better soon, "*inshallah*," Wafa said. If her mother sensed what Wafa was about to do, she didn't let on, she insisted.

As the day of her operation approached, Wafa grew despondent. She had gone to a safe house in Gaza twice with young men who picked her up in a car on a corner near her home. Being in the company of men who were not family members was religiously and culturally forbidden in conservative Palestine. She initially feaired they would "harm my dignity as a woman," she told me. Instead, they escorted her to a nondescript house on the edge of her city where she was asked to try on the explosive pants, test the detonator—a gift to the Al-Aqsa group from its ostensible rival, Hamas—and videotape a political statement about the need to kill Jews. "I didn't feel that way; I told them I wanted to say something else," she said.

Ultimately, however, she complied. She was taped reading the statement and holding a Kalashnikov—for the first time ever, she says. "It was heavy."

The day before her operation, she kept to herself, cried, prayed, and tried cheering herself up by serenading her two pet canaries with a song she sang for me that morning in prison—a popular prisoner anthem in many Arab countries. "I am running away from my cage, said the bird," as Wafa began humming.

"And the bird said: Hide me with you . . . as a tear came out to his eye.

And he said his wings are broken,

And he can no longer fly."

The morning before her attack, she woke up in terror. She called Abul Khair to tell him she had changed her mind. "But they threatened me," she said. "They said they would bring the belt to my house and explode it on me." She relented and accompanied them to the safe house, she said, where she spent the night before the attack.

The day of her attack, June 21 , 2005, "was the hardest day of my life." She had failed at this as she had "so many other opportunities in my life."

She expected little now, she told me. No one was helping her; no group was paying or supporting her parents, she said. One day, she hoped to marry, but her pained expression suggested she knew this was unlikely. Perhaps she would be able to have her burns treated, she said. She would replace the birds, which had died since she went to jail.

While Shefa'a al-Qudsi's story of her failed suicide bombing was consistent over time with what she had told her Israeli interrogators soon after her arrest, Wafa's account was not. Who was the real Wafa al-Biss: the proud patriotic bomber who boasted of her desire to slaughter Jews, even babies, at the hospital that had saved her life? Or the tearful victim of a sophisticated martyrdom recruiting organization who had failed to kill herself, if not others, only because of a defective detonator? Which al-Biss was I to believe?

Smadar Perry, a journalist for the Israeli newspaper Yediot Ahranot who has interviewed over a dozen would-be male and female martyrs in her many trips to Israeli prisons and detention centers, told me that what these prisoners say soon after their arrest is usually more reliable than what they are encouraged to say later on by fellow inmates and political mentors in jail.

What Wafa al-Biss omitted from her saga, however, shows how hard it is to understand the motives of suicide bombers and how complex those motives can be. She still had enough pride or shame to conceal from me facts that would have highlighted her despair. For unlike al-Qudsi, she was not motivated by the nationalist and religious reasons she claimed soon after her arrest. And it was not her long-standing "dream" to become a martyr. Nor did she act primarily because of Israel's occupation, though the Al-Aqsa Martyr's Brigades, which had given her the bomb, driven her to the crossing, and shown her how to blow herself up, would have us beUeve that. Rather, she acted in large part because those she had loved and trusted the most had abandoned her.

She did not tell me, for instance, as NBC News reported a few days after her arrest and press conference, that she had been engaged to be married, or that her fiance had broken off their engagement after her disfiguring accident. Nor did she say that, according to a Palestinian friend whose son Wafa had befriended at Soroka Hospital, she had resisted leaving after her three-month stay. Wafa's friend recalled how she had to be removed on a stretcher, crying and pleading not to be returned home.

In Gaza, she grew ever more despondent. While Israeli doctors at Soroka had strongly recommended counseling, her brothers had objected: neighbors might think she was crazy, bringing further shame upon the family.

Finally, although Wafa had told me her parents knew nothing of her plans, this, too, conflicted with what she told Israeli interrogators. Security sources told me that soon after her arrest she told them that although her parents had initially disapproved of her mission, they ultimately encouraged her. The video she told me had been made in the Al-Aqsa safe house, for instance, was actually taped on the second floor of her own home, with her parents' approval. Her own mother had helped her dress the morning of her attack. When the zipper of the explosive-laden pants tore as she was putting them on, her mother sewed it back up.

Wafa Al-Biss, the ultimate victim, is the exception among suicide terrorists, says Yoram Schweitzer, an Israeli terrorism expert. "I reject the notion that all female suicide bombers are 'damaged goods,'" he told me over coffee at the Tel Aviv University's Jaffee Center for Strategic Studies. Only a tiny minority, he said, is really coerced into committing suicide. "Most are true volunteers. Men and women alike clamor, to do this. I also reject the argument that women are more easily manipulated than men."

If anything, female suicide bombers, statistics show, tend to be better educated than their male counterparts. Between 30 percent and 40 percent of them have attended university. "They are the smarter of these smart weapons," says Anat Berko, an Israeli criminologist whose interviewed suicide bombers and those who sent them for her new book, *The Path to Paradise* (Praeger, 2007).

Now that suicide bombing has spread to some 32 groups in 28 countries, says Ami Pedahzur, an Israeli expert at the University of Texas, most counterterrorism experts have discarded the earlier "profiles" they assembled of the "average" suicide bomber. In the first wave of modern suicide bombing, which started against American and other western targets in Lebanon in the early 1980's, suicide bombers tended to be mostly young, male, and single. That is no longer the case.

The face of modern terrorism, and of suicide bombing in particular, is increasingly female. Though still a minority among suicide bombers in Israel and Iraq, the growing number of women willing to volunteer for such missions is especially evident in non-Palestinian and non-Islamic secular movements. Christoph Reuter, the German author of *My Life Is a Weapon: A Modern History of Suicide Bombing* (Princeton University Press, 2004), notes that one-third of the estimated 10,000 Tamil Tiger cadres in Sri Lanka have been female. Among suicide commandos, female participation is close to 60 percent.

The same is true for the PKK, the Kurdistan Workers' Party, the largely secular Muslim militants who have been battling Turkey since the 1970s for Kurdish rights and autonomy. Eleven out of some 15 suicide bombings staged by the PKK since 1996 were conducted by women, as were three out of six foiled attacks. In Chechnya, women have conducted 43 percent of the attacks since suicide missions began there in 2000.

Even in Israel, where the total number of such attacks declined sharply in 2006, Reuven Ehrlich, who directs the Intelligence and Terrorist Information Center in Tel Aviv, reports in a recent study that a woman conducted one of the four suicide attacks.

Between 1985 and 2006, Schweitzer says, 220 women suicide bombers have accounted for 15 percent of the total number of successful or attempted attacks throughout the world. In 2006, alone, women were enlisted for suicide raids from Belgium, India, Iraq, Turkey, and the West Bank territories, he writes in *Female Suicide Bombers: Dying for Equality* (Jaffee Center for Strategic Studies, August 2006). Indeed, the phenomenon appears to be "contagious," especially among women, concludes Mia Bloom, an American expert.

Even in death, inequality endures: A family is usually paid far less for a woman's suicide than for a man's.

Bloom and Schweitzer caution that the increase in women suicide bombers reflects neither a progressive attitude towards women nor gender equality in the religious, revolutionary, and national liberation movements that promote such terror. Women continue to play a distinctly marginal role in most of these groups. Even in death, inequality endures: A Palestinian family, for instance, is usually paid far less for a woman's suicide death than for a man's. And despite efforts to honize their sacrifice and portray them as heroines, Schweitzer concludes, women serve mainly as "pawns and sacrificial lambs."

This perverse "feminization" of suicide attacks also undercuts the theory that women are more likely to choose peaceful mechanisms for conflict resolution than men. In her influential book, *Dying to Kill* (Columbia University Press, 2005). Bloom dismisses the notion that women are somehow inherently more inclined towards moderation. "But while male suicide bombers seem to be motivated by religious or nationalist fanaticism," she argues, female operatives, in Palestine and elsewhere, "appear more often motivated by very personal reasons." This was certainly the case for Shefa'a al-Qudsi, and even more dramatically for Wafa al-Biss, who seemed to have been driven by a "cocktail" of motives—personal distress and shame, a quest for revenge and enhanced social status for themselves and their families, nationalism, hatred of occupation, religious ideology, and political culture. Louise Richardson, a lecturer at Harvard, sums it up in what she calls the three "R'S"—"exacting revenge, attaining renown, and eliciting a reaction."

Although both al-Qudsi and al-Biss sprinkled their speech with references to Islam and what it permitted or banned, neither said she was particularly devout; nor did the allure of Islamic paradise seem to hold much appeal. Both appeared focused on how their families and friends would react to their deed rather than on the prospect of eternal pleasures, such as the proverbial 72 black-eyed virgins who are said to await their male counterparts if they succeed. Al-Biss scoffed at the very notion of paradise. "I knew I was not going to heaven," she told me, "and that all the other martyrs were not going there either."

Al-Qudsi's vision of her eternal reward was consistent with the empowerment she felt as the mistress of her own failed martyrdom mission. In paradise, she said, she would not only become the wife of a martyr, she would be able to choose which martyr she married.

> **In paradise, she said, she would not only become the wife of a martyr, she would choose which martyr she married.**

The prospect of choice is especially seductive in a culture that offers women so few of them. In such rigid, unforgiving societies in which a single transgression, real or even rumored, particularly by a woman, can result in the loss of family honor, a chance to marry, and occasionally even death at the hands of outraged relatives, choosing to redeem one-self through a suicide mission does not seem so terrible, or irrational an alternative.

What also seems clear—based on my interviews with the two would-be bombers and a survey of the scholarly literature—is that no matter how desperate they may be, such vulnerable, disposable young women and men do not act in a vacuum. It takes a sophisticated organization to launch such missions and political, social, and religious approbation to sanction them. Someone must recruit, train, arm, finance, and dispatch a volunteer *jihadi*. Bombs and explosive vests must be made, safe houses established, reliable drivers and escorts found, media teams ordered to write and videotape the bomber's final statements. Friends and family, schools and mosques where they meet, must be complicit. It takes what journalist Anne Marie Oliver calls a "martyrdom machine" to produce people willing to sacrifice their lives in the numbers we have seen in Palestine and Iraq today. And it takes an entire society, not merely a cult, to promote the culture of death that has taken root in Palestine. Encouraged by the ostensibly secular Palestine Authority and the allegedly religious-inspired Hamas alike, soccer tournaments are named after "martyrs." Parents dress their babies up as suicide bombers and photograph them in fancy studios. Posters bearing the martyrs' faces are plastered on walls of stores and schools in every town and village. Saudi diplomats write poems in their honor while children exchange "martyr cards."

While scholars dispute what causes suicide attacks and how best to prevent them, they agree that the tactic itself—what Diego Gambetta of Oxford's Nuffield College calls the "defining act of political violence of our age"—has spread so far and so fast, among secular and religious groups alike, because it is effective. The 9/11 attacks led many Americans to equate suicide bombing with Islamic militants, but secular groups have used the tactic with equal tenacity.

Though still rare in the universe of armed conflicts, says Robert A. Pape of the University of Chicago, suicide bombing has been 12 times deadlier than any other form of terrorism. While such attacks constituted 3 percent of terrorist acts between 1980 to 2003, they caused 48 percent of terrorism deaths, excluding September 11.

While the average shooting attack between 1980 and June 2005 killed 3.32 people and remote control bombs killed an average of 6.92 people per attack, suicide bombers wearing explosive belts claimed an average of 81.48 victims. If the bomber was driving an explosive-laden car, as are so many in Iraq, says Ami Pedahzur, the average soared to 97.81 victims.

The upward trend that began in 1999 has continued to grow exponentially in some places. Between 1981 and the end of 2003, there were 535 successful suicide missions. But in just two years—from January 2004 to December 2005—there were no less than 555 successful attacks, 84 percent of which took place in Iraq.

The experts, divided over what causes this pernicious form of terrorism, are even more at odds over how to prevent it. Pape argues that because suicide attacks are not a religious phenomenon but mainly "a response to foreign occupation," the most obvious solution is withdrawal from disputed territory. Suicide attacks in Lebanon virtually ended after Israel withdrew in 2000, he notes, and they also declined dramatically after Israel's unilateral withdrawal two years ago from Gaza two years ago. But the best evidence of his thesis, he claims, is Iraq. The country that had no suicide attacks before the U.S. invasion had 20 in 2003. And since American forces have been stationed there, Iraq's rate of suicide bombings has doubled each year. The only way to stop them, he argues, is to withdraw American forces there.

Though his analysis seems statistically compelling, few scholars agree with him. Assaf Moghadam, a German-Iranian scholar at Harvard's Olin Institute in Cambridge, and Mohammed Hafez, at the University of Missouri, argue that territorial struggle does not explain movements like al Qaeda or their increasing tendency to cross geographic boundaries and conduct missions along sectarian lines as in Iraq. These now "globalized" suicide attacks are truly transnational in nature and aspiration.

Nor would unilateral withdrawal from the West Bank—which few consider a politically viable option for Israel—be likely to satisfy Hamas or Islamic Jihad, since they claim all Israeli territory as their own. Yes, says Bruce Hoffman, a leading terrorism expert at Georgetown University, suicide missions dropped both in Lebanon and Gaza after Israel unilaterally withdrew. But in the absence of Israeli forces, Hezbollah in Lebanon and Hamas in Gaza imported, produced and used vast arsenals of rockets and missiles against Israel, built defensive tunnels and infrastructure to better counter Israeli strikes, and intensified the training of fighters and jihadis for future confrontations. "Militant Islamists switched tactics after Israel's withdrawal," Hoffman said. "It sent rockets rather than people to kill. It did not stop fighting."

Israeli security officials have, in fact, dramatically reduced the number of suicide attacks and casualties since their peak in 2002 by resorting to other controversial measures. Ehrlich notes that while 22 civilians were killed in 2005 (and 55 in 2004), 15 people were killed in such attacks and 104 wounded in 2006.

Israel's extension of its security fence—the much loathed "Wall" to Palestinians—has reduced suicide attacks.

Many Israeli and American terrorism experts assert that Israel's extension of its security fence and buffer zone—the much loathed "Wall" to Palestinians—to cover roughly half of the border between Israeli and Palestinian territory has not only reduced suicide attacks—at least temporarily—but all violent and property crime, an assertion heatedly challenged by Palestinians. Second, Israel has significantly increased the number of Palestinians it detains on suspicion of terrorist activities: whereas 4,532 Palestinians were arrested in 2005, 6,968 suspects were detained last year.

"It's the intel, stupid," says Hoffman. Israel has managed to reduce the rate of attacks by penetrating Palestinian bombing networks and stopping them before they occur. Withdrawing from territory absent a political solution, he fears, may make it harder for Israel to collect such vital information.

But scholars like Mia Bloom worry about the longer-term impact of such policies. Yes, harsh Israeli counterterror measures such as the use of targeted assassination, increasing detentions, and building a wall appear to have stemmed suicide terror in the short run. Yet over time, she argues, such heavy-handed tactics will only further humiliate and enrage Palestinians, providing ever more recruits for martyrdom missions. If the ultimate challenge is to make the Shefa'a al-Qudsi's and Wafa al-Biss's of Palestine forgo suicide terror and make their sacrifice unacceptable to Palestinian society, only a political compromise satisfactory to the key parties is likely to succeed. Between the Oslo peace accords of 1993 until the autumn of 2000, Palestinian support for suicide terror never exceeded one-third of the population, she notes. Today, that figure is well over 80 percent.

What lies ahead for the United States abroad and at home is even harder to project, and not surprisingly, equally divisive among scholars. Israeli-style "walls" in Iraq and Afghanistan will not keep out militants opposed to America's presence or policies there or contain Iraq's deadly sectarian violence that so far shows little sign of abating. A political compromise acceptable to the major factions, or neighbors who feed various insurgents, has so far proven elusive. At home, Americans have yet to adopt a psychology of what one Israeli security official called "hardening your hearts as well as our targets" when terrorists strike. Israeli security takes pride in restoring "normal" life in Israel within hours after a suicide attack. Many Americans, by contrast, remain traumatized by the September 11 attacks.

On the other hand, many Israeli, Arab, and American scholars and security officials doubt that America is likely to endure domestically the waves of suicide terror that Israeli has weathered. Gil Kleiman, a former superintendent of the Israeli National Police who was partly raised in the U.S., says, "you need to control geographic and political territory to use the suicide weapon effectively. That space does not exist in America." Yes, non-Islamic fanatics, such as Timothy McVeigh, the right-wing militiaman whose 1995 Oklahoma bombing attack killed more Americans domestically than any other single terrorist strike prior to 9/11, have an infrastructure and friendly territory in which to work, build, and proselytize, Hoffman acknowledges. And McVeigh, in fact, contemplated a suicide strike against his target until he discovered how vulnerable it was.

Immunity to jihadist ideology, to the culture of death gripping Palestine and Iraq, is still our nation's most enviable defense.

Yet Hoffman argues that for all their faults, the counterterrorism measures adopted since 9/11 make it harder to conduct such an attack today than it was before. Al Qaeda still appears to lack an infrastructure in this country. Nor does the United States have the vast unassimilated foreign Muslim populations that have been radicalized in Europe and may be capable of launching sustained attacks.

Brian M. Jenkins of the Rand Corporation, notes that with a population of 350 million, Europe is home to between 30 and 50 million Muslims. By 2050, one-third of all children born there will Muslim. The U.S., by contrast, with 300 million people, has about 4.7 million Muslims, many of them native Americans. And of the 3.5 million Arab-Americans, fewer than 25 percent are Muslim. "Can we see individuals or a small cluster who self radicalize and carry out even a devastating attack in this country? Yes, clearly," he told me. "The small conspiracy likely to lead to one-off attacks is always possible, maybe even likely. But I see nothing so far that would support a campaign such as what we have seen in the occupied territories or Iraq."

Of course, even a "one-off" attack in the United States involving a weapon of mass destruction, which al Qaeda and like-minded militants have repeatedly sought to acquire and would not hesitate to use, would be psychologically devastating to Americans. And as I left Hasharon prison, it was hard not to be shaken by my meetings with al-Qudsi and al-Biss—by their despair-driven determination, their plight, and finally, the enormity of what they had tried to do. The fact that neither was a religious extremist nor obviously deranged suggested that the reservoir of potential suicide bombers might be larger than many Americans appreciate. But while complacency about such terrorism was a luxury Americans could ill-afford, a panicky overreaction might jeopardize the very immunity to jihadist ideology, to the culture of death gripping Palestine and Iraq, that is still our nation's best, most enviable defense.

JUDITH MILLER is a journalist who writes about national security issues. She is the author of *God Has Ninety-Nine Names: Reporting From a Militant Middle East* (Simon and Schuster, 1996), among other books.

From *Policy Review*, June/July 2007, pp. 43–58. Copyright © 2007 by Judith Miller. Reprinted by permission of The Hoover Institution, Stanford University and Judith Miller. www.policyreview.org

Picked Last: Women and Terrorism

ALISA STACK-O'CONNOR

Scholars date the genesis of modern terrorism to the People's Will in Russia in the late 1800s.[1] If terrorism's Garden of Eden was indeed Russia, then Vera Zasulich was Eve. On January 24, 1878, Zasulich shot the Governor General of St. Petersburg. She was arrested and tried for attempted murder. Although this was not her first arrest—she had been in prison, banished, and under police supervision since 1869 for her political activities—two prosecutors refused to try her for the shooting.[2] She was ultimately acquitted and left Russia, but remained involved in the revolutionary movement, writing for two Marxist publications.

Although times have changed since Zasulich was active, in examining how and why terrorist groups employ women, many things remain the same. For example, in pre-revolutionary Russia, women were less likely to be arrested, and when they were, they were not taken seriously[3] or were forgiven, as was Zasulich. While her colleagues admired her act of violence, they had less respect for her intellect, reflecting a typical assumption that women act out of emotion rather than a rational political program.[4]

Women's roles in Russian revolutionary groups increased when the number of men available for political activism was reduced by the Russo-Japanese War and security measures.[5] These women had the reputation of personal, rather than ideological, dedication to the cause, leading to the belief that they were more willing to die than their male comrades.

These observations reflect a profound ambivalence about women and political violence. This article examines Chechen, Palestinian, and Tamil terrorist groups to discover how and why such groups employ women. Three themes about women's entry into and roles in these groups emerge:

- Terrorist attacks by women have unique propaganda value.
- Women have to fight for their right to fight.
- Groups overcome cultural resistance to women's involvement when tactics require it or they face a shortage of males.

There is little written about female terrorists. Most works on female violence look at women as victims, not perpetrators. Recent high-profile attacks involving female perpetrators—such as the 2004 Beslan hostage-taking and the April 2006 attack on Lieutenant General Sarath Fonseka, head of the Sri Lankan army—have sparked some academic and policy interest in the subject. The few works on female terrorism tend to focus on women's motivations for violence. This article, however, examines the groups' motivations for employing women.

Additionally, it offers proposals for policymakers to consider in combating terrorism.

Most works on female violence look at women as victims, not perpetrators.

Female Terrorism as Propaganda

Terrorism has been called "propaganda of the deed."[6] When women do the deed, the story often becomes more about women than terrorism. This dynamic is particularly evident in the Russian-Chechen conflict. Until the hostage-taking at the Dubrovka theater in Moscow in October 2002, Chechen women were viewed primarily as victims of the Russian-Chechen wars. In the theater seizure, they emerged in the Russian and Western press as vicious, sympathetic, strong, fanatical, foolish, and weak, often in the same portrayal.

Two images come to the fore in media reporting on Chechen female terrorists. First, there is the "black widow," a suicide bomber who is driven to terrorism after the deaths of the men in her life. Second, there is the "zombie," who is forced or tricked into terrorism by Chechen men. Although the Chechen groups did not coin the terms *black widow* and *zombie* to describe their female members, their leaders, such as the recently killed Shamil Basayev, have played up the black widow image, emphasizing victimization. The zombie image is generally used by the Russian government and media to discredit the Chechen insurgent and terrorist groups.

The zombies tend to receive more sensational press coverage. The best example of a zombie is Zarema Muzhikhoeva. On July 9, 2003, Muzhikhoeva failed to set off her bomb at a Moscow cafe. She was arrested and has been in custody ever since. The Russian Federal Security Service released some of its interviews with her and also allowed a televised interview.[7] Some of Muzhikhoeva's statements contradict each other. However, her basic life story stays fairly constant: she was married in her teens and had a child. Her husband died fighting the Russians, and she and her child then became the responsibility of her husband's family. Desperate either to escape servitude to her in-laws or avoid marrying her brother-in-law, Muzhikhoeva ran away, leaving her child. When she could not find work, she borrowed money. When she could not repay her debt, she felt driven to become a suicide bomber. According to Muzhikhoeva's account, she went to a terrorist camp in the mountains of Chechnya in March 2003, where Arabs provided instruction on fighting and Islam. She reported being beaten for dressing inappropriately and having sex with the camp leader. She also reported that other women in the camp were raped, beaten, and drugged. After a month of training, she was sent to Moscow to conduct an attack. Zombie stories such as Muzhikhoeva's are attention-grabbing, benefiting Chechen objectives, and explain away women's violence, benefiting the Russian government.

Although the zombie depiction is less flattering to individual women than the black widow stereotype, both have similar effects on the public inside and outside of Russia. The Chechens gained much attention and some sympathy from terrorist attacks by women.[8] In a July 2003 survey, the Public Opinion Foundation of the All-Russia Center for the Study of Public Opinion found that 84 percent of Russians surveyed believed female suicide bombers were controlled by someone else (zombies); only 3 percent believed the women acted independently.[9] Similarly, Western authors have blamed Russian actions for forcing women into terrorism.[10] In contrast, there is little writing about the desperation of men who have lost wives, mothers, and sisters to excuse or explain the Chechen call to arms. Women terrorists serve a uniquely feminine role in propaganda by playing the victims even when they are the perpetrators.

Female Palestinian suicide bombers have been depicted in much the same way as the zombies and black widows. As in the Russian case, the Israeli government has not hesitated to use women's personal stories to discredit them and the movements they worked for. Palestinian groups, unlike their Chechen counterparts, have been more active in using women's stories for the group's benefit. Ayat Akhras, for example, an 18-year-old female, blew herself up outside a Jerusalem supermarket on March 3, 2002, in an attack claimed by Al Aqsa Martyr's Brigade. Her attack illustrates the propaganda value of female terrorists in shaming Arab men into action. In her martyr video, she states, "I am going to fight instead of the sleeping Arab armies who are watching Palestinian girls fighting alone; it is an *intefadeh* until victory."[11]

In both the Palestinian and Chechen cases, the propaganda effect of women's attacks does not appear to be a factor in group planning; rather, it is an externality provided by the media. The Liberation Tigers of Tamil Eelam (LTTE or Tamil Tigers), on the other hand, have been highly successful in employing women in propaganda. The LTTE allows active female fighters to meet with the press, publishes books about its female guerrillas (the Freedom Birds), makes films about them, and holds public events to commemorate them. It is also careful to separate the group's guerrilla and terrorist activities. Unlike the Chechen and Palestinian groups, the LTTE does not acknowledge suicide attacks. Instead, it promotes the Freedom Birds, showing them as equal to male fighters and liberated from cultural oppression through fighting for the organization.

In all three cases, the media coverage of terrorist events differs based on whether a male or female conducts the act. Media coverage of a female terrorist tends to focus on the woman's nonpolitical motivations (for example, death of a male family member), her vulnerability to recruitment because of her personal life (for example, promiscuity), and her basically peaceful and nurturing character. The coverage of male terrorists, on the other hand, generally focuses on the act committed. As terrorists need media attention to spread their message, the unique portrayals of females are one of the important factors in women's employment in terrorist attacks.

With the exception of the LTTE, it seems male terrorists and insurgent leaders are unaware of the propaganda benefits of female attacks; however, whether they plan for it or not, the media create it for free. Because terrorist leaders may not recognize the propaganda value, it cannot by itself explain why terrorists would want to use women. For most groups, the sympathy or increased attention is an externality realized only after women are involved in the group and its violence.

Fighting to Fight

Like women entering legitimate militaries and the labor force in general, females have to demonstrate great determination in gaining access to terrorist groups. In the Palestinian, Chechen, and Tamil cases, they have asked for active roles in political violence before groups invite them to take part. This trend is most evident in the Palestinian case, particularly in Leila Khaled's story. Denied a fighter's role in the Arab Nationalist Movement and then Fatah, Khaled kept searching for a group that would allow her to fight until the Popular Front for the Liberation for Palestine (PFLP) put her into guerrilla training. She hijacked aircraft in 1969 and 1970 for the PFLP, eventually becoming active in the group's leadership. She garnered international media attention after her foiled 1970 hijacking landed her in jail in the United Kingdom. Like the attention to Chechen women more than 30 years later, the media focused on Khaled's beauty and youth, not her politics.

> **The propaganda effect of women's attacks does not appear to be a factor in group planning; rather, it is an externality provided by the media.**

Her fame and involvement in the political leadership and tactical operations of the PFLP are not typical of women participating in Palestinian militancy. Most were involved in support roles and on the fringe of groups. In addition to a male cultural aversion to bringing women into militant groups, social demands such as raising children have made participation difficult. Great individual effort has been required to overcome cultural barriers. The PFLP recognized Khaled's popular appeal and promoted her and her story to gain attention, legitimacy, and support, but it was her initiative that brought her to the organization.

In the years since Khaled's hijackings, women's involvement in Palestinian terrorism has been either inconsistent or invisible. Even after proving their success as hijackers, bombers, and cover for men, women have to remind terrorist leaders of their tactical usefulness. It has been especially difficult for them to find active fighting roles in Hamas and Palestinian Islamic Jihad (PIJ). Potential female suicide bombers have been turned down by Hamas but have kept searching until secular organizations accepted them. Despite the tactical and propaganda benefits demonstrated by secular female suicide bombers in 2002, Hamas and PIJ struggled to reconcile conservative beliefs with evolving terrorist tactics. By 2003, however, PIJ believed the operational gains outweighed the social costs and began actively recruiting women for suicide bombings.[12] Leader Ramadan Abdallah Shallah explained the ideological and organizational adjustments the group had to make to accommodate female suicide bombers:

> The Shari'ah or religious judgment also deems that if there are sufficient numbers of men to carry out jihad, it is not preferable for women to carry out the jihad. The reason is to keep the woman away from any kind of harm.... Every operation is scrutinized and if the female ... might be taken prisoner or face harm ... it would not be preferable for the woman to carry out the operation. But if the Mujahidin estimate that the operation would not be fit for or carried out except by a woman because of the circumstances of disguise and reaching the target necessitate it, then we would not object.[13]

Similarly, Sheikh Ahmed Ismail Yassin, founder of Hamas, stated that his organization did not need women in its jihad because "The woman is the second defense line in the resistance of the occupation."[14] Religiously based terrorists are often thought to be irrational and fanatical in their devotion to violence. Both Shallah's and Yassin's statements, however, show rational and practical approaches. Men are preferred if available. But if only a woman can get to a target, then a woman should be used.

Tamil women faced similar barriers in the LTTE. While the group credits its leader, Vellupillai Prabhakaran, for including females, both supporters and detractors acknowledge that women were asking to fight, and were fighting for other Tamil groups, before the LTTE began training them for combat in 1984. The Freedom Birds were organized as a result of group needs and women's initiative. Once in the organization, Freedom Birds say they must prove themselves continually. In most cases, there must be a practical reason for terrorist groups to decide to use women in political violence. Female demands for operational roles are insufficient to overcome cultural practices, even among groups such as the PFLP and LTTE that claim women's liberation as part of their cause.

If only a woman can get to a target, then a woman should be used.

Overcoming Cultural Resistance

One reason women must fight for involvement in politics and violence is that, in many societies, women's roles are limited to wife and mother. The LTTE is an example of this reality. It took the group 12 years to admit women into fighting roles, and it had difficulty determining how to incorporate them. The group is one of the few terrorist/insurgent bodies in the world with explicit rules on cadres' romantic lives and when they can marry. It also experimented with how to train women and employ them in combat. The difficulty of deciding whether the Freedom Birds should cut their hair to help them fight is emblematic of the tension the group faces between the necessity of having women directly involved in political violence and preservation of the Tamil culture. At each turn, the LTTE had to weigh how using females in combat and terrorism would affect the group's discipline, ability to fight, and popular support. Its decisions were a result of trial and error.

Necessity appears to help terrorist leaders overcome biases about women. A shortage of male volunteers may have encouraged Palestinian, Chechen, and Tamil groups to involve women in attacks. Given the difficulty of obtaining reliable population statistics for the areas in conflict, it is hard to prove that one of the elements in an organization's decision is a shortage of men. However, in these cases, the number of men available for terrorist operations has been reduced by outward labor migration, a lack of male volunteers, and arrests, harassment, and investigations of men.

Women, on the other hand, can be left in conflict zones and can move between cities without generating suspicion from security services. For example, in the 1980s, the Sri Lankan government targeted Tamil males between the ages of 14 and 40 for interrogation and detention.[15] In 1986, when women began fighting in the Freedom Birds, the government detained about 3,000 Tamil men.[16] Additionally, males were targets for recruitment, interrogation, and detention by competing Tamil groups. Consequently, many males fled the country.[17]

Decisions not to employ women in attacks are shaped by culture, but cultural prohibitions can be overcome by practical requirements.

Target assessment may also have helped terrorist leaders overcome cultural biases. For instance, on January 14, 2004, Reem al-Reyashi detonated a suicide bomb at a border crossing in Jerusalem. After the attack, Sheikh Yassin stated that Hamas decided to use a female attacker due to the increasing operational difficulties of getting men to their targets.[18] Even in traditional societies, women's household duties place them in markets and other public places, allowing them to blend with daily life. They have more flexibility in their dress than men. These factors make them less noticeable and less threatening to security services.

In the Palestinian, Chechen, and Tamil cases, terrorist groups did not begin their activities with women in operational roles. Women became involved only when men were unavailable, in part because of states' security measures. The interaction and learning that occur between terrorist groups and states are important to understanding terrorist actions, particularly why groups would want women.

State Responses

Decisions not to employ women in attacks are shaped by culture, but cultural prohibitions can be overcome by practical requirements. The leaders of Hamas, PIJ, and the LTTE have been explicit in explaining that women are employed when the target necessitates it. As noted above, men tend to be the preferred option for these groups, and women are usually employed when there are not sufficient men for operations or males cannot reach the targets. These factors—manpower and access to targets—are influenced by state actions.

With all three groups, it is impossible with present data to show direct cause and effect between specific state actions and terrorists' decisions to use women. For example, in the 3 months prior to Wafa Idris' January 2002 suicide bombing in Jerusalem, there were at least 13 major terrorist attacks, including suicide bombings inside Israel by male Hamas, PIJ, and Fatah members. There was no change in Israeli security practices that prevented male terrorists from reaching targets and thus forcing Al Aqsa to employ women. Yet it is likely that state actions and policies to combat terrorism had an influence on groups' decisions to change their practices. Indeed, Hamas and PIJ are explicit about picking the right person based on assessment of targets.

Security services' expectations, and occasionally official "profiles" of terrorists, made it easy for governments to focus on men, which may have encouraged groups to employ women. Early in each conflict, states expected terrorists to be young and male. Women were not part of the profile despite evidence of their involvement in all three conflicts. *Mirror imaging* (assuming the adversary's behavior is the same as one's own) may be partly to blame for states' ignoring the possibility of female terrorists. When the terror campaigns began, these governments did not regularly include significant numbers of women in operational roles in the military, police, intelligence, and other government jobs. They may have assumed that terrorists would act similarly.

States also viewed the cultures from which their adversaries came as so repressive toward women that terrorists would not allow their involvement. The infrequency of female attacks and the invisibility of women in groups could have reinforced these assumptions.

At some point in each conflict, however, states' expectations and assumptions changed. In the Russian-Chechen conflict, Chechen men between the ages of 16 and 60 have been the targets of detention and interrogation. As in Sri Lanka, Russian forces took control of villages to "cleanse" them by removing the young men for interrogations, from which many did not return. Unlike Sri Lanka and Israel, Russia has taken steps aimed specifically at female terrorists, most notably expanding cleansing operations to include them. According to one estimate, about 100 women have disappeared in Chechnya since the 2002 Dubrovka hostage-taking.[19] In 2003, the Ministry of Internal Affairs issued a directive to search women in headscarves and other traditional Muslim clothing.[20]

Moscow has not been insensitive to the possibility that targeting women may produce more terrorists of both genders, and its response has taken into account the unique propaganda value of women. In statements explaining why females are targeted, Russian officials emphasize that Chechen groups prey on women in mourning to make them "zombies." With this argument, detentions are meant to protect both Chechen women from becoming zombies and Russian society from the zombies. Federal Security Service officials also claimed that use of women in attacks indicated that the terrorist groups were defeated.[21]

Chechen terrorists' use of women may represent some success by Russian security services in decreasing the number of men available to the groups and their ability to reach targets. Furthermore, the government, through its influence over the media, has been able to take advantage of the unique propaganda tools that female terrorists offer in its strategy to defeat Chechen terrorism.

Israel has also taken advantage of women's particular propaganda value for counterterrorism. The Foreign Ministry has published reports on female suicide bombers, emphasizing the terrorists groups' desire to exploit vulnerable women. The government has published descriptions of both successful and unsuccessful suicide bombers to illustrate the women's personal problems and how male terrorists took advantage of them. Perhaps most important for this study, Israel stopped profiling individuals and started profiling circumstances—that is, looking for anomalies in behavior or situations as an indication of a terrorist attack rather than trying to identify a person or the type of person who could be a terrorist.

> **The lesson is not only to add women to an existing profile, but also to recognize the diversity of the threat.**

The government has also tried to balance the need to conduct searches while not further inflaming Palestinian anger by touching Palestinian women. As a partial solution, Israel has included female soldiers and police officers at checkpoints and in interrogations. Because not every checkpoint can be covered, technologies such as X-ray wands have been used.

Sri Lanka has taken a similar approach in confronting female terrorists. As in Israel, it includes women in the police and military. Again, there are not enough women to cover all security checkpoints. Sri Lanka has been willing to negotiate with the Tamil Tigers and maintain ceasefire agreements. Unlike Israel, however, the government does not control all its territory. The LTTE effectively runs many communities in northern and eastern Sri Lanka, complicating counterinsurgency operations.

In all these cases, efforts by governments often increased tensions in the populations they sought to control. The states' actions reduced the number of men available through arrest, detention, and death, perhaps increasing women's motivations for political violence while making them attractive to terrorist groups. Additionally, the decision to search men but not women at checkpoints may have encouraged groups to employ women.

Policy Implications

The actions of the three states are important for understanding terrorists' decisions about the use of women in terrorism and for combating terrorism. First, as in studies of serial killers that drew only on male murderers, studies of individual terrorists have focused only on male terrorists. This emphasis, combined with assumptions about the female nature, created a popular and sometimes official profile of terrorists as young and male. Women's repeated involvement should be a signal that there is no standard terrorist. The first lesson Russia, Israel, and Sri Lanka learned from female terrorism was that women represented a threat. The lesson is not only to add women to an existing profile, as Russia has, but also to recognize the diversity of the threat. The Israeli approach of looking for anomalies in situations is time- and personnel-intensive but offers more promise than attempting to describe all possible individuals who could be terrorists.

Second, just as groups can gain from sympathetic media portrayals of women terrorists, governments can use groups' ambivalence about female members to state advantage. Israel and Russia use stories of socially marginal women being exploited by men to discredit terrorist groups and explain away female violence. By making the women anomalies in the public mind, states reinforce the idea that they are in control and the public need not fear. These stories could be further exploited to delegitimize and fracture terrorist groups. The LTTE's policies on members' sexual behavior show the difficulty some groups have integrating women. Using propaganda about the group's sexual practices, as in Russia, can both discredit the group and exacerbate mistrust between members.

Finally, the decision by a group to employ women may be a sign that the state's efforts to combat terrorism are having an effect. The LTTE as well as Palestinian and Chechen groups turned to women only when they had to. If that is true with other groups, evidence of the use of women by terrorists may open more policy choices to a government—such as negotiations or incentives to individuals to renounce terrorism—because the group is weakened.

Female participation offers both states and terrorist groups unique options. However, policymakers should be realistic; women remain the minority. While their roles may be limited, women are important elements of groups and should not be overlooked. Wives know where their husbands are and with whom they meet. Mothers teach their children violence. Sisters, girlfriends, and female comrades enable men to get to their targets. Female terrorists likely know and do more than some security forces or terrorist groups give them credit for.

After al Qaeda's attacks on the United States in 2001, much has been made of terrorists' ability to innovate. Just as states and publics must be wary of underestimating terrorists, they must be cautious of deifying them. The employment of women by terrorist groups in Chechnya, Israel and the Occupied Territories, and Sri Lanka is an example of the limits of terrorists' thinking. Like states, these groups are bound by cultural expectations, demographics, public support, and the international context. Their limited use of women illustrates their strengths and shortcomings. Further exploration of this topic may provide greater insights for governments in combating terrorism.

Notes

1. For example, see Walter Laqueur and Yonah Alexander, eds., *The Terrorism Reader* (New York: Nal Penguin, 1987), 48. David Rapoport, "The Four Waves of Modern Terrorism," in *Attacking Terrorism,* ed. Audrey Kurth Cronin and James M. Ludes (Washington, DC: Georgetown University Press, 2004), 47. For an alternate view of the origins of modern terrorism, see Lindsay Clutterbuck, "The Progenitors of Terrorism: Russian Revolutionaries or Extreme Irish Republicans?" *Terrorism and Political Violence* 16, no. 1 (Spring 2004), 155–156.

2. Samuel Kucherov, "The Case of Vera Zasulich," *Russian Review* 11, no. 2 (April 1952), 87.

3. Cathy Porter, *Women in Revolutionary Russia* (New York: Cambridge University Press, 1987), 13.

4. Jay Bergman, "The Political Thought of Vera Zasulich," *Slavic Review* 38, no. 2 (June 1979), 244.

5. Porter, 15–17.

6. See, for example, Walter Laqueur, *The New Terrorism* (New York: Oxford University Press, 1999), 43; and J.B.S. Hardman, "Terrorism: A Summing Up in the 1930s," *The Terrorism Reader,* 227.

7. "Russian TV Interview Jailed Would-Be Suicide Bomber," RenTV, June 24, 2004, FBIS CEP20040721000353.

8. Russian opinion surveys indicate positive attitudes toward Chechens. See Public Opinion Foundation Database, "Attitude to Chechens: Pity and Fear," January 30, 2003, available at <http://bd.english.fom.ru/report/cat/societas/Chechnya/chechenian/ed030429>.

9. Public Opinion Foundation Database, "The terrorist attack in Tushino—"they want to face us down," July 15, 2003, available at <http://bd.english.fom.ru/report/map/ed032826>.

10. See, for example, Genevieve Sheehan, "Rebel Republic," *Harvard International Review* 25, no. 3 (Fall 2003), 14.

11. Ibrahim Hazboun, "Eighteen-year-old woman is latest suicide bomber," The Associated Press, March 29, 2002.

12. Yoni Fighel, "Palestinian Islamic Jihad and Female Suicide Bombers," International Policy Institute for Counter-Terrorism, October 6, 2003, available at <www.ict.org.ll/articles/articledet.cfm?articleid=499>.

13. "Islamic Jihad Leader Views Israeli Raid on Syria, Suicide Operations," Al-Arabiyah Television, October 5, 2003, FBIS GMP20031006000207.

14. "Hamas Founder Opines on Participation of Palestinian Women in Suicide Bombings," *Al-Sharq al-Awsat,* February 2, 2002, 8, FBIS 20020202000123.

15. Rajan Hoole et al., *The Broken Palmyra* (Claremont, CA: The Sri Lankan Studies Institute, 1988), 308.

16. Edgar O'Ballance, *The Cyanide War: Tamil Insurrection in Sri Lanka, 1973–88* (London: Brassey's UK, 1990), 68.

17. By 2002, an estimated 500,000 people had fled Sri Lanka, and about 600,000 were internally displaced. Miranda Allison, "Cogs in the Wheel? Women in the Liberation Tigers of Tamil Eelam," *Civil Wars* 6, no. 4 (Winter 2003), 38.

18. "Hamas uses female suicide bomber and threatens escalation," Jane's Terrorism and Insurgency Center, January 14, 2004.
19. Mark Franchetti, "Russians hunt down potential 'black widows,'" *The Australian,* September 27, 2004, 14.
20. "Russia: MVD Confirms Nationwide Operation to Check Muslim Women," *Moscow Gazeta,* July 23, 2003, FBIS CEP20030724000198.
21. "Russia: FSB Says Desperate Militants Enlisting Female Suicide Bombers," *ITAR—TASS,* July 10, 2003, FBIS CEP20030710000164.

From *Joint Force Quarterly,* Issue 44, 1st Quarter 2007, pp. 95–100. Published in 2007 by National Defense University Press. www.ndu.edu

UNIT 9
Government Response

Unit Selections

34. **The Eye of the Storm,** Kevin Whitelaw
35. **Port Security Is Still a House of Cards,** Stephen E. Flynn
36. **Are We Ready Yet?,** Christopher Conte
37. **Held Without Trial in the USA,** A.C. Thompson

Key Points to Consider

- What is the role of the National Counterterrorism Center?
- How can security at U.S. port facilities be improved?
- What effect have preparations for bioterrorism had on our public health system?
- Should individuals who are labeled "enemy combatant" have legal rights?

Student Web Site
www.mhcls.com/online

Internet References
Further information regarding these Web sites may be found in this book's preface or online.

Counter-Terrorism Page
http://counterterrorism.com

ReliefWeb
http://www.reliefweb.int

The South Asian Terrorism Portal
http://www.satp.org/

Royalty-Free/CORBIS

Government response to terrorism is multifaceted and complex. Choices about domestic spending, the use of military force, and long-term foreign policy objectives are increasingly shaped by our commitment to a Global War on Terrorism.

While counterterrorism spending has increased significantly since 9/11, choices about how this money is to be used have become more difficult as various constituencies lobby to have their voices heard. As policymakers struggle to allay public concerns, choices between spending for security today and preparing for the threats of the future have become more difficult. The tragedy of September 11 and the subsequent anthrax attacks have fueled fears about catastrophic terrorism. This makes choices about public policy priorities even more difficult. Given limited resources, should governments focus their efforts on existing crises and the most likely threats, or should they focus their resources on countless potential vulnerabilities and catastrophic threats, which many experts agree may be possible but not likely? Ideally governments should do both. Realistically, even in a resource-rich environment, governments have to make choices.

Decisions about when or how to use military force are equally complex. Should governments adopt preemptive or defensive postures? Should governments focus their resources on state sponsors of terrorism, or should they focus their efforts on capturing or killing the leaders of existing terrorist groups? Does the long-term deployment of a military force to a foreign country increase or reduce the threat of terrorism? Should nonproliferation be a priority in the war on terrorism?

Finally, it is important to note that the U.S. commitment to a global war on terrorism has not only an impact on long-term U.S. foreign policy objectives but also the foreign policies of others. There is an opportunity cost to foreign policy decisions. By prioritizing a particular set of objectives, governments inevitably sacrifice others. This impacts not only our policies but also the policies of others. By making terrorism a policy priority we influence and shape the policies of others, as states may act in support of U.S. policy or take advantage of the vacuums created by such policies.

This unit examines the methods and policies governments use to respond to the threat of international terrorism. In the first article, Kevin Whitelaw provides a first look into the day-to-day activities of the National Counterterrorism Center. He identifies some of the problems that its staff has encountered. Next, Stephen Flynn argues that port security should be placed higher on the U.S. government's list of priorities and criticizes ongoing efforts to secure domestic ports and monitor foreign points of origin. Flynn highlights three important weaknesses of the maritime security apparatus and offers policy recommendations designed to address these issues. The third article discusses efforts by various public health agencies to prepare local communities for bioterrorism. In the article, Christopher Conte argues that preparations for bioterrorism are drawing resources away from more prevalent health crises. Finally, A.C. Thompson discusses the case of Ali Saleh Kahlah al-Marri, a man accused of collaboration with al-Qaeda. Labeled an "enemy combatant" four years ago, al-Marri was stripped of all legal rights, including the right to trial.

The Eye of the Storm

In a secret, high-tech spy hub near Washington, the war on terror is 24-7.

KEVIN WHITELAW

Every weekday at 8 A.M., Kevin Brock hefts a thick white ring binder onto a sleek, oval conference table. Labeled "Read Book," the deceptively plain folder houses the "Threat Matrix," a top-secret compendium of the most troubling reports of possible terrorist activity, drawn from the nation's 16 intelligence agencies. It is thicker than usual on a recent Monday morning, packed with 66 separate items that came in over the weekend. Brock, the principal deputy director of the National Counterterrorism Center, is about to brief some of the government's most senior officials on the latest threat information.

First, though, he must sort through the reports, most of which are vague—and sometimes little more than anonymous tips. Many are false alarms. ("If we could eliminate all the jilted lovers and ex-spouses," Brock says later, cracking a smile, "we would greatly reduce the number of threats we receive on a daily basis.") But some of the nuggets—coming from CIA operatives, FBI sources, or reliable foreign spy agencies—must be taken seriously. Brock, after meeting with the leadership of the counterterrorism center, decided to present 18 of the threat reports at the 8 A.M. videoconference.

Facing a wall of secure video feeds, Brock watches top leaders from a dozen key players gather—the CIA, the FBI, the eavesdroppers at the National Security Agency, even the White House. A briefer from the center, running through the 18 items, discusses possible terrorist action in south Asia, Southeast Asia, the Middle East, even inside the United States. Brock raises the recent release of a videotape showing two of the September 11 hijackers smiling for the camera. He pays particular attention to overseas threats that have a possible domestic angle. "NCTC was created to . . . ensure the handshake occurs between international intelligence collection and the FBI or others within the country to take action," says Brock, a career FBI agent. "And we're seeing that take place on almost a daily basis."

"No Boundaries"

Housed in an unmarked office complex in Northern Virginia, the National Counterterrorism Center has become the centerpiece of reform efforts to integrate the far-flung intelligence community. The NCTC was created in the wake of the September 11 attacks to reduce the gulf between America's spy agencies and domestic law enforcement. With more than 30 separate, highly classified government networks pumping information into NCTC headquarters, it has unfettered access to the crown jewels of the U.S. intelligence community—including raw cables from CIA spies and detailed FBI case files. One congressional staffer with knowledge of intelligence matters calls it a "miracle," only half joking. "We're the only place in the U.S. government where all that information comes together," says retired Vice Adm. Scott Redd, the center's director. "There are no boundaries in this business."

Inside and outside the intelligence world, however, people are still confused about what the two-year-old organization is supposed to do—and what it's not. *U.S. News* was granted unprecedented access to the senior leadership of the NCTC, which is supposed to become the primary hub for tracking and analyzing the terrorist threat. Director of National Intelligence John Negroponte calls it the single biggest change during his 18 months in office. "The center is really looked to as the principal source of analysis of these kinds of developments," Negroponte tells *U.S. News*. The NCTC is still building up its ranks, but already it is butting up against the other agencies that work on terrorism, particularly the CIA, which has run its own Counter-Terrorism Center since 1986.

Number of analysts with access to NCTC's secure website, NCTC Online: 6,000

The 2004 law that formalized the NCTC also gives it a "strategic operational planning" role, which has taken some time to define. In some ways, it's easier to explain what it isn't. Redd is quick to say that, unlike in the popular TV spy show *24*, they don't go after any terrorists themselves. "Jack Bauer doesn't live here," he says.

NCTC officials might not be prowling dark alleyways in Cairo or camping out in Pakistan's lawless borderlands. But the NCTC is, for the first time, trying to make sure that all the operational agencies don't unwittingly trip over one another in the field. "NCTC is not directing operations," says Brock. "We're here just to kind of act as the air traffic controller and make sure everybody is talking." Most of this work is so highly classified that it is difficult to discuss, but Brock tries to describe a recent example in general terms. During the daily 8 A.M. videoconference earlier this year, one intelligence agency announced that it had an imminent opportunity to capture a key terrorist suspect in a Middle Eastern country. Another agency piped up, warning that a productive source of intelligence might be lost if the suspect were nabbed. Brock asked the two agencies to work it out themselves, which they did (although Brock declined to describe how).

Disney-Esque

NCTC officials also monitor unfolding plots and investigations, producing continually updated reports called Threat Threads on the most dangerous cases. There are as many as a dozen Threat Threads at any given time; on a recent Monday, the NCTC was tracking 11 different threats. A Thread report came in handy when, for example, the NCTC was coordinating the fast-moving investigation into this summer's alleged plot in Britain to blow up as many as 10 aircraft using liquid explosives. At first, officials had been following the investigation from a distance, because it appeared to be a largely U.K. plot.

But after receiving what officials call "a very specific piece of intelligence" that the suspected plotters were targeting airplanes heading for the United States, the NCTC swung into high gear. Redd was at the White House every day as the investigation built to a climax. At the same time, his aides were helping to coordinate how much information was released to officials at key government agencies, particularly the Department of Homeland Security and its Transportation Security Administration. "They don't need to know what we know about what's going on in Pakistan," says Redd. "But they very much want to know what data we have to be on the lookout for and how does this change our screening procedures."

The NCTC's showpiece is its 24-hour operations center. Designed with input from, among others, Walt Disney's Imagineers, it looks like a film director's version of a high-tech government command post. Giant screens dominate the front of the room, displaying anything from broadcast of an Arab satellite news channel or the radar map over New York City to a highly classified live feed from an armed Predator drone over Afghanistan. An NCTC watch team of at least a dozen people is on duty at all times, while the FBI and the CIA each maintain their own independent terrorism watch centers in the same space. "We are getting paid to say who knows about this information we've just come across, who needs to know about it, and what are they doing about it," says Don Loren, a retired naval officer who runs the operations center.

"Historic Baggage"

Every watch officer can, in theory, access any piece of counterterrorism intelligence in the entire U.S. government. "We're pretty much the cutting edge," says an air marshal from the TSA assigned to the watch center for the past 18 months. "We're the first ones to see it, and we push it to wherever it needs to go." There are limits, however: To send a piece of raw intelligence from an agency's operational files out to the rest of the community, an NCTC official must first secure the permission of the agency that issued it.

The bulk of the NCTC's work remains on the analysis side. But the road to becoming the hub for U.S. counterterrorism analysis has been rocky. The NCTC (and its predecessor organization, the Terrorist Threat Integration Center) got off to a slow start. "Initially, there was a reluctance on the part of government agencies to let people from other agencies have access to their networks," says John Brennan, who founded the Threat Integration Center and ran the NCTC for its first year. "A lot of people didn't understand what NCTC's mission was."

Getting enough experienced analysts was another problem, and the NCTC had several early tussles over personnel with the CIA's CounterTerrorism Center. Officials insist the wrinkles have largely been ironed out. Negroponte, the director of national intelligence, took the first big step last year when he ordered some 90 CIA analysts to move over to the NCTC. Gen. Michael Hayden's arrival as CIA director (after a stint as the deputy DNI) helped to further cement NCTC's status. Almost immediately, Hayden dispatched an additional 28 analysts to NCTC, and he has pledged to send over 50 more in the next year.

Some critics worry that taking analysts from the CIA could harm the ability of its own CounterTerrorism Center to use analysis to target operations aimed at capturing or killing terrorists. But officials insist that, if anything, the new structure frees up the CIA's center from much of the broader analytical work. "I actually think that NCTC may offer us better opportunities to support all the elements of national power because an awful lot of our activity here, quite legitimately and quite naturally, was focused in on supporting our operations," Hayden tells *U.S. News*. "We can't take all of America's analytic expertise and hard-wire it to any kill or capture operation. So I was willing to take the risk of shifting some of the weight of our analytic force from here to NCTC." Another factor is the civil liberties concern of giving the CIA, which is barred from domestic spying, access to law enforcement case files. Hayden says that it is better to bridge that gap "in a new location, without any historic baggage to worry about."

This summer, the CIA and the NCTC also agreed to adhere to what officials call "lanes in the road," which lay out who is responsible for reporting on which general areas. It's a tough balancing act, between reducing overlap on one side and ensuring competitive analysis on the other. "The worst thing in the world would be to have one gigantic organization that did all the thinking on counterterrorism for the entire government because the 'groupthink' syndrome comes into play," says Andy Liepman, a career CIA official who now manages the 200 analysts inside the NCTC.

Liepman's most active analysts work in the Al Qaeda and Sunni Affiliates group. One team in the group is dedicated solely to al Qaeda's plotting inside the United States. "Most of the [homeland] plots we believe are credible have in their ancestry an al Qaeda brain," says Liepman. Other groups look at all the other terrorist organizations, as well as their interest in weapons of mass destruction. A fourth tracks the logistical aspects of terrorism, including travel, financing, and communications. "You can't just disrupt the attack," says Redd. "You have to go after every element of that life cycle."

Critics have faulted the NCTC for weak analysis on longer-term strategic topics, such as which factors in Islamic societies help generate more terrorists. Part of it is a staffing problem—there is just so much demand for the tactical work of chasing terrorism suspects. "We have not been able to work the long-term strategic issues to our satisfaction," says Dawn Scalici, a veteran CIA officer who is the deputy director for mission management at the NCTC. "We're stretched pretty thin." Eventually, NCTC officials plan to double the number of analysts. For now, more than half of the 200 analysts have less than three years' experience working on counterterrorism issues. "The fact is that they don't have the culture of analysis that the CIA has built up over decades," says a recently retired intelligence analyst. "They need to develop the analytic tradecraft."

Number of intelligence cables and reports on NCTC Online: 6 million

The NCTC's analysts do have one tremendous advantage-wide access to both domestic and foreign raw intelligence traffic. But their physical isolation from the bulk of the CIA's regional and cultural experts could make it more difficult to detect emerging threats. "The analysts are further away from many of the specialists in the intelligence community," says Paul Pillar, a 30-year veteran of the CIA who once served as the deputy chief of its CounterTerrorism Center. "Consultation with them would be essential to help have early warning." Liepman counters that much of that contact is already happening in secure online forums these days. "There is a very good, very healthy, substantive discussion going on now between people who follow Hezbollah and people who follow Iran," he says. "Just because they are not at NCTC or in the counterterrorism community, it doesn't mean they don't have a voice."

The technological challenges have been daunting. When *U.S. News* visited the Terrorist Threat Integration Center three years ago, then director Brennan had five different computers under his desk to access all the different agencies' networks. That problem remains, and, if anything, is even worse now that the NCTC has even greater access to data. In fact, with more than 30 computer networks wired into the NCTC, analysts in the operations center have to use multiple desks to access them all—the switching equipment they use to toggle between networks can accommodate a maximum of only nine systems. Also, analysts cannot yet search all the networks at the same time with a single command. That technology, says Chief Information Officer Bill Spalding, is still "a couple of years away."

"The Fight of a Generation"

The deluge of information is intimidating. The NCTC maintains the intelligence community's ever expanding central repository of suspected terrorists, called the Terrorist Identities Datamart Environment (which is used to feed several terrorist watch lists, including the TSA's no-fly list). Russ Travers, a career Defense Intelligence Agency official, manages a youthful team of 80 analysts who sort through the mass of reporting on possible terrorist names. Every day, the NCTC receives as many as 2,000 cables—containing some 5,000 to 7,000 names. The database has quadrupled to 400,000 names in three years (although about 100,000 of the names are aliases). Further complicating the task is the fragmentary, often contradictory, nature of the intelligence and the language barrier. "Right away, you run into the whole problem with Arab names," says Travers. "Trying to sort out this 'Mohammed Mohammed' from that 'Mohammed Mohammed' can be a tremendous challenge for these young people."

Perhaps the most ambitious part of the NCTC's mission is its strategic operational planning function. As the "mission manager" for terrorism, the NCTC is supposed to work with the newly created DNI's office, which is charged with reforming the intelligence community, to eliminate gaps in the U.S. counterterrorism effort as well as unnecessary overlap. Without direct command authority, however, the NCTC will have to rely on the DNI's influence over the budget to help push change. It is unclear just how much clout either organization will have.

The NCTC has already issued several plans, including the first National Action Plan to Combat Foreign Fighters in Iraq, completed in June. Officials are now working on another, to counter terrorists' use of the Internet. The most comprehensive effort is the now completed National Implementation Plan, a nearly 200-page document that has become the de facto war plan for the struggle against terrorism. Signed by President Bush in June, the classified plan assigns a lead agency to each of more than 500 different tasks related to the war on terrorism. Some of them are obvious, such as the FBI's lead role in hunting terrorists at home. Others relate to the war of ideas and the need to quell violent Islamic extremism, an area where the State Department has many of the lead roles. The new plan tries to take a broader view, including goals like bolstering educational institutions that focus on Islam and the Muslim world. "This is the fight of a generation," says Vice Adm. Bert Calland, a former deputy CIA director who is now the deputy director for strategic operational planning at the NCTC. "We need to start establishing processes and capabilities with that in mind." Many experts are skeptical; previous efforts by the Bush administration to do outreach to the Muslim world have foundered.

"Radicalization"

At the same time, the terrorist threat and the al Qaeda network have become increasingly diffuse. NCTC's analytical director Liepman says that the most credible terrorist plotting appears to have some al Qaeda link back to Pakistan and Afghanistan, but officials are increasingly worried about individual extremists—particularly Muslim men already living here who may be drawn to jihad but who have no ties to known terrorist groups. "In looking at threat reporting on a daily basis, you tend to get a sense of issues of concern and things that might help us understand where radicalization is taking place, why it's taking place, and what we need to be worried about in the future," says principal deputy director Brock. "Radicalization happens in different ways, at different times, with different people, and that's what makes it such a difficult problem."

Redd offers a simple, if unsettling, way to measure their success: "Do the 5-year-olds of today turn into terrorists or do they decide there is something better out there?"

Port Security Is Still a House of Cards

STEPHEN E. FLYNN

As one of the world's busiest ports, it is fitting that Hong Kong played host to the World Trade Organization's December 2005 meeting. After all, seaports serve as the on- and off-ramps for the vast majority of traded goods. Still, the leaders of the 145 delegations that convened in Hong Kong undoubtedly did not have much more than a sightseer's interest in the host city's magnificent and frenetic harbor. For the most part, finance and trade ministers see trade liberalization as involving efforts to negotiate rules that open markets and level the playing field. They take as a given the availability of transportation infrastructures that physically link markets separated by vast distances.

But the days when policy makers could take safe transportation for granted are long past. The Sept. 11, 2001 attacks on New York and subsequent attacks on Madrid and London show that transport systems have become favored targets for terrorist organizations. It is only a matter of time before terrorists breach the superficial security measures in place to protect the ports, ships and the millions of intermodal containers that link global producers to consumers.

Should that breach involve a weapon of mass destruction, the United States and other countries will likely raise the port security alert system to its highest level, while investigators sort out what happened and establish whether or not a follow-on attack is likely. In the interim, the flow of all inbound traffic will be slowed so that the entire intermodal container system will grind to a halt. In economic terms, the costs associated with managing the attack's aftermath will substantially dwarf the actual destruction from the terrorist event itself.

Fortunately, there are pragmatic measures that governments and the private sector can pursue right now that would substantially enhance the integrity and resilience of global trade lanes. Trade security can be improved with modest upfront investments that enhance supply chain visibility and accountability, allowing companies to better manage the choreography of global logistics—and, in the process, improve their financial returns. In short, there is both a public safety imperative and a powerful economic case for advancing trade security.

A Brittle System

Though advocates for more open global markets rarely acknowledge it, when it comes to converting free trade from theory to practice the now-ubiquitous cargo container deserves a great deal of credit. On any given day, millions of containers carrying up to 32 tons of goods each are moving on trucks, trains and ships. These movements have become remarkably affordable, efficient, and reliable, resulting in increasingly complex and economically expedient global supply chains for manufacturers and retailers.

From a commercial standpoint, this has been all for the good. But there is a problem: as enterprises' dependence on the intermodal transportation system rises, they become extremely vulnerable to the consequences of a disruption in the system. To appreciate why that is so requires a brief primer on how that system has evolved.

Arguably, one of the most unheralded revolutions of the 20th century was the widespread adoption of the cargo container to move manufactured and perishable goods around the planet. In the middle of the last century, shipping most goods was labor intensive: items had to be individually moved from a loading dock at a factory to the back of a truck and then offloaded and reloaded onto a ship. Upon arrival in a foreign port, cargo had to be removed by longshoremen from the ship's holds, then moved to dock warehouses where the shipments would be examined by customs inspectors. Then they were loaded onto another transportation conveyance to be delivered to their final destination. This constant packing and repacking was inefficient and costly. It also routinely involved damage and theft. As a practical matter, this clumsy process was a barrier to trade.

The cargo container changed all that. Now goods can be placed in a container at a factory and be moved from one mode of transportation to another without being manually handled by intermediaries along the way. Larger vessels can be built to carry several thousand containers in a single voyage. In short, as global trade liberalization accelerated, the transportation system was able to accommodate the growing number of buyers and sellers.

Arguably, East Asia has been the biggest beneficiary of this transportation revolution. Despite the distance between Asia and the U.S., a container can be shipped from Hong Kong, Shanghai, or Singapore to the West Coast for roughly $4,000. This cost represents a small fraction of the $66,000 average value of goods in each container that is destined for the U.S.

However, multiple port closures in the U.S. and elsewhere would quickly throw this system into chaos. U.S.-bound container ships would be stuck in docks, unable to unload their cargo. Marine terminals would have to close their gates to all incoming containers since they would have no place to store them. Perishable cargo would spoil. Soon, factories would be idle and retailers' shelves bare.

In short, a terrorist event involving the intermodal transportation system could lead to unprecedented disruption of the global trade system, and East Asia has the most to lose.

What Has Been Done?

The possibility that terrorists could compromise the maritime and intermodal transportation system has led several U.S. agencies to pursue initiatives to manage this risk. The U.S. Coast Guard chose to take a primarily multilateral approach by working through the London-based International Maritime Organization to establish new international standards for improving security practices on vessels and within ports, known as the International Ship and Port Facility Code (ISPS). As of July 1, 2004, each member state was obliged to certify that the ships that fly their flag or the facilities under their jurisdiction are code-compliant.

The Coast Guard also requires that ships destined for the U.S. provide a notice of their arrival a minimum of 96 hours in advance and include a description of their cargoes as well as a crew and passenger list. The agency then assesses the potential risk the vessel might pose. If the available intelligence indicates a pre-arrival security check may be warranted, it arranges to intercept the ship at sea or as it enters the harbor in order to conduct an inspection.

The new U.S. Customs and Border Protection Agency (CBP), which was established within the Department of Homeland Security, mandated that ocean carriers must electronically file cargo manifests outlining the contents of U.S.-bound containers 24 hours in advance of their being loaded overseas. These manifests are then analyzed against the intelligence databases at CBP's National Targeting Center to determine if the container may pose a risk.

If so, it will likely be inspected overseas before it is loaded on a U.S.-bound ship under a new protocol called the Container Security Initiative (CSI). As of November 2005, there were 41 CSI port agreements in place where the host country permits U.S. customs inspectors to operate within its jurisdiction and agrees to pre-loading inspections of any targeted containers.

Decisions about which containers will not be subjected to an inspection are informed by an importer's willingness to participate in another post-9/11 initiative, known as the Customs-Trade Partnership Against Terrorism (C-TPAT). C-TPAT importers and transportation companies agree voluntarily to conduct self-assessments of their company operations and supply chains, and then put in place security measures to address any security vulnerabilities they find. At the multilateral level, U.S. customs authorities have worked with the Brussels-based World Customs Organization on establishing a new framework to improve trade security for all countries.

In addition to these Coast Guard and Customs initiatives, the U.S. Department of Energy and Department of Defense have developed their own programs aimed at the potential threat of weapons of mass destruction. They have been focused primarily on developing the means to detect a "dirty bomb" or a nuclear weapon.

The Energy Department has been funding and deploying radiation sensors in many of the world's largest ports as a part of a program called the Megaport Initiative. These sensors are designed to detect radioactive material within containers. The Pentagon has undertaken a counterproliferation initiative that involves obtaining permission from seafaring countries to allow specially trained U.S Navy boarding teams to conduct inspections of a flag vessel on the seas when there is intelligence that points to the possibility that nuclear material or a weapon may be part of the ship's cargo.

Finally, in September 2005, the White House weighed in with its new National Maritime Security Strategy. This purports to "present a comprehensive national effort to promote global economic stability and protect legitimate activities while preventing hostile or illegal acts within the maritime domain."

A House of Cards

Ostensibly, the flurry of U.S. government initiatives since 9/11 suggests substantial progress is being made in securing the global trade and transportation system. Unfortunately, all this activity should not be confused with real capability. For one thing, the approach has been piecemeal, with each agency pursuing its signature program with little regard for other initiatives. There are also vast disparities in the resources that the agencies have been allocated, ranging from an $800 million budget for the Department of Energy's Megaport initiative to no additional funding for the Coast Guard to support its congressionally mandated compliance to the ISPS Code. Even more problematic are some of the questionable assumptions about the nature of the terrorist threat that underpin these programs.

East Asia has the most to lose if a terrorist event disrupts the global trading system.

In an effort to secure funding and public support, agency heads and the White House have oversold the contributions of these new initiatives. Against a backdrop of inflated and unrealistic expectations, the public is likely to be highly skeptical of official assurances in the aftermath of a terrorist attack involving the intermodal transportation system. Scrambling for fresh alternatives to reassure anxious and angry citizens, the White House and Congress are likely to impose Draconian inspection protocols that dramatically raise costs and disrupt crossborder trade flows.

The new risk-management programs advanced by the CBP are especially vulnerable to being discredited, should terrorists succeed at turning a container into a poor man's missile. Before stepping down as commissioner in late November 2005, Robert Bonner repeatedly stated in public and before Congress that his inspectors were "inspecting 100% of the right 5% of containers." That implies the CBP's intelligence and analytical tools can be relied upon to pinpoint dangerous containers.

Former Commissioner Bonner is correct in identifying only a tiny percentage of containers as potential security risks. Unfortunately, CBP's risk-management framework is not up to the task of reliably identifying them, much less screening the low- or medium-risk cargoes that constitute the majority of containerized shipments and pass mostly uninspected into U.S. ports. There is very little counterterrorism intelligence available to support the agency's targeting system.

That leaves customs inspectors to rely primarily on their past experience in identifying criminal or regulatory misconduct to determine if a containerized shipment might potentially be compromised. This does not inspire confidence, given that the U.S. Congress's watchdog, the Government Accountability Office (GAO), and the U.S. Department of Homeland Security's own inspector general have documented glaring weaknesses with current customs targeting practices.

Prior to 9/11, the cornerstone of the risk-assessment framework used by customs inspectors was to identify "known shippers" that had an established track record of engaging in legitimate commercial activity. After 9/11, the agency expanded that model by extracting a commitment from shippers to follow the supply chain security practices outlined in C-TPAT. As long as there is no specific intelligence to tell inspectors otherwise, shipments from C-TPAT-compliant companies are viewed as low-risk.

The problem with this method is that it is designed to fight conventional crime; such an approach is not necessarily effective in combating determined terrorists. An attack involving a weapon of mass destruction differs in three important ways from organized criminal activity.

First, it is likely to be a one-time operation, and most private company security measures are not designed to prevent single-event infractions. Instead, corporate security officers try to detect infractions when they occur, conduct investigations *after* the fact, and adapt precautionary strategies accordingly.

Second, terrorists will likely target a legitimate company with a well-known brand name precisely because they can count on these shipments entering the U.S. with negligible or no inspection. It is no secret which companies are viewed by U.S. customs inspectors as "trusted" shippers; many companies enlisted in C-TPAT have advertised their participation. All a terrorist organization needs to do is find a single weak link within a "trusted" shipper's complex supply chain, such as a poorly paid truck driver taking a container from a remote factory to a port. They can then gain access to the container in one of the half-dozen ways well known to experienced smugglers.

Third, this terrorist threat is unique in terms of the severity of the economic disruption. If a weapon of mass destruction arrives in the U.S., especially if it enters via a trusted shipper, the risk-management system that customs authorities rely on will come under intense scrutiny. In the interim, it will become impossible to treat crossborder shipments by other trusted shippers as low-risk. When every container is assumed to be potentially high-risk, everything must be examined, freezing the worldwide intermodal transportation system. The credibility of the ISPS code as a risk-detection tool is not likely to survive the aftermath of such a maritime terrorist attack, and its collapse could exacerbate a climate of insecurity that could likely exist after a successful attack.

Moreover, the radiation-detection technology currently used in the world's ports by the Coast Guard and Customs and Border Protection Agency is not adequately capable of detecting a nuclear weapon or a lightly shielded dirty bomb. This is because nuclear weapons are extremely well-shielded and give off very little radioactivity. If terrorists obtained a dirty bomb and put it in a box lined with lead, it's unlikely radiation sensors would detect the bomb's low levels of radioactivity.

The flaws in detection technology require the Pentagon's counterproliferation teams to physically board container ships at sea to determine if they are carrying weapons of mass destruction. Even if there were enough trained boarding teams to perform these inspections on a regular basis—and there are not—there is still the practical problem of inspecting the contents of cargo containers at sea. Such inspections are almost impossible because containers are so closely packed on a container ship that they are often simply inaccessible. This factor, when added to the sheer number of containers on each ship—upwards of 3,000—guarantees that in the absence of very detailed intelligence, inspectors will be able to perform only the most superficial of examinations.

In the end, the U.S. government's container-security policy resembles a house of cards. In all likelihood, any terrorist attack on U.S. soil that involved a maritime container would come in contact with most, or even all, of the existing maritime security protocols. Consequently, a successful seaborne attack would implicate the entire security regime, generating tremendous political pressure to abandon it.

The Way Ahead

We can do better. The Association of Southeast Asian Nations should work with the U.S. and the European Union in authorizing third parties to conduct validation audits in accordance with the security protocols outlined in the International Ship and Port Facility Security Code and the World Customs Organization's new framework for security and trade facilitation.

A multilateral auditing organization made up of experienced inspectors should be created to periodically audit the third party auditors. This organization also should be charged with investigating major incidents and recommending appropriate changes to established security protocols.

To minimize the risk that containers will be targeted between the factory and loading port, governments should create incentives for the speedy adoption of technical standards developed by the International Standards Organization for tracking a container and monitoring its integrity. The technology now used by the U.S. Department of Defense for the global movement of military goods can provide a model for such a regime.

Asean and the EU should also endorse a pilot project being sponsored by the Container Terminal Operators Association (CTOA) of Hong Kong, in which every container that arrives passes through a gamma-ray content-scanning machine, as well as a radiation portal to record the levels of radioactivity within the container. Optical character recognition cameras then photograph the number painted on several sides of the container. These scanned images, radiation profiles, and digital photos are then stored in a database where they can be immediately retrieved if necessary.

The marine terminals in Hong Kong have invested in this system because they hope that a 100% scanning regime will deter a terrorist organization from placing a weapon of mass destruction in a container passing through their port facilities. Since each container's contents are scanned, if a terrorist tries to shield radioactive material to defeat the radiation portals, it will be relatively easy to detect the shielding material because of its density.

Another reason for making this investment is to minimize the disruption associated with targeting containers for portside inspection. The system allows the container to receive a remote preliminary inspection without the container leaving the marine terminal.

By maintaining a record of each container's contents, the port is able to provide government authorities with a forensic tool that can aid a follow-up investigation should a container with a weapon of mass destruction still slip through. This tool would allow authorities to quickly isolate the point in the supply chain where the security compromise took place, thereby minimizing the chance for a port-wide shut-down. By scanning every container, the marine terminals in Hong Kong are well-positioned to indemnify the port for security breaches. As a result, a terrorist would be unable to successfully generate enough fear and uncertainty to warrant disrupting the global trade system.

This low-cost inspection system is being carried out without impeding the operations of busy marine terminals. It could be put in place in every major container port in the world at a cost of $1.5 billion, or approximately $15 per container. Once such a system is operating globally, each nation would be in a position to monitor its exports and to check their imports against the images first collected at the loading port.

The total cost of third-party compliance inspections, deploying "smart" containers, and operating a cargo scanning system such as Hong Kong's is likely to reach $50 to $100 per container depending on the number of containers an importer has and the complexity of its supply chain. Even if the final price tag came in at $100 additional cost per container, it would raise the average price of cargo moved by, say, Wal-Mart or Target by only 0.06%. What importers and consumers are getting in return is the reduced risk of a catastrophic terrorist attack and its economic consequences.

In short, such an investment would allow container security to move from the current "trust, but don't verify" system to a more robust "trust but verify" regime. That would bring benefits to everyone but criminals and terrorists.

MR. FLYNN is the Jeane J. Kirkpatrick senior fellow for national security studies at the Council on Foreign Relations and author of *America the Vulnerable* (HarperCollins, 2005).

From *Far Eastern Economic Review*, January/February 2006, pp. 5–11. Copyright © 2006 by Far Eastern Economic Review. Reprinted by permission of Far Eastern Economic Review via the Copyright Clearance Center.

Are We Ready Yet?

We're building our defenses against bioterrorism, but we face growing questions about costs and priorities.

CHRISTOPHER CONTE

Patrick Libbey likes to be positive. When the executive director of the National Association of County and City Health Officials is asked about how ready state and local governments are to respond to bioterrorism—it's a question he hears frequently—he'll tell you, "Significant progress has been made."

It's true. As the nation moves into its fifth year of a crash effort to build defenses against a possible bioterrorist attack, states have developed a wide range of emergency plans, conducted numerous exercises, and modernized their information and communications systems. But Libbey is not really satisfied with his answer. That's because there is no "consistent measure of where we are or where we need to be," he says. "That is probably our largest failing since the whole push began."

Libbey is not alone. George Hardy, executive director of the Association of State and Territorial Health Officers, sings a similar refrain. "It is absolutely critical that we develop some metrics," Hardy says. "We need accountability indicators for federal funds that are going out, and we need indicators for the overall level of community preparedness."

The two men, who together represent public health agencies serving the majority of Americans, no doubt have complex motives in pressing for standards to gauge preparedness efforts. On one hand, they are eager to keep federal bioterrorism funds—the first significant influx of new money into the public health system in decades—flowing. Many state and local public health agencies have launched ambitious infrastructure-building efforts on the expectation that bioterrorism readiness will continue to be a federal priority, and they clearly would like more support. Although the federal government has been sinking $1 billion annually into public health readiness, researchers at the RAND Corp. recently concluded from an assessment of California public health agencies that spending is only one-third to one-half of what local officials believe is needed.

At the same time, Libbey and Hardy also may be eager to draw some boundaries around bioterrorism-preparedness activities. The emphasis on preparing for mass-casualty incidents is diverting attention from other mounting public health problems—such as diabetes, tuberculosis and sexually-transmitted diseases—that may be relegated to the back burner for some time to come. "Our initial response to building emergency capacity was to treat the problem as if it were an emergency," Libbey says. "We thought we would drop everything we were doing, tend to the problem, and then everything would go back to normal. But there isn't the old 'normal' to go back to. Emergency preparedness is now part of our ongoing work."

All of this suggests that Americans are due for some serious soul-searching about what to expect from their public health system. What does it mean to be prepared? How do we balance the goal of making people safer with keeping them healthier? And what are the long-term implications of the growing role Washington is assuming in shaping a public health system that traditionally has been local in nature?

Mixed Results

Until recently, most health departments have been too busy trying to get a seat at the emergency-planning table to spend much time on such big-picture questions. "We spent the first year or more just building relationships," notes Darren Collins, director for the DeKalb County, Georgia, Board of Health's Center for Public Health Preparedness. That effort, at least, has paid off. Before 2001, public health departments rarely played a role in disaster planning. But now, they are integral players in most local emergency planning teams, serving on—and in some cases leading—unified incident command systems that can be activated any time there is an emergency. "We have much greater visibility in the community now," says Martin Fenstersheib, the health officer for Santa Clara County, just south of San Francisco. "With the advent of biological issues, we are now in at the top among first responders."

Along the way, public health agencies have acquired many new tools. Public health workers in Santa Clara County, for instance, now have "go-kits"—duffle bags containing personal protective gear, cameras, computers, specimen-gathering equipment and other tools to help them diagnose health problems in the field. The county also issues packs of laminated cards and reference materials so doctors can quickly recognize outbreaks of anthrax, smallpox, plague or Ricin toxin.

North Carolina's Health Department uses the Internet to review hospital admission records and check on the availability of hospital beds in real time—capabilities that could help it detect disease outbreaks more quickly and respond more effectively to mass-casualty situations. The state also has seven Public Health Regional Surveillance Teams, each consisting of a physician, an epidemiologist, an industrial hygienist and a field veterinary officer. A team can be deployed anywhere in the state in an emergency.

Montgomery County, Maryland, has been training public works and other county employees, as well as lay educators, parish nurses and other medical professionals, to serve as volunteers in emergencies, and it is helping schools, nursing homes and group homes make their own preparations to respond to emergencies. "In a crisis, we won't be able to get to people right away," says Kay Aaby, project coordinator at the county's Department of Health and Human Services. "They have to know how to shelter in place."

Should a pandemic of influenza hit, the Seattle-King County public health department has procedures for imposing a large-scale quarantine. It has identified a facility where sick people could be isolated from the general population. The department also is working with area governments and businesses to plan how they will keep operating during a pandemic, in which absenteeism could run as high as 30 percent.

Despite such progress, however, most public health officials concede the country still is not ready for a public health calamity. One reason for the gap is the sheer magnitude of the job and the dearth of trained personnel to do it. While public health laboratories have acquired a lot of new equipment in the past four years, more than half say they don't have enough scientists to run tests for anthrax or plague, and a majority lack sufficient capabilities to test for chemical terrorism, according to a report issued last year by Trust for America's Health, a public health advocacy group.

Similarly, two-thirds of the states still don't use the Internet to contribute to a national database on disease outbreaks—a capacity the federal Centers for Disease Control and Prevention believes would greatly increase the public health system's ability to identify and stamp out harmful biological agents. "A lot of gears are moving, but they aren't meshing together," says Shelley Hearne, TFAH's executive director. "The jalopy has gotten better oil and faster wheels, but it is not a race car that can get you from zero to 60 when you give it a good push on the gas."

Meanwhile, low pay and an aging workforce are complicating efforts to bolster public health staffs. Some 30 of 37 states that responded to a 2003 survey conducted by the Association of State and Territorial Health Officers reported shortages of public health nurses, 15 lacked enough epidemiologists, 11 didn't have as many laboratory workers as they need, and 11 others said they are shy of environmental specialists. And it may become difficult to stay even, let alone get ahead. The average age of public health workers is 46, compared with 40 for the overall U.S. workforce, and retirement rates are projected to run as high as 45 percent over the next five years.

Low pay and an aging work force are complicating much-needed efforts to bolster the public health system.

Perhaps most important, there is growing concern among some public health officials about the impact preparedness efforts have had on our ability to deal with our chronic health problems. RAND researchers have noted that the increased emphasis on bioterrorism has led to retrenchments in programs to control sexually-transmitted diseases and tuberculosis, as well as teen pregnancy-prevention programs. In Madison County, North Carolina, public health nurse Jan Lounsbury had to drop work on programs to discourage smoking and promote exercise and better nutrition when she became bioterrorism planner for the county, in the state's western mountains. "Health promotion has been put on the back burner," says Lounsbury. And Russell Jones, a state epidemiologist based in Temple, Texas, warns that budget cuts have left the Lone Star State seriously vulnerable to an outbreak of pertussis (it had one several years ago). "In bioterrorism, we're adequate," Jones says. But otherwise, "if something bad happens, we are not prepared."

The New York-based Century Foundation, meanwhile, has questioned the cost-effectiveness of syndromic surveillance, a glitzy new technology that has gotten a big boost thanks to bioterrorism funding. It involves amassing a wide range of information, such as hospital admission forms, 911 calls, over-the-counter drug sales, school absenteeism figures and more, into a single database that allows analysts to look for clusters of symptoms that might indicate the beginning of a new disease outbreak. But it's expensive—New York City's system, widely considered the state of the art, costs $1.5 million annually, or about $4,000 a day—and so far largely unproven. "If it is sensitive enough to catch the few additional cases that may be the harbinger of a bioterrorist attack, it is likely to generate many false alarms as well and to command scarce resources," the foundation warns.

Defining Moments

One of the most glaring deficiencies in the public health system today is a serious gap between many health departments and the communities they serve. When RAND researchers assessed California public health departments, for instance, they noted that many local health departments have shockingly little information about their own communities. "In some jurisdictions," the analysts wrote, "representatives from police and fire departments appeared to have better knowledge of vulnerable populations than the health departments had."

Although this problem didn't begin with the national push for bioterrorism readiness, it hasn't been helped by it either. Some public health officials believe it may be a major reason why we are less safe than we need to be. That is the view of leaders of the Alameda County Public Health Department in California (it's unknown whether the department was part of the RAND study, which was conducted under a pledge of confidentiality). The department has devoted considerable time and effort to reaching out to neighborhoods. Most of its public health nurses work out of satellite offices in various communities, not out of the department's office in downtown Oakland. In some low-income communities, public health workers have gone door-to-door to survey residents, organize community meetings and otherwise help neighbors learn how to address common concerns. Public Health Director Arnold Perkins believes such "capacity building" will improve health in the targeted communities by reducing the myriad tensions and sense of isolation that significantly contribute to problems ranging from high infant mortality to heart disease, hypertension and asthma.

When federal bioterrorism funds began flowing to Alameda County, the department worked hard to integrate them into its ongoing activities, rather than let them be a diversion. One solution was to provide special "survival kits"—first aid items, food bars, water boxes, thermal blankets, ponchos, water purification tablets, dust masks, vinyl gloves and a combination radio-siren-flashlight—to people in the troubled communities in return for their participation in the capacity-building effort.

Are the kits just a clever subversion of a federal program? Not according to Anthony Iton, the county health officer. People in low-income neighborhoods have too many daily concerns—many lack health insurance or have high blood pressure; the local food stores sell liquor and junk food rather than fresh fruit and vegetables; and the neighborhood park has been taken over by drug dealers—to spend much time worrying about bioterrorism. By lacing information and self-help tools about bioterrorism into a broader effort to address residents' concerns, the department believes it has a better chance of getting its message across than if it tried to deal with preparedness separately. Moreover, by showing people that it is working to make their daily lives better, the health department is increasing the chances they will cooperate with it in an emergency—by staying home to slow the spread of a new virus or by coming to a mass inoculation site, for instance. "It's all about trust," says Iton. "If people don't trust us, they won't follow our instructions in emergencies."

Iton contends that the health department's work with poor neighborhoods effectively addresses one of the weakest links in current bioterrorism defenses. Most epidemics take root first in poor communities and then spread from there. In affluent communities, people are quick to see doctors if they get sick, increasing the chances that any new epidemic will be quickly detected. But in poor communities, people avoid going to doctors because they lack health insurance, can't afford to pay for health care or distrust mainstream institutions. That gives germs a better chance to incubate and spread. And because low-income people often commute from their homes to places such as airport concession stands, where diverse people commingle, these bugs have abundant opportunities to leap to the population at large. "Lack of health insurance, unfamiliarity with diseases and what to do about them, and the fact that the health care system turns poor people away—those are our greatest causes of vulnerability to bioterrorism in Alameda County," Iton argues.

Federal agencies aren't likely to accept as expansive a definition of emergency preparedness as Iton's views imply are necessary. To be sure, the Bush administration does view preparedness in broader terms today than it did a few years ago. When the U.S. Department of Homeland Security recently issued a "target capabilities list" for emergency planning, for instance, it identified 15 possible health calamities that would have "national significance"—including some, such as pandemic flu and major earthquakes and hurricanes, that aren't terrorism-related. But the list doesn't include lack of health insurance or community cohesion.

Nor does a list of 62 "critical tasks" and 34 performance measures recently issued by the CDC in response to calls for clearer standards to govern emergency public health preparations. Some of the proposed performance measures are highly specific (one says, for instance, that health departments should be able to bring the "initial wave" of personnel on board to conduct emergency operations within 90 minutes). Others deal with preparedness quite broadly (a knowledgeable public health professional should be available to answer a call reporting a suspicious disease within 15 minutes). But the CDC rules don't go so far as to tackle community capacity-building or require public health departments to spend more time meeting constituents in their own neighborhoods.

The current federal rules won't be the final world on preparedness; the CDC has pledged to meet with major players in the bioterrorism-preparedness arena to discuss them in detail. But the rules nevertheless represent a significant assertion of federal influence in a field that has generally been a state and local responsibility—one that nudges local health departments more in the direction of emergency preparedness. Given the absence of similar pressures to address other long-standing public health concerns, it's easy to imagine that local health departments' ability to deal with non-emergency health problems will become even more attenuated. So here's a word of advice to NACCHO's Libbey, ASTHO's Hardy and other state and local representatives who will be discussing the issues with Washington in the months ahead: Be careful what you ask for.

CHRISTOPHER CONTE can be reached at crconte@earthlink.net

From *Outlook*, October 2005, pp. A2–A6. Copyright © 2005 by Congressional Quarterly, Inc. Reprinted by permission of Congressional Quarterly, Inc via the Copyright Clearance Center.

Held Without Trial in the USA

A.C. THOMPSON

The Man

How to describe Ali Saleh Kahlah al-Marri? The basic bio is easy. He's a native of Qatar, a member of a prominent Arab tribe. Forty-one years old with a mess of coal hair and a beard speckled with gray. Married with five children. Holds a degree in business administration from a small university in Illinois.

And since 2001, when U.S. government agents grabbed al-Marri and accused him of plotting heinous crimes against America, he's been one of the Bush Administration's prize prisoners, a trophy captured during the War on Terror.

After reciting these facts, rendering a portrait of the man becomes a challenge—the U.S. government has thrust him into a vortex, a place from which only minuscule fragments of information dribble out.

Some three-and-a-half years ago, the Pentagon effectively disappeared al-Marri, dubbing him an "enemy combatant" and confining him to a solitary cell in the military brig at the Charleston Naval Weapons Station in South Carolina. For seventeen interrogation-heavy months, his captors barred him even from talking to his attorneys. Now his attorneys are the only ones he can talk to.

Citing security concerns, the Defense Department refused to let this reporter interview al-Marri, or even visit the brig to get a sense of how the facility operates. "There are no media visits due to the unique circumstance that an alleged Al Qaeda operative is being held there," says Defense spokesman Navy Commander J. D. Gordon. "There are a wide variety of operational security concerns."

Thus we know very, very little about al-Marri. What does his voice sound like? Is it smooth or raspy? Is it a deep baritone or whiny and high-pitched or somewhere in between? What about his eyes? Do they flit around anxiously? Do they lock onto the person he's conversing with? Does he cast them sullenly towards the floor?

We can't tell you.

Is he, as the government contends, an Al Qaeda operative connected to the 9/11 attacks, a guy who surreptitiously moved around money for jihadists and cooked up chemical warfare recipes on his home computer?

We can't tell you.

Could he be innocent, a victim of this paranoid age?

We can't tell you.

Despite the informational blackout, we *can* tell you this: Experts outside the armed forces characterize the conditions of al-Marri's incarceration which he shared with alleged dirty-bomb schemer Jose Padilla until Padilla was criminally charged—as a subtle brand of torture. Pentagon investigators found problems with the treatment of enemy combatants at the South Carolina brig, according to an internal report obtained by *The Progressive*.

Now, thanks to recent moves by the Administration of George W. Bush—moves that reflect a drastic restructuring of the American justice system—al-Marri could languish in this purgatory for decades to come without facing any sort of trial.

Pentagon officials have "never admitted that he has any rights, including the right not to be tortured," says Jonathan Hafetz, one of al-Marri's lawyers. "They've created a black hole where he has no rights."

The Arrest

With the government gagging al-Marri and disseminating little information about him, we've got to rely heavily on the court record hundreds of pages of paperwork filed in four different federal courthouses—to tell his story.

> **Al-Marri could languish in this purgatory for decades to come without facing any sort of trial. "They've created a black hole where he has no rights."**

One key document is an affidavit written up days after September 11, 2001, by Nicholas Zambeck, a special agent with the FBI. That document makes for chilling reading, accusing al-Marri of running a sophisticated credit card fraud operation, and implying he may have somehow been involved in raising or circulating money for the world's most notorious terrorist group.

At the time in question, al-Marri was dwelling in Peoria, Illinois, and working on a master's in computer science at Bradley University, the same school he'd attended while earning a BA in business in 1991.

While he claimed to be studying, al-Marri was actually living in a motel and using a fake name to open a trio of bank accounts for a fake company called AAA Carpet, according to Zambeck and the FBI. The bureau also alleges that al-Marri opened an account with a credit card processing firm, allowing AAA Carpet to conduct credit card transactions. That account was purportedly used to siphon money from twelve stolen credit cards, although agents reportedly discovered evidence of a much larger scam—more than 1,000 credit card numbers on al-Marri's laptop computer.

When digital analysts with the FBI scrolled through the files on al-Marri's computer they came across a host of unsettling material, according to Zambeck: audio lectures by Osama bin Laden and his fellow jihadists; photos of the 9/11 attacks; a folder marked "chem" filled with data on deadly chemicals; bookmarked websites about weaponry, computer hacking, phony IDs, and satellite equipment.

What Zambeck and company portray as a direct connection to Al Qaeda comes in the form of several phone calls allegedly made by al-Marri to a phone number in the United Arab Emirates.

The phone number in the Emirates allegedly belonged to Mustafa Ahmed al-Hawsawi. The 9/11 Commission describes al-Hawsawi as someone who had "worked on Al Qaeda's media committee" and as a "financial and travel" planner for the attacks on Manhattan. When federal prosecutors tried the so-called twentieth hijacker Zacarias Moussaoui, they labeled al-Hawsawi a "co-conspirator." Allegedly, he helped the hijackers travel from Pakistan to the Emirates and on to the U.S. in preparation for the attacks.

After the FBI arrested al-Marri in December 2001, prosecutors charged him with seven criminal offenses, including unauthorized possession of credit card numbers, making false statements to a bank, and using a phony ID to scam a bank.

His lawyers insist the government has hyped the case against him. "There's been no evidence presented" that al-Marri is an Al Qaeda operative or ally, says Hafetz, an attorney with the Brennan Center for Justice at NYU School of Law, and one of several lawyers working on al-Marri's case. Hafetz adds, "He's asserted his innocence."

Under normal circumstances, a jury would have considered his guilt or innocence by now, a half-decade later, and rendered a verdict, pushing al-Marri into a prison sentence or cutting him loose. But these are not normal times.

The Shift and the Treatment

After a string of court hearings in the *United States of America v. Ali Saleh Kahlah al-Marri,* the Bush Administration, in 2003, switched tacks. A month before al-Marri was to stand trial in Illinois, the President, with a stroke of the executive pen, wiped the case out of existence. Saying al-Marri "represents a continuing, present, and grave danger" to the country, Bush labeled al-Marri an "enemy combatant" and turned him over to the Defense Department. Instantly, the strictures of the criminal justice system no longer applied. Fundamental rights were out the window: al-Marri could now be held indefinitely without charge in a military prison, could be denied a lawyer, could be denied not only a speedy trial but any trial.

Thus began his habitation of a nine-by-six concrete cell in the naval brig in Charleston.

While progressives and liberals raised concerns about the hundreds shipped from the battlefields of Afghanistan and Iraq to the prison camp in Guantanamo Bay, Cuba, few realized that right here on American soil al-Marri was facing a similar fate—jailed without charge.

For the first seventeen months of al-Marri's incarceration in Charleston, the Defense Department did not allow Hafetz and al-Marri's other attorneys to communicate with him in any way. He had no contact with family, friends, or anyone other than government personnel.

After many months of interrogation, al-Marri finally got to see his lawyers. He quickly filed a lawsuit alleging that he'd been subjected to torturous living conditions. According to the suit, al-Marri "has suffered inhumane, degrading, and physically and psychologically abusive treatment at the brig in violation of this country's most basic laws and fundamental norms."

Hafetz says aside from some sporadic recreation periods, his client is kept caged in his cell twenty-four hours a day, seven days a week, and surveilled constantly by a video camera.

For much of his time, al-Marri has had nothing in his cell but a thin mattress and blanket, although at times he didn't even have those items. When he leaves his cell now, the isolation continues, Hafetz says. He's cuffed and shackled, and his ears are sometimes covered with noise-diffusing headphones, his eyes shielded by opaque goggles.

"He had no books, no magazines, nothing. He was in a black box," recalls Hafetz. "The isolation is very, very detrimental to him and clearly unconstitutional. He has not had any contact with anyone but his attorneys for the past three years. He hasn't been able to talk to his wife and five children."

Commander Gordon gives this response: "The government in the strongest terms denies allegations of torture, allegations made without support and without citing a shred of record evidence. It is our policy to treat all detainees humanely."

After the lawyers started agitating over his conditions, al-Marri began to get letters from his wife and children in Qatar, although the missives are thoroughly redacted. He's now able to read newspapers, as well, but those, too, are heavily censored.

The Report

A high-level Pentagon report obtained by *The Progressive* reveals that all has not been right at the South Carolina brig. The report, dated May 11, 2004, is entitled: "Brief to the Secretary of Defense on Treatment of Enemy Combatants Detained at Naval Station Guantanamo Bay, Cuba, and Naval Consolidated Brig Charleston." It was written by Naval Vice Admiral A. T. Church III and by Marine Brigadier General D. D. Thiessen. Its task: "Ensure Department of Defense orders concerning proper treatment of enemy combatants."

They found numerous problems at both facilities. At Charleston, where al-Marri was held, these included the following citations:

"One detainee has Koran removed from cell as part of JFCOM [Joint Forces Command] interrogation plan. Muslim chaplain not available."

"One detainee in Charleston has mattress removed as part of JFCOM-approved interrogation plan."

"One detainee in each location currently not authorized ICRC [Red Cross] visits due to interrogation plans in progress."

"One detainee in Charleston has Koran, mattress, and pillow removed and is fed cold MREs as part of interrogation plan." (This citation had a footnote that added: "After completion of current interrogation," removal of the Koran as an incentive "will no longer be used at Charleston.")

"Limited number and unique status of detainees in Charleston precludes interaction with other detainees. Argument could be made that this constitutes isolation."

In the "Summary of Findings," it added about Charleston: "Christian chaplain used to provide socialization, but could be perceived as forced proselytization."

For all these problems, the report nevertheless concluded: "No evidence of noncompliance with DoD orders at either facility." The authors did take as an assumption, they wrote, that "treatment provided for in Presidential and SECDEF orders constitutes 'humane treatment.'"

The Law

After President Bush shipped al-Marri to South Carolina, his plan to try al-Marri and other detainees in military commissions hit a serious snag. In a series of decisions, the U.S. Supreme Court invalidated the commissions, saying they trampled on basic legal protections and military justice rules, and violated the 1949 Geneva Convention. Last fall, Congress passed—and Bush signed—the Military Commissions Act, a legal rewrite intended to appease the high court.

The Military Commissions Act throws open the door for the use of secret evidence and coercive interrogation tactics. It also suspends habeas corpus for noncitizens, including legal residents. A cornerstone of the American justice system, habeas corpus is the legal doctrine allowing prisoners to challenge their confinement in court.

Even though al-Marri could now be tried by a military commission, there's no guarantee of that actually happening. And it's not clear that a military commission would try al-Marri in a transparent, public process.

The problem, says Beth Hillman, a former air force officer and professor at the Rutgers School of Law at Camden, is that the Military Commissions Act, in contrast to the rules governing criminal prosecutions, sets no timeline for bringing charges. "If the MCA stands as written, the U.S. government has little motivation to move forward in pressing charges," argues Hillman. "I hope that political pressure will intervene and force a solution, but the legal situation under the MCA gives detainees like al-Marri no reason to hope for either release or trial."

There are two ways to look at the al-Marri narrative. He may truly be the cunning, ruthless character the government has made him out to be. Or he may not. Without a public trial, we'll never know whether al-Marri really is a terrorist, whether he truly was collaborating with bin Laden's minions who attacked the towers.

Hafetz says his client is eager to have his day in criminal court. "Why are they so afraid to go in front of a judge? They're running scared of having a court hearing. To me that speaks volumes," he says. "Part of the purpose of a trial is to get the truth out, to expose what happened."

The case "raises fundamental questions about America and how it values its traditions," Hafetz continues. "Since the nation's founding, we've held that people accused of a crime deserve a trial."

When Ali Saleh Kahlah al-Marri closes his eyes in his blank-walled cell, under the surveillance camera, what does he dream about?

We can't tell you.

Based in San Francisco, **A.C. THOMPSON** is a staff writer with SF Weekly and co-author, with Trevor Paglen, of *Torture Taxi: On the Trail on the CIA's Rendition Flights*.

UNIT 10
Future Threats

Unit Selections
38. **From the War on Terror to Global Counterinsurgency,** Bruce Hoffman
39. **The Terrorism to Come,** Walter Laqueur

Key Points to Consider
- Can Al Qaeda be defeated?
- How great is the risk of a "nuclear 9/11"?
- Can the war on terrorism be won?

Student Web Site
www.mhcls.com/online

Internet References
Further information regarding these Web sites may be found in this book's preface or online.

Centers for Disease Control and Prevention—Bioterrorism
   http://www.bt.cdc.gov
Nuclear Terrorism
   http://www.nci.org/nci/nci.nt.htm

U.S. Air Force photo by Staff Sgt. Derrick C. Goode

Terrorism will, undoubtedly, remain a major policy issue for the United States well into this 21st century. Opinions as to what future perpetrators will look like and what methods they will pursue continue to vary. While some argue that the traditional methods of terrorism, such as bombing, kidnapping, and hostage taking will continue to dominate this millennium, others warn that weapons of mass destruction or weapons of mass disruption, such as biological and chemical weapons, or even nuclear or radiological weapons, will be the weapons of choice for terrorists in the future.

Experts believe that there are certain trends that will characterize international terrorism in the coming years. Some scholars predict that the continuing rise of Islamic extremists will give rise to a new generation of violent, anti-American terrorists. Others warn of a rejuvenation of left-wing terrorism in Europe. Most believe that the tactics employed by terrorists will be more complex. Future terrorism will likely cause more casualties and will involve the use of weapons of mass destruction.

In the first of two articles in this unit, Bruce Hoffman describes a shift in Al Qaeda's operations. He argues that the U.S. Government must "adjust and adapt its strategy, resources, and tactics" to counter the threat. Next, Walter Laqueur in "The Terrorism to Come," treats the reader to a sweeping overview of modern terrorism. He then closes with a hard dose of realism, arguing that ". . . there can be no victory, only an uphill struggle, at times successful, at others not."

From the War on Terror to Global Counterinsurgency

"Not only is Al Qaeda alive and kicking, but it is still actively planning, supporting, and perhaps even directing terrorist attacks on a global canvas."

BRUCE HOFFMAN

Al Qaeda's obituary has been written often since 9-11. "Al Qaeda's Top Primed to Collapse, US Says," trumpeted a *Washington Post* headline two weeks after Khalid Sheikh Mohammed, the mastermind behind the 9-11 attacks, was arrested in March 2003. "I believe the tide has turned in terms of Al Qaeda," said Congressman Porter J. Goss, then-chairman of the US House of Representatives Intelligence Committee and himself a former case officer for the CIA who became its director a year later. "We've got them nailed," an unidentified intelligence expert was quoted, who still more expansively declared, "We're close to dismantling them."

These upbeat assessments continued the following month with the nearly bloodless capture of Baghdad and the failure of Al Qaeda to make good on threats of renewed attacks in retaliation for invasion. Citing administration sources, an April 2003 article in *The Washington Times* reported the prevailing view in official Washington that Al Qaeda's "failure to carry out a successful strike during the US-led military campaign to topple Saddam Hussein has raised questions about their ability to carry out major new attacks."

Despite major terrorist attacks in Jakarta and Istanbul during the latter half of that same year and the escalating insurgency in Iraq, this optimism carried into 2004. "The Al Qaeda of the 9-11 period is under catastrophic stress," Cofer Black, the US State Department's counterterrorism coordinator, declared. "They are being hunted down, their days are numbered."

Then came the Madrid bombings on March 11, 2004, and the deaths of 191 people. The most accurate assessment, perhaps, was therefore the one offered by Al Qaeda itself. "The Americans," Thabet bin Qais, a spokesperson for the movement, said in May 2003, "only have predications and old intelligence left. It will take them a long time to understand the new form of Al Qaeda." Admittedly, while the first part of bin Qais's assertion was not correct, there is more than a grain of truth to the second part. More than three years later Americans are indeed still struggling to understand the changing character and nature of Al Qaeda and the shifting dimensions of the terrorist threat as it has evolved since 9-11.

Today, Al Qaeda is still frequently spoken of as if it were in retreat: a broken and beaten organization, incapable of mounting further attacks on its own, and instead having devolved operational authority either to its various affiliates and associates or to entirely organically produced, homegrown terrorist entities. Nothing could be further from the truth. Al Qaeda in fact is on the march. It has regrouped and reorganized from the setbacks meted out to it by the United States and its coalition partners and allies during the initial phases of the global war on terrorism. It is marshalling its forces to continue the epic struggle begun some 10 years ago.

According to Plan

Al Qaeda is now functioning exactly as its founder and leader, Osama bin Laden, envisioned it. On the one hand, true to the meaning of the Arabic word for the "base of operation" or "foundation" (or, as other translations have it, the "precept" or "method"), Al Qaeda serves as the base or foundation from which worldwide Islamic revolution can be waged. It simultaneously inspires, motivates, and animates radicalized Muslims to join the movement's fight. On the other hand, it continues to exercise core operational and command and control capabilities, directing the implementation of terrorist attacks.

The Al Qaeda of today combines, as it always has, both a "bottom up" approach (encouraging independent thought and action from low or lower-level operatives) and a "top down" approach (issuing orders and still coordinating a far-flung terrorist enterprise with both highly synchronized and autonomous moving parts). Mixing and matching organizational and operational styles whether dictated by particular missions or imposed by circumstances, the Al Qaeda movement, accordingly, can perhaps most usefully be conceptualized as comprising four distinct, though not mutually exclusive, dimensions. In descending order of sophistication, they are: Al Qaeda Central, Al Qaeda Affiliates and Associates, Al Qaeda Locals, and the Al Qaeda Network.

The first category, Al Qaeda Central, comprises the remnants of the pre–9-11 Al Qaeda organization. Although its core leadership includes some of the familiar, established commanders of the past, a number of new players have advanced through the ranks as a result of the death or capture of key Al Qaeda senior-level managers such as Abu Atef, KSM, Hambali, and, more recently, Abu Faraj al-Libi and Abu Hamza Rabia. It is believed that this hard core remains centered in or around the Afghanistan and Pakistan border region and continues to exert actual coordination, if not some direct command and control capability, in commissioning attacks, directing surveillance and collating reconnaissance, planning operations, and approving their execution.

This category comes closest to the Al Qaeda operational model evident in the 1998 East Africa embassy bombings and the 9-11 attacks. Such high-value "spectacular" attacks are entrusted only to Al Qaeda's professional cadre: the most dedicated, committed, and absolutely reliable element of the movement. Previous patterns suggest that these "professional" terrorists are deployed in predetermined and carefully selected teams. They will also have been provided with very specific targeting instructions.

In some cases, such as the East Africa bombings, they may establish contact with, and enlist the assistance of, local sympathizers and supporters. This will be solely for logistical purposes or to enlist these locals to actually execute the attacks. The operation, however, will be planned and directed by the "professional" element with the locals clearly subordinate and playing strictly a supporting, albeit a critical, role.

The movement's second category is Al Qaeda Affiliates and Associates. It embraces formally established insurgent or terrorist groups that over the years have benefited from bin Laden's largesse and spiritual guidance, or have received training, arms, money, and other assistance from Al Qaeda. Among the recipients of this assistance have been terrorist groups and insurgent forces in Uzbekistan, Indonesia, Morocco, the Philippines, Bosnia, and Kashmir, among other places.

By supporting these groups, bin Laden's intentions were threefold. He sought to co-opt these movements' mostly local agendas and channel their efforts toward the cause of global jihad. In addition, he hoped to create a jihadi "critical mass" from these disparate, geographically scattered movements that would one day coalesce into a single, unstoppable force. And, finally, he wanted to foster a dependent relationship whereby, as a quid pro quo for prior Al Qaeda support, these movements would either undertake attacks at Al Qaeda's behest or provide essential local, logistical, and other support to facilitate strikes by the Al Qaeda "professional" cadre.

This affiliate category includes groups such as: al-Ittihad al-Islami (AIAI), the late Abu Musab Zarqawi's Al Qaeda in Mesopotamia (formerly Jamaat al Tawhid wa'l Jihad), Asbat al-Ansar, Ansar al Islam, the Islamic Army of Aden, the Islamic Movement of Uzbekistan (IMU), Jemaah Islamiya (JI), the Libyan Islamic Fighting Group (LIFG), the Moro Islamic Liberation Front (MILF), the Salafist Group for Call and Combat (GSPC), and the various Kashmiri Islamic groups based in Pakistan—for example, Harakat ul Mujahidin (HUM), Jaish-e-Mohammed (JEM), Laskar-e-Tayyiba (LET), and Laskar i Jhangvi (LIJ). Both the number and geographical diversity of these entities offer proof of Al Qaeda's continued influence and vitality.

Fresh Recruits

What I call Al Qaeda Locals comprise the third category. These are dispersed cells of Al Qaeda adherents who have or have had some direct connection with Al Qaeda—no matter how tenuous or evanescent. They appear to fall into two subcategories.

One is made up of individuals who have had some prior terrorism experience—having engaged in a previous jihadi campaign in Algeria, the Balkans, Chechnya, or more recently in Iraq; or having trained in an Al Qaeda facility, whether in Afghanistan, Yemen, or Sudan before 9-11. An example of this kind of individual is Ahmed Ressam, who was arrested in December 1999 at Port Angeles, Washington, shortly after he had entered the United States from Canada. Ressam had belonged to Algeria's Armed Islamic Group (GIA). After being recruited to Al Qaeda, he was provided with a modicum of basic terrorist training in Afghanistan.

In contrast to the core professional cadre, however, Ressam was given very nonspecific, virtually open-ended targeting instructions before being dispatched to North America. Also, unlike the well-funded professional cadre, Ressam was given only $12,000 in "seed money" and instructed to raise the rest of his operational funds from petty thievery. He was told to recruit members for his terrorist cell from among the expatriate Muslim communities in Canada and the United States.

The other subcategory of Al Qaeda Locals conforms to the profile of the four British Muslims responsible for the July 7, 2005, bombings of mass transit targets in London. In contrast to Ressam, none of the London bombers had previously fought in any of the contemporary, iconic Muslim conflicts (Algeria, Chechnya, Kashmir, Bosnia, Afghanistan, Iraq), nor is there conclusive evidence of their having received any training in an Al Qaeda camp in Afghanistan, Yemen, or Sudan before 9-11. Rather, at least the two ringleaders of the London cell were recruited locally, brought to Pakistan for training, and then returned to their homeland with both an attack plan and the knowledge to implement it. They recruited others locally as needed into the cell and undertook a relatively simple but nonetheless sophisticated and highly consequential attack.

In both of these subcategories, the terrorists will have some link with Al Qaeda. Their current relationship and communication with a central Al Qaeda command and control apparatus may be either active or dormant, and similarly their targeting choices may either be specifically directed or else entirely left to the cell to decide. The distinguishing characteristic of these operatives is that there is a previous direct connection of some kind with Al Qaeda.

The movement's fourth and final category is the Al Qaeda Network. These are homegrown Islamic radicals—from North Africa, the Middle East, and South and Southeast Asia—as well as local converts to Islam who mainly live in Europe and Africa, and perhaps Latin America and North America as well. They are like-minded locals who have no direct connection with Al Qaeda, but who gravitate toward each other to plan and mount terrorist attacks in solidarity with or support of Al Qaeda's radical jihadi agenda.

Like the Al Qaeda Locals, they are motivated by a shared sense of enmity and grievance toward the United States and the West in general and toward their host nations in particular. In this instance the relationship with Al Qaeda is more inspirational than actual, abetted by profound rage over the US invasion and occupation of Iraq and the oppression of Muslims in Palestine, Kashmir, Chechnya, and elsewhere.

Critically, these individuals are neither directly members of a known, organized terrorist group nor necessarily even a very cohesive entity unto themselves. Examples of this category include the so-called Hofstad Group in the Netherlands, a member of whom (Mohammed Bouyeri) murdered the Dutch filmmaker Theo Van Gogh in Amsterdam in November 2004.

Americans might cloak themselves in a false sense of security based on faulty assumptions or wishful thinking.

Europe's "Unknown Unknown"

The most salient threat posed by these four categories continues to come from Al Qaeda Central and from its affiliates and associates. However, an additional and equally challenging threat is now posed by less discernible and more unpredictable entities drawn from the vast Muslim diaspora in Europe. As far back as 2001, for example, the Netherlands' intelligence and security services had detected increased terrorist recruitment efforts among Muslim youth living in the Netherlands who, it was previously assumed, had been completely assimilated into Dutch society and culture.

Thus, representatives of Muslim extremist organizations—including, presumably, Al Qaeda—had already succeeded in embedding themselves in, and drawing new sources of support from, receptive elements within established diaspora communities. In this way, new recruits could be drawn into the movement who likely had not previously come under the scrutiny of local or national law enforcement agencies.

This new category of terrorist has proved more difficult for authorities in these countries to track and anticipate. The director of Government Communications Headquarters, Britain's equivalent of America's National Security Agency, admitted this in testimony before a parliamentary committee investigating the London bombings. "We had said before July [2005]," Sir David Pepper noted, that "there are probably groups out there that we do not know anything about, and because we do not know anything about them we do not know how many there are. What happened in July was a demonstration that there were . . . conspiracies going on about which we essentially knew nothing, and that rather sharpens the perception of how big, if I can use [outgoing Secretary of Defense Donald] Rumsfeld's term, the unknown unknown was."

This adversary, comprising hitherto unknown cells, is difficult if not impossible to profile effectively. Some members of these cells may be marginalized individuals working in menial jobs from the lower socioeconomic strata of society, perhaps with long criminal records or histories of juvenile delinquency. Others, however, may come from solidly middle and upper-middle class backgrounds, with university and perhaps even graduate degrees and prior passions for cars, sports, rock music, and other completely secular, material interests.

In the case of radicalized British Muslims, for instance, we have seen since 9-11 the emergence of terrorists of South Asian and North African descent, as well as some hailing from the Middle East and the Caribbean. They have included lifelong devout Muslims as well as recent converts, individuals from the margins of society who made a living as thieves or from drug dealing, and students at the London School Economics, one of Britain's premiere universities.

What they will have in common is a combination of a deep commitment to their faith, often recently rediscovered; admiration of bin Laden for the cathartic blow struck against America on 9-11; hatred of the United States and the West; and a profoundly shared sense of alienation from their host countries.

"There appear to be a number of common features to this grooming," a report by the Intelligence and Security Committee of the British House of Commons concluded. "In the early stages, group conversation may be around being a good Muslim and staying away from drugs and crime, with no hint of an extremist agenda. Gradually individuals may be exposed to propaganda about perceived injustices to Muslims across the world, with international conflict involving Muslims interpreted as examples of widespread war against Islam; leaders of the Muslim world perceived as corrupt and non-Islamic; with some domestic policies added as 'evidence' of a persecuted Islam; and conspiracy theories abounding."

"They will then move on," the committee's report continued, "to what the extremists claim is religious justification for violent jihad in the Quran and the Hadith . . . and—if suicide attacks are the intention—the importance of martyrdom in demonstrating commitment to Islam and the rewards in Paradise for martyrs; before directly inviting an individual to engage in terrorism. There is little evidence of overt compulsion. The extremists appear rather to rely on the development of individual commitment and group bonding and solidarity."

These new recruits are the anonymous cogs in the worldwide Al Qaeda enterprise and include both longstanding residents and new immigrants found across Europe, but specifically in countries with large expatriate Muslim populations such as

Britain, Spain, France, Germany, Italy, the Netherlands, and Belgium.

Wishful Thinking

The United Kingdom rightly prides itself on decades-long experience and detailed knowledge of effectively countering a variety of terrorist threats. Over the past dozen years, the UK homeland itself has been subject to attack from adversaries that include the Provisional Irish Republican Army, renegade Palestinian factions, and, both before and since 9-11, Al Qaeda as well. Yet, despite Britain's formidable counterterrorist capabilities and unrivaled expertise, only a month before the July 2005 London bombings, its Joint Terrorism Assessment Center concluded that, "at present there is not a group with both the current intent and the capability to attack in the UK." The center consequently downgraded the overall threat level for the country.

More astonishing perhaps was the dismissal of the prospect of suicide attacks occurring in the United Kingdom, despite the emerging global pattern of terrorism in this respect and the involvement of several British nationals in both attempted and successful suicide attacks elsewhere. Seventy-eight percent of all the suicide terrorist incidents perpetrated between 1968 and 2004 had occurred in the years following 9-11. And the dominant force behind this trend is religion—specifically, groups and individuals identifying themselves as Islamic.

Of the 35 terrorist organizations currently employing suicide tactics, 31 are Islamic. These movements, moreover, have been responsible for 81 percent of all suicide attacks since 9-11. To date, suicide attacks have taken place in at least two dozen countries, including the United Kingdom, Israel, Sri Lanka, Russia, Lebanon, Turkey, Italy, Indonesia, Pakistan, Colombia, Argentina, Kenya, Tanzania, Croatia, Morocco, Singapore, the Philippines, Saudi Arabia, Kuwait, and Iraq. By comparison, at the dawn of the modern era of religious terrorism some 20 years ago, this was a phenomenon confined exclusively to two countries—Lebanon and Kuwait—and employed by less than a half dozen groups.

Yet, only four months before the 7-7 bombings, the Joint Intelligence Committee, Britain's most senior intelligence assessment and evaluation body, judged that "such attacks would not become the norm within Europe." This judgment, coupled with the testimony of Dame Eliza Manningham-Buller, the director general of the Security Service (MI-5), prompted the aforementioned parliamentary committee to conclude that "it was a surprise that the first big attack in the UK for 10 years was a suicide attack."

The point of this discussion is most certainly not to criticize Washington's principal ally in the war on terrorism but rather to highlight the immense difficulties and vast uncertainties concerning countering terrorism today, problems that have confounded even the enormously professional and experienced British intelligence and security services. In so fluid and dynamic a terrorism environment as exists today, there is a danger that Americans might similarly cloak themselves in a false sense of security based on faulty assumptions or wishful thinking.

Indeed, Americans' appreciation and understanding of the current Al Qaeda threat further underscore these perils. Both at the time of the London bombings and since, a misconception has frequently been perpetuated that this was entirely an organic or homegrown phenomenon of self-radicalized, self-selected terrorists. Such arguments often were cited in support of the view that entirely homegrown threats had superseded those posed by Al Qaeda; that Al Qaeda itself was no longer a consequential, active, terrorist force; and, accordingly, that the threat had both changed and perhaps even receded.

Produced in Pakistan?

The evidence that has come to light since the London bombings points to the opposite conclusion: not only is Al Qaeda alive and kicking, but it is still actively planning, supporting, and perhaps even directing terrorist attacks on a global canvas.

Issues of classification and sensitive collection prevent a full description and account of this evidence of active Al Qaeda involvement in the London attacks. However, suffice it to say that what is publicly known and has been reported in unclassified sources clearly points to such involvement.

For instance, the report by the parliament's Intelligence and Security Committee noted that "investigations since July have shown that the group [the four London bombers] was in contact with others involved in extremism in the UK. . . . Siddique Khan [the group's ringleader] is now known to have visited Pakistan in 2003 and to have spent several months there with Shazad Tanweer [another bomber] between November 2004 and February 2005. It has not yet been established who they met in Pakistan, but it is assessed as likely that they had some contact with Al Qaeda figures."

The effectiveness of US strategy will be based on the capacity to think like a networked enemy.

More compelling, albeit for the moment necessarily circumstantial, evidence may be found in the "martyrdom" videos made by Khan and Tanweer some time while they were in Pakistan between November 2004 and February 2005. Like all of bin Laden's most important videotaped statements and appearances, the Khan and Tanweer statements were both professionally produced and released by Al Qaeda's perennially active communications department.

The first of the two videos, of Khan, was broadcast on the Qatar-based Arabic-language news station al Jazeera on September 1, 2005. It is worth exploring the content of this video since it accurately encapsulates the essence of European Muslim radicalism today. Khan's statement is noteworthy for several reasons.

For one, he professes his preeminent allegiance to and identification with his religion and the umma—the worldwide Muslim community. Hence, unlike most Western conceptions of identity and allegiance that are rooted to the nation or state, Khan's is exclusively to a theology. Second, like all terrorists before him, Khan frames his choice of tactic and justifies his actions in ineluctably defensive terms. He describes his struggle as an intrinsically defensive one and his act as a response to the repeated depredations and unmitigated aggression of the West that have been directed against Muslims worldwide.

Third, Khan's words and demeanor display a sense of individual empowerment and catharsis. He shows an intense desire for vengeance and martyrdom, the latter of which he regards as "supreme evidence" of his religious commitment. And, finally, Khan's statement includes laudatory comments about bin Laden and his deputy, Ayman al-Zawahiri.

Not Enough Bullets

Al Qaeda and the threat that it poses cannot be defeated through military means alone. Yet America's policy to date has been predominantly weighted toward the tactical "kill or capture" approach and metric. This assumes that a traditional center of gravity exists, whether the target is Al Qaeda or the insurgency in Iraq, and that this target simply needs to be destroyed so that global terrorism or the Iraqi insurgency will end.

> **Al Qaeda in fact is on the march. It is marshalling its forces to continue the epic struggle begun some 10 years ago.**

In fact, America's adversaries today are much more elusive and complicated, and less amenable to kinetic solutions. As one us intelligence officer with vast experience in this realm acerbically told me nearly two years ago: "We don't have enough bullets to kill them all."

Accordingly, a new approach is vital. Its success will depend on a strategy that combines the tactical elements of systematically destroying and weakening enemy capabilities (the "kill or capture" approach) alongside the equally critical, broader strategic imperative of breaking the cycle of terrorist recruitment and insurgent replenishment that has respectively sustained both Al Qaeda's continued campaign and the ongoing conflict in Iraq. A successful strategy will be one that also thinks and plans ahead with a view toward addressing threats likely to be posed by the terrorist and insurgent generation beyond the current one.

At the foundation of such a dynamic and adaptive strategy must be the axiom that effectively countering terrorism as well as insurgency is not exclusively a military endeavor but also involves parallel political, social, economic, and ideological activities. This timeless principle of countering insurgency was first defined by Field Marshal Sir Gerald Templer in Malaya more than 50 years ago. "The shooting side of the business is only 25 percent of the trouble and the other 75 percent lies in getting the people of this country behind us," Templer famously wrote in 1952.

Rather than viewing the fundamental organizing principle of US national defense strategy in this unconventional realm as a global war on terror, it may be more useful to re-conceptualize it in terms of a global counterinsurgency. Such an approach would knit together the equally critical political, economic, diplomatic, and developmental sides inherent to the successful prosecution of counter-insurgency with the existing, dominant military side of the equation.

This approach would necessarily be built on a more integrated, systems approach to a complex problem that is at once operationally durable, evolutionary, and elusive in character. Greater attention to this integration of US capabilities would provide recognition of the importance of endowing a global counterinsurgency with an overriding and comprehensive, multidimensional policy. Ideally, this policy would embrace several elements, including a clear strategy, a defined structure for implementing it, and both a vision of intergovernment agency cooperation and the unified effort to guide it.

It would have particular benefit in the gathering and exploitation of "actionable" intelligence. By updating and streamlining interagency counterterrorism and counterinsurgency systems and procedures both strategically and operationally among the Department of Defense, the Department of State, and the intelligence community, actionable intelligence could likely be acquired, analyzed, and disseminated faster and operations mounted more quickly.

A more focused and strengthened interagency process would also facilitate the coordination of key themes and messages and the development and execution of long-term "hearts and minds" initiatives.

Think Like the Enemy

The US government, in sum, will need to adjust and adapt its strategy, resources, and tactics to formidable opponents that, as we have seen, are widely dispersed and decentralized and whose many destructive parts are autonomous, mobile, and themselves highly adaptive. In this respect, even the best strategy will be proved inadequate if military and civilian agency leaders are not prepared to engage successfully within ambiguous environments and reorient their organizational culture to deal with irregular threats.

A successful global counterinsurgency transcends the need for better tactical intelligence or new organizations. It is fundamentally about transforming the attitudes and mindsets of leaders so that they have the capacity to take decisive yet thoughtful action against terrorists and/or insurgents in uncertain or unclear situations based on a common vision, policy, and strategy.

In addition to traditional "hard" military skills of "kill or capture" and destruction and attrition, "soft" skills such as information operations, negotiation, psychology, social and cultural anthropology, foreign area studies, complexity theory, and systems management will become increasingly important in the ambiguous and dynamic environment in which irregular adversaries circulate.

By combating irregular adversaries in a more collaborative manner with key civilian agencies, military planners can better share critical information, track the various moving parts in terrorist/ insurgency networks, and develop a comprehensive picture of this enemy—including their supporters, nodes of support, organizational and operational systems, processes, and plans. With this information in hand, the United States would then be better prepared to systematically disrupt or defeat all of the critical nodes that support the entire terrorist/insurgent network.

An equally critical dimension of this process will be aligning the training of host-nation counterparts with the global war on terror/global counterinsurgency operations: building synergy, avoiding duplication of effort, ensuring that training leads to operational effectiveness, and ensuring that the US interagency team and approach are in complete harmony.

The effectiveness of US strategy will be based on the capacity to think like a networked enemy, in anticipation of how it may act in a variety of situations, aided by different resources. This goal requires that the American national security structure in turn organize itself for maximum efficiency, information sharing, and the ability to function quickly and effectively under new operational definitions. With this understanding in mind, the new approach would need to take into account several factors critical to effectively waging a global counterinsurgency.

The Shark in the Water

Success depends, first, on separating the enemy from the populace that provides support and sustenance. This, in turn, entails three basic missions: denial of enemy sanctuary; elimination of enemy freedom of movement; and denial of enemy resources and support. In addition, the enemy must be identified and neutralized. And a secure environment must be created, progressing from local to regional to global arenas.

A successful global counterinsurgency also requires ongoing and effective neutralization of the enemy's propaganda through the planning and execution of comprehensive, integrated information operations and a holistic civil affairs campaign in harmony with the other tasks. Finally, interagency efforts are needed to build effective and responsible civil governance mechanisms that eliminate the fundamental causes of terrorism and insurgency.

Al Qaeda may be compared to the archetypal shark in the water that must keep moving forward— no matter how slowly or incrementally—or die. In Al Qaeda's context, this means adapting to the countermeasures of the United States and its allies while simultaneously searching to identify new targets and vulnerabilities. In this respect, Al Qaeda's capacity to continue to prosecute this struggle is a direct reflection of both the movement's resiliency and the continued resonance of its ideology.

Likewise, if the threat facing America and the West is constantly changing and evolving, so must their policies and responses be regularly reviewed, updated, and adjusted. In this struggle, Americans cannot afford to rest on past laurels. They cannot remain content with security that may have been effective yesterday and today, but that might well prove inadequate tomorrow given this process of terrorist evolution and adaptation.

Al Qaeda's operational durability thus has enormous importance for US counterterrorism strategy and policy. Because Al Qaeda has this malleable resiliency, it cannot be destroyed or defeated in a single tactical, military engagement or series of engagements—much less ones exclusively dependent on the application of conventional forces and firepower. To a significant degree, Washington's ability to carry out such missions effectively will depend on its ability to adjust strategies to changes in the nature and character of its adversaries.

BRUCE HOFFMAN *is a professor at Georgetown University's Edmund A. Walsh School of Foreign Service. He is the author of* Inside Terrorism *(Columbia University Press, 2nd edition, 2006).*

Reprinted from *Current History,* December 2006, pp. 423–429. Copyright © 2006 by Current History, Inc. Reprinted with permission.

The Terrorism to Come

WALTER LAQUEUR

Terrorism has become over a number of years the topic of ceaseless comment, debate, controversy, and search for roots and motives, and it figures on top of the national and international agenda. It is also at present one of the most highly emotionally charged topics of public debate, though quite why this should be the case is not entirely clear, because the overwhelming majority of participants do not sympathize with terrorism.

Confusion prevails, but confusion alone does not explain the emotions. There is always confusion when a new international phenomenon appears on the scene. This was the case, for instance, when communism first appeared (it was thought to be aiming largely at the nationalization of women and the burning of priests) and also fascism. But terrorism is not an unprecedented phenomenon; it is as old as the hills.

Thirty years ago, when the terrorism debate got underway, it was widely asserted that terrorism was basically a left-wing revolutionary movement caused by oppression and exploitation. Hence the conclusion: Find a political and social solution, remedy the underlying evil—no oppression, no terrorism. The argument about the left-wing character of terrorism is no longer frequently heard, but the belief in a fatal link between poverty and violence has persisted. Whenever a major terrorist attack has taken place, one has heard appeals from high and low to provide credits and loans, to deal at long last with the deeper, true causes of terrorism, the roots rather than the symptoms and outward manifestations. And these roots are believed to be poverty, unemployment, backwardness, and inequality.

It is not too difficult to examine whether there is such a correlation between poverty and terrorism, and all the investigations have shown that this is not the case. The experts have maintained for a long time that poverty does not cause terrorism and prosperity does not cure it. In the world's 50 poorest countries there is little or no terrorism. A study by scholars Alan Krueger and Jitka Maleckova reached the conclusion that the terrorists are not poor people and do not come from poor societies. A Harvard economist has shown that economic growth is closely related to a society's ability to manage conflicts. More recently, a study of India has demonstrated that terrorism in the subcontinent has occurred in the most prosperous (Punjab) and most egalitarian (Kashmir, with a poverty ratio of 3.5 compared with the national average of 26 percent) regions and that, on the other hand, the poorest regions such as North Bihar have been free of terrorism. In the Arab countries (such as Egypt and Saudi Arabia, but also in North Africa), the terrorists originated not in the poorest and most neglected districts but hailed from places with concentrations of radical preachers. The backwardness, if any, was intellectual and cultural—not economic and social.

It is no secret that terrorists operating in Europe and America are usually of middle-class origin.

These findings, however, have had little impact on public opinion (or on many politicians), and it is not difficult to see why. There is the general feeling that poverty and backwardness with all their concomitants are bad—and that there is an urgent need to do much more about these problems. Hence the inclination to couple the two issues and the belief that if the (comparatively) wealthy Western nations would contribute much more to the development and welfare of the less fortunate, in cooperation with their governments, this would be in a long-term perspective the best, perhaps the only, effective way to solve the terrorist problem.

Reducing poverty in the Third World is a moral as well as a political and economic imperative, but to expect from it a decisive change in the foreseeable future as far as terrorism is concerned is unrealistic, to say the least. It ignores both the causes of backwardness and poverty and the motives for terrorism.

Poverty combined with youth unemployment does create a social and psychological climate in which Islamism and various populist and religious sects flourish, which in turn provide some of the footfolk for violent groups in internal conflicts. According to some projections, the number of young unemployed in the Arab world and North Africa could reach 50 million in two decades. Such a situation will not be conducive to political stability; it will increase the demographic pressure on Europe, since according to polls a majority of these young people want to emigrate. Politically, the populist discontent will be directed against the rulers—Islamist in Iran, moderate in countries such as Egypt, Jordan, or Morocco. But how to help the failed economies of the Middle East and North Africa? What are the reasons for backwardness and stagnation in this part of the world? The countries that have made economic progress—such as China and India, Korea and Taiwan, Malaysia and Turkey—did so without massive foreign help.

All this points to a deep malaise and impending danger, but not to a direct link between the economic situation and international terrorism. There is of course a negative link: Terrorists will not hesitate to bring about a further aggravation in the situation; they certainly did great harm to the tourist industries in Bali and Egypt, in Palestine, Jordan, and Morocco. One of the main targets of terrorism in Iraq was the oil industry. It is no longer a secret that the carriers of international terrorism operating in Europe and America hail not from the poor, downtrodden, and unemployed but are usually of middle-class origin.

The Local Element

The link between terrorism and nationalist, ethnic, religious, and tribal conflict is far more tangible. These instances of terrorism are many and need not be enumerated in detail. Solving these conflicts would probably bring about a certain reduction in the incidence of terrorism. But the conflicts are many, and if some of them have been defused in recent years, other, new ones have emerged. Nor are the issues usually clear-cut or the bones of contention easy to define—let alone to solve.

If the issue at stake is a certain territory or the demand for autonomy, a compromise through negotiations might be achieved. But it ought to be recalled that al Qaeda was founded and September 11 occurred not because of a territorial dispute or the feeling of national oppression but because of a religious commandment—jihad and the establishment of *shari'ah*. Terrorist attacks in Central Asia and Morocco, in Saudi Arabia, Algeria, and partly in Iraq were directed against fellow Muslims, not against infidels. Appeasement may work in individual cases, but terrorist groups with global ambitions cannot be appeased by territorial concessions.

As in the war against poverty, the initiatives to solve local conflicts are overdue and should be welcomed. In an ideal world, the United Nations would be the main conflict resolver, but so far the record of the U.N. has been more than modest, and it is unlikely that this will change in the foreseeable future. Making peace is not an easy option; it involves funds and in some cases the stationing of armed forces. There is no great international crush to join the ranks of the volunteers: China, Russia, and Europe do not want to be bothered, and the United States is overstretched. In brief, as is so often the case, a fresh impetus is likely to occur only if the situation gets considerably worse and if the interests of some of the powers in restoring order happen to coincide.

Lastly, there should be no illusions with regard to the wider effect of a peaceful solution of one conflict or another. To give but one obvious example: Peace (or at least the absence of war) between Israel and the Palestinians would be a blessing for those concerned. It may be necessary to impose a solution since the chances of making any progress in this direction are nil but for some outside intervention. However, the assumption that a solution of a local conflict (even one of great symbolic importance) would have a dramatic effect in other parts of the world is unfounded. Osama bin Laden did not go to war because of Gaza and Nablus; he did not send his warriors to fight in Palestine. Even the disappearance of the "Zionist entity" would not have a significant impact on his supporters, except perhaps to provide encouragement for further action.

Osama bin Laden did not go to war because of Gaza and Nablus.

Such a warning against illusions is called for because there is a great deal of wishful thinking and naïveté in this respect—a belief in quick fixes and miracle solutions: If only there would be peace between Israelis and Palestinians, all the other conflicts would become manageable. But the problems are as much in Europe, Asia, and Africa as in the Middle East; there is a great deal of free-floating aggression which could (and probably would) easily turn in other directions once one conflict has been defused.

It seems likely, for instance, that in the years to come the struggle against the "near enemy" (the governments of the Arab and some non-Arab Muslim countries) will again feature prominently. There has been for some time a truce on the part of al Qaeda and related groups, partly for strategic reasons (to concentrate on the fight against America and the West) and partly because attacks against fellow Muslims, even if they are considered apostates, are bound to be less popular than fighting the infidels. But this truce, as events in Saudi Arabia and elsewhere show, may be coming to an end.

Tackling these supposed sources of terrorism, even for the wrong reasons, will do no harm and may bring some good. But it does not bring us any nearer to an understanding of the real sources of terrorism, a field that has become something akin to a circus ground for riding hobbyhorses and peddling preconceived notions.

How to explain the fact that in an inordinate number of instances where there has been a great deal of explosive material, there has been no terrorism? The gypsies of Europe certainly had many grievances and the Dalets (untouchables) of India and other Asian countries even more. But there has been no terrorism on their part—just as the Chechens have been up in arms but not the Tartars of Russia, the Basque but not the Catalans of Spain. The list could easily be lengthened.

Accident may play a role (the absence or presence of a militant leadership), but there could also be a cultural-psychological predisposition. How to explain that out of 100 militants believing with equal intensity in the justice of their cause, only a very few will actually engage in terrorist actions? And out of this small minority even fewer will be willing to sacrifice their lives as suicide bombers? Imponderable factors might be involved: indoctrination but also psychological motives. Neither economic nor political analysis will be of much help in gaining an understanding, and it may not be sheer accident that there has been great reluctance to explore this political-intellectual minefield.

The Focus on Islamist Terrorism

To make predictions about the future course of terrorism is even more risky than political predictions in general. We are dealing here not with mass movements but small—sometimes very small—groups of people, and there is no known way at present to account for the movement of small particles either in the physical world or in human societies.

It is certain that terrorism will continue to operate. At the present time almost all attention is focused on Islamist terrorism, but it is useful to remember from time to time that this was not always the case—even less than 30 years ago—and that there are a great many conflicts, perceived oppressions, and other causes calling for radical action in the world which may come to the fore in the years to come. These need not even be major conflicts in an age in which small groups will have access to weapons of mass destruction.

At present, Islamist terrorism all but monopolizes our attention, and it certainly has not yet run its course. But it is unlikely that its present fanaticism will last forever; religious-nationalist fervor does not constantly burn with the same intensity. There is a phenomenon known in Egypt as "Salafi burnout," the mellowing of radical young people, the weakening of the original fanatical impetus. Like all other movements in history, messianic groups are subject to routinization, to the circulation of generations, to changing political circumstances, and to sudden or gradual changes in the intensity of religious belief. This could happen as a result of either victories or defeats. One day, it might be possible to appease militant Islamism—though hardly in a period of burning aggression when confidence and faith in global victory have not yet been broken.

More likely the terrorist impetus will decline as a result of setbacks. Fanaticism, as history shows, is not easy to transfer from one generation to the next; attacks will continue, and some will be crowned with success (perhaps spectacular success), but many will not. When Alfred Nobel invented dynamite, many terrorists thought that this was the answer to their prayers, but theirs was a false hope. The trust put today in that new invincible weapon, namely suicide terrorism, may in the end be equally misplaced. Even the use of weapons of mass destruction might not be the terrorist panacea some believe it will be. Perhaps their effect will be less deadly than anticipated; perhaps it will be so destructive as to be considered counterproductive. Statistics show that in the terrorist attacks over the past decade, considerably more Muslims were killed than infidels. Since terrorists do not operate in a vacuum, this is bound to lead to dissent among their followers and even among the fanatical preachers.

Over the past decade, more Muslims were killed in terrorist attacks than infidels.

There are likely to be splits among the terrorist groups even though their structure is not highly centralized. In brief, there is a probability that a united terrorist front will not last. It is unlikely that Osama and his close followers will be challenged on theological grounds, but there has been criticism for tactical reasons: Assuming that America and the West in general are in a state of decline, why did he not have more patience? Why did he have to launch a big attack while the infidels were still in a position to retaliate massively?

Some leading students of Islam have argued for a long time that radical Islamism passed its peak years ago and that its downfall and disappearance are only a question of time, perhaps not much time. It is true that societies that were exposed to the rule of fundamentalist fanatics (such as Iran) or to radical Islamist attack (such as Algeria) have been immunized to a certain extent. However, in a country of 60 million, some fanatics can always be found; as these lines are written, volunteers for suicide missions are being enlisted in Teheran and other cities of Iran. In any case, many countries have not yet undergone such first-hand experience; for them the rule of the *shari'ah* and the restoration of the caliphate are still brilliant dreams. By and large, therefore, the predictions about the impending demise of Islamism have been premature, while no doubt correct in the long run. Nor do we know what will follow. An interesting study on what happens "when prophecy fails" (by Leon Festinger) was published not long after World War II. We now need a similar study on the likely circumstances and consequences of the failure of fanaticism. The history of religions (and political religions) offers some clues, as does the history of terrorism.

These, then, are the likely perspectives for the more distant future. But in a shorter-term perspective the danger remains acute and may, in fact, grow. Where and when are terrorist attacks most likely to occur? They will not necessarily be directed against the greatest and most dangerous enemy as perceived by the terrorist gurus. Much depends on where terrorists are strong and believe the enemy to be weak. That terrorist attacks are likely to continue in the Middle East goes without saying; other main danger zones are Central Asia and, above all, Pakistan.

The founders of Pakistan were secular politicians. The religious establishment and in particular the extremists among the Indian Muslims had opposed the emergence of the state. But once Pakistan came into being, they began to try with considerable success to dominate it. Their alternative educational system, the many thousand madrassas, became the breeding ground for jihad fighters. Ayub Khan, the first military ruler, tried to break their stranglehold but failed. Subsequent rulers, military and civilian, have not even tried. It is more than doubtful whether Pervez Musharraf will have any success in limiting their power. The tens of thousands of graduates they annually produce formed the backbone of the Taliban. Their leaders will find employment for them at home and in Central Asia, even if there is a deescalation in tensions with India over Kashmir. Their most radical leaders aim at the destruction of India. Given Pakistan's internal weakness this may appear more than a little fanciful, but their destructive power is still considerable, and they can count on certain sympathies in the army and the intelligence service. A failed Pakistan with nuclear weapons at its disposal would be a major nightmare. Still, Pakistani terrorism—like Palestinian and Middle Eastern in general—remains territorial, likely to be limited to the subcontinent and Central Asia.

Battlefield Europe

Europe is probably the most vulnerable battlefield. To carry out operations in Europe and America, talents are needed that are not normally found among those who have no direct personal experience of life in the West. The Pakistani diaspora has not been very active in the terrorist field, except for a few militants in the United Kingdom.

Western Europe has become over a number of years the main base of terrorist support groups. This process has been facilitated by the growth of Muslim communities, the growing tensions with the native population, and the relative freedom with which radicals could organize in certain mosques and cultural organizations. Indoctrination was provided by militants who came to these countries as religious dignitaries. This freedom of action was considerably greater than that enjoyed in the Arab and Muslim world; not a few terrorists convicted of capital crimes in countries such as Egypt, Jordan, Morocco, and Algeria were given political asylum in Europe. True, there were some arrests and closer controls after September 11, but given the legal and political restrictions under which the European security services were laboring, effective counteraction was still exceedingly difficult.

West European governments have been frequently criticized for not having done enough to integrate Muslim newcomers into their societies, but cultural and social integration was certainly not what the newcomers wanted. They wanted to preserve their religious and ethnic identity and their way of life, and they resented intervention by secular authorities. In its great majority, the first generation of immigrants wanted to live in peace and quiet and to make a living for their families. But today they no longer have much control over their offspring.

> **Non-Muslims began to feel threatened in streets they could once walk without fear.**

This is a common phenomenon all over the world: the radicalization of the second generation of immigrants. This generation has been superficially acculturated (speaking fluently the language of the host country) yet at the same time feels resentment and hostility more acutely. It is not necessarily the power of the fundamentalist message (the young are not the most pious believers when it comes to carrying out all the religious commandments) which inspires many of the younger radical activists or sympathizers. It is the feeling of deep resentment because, unlike immigrants from other parts of the world, they could not successfully compete in the educational field, nor quite often make it at the work place. Feelings of being excluded, sexual repression (a taboo subject in this context), and other factors led to free-floating aggression and crime directed against the authorities and their neighbors.

As a result, non-Muslims began to feel threatened in streets they could once walk without fear. They came to regard the new immigrants as antisocial elements who wanted to change the traditional character of their homeland and their way of life, and consequently tensions continued to increase. Pressure on European governments is growing from all sides, right and left, to stop immigration and to restore law and order.

This, in briefest outline, is the milieu in which Islamist terrorism and terrorist support groups in Western Europe developed. There is little reason to assume that this trend will fundamentally change in the near future. On the contrary, the more the young generation of immigrants asserts itself, the more violence occurs in the streets, and the more terrorist attacks take place, the greater the anti-Muslim resentment on the part of the rest of the population. The rapid demographic growth of the Muslim communities further strengthens the impression among the old residents that they are swamped and deprived of their rights in their own homeland, not even entitled to speak the truth about the prevailing situation (such as, for instance, to reveal the statistics of prison inmates with Muslim backgrounds). Hence the violent reaction in even the most liberal European countries such as the Netherlands, Belgium, and Denmark. The fear of the veil turns into the fear that in the foreseeable future they too, having become a minority, will be compelled to conform to the commandments of another religion and culture.

True, the number of extremists is still very small. Among British Muslims, for instance, only 13 percent have expressed sympathy and support for terrorist attacks. But this still amounts to several hundred thousands, far more than needed for staging a terrorist campaign. The figure is suspect in any case because not all of those sharing radical views will openly express them to strangers, for reasons that hardly need be elaborated. Lastly, such a minority will not feel isolated in their own community as long as the majority remains silent—which has been the case in France and most other European countries.

> **Extremists may be repelled by the decadence of the society facing them, but they are also attracted by it.**

The prospects for terrorism based on a substantial Islamist periphery could hardly appear to be more promising, but there are certain circumstances that make the picture appear somewhat less threatening. The tensions are not equally strong in all countries. They are less palpably felt in Germany and Britain than in France and the Netherlands. Muslims in Germany are predominantly of Turkish origin and have (always with some exceptions) shown less inclination to take violent action than communities mainly composed of Arab and North African immigrants.

If acculturation and integration has been a failure in the short run, prospects are less hopeless in a longer perspective. The temptations of Western civilization are corrosive; young Muslims cannot be kept in a hermetically sealed ghetto (even though a strong attempt is made). They are disgusted and repelled by alcohol, loose morals, general decadence, and all the other wickedness of the society facing them, but they are at the same time fascinated and attracted by them. This is bound to affect their activist fervor, and they will be exposed not only to the negative aspects of the world surrounding them but also its values. Other religions had to face these temptations over the ages and by and large have been fighting a losing battle.

It is often forgotten that only a relatively short period passed from the primitive beginnings of Islam in the Arabian desert to the splendor and luxury (and learning and poetry) of Harun al Rashid's Baghdad—from the austerity of the Koran to the not-so-austere Arabian Nights. The pulse of contemporary history is beating much faster, but is it beating fast enough? For it is a race against time. The advent of megaterrorism and the access to weapons of mass destruction is dangerous enough, but coupled with fanaticism it generates scenarios too unpleasant even to contemplate.

Enduring Asymmetry

There can be no final victory in the fight against terrorism, for terrorism (rather than full-scale war) is the contemporary manifestation of conflict, and conflict will not disappear from earth as far as one can look ahead and human nature has not undergone a basic change. But it will be in our power to make life for terrorists and potential terrorists much more difficult.

Who ought to conduct the struggle against terrorism? Obviously, the military should play only a limited role in this context, and not only because it has not been trained for this purpose. The military may have to be called in for restoring order in countries that have failed to function and have become terrorist havens. It may have to intervene to prevent or stop massacres. It may be needed to deliver blows against terrorist concentrations. But these are not the most typical or frequent terrorist situations.

The key role in asymmetric warfare (a redundant new term for something that has been known for many centuries) should be played by intelligence and security services that may need a military arm.

As far as terrorism and also guerrilla warfare are concerned, there can be no general, overall doctrine in the way that Clausewitz or Jomini and others developed a regular warfare philosophy. An airplane or a battleship do not change their character wherever they operate, but the character of terrorism and guerrilla warfare depends largely on the motivations of those engaging in it and the conditions under which it takes place. Over the past centuries rules and laws of war have developed, and even earlier on there were certain rules that were by and large adhered to.

But terrorists cannot possibly accept these rules. It would be suicidal from their point of view if, to give but one example, they were to wear uniforms or other distinguishing marks. The essence of their operations rests on hiding their identities. On the other hand, they and their well-wishers insist that when captured, they should enjoy all the rights and benefits accorded to belligerents, that they be humanely treated, even paid some money and released after the end of hostilities. When regular soldiers do not stick to the rules of warfare, killing or maiming prisoners, carrying out massacres, taking hostages or committing crimes against the civilian population, they will be treated as war criminals.

If terrorists behaved according to these norms they would have little if any chance of success; the essence of terrorist operations now is indiscriminate attacks against civilians. But governments defending themselves against terrorism are widely expected not to behave in a similar way but to adhere to international law as it developed in conditions quite different from those prevailing today.

Terrorism does not accept laws and rules, whereas governments are bound by them; this, in briefest outline, is asymmetric warfare. If governments were to behave in a similar way, not feeling bound by existing rules and laws such as those against the killing of prisoners, this would be bitterly denounced. When the late Syrian President Hafez Assad faced an insurgency (and an attempted assassination) on the part of the Muslim Brotherhood in the city of Hama in 1980, his soldiers massacred some 20,000 inhabitants. This put an end to all ideas of terrorism and guerrilla warfare.

Such behavior on the part of democratic governments would be denounced as barbaric, a relapse into the practices of long-gone pre-civilized days. But if governments accept the principle of asymmetric warfare they will be severely, possibly fatally, handicapped. They cannot accept that terrorists are protected by the Geneva Conventions, which would mean, among other things, that they should be paid a salary while in captivity. Should they be regarded like the pirates of a bygone age as *hostes generis humani,* enemies of humankind, and be treated according to the principle of *a un corsaire, un corsaire et demi*—"to catch a thief, it takes a thief," to quote one of Karl Marx's favorite sayings?

Should terrorists be regarded, like pirates of a bygone age, as enemies of humankind?

The problem will not arise if the terrorist group is small and not very dangerous. In this case normal legal procedures will be sufficient to deal with the problem (but even this is not quite certain once weapons of mass destruction become more readily accessible). Nor will the issue of shedding legal restraint arise if the issues at stake are of marginal importance, if in other words no core interests of the governments involved are concerned. If, on the other hand, the very survival of a society is at stake, it is most unlikely that governments will be impeded in their defense by laws and norms belonging to a bygone (and more humane) age.

It is often argued that such action is counterproductive because terrorism cannot be defeated by weapons alone, but is a struggle for the hearts and minds of people, a confrontation of ideas (or ideologies). If it were only that easy. It is not the terrorist ideas which cause the damage, but their weapons. Each case is different, but many terrorist groups do not have any specific idea or ideology, but a fervent belief, be it of a religious character or of a political religion. They fight for demands, territorial or otherwise, that seem to them self-evident, and they want to defeat their enemies. They are not open to dialogue or rational debate. When Mussolini was asked about his program by the socialists during the early days of fascism, he said that his program was to smash the skulls of the socialists.

Experience teaches that a little force is indeed counterproductive except in instances where small groups are involved. The use of massive, overwhelming force, on the other hand, is usually effective. But the use of massive force is almost always unpopular at home and abroad, and it will be applied only if core interests of the state are involved. To give but one example: The Russian government could deport the Chechens (or a significant portion), thus solving the problem according to the Stalinist pattern. If the Chechens were to threaten Moscow or St. Petersburg or the functioning of the Russian state or its fuel supply, there is but little doubt that such measures would be taken by the Russian or indeed any other government. But as long as the threat is only a marginal and peripheral one, the price to be paid for the application of massive force will be considered too high.

Two lessons follow: First, governments should launch an antiterrorist campaign only if they are able and willing to apply massive force if need be. Second, terrorists have to ask themselves whether it is in their own best interest to cross the line between nuisance operations and attacks that threaten the vital interests of their enemies and will inevitably lead to massive counterblows.

Terrorists want total war—not in the sense that they will (or could) mobilize unlimited resources; in this respect their possibilities are limited. But they want their attacks to be unfettered by laws, norms, regulations, and conventions. In the terrorist conception of warfare there is no room for the Red Cross.

Love or Respect?

The why-do-they-hate-us question is raised in this context, along with the question of what could be done about it—that is, the use of soft power in combating terrorism. Disturbing figures have been published about the low (and decreasing) popularity of America in foreign parts. Yet it is too often forgotten that international relations is not a popularity contest and that big and powerful countries have always been feared, resented, and envied; in short, they have not been loved. This has been the case since the days of the Assyrians and the Roman Empire. Neither the Ottoman nor the Spanish Empire, the Chinese, the Russian, nor the Japanese was ever popular. British sports were emulated in the colonies and French culture impressed the local elites in North Africa and Indochina, but this did not lead to political support, let alone identification with the rulers. Had there been public opinion polls in the days of Alexander the Great (let alone Ghengis Khan), the results, one suspects, would have been quite negative.

Big powers have been respected and feared but not loved for good reasons—even if benevolent, tactful, and on their best behavior, they were threatening simply because of their very existence. Smaller nations could not feel comfortable, especially if they were located close to them. This was the case even in times when there was more than one big power (which allowed for the possibility of playing one against the other). It is all the more so at a time when only one superpower is left and the perceived threat looms even larger.

There is no known way for a big power to reduce this feeling on the part of other, smaller countries—short of committing suicide or, at the very least, by somehow becoming weaker and less threatening. A moderate and intelligent policy on the part of the great power, concessions, and good deeds may mitigate somewhat the perceived threat, but it cannot remove it, because potentially the big power remains dangerous. It could always change its policy and become nasty, arrogant, and aggressive. These are the unfortunate facts of international life.

Soft power is important but has its limitations. Joseph S. Nye has described it as based on culture and political ideas, as influenced by the seductiveness of democracy, human rights, and individual opportunity. This is a powerful argument, and it is true that Washington has seldom used all its opportunities, the public diplomacy budget being about one-quarter of one percentage point of the defense budget. But the question is always to be asked: Who is to be influenced by our values and ideas? They could be quite effective in Europe, less so in a country like Russia, and not at all among the radical Islamists who abhor democracy (for all sovereignty rests with Allah rather than the people), who believe that human rights and tolerance are imperialist inventions, and who want to have nothing to do with deeper Western values which are not those of the Koran as they interpret it.

Big, powerful countries have always been feared, resented, and envied.

The work of the American radio stations during the Cold War ought to be recalled. They operated against much resistance at home but certainly had an impact on public opinion in Eastern Europe; according to evidence later received, even the Beatles had an influence on the younger generation in the Soviet Union. But, at present, radio and television has to be beamed to an audience 70 percent of which firmly believes that the operations of September 11 were staged by the Mossad. Such an audience will not be impressed by exposure to Western pop culture or a truthful, matter-of-fact coverage of the news. These societies may be vulnerable to covert manipulation of the kind conducted by the British government during World War II: black (or at least gray) propaganda, rumors, half-truths, and outright lies. Societies steeped in belief in conspiracy theories will give credence to even the wildest rumors. But it is easy to imagine how an attempt to generate such propaganda would be received at home: It would be utterly rejected. Democratic countries are not able to engage in such practices except in a case of a major emergency, which at the present time has not yet arisen.

Big powers will never be loved, but in the terrorist context it is essential that they should be respected. As bin Laden's declarations prior to September 11 show, it was lack of respect for America that made him launch his attacks; he felt certain that the risk he was running was small, for the United States was a paper tiger, lacking both the will and the capability to strike back. After all, the Americans ran from Beirut in the 1980s and from Mogadishu in 1993 after only a few attacks, and there was every reason to believe that they would do so again.

Response in Proportion to Threat

Life could be made more difficult for terrorists by imposing more controls and restrictions wherever useful. But neither the rules of national nor those of international law are adequate to deal with terrorism. Many terrorists or suspected terrorists have been detained in America and in Europe, but only a handful have been put on trial and convicted, because inadmissible evidence was submitted or the authorities were reluctant to reveal the sources of their information—and thus lose those sources. As a result, many who were almost certainly involved in terrorist operations were never arrested, while others were acquitted or released from detention.

As for those who are still detained, there have been loud protests against a violation of elementary human rights. Activists have argued that the real danger is not terrorism (the extent and the consequences of which have been greatly exaggerated) but the war against terrorism. Is it not true that American society could survive a disaster on the scale of September 11 even if it occurred once a year? Should free societies so easily give up their freedoms, which have been fought for and achieved over many centuries?

Some have foretold the coming of fascism in America (and to a lesser extent in Europe); others have predicted an authoritarian regime gradually introduced by governments cleverly exploiting the present situation for their own anti-democratic purposes. And it is quite likely indeed that among those detained there have been and are innocent people and that some of the controls introduced have interfered with human rights. However, there is much reason to think that to combat terrorism effectively, considerably more stringent measures will be needed than those presently in force.

But these measures can be adopted only if there is overwhelming public support, and it would be unwise even to try to push them through until the learning process about the danger of terrorism in an age of weapons of mass destruction has made further progress. Time will tell. If devastating attacks do not occur, stringent anti-terrorist measures will not be necessary. But if they do happen, the demand for effective countermeasures will be overwhelming. One could perhaps argue that further limitations of freedom are bound to be ineffective because terrorist groups are likely to be small or very small in the future and therefore likely to slip through safety nets. This is indeed a danger—but the advice to abstain from safety measures is a counsel of despair unlikely to be accepted.

There are political reasons to use these restrictions with caution, because Muslim groups are bound to be under special scrutiny and every precaution should be taken not to antagonize moderate elements in this community. Muslim organizations in Britain have complained that a young Pakistani or Arab is 10 times more likely to be stopped and interrogated by the police than other youths. The same is true for France and other countries. But the police, after all, have some reasons to be particularly interested in these young people rather than those from other groups. It will not be easy to find a just and easy way out of the dilemma, and those who have to deal with it are not to be envied.

It could well be that, as far as the recent past is concerned, the danger of terrorism has been overstated. In the two world wars, more people were sometimes killed and more material damage caused in a few hours than through all the terrorist attacks in a recent year. True, our societies have since become more vulnerable and also far more sensitive regarding the loss of life, but the real issue at stake is not the attacks of the past few years but the coming dangers. Megaterrorism has not yet arrived; even 9-11 was a stage in between old-fashioned terrorism and the shape of things to come: the use of weapons of mass destruction.

The real issue at stake is not the attacks of the past few years but the coming dangers.

The idea that such weapons should be used goes back at least 150 years. It was first enunciated by Karl Heinzen, a German radical—later a resident of Louisville, Kentucky and Boston, Massachusetts—soon after some Irish militants considered the use of poison gas in the British Parliament. But these were fantasies by a few eccentrics, too farfetched even for the science fiction writers of the day.

Today these have become real possibilities. For the first time in human history very small groups have, or will have, the potential to cause immense destruction. In a situation such as the present one there is always the danger of focusing entirely on the situation at hand—radical nationalist or religious groups with whom political solutions may be found. There is a danger of concentrating on Islamism and forgetting that the problem is a far wider one. Political solutions to deal with their grievances may sometimes be possible, but frequently they are not. Today's terrorists, in their majority, are not diplomats eager to negotiate or to find compromises. And even if some of them would be satisfied with less than total victory and the annihilation of the enemy, there will always be a more radical group eager to continue the struggle.

This was always the case, but in the past it mattered little: If some Irish radicals wanted to continue the struggle against the British in 1921-22, even after the mainstream rebels had signed a treaty with the British government which gave them a free state, they were quickly defeated. Today even small groups matter a great deal precisely because of their enormous potential destructive power, their relative independence, the fact that they are not rational actors, and the possibility that their motivation may not be political in the first place.

Perhaps the scenario is too pessimistic; perhaps the weapons of mass destruction, for whatever reason, will never be used. But it would be the first time in human history that such arms, once invented, had not been used. In the last resort, the problem is, of course, the human condition.

In 1932, when Einstein attempted to induce Freud to support pacifism, Freud replied that there was no likelihood of suppressing humanity's aggressive tendencies. If there was any reason for hope, it was that people would turn away on rational grounds—that war had become too destructive, that there was no scope anymore in war for acts of heroism according to the old ideals.

Freud was partly correct: War (at least between great powers) has become far less likely for rational reasons. But his argument does not apply to terrorism motivated mainly not by political or economic interests, based not just on aggression but also on fanaticism with an admixture of madness.

Terrorism, therefore, will continue—not perhaps with the same intensity at all times, and some parts of the globe may be spared altogether. But there can be no victory, only an uphill struggle, at times successful, at others not.

WALTER LAQUEUR is co-chair of the International Research Council at the Center for Strategic and International Studies. He is the author of some of the basic texts on terrorism, most recently *Voices of Terror* (Reed Publishing, 2004). The present article is part of a larger project; the author wishes to thank the Earhart Foundation for its support.

From *Policy Review,* August/September 2004, pp. 49–64. Copyright © 2004 by Walter Laqueur. Reprinted by permission of the author and Policy Review.

Test-Your-Knowledge Form

We encourage you to photocopy and use this page as a tool to assess how the articles in *Annual Editions* expand on the information in your textbook. By reflecting on the articles you will gain enhanced text information. You can also access this useful form on a product's book support Web site at *http://www.mhcls.com/online/*.

NAME: DATE:

TITLE AND NUMBER OF ARTICLE:

BRIEFLY STATE THE MAIN IDEA OF THIS ARTICLE:

LIST THREE IMPORTANT FACTS THAT THE AUTHOR USES TO SUPPORT THE MAIN IDEA:

WHAT INFORMATION OR IDEAS DISCUSSED IN THIS ARTICLE ARE ALSO DISCUSSED IN YOUR TEXTBOOK OR OTHER READINGS THAT YOU HAVE DONE? LIST THE TEXTBOOK CHAPTERS AND PAGE NUMBERS:

LIST ANY EXAMPLES OF BIAS OR FAULTY REASONING THAT YOU FOUND IN THE ARTICLE:

LIST ANY NEW TERMS/CONCEPTS THAT WERE DISCUSSED IN THE ARTICLE, AND WRITE A SHORT DEFINITION:

We Want Your Advice

ANNUAL EDITIONS revisions depend on two major opinion sources: one is our Advisory Board, listed in the front of this volume, which works with us in scanning the thousands of articles published in the public press each year; the other is you—the person actually using the book. Please help us and the users of the next edition by completing the prepaid article rating form on this page and returning it to us. Thank you for your help!

ANNUAL EDITIONS: Violence and Terrorism 08/09

ARTICLE RATING FORM

Here is an opportunity for you to have direct input into the next revision of this volume.
We would like you to rate each of the articles listed below, using the following scale:

1. **Excellent: should definitely be retained**
2. **Above average: should probably be retained**
3. **Below average: should probably be deleted**
4. **Poor: should definitely be deleted**

Your ratings will play a vital part in the next revision.
Please mail this prepaid form to us as soon as possible.
Thanks for your help!

RATING	ARTICLE	RATING	ARTICLE
	1. Ghosts of Our Past		21. José Padilla and the War on Rights
	2. An Essay on Terrorism		22. A Violent Episode in the Virtual World
	3. The Origins of the New Terrorism		23. Terror's Server
	4. The Myth of the Invincible Terrorist		24. The Globe of Villages
	5. Paying for Terror		25. Congress and the "YouTube War"
	6. Toy Soldiers		26. Qutbism: An Ideology of Islamic-Fascism
	7. Iran's Suicide Brigades		27. The Madrassa Scapegoat
	8. Hizballah and Syria		28. Holy Orders
	9. Guerrilla Nation		29. Female Suicide Bombers: A Global Trend
	10. The Growing Syrian Missile Threat: Syria after Lebanon		30. Cross-Regional Trends in Female Terrorism
	11. Colombia and the United States: From Counternarcotics to Counterterrorism		31. Explosive Baggage: Female Palestinian Suicide Bombers and the Rhetoric of Emotion
	12. Wounded But Still Dangerous		32. The Bomb Under the Abaya
	13. Peace at Last?		33. Picked Last: Women and Terrorism
	14. Root Causes of Chechen Terror		34. The Eye of the Storm
	15. End of Terrorism?		35. Port Security Is Still a House of Cards
	16. Homegrown Terror		36. Are We Ready Yet?
	17. Green Rage		37. Held Without Trial in the USA
	18. Echoes of the Future		38. From the War on Terror to Global Counterinsurgency
	19. Casting a Wider Net		39. The Terrorism to Come
	20. Speaking for the Animals, or the Terrorists?		

ANNUAL EDITIONS: VIOLENCE AND TERRORISM 08/09

BUSINESS REPLY MAIL
FIRST CLASS MAIL PERMIT NO. 551 DUBUQUE IA

POSTAGE WILL BE PAID BY ADDRESSEE

McGraw-Hill Contemporary Learning Series
501 BELL STREET
DUBUQUE, IA 52001

NO POSTAGE
NECESSARY
IF MAILED
IN THE
UNITED STATES

ABOUT YOU

Name

Date

Are you a teacher? ☐ A student? ☐
Your school's name

Department

Address

City

State

Zip

School telephone #

YOUR COMMENTS ARE IMPORTANT TO US!

Please fill in the following information:
For which course did you use this book?

Did you use a text with this ANNUAL EDITION? ☐ yes ☐ no
What was the title of the text?

What are your general reactions to the Annual Editions concept?

Have you read any pertinent articles recently that you think should be included in the next edition? Explain.

Are there any articles that you feel should be replaced in the next edition? Why?

Are there any World Wide Web sites that you feel should be included in the next edition? Please annotate.

May we contact you for editorial input? ☐ yes ☐ no
May we quote your comments? ☐ yes ☐ no